C0-AUL-876

# PROBLEMS OF THE PACIFIC

THE UNIVERSITY OF CHICAGO PRESS
CHICAGO, ILLINOIS

THE BAKER & TAYLOR COMPANY
NEW YORK

THE MACMILLAN COMPANY OF CANADA, LIMITED
TORONTO

THE CAMBRIDGE UNIVERSITY PRESS
LONDON

THE MARUZEN-KABUSHIKI-KAISHA
TOKYO, OSAKA, KYOTO, FUKUOKA, SENDAI

THE COMMERCIAL PRESS, LIMITED
SHANGHAI

# PROBLEMS OF THE PACIFIC

Proceedings of the Second Conference of the Institute of Pacific Relations, Honolulu, Hawaii, July 15 to 29, 1927

EDITED BY

J. B. CONDLIFFE, M.A., D.Sc. (N.Z.)

*Formerly Professor of Economics, Canterbury College, Christ Church, New Zealand*

THE UNIVERSITY OF CHICAGO PRESS
CHICAGO, ILLINOIS

COMPOSED AND PRINTED BY THE UNIVERSITY OF
CHICAGO PRESS, CHICAGO, ILLINOIS, U.S.A.

## FOREWORD

This book portrays the encounter of representatives of diverse civilizations who met to confer in the middle of the Pacific in the summer of 1927 upon matters of mutual concern. Opinions were exchanged, facts were examined, fears, hopes, and prejudices frankly aired, and friendships formed between members of nine of the leading peoples living in, or having great interests in, the Pacific area.

The book also reflects an intensely human experience. The attempt of men and women of conflicting interests and different backgrounds, with various social, economic, and political concepts of life, to find out whether it is possible to live together harmoniously in a world that is constantly growing smaller. These people wished to study the factors that underlie racial contacts and the adjustment of conflicting interests and to examine the possibility of creating a new type of international community in the Pacific area built upon reciprocity and mutual understanding.

The book is the story of a democratic procedure applied to international relations. The Conference was unofficial. The members represented no governments or governmental or private interests. Though well acquainted with the matters discussed and their governments' policies in relation to these matters, the members spoke for themselves alone. They came under no instructions. Compromise, barter, the giving a *quid pro quo* were absent. Thinking did not stop where the interests of the other party were concerned, but minds were free to think with the other party to his conclusions and so get the reasons for his point of view.

People within the Pacific countries of widely contrasted viewpoints and types of mind attended the Conference. The national groups represented no *bloc* opinion or sympathies. The liberal and conservative, idealist and materialist, labor leader and capitalist, internationalist and nationalist were present and stated their opinions. The Conference assembled a fair cross-section of the unofficial experience, expert knowledge, and representative opinion of the various countries and focused it upon a program of extraordinary interest and difficulty.

The chief characteristic of the meeting, however, centered upon facts: the collection, exchange, discussion, and analysis of facts related to the big problems of this part of the world. The members all shared in a thirst for new data —data that would throw light on obscure and difficult situations—and they also shared in a willingness to readjust their attitudes and opinions on the basis of such data. Viewed from this angle the Conference was a success. At its close, a distinguished member of the British group said: "I have learned more during these two weeks than in any similar period since the Paris conference."

THE INSTITUTE OF PACIFIC RELATIONS

The Institute of Pacific Relations is an unofficial organization which aims at the improvement of the relations between the peoples of the Pacific area.

The Institute functions as an international shock-absorber, fact-finder, and interpreter. It centers its efforts upon a study of the conditions of the Pacific peoples and the discovery of the facts that underlie the chief areas of friction in this region, and it encourages the study and discussion of such facts by the people who are primarily concerned.

The Institute holds biennial conferences, stimulates research, and disseminates information.

The Institute is directed by a Pacific Council, to which each of its constituent national units elects a member. The present membership of the Council is as follows:

Ray Lyman Wilbur, United States, chairman; Junnosuke Inouye, Japan, first vice-chairman; David Z. T. Yui, China, second vice-chairman; Frank C. Atherton, Hawaii, treasurer; Sir Mungo McCallum, Australia; Sir Robert Borden, Canada; Sir James Allen, New Zealand.

The work of the Institute is conducted by a permanent Secretariat, with headquarters in Honolulu, which is responsible for the preparation and conduct of conferences, the promotion of research, the exchange of information, and the maintenance of *liaison* between the national units.

The Institute has no connection with any government. It is non-sectarian, non-controversial, and non-propagandist. It is not a pacifist society.

The Institute derives its support from research foundations and from private contributions. The national units are autonomous and self-supporting and are organized in each country on the basis of a central constitution in the framing of which they have shared.

The origin of the Institute of Pacific Relations is traced to a group of business and professional men in Hawaii. In this advanced frontier of America, the prosperity and even the existence of the island community depends upon the good will and friendly relations of the nations of the Pacific. Moreover, in these islands there has been going on for one hundred years a fairly successful experiment in building a mutually dependent and friendly community from many diverse races and cultures.

If such a community is possible in the island world, why not in the larger area, ran the argument. Hence the proposal that representatives of the various peoples around the Pacific rim should come together to talk over the matter.

This proposal was carried out in the first conference of the Institute, which met in Honolulu July 1–15, 1925. The organizing committees of the Conference in a majority of the participating countries were nominated by the national councils of the Young Men's Christian Association. At the opening of the Conference, however, these committees handed over their responsibilities to the Conference Executive Committee, which took charge of the meeting and under which a Committee on Permanent Organization was formed. The first Conference was attended by 111 people from eight of the countries of the Pacific area: Australia, Canada, China, Korea, Japan, New Zealand, Philippines, and United States. Leaders of public opinion and scholars from these widely scattered countries met in person, exchanged points of view upon the problems of the Pacific, and determined a program of action. A permanent Institute was formed, with branches in the various countries; a Secretariat with headquarters in Honolulu was established, and practical steps were taken for keeping contact between the various branches. An agreement was reached as to the outstanding problems of difficulty and the most important topics for research, and it was decided to hold a second conference in 1927 for examining together these questions in the light of whatever pertinent factual material could be assembled in the intervening period.

## THE 1927 CONFERENCE

The second conference of the Institute of Pacific Relations assembled at Honolulu on July 15, 1927. Its members were appointed by the national councils of the Institute in Australia, Canada, China, Japan, New Zealand, and the United States, and by local groups (acting with the consent of the national councils concerned) in Hawaii, Korea, and the Philippines. Upon the invitation of the Pacific Council, the Royal Institute of International Affairs took the initiative in organizing a group of individuals from Great Britain. Members of the League of Nations Secretariat and of the International Labor Office also attended as unofficial observers. The total membership of the Conference was 137, made up as follows: Australia, 5; Canada, 13; China, 14; Great Britain, 14; Hawaii, 15; Japan, 18; Korea, 3; New Zealand, 5; Philippines, 3; United States, 44; League of Nations, 2; International Labor Office, 1. A full list of members is printed as an Appendix to these proceedings.

At the invitation of Mr. Frank C. Atherton, the chairman of the Executive Committee, members attended an opening luncheon at the Royal Hawaiian Hotel, where they were informally welcomed by Mr. Atherton and Hon. Wallace R. Farrington, governor of the Territory of Hawaii. Replies to the addresses of welcome were made by Dr. Ray Lyman Wilbur, Chairman of the Pacific Council of the Institute, by Sir Frederick Whyte, for the British group, Dr. Masataro Sawayanagi, for the Japanese group and Dr. David Z. T. Yui, for the Chinese group.

The formal opening of the Conference was held the same evening at Punahou School under the chairmanship of President Ray Lyman Wilbur of Stanford University. At this session three introductory lectures were delivered, "The Geography of the Pacific," by Dr. Herbert E. Gregory, "The Races of the Pacific," by Dr. Peter Buck, and "The Pacific Problem as I See It," by Mr. Chester H. Rowell. The first two of these addresses are printed in Documents, Sections 1 and 2.

On Saturday, July 16, the Report of the Committee on Permanent Organization, covering the two-year period since the preceding conference was presented by the general secretary of the Institute, Mr. J. Merle Davis, and formal opening statements were made by the various group leaders, summarizing the attitudes of their countries toward Pacific problems, with special reference to the events of the last two years. These opening statements are published as Part 1 of this report.

During the evening of Sunday, July 17, members of the various national groups made fifteen-minute statements concerning the aims and aspirations of their countries. These statements are published in the *Institute News Bulletin* for October and November, 1927.

The main program of the Conference was begun on Monday, July 18, when four round tables met simultaneously to discuss the external political problems of China. The full program appears as Appendix B.

By common consent the first three days of round-table discussions were devoted exclusively to the consideration of the external political relations of China. The procedure of these round tables may be used to illustrate the method of discussion adopted with some variations throughout the Conference. For the discussions on China the membership of the Conference was divided as evenly as possible into four round tables, due regard being paid to the distribution of group membership and also to expert knowledge. The round tables were presided over by chairmen who were chosen primarily for their ability as presiding officers, rather than as experts on the subjects under discussion. A secretary was designated for each round table to assist the chairman and also to direct the stenographic recorder.

The group of chairmen and secretaries worked out a series of questions for discussion and prepared brief lists of references to sources and data material. After each session the officers of the round tables met to report the trend of the discussions and to compare notes. During the three days' discussions on China each round table met in seven sessions of an hour and a half each. There were in addition two evening sessions in which the whole membership of the Conference met as a forum to consider the reports of the chairmen of the round tables. The round tables and a part of the forums were closed to visitors and to the press. In these ways a definite effort was made toward sustained group discussion and frank exchange of opinion. With the exception of "The Future of the Institute," in which the verbatim discussions of the round tables are reproduced, the stenographic reports have been summarized so as to indicate the main trend of the discussions without using the names of the participants.

The discussions throughout the Conference were based upon data material forwarded by the various national councils, and upon data papers written by members at the Conference and circulated in mimeographed form. A selection of this material is printed in the third part of this record of proceedings. A full list of titles is appended. The list of references used by each round table is printed with each chapter, and reference is also made to the relevant source material wherever necessary in the text. While the source material is printed in this record separately from the summary of the round-table discussions, it should be emphasized that this separation is merely for convenience in printing. The discussions were based on the source material, there was constant reference to relevant documents, and much of the value of the discussion lay in the elucidation, amplification, and explanation of these documents. The various parts of this record, therefore, should be regarded as complementary.

For assistance in determining the general plan of the report and in the selection of documents for publication the editors are much indebted to Professors Quincy Wright, Robert E. Park, and Charles E. Merriam, of the University of Chicago.

Special acknowledgment should also be made of the valuable interpretive papers contributed to the documentary section of the report by Professor William H. Kilpatrick, of Teachers' College, Columbia University, and Mr. Herbert Croly, editor of the *New Republic*, New York City. Mr. Croly's article, entitled "The Human Potential in Pacific Politics," is a reprint from the October 5 issue of the *New Republic*.

J. Merle Davis
*General Secretary, Institute of Pacific Relations*

Honolulu, Hawaii
November, 1927

## CONTENTS

## LIST OF MAPS, DIAGRAMS, ETC.

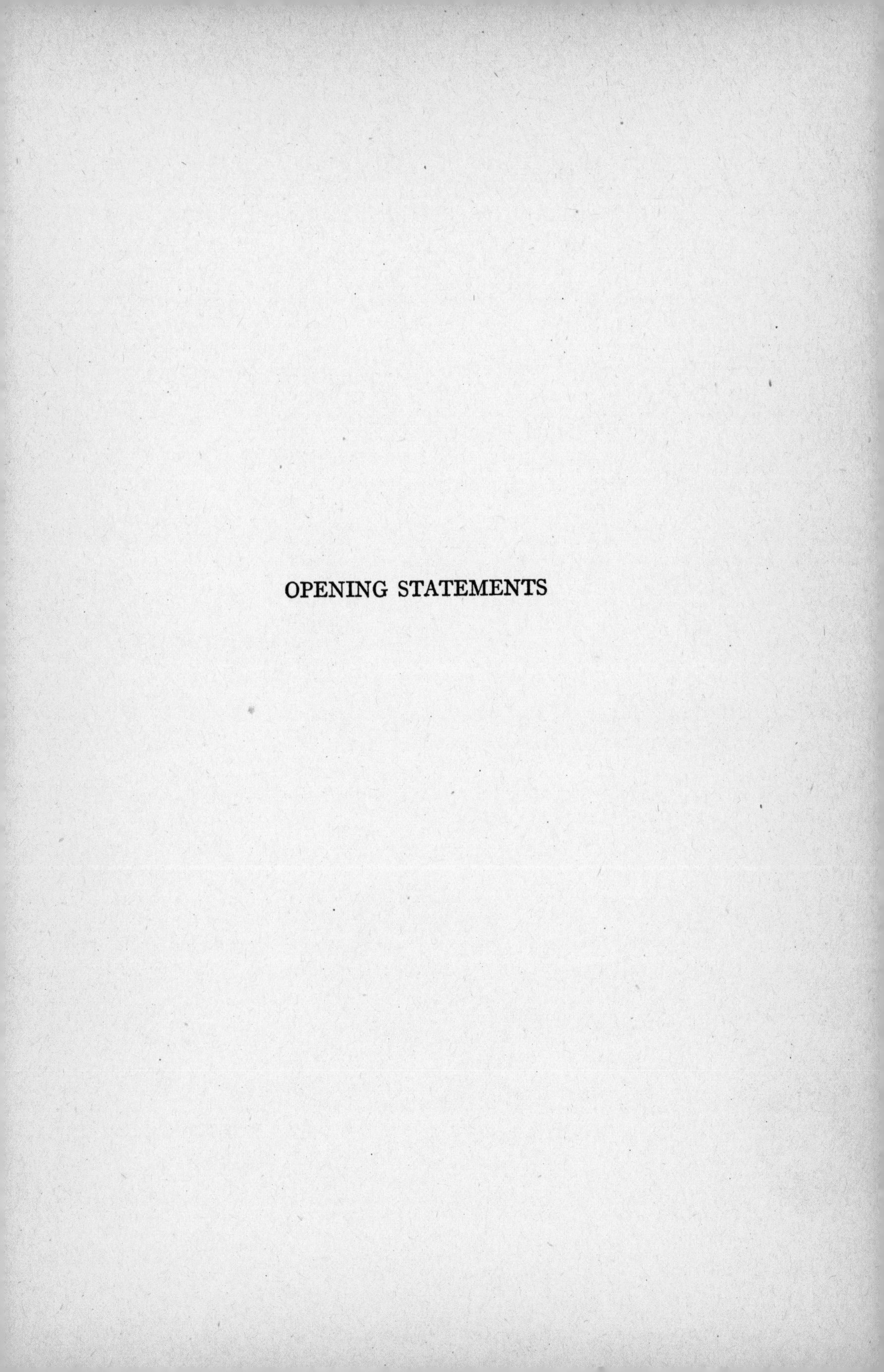

OPENING STATEMENTS

# THE VIEWPOINT OF AUSTRALIA ON PACIFIC AFFAIRS

HON. F. W. EGGLESTON
Formerly Attorney-General and Minister of Railways for Victoria

In speaking on behalf of the Australian delegation I want in the first place to say that we regard it as a great privilege to be participating in the Conference and to collaborate with the many distinguished men and women who are gathered here to further the objects of this Institute. The beautiful spot in which we meet stimulates our imagination and encourages those aspirations of mutual good will which must be present if these objectives are to be realized. Even if the Institute were unable to succeed at once, the friendships which we make here will remain assets out of which good must grow. There has never been any doubt about Australian interest in the aims of this organization. Australia is a lonely outpost in the most isolated area of the world. We are attempting to build up a society based on the institutions that we have inherited. Our isolation and our aspirations combine to make us acutely conscious of our environment. More than most young nations we have a sense of international tendencies and possibilities. We realize our interest in the Pacific and the movements which are likely to take place among the peoples surrounding that ocean.

In this address I am endeavoring to interpret to the Conference the aspirations of the Australian people and the ideas which are generally held as to the way in which the Pacific problems relevant to us should be solved. But of course such interpretations can only be an approximation. Australians do not all think alike. I will give my view as to general tendencies in which the group is in general accord. There will of course be many Australians who would hold different opinions. Members of the Australian group differ among themselves. It is, I think, necessary to emphasize the unofficial character of Australian representation here. I have no official position. I emphasize this because lists of delegates, with an unfortunate reference to an unhappy past in which I was a politician, have referred to offices which I held in the state of Victoria. But I have never had any official connection with the handling of foreign affairs. I speak therefore, not as an official or politician, not even as an ex-official or ex-politician, but as a student and citizen. Finally, I have endeavored to make this statement of the Australian point of view as comprehensive as possible. I have endeavored to give a reasoned account of our attitude—an attitude which either has our individual support or at any rate is believed by me to be the only attitude which the Australian people will support as a whole. In doing this I have covered a large field and have had to condense severely. I am afraid that this may possibly give my paper a dogmatic tone. Such an impression would be misleading. I have had to make my statements in a summary way, but in doing this I do not wish to suggest that we do not realize that they are controversial or that we are not prepared to discuss them in the freest and most candid manner.

It is frequently said that the Pacific is the area in which the next war will take place. In my opinion such a statement is as misleading as it is mischievous. No war is inevitable. The Pacific has problems of immense complexity. On the other hand there are factors in the Pacific situation which can be used to secure peaceful solutions. Pacific nations are widely separated by the ocean. They are not crowded together like European countries. Do not let us argue from European analogies or be dominated by a European psychology in these matters. The spaciousness of the Pacific is a factor of safety. If there is no bankruptcy of statesmanship, the Pacific should be made an area pacific in fact as well as name.

The objective of Australian policy should be peace. I will even admit that it is necessarily pacific. War in the Pacific cannot be of advantage to Australia. Australia is a sincere member of the League of Nations, and is willing to act up to the obligations involved in its membership. It is also, I believe, the universal sentiment of Australians that their relationship with the British Empire should remain unimpaired. We believe that the British Empire has been and is one of the greatest agencies for world-peace. The Empire has a form of organization which is puzzling to plain men like myself, although its subtleties afford special satisfaction to constitutional lawyers and students of political science. But whatever it may be, it is in my opinion the overwhelming feeling in Australia that we should co-operate with the British government in formulating common policy. It might be a disturbing influence in the relations of Pacific nations, and in the discussion of them in a conference like this, if it were believed that British and Australian policy were likely to pursue different courses, and that Australia could be diverted into different affiliations. In my opinion that could not take place.

As a member of the League of Nations, Australia undertook a definite share of responsibility in accepting the mandate for certain Pacific islands. In our opinion and in the opinion of the Mandate Commission it has acted up to the obligations involved. These territories are managed primarily in the interests of the natives, it being thought that economic development is definitely favorable to native interests, provided these interests are carefully safeguarded. I am not concerned to deny that criticisms have been made of our management. I have been a free critic myself. The critical spirit in these things is acute in Australia and I think it can be asserted with truth that the right course has only to be demonstrated for it to be adopted. One vexed point has been the application of the shipping laws of the Commonwealth to the territory so as to treat voyages there on the basis of coastal trade. This was terminated in 1925. The demand of other alien races to be permitted in the territory is one that should be decided in the interest of the native race. It should be the objective of policy to maintain the native races in their homeland and develop them to a higher stage.

The expropriation and sale of German properties in the Pacific has now been completed. Difference of opinion may exist as to the justice of expropriation and the manner in which it and the sale was carried out, but Australia, I believe, acted within the limits authorized by the treaty and according to the methods of strict business dealing. It was freely asserted at one time that certain interests would be favored. This suspicion has I think not been justified.

The main problem before the Australian people is an internal one: that of the development of our continent. I have hope that peace in the Pacific will enable us to concentrate on this problem. It is no simple task. Some people appear to believe that Australia is a kind of vacuum into which the human race would rush if it were permitted. This is not correct. It is not a country which at the present stage is capable of absorbing large numbers of people in a short time. Its settlement problems are special and are complicated at every stage by difficulties of climate, soil, power, and markets. The early navigators found it uninviting and no attempt was made to settle it for two centuries after it was first discovered.

Australia as it exists was built up by the pioneering genius of a British people and the almost unlimited supplies of British capital which enabled these pioneering problems to be settled. The gold discoveries were a temporary factor in this economic development, and the Merino sheep improved by the Australian breeder a permanent one. It is commonly believed that this settlement is unduly retarded and that other people could develop the country quicker. This is not true. About one-third of the continent has less than a 10-inch rainfall. Of this area a large proportion is practically useless and has no inhabitants. The remaining area under 10 inches produces a large quantity of wool which is a very considerable proportion of the wealth of Australia. Here the Merino sheep is held in large flocks ranging over vast areas, involving an amount of labor which is trifling. Settlement requires large amounts of capital owing to climatic risks. It is not a problem for the poor immigrant. The population in the area of Australia where the rainfall is under 10 inches is 24,000. No intensification of pastoral industry, the only industry possible, could add appreciably to this number. Colored labor is considered by some people indispensable in cases where tropical agriculture is undertaken. Curiously enough, although one-third of Australia is in the tropics, agriculture is impossible for climatic reasons in most of that area, and is only carried on with success in a few patches on the east coast of Queensland. Here white labor is used with satisfactory results, though as a fact the industries are heavily protected in various ways.

It is said that our social and industrial standards are unduly high and retard settlement by making it unduly expensive. On the other hand those standards constitute the main attraction to the immigrants. The parts of Australia within the temperate zone capable of agricultural development consist of a large area on the east and southeast corner of the continent and another on the southwest corner. This rarely extends to as much as 400 miles from the coast.

A comparison of the area in Australia having an agricultural climate with that of the United States is interesting. The latter country has 2,400,000 square miles of such land, of which one-third has a rainfall of over 40 inches. The Australian land of similar climate is 715,000 square miles, of which 80,000 has a rainfall of over 40 inches. The land in the United States is probably richer on the whole, and the rainfall more reliable. Under the circumstances the Australian development cannot be regarded as unsatisfactory. The area of unutilized agricultural land is, according to Professor Griffith Taylor, far higher in the United States than in Australia.

The sort of development of which Australia is capable in the future is a normal expansion of the present population by improvement in methods, by means of careful scientific research, and by evolving industrial possibilities. For this development it is necessary that large increases of capital shall be provided, either by immigrants, by the savings of the present population, or by borrowing from wealthier countries. The question as to whether a rate of increase of population is sufficient must be judged by comparison with other nations, remembering that the possible rate of increase is a function of the present number. Looked at from this point of view, the rate of development of Australia is more than satisfactory. It has one of the highest increase rates in the world. The natural increase is 1.5 per cent. The increase by immigration is .5 per cent, making a total of 2 per cent. This is quite a remarkable result, and is, as it seems to me, a sufficient answer to those who accuse us of retarding increase by immigration restrictions, or suggest that other nations could accelerate the increase. Scientific observers in Australia believe that this rate of increase cannot be largely accelerated without courting failure and consequent retardation.

Australians feel strongly that as they have, by their own efforts, created a prosperous and unique commonwealth out of elements which have been difficult and were considered unpromising, they are entitled to control its growth in the future for the people which built it up and to develop it so that their traditions and institutions can be preserved.

It does not seem necessary to defend the proposition that a nation is entitled to build up its population of the elements which it thinks best, for such an aspiration is generally acknowledged as legitimate, or is, at any rate, practiced wherever it is thought necessary. It was the policy of the United States at a stage when the menace of a competing race was trifling owing to the large population already established. After the experience of the last century in Europe it would be a foolhardy act to guide world-development in such a way as to leave room for racial conflict in new countries. We proceed on the assumption that the development we have started will be continued under the same conditions. Immigration from Great Britain is assisted, that from some European countries is controlled under a quota system, but generally it may be said that our policy is directed to prevent the flooding of Australia by immigrants whom it would be impossible to assimilate in a reasonable period of time. I repeat what has often been said before that this policy is not based upon ideas of race superiority or race prejudice, though race prejudice of an acute kind might speedily develop if immigrants with very different points of view were permitted to enter. Our policy is based partly on the idea that our economic standards cannot be maintained if we have to compete with people having very different standards. But it must also be realized that the urge for democracy is the desire to govern one's self according to the ideas and through the institutions one holds in common with one's neighbors. This is what self-government means to the average man. If he finds himself associated with strangers who will insist on the dominance of ideas radically different, his views on democracy and his political methods change. As a rule he determines that the other group will not dominate, and so conflict is started. The tendency toward democratic institutions is then, I believe, generally associated with a tendency to segregate into groups having similar ideas and institutions.

We are bound, in my opinion, to give full rights of citizenship and of economic developments to all who are admitted. There is a corresponding duty, however, on the immigrant to accept full citizenship, assume a new loyalty, and co-operate for the common good. Allegiance to the old state and the tendency to form separate enclaves should in my opinion be abandoned. In Australia the principle of giving full citizenship to all immigrants is very nearly complete. There are but few instances in which discrimination still exists, and a great advance has been made during the last few years. Details of the present position and of the agreements which control immigration with several countries are available in the Australian delegation.

Another ideal of the Australian people is for a balanced economy, and we seek to secure this by protective tariffs. This is challenged by those who say that the raw materials of Australia should be available and our markets open for the world. As a matter of fact the protective policy has not up to the present made an appreciable difference to our export of raw materials, and would only do so if our policy resulted in a large shift of population to Australia. In such a case of course a larger share of our own materials would be consumed on the spot. But if this took place our policy would surely have served a useful purpose. If the populations could be readjusted and grouped more nearly around the resources of the world, the world would be more stable. But in any case, whether our policy could be justified on high grounds or not, there is an irresistible urge for a balanced economy. The idea of a continent devoted entirely to primary industry and politically controlled by the farmer is not palatable to the majority of Australians. Under such a régime the population would rapidly become stationary. It would be a poor market. The ratio of exports to production would reach to about 80–90 per cent. Australian economic life would not be self-determined. It would depend on circumstances beyond our own control. Protection is a crude instrument liable to all sorts of abuse, but it is an effective instrument of economic integration. It involves sacrifice, but tends to produce a balanced economy. Only with such an economy do we believe that we could increase our population rapidly. I am not concerned to deny that our present tariff is defeating itself by its exaggeration and universality. Where everybody is protected, nobody is benefited. There is a definite movement in my opinion toward a lower and more effective tariff.

I am aware that the interest of the Conference is not very much centered upon the subjects which I have mentioned. The problem we will be chiefly considering is how China is to settle her own problems. On this I am afraid that we cannot offer any contributions. There are many distinguished people here who know how it should be done, and we hope to listen and profit by the debate. There is only one small caveat which I should like to put in, and that is, that this is not merely an institute of Far-Eastern relations, but a wider one for all Pacific relations. I ask that the wider aspect shall not be lost sight of in discussing the most important and the most engrossing subject of China. I would also suggest that a solution of some Far-Eastern questions may be found in the islands of the Pacific. I would be very much disappointed if this Institute did not provide for research and discussion on the development of the Pacific islands and the ethnology of Pacific races. Tropical disease, the agricultural and developmental problems of the islands, are questions of the utmost importance for this Institute. I have dwelt in this paper very largely on Australia's problems because I considered that in doing so I was faithful to the Institute idea. Our Commonwealth, however, has many other interests. It has in particular carried out a series of most interesting experiments in advanced democracy. The aim or ideal of this movement may be summed up as an attempt to emphasize and exalt the human factor in social, economic, and political life, to protect it from exploitation, liberate it from old customs and dominations, and promote its freedom and happiness. A number of experiments have been tried which older schools of thought condemn. Many of these, however, are being imitated in other parts of the world. The offices of government are, not only theoretically, but actually, open to all sections of the community. The workingman has had a considerable share of political power and is responsible to some extent for our Commonwealth as it now exists. There is radical difference of opinion in Australia as to various phases of this development. But there is an agreement, I think, as to our ideal, and there is little doubt as to our freedom, happiness, and prosperity. What is needed at the present time is a careful survey of our political and economic development, a scientific appraisal of the result of our experiment, a comparison with results in other countries, and a judgment of their value. For such a survey the criticism of thinkers of all nations is needed. It is a most pleasing feature of this Institute that the prosperity, the policy, the special developments, and the ideals of each Pacific country are the interest of all. The Australian delegation hopes that one happy result of these meetings will be an increased interest in our Commonwealth, and that the memories of this beautiful spot, of the hospitalities received here and the friendships made may be renewed through the visits of members of this Conference to Australia.

# CANADA AND PACIFIC RELATIONS

SIR ARTHUR W. CURRIE, G.C.M.G., K.C.B.
Principal and Vice-Chancellor, McGill University

It is my proud privilege this morning to supplement the excellent statement submitted by Mr. John Nelson in 1925, setting forth the interest Canada has in all those objects for the achievement of which this Institute of Pacific Relations was formed.

Every nation and civilization exists for the purpose of making a distinctive contribution all its own to the whole of human history; my country believes that it can make a contribution to the settlement of Pacific problems, but the nature of its contribution is determined by certain interesting features in the life and history of the Canadian people.

In the first place, Canada is perhaps the first political community—certainly the first political community drawn on a large scale—to achieve national autonomy without a revolution or war of any kind. This fact is of fundamental importance to anyone who would understand the spirit of the Canadian people. As a result of this fact the people of Canada entertain, at the present beginning of their national history, no ancient grudges, prejudices, or bitternesses of any kind. Hatred or jealousy of other nations find no place in their national sentiments or in their patriotism to their own country. The people of Canada are clearly conscious of this fact and are determined to make it a keynote of their national history. Hence our interest in the League of Nations, and the propriety of our participation in this Conference.

Canada has been schooled in peace. Within her borders two races, French and Anglo-Saxon, with centuries of antagonisms, centuries of conflict, left behind, live together in peace and harmony, each maintaining its own language, its own traditional religion, its national customs, and its civil law. Membership in the British Commonwealth of Nations has taught international co-operation, while the hundred years of peace on our three thousand miles of United States border has been a practical demonstration of the possibilities of sympathetic contact without loss of national identity. The existence of this—three thousand miles of frontier unprotected by a fortress or unguarded by a single sentry—has profoundly influenced the consciousness of the Canadian people and is itself the world's most significant prophecy that *force* may be replaced by mutual good will.

Canada's loyalty to, and affection for, the Motherland, her proud and happy relations with all other parts of the Empire, her intimacy with, and unvarying and unflinching friendship for, her great and powerful neighbor, the United States of America, the presence of interracial problems and traditions within her own borders, her peculiar geographical position and formation, forming as it does an international highway between the Occident and the Orient, between Europe and Asia, are all factors conspiring to create among the people of Canada an international sentiment and sympathy of profound importance and promise.

There have always been writers and critics, like Goldwin Smith of honored and respected memory, who have maintained that this Canadian venture in nation-making is impossible and doomed to failure. The Canadian people, however, are determined to achieve it, and the sixty years of remarkable progress since the union of the Canadian provinces was first designed clearly indicate at present that the attempt will prove successful.

With the development of Pacific trade, which bids fair soon to rival that of the Atlantic, North America becomes the center of the world's commerce, and Canada lies closest to Asia and to Europe. This gives to her Pacific seaboard a significance highly important and not always fully appreciated. On it she has one of the finest climates in the world, and innumerable harbors of magnificent proportions. Immediately behind the coast line lie the mountain areas with their uncalculated natural resources in timber, coal, gold, silver, lead, in water-power, in great agricultural areas in the valleys, while behind and beyond these mountains lies perhaps the world's greatest northern food-producing hinterland.

The center of population and industry in Canada will undoubtedly continue to move westward. Witness the fact that last year nearly 50,000,000 bushels of wheat were shipped out of Vancouver Harbor to the markets of Europe and the Orient, whereas five years ago such shipments were unknown. Merchants of British Columbia and the prairie provinces are beginning largely to import their merchandise via the Panama Canal. In fact our trade in the Pacific is vastly on the increase. Two-thirds of Canada's imports, and approximately one-half her exports, are with countries bordering on the Pacific. With New Zealand and Australia Canada shares the leading position among all nations of the world in per capita foreign trade, more especially in export.

While a large portion of the before-mentioned trade is with the United States, there has nevertheless been a very rapid growth during the post-war period in Canada's commerce with other Pacific countries, notably China, Japan, and the two Australasian dominions. Our exports to China during 1926 amounted to nearly one-half the total for the whole preceding fifty years. In spite of present unsettled conditions there is every prospect of China's becoming in the near future one of our greatest export markets. Japan is our third-greatest foreign customer. Several factors have contributed materially to this commercial progress. The excellent transpacific steamship services, not the least of which is that provided by the Canadian Pacific Railway, has helped to draw attention to Canada's strategic position on the shortest and most direct water route from Asia to North America and Europe. The terminal facilities at Vancouver which were provided for the Panama Canal route have also served for the increasing wheat and flour requirements of China and Japan.

Since our last Conference Prince Rupert has also become prominent as a grain port for the Far East, being, as it is, one day's sailing nearer the Orient than any other North American terminus. The trade between Canada and Japan and China has one distinct advantage which encourages the belief that it will continue to grow to much greater proportions, namely, that it is non-competitive as far as the respective parties are concerned. The commodities imported from the Far East do not compete with our home industries, with the possible exception of egg products, while Canadian hard wheat, lumber, news print, zinc, lead, silver, and nickel will be needed in increasing quantities in the progressive industrialization of the Orient, notably China.

And now let me proceed to the much misunderstood attitude of Canada toward unrestricted immigration from oriental countries. To appreciate how dearly the Canadian people cherish their heritage it is necessary to outline briefly their hard struggle in the making of a nation. We are celebrating this year in Canada the sixtieth anniversary of confederation. Now sixty years, while long in the life of the individual, is a relatively short period in the life of a nation and so our Dominion is a comparatively young land.

Every student of history knows that the Dominion of Canada was formed in 1867 by the union of the three British provinces in North America—Canada, Nova Scotia, and New Brunswick. The other provinces now in the Dominion joined later. The dream of confederation before its ultimate realization was a long, long dream. Britain lost in 1776 the chief part of her eighteenth-century empire. Britain did not lose thereby her place in the North American Continent. The American colonies determined to try their experiment of autonomy in separation from the Empire, but the colonies that now form Canada resolved to try the experiment of free self-government within the Empire and under the British flag. It was a new experiment in nation-making, this attempt—to establish a free national government in the parts of Britain overseas, to secure essential autonomy, and at the same time to retain membership in the larger British Commonwealth.

It was a difficult task because of widely scattered parts, the diversity of the peoples and institutions, the barriers of language, and the difference of nationality and creed. The idea had long existed, but difficulties always stood in the way of its fruition. There was the Rebellion of 1837 which attempted to secure by force the system of responsible government which the provinces had hoped to secure by peaceful means. Lord Durham was sent from England soon after to investigate the problem and suggest a remedy. Even he had little faith in confederation, and another quarter of a century was to elapse before such a dream became a reality.

Those were twenty-five troubled years in Canada's making of a nation. There was much violent friction between the so-called "patriots" and the so-called "reformers," principally over the Rebellion Losses Bill. There were riots and the burning of the parliament buildings in Montreal. There was obvious disruption in the sparsely settled provinces which, because of their scanty population and proximity to a rapidly growing and powerful neighbor, could ill afford disunion. There was economic depression, resulting from Britain's changed policy regarding trade with the colonies. The "hungry forties" forced the cancellation of the preferential privileges. The maintenance of British connection was seriously threatened. The bonds of Empire were severely tried, and the annexation movement appeared, supported by hundreds of Canada's most influential citizens, all of British descent.

There was the further trade depression caused by the non-renewal of the Reciprocity Treaty with the United States. There was the unfriendly attitude of the northern states, victorious after the Civil War—unfriendly because of Britain's alleged sympathy with the South. The man from Nova Scotia was a foreigner in New Brunswick, much more so in Ontario. A custom's barrier, a tariff wall around each colony, kept out the intruding trader. Then came political deadlock between Upper and Lower Canada, caused largely by the difference of race and creed and language, and the bitterness of parties. The mother-country was indifferent. Statesmen complained that Canada had no constitution, but the dicta of the ever changing occupants of Downing Street sections of the press were bitterly hostile to the idea of confederation, and altogether there were years of struggle and opposition not unmixed with bitterness. The road was one of innumerable pitfalls, but triumph finally came and confederation finally emerged.

It is in the light of this historical perspective that one must approach that phase of its evolution which has to do with the relations of Canada with the Orient in the matter of immigration. Canada's oriental relations are not to be judged apart from the main current of Canadian history, and the point to be emphasized above all others in this Conference is that the history of Canada is so utterly unlike that of the Orient as to make comparisons difficult to appreciate fairly.

This year is only the sixtieth year of confederation. Imagine how little that brief period means in the millenniums of China. Yet in this brief period we have not only to win for confederation half a continent; we have to work out with variant strains of people, especially the French and English nationalities, those institutions of liberty and freedom which will also preserve our heritage.

The question of oriental immigration is a part of this problem. There is a natural and inevitable reluctance, a definite and instinctive recoil from the possibility of the creation in our midst of unassimilable units socially and culturally connected with a heritage in which the rest of the nation has no part.

Whatever there is of difficulty in racial relations is to be considered, not on the basis of race antipathy or race prejudice, despite what statements may be made to the contrary. There is a real concern in Canada for the maintenance of those traditions and institutions for which our people struggled through long and weary years and which embody what they now hold most dear. Just how far the intermingling and intermarrying of races of different colors and civilizations should be permitted in any one community is something that can only be amicably settled by long and patient periods of trial and error. The people of Canada, particularly the people of British Columbia, naturally fear that if the door on the Pacific were thrown wide open to the people of the Orient serious difficulties and dangers might result in the future.

It is obvious too from what I have said of the peculiar formation of Canada, of its history and experiences, that her people must remain intensely loyal, man to man, from sea to sea, if the Canadian venture in nation-making is to prove successful. Should any one distinctive group be allowed to settle too largely in any one province, the result we honestly fear might prove disastrous and the whole difficult undertaking brought to failure. Let me in closing my remarks on this question of immigration repeat that none of Canada's distinctive aims and purposes is based on jealousy or dislike of other nations. I must add that the Gentlemen's Agreement, which regulates the incoming of Japanese, has been most faithfully observed, not only in the letter, but in the spirit of the arrangement. The fact that the 400 quota has been materially reduced by mutual agreement does not alter the good feeling which exists between the two countries. Canada has not forgotten the 200 Japanese who served with distinction in the Canadian forces during the war.

Let me now make brief reference to Canada's cultural contacts with the peoples of the Orient. While Canadian churches for over fifty years have carried on missionary activities in the Far East, have established schools, colleges, and hospitals in Japan, Korea, and China, it is only in the last few years that the cultural assets of these countries have begun to be appreciated in Canada. The Gest Chinese Research Library at McGill University, while containing only thirty-five thousand volumes at present, is nevertheless one which rivals those of the British Museum and the Congressional Library at Washington. Every effort is being made to render it as complete as any outside of China.

In addition to this, the Royal Museum associated with the University of Toronto contains one of the finest collections of Chinese art in existence, especially of the Ming and pre-Ming periods. The organization of a School of Chinese Studies at McGill University is a further indication of the growing interest in the old cultures and in the present progress of Oriental nations.

And now I come to my final point. A very important phase of Canada's relation to Pacific problems arises because of her place as a member of the British Commonwealth of Nations. The Imperial Conference of 1926 codified the series of unwritten understandings between the various members of the British Commonwealth which have been arrived at through the experience of years. By decision of the Conference Great Britain and the dominions are defined at the outset as "autonomous communities within the British Empire, equal in status, in no way subordinate one to another in any aspect of their domestic or external affairs, though united by common allegiance to the crown and freely associated as members of the British Commonwealth of Nations."

This means that the rapidly extending interests of Canada in the commerce, the cultural contacts, the missionary activities, and the migrations from Pacific lands to its shores will be viewed in the first place by their bearing upon the national interests of Canada. In the realm of commerce Canada will become more and more a rival of Great Britain and the other British dominions, and will shape its tariffs and trade policies with primary regard to its own national interests. The same is true of its immigration policies and its attitude to the racial and religious problems of the Pacific.

Yet because of the close spiritual union between the members of the Commonwealth no policy which would prove seriously detrimental to any other member of our Commonwealth could receive the support of the Canadian people, unless it were clearly evident that to refuse to adopt such a policy would be fatal to Canadian interests. The close affinity in traditions and aspirations between the members of our Commonwealth has allowed Canada to play an important rôle in determining the general attitude of the other members of the Empire to the problems of the Pacific.

Furthermore, because of the central position of Great Britain in the British Commonwealth of Nations and her widespread interests in all parts of the world, the Canadian people have begun to think internationally and ask the privilege of co-operating in any effort that has for its purpose the attainment of world-peace and the security of world-progress. Lying as Canada does along the entire northern boundary of the great republic of the United States and forming the great highway between Great Britain and the Orient and the Australasian dominions, her position as an interpreter of the United States to the British People and of British institutions to the United States and to the Orient is one of first-rate importance.

Thus as an autonomous nation of the shores of the Pacific, working out its own destiny and considering primarily its own interests, consonant with those of the great empire of which it forms a part, and as an increasingly important member of the British Commonwealth of Nations, Canada's place in Pacific affairs is undoubted, and will increase vastly in significance in the great era of Pacific development which is just beginning.

The problems of the Pacific are many and difficult, but they are not insoluble if we approach them in the spirit so eloquently portrayed by the distinguished Chinese statesman who addressed us at the luncheon yesterday. The view of the Canadian people is that in the solution of these problems we have a safe guide, an unfailing light, if we remember that faith is better than doubt, and love is better than hate.

# CHINA AND PACIFIC RELATIONS DURING 1925–27

DR. DAVID Z. T. YUI
General Secretary of the National Committee of Young Men's Christian Associations of China

I take great pleasure in extending to the Institute and to the delegates of different countries gathered at this Institute the heartiest greetings of the people of China. The Book of Odes, which has been exerting a strong influence in our country for thousands of years, teaches us that "friendship should culminate in mutual fidelity." Friends, the greetings which I am bringing are not mere formality, but are from the bottom of the hearts of our people. You will please receive them in the same spirit.

Our people also deeply appreciate the fact that at this Institute all delegates not only meet on an absolutely equal basis, but are capable of discussing and are going to discuss all Pacific problems and relations in a frank, unreserved, fair-minded, constructive, and fraternal spirit. We are here not to represent our own governments or any particular political, social, or religious organizations, nor to have any axe to grind. We meet at this paradise to exchange our ideas and experiences, to face the facts in any given problem and to understand them, to dream dreams together for a better world in which we shall truly live and let live, and, through mutual understanding and co-operation, to evolve a plan or plans whereby our dreams will be fully realized and the Pacific relations will be placed on a sincerely pacific basis. Friends, the delegates from China have come in this spirit and with this hope, and we know we shall not be disappointed.

During the period between this and the last Institute much water has passed under the bridge in China. I shall not take the time to dwell on "those points on which my countrymen feel that they have been mistreated, and those in reference to which they think they are misunderstood and perhaps censured." Nor shall I try to classify our internal and external problems and present them as such. In my humble judgment it will be better for me quickly to pass in review the important events which have taken place in China during the last two years and which will profoundly influence the Pacific relations. In this brief presentation I shall be sparse in my remarks about each event, and shall especially reserve my judgment concerning the right or wrong of each case. What we are aiming at is that as a result of our study and discussion together we may better understand them and discover some proper and satisfactory solution for them.

### 1. INCIDENTS

First, I shall briefly touch upon the several incidents which, whether settled or not, constitute important factors in China's present foreign relations:

*a*) *The May 30th Incident,* according to the foreign governments concerned, was already settled by the International Commission of Judicial Inquiry in Shanghai in the winter of 1925. As the Chinese government, however, did not participate in the inquiry, the incident is still looked upon by the Chinese people as a case outstanding.

*b*) *The Shameen Incident,* which happened in Canton in June, 1925, is another unsettled case which will require attention.

*c*) *The Wanhsien Incident,* which even according to the reports published in the foreign papers in China caused many casualties among the innocent Chinese people in Wanhsien and seriously damaged the business section of that city has to this day not been taken up in negotiations.

*d*) *The Taku Incident* may be looked upon as a closed affair. But its settlement under an ultimatum by the foreign powers and the large number of student lives lost in Peking in connection with this incident are still being resented by the Chinese people.

*e*) *The Nanking Incident* is awaiting negotiations. From the viewpoint of friendship, our people have already expressed our regret over the incident to the people of the different countries concerned. We are confident that as soon as the true situation is revealed, full justice will be meted out and suitable reparations made.

### 2. CONFERENCES

Next, I shall call the attention of the Institute to the two important conferences which were really instituted at the Washington Conferences 1921–22, and which were, as we know, prevented from taking place until the winter of 1925 and the spring of 1926.

*a*) *The Tariff Conference* was started in Peking with an exceedingly hopeful note. What the Chinese people wanted was complete tariff autonomy, which should be restored at as early a date as possible. For a time it looked as if the tariff autonomy might be achieved by January 1, 1929, although it was known to be somewhat complicated by the question of abolishing the likin system. The representatives at the Conference did not seem to have any argument against the demand for tariff autonomy. In fact, they all professed to be in favor of it. Pretty soon dark clouds arose from various directions, which I do not propose to take up now—China's civil war is one of the clouds—and which finally made the Tariff Conference a mere abortive attempt. The Chinese people remain unsatisfied and dissatisfied.

*b*) *The Extrality Conference* was held at a very unfortunate time in our country. Our codes were carefully examined in Peking, and received the approbation of the Conference. But our civil strife did not give the Conference an adequate chance to study and investigate the administration of justice in different parts of China. Anyway, the Conference has already made its formal report, and we have to wait for what the future may bring to us. Meanwhile, extrality privileges are still being fully enjoyed by the foreigners in China.

I should not fail to mention in this connection the rendition of the Mixed Court in Shanghai which had been under negotiations for many years, but which was consummated last year. In its place the Chinese Provisional Court was organized. It is much too early to pass any judgment on this new court. However, it is important to point out that some of our best legally trained and judicially experienced men are now taking charge, and we have confidence in them.

### 3. GOVERNMENTAL MEMORANDA

During the past eight months several governments have issued memoranda in which their policies toward the situation have been enunciated. I shall try briefly to state the impression which these memoranda have made on the minds of the different people concerned.

*a*) *The British memoranda.* The British government issued its first memorandum last December in which the 2½ per cent surtax was conceded and an assurance of friendly treatment was given. This memorandum failed to receive a response from the Chinese people for the simple reason that it came six months too late. The 2½ per cent surtax was already being collected by Canton. Later the British government published a second memorandum which was intended to manifest a more conciliatory and friendly spirit, but the good effects of which were almost entirely obscured by the dispatch of troops to China by the British government at that time. Although the Willingdon Commission Report is not to be regarded as another memorandum, yet I wish to call the attention of the Institute to it and to say that the findings, when finally carried out, may help greatly to restore the cordial relations between the two countries.

*b*) *The American memorandum.* Shortly after the first British memorandum came out the American government, in a long statement, defined its China policy. The Chinese people were impressed by the great legal care with which the document was prepared. It was felt, however, that the memorandum did not make plain enough the true friendship which the American people have for China and the Chinese people in their struggle to reconstruct their nation on democratic lines.

*c*) *The Japanese memoranda.* Baron Shidehara, in the speech which he delivered before the Japanese Imperial Diet on January 18, 1927, declared his government's policy in regard to the relations between China and Japan. A favorable impression was created at the time, but unfortunately it was almost completely annulled by the recent Tanaka pronouncement and action.

*d*) *The Chinese memoranda.* Meanwhile, memoranda were issued by Hankow, Peking, and Nanking, each announcing its policy and guaranteeing protection to foreign life and property within its jurisdiction. These memoranda did not succeed any better because the evacuation of foreigners on a large scale and the dispatch of foreign troops and gunboats continued without interruption.

### 4. FOREIGN TROOPS AND GUNBOATS

We have today in China thousands of foreign troops and between one and two hundred foreign gunboats. China has been charged as being unable to offer protection. "For defensive purposes," as announced, the British government has sent over 30,000 soldiers to Shanghai; the Japanese government has dispatched several thousand to Shantung; and the other foreign governments have also done whatever they claimed their own interests demanded. On the other hand, the Chinese people are convinced that whatever danger there may be to foreign life and property in the course of our revolution can scarcely be used to justify the action of the foreign governments in dispatching their troops and gunboats to Chinese territory, which is a distinct infringement of our sovereignty. Likewise, they can hardly be led to believe that China exists mainly for her foreign trade. To reduce this question to the simplest terms, the presence of so many foreign troops and gunboats in Chinese territory at a time when the revolution in China is finding itself seriously threatened from without as well as within and when the nationalistic feeling is running high can hardly be denied as a most serious problem which requires immediate attention.

### 5. FOREIGN CONCESSIONS

I wish to call the attention of the Institute to (*a*) the Chen-O'Mally Agreement, by means of which the retrocession of the British concessions in Hankow and Kiukiang was sealed; (*b*) the conference between the Chinese and the British authorities in North China which might result in an agreement in regard to the British concession in Tientsin; and (*c*) the voluntary retrocession of its concession also in Tientsin by the Belgian government. These acts and agreements have been looked upon by my people, not as signs of weakness, but as an evidence of a new helpful and hopeful spirit in our mutual relations. The satisfactory progress already achieved should encourage us hopefully to seek for and to arrive at the proper solution for the other foreign concessions and settlements in China.

### 6. TREATIES

The Chinese people are themselves divided on a number of issues, but they are absolutely united in demanding and working for the abrogation of the unequal treaties. I am glad to point out that today not a few of the foreign governments look upon the old treaties as "antiquated and unsuited to modern conditions," and regard the demand for revision as "fundamentally reasonable," and have expressed their readiness to negotiate "with a China which is under one central government" or "with the contending governments even in the midst of the civil war." The Sino-Belgian Treaty has already been abrogated, and there have been a number of meetings with the object of forming a new treaty. The Sino-Japanese Treaty, the Sino-French Treaty, and the Sino-Spanish Treaty have all expired recently and several other treaties will expire within the next few years. I wish to point out that the abrogation of the old treaties and the formation of new ones on an equal and reciprocal basis constitutes the key to the solution of many problems in the relations between China and the foreign governments concerned. The sooner this work is started the better.

### 7. UNIFICATION OF CHINA

I must not give the Institute the wrong impression, that the Chinese people are charging up all our national ills and difficulties to the unsatisfactory foreign relations. We do not for a moment believe that the political unification of China will follow at once the abrogation of the unequal treaties and the signing of new and equal treaties. Effective internal unification will require more than this. Our true position is that we must solve our external and internal problems at the same time, as often they have most intricate and inseparable relations. To be sure, the Nationalist movement, which is the most hopeful movement in China today, has been working hard on these problems and also winning the confidence and increasing support of our people throughout the whole country.

*a*) *Northern expedition.* During the past two years the northern expedition of the Nationalist government has made phenominal progress. City after city, province after province, have yielded to the revolutionary army, or, more properly, themselves have embraced the revolutionary cause. Three weeks ago there had come under the jurisdiction of the Nationalists almost all of China, excepting only the northeastern section which was then comprised of northern Shantung, Chihli, Manchuria, and one or two special areas. By now the northern expedition may be much nearer its goal, and will reach it soon if it encounters no foreign intervention.

*b*) *Communistic influence.* This northern expedition the Communists within the Kuomintang greatly helped, but they also almost ruined it. It was due in no small measure to the splendid organization and fearless spirit of the Communists that the expeditionary force was driven over the mountains of Hunan and Kiangsi to the Yangtze Valley in a few months. At the same time the outrages instigated by the Communists at Nanking last March and the subsequent split between the Kuomintang and the Communist party resulted in rival governments at Hankow and Nanking and nearly wrecked an early unification of our country. Though the dangerous communistic influence still obtains in certain sections, yet its days seem to be numbered.

*c*) *New advance.* Up to less than a month ago Marshal Feng Yu-Hsiang was labeled "red" by the enemies of the Nationalist movement and was proclaimed by them as a staunch supporter of the communistic régime in Hankow, ready to attack both Nanking and Peking. At that time communication between Marshal Feng and the rest of China was almost completely cut off. Recently, at the Conference at Hsuchow, which is situated at a strategic junction of the Tientsin-Pukow and the Lunghai railways in northern Kiangsu, not only the myth of Marshal Feng's color was absolutely cleared up, but he and Marshal Chiang Kai-shek and all the important leaders of Nanking joined hands and pledged themselves, on the one hand, to clean up the Communist element within their own jurisdiction, and on the other hand, to complete within a short time the Northern expedition. While fortunes of war are uncertain, it will be difficult for such united efforts not to succeed in this new advance.

*d*) *The will of the Chinese people.* The strength of the will of the Chinese people has demonstrated itself time and again even in the brief history of our Republic. Those who have gone against this will have been defeated and finally eliminated, and those who have respected and obeyed it have met with success even in the midst of great odds. Any man who has been studying the situation in China cannot fail to discover the will of the Chinese people, viz., to unify our country politically through the proper and adequate solution of our internal and external problems. From experience, our people see clearly that to solve these problems we must not rely too much on force, but we must depend upon civil administration and peaceful measures. When 400,000,000 Chinese people make up their minds firmly enough on these matters, what force have we to resist or oppose them?

## CONCLUSION

Friends, I have, in a spirit of utmost sincerity, set before you the things which have happened in my country during the past two years and which cannot but have a profound influence on the Pacific relations. I have not passed judgment on them, and there is no necessity for it. Do we not agree, however, that we must study and discuss them, and if possible, reach some common understanding which will be capable of facilitating their early and satisfactory solution? During the next two weeks this company of true internationalists, and therefore sincere nationalists, will surely be able better to understand our Pacific problems, and through mutual understanding and co-operation greatly to improve our Pacific relations. May our efforts not cease until our common goal is reached!

## OPENING STATEMENT FOR THE BRITISH GROUP

SIR FREDERICK WHYTE, K.C.S.I.
Formerly President, National Indian Legislative Assembly

It has become a commonplace in recent times to say that the future of peace and war lies in the Pacific. Viewing the entire world-scene it would be truer to say that whereas Europe has hitherto been the center of the world and still remains its most important political area, the Eastern Hemisphere has emerged to challenge the predominance of the West, and that the world of international affairs now revolves upon the two poles of Orient and Occident. The polar simile is here used to convey the idea that if these two areas are in fact poles apart, they are not isolated, and they can be—nay, must be—regarded as decisive factors, influencing each other in the equilibrium of the whole. By their action and reaction the future growth of the entire globe will be decided.

Now, the United States of America, in virtue of their geographical position, their immense resources, and their potential political power, and the British Commonwealth, in virtue of its world-wide character, stand in a position of peculiar influence and responsibility. These two, above all other nations, can influence and are influenced by every current that passes between the two poles of East and West, and therefore the policy pursued by their government, either independently or in co-operation, may well prove to be the decisive factor in establishing a true equilibrium. In laying down the preliminary axiom we are only concerned with the whole international situation, and the position assigned to Britain and America does not imply any derogation whatsoever from the sovereign importance within their own sphere of the political action of China and Japan. It is none the less incontrovertible that the peoples of America and the British Commonwealth stand in a position of responsibility which they cannot evade.

The policy pursued by all concerned is therefore a matter of urgent concern, and since the policy of every nation is undergoing substantial changes it is important to study the facts which have influenced the alterations in policy. We here are not concerned with the execution of policy, nor are we responsible for the diplomatic action of our respective governments. We are therefore able to seek the truth in all things. It is the proclaimed function of the Institute of Pacific Relations (*a*) to search for the facts out of which all policy is born, and (*b*) when the facts are known, to examine all national policies without prejudice in order to see whether they really correspond with the facts. To the fulfilment of that function we of the British delegation will contribute all that lies in our power. We shall put all our cards on the table, eschewing propaganda and offering our cordial co-operation to all.

Before I come to the main text of this statement, let me say that I can offer you here only my own interpretation of British ideals and British policy. Nevertheless, what you are about to hear represents broadly the consensus of opinion in a mixed group containing members of all parties and of no party in Great Britain. Moreover, it may claim to express the general opinion of those, a vast and growing number, who look to the future and not to the past. I am in no sense an official voice, nor do I claim to be representative in any but a general sense.

Pacific relations are of many kinds, and, as the program of the Institute shows, they are to be treated in many different ways. But they find the center of their interest in the political sphere because in that sphere national policies meet in those contacts that produce peace and war.

There is a general sense, no doubt, in which everything that pertains to the Pacific Ocean has an interest for Great Britain. Britain is a world-power, with territorial possessions in the Pacific. In Fiji she has a point of real contact where Polynesia, China, and India meet, and a study in land tenure in which her mistakes are as instructive as her successes. In the New Hebrides, and at a hundred lesser points, she has political and commercial interests. In Hongkong she holds an island possession in which she has created a wide and safe gateway for European trade in China. In Singapore, which looks out upon the narrow waters that join the Indian and Pacific oceans, she has made a great entrepôt of trade for all nations. And upon the surface of this great ocean itself her merchant ships move to and fro in such numbers that peace in the Pacific is the greatest of her mercantile interests. She is thus a trading power with interests everywhere. Moreover, she is a partner in the British Commonwealth, with three other partners vitally concerned in the Pacific. Questions arising out of this partnership I leave on one side because they will be more appropriately treated by the representatives of Canada, Australia, and New Zealand. Questions of trade, except where they are interwoven with political interests, are a special subject that will be treated at one round table or another. It is therefore Pacific relations as a political subject, with special regard to contemporary China, that are our concern here.

Our special regard for contemporary China, however, cannot lead us to minimize or misinterpret the well-nigh decisive importance of Japan. The proximity of Japan to China, and the vital needs of the Japanese people, combine to give Japanese policy a significance in the future political development of the Far East which is so obvious that it requires no emphasis. Moreover, in present circumstances the policy of Japan is influenced, like the policy of all other nations, by changing conditions in China; and while the ultimate aim remains substantially the same, the method pursued by her appears to have altered in several important respects. With the ultimate aim, which is to secure access to the natural resources necessary for the livelihood of her people, no one can fail to sympathize. Apart from method, which varies from time to time, and has sometimes been open to serious objection, there is no fundamental reason in Japanese policy which should prevent all concerned from reaching a permanent and constructive agreement on the basis of the Four Power Treaty signed at Washington in 1922.

I am aware that some of my Japanese friends regard that treaty as the decent shroud which incloses the corpse of the Anglo-Japanese Alliance, but I suggest that it is something more. There are no doubt reasons to regret the ending of the Alliance. Without it the world might have been plunged into general war twenty years ago, for the Russo-Japanese conflict could hardly have been localized if Great Britain had not given public notice that any power which attempted to widen the area of hostilities would automatically find itself at war with her. The Japanese treaty was not merely a warning to Russia that there were limits to her aggression in the Orient; it was Lord Salisbury's safest insurance against something that threatened to become a world-war. The Alliance served a vital purpose in its beginning; it promoted much that was good both in British and in Japanese policy during its life, and it performed unforgetable services in the World War. None the less, its record was defaced by serious blemishes which the impartial observer has often and rightly singled out for severe reprobation. The War itself radically changed the conditions which originally gave it birth and it could only have continued to exist in the absence of something better.

To the question, "Is the Four Power Treaty better than the Anglo-Japanese Treaty which it replaces?" the answer must surely be "yes." But this affirmative answer, let us admit, is only in respect of the promise that the Washington Treaty seems to contain as well as the substance of its actual clauses. To put it in another way, and looking at it from an objective and international point of view, there are fewer objections to the Four Power Treaty than to the former Alliance. And conversely, the Four Power Treaty holds a greater promise of good than the other. I should be the first to regret the Alliance if I thought that the Four Powers were not prepared to develop upon the foundation of their treaty a new and more permanent structure of peace. Therefore if we are asked to approve of the policy which brought the Alliance to an end and put the new quadruped in its place, we can only give a conditional approval, conditional on the nature of the constructive policy which the four Pacific powers can be persuaded to pursue in common.

Finally, Japan and Great Britain stand in a new relation to each other in virtue of their common membership in the League of Nations. They have both assumed new obligations under the Covenant of the League which in some ways are more extensive than any which the Anglo-Japanese Treaty contained.

So leaving for the moment the Japanese aspect, we come to China. Now the policy of today, which springs from a sincere recognition of Chinese rights, can only be appreciated if it is placed in its historical setting. It was for the purpose of depicting this background in broad strokes that the little book entitled *China and Foreign Powers* was prepared and distributed to the members of this Conference. As a historical introduction it does not claim to be exhaustive, and my British colleagues and I will welcome any suggestion for its improvement. In proceeding to the description of British policy in China I will ask you to allow me to assume that you are aware of the general outline of its contents.

British policy in China took a new turn at, or perhaps I should say after, the Washington Conference of 1921–22. The treaties signed at that time committed the powers to certain principles of which you are all aware. The acceptance of these principles represented a real new departure for some of the powers, while for others these principles were only the restatement of a policy which the latter had already pursued for some time. But Washington, however important in substance or in theory, was only the first step. We are here concerned with the development of the Washington policy in action. Now, for Great Britain, what was that development? I leave on one side, for the moment, *but only for the moment,* any attempt to explain why the next steps in the Washington policy were delayed for several years. I do so because I can best use the time available this morning in describing what British policy is now. And for this purpose we will go to the source in the explicit and sincere declarations of the British government. In September, 1925, Sir Austen Chamberlain said:

> Our only wish is for a strong, united, independent, orderly and prosperous China. We, on our side, will contribute all we can; we are ready to meet China halfway. We are ready to relinquish special rights just in proportion as the Chinese Government can assure to our nationals the due enjoyment of the ordinary rights of foreigners in their country.

Now, governments, alas, move slowly; and events never wait for them. It took the British government some time to put that statement into action; but when it was put into action the policy was such as commanded the almost unanimous support of the British nation. And I hope that a clearer knowledge of what that policy is may dispel some of the misunderstandings which now impede its progress. Here is the policy in the measured words of the British memorandum to the Washington Treaty powers, dated December 18, 1926.

> His Majesty's Government propose that these Governments shall issue a statement setting forth the essential facts of the situation; declaring their readiness to negotiate on treaty revision and all other outstanding questions as soon as the Chinese themselves have constituted a Government with authority to negotiate; and stating their intention pending the establishment of such a Government to pursue a construc-

tive policy in harmony with the spirit of the Washington Conference but developed and adapted to meet the altered circumstances of the present time.

His Majesty's Government propose that the Powers should make it clear that in their constructive policy they desire to go as far as possible toward meeting the legitimate aspirations of the Chinese nation. They should abandon the idea that the economic and political development of China can only be secured under foreign tutelage, and should declare their readiness to recognize her right to the enjoyment of tariff autonomy as soon as she herself has settled and promulgated a new national tariff. They expressly disclaim any intention of forcing foreign control upon an unwilling China. While calling upon China to maintain that respect for the sanctity of treaties which is the primary obligation common to all civilized States, the Powers should yet recognize both the essential justice of the Chinese claim for treaty revision and the difficulty under present conditions of negotiating new treaties in place of the old, and they should therefore modify their traditional attitude of rigid insistence on the strict letter of treaty rights. During this possibly very prolonged period of uncertainty the Powers can only, in the view of His Majesty's Government, adopt an expectant attitude and endeavour to shape developments so far as possible in conformity with the realities of the situation so that ultimately, when treaty revision becomes possible, it will be found that part at least of the revision has already been effected on satisfactory lines. It would therefore be wise to abandon the policy of ineffective protest over minor matters, reserving protest—which should then be made effective by united action—only for cases where vital interests are at stake. Every case should be considered on its merits and the declaration should show that the Powers are prepared to consider in a sympathetic spirit any reasonable proposals that the Chinese authorities, wherever situated, may make, even if contrary to strict interpretation of treaty rights, in return for fair and considerate treatment of foreign interests by them. The declaration should show that it is the policy of the Powers to endeavour to maintain harmonious relations with China without waiting for or insisting on the prior establishment of a strong Central Government.

Now here is a new departure. It is new because hitherto the treaty powers have always endeavored to act together, and have always lost valuable time, irrecoverably, in the attempt to agree beforehand what they should do. The needs of the time were too urgent to allow of any such delay, and therefore the British government determined to go ahead along a very difficult road.

It is also new for another reason. Governments do not usually attempt to deal with any authority in any nation that is not the established and authentic government wielding full sovereign power over its subjects. I say deliberately, "usually"! But here we are face to face with the unusual. The British government acknowledges that the present situation is unusual and has acted accordingly. It does not wait for or insist upon the establishment of a strong central government in China before putting its policy into practice. And here let us give you the British Foreign Minister's words once more:

There is no such Government in China today. But the demand for treaty revision is becoming—or has become—so insistent, and is fundamentally so reasonable, that, in spite of all the difficulties involved by the prevailing dissensions among the Chinese, we must try to negotiate this change with the contending Governments, even in the midst of civil war. That this was our intention was made perfectly clear in the Memorandum of British policy which was published on December 26. It is difficult, in such circumstances, to pursue the policy, but we shall persevere in the attempt because we feel that it is the right, and the only right, thing to do.

One more quotation, before I proceed to show how Great Britain has endeavored to put her pledges into action. At the same meeting in Birmingham, on January 29, 1927, Sir Austen Chamberlain used the following words:

I have reminded you that in 1925 I said that we would meet China halfway. You will see, from what I have said, that we are going more than halfway, but I am certain that this is a right and wise course. We do not disguise from ourselves the inconveniences and the difficulties of the moment, but we are thinking of our relations with China for the next 100 years.

His Majesty's Government will not be deflected from their policy of patient conciliation, nor will their efforts to reach satisfactory agreements with the Chinese authorities in any degree slacken or cease. On the contrary, I heartily welcome and I reciprocate the desire expressed in his recent declaration by the Nationalist Minister for Foreign Affairs for a settlement of treaty and other cognate questions on the basis of economic equality and mutual respect for each other's political and territorial sovereignty.

Now declarations are only words. Their significance is seen in the acts which follow words. What are those acts which give British policy their significance today?

1. Great Britain has negotiated the rendition of Wei hai wei, and the agreement only awaits the signature of a competent Chinese authority.

2. Great Britain has signed an agreement with the Nationalist government for the transformation of her concession at Hankow into a self-governing municipality, and has done the same at Kiukiang.

3. Great Britain is now negotiating regarding the concession at Tientsin.

4. Great Britain has, in company with the other powers, restored the Mixed Court in Shanghai to Chinese control.

5. Great Britain has relinquished her share in the Boxer Indemnity, has accepted the principle of tariff autonomy, and has undertaken to negotiate new treaties with China on the basis of economic equality and mutual respect for each other's political and territorial sovereignty.

Why do I recite these well-known facts? To show you that the pledges of the British nation are real. These things are not the end; they are only the beginning of our new relation with China. They are not the proposals merely of our party in Great Britain. They have behind them the united mind of my countrymen. May I ask you to make them the starting-point of our work in this conference? They are but the first steps on the road of new relations between China and Great Britain; and I hope to learn from the discussions in our round tables next week how we may proceed farther and faster along that road.

We are here to learn, by the formation of new friendships and by sincere discussion, how the friction between two great civilizations may be abated and how co-operation may eventually take its place.

My friends, I see beyond the political troubles of today an era in our relations with China in which we shall be equal not only in intention but in fact. The movements and counter-movements which so confuse us in the China of 1927, the violence with which the national spirit is being generated before our very eyes, the incidents which arise out of the present revolution: these things, all of them, create problems for governments and often produce most unhappy results; but these things, all of them, are unfailing signs of life; and we know that when a nation is reborn the pangs of its new birth are extreme. New China, we salute; New China in promise, in process of creation; and, if there is a part which, under providence, we can play in promoting her new growth, we shall gladly play it.

# THE GENERAL FEATURES OF PACIFIC RELATIONS AS VIEWED BY JAPAN

DR. MASATARO SAWAYANAGI
President, Imperial Educational Association of Japan

We members of the Japanese group have come to this conference with high expectations. We gained much from the first session in 1925, but we hope for more from this second session. We have come to learn far more than to teach. We are simply a group of individuals, like the rest of you, and it is needless to add that we do not represent our government. Furthermore, we are not agreed among ourselves on many of the questions here to be discussed. In what I am now about to say, for example, I am not representing the unanimous opinion of my fellow-members. But I venture to speak my own view with the utmost frankness in the expectation that members from other countries will be equally frank. This Institute, I believe, is one place where everyone is supposed to have been immunized against having either his national or personal feelings hurt.

The Pacific Ocean is gradually becoming the center of the world, and Japan has become firmly lodged in the thinking of internationally minded people as one of the important Pacific powers. As such, Japan's future is inseparably linked with the slowly unfolding destiny of the great Pacific area.

If we look back only seventy years, however, we have to admit that our point of view was regrettably different. Before she was opened to the world's intercourse, Japan entertained a curious self-consciousness that she was the most enlightened nation in the world. But when the closed gate was swung open and the flood of Western civilization flowed in, we were brought face to face with the achievements of the Western countries and we were challenged with a new situation, namely, that Japan was far behind the West in various frontiers of human progress. How to adjust herself to this challenging situation and how to overtake the Western nations and thenceforth keep in step with them thus became the task to which the whole nation, government and people alike, addressed itself.

The seventy years of strenuous struggle which followed, in the course of which Japan left no stone unturned in learning things Western, spelled the astonishing achievements of the Meiji and Taisho eras. With sheer force of determination and unceasing effort through half a century, Japan rightfully earned the place she coveted in the comity of the great powers. As a result, Japan has replaced her sense of inferiority to Western nations by a realization that she could appreciate and master the secrets of the West.

The first fruit of this belief was the discovery by the leaders that Japan commands a strategic position in the blending of two distinctive systems of culture, the harmonization of the Western and Eastern civilizations. In fact, modern Japan is a child whose grandfather was the Eastern civilization which came from India and China and whose father was the Western civilization which came from Europe and America. Being still a child, Japan has as yet very little to contribute toward the happiness and cultural attainment of the world. But she is perfectly aware of her indebtedness to these cultural creditor-nations. What has Japan in store to contribute to them in repayment of her debt?

In answering this question some Japanese maintain that the chief characteristic of the Western civilization is material, that Japan represents the essence of the Eastern civilization which is spiritual, and that therefore she can communicate spiritual things to the West. I for one disclaim such an attitude. On the other hand, I believe with the majority of our thinking people that Japan is in the position to create a richer and more balanced civilization by harmoniously combining the best of the two civilizations, spiritual and material. This is and must remain the real mission of Japan as a Pacific power, and herein lie Japan's cultural aspirations.

Whichever course this supreme endeavor may take in the future, I am fully convinced of one thing: that we must follow the slow but steady road of peaceful procedure. By means of new achievements and discoveries in art and sciences, and new development in political and social as well as industrial fields, we are determined to do our best in repaying our cultural debt to our sister nations of the world.

If we now look closer into the present condition in Japan one cannot overlook the amazing advance in the material comforts of life which the Japanese people have made during the same period of seventy years. This is best exemplified in the elevation of the standard of her living. At the same time the population has increased with leaps and bounds. As a result of these two phenomena Japan is today facing a series of acute problems, of which the greatest is undoubtedly the problem of population and food supply.

Of all the methods proposed in meeting this problem, such as emigration, industrialization, further intensification of agriculture, birth control, and others, the one which is most vital to Japan and on which the Japanese people are most sensitive is the first, the question of emigration. However, as we look over the world-situation from this angle, the density of population in Europe is nearly as great as Japan, and it is only in the Pacific countries, especially in Australia and North and South America, that there are vest territories still undeveloped and sparsely settled. And in almost all these countries Japan faces the stone wall of exclusion. Before Japan realized the serious pressure of her population and the limitation of her food supply the doors of these countries were wide open; now when she is eagerly trying to alleviate the pressure, these doors have been shut in her face.

Before I go farther, however, I wish to affirm emphatically that we are not trying to reopen the immigration issue at this time. Our government fully respects the sovereign right of nations to enact exclusion laws, but only questions the right of enacting discriminatory laws on the basis of race. On the other hand, Japan humbly expects other nations to respect her honor and sovereignty in the same degree that she respects their sovereignty, and, when her honor is at stake, she feels that she has the sovereign right to protest against invidious discrimination. In short, the issue is not so much the question of sovereign right to exclude certain racial groups as respect or disrespect toward another sovereign state which is jealous of her dignity.

In trying to solve this difficult problem of population we are certain of one thing: Japan will never resort to arms on account of the immigration issue. It is true in Japan as in all other countries that a few chauvinists may be found who are voicing such an idea; but the intelligentsia and the general public will never hearken to their opinion. In fact, Japan, like her sister nations of the East, has long been and will remain a peace-loving nation, and will never entertain the thought of going to war over the question of population.

I am also convinced of another and perhaps more important thing. The only satisfactory method of solving the problem of immigration is, not through discriminatory legislation, but through the recognition by the nations bordering on the Pacific Ocean of the natural right of immigration. We are living in the new day when the notion of unlimited individualism is undergoing a decided change and the spirit of social sharing and co-operation is gradually gaining ground. I believe that the natural right of all humankind to share the resources of the world on some equitable basis and to enjoy freedom of movement and residence will be recognized by the thinking leaders of all progressive lands. This recognition will come, however, not simply as a desire to relieve the pressure of population, but as a result of unreserved acceptance of justice and fair play as fundamental principles of international and interracial relations. Naturally, I believe that it will be realized first in the most progressive and enlightened country. Already the dawn of such a day is being voiced by far sighted thinkers. Japan will patiently await the coming of that day because, after weighing various proposed solutions, it seems to me to be the most rational and the only lasting solution.

In realizing the natural right of migration, however, we confront several barriers, often labeled, "reasons" for exclusion. The most widely discussed one is the standard of living. But the standard of living is a matter of adjustment, and not of dogmatic, unvarying principle, as witness the history of all migrations of races. Here comes into play an important principle, namely, if the same standard of living as obtains in a receiving country is maintained by immigrants coming from a country with a lower standard of living, then there is no just economic ground for denying to them the right of immigration.

The countries bordering the Pacific Ocean embrace two mighty branches of the human race, the white and the yellow or brown. They are mighty races, proud of their past and ambitious for the future. On the part of the white race, at least, a strong feeling has developed that only by artificial barriers can their racial identity be maintained. A sense of racial superiority has grown up and has denied the natural right of migration. The fetish of race superiority, even more than economic standards, is, I believe, the determining factor in the American exclusion law; even in Australia the dictation test seems to me merely a scheme to dress up the discriminatory immigration policy in a transparent disguise. The intrinsic superiority or inferiority of races is a fable, with the possible exception of some of the vanishing races, unsupported by anthropology, psychology, and sociology. It is a matter of sentiment rather than of reason, and we can remove the unnecessary fear and sentimentalism through education based upon scientific investigation. Here again we look to such an impartial group as this Institute for a priceless contribution.

The difficulty of cultural assimilation is another barrier which is often invoked to retard the realization of the natural right of migration. The belief in the non-assimilability of certain races is again the product of dogmatism and ignorance. In spite of the charges very often brought against the Japanese that they resist assimilation, their assimilability has been conclusively proved in various ways. The Survey of Race Relations on the Pacific Coast, for example, has gathered many cases showing that the second generation of Japanese are well-nigh completely assimilated to American life in a comparatively short time. The cultural absorption of Western elements by modern Japan as a whole is another convincing illustration. Thus we can see that the charge of the non-assimilability of Japanese has been a rash and unsupported generalization; we only need to study this question more impartially in order to reach a rational conclusion.

I purposely left the problem of China to the last, not because it is unimportant, but because what I wanted to say is simple and clear. The liberal element in Japan is heartily in sympathy with the difficulties which China is facing today, and I wish to extend our hand of unreserved co-operation in realizing the aspirations of New China.

So I return to where I began. Japan is today rightfully called a Pacific power and her future is inseparably bound up with the destinies of her fellow-nations of the Pacific Basin. As we face the future we are spellbound with the magnitude of our task. On the one hand we hope to create a richer and better-balanced civilization embodying the best gifts of both East and West. On the other hand we are facing the difficult task of solving our population and food problems which can be done only through the tolerance and enlightened co-operation of all the nations bordering the Pacific. Herein lies our chief interest in the work of the Institute of Pacific Relations.

# PACIFIC RELATIONS FROM THE VIEWPOINT OF THE KOREAN GROUP

MISS HELEN K. KIM
Dean of Ewha College, Seoul

The Korean delegation brings hearty greetings and congratulations from the Korean Council on Pacific Relations and from the people at large to the members of the Institute of Pacific Relations, our brothers and sisters from Australia, Canada, China, Great Britain, Hawaii, Japan, New Zealand, Philippine Islands, and the United States of America. We take an unusual delight in attending this conference. A sentence in the report of the Committee on Permanent Organization made our coming possible. The sentence reads as follows: "The Institute of Pacific Relations is a body of men and women deeply interested in the Pacific area, who meet and work, not as representatives of their Governments, or of any other organizations, but as individuals in order to promote the well-being of the peoples concerned." We are happy, not only because we can attend the Institute, but also because we are assured of the fact that the Institute is going to keep up the fraternal spirit in which it was originated. And being one with you in spirit and aims, we will participate in words when fitting and in silence when expedient.

The world around the Pacific area is endeavoring to find a new way of life, a way which will put an end to present evils such as poverty, misunderstanding, and injustice, and a way which will create peace, good will, and co-operation among mankind. Such a purpose brought the peoples together more than once in the past; but why the non-achievement? Our remote ancestors let superstition guide their action. Then later on in the course of evolution they allowed unexamined and uncriticized emotions direct their lives. And even now we are not wholly emancipated from that error. But these stages have been stepping-stones to a higher level on which we aspire to stand. And that new way is to have our highest ethical ideals guide the actions of our peoples. And that higher level is where we let the ethical standards judge the peoples. It is not the test of physical force and material goods that should determine who the powers of the world are, but rather how much a people can endure, serve, and sacrifice. Patience, service, and sacrifice in the real sense are going to be more and more recognized as the qualifications for world-citizenship. When the ethical standard becomes the compass of the world's life many of our present-day problems will be solved. The legal rights of possession, although generally recognized at the present time, are so prickly that they hurt our feelings and work against international friendship. But when we prefer the moral rights to the legal such questions as immigration and food supply will be answered, in their feeling aspects at least. The new world of peace is waiting for the Institute of Pacific Relations to initiate the usage of the ethical standard into all international relationships. And we feel in our humble way that Korea can take a definite stand of recognizing such a standard.

Korea's history of over four thousand years without a single record of an aggressive war waged against another people, together with her educational system centering around the ethical texts, vindicate her stand. One may think that the reason why Korea could never invade another people was because she never had the military strength to do so. Let history itself speak. In 591 A.D. when an army of 1,130,000 soldiers invaded the country, the Korean army under General Ulji Moonduk defeated them at one attempt. Again in 1592 A.D. Admiral Ye Soonsin totally defeated the naval invaders on the Korean Strait. Wars fought for protective purposes show that Koreans could invade and exploit another people if they wanted to. But they never did, and this was not an accident. Their peace-loving nature kept them from such an inhuman act as war, except for self-protection. From the beginning to the end of a child's education he was taught and drilled in virtues such as loyalty, filial piety, trustworthiness, obedience, patience, kindness and respect for the elder. The core of our education was ethical. And no matter how clever and skilful a person might be, if he lacked these virtues and shirked his responsibility the decent people would have nothing to do with him. Virtue was the first requisite for success in all the walks of life from butchery to kingship. Korea's complete disarmament and her zeal for the ideals of peace and brotherhood at the present, as well as in the past, assure her stand at least in the near future. Not a single sword nor a gun, not a single submarine nor an aeroplane do the Korean people have in their possession. And none of our youth is being wasted in training to kill human brothers. In spite of the factors that have brought us to such a state we are proud of the fact. We are disarmed and we challenge the world to disarm completely and work out justice, peace, and universal brotherhood with reason and love.

Within the last year two very significant organizations of the people came into existence which tell something about developments since the last session of the Institute of Pacific Relations. First is Sin-kan Hoi, which has the three following items in its purpose: (1) We will endeavor to quicken the political and economic sense of the people. (2) We will intensify the spirit of unity of our people. (3) We will not under any circumstances recognize opportunism. Any man or woman above twenty years of age can become a member provided that he or she is in sympathy with its purpose. And last June when we left Korea it already had after four and a half months' existence thirty local chapters and a membership of three thousand. Secondly, there is Kun-woo Hoi, which has for its purpose the unification and uplift of the status of women of Korea. It is a feminist movement with an educational program as the starting-point. Membership is allowed to any woman of higher education who is in sympathy with its purpose. In both of these organizations, socialists and nationalists, Christians and Confucianists, Buddhists and Chundoists[1] are pooling their experiences, their material, and mental resources to carry on a common project. It is generally realized that nothing short of united efforts will enable us to overcome the insurmountable difficulties lying in the way of better days. The church organizations are also working for union, which will mean stronger and more efficient machinery for bringing in the Kingdom of God. And all these efforts have in view the common object of making Korea a valuable member of the world.

The rest of the paper is going to be devoted to telling you only one of our outstanding problems. That is the problem of the economic reconstruction of Korea. The Korean population in Korea is 18,543,000. Out of that, 14,600,000 people are farmers. In other words, 80 per cent of the whole comprise the agricultural population. The average yearly income of each farmer is 13 mal[2] of grain, of which 8 mal is consumed for food and only 5 mal, twenty yen or ten dollars, is left for clothing, shelter, medicine, education, etc. Two-thirds of that agricultural population are tenants tilling somebody else's land. In order to improve the land and to increase the production there will have to be a way of making it possible for tenants to own their land. Both in Ireland and in Denmark during the last quarter of the nineteenth century bills have been passed to lay aside each year a big sum of money from the imperial treasury to loan to the tenants on low interest so as to enable them to pay back the principal and interest and gradually come to own the land in a reasonable number of years. The McNary-Haugen bill, or farmer's relief bill of the United States, which I understand did not pass Congress, is also to protect farmers. But no help of such kind is given to poor Korean peasants. They toil and suffer without a hopeful outlook for the future. Nevertheless, although very meager, there have been in the last two years certain steps taken by the people, definitely by the Y.M.C.A., to help the peasants improve their opportunities by teaching them the elementary but necessary knowledge of modern farming and the necessity for co-operative movements among themselves.

However, no matter what amazing improvements are brought about, the land of Korea is not big enough for all the agricultural population depending upon the soil for their living. The Korean population is also increasing. The statistics of 1925 show that the birth-rate was 38.4 per cent, the death-rate 20.7 per cent, making the increase 17.7 per cent. It is needless to say at this point that plans, if there are any, for moving other peoples into Korea are unreason-

[1] Chundoism is an indigenous religion in Korea, religion of the way of Heaven.

[2] Two mal is equal to one bushel.

able. When other industries are developed and the economic reconstruction is completed enabling us to guarantee a comfortable living to immigrants we will invite them in gladly. But at the present time even among our own farmers at least 20–30 per cent will have to be converted to some other industry. This also necessitates some organized financial backing. But the whole field of economics of the Korean people is in a chaotic and perilous condition, not organized and not systematized. And this economic problem is not a question of determining comfort nor culture for the Korean people, but it is a question of existence or subsidence to gradual disappearance. The solution of a great many other problems hinges on this.

History and the recent excavations show that when the Koreans navigated their own ship they somehow managed to find leisure to make inventions such as the printing press and iron turtle-boat and to produce magnificent and exquisite pieces of music, poetry, painting, sculpture, architecture, pottery, and other fineries. But now they are so absorbed and troubled about finding the means and ways of their physical sustenance that their innate possibilities and capacities are laid aside undeveloped and unrealized. The fullest development of the Korean people is also an enrichment of all peoples around the Pacific. And our welfare means your welfare as much as your welfare means our welfare. So we claim your brotherly co-operation in hastening the better days for Koreans which we know are coming. And we humbly offer ourselves for any service we are capable of rendering in solution of your problems.

# A NEW ZEALAND OUTLOOK ON PACIFIC AFFAIRS

WALTER NASH
Secretary of the New Zealand Labor Party

New Zealand is an integral part of the British Commonwealth of Nations. Its outlook upon both internal and external problems is deeply affected by its relationship with the other nations within that Commonwealth, and by its view of the obligations which membership in that Commonwealth involves. No account of New Zealand's political and economic problems and points of view would give a true perspective unless it emphasized the close relation which exists between New Zealand and the mother country.

New Zealand is essentially British in tradition, population, and outlook. Its early settlers were drawn from some of the finest elements in English society, and the earliest settlements were founded to a great extent under the auspices of religious organizations, especially the Church of England and the Free Church of Scotland. Other organized settlements were carried out under the Wakefield system. Under all these schemes of settlement high regard was paid to the character of the immigrant and care was exercised in his selection. These immigrants carried with them British traditions and British ways of life, so that each young community became almost a facsimile of the communities in England and Scotland from which they had sprung. Many of them, in deciding to emigrate, were no doubt influenced by a desire to lead a fuller, freer, and less circumscribed life than was possible for them in their native country. This desire was not grounded in any deep-seated sense of injustice at home such as impelled some emigration from Britain. These circumstances, coupled with the fact that the immigrants found themselves in a country of equable climate and fertile soil and one capable of comparatively easy economic development, provided an atmosphere especially favorable for the maintenance of English standards and ideals in their new country, and also enabled the newcomers to advance along the lines of political democracy and social experiment.

But in spite of the strong attachment between New Zealand and Britain, New Zealand would strongly resent any interference in her internal affairs on the part of the British government; and, as in the case of all the British dominions, Great Britain recognizes our right to complete local autonomy. In matters of foreign policy New Zealand rarely questions the attitude or policy of Great Britain. This support of British foreign policy is illustrated by the attitude of New Zealand toward the development of the naval base at Singapore. This question, together with questions arising out of the industrialization of the

East and the exploitation of the resources of tropical and subtropical islands of the Pacific, are the chief matters involving external policy which concern pacific relations.

Opinion in New Zealand at the present time supports the declared policy of the British government with regard to the Singapore base. The arguments upon which support of the base is founded are briefly: (1) that the British fleet is one of the great securities for the peace of the world; (2) that this security can only be maintained by providing the fleet with means to operate effectively; (3) that a naval base at Singapore is the one place from which the fleet can operate effectively in the Pacific area; (4) that if you exclude the Pacific from the area in which the British fleet is effective you exclude one of the greatest instruments for maintaining world-peace.

If it is admitted that it is desirable to make the British navy an effective instrument in the Pacific, then a naval base is necessary and Singapore is probably the most convenient place. Opponents of the base, however, state that the price of the instrument may be too great. It is said that a naval base for merely defensive purposes is not possible, and accepting this argument implies that it is essential for the base to be an instrument of offensive possibility. The best defense is often attack. It is also said that Singapore must be so constructed as to enable the British navy to function effectively in the Pacific.

If the case for the establishment of the base is accepted and the argument of the efficiency of the British navy as a peace instrument admitted, then it is correct to say that it would afford a complete defense to Australia and New Zealand. This is the reason why the New Zealand government has agreed—subject to confirmation by Parliament—to contribute, over a period of years, a million pounds toward the cost of the base. The urge behind the New Zealand government is purely one of defense. It believes that the development of the naval base at Singapore is essential and necessary to the well-being of New Zealand, and admitting this, it is correct and in order for New Zealand to make some contribution towards the cost. Believing that the policy of the government is purely for defensive purposes, a majority of New Zealanders support its policy.

The decision to make the contribution has been announced by the government. It is subject to confirmation by Parliament. A number of protests have been made against the government's action. The leader of the opposition in Parliament has issued a statement opposing the government's decision, but it is reasonable to assume that the government policy would be approved by a majority of New Zealand citizens.

### INDUSTRIALIZATION OF THE EAST

The next problem of outstanding importance is the rapid industrialization of the Eastern countries. Its particular interest to New Zealand is its effect on the markets of our primary produce. Ninety-four per cent of New Zealand's exports are supplied by the pastoral industries, and 80 per cent of our exports go to Great Britain. The price of these products is largely determined by the purchasing power of the British workers. The purchasing power of the British workers is largely determined by the demand from overseas for Britain's industrial products. The East has been one of the main customers for these products. As this demand declines, so will the price of our products be ill affected. The problem may be solved by a readjustment of exports, which may be satisfactory in the long run, but the transitory period generally means dislocation and loss. Our direct trade with the East—Japan and China—is very small, consisting mainly of wool exported to Japan and the import of manufactured articles in exchange. Improved communications, transportation, and mail are automatically drawing the East closer to New Zealand, and with wise administration this should be all for the good.

The development of the natural resources of the Pacific islands during the next ten years will need all the care and wisdom available to our statesmen. New Zealand is responsible for the government of the Cook Islands, Niue, and western Samoa. The problem to be faced is a complex one. The soils and climate of the islands render them particularly suitable for the production of tropical fruits. Tropical fruits are required by the older countries. The production of these fruits requires labor. The labor available at present is not sufficient profitably to exploit the resources. The introduction of more virile labor from overseas has tended to accentuate the problem. The native who previously worked a little has then a tendency to work still less. The exploitation of imported labor has not always been under the best of conditions. If the imported laborer survives he will displace the native—which means ultimate extinction for the latter.

Another question arising is as to the right of the exploiting newcomers to take over the natural resources and to say in effect to the native: "Unless you work in my way, your lands will be taken from you, and your race will die." The native has lived, is living, and can live without the white man. Under normal conditions his natural aptitude, his customs, and his spirit of adventure will enable him to overcome his present environment, and in equity the duty of the white races is to determine how best they can assist the native.

An answer is required to the question, "By what means can the white races assist the natives of the Pacific to a fuller life?"

The policy of New Zealand is to foster and encourage the native to use his own land and to adjust his customs and means of obtaining a livelihood to something more approximating the standards and methods of the twentieth century. To do this will take time, but every effort is being made to try it out. All parties in Parliament are agreed as to the justice and need of assisting the native to develop his own country. As far as possible, and as soon as possible, the natural resources of the islands of the Pacific should be made available to the world; and the New Zealand government is doing all that is possible to realize this end.

In western Samoa at the present time a difference of opinion has arisen regarding the methods of securing the efficient administration of the islands. The New Zealand government has through its administration taken power to deport persons who so act as to interfere with the normal course of government, which may stir up strife in the islands to the disadvantage of all. There has been much criticism of the administration methods, but all parties in Parliament are agreed that the interests of the natives are paramount. Mr. H. E. Holland, M.P., leader of the opposition in the New Zealand Parliament, speaking in the House of Representatives last month (while attacking the government policy) said: "So far as I am concerned, I will stand every time against whatever is detrimental to the interests of the Samoans." Referring to the administration of the islands, he said that when it was standing for the interests of the natives against any other section he would be pleased to support it.

The value of these statements is enhanced by the fact that they are made by the most ardent critic and opponent of the present government in New Zealand.

### UNEMPLOYMENT

The extent of unemployment in New Zealand today is greater than for any period during the past twenty years, and the position has become so acute that the central government and local governing authorities have instituted relief works.

The wages to be paid on these works have been the subject of much criticism and controversy. The officials of the labor unions and labor members of Parliament have strenuously fought the alleged low rates effected, contending that they menace the standard of living and working conditions which have operated for so many years.

The unemployment situation has been accentuated by immigration, the arrivals during the past five years exceeding 70,000 and showing a net increase of over 60,000, the proportion per head of population being greater than for any other British dominion. The large number of arrivals was due to the government policy of assisted immigration, under which the governments of New Zealand and Great Britain paid either in full or in part the boat fares of certain types of immigrants. The result of this policy has so effected the labor market that assisted immigration has been suspended for some months, and the government a short time ago announced that it had been suspended until September of the present year.

There is no policy of exclusion for the British emigrant. All parties are agreed that ultimately there will be room in New Zealand for a larger population, but the free incoming of large numbers of persons from overseas at the present time will reduce the standard of living, which the present Prime Minister says no party desires to do, and in this respect the opposition is in complete accord.

The present standard of living in New Zealand can only be maintained by careful organization of the natural resources of the dominion, which must be precedent to immigration. This organization must be in the direction of better utilization of the land resources of the dominion, and this ultilization is complicated by the fact that during the past few years the land in occupation has slightly declined. This is largely due to the speculation in land which took place during the post-war boom period.

The price of land with butter at 224 shillings per cwt. is much higher than when butter is at 168 shillings per cwt. When butter prices rose, land prices advanced; and when butter prices declined, the land could not be profitably used at the price paid. Land settlement is now one of the major internal problems.

We have a magnificent country, with climate of the best and land of unsurpassed productivity, but speculation in land values has created a problem difficult to solve; and while there are some who feel that the present difficulties of land settlement will continue while speculation is allowed, yet the government is taking every step from research and educational viewpoints to exploit scientifically its land resources.

We are of the opinion that the co-ordination of the marketing of our primary products is of supreme importance, and steps in this direction have already been made by the setting up of boards to control the export of meat, dairy produce, honey, and fruit. Established by way of experiment, these boards have rendered splendid service to the producers in New Zealand, and with minor exceptions are approved by the whole of the people.

### TARIFF POLICY

For a brief period I wish to refer to the policy pursued by the government when determining what duties, if any, should be levied on imports into the dominion. The tariff policy of New Zealand may be set out under the following headings: (1) to extend preference to Britain and her dominions; (2) to provide machinery for reciprocal or special tariffs to meet the policies of other countries; (3) to maintain the protection granted to industries already established; (4) to admit free of duty raw materials which cannot be economically produced in the country; (5) to provide machinery to prevent dumping or unfair competition with industries established in New Zealand; (6) to grant protection to new industries only where it can be shown that a substantial amount of capital is invested, that the industry is fully equipped with the most modern appliances, that its output is likely to form a reasonable proportion of the total needs of the dominion, and that the goods produced are reasonably comparable with those produced abroad.

The tariff law provides for an intermediate tariff for countries which give specially favored treatment to New Zealand, but it has not been put into operation. The policy is founded on the principle that in the first stage the commercial intercourse of young nations with more advanced nations should be welcomed. In the second stage the young manufacturing industries of the country should be fostered by import duties which they are beginning to be able to make, and in the third stage protection, having done its work, should disappear.

New Zealand, though still young, comes within the scope of the second stage, and it is on this basis that the present policy is founded.

One of the main reasons given by a tariff commission—which reported to the government in 1921—for advocating protection was the unfair competition from low-paid labor in overseas countries with goods made in New Zealand under conditions regulated by the Arbitration Court. The state, so the report said, takes a prominent part in regulating labor conditions in order to keep the standard of living high, and the industries should be given some compensatng advantage by tariff protection. New Zealand will take all steps necessary to protect its present comparatively high standard of living and labor conditions.

New Zealand has in the past been a country of experiments. It was one of the first countries to institute old-age pensions. It was the first country to grant full electoral rights to women. It has a State Advances Department from which money is advanced at practically cost price to farmers for productive purposes, and to workers for house-building. It operates two state coal mines and runs all the railway systems. It conducts fire, accident, and life insurance.

In spirit the country is intensely British—some say more British than the British. We look at most problems through British spectacles. In trade, intercourse, migration, and finance we look 13,000 miles overseas to the motherland. It may be that we carry this policy to too great an extreme, but you will find in nearly all circles that England, Scotland, Ireland, and Wales are referred to as "Home" and the "Old Country."

Our relations with the Maori are the best. He is represented in the Houses of Parliament. A member of the race has been acting prime minister. You were all privileged last night to hear one of its distinguished sons in Dr. Buck, of whom we are so proud, but there are others: Sir James Carroll, Hon. A. T. Ngata, and Sir Maui Pomare would grace any gathering of any race or any nation.

If then the policy of New Zealand has won the co-operation and good will of the native, and the Briton and the Polynesian can go forward together in the march of the nations, I suggest Mr. Chairman, ladies and gentlemen, that New Zealand is a child that may well grow into a great and powerful nation. Not powerful by the might of its navy, or strength of its army, but powerful in that it was able to point out the way by which people of different color have realized that each is essential to all, and that the right of the individual to develop and express his or her personality to the full is the supreme right of all the individuals of all nations.

# PRESENT-DAY PROBLEMS OF THE PHILIPPINES

JUDGE FRED C. FISHER
Former Justice of the Supreme Court of the Philippines

As a preliminary to this brief statement of the problems which now confront the American and Filipino peoples with respect to their relations to one another, I wish to disclaim any authority to act as the spokesman of any group whatever. The views expressed are offered as my own, based upon an experience of nearly thirty years of active life in the Philippine Islands.

## THE BACKGROUND

The Philippine Archipelago is a group of islands with a combined area of some 114,000 square miles, lying to the southeast of Asia, wholly within the tropics. Two-thirds of that area is contained in the great islands of Luzon and Mindanao. The native people are almost exclusively of the Malay race, but there is an important element—nearly 8 per cent of the population—of people of mixed blood, principally Chinese and Spanish half-castes and their descendants. The population is now estimated at approximately eleven million, an increase of nearly four million since the cessation of Spanish sovereignty in 1898. This includes about six hundred thousand pagan people, dwelling in the mountainous regions, still at a very low stage of development, and the four or five hundred thousand Mohammedan inhabitants of Mindanao and Jolo. The term "Filipino" will be used in this paper generally to designate the native inhabitants of the Philippines other than the pagan primitives and the Mohammedans. The Filipinos depend almost exclusively upon agriculture. There is some mining and manufacture, but these activities are as yet of little relative importance.

A little more than half the area of the country is under forest. The land now under cultivation is not more than a third of the available area. Some twenty million acres of agricultural land are still available for settlement.

## THE CIVILIZATION OF THE FILIPINOS

The Filipinos differ radically from all other nations of the Orient in that they are Christians and that their civilization is essentially Occidental. When the Spaniards took the Philippines the native occupants of the lowlands had advanced far beyond the stage of savagery; but they had nothing even remotely approaching national unity. They made no concerted resistance to the establishment of Spanish sovereignty, and readily accepted the teachings of the newcomers, including their religion. For over three hundred years the Filipinos had either no education at all, or such only as they received from the Spaniards. During the latter half of the nineteenth century increasing numbers of Filipinos of the wealthier classes graduated from Spanish schools and colleges in the Islands, and many of them went to Spain to study. Their only intellectual contacts were with Europeans, through the medium of the Spanish language. There was practically nothing available in print in the native dialects, and they were completely out of touch with other Orientals. It was to the small Europeanized nucleus of educated Filipinos that their unlettered fellow-countrymen looked for leadership. Unlike other Oriental countries, there were in the Philippines no indigenous political institutions to constitute an obstacle to the acceptance of the principles and form of government which the Americans offered in place of the military and ecclesiastical oligarchy by which the Spaniards had governed the country. There was no native nobility or aristocracy as a ruling class. Lowly origin and early poverty were not barriers to success, then or now. The social position of the Filipino woman was practically one of equality with men.

### FUNDAMENTAL NEEDS

The situation, when order was restored after the period of war which followed the assumption of sovereignty over the Philippines by the United States, was that the people of the country were as a whole poor and ignorant, but eager to learn. They were the helpless victims of epidemic and endemic preventable disease. They possessed a country sparsely populated except in a few regions, rich in potential resources, but undeveloped. An epidemic of rinderpest had swept away over 80 per cent of their work animals. Their trade, domestic and foreign, was in alien hands. They were without a common language. They were ambitious to achieve political independence, but were without the men, the means, or the experience to maintain successfully an independent republican government. Their fundamental problems, then, were those relating to (1) education, (2) sanitation, and (3) economic development. These are the most important problems of the Filipinos today.

### EDUCATION

At the end of the nineteenth century the Filipinos as a whole were woefully ignorant. Outside of Manila, Iloilo, and Cebu very few could speak Spanish, and illiteracy was the prevailing condition. This, however, was due only to lack of opportunity. At all times since the establishment of the American government in the Philippines the Filipinos have been quick to profit by the facilities for education made available to them under the new order. It is to the everlasting credit of the educated Filipinos that they have always been earnestly anxious to give their less fortunate fellow-countrymen the benefits of instruction. The Philippine legislature is liberal in the appropriation of money for schools. Today over 27,000 teachers are employed in the public schools of the Islands, teaching over a million children. Thousands of Filipinos are now able to speak English well, and a much larger number have a fair working knowledge of it. Hundreds of students are enrolled in the universities. The last census (1918) gives a percentage of literacy of over 60 per cent among the people ten years old or over.

Nevertheless, while much has been accomplished, much more remains to be done. Less than half the children of school age are in school. Few of those who enter school remain more than three or four years. Of the 27,000 teachers in the schools, the Americans number little more than three hundred. Less than 5 per cent of the Filipino teachers are graduates of normal schools, colleges, or universities, and only a fraction over 10 per cent have gone through high school. A very large number have had no high-school training at all. The total number of students graduated from the government high schools from 1900 to 1925 was only 15,500. While the percentage of absolute illiteracy has been greatly reduced, comparatively few of the people who are able to read and write do either. The total circulation per issue of periodicals, daily, weekly, and monthly, in the Philippines in 1924 was approximately 150,000 for a population of eleven million: one paper for each 80 persons.

### SANITATION

While the climate of the Philippines is good, people and animals alike are subject to many tropical diseases. Smallpox, cholera, bubonic plague, leprosy, tuberculosis, malaria, and dysentery are enemies which must be fought unceasingly. Rinderpest, anthrax, and foot-and-mouth disease constantly threaten domestic cattle. American sanitary science has won many a victory over these enemies and saved countless lives; but the constant vigilance of trained men and the intelligent co-operation of the people are necessary elements in the endless battle with disease. Such co-operation cannot be expected unless the foundation is laid by the education of the masses. Disease and ignorance go hand in hand.

### ECONOMIC DEVELOPMENT

The proper development of the economic resources of the country is essential to the spread of education and the successful prosecution of the war on disease. Both involve a steady advance in the standard of living of the people. There has indeed been a marked improvement in this regard in the last twenty-five years, but the advance has not been what it should have been. The Philippines is an agricultural country. It produces export crops—principally sugar, hemp, copra, and tobacco—and imports manufactured goods and foodstuffs. In 1895, the last normal year before the Philippine Revolution, the total foreign trade was about $30,000,000. In 1926 it was about $258,000,000. The total exports for that year were a little more than $141,000,000, less than $13.00

per capita. In the same year Porto Rico, with a population of only 1,300,000, exported products worth over $99,000,000. Hawaii, with a population of less than 350,000, in 1926 exported to the United States sugar and pineapples valued at over $100,000,000. Cuba, with a population of about 3,500,000, sent to the United States alone in 1925–26 exports worth nearly $228,000,000. If the resources of the Philippines were as well developed as those of Porto Rico and Cuba, its per capita export production would be about five times what it is.

### LACK OF CAPITAL

The principal reason why the Philippines has lagged behind in the development of the natural resources with which it is so richly endowed is that capital has not been attracted to the country. The present total investment of American and foreign capital in the Philippines, including the government bonds outstanding, is not much over $200,000,000; while Cuba, with a third of our area and population, has absorbed nearly a billion and a half dollars of American and British capital.

The reason why capital has been withheld from the Philippines while flowing freely into other countries is to be found in the prevailing uncertainty as to the political future of the country. At present Philippine exports are admitted to the American markets free of duty. If it were certain that this condition would continue and the protection of an orderly and just government could be assured it is reasonable to assume that the capital necessary to the development of the country would flow in, and that the resulting increased national wealth would make possible a further improvement in the standard of living and supply the additional revenue necessary to enable the Philippine government to improve and extend its educational system and its public health services.

### THE INDEPENDENCE ISSUE

The uncertainty as to the future which is thus retarding development is due to the insistent demand of the political leaders of the Filipino people for complete and immediate independence from the United States and the failure or inability of our government to make a definite and authoritative statement of its policy in the matter. This demand is voiced on every possible occasion by the Philippine legislature, and for years the attitude of that body has been unfavorable to the introduction of American and other foreign capital, because of the fear that such foreign interests would tend to oppose the attainment of this political ideal. The attitude of the legislature has been that it is better to forego the present enjoyment of enhanced material prosperity than to risk an indefinite postponement of complete independence.

### THE CONFLICT WITH THE EXECUTIVE

Under the form of government which the Congress of the United States has established in the Philippines the legislative power, with certain limitations, is vested in an elective senate and house of representatives, and the executive power is vested in a governor-general appointed by the president of the United States, and subordinate officials subject to his control. The result of this arrangement has been of late years, as it was inevitably bound to be, a constant effort on the part of the legislature to encroach upon and restrict the power vested by the organic law in the insular chief executive. This attempt has been vigorously opposed by the present incumbent of the highest executive office. He has insisted that it is his duty to exercise, directly or by efficient supervision, the executive authority vested in him by the organic law by which the Philippine government was created by Congress; and he has resumed some of the executive powers, inherent in his office, which had been abdicated by his predecessor. In this he has been upheld by a recent important decision of the Philippine Supreme Court. The result of the governor's action has been a conflict between the executive and legislative branches of the insular government which has brought practically all constructive legislation to a standstill. The governor-general freely exercises his veto power, and the Legislature retaliates by a systematic rejection of nearly every measure which the governor advocates, and by making full use of the power vested in the Senate to withhold approval of his nominations of officials whom he is authorized to appoint.

### THE SOLUTION

It is obvious, therefore, that the economic problem of the Philippines is but a part of the overshadowing political problem. Would the grant of immediate and complete independence be the proper solution? The Filipino political leaders insist vehemently that the question is not now open to debate; that the United States, in the preamble to the Jones Law, promised to grant independence to the Philippines as soon as a stable government could be established in the Islands, and that such a government now exists. Indeed, it is contended by one of the Filipino representatives in Congress, in a speech reported in the *Congressional Record* of March 12, 1927, that such a stable government has existed ever since the Jones Law was put into effect, and that therefore the United States has now been eleven years in default in the performance of its promise!

The position of the present American national administration, as expressed by President Coolidge, is that the Filipino people have neither the political experience nor the economic resources which would enable them, at the present stage of their development, to maintain a successful independent republican government. The fact that the present government of the Philippine Islands, backed by the power of the United States, possesses stability does not in itself constitute proof that a stable government can be established at this time if our support were to be withdrawn. What conditions must exist to warrant the belief that such a government can be established, and what degree of stability may reasonably be required, are matters essentially debatable. They have been debated for years, most vigorously. Much heat has been engendered in the process, and but little else has been accomplished.

The great majority of the American residents of the Philippines are opposed to the demand of the Filipino leaders for immediate independence. Many of them believe that independence should never be granted, and advocate permanent annexation. Unfortunately, many of the most outspoken advocates of this extreme policy are scornful and contempuous of the Filipinos in the expression of their opinions. This naturally leads to retaliation, and irritatingly provocative assertions are often made by the more radical of the Filipino political leaders. The inevitable result of such utterances is to make co-operation increasingly difficult.

The existing irritation is, I believe, greatly increased by statements frequently made by American opponents of the plea of the Filipinos tending to create the impression that the demand for independence is limited largely to the professional politicians and is voiced by them for selfish motives only. This is not in accordance with my observations. True it is that the vast majority of the Filipinos are today, because of their lack of education, unable to form an intelligent opinion regarding the effect which independence might have upon them; and that if left to their own devices they might be perfectly satisfied as they are. It is a significant fact, however, that the articulate Filipinos almost unanimously desire independence and say so. Some of them want independence with more or less protection from the United States; others are willing to postpone it for a time; recently there have been many public expressions of Filipino opinion favorable to a further extension of the period of preparation; but most of them want independence *now*.

Some visitors to the Philippines, and some Americans resident there, record the experience of being told in confidence by numbers of well-to-do Filipinos that independence is not desired by them and their class. Such has not been my experience. For many years I have been in close and friendly contact with Filipinos of the property-owning, professional, and business classes. From very few of them indeed have I heard any expression of desire for an indefinite continuance of the existing relations between their country and the United States, and from fewer still an expression of a desire for its perpetuation. My experience leads me to believe that the desire for immediate and complete independence, regardless of consequences, is almost unanimous among literate Filipinos of all ranks. It is not, with most of them, a matter of reasoned opinion. It is a sentiment—an ideal. The political leaders help to keep the sentiment constantly in mind, but it is not a thing of their creation. Nor is it fair to say—although one often hears it said—that all the political leaders are animated by selfish motives in their advocacy of independence. Most of them, I am convinced, are absolutely sincere in their believe that they are performing a patriotic duty in keeping up the agitation. Whether such a course of procedure, and the sentiment behind it, are wise or unwise is another matter; but the widespread and deep-rooted existence of a desire on the part of the Filipinos for independence is a *fact*—a most important fact—which must be kept constantly in mind in dealing with the Philippine problem.

The ambition to attain political independence is the most vital of all the forces now operating to arouse the Filipino people from the apathy of ignorance and poverty. They have been encouraged to entertain it by the frequent utterances of our own political leaders and by Congress in the preamble to the Jones Law. They are entitled to a sympathetic consideration by us of their desire, whether we agree with them or not. Conversely, the Filipinos should not allow their eagerness and their impatience to create the erroneous belief, apparently entertained by so many of them, that their only friends among Americans and foreigners are those who encourage them in their desire to break at once the tie which binds them to the United States.

### THE DANGERS OF INDEPENDENCE

It would be absurd to contend that the Filipinos are now the victims of oppression by the United States. They have complete control of the legislature, hold nearly all the judicial and executive offices of the insular government, and fill by election all provincial and municipal offices. Of the 15,000-odd persons in the Philippine Insular Civil Service at the end of 1924, only 526 were Americans, including 325 teachers. It is obvious therefore that the Filipinization of the public service has been carried to a high degree at the cost, it must be said, of increased expenditure and some decrease in efficiency. The provincial Filipino rarely sees an American and hardly ever comes into direct contact with an American official. It is quite evident, therefore, that the demand for independence cannot be justified upon the ground of any irritating interference with the daily life of the people by an alien official class.

There can be no doubt that the "stable government" which the American people—or at least those who give any thought to the subject—desire to see established in the Philippines is a self-governing republic, resting upon the foundation of intelligent appreciation by the people at large of their rights and duties. At present such a government would be an impossibility in the Philippines. The essential element, a well-informed public opinion, is wholly lacking. It could not possibly exist in a country in which the people as a whole read little or nothing. Under such conditions the natural tendency would be to establish an autocracy or an oligarchy, beneficent or otherwise. It can safely be said that this is not the kind of government which their American friends wish to give the Filipino people. I believe their attitude was fairly expressed by President Taft, while secretary of war, in a speech made in 1905, in which he said on this subject:

Enjoying as Americans do a government of free institutions, a government of liberty regulated by law, a republican form of government resting in its last analysis upon an intelligent public opinion, they do not think that their duty to the whole Filipino people can be discharged without preparing that people to maintain a stable, popular government in which shall be secured the civil liberty of all. They do not conceive that they have the right to relieve themselves of the burden of wardship or guardianiship of this whole people by attempting to assign the burden of government to a small element of that people, however confident that educated element may be of its ability to carry on a government for the Filipino people.

Many of the educated Filipinos of today make the objection that such a standard is too high, and cannot reasonably be required. Perhaps it is. It may well be that Americans are wrong in their belief that a democracy is the best form of government for the Filipinos. They might conceivably be quite contented now under an autocracy or an oligarchy of their own people; and it is certain that under existing conditions they would not be likely to achieve self-government thereafter by their unaided efforts. The attempt to establish a self-governing democracy in the Philippines may be foredoomed to failure, however prolonged be the period of preparation; but unless a far better foundation is provided than that which now exists, we shall never know whether it would have succeeded or not. Most of the Americans who have given careful consideration to the subject are unwilling to expose the work of a generation to almost certain destruction by allowing it to be subjected to perils which it is not yet prepared to encounter.

Many qualified observers are strongly inclined to believe the experiment may succeed, if patiently continued. There are hundreds of educated and cultured Filipinos well qualified individually for self-government and intelligent public service, but they are relatively but a handful. When such men are to be found by the tens of thousands it may be safe to try the experiment; but that day has not yet come. But even if we were to assume that the Filipinos would be satisfied with the kind of government which their present ruling classes would give them, have they the economic resources to maintain it?

The present revenues of the Philippine government could not be materially increased, in the present stage of development of the country, without imposing an intolerable burden on the people. An independent Philippine government would inevitably undertake expenditures for an army and navy, and for diplomatic and consular representation, which would involve outlays which could be met only by diverting to these uses money needed for education, sanitation, and public works. The standard of living would be of necessity reduced if Philippine products which now enter the American markets free of duty were subjected to the same tariffs as other foreign goods. The Philippine government is now able to borrow money at very favorable interest rates. What would it pay without the backing of the United States?

The development of economic resources is essentially a business undertaking. The Filipino people have produced many clever professional men, but so far, as a race, they have displayed no commercial genius. Trade and commerce have always been open to them, but the business of the Philippines has been done, and is still being done, by foreigners. The retail trade throughout the country is almost entirely in the hands of the Chinese. There is not a single bank in operation financed by Filipino private capital and managed by Filipinos. The attempt to develop natural resources by means of government-owned corporations has been a complete and costly failure. Economic independence is essential to successful political independence; and it is obvious that the Filipinos must develop a competent commercial class of their own before they can achieve that economic independence. This will require time—and the work has hardly begun.

### PRESSURE FROM WITHOUT

The Philippines are distant only a few hours' steaming from the most densely overpopulated countries in Asia. They have vast areas of unoccupied agricultural land, immense tracts of valuable forest, great deposits of iron ore. The Filipinos naturally and properly hope to preserve these resources as the heritage of their descendants. So far they have been protected from an overwhelming influx of immigrants from adjacent countries by the laws established and maintained first by Spain and later by the United States. The Filipinos realize that they could not compete successfully with their overseas neighbors, and have frequently and emphatically opposed all suggestions for a modification of the existing exclusionary policy. It is to be feared that unrestricted immigration would result in their ultimate elimination or absorption. As compared with their neighbors to the north and the west, the Filipinos, left to their own resources, would be woefully weak. Is it reasonably to be expected that an independent Philippines would be permitted to enforce the policy of restricted immigration which is absolutely essential to the preservation of the Filipinos as a race?

### THE FUTURE

No one able to compare present conditions in the Philippines with the state of affairs which existed at the beginning of the century can fail to be impressed with the benefits which the Filipinos have derived from their contact with the United States. They have made great progress in the establishment of the conditions essential to national existence, and they will continue to progress unless their development is arrested. If they continue to enjoy the protection of the United States during this period of development there is every reason to believe that progress will continue at a rate which will depend only upon their own efforts and the degree of their co-operation with us. Independence now would at best be an experiment, fraught with great peril. Its failure might be fatal. There are no indications that the American people are persuaded now, or that they are likely to be persuaded in the near future, that the Philippines are ready to assume the responsibilities of political independence. This, I believe, is not due to a lack of sympathy with the aspiration of the Filipinos, or to a belief that they are incapable of attaining it in the fulness of time; although perhaps some doubt has been engendered by the recent insistent demands for *independence* or *nothing,* and the rejection of all suggestions for further orderly and gradual development of national resources and skill in self-government under the American flag.

In a recent official statement of his views on the subject, in connection with his veto of the bill passed by the Philippine legislature to ascertain by a plebiscite the desires of the Filipino people with regard to independence, President Coolidge said:

> The ability of a people to govern themselves is not easily attained. History is filled with failures of popular government. It cannot be learned from books; it is not a matter of eloquent phrases. Liberty, freedom, independence are not mere words, the repetition of which brings fulfilment. They demand long, arduous, self-sacrificing preparation. Education, knowledge, experience, sound public opinion, intelligent participation by the great body of the people—these things are essential. The degree in which they are possessed determines the capability of a people to govern themselves. In frankness and with the utmost friendliness, I must state my sincere conviction that the people of the Philippine Islands have not as yet attained the capability of full self-government. . . . . Demonstration of the ability to carry on successfully the large powers of government already possessed would be far more convincing than continued agitation for complete independence.

If the opinion so expressed by the President is indeed the opinion of the American people it would be helpful if it were embodied in an official declaration of policy by Congress. I believe it should be coupled with an equally formal and emphatic declaration of the adherence of our government to the policy of granting ultimate complete independence when the Filipino people are prepared for it (if they then still desire it), and a statement of the minimum definite economic and educational standards to be attained before the matter of independence be again considered. There would be no inconsistency with the preamble to the Jones Law in such a statement. It would be nothing but a legislative interpretation of the preamble, and would make definite that which is now indefinite. If such a definite declaration of policy were to be made, the present clamorous demand for immediate independence might in time be abandoned or greatly diminished. Its present insistence is, I believe, very largely due to the fear that if independence is not attained shortly, all hope for it might as well be abandoned. A formal and authoritative official declaration of such a definite, unambiguous policy as that herein advocated, coupled, as the opportunities arise, with actual demonstrations of its sincerity, would tend to allay that fear and would operate increasingly as an incentive to the conservative and moderate intelligent elements of the population to organize and to formulate a constructive policy of intelligent co-operation by the Filipino people with their American friends, official and unofficial, looking to the orderly development of the material, mental, and spiritual resources of the Philippines, with complete insular autonomy under American sovereignty as the first objective, and national independence as the *ultimate* goal.

# AN INTERPRETATION OF AMERICA IN PACIFIC RELATIONS

RAY LYMAN WILBUR
President of Stanford University, California

The forces in the background of American life are so immense in volume and so extensive in range that it is difficult for America to understand itself, let alone interpret itself to other countries. In the course of a little more than a century the United States has absorbed one of the greatest and most diverse migrations of people in the history of the world, and has developed the resources of one of the great continents. During this period it has seen the growth of modern science and has used its discoveries in a practical way in the handling of, and sometimes the exploitation of, natural resources of untold value. It has had as its political mainspring the idea of government by the people, or, as Abraham Lincoln put it, "government of the people, for the people, by the people." Control has been invested in a majority at frequent popular elections, with universal suffrage extended in recent years to women voters.

To understand America's foreign policy it is necessary to review the history of its origin as a nation. The early colonists coming from Europe developed in New England, New York, Pennsylvania, Virginia, and the South and the now West certain established habits of thought which led to the break with England, the principal mother country. The simple, practical, astute Benjamin Franklin symbolized the American style of democracy among the aristocratic forces of Europe. He did much to develop the attitudes of Americans to foreign governments. He had full confidence in the capacity of the people to work out their own problems. He believed that the government should be kept responsive to the will of the people. This was in part his reaction to his European experience, where he saw established governments sheltering those who were exploiting their fellow-citizens, distant colonies, and the government itself.

When through him and those who followed him recognition of the new United States was established there was left a prejudice against so-called "entangling alliances" and a feeling of aggressive independence was ingrafted upon the thinking of the American people. The Declaration of Independence itself was an appeal for independent sovereignty which carried with it, unconsciously perhaps, definite antagonisms and oppositions to other nations. The country felt that it had come up through the tangle of the European web, had broken its bonds, and that it must beware of anything approaching control or dictation from the outside. Used as it has been in the education of successive generations of Americans, the stimulating spirit of the Declaration of Independence has profoundly influenced the thinking of the average citizen and has instilled in his blood a patriotic fervor accompanied by a readiness to suspect any overture of a foreign country as a part of building up new and perhaps dangerous bonds.

In order to establish itself the new Republic had to work out by a series of compromises a combination of the separate colonies and to develop a strong centralized government in Washington. When this was once done the march to conquer the great continent began, with those inevitable differences of opinion, custom, and economic situation which led to the great Civil War, with the settlement of which the unity of the country was definitely established.

There has been a constant faith in the American people in self-government, majority rule, public education, and the maintenance of conditions by which any individual could rise to any height through his own quality and efforts. In spite of the attitude taken toward the American Indian and the Negro, class distinctions as such have not existed. It is doubtful if any other people in history has increased in wealth and in numbers at such a rate as America has experienced in the last hundred years. To absorb individuals of all ages, various religious beliefs, with marked differences in experience with government and with the most diverse attitudes toward constituted authority into the rapidly expanding American communities, and to make them American in their reactions, was a supreme task which has been accomplished to a remarkable degree.

The influence of mass migrations from different countries has had a profound effect upon the foreign policies of the United States. There has been an unconscious reaction in the presence of large minorities of different national origins where the adults often failed to learn the English language and maintained a foreign press which has developed very definite, and not unfounded, fears of foreign influence being exerted in American affairs. This is one of the reasons for the slogan "America first," and explains to a considerable extent the delay in the ratification of the League of Nations compact. Appeals to the prejudice of nationals has been a part of local and national elections. With large blocks of Irish, German, Swedish, or other votes in many states capable of determining close elections between the two parties, the growth of a sensitive attitude on the part of the Americans is not difficult to understand.

To play upon the prejudices of the fearful and the uninformed by bringing up foreign bogies of various sorts has been a favorite method of attempting to win American elections. In America too, as elsewhere, it has been much easier to attract the attentions of the voters to distant problems associated with foreign governments and incapable of accurate understanding, and where the politician could talk freely without responsibility, than to meet the important and responsible local and national issues. There has been no good opportunity to work out a consistent, long-time foreign policy for the United States. With the change of government every four years, with a policy fairly well established of placing new men of affairs as ambassadors in foreign countries with each change of administration, no adequate opportunity for carrying on traditional or agreed-upon programs is possible. In general, the idea in the American foreign service has been to secure men to represent America who would be responsive to the currents of American life rather than those who by living abroad over a series of years might acquire a suspected foreign or international viewpoint.

Throughout its history there has been a firm faith in the American people in their form of government, and a feeling that all other peoples and nations were struggling, perhaps unconsciously, toward a similar form of democratic government and away from monarchical rule. In fact, crowned heads have been looked upon as an evidence of incomplete development. Nevertheless there has been a respect and desire for strong leadership on the part of those men elected to high office. The American likes to vote *for* and *against* individuals and issues. There has been also a constant struggle between the democratic ideal and sound, practical, and efficient government. Our steps upward can be viewed as a series of compromises between these two main issues. A rapidly developing economic and industrial life alongside of a well-established and growing rural life has played a large part in this conflict.

In a broad way the House of Representatives, elected as it is on the basis of population, represents the cities of the United States; and the Senate, elected by states, represents the rural population or the farmers. Since all treaties are subject to ratification by the Senate, the ratification of foreign policy depends primarily upon the sentiment of the agrarian population. Much of this population is distant from the coasts and is definitely provincial and local in its outlook. While there has been a marked change in the last decade in this regard there is still the necessity of bringing the whole people up to a new level of appreciation of foreign countries and international responsibilities if America is to take its proper place among the nations of the world. With a literate population, with the great spread of the American newspaper and the part which the newspaper plays in everyday politics there are great difficulties in the way of establishing a satisfactory understanding of world-problems.

### IMMIGRATION

Staggered by attempts to digest and assimilate large groups of immigrants, a change in attitude toward the new citizen from a foreign land has brought about the immigration laws. This has been an attempt to maintain the integrity of America. The tendency of many immigrants to think in terms of the home country and of America as a place to be exploited for the benefit of the individual and of the home country has developed a definite fear of permitting immigration from any country beyond a certain limited number which seem likely to be absorbed without undue conflict into American life.

America's experience with immigrants from European countries materially influenced the procedure followed toward those who came from Asia at a later period. The differences in race and culture and habits made it easier to focus attention upon them and to take more specific action. In spite of the discriminations that have already been put into effect there is a growing tendency on the part of the American people to deal on an equal basis with the inhabitants of all countries, but to insist firmly upon the right of America to determine its own future population. While I think it is true that, due to the old slavery experience, Africans have been looked down upon, this has not applied to other races to any greater extent than is inevitable in all national and international relations where there is a certain amount of lack of understanding.

I think it is safe to presume that the forces operating in American life at the present time will lead to the recognition that, while the people of other nations and other races may be different, they are in no sense inferior, and that all must be treated on a uniform plan. There is sound reason for the hope that the quota basis may eventually be extended to the inhabitants of all countries, including those of Asia. A more humble attitude on the part of Americans is replacing the rather flamboyant self-adulation characteristic of new peoples and new countries. We have had to deal too with the second-generation foreigner, who has often been even more ardent in his Americanism and in his desire to keep others out than are the descendants of the older generations.

### TERRITORIAL EXPANSION

The United States of America has shown throughout its whole history a tendency to expand its territory. Its normal growth from the Atlantic to the Pacific Coast was followed by the purchase of Alaska from Russia, the acquisition of the Hawaiian Islands, and the purchase of the Philippines from Spain. Its relationship to the Panama Canal zone and to some of the islands of the West Indies, and certain of its actions in connection with the Monroe Doctrine, might lead to an assumption that these acquisitions were due to a strong imperialistic program. The conduct of the American government toward the Philippines, the renunciation of any territorial advantage following the great war, and the willingness with which the Americans have spent large sums in connection with the development of the peoples more or less under their sovereignty point in another direction.

It is impossible to define the great surges which come in the life of a people which carry them into new territory, or to prophesy as to just what the future will hold. I am confident that the general American attitude is not imperialistic. There is a faith in the democratic ideal and a faith that the American form of government and of general education will lead other countries to those advances which have meant so much in the life of America. The general desire is that other nations and other groups will develop their people and their resources, and that a brotherly relationship may be established with all bordering nations and all neighboring peoples. The century-old association with Canada represents the ideal type of relation to a foreign country toward which the American is aspiring.

The long experience of the nation with the Monroe Doctrine and the many difficulties of its application to the rapid changes in two new continents, together with the attitudes toward Europe which were matured throughout a century and were, except for the time being, not materially modified by the World War, has developed certain handicaps with which the problems of the Pacific area are approached by the United States. When we turn to the outlook on the Pacific as far as the United States is concerned one can sense now the feeling that America realizes that it is reaching its maturity and that it must view its foreign relations from a new standpoint of responsibility. The expanding wealth of the American people, the development of the merchant marine, the increase in foreign trade, and the spread of American capital into all parts of the world have suddenly brought home this responsibility. Just as many new enterprises in America were developed through European capital, so America now finds its capital developing other countries. The long seasoning process by which European capital, particularly that of Great Brtain, discovered methods for handling foreign business has not as yet been gone through.

America suddenly finds itself with interests of all sorts in Mexico, Central America, South America, Japan and China, and elsewhere, and it is conscious of new relations with Australia, New Zealand, Canada, and the islands of the Pacific, and is trying to discover some consistent method for handling the difficulties arising therefrom. The policy of America can be classified as a mixture of idealism and selfishness. The consistent support of missions, the generous gifts to those in need in various parts of the world, and the desire to be of some real service is a definite part of American thought and action. In America there has been a rapid increase in the standards of living, rapid absorption of wealth by increasing numbers of the population, and a practical understanding of economic affairs that has put the financial question forward in much of American life.

It is natural enough that in a population where there is rapid expansion in wealth there should be a tendency to look "through the pocket" at problems, particularly foreign ones. With increasing maturity of the American people there has grown up a larger percentage of individuals with a broader outlook, who have enough time free from the turmoil of business and other life to view world-problems in a more comprehensive way and to endeavor to meet them as great human issues rather than from a strictly selfish or nationalistic viewpoint. There is being built up, on the basis of international law and upon the machinery of all sorts of international contact, an intercontinental and world-relationship which is growing each year in its importance. Isolation of any single progressive nation is now out of the question. While the distances are great in the Pacific, transportation of ideas, goods, and men is going forward at such a rapid rate that this world feeling or sense of interrelation between peoples and nations is bound to grow. This has to be borne in mind in interpreting America's relation to some of the more immediate pressing questions concerning the Pacific countries.

### CHINA

The amount of interest shown by the American people in the development of China is one of the outstanding social phenomena of this decade. There is a strong sense of sympathy felt for a people struggling to develop a form of political organization, not dissimilar to that of the United States, on the basis of its age-old culture. The development of a nationalistic spirit in China, replacing the former indifference which the American could never understand, has been viewed with the heartiest approval. It is evident that the day of concessions and of rights of extraterritoriality is rapidly passing, and the general hope in America, a hope universally expressed, is that this transition stage may be gone through promptly without material losses of life and property, and that the sovereignty of a great people may be re-established throughout its whole territory and along the lines of peace and prosperity. There is general recognition of the patience required by all while the painful steps of early democratic nationhood are being taken. America knows by hard experience the difficulty of achieving unity and efficient popular government.

### RUSSIA

The Americans have looked upon the recent Russian experience on the Pacific, as well as in Europe, with perplexity. They have been baffled by the tendency toward destruction which has characterized the last ten years in that country and the mischievous activities in other countries of some of its adherents. Instinctively they have felt a natural hostility to bolshevism as they have understood it. A minority control of a nation by a party or a class which pulls down those who have risen or who rise above the ordinary level in the intellectual field or in the accumulation of property acquired through industry or skill is abhorrent to American thinking. The clash in Western Asia of the American idea of majority rule and equal opportunity for all to rise to any level which their capacities make possible and that of the Russian minority rule and dead level of society concept is one of the great present conflicts in the field of human relationships.

### JAPAN

There has been a steady increase in admiration of the great achievements of the Japanese people. Their rapid advance in what the American thinks of as progress in civilization and the high qualities shown in the face of disaster have made a profound impression. The patience and friendliness shown by the Japanese people in the delicate subject of immigration has enhanced the respect of America for Japan and brightened the prospects for a mutually satisfactory solution.

PHILIPPINES

The enthusiastic confidence with which the American government entered upon the program of education for the people of the Philippines has been tempered by the realization that it takes time for modern representative popular government to become reasonably efficient. America at present has a parental attitude toward the people of these Islands and is in the mood of the father of an ambitious adolescent boy who is not yet thought to be capable of making his own way in the world, but who needs more training and education.

BRITISH COMMONWEALTH OF NATIONS

Canada, to the American mind, is taking more and more the place of a twin nation to the United States, working out a destiny similar to our own.

Australia and New Zealand seem closer to America than ever before. As constituent members of the British Commonwealth of Nations, the place they are taking in the life of the Pacific is accepted as the natural outgrowth of their history.

In conclusion I think it is just to say that one cannot understand the American attitude in the Pacific or elsewhere unless he grasps the confidence of the American in his own form of government, in his ideals, and in education as a method of developing the future of a nation. The American feels that the general ideas in use in the government of his country are sound and that they have worked well in spite of many inadequacies. The high standard of living, the uniform contentment and general happiness of the people, are associated in the mind of the American citizen with the penetration of certain ideas and ideals into the lives of the whole people. I think it is fair to say that the ultimate aim of the American people, viewed as a whole, is not to accumulate mere wealth and power or to exploit the world in the development of a great imperialistic design, but to offer some form of world-service as its contribution to human welfare.

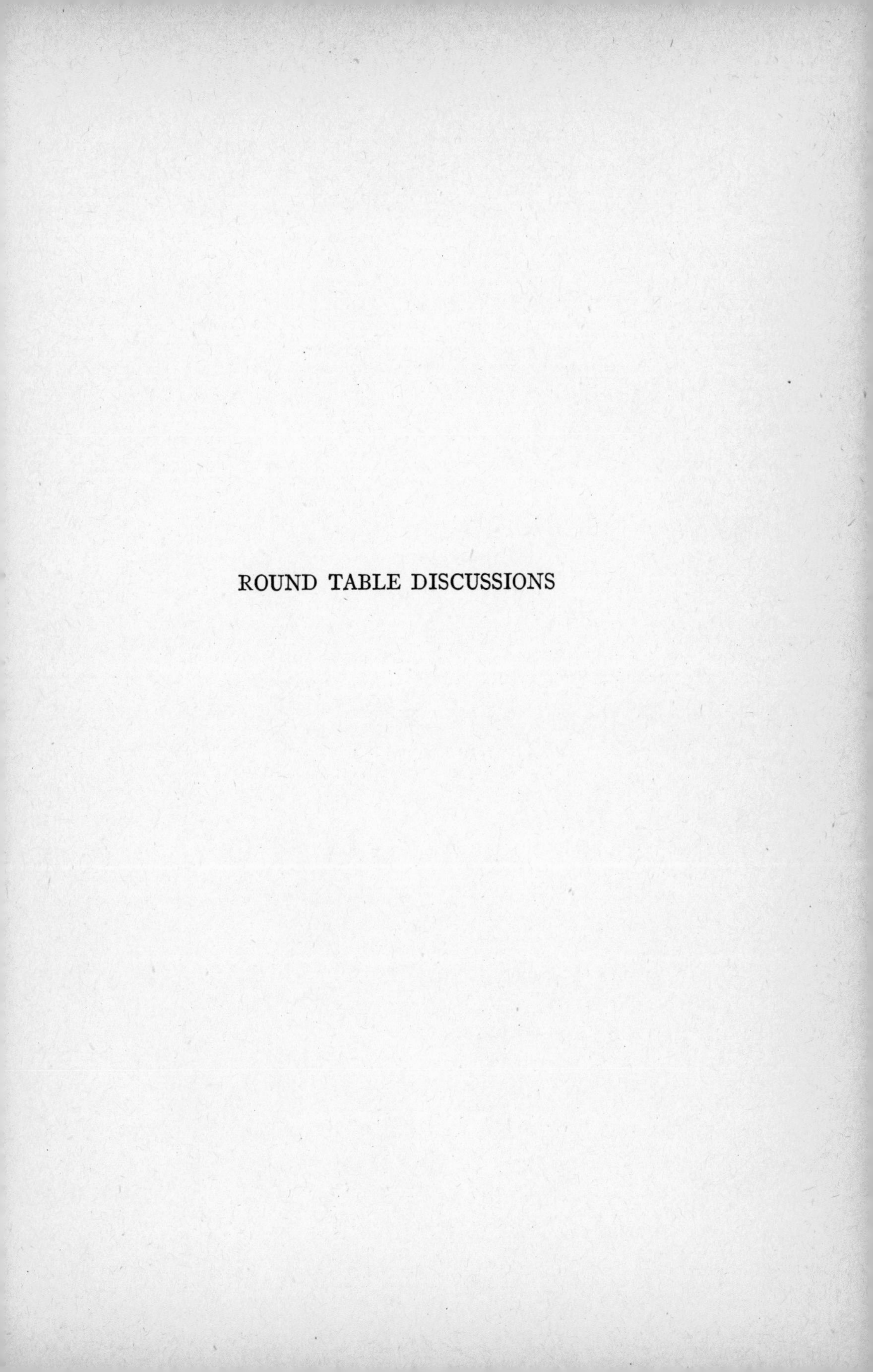

# ROUND TABLE DISCUSSIONS

## TARIFF AUTONOMY IN CHINA

### 1. QUESTIONS FOR DISCUSSION

1. What if any additional facts are necessary to supplement the statement submitted with regard to the present tariff situation?
2. What are the conditions necessary for the successful exercise by China of tariff autonomy?
3. What is the relation, if any, between the exercise of tariff autonomy and the maintenance of the existing customs administration?
4. What difficulties does the problem of Likin present from (*a*) the fiscal point of view, and (*b*) the administrative point of view?

### 2. SUMMARY OF ROUND-TABLE DISCUSSIONS

CHAIRMEN AND SECRETARIES

Round Table I
*Chairman:* KENZO TAKAYANAGI
*Secretary:* H. DUNCAN HALL

Round Table II
*Chairman:* SIR ARTHUR CURRIE
*Secretary:* KARL C. LEEBRICK

Round Table III
*Chairman:* WILLIAM H. KILPATRICK
*Secretary:* MALCOLM MACDONALD

Round Table IV
*Chairman:* GEORGE H. BLAKESLEE
*Secretary:* DANIEL J. FLEMING

#### I. HISTORICAL[1]

Origin of tariff control

China's autonomy in tariff matters was definitely limited by the Treaty of Nanking (1842), which closed the so-called "opium war." In that treaty China made an agreement with Great Britain to open five ports to foreign trade and to levy a "fair and regular tariff of export and import customs and other dues," upon payment of which, and of a further amount to cover transit dues, British merchandise should become free to be conveyed by Chinese merchants to the interior of China. In the following year the governments of China and Britain agreed upon a tariff schedule on the basis of approximately 5 per cent ad valorem duties on imports and exports. It was agreed at the same time that transit dues should be levied at the moderate scale then prevailing.

[1] Cf. Bau, Documents, Section 3, below; Hornbeck, pp. 458–68, 491–94; Whyte, pp. 3–7, 34, 40–46.

The transit dues payable were complicated by the imposition of the new tax upon goods in process of conveyance which was inaugurated to provide extra revenue in the early years of the Taiping Rebellion. This new tax, called likin, spread throughout China, and the charges levied under that name have also been multiplied until they now form a variety of taxes collected upon internal trade.[2]

Likin

It was during the Taiping Rebellion also and the consequent disorganization that Chinese officials in 1854 asked foreign officials to assist in the creation of what has since become the Chinese Maritime Customs Administration.[3]

The Chinese maritime customs

In 1858 new treaties were concluded at Tientsin providing for new tariff schedules and commutation of transit dues, including likin, by the payment of a single charge at the rate of 2½ per cent ad valorem. The new schedules, which were agreed upon at Shanghai in the same year, consisted mainly of specific rates of duty calculated on the basis of 5 per cent of the values of the goods then prevailing. The tariff rules agreed upon at the same time provided a legal basis also for the customs administration.[4] No important changes were made either in the tariff schedules or the tariff rules until, in pursuance of the protocol of 1901, the schedules were revised in 1902 to allow for the higher level of prices and make the specific rates approximate an effective 5 per cent.[5]

The MacKay Treaty, 1902

In 1902 Britain concluded with China the Mackay Treaty, which provided, *inter alia,* for the abolition of likin and other transit duties and broadly for the raising of existing import duties from 5 per cent, plus 2½ per cent, to 12½ per cent, and of export duties to 7½ per cent. In the following year similar treaties were concluded with China by the United States and Japan, and in 1908 one with Sweden; but the other treaty powers did not follow suit, and these provisions of that group of treaties therefore never became effective.[6]

The treaty powers

This failure to effect a revision agreed upon by the powers principally concerned draws attention to one of the chief difficulties which China has to face in her external relationships. The British treaty of 1843 included a "most-favored-nation clause" of the type common in treaties affecting international trade.[7] Practically all of the treaties effected with China since that date have included a similar provision, with the result that China is apparently under the necessity of negotiating with no less than sixteen separate powers if she desires amendment of her tariff schedules. The sixteen powers concerned at the present time are Belgium, Brazil, Denmark, France, Great Britain, Italy, Japan, Mexico, Netherlands, Norway, Peru, Portugal, Spain, Sweden, Switzerland, and the United States.[8] Four other powers, Germany, Austria, Hungary, and Rus-

[2] Bau, *op. cit.;* Hornbeck, p. 460.

[3] Bau, *op. cit.;* Hornbeck, pp. 460, 496–97.

[4] Bau, *op. cit.;* Hornbeck, pp. 461, 502; Whyte, pp. 9–11.

[5] Hornbeck, p. 461.

[6] Whyte, p. 13; Hornbeck, pp. 503–14.

[7] Hornbeck, pp. 447–49.

[8] Hornbeck, p. 448, n. 6.

sia, no longer have extra-territorial rights, their treaties having been abrogated;[9] but in practice their trade is subjected to the same tariff charges as is that of the so-called "treaty powers."

The Chinese delegation to the Peace Conference at Versailles presented a program for the restoration of tariff autonomy to China by successive stages, but this program was not incorporated in the Treaty of Versailles and is now abandoned by the Chinese, who have announced their intention to establish immediate and unconditional tariff autonomy on January 1, 1929.[10]

**The tariff conference, 1925**

At the Washington Conference it was agreed by the nine powers concerned—China, Belgium, the British Empire, France, Italy, Japan, Netherlands, Portugal, and the United States—that the tariff schedules should be revised and that China should levy certain surtaxes and that a special tariff conference should be held to make arrangements for authorizing the surtaxes.[11] The Tariff Revision Commission met at Shanghai in 1922 and published a revised tariff schedule, but delays in the ratification of the Washington treaties delayed the assembling of the special conference which finally met in Peking on October 26, 1925. After nine months' effort this conference adjourned without formal action, owing to the conditions of civil war in and about Peking and to the declaration by the Canton government and by General Feng that no agreement concluded with the Peking government would be recognized by the Nationalist parties. The conference adjourned inconclusively on June 23, 1926, by common consent and without formal action. It was made clear by the foreign delegations and it was the general understanding that when the Chinese delegation felt itself in a position to call for the reconvening of the conference it should do so.[12]

## II. THE CHINESE DEMANDS[13]

Discussing the present situation in the light of these historical facts, the Chinese spokesmen in the Round Tables felt that the existing tariff treaties were objectionable from many points of view. In the first place they are inconsistent with China's sovereignty as an independent power. This limitation of sovereignty has important practical as well as sentimental aspects. The possibility of a stable central government in China depends obviously upon the possession of sufficient and certain sources of revenue. One of the best and simplest sources of revenue in a country which lacks administrative machinery, as does China, is the customs tariff. At the present time the rates of duty are fixed by treaty and are unalterable except by the most cumbrous diplomatic procedure;

**Lack of revenue**

[9] Whyte, pp. 28–34; Hornbeck, pp. 475–77, 516–22; Bau, Documents, Section 6, Nos. I and II.

[10] Bau, *op. cit.;* Whyte, pp. 16–22, 46–47.

[11] Bau, *op. cit.;* Hornbeck, pp. 462, 523–39.

[12] Bau, *op. cit.;* Hornbeck, pp. 463–65.

[13] Bau, *op. cit.;* also Documents, VIII and IX.

they are inadequate to provide the revenue necessary for modern governmental expenditure and are largely hypothecated for the service of loans, many of which are in themselves a source of irritation to the Chinese people as having been contracted by previous governments for purposes which are considered now to have been illegitimate.

Moreover, with the present tariff schedules and a uniform flat rate of duty it is impossible to build anything approaching a scientific tariff. Graduated taxes on luxuries and protective duties upon goods which compete with local industries are alike impossible. The latter fact is a source of much concern since the rapid development of trade in recent years has disturbed the equilibrium of Chinese industry and more latterly, since the beginnings of factory industry in China itself.

or protection

The difficulty of securing uniformity of agreement among the treaty powers is so great that the Chinese, while recognizing the wisdom of upholding and extending the force of international law, are reluctant to enter upon another series of protracted multilateral conferences. Their view is that concessions by the powers are made unwillingly and lag behind the necessities of the situation until the Chinese have reached the limit of patience and complete disintegration seems imminent. Historically speaking, in the Chinese view, the powers have taken advantage of every possible technicality to delay the restoration of China's rights. They ask for the recognition of China's autonomy, without conditions, as a right. They feel that there is no generosity on the part of the powers in conceding what belongs to another sovereign state.

Diplomatic delay

The reply to this argument is that the facts of modern industry and trade must be recognized. The economic systems of the foreign countries are involved. Any change made in trading relationships will affect the welfare of the peoples of those countries. In the case of Great Britain, and even more of Japan, the economic consequences of such a change would be of such importance as to warrant the most careful consideration by the governments concerned. China is an important power—especially from the point of view of commerce—and her actions are of more far-reaching importance than might be the actions of a smaller country in like circumstances.

The general position, particularly of the United States, at the special conference was that the promise of extra revenue from surtaxes made at the Washington Conference should first be redeemed, that the conference should then arrange for further increases in rates, and proceed, having recognized China's right, to complete tariff autonomy and to make detailed plans for the resumption of that right after an interim period.

The Chinese, on the other hand, looking forward to early unification of their governments with a confidence which was not fully shared by their fellow-members in the Round Tables, tended to be impatient of delay or of anything that savored of the reopening of prolonged and possibly inconclusive negotia-

The Chinese policy

tions. They were frankly suspicious of the fair words of the powers as expressed in recent official statements and demanded action in place of promises. They asked for an immediate and full abolition of foreign privileges and the substitution of a relationship of equal treatment and reciprocity. The example of Russia in giving up concessions and other privileges has encouraged this attitude. The success of Turkey in first abolishing extra-territorial privileges and later getting her action validated by the Treaty of Lausanne has also not been without effect.

The state of civil war contemporaneous with revolution in the widest sense of the word, bringing in its train disunity of government and breakdown of administration, does not obscure in the minds of the Chinese the essential unanimity of the Chinese people on matters of foreign policy and national status. The various factions differ on matters of domestic policy and personal rivalries, but in matters of foreign policy reflect the same general attitude of nationalism which is the inevitable result of a widespread and increasing determination among the educated classes of China to regain for their country its national status.

### III. THE TARIFF TREATIES IN INTERNATIONAL LAW

The position in international law of the treaties which at present limit China's autonomy in tariff matters seems clear. Tariff schedules and their administration are usually recognized as domestic questions, but the Permanent Court of International Justice has ruled that any domestic question becomes international the moment it is covered by a treaty. The Chinese tariff today is governed by treaties made between China and certain powers establishing and recognizing tariff schedules. Other powers have the right, by virtue of most-favored-nation clauses in their treaties with China to have their merchandise come under these schedules; but such powers would seem to have no voice in any negotiations which might be started for establishing new tariff schedules.

**Validity of the tariff treaties**

The fact that coercion of the state may have been a factor in concluding a treaty is not considered a ground in international law for holding that treaty to be void. If it were so it would be impossible to terminate a war by making a treaty. Treaties, to be valid, must receive proper formal ratification by all parties concerned, but this does not necessarily imply absence of coercion. The Chinese tariff treaties have been formally ratified by the proper authorities. In the strict interpretation of international law, therefore, the treaties are valid. It is common in treaties to have a provision that after a certain period either party may denounce the arrangement by giving stated notice, but in most of the Chinese tariff treaties there is no express provision for denunciation by China. China has recently denounced the Belgian treaty of 1865 on the ground that the right of denunciation, expressly given to Belgium, should be held to be reciprocally applicable by China. A case to test the validity of this action was brought before the Permanent Court of International Justice by Belgium, but hearing has several times been postponed at request of the parties pending negotiation of a new treaty.

**Abrogation of German and Austrian treaties**

China has also invoked the legal principle, *rebus sic stantibus,* on the ground that conditions have changed and consequently the treaties have become obsolete. This principle is usually given a narrow interpretation by international lawyers, and its invocation inevitably arouses serious controversy. War, however, is recognized as coming within this condition as a ground for terminating most treaties. This principle was invoked by China when she entered the World War, and her consequent abrogation of the treaties with Germany and Austria-Hungary has been recognized by the other powers. The abandonment of old treaty commitments by the Soviet government after the revolution in Russia on the ground of changed conditions is still a source of serious controversy. The abolition of extra-territoriality by Turkey was subsequently validated by the Treaty of Lausanne.

The lawful way to terminate the treaties is by agreement of the parties concerned. This, however, involves in regard to the China treaties a measure of collective action which is difficult to obtain. As stated before, the Mackay Treaty, negotiated between Great Britain and China in 1902 for the amendment of the tariff schedules, and the similar treaties negotiated by two other powers in the following year and a third later, made their tariff provisions conditional upon the conclusion by China of similar agreements with the other powers concerned, including those entitled to most-favored-nation treatment. These provisions of those treaties have consequently never come into effect.

The Washington Conference made provision for the holding of the recent Special Tariff Conference in Peking to meet the conditions of the Mackay Treaty, but did not provide for termination of the existing treaties. At this conference the powers assented on November 19, 1925, to a resolution recognizing the principle of tariff autonomy, but this resolution was intended to be incorporated in a treaty which would take the place of the present treaties, and the new treaty was not negotiated.

**The sanctity of international law**

While this appears to be the position of the treaties in international law, the Chinese spokesmen and many others were impressed by the seriousness and urgency of the present situation in China and anxious to avoid any further prolonged delays arising out of needless technicalities. A violation of treaty obligations, it was recognized, would tend to weaken China's international position from the point of view of international law and to weaken the beginnings of international co-operation laid in the Pacific by the Washington Conference. This constitutes a major reason for the co-operative policy pursued by the powers in recent years and for the reluctance of powers who are sympathetic with China's aspirations to proceed to independent bilateral negotiations with her.[14]

At the same time it must be recognized that the temper of China is such

[14] Whyte, p. 53.

that to insist upon keeping her tied by technicalities might under certain circumstances be the quickest way to force her to violate the treaties. The leaders of young China are extremely suspicious of any further suggestions for international conferences. It is too easy, they feel, for such conferences to become lost in a maze of legal difficulties. Meanwhile, the necessity for action is, they feel, urgent. The beginnings of industrialization and the rapid increase in the importation of manufactured goods which compete with the handicraft industries of China have created an industrial situation in which tariff autonomy seems more desirable than ever.

Some new international machinery or legal device would seem necessary to meet the tariff situation, or in the alternative China must be recognized to have a moral right to terminate the treaties, when she is in a position to do so, by methods which are not fully approved by international law. The Chinese representative at Geneva has attempted to bring the treaties to the attention of the League of Nations under Article 19 of the Covenant, but without success. This article provides that a treaty which has become obsolete may be presented to the Assembly for discussion. In practice, however, the League has given a very restricted interpretation to that article. The fact that the United States is not a member of the League also renders it very difficult to use League machinery for such a purpose.[15]

**Treaties under the League Covenant**

The Washington Conference attempted to provide means for treaty adjustments by setting up the machinery for revision of tariff schedules, as in 1922, and for the special conference which met in Peking during 1925–26. If the nine powers at this conference, however, had definitely agreed upon tariff autonomy, it would still have been necessary to get the assent of several other powers who claim a voice on the basis of most-favored-nation clauses. The chief obstacle at the present moment to any such procedure is obviously the lack of a stable government in China itself. The position of the British government in this respect was made clear by Sir Austen Chamberlain in his memorandum of December 18, 1926.[16]

## IV. THE ATTITUDE OF THE POWERS

**A way out**

It is probable that any government in China strong enough to secure international recognition could escape from the legal difficulties sketched in the preceding by comparatively simple diplomatic procedure. If such a government prepared and promulgated definite and detailed tariff rates and schedules these could be transmitted by the Chinese Foreign Office with covering notes to the foreign offices of the other powers concerned. The acceptance of the new tariff could then be signified by similar notes. This would be the simplest form of diplomatic procedure. As far as the attitude of the chief powers concerned can be interpreted from recent official statements, it seems likely that Great Britain,

[15] Whyte, pp. 61–65.

[16] Whyte, p. 50, par. 7.

the United States, and Japan would all be ready to accept any reasonable tariff which was notified to them in this way. The position of China in the matter is apparently determined by the circular letter to the legations at Peking on January 13, 1926, to the effect that China intends to exercise tariff autonomy on January 1, 1929.[17] The Nanking government has expressed its willingness to negotiate tariffs with the powers in the meantime.

Two days before the Conference opened in Peking the Provisional Chief Executive made public a brief national tariff law and thereby established the technical position that such a tariff law was in existence.[18] The amplification and elaboration of this statement into proper scientific tariff schedule and regulations, and the presentation of the Chinese national tariff, as thus elaborated, to the foreign offices of the treaty powers is the alternative procedure to the negotiation of separate tariffs with each government. Such a presentation, followed by an interchange of notes, would give an opportunity to the powers to fulfil the promises they have already made to recognize China's tariff autonomy upon the fulfilment of certain simple conditions, the chief of which is the existence of a national, certain, and non-discriminatory tariff. The signatories of the Nine Power Treaty entered into at the Washington Conference, including China, are committed to the principle of the open door and non-discrimination.

The necessity for non-discrimination

China at present has the right to levy what import taxes she desires upon goods from Germany and Austria, but by the agreement between China and Germany of May 20, 1921, she has agreed that no duty higher than those paid by other nations shall be charged.[19] In this agreement, therefore, China has laid down the principle of non-discrimination. It is to be remembered, however, that this Sino-German agreement differs from the so-called "unequal treaties" since it is an agreement entered into freely by the Chinese government rather than a treaty forced upon China as a result of war or threats of war. It is claimed by the Chinese that in consequence German and Austrian traders are able to do business in parts of China that are closed to their rivals. Any treaty entered into separately which resulted in more favorable rates being granted to one power than to others would violate the obligations of the Washington Treaty as well as the most-favored-nation clauses of the existing treaties.

America and the Washington treaties

The United States government in particular sets great store by the Washington treaties and is disposed to regard them as an interlocking set of solemn engagements to be treated as a bloc or an entirety. In particular the American government appears to stand by the Nine Power Treaty with regard to the policy concerning China, and by the tariff treaty and other agreements entered into at Washington. It does not wish to handle the problem of China in an opportunistic manner. It was for this reason apparently that the United States gov-

[17] Bau, *op. cit.*, also Documents, No. IX.

[18] Bau, *op. cit.*

[19] Text, given in Hornbeck, p. 518.

ernment wished the recent tariff Conference at Peking to proceed first to the execution of the agreement arrived at in the Washington discussions before taking up the question of any further increases in duties or the general question of tariff autonomy.[20]

The British attitude appears to be as follows:[21] Sir Austen Chamberlain's statement of December 18, 1926, was prepared primarily with regard to concessions in China, but the general principle was laid down that Britain was prepared to negotiate with China on all outstanding questions wherever possible. Sir Austen Chamberlain stated plainly that the British government was prepared to revise the treaties with China if and when there was a stable government functioning in China. There is no such government today, but Great Britain has nevertheless gone ahead with this policy. An agreement was negotiated with the Hankow government which subsequently became divided into two factions.[22] The minister with whom the British government had negotiated became the representative of a faction instead of the foreign minister of a government. The British government, however, has accepted the principle of tariff autonomy and will instruct all British nationals in China to pay all taxes in China upon the fulfilment of two conditions: certainty of tariff charges and non-discrimination.

British members of the Round Tables pointed out that the original tariff trouble in China arose from the fact that foreign merchants hardly knew what at any moment would be the rates of duty levied upon imports. The British and other foreign governments attach great importance to the provision of definite and certain tariff schedules and stable administration. It is not only desirable that there be unified customs administration; there must be a definite, ascertainable, and certain authority for that administration. The British memorandum of December 18, 1926,[23] referred to "Chinese authority wherever situated," and "most competent Chinese authorities." These phrases, however applicable to negotiations concerning concessions and other extra-territorial privileges, must be read in connection with the later statement[24] as far as tariff autonomy is concerned. The Washington Treaty to which Britain was a signatory laid down the principle of uniform rates of duty at all the frontiers. It would not be possible to negotiate separate tariffs with different governments in China. Great Britain and China, as well as the other signatories to the Washington Treaty, are definitely committed to the principle of a uniform national tariff. The external obligations of China in respect of loans contracted upon the credit of a national Chinese government and secured upon the customs revenues of an undivided China must be considered in this connection.

[20] See Hornbeck, pp. 480–90, 550–55, 561–66; Bau, *op. cit.*, Documents, No. VII.

[21] Whyte, pp. 34–38, 49–64; Hornbeck, pp. 556–60; Bau, *op. cit.*

[22] Whyte, pp. 65–72; Bau, Documents, No. XI.

[23] Whyte, pp. 51, 54.

[24] Whyte, p. 57, par. 3.

The preparation and promulgation of a detailed and comprehensive national tariff law would therefore seem to be a necessary precondition of tariff autonomy. The preparation of such a law is a matter requiring expert study over a long period. The incidence of the new duties proposed and the economic effect of tariff changes, both within China and abroad, present intricate and difficult problems. For some years there has been no legislature in China. Laws are promulgated by presidential decree, but for many months past there has been no president in office. Political influences are, however, bound to enter into the making of any tariff, particularly if and when there is a popular legislature. The detailed formulation of a new tariff is greatly complicated by such political influences. Any new tariff must also take careful account of the incidence of increased taxation upon the Chinese consumer and importer. It must further reckon with the demands of infant Chinese industries for tariff protection. On the other hand, it appears probable that China will need a great deal of foreign capital, and the possibility of obtaining this capital will be greatly affected by the nature of the tariff which China puts into operation. The present tariff law promulgated on October 24, 1925, is clearly inadequate and impracticable. It is in fact a declaration of policy in the form of a tariff law, which, before it can be applied to foreign goods entering China, will have to be elaborated in the form of clauses and schedules giving specific rates of duty upon detailed classes of imports.

**A detailed national tariff**

The experience of other countries in this connection indicates clearly the necessity for expert study of the economic problems involved in the formulation of a new tariff. The elaborate investigation made recently in India, involving as it did a considerable political element, is especially relevant to the present situation in China. The chief difference lies in the stability of a strong central government in India as contrasted with the disorganization of civil war and revolution in China.

**Requires expert preparation**

It is obvious that the reception which is accorded by the powers to any effort at Tariff autonomy on the part of the Chinese government or governments will depend very largely upon the nature of the tariff which is actually put into force. While technically it may be claimed that any attempt by the powers to scrutinize and influence this tariff is an infringement of China's autonomy, it is obvious that China can best achieve the purposes for which she desires tariff autonomy if it is carried out with the consent and good will and confidence of the traders immediately concerned and of their national governments.

The official position of the Japanese government does not differ from that of Great Britain and the United States as far as recognition of the general principle of tariff autonomy is concerned.[25] Japan, however, is more vitally dependent upon the Chinese market than any other power. She has also passed very recently through the experience of regaining tariff autonomy for herself. In

**Japanese experience**

[25] Cf. Documents, Sections 7 and 8; Bau, *op. cit.;* Hornbeck, pp. 548–49.

that process there was an interim period of twelve years after the principle of tariff autonomy had been recognized during which there were special conventional tariffs in operation. This experience has prompted Japanese statesmen to suggest a similar arrangement during a transitional period in China. Their suggestion apparently caused some confusion in the press at the time it was made. It was interpreted to mean that Japan sought a special reciprocity agreement that would admit certain Japanese goods to China at rates of duty lower than those imposed upon similar goods from other countries.

The Japanese suggestion, however, was interpreted by Japanese spokesmen in the Round Tables rather as a request for definite rates upon certain low-grade goods which are of special importance to the trade between China and Japan. It was intended that the same rates of duty should be applied to similar goods coming from other countries. There is, therefore, no discrimination intended, but it was pointed out that there might be some prospect of the arrangement resulting in unfair indirect competition with higher grade varieties of similar goods not subject to special treatment and of greater importance to other exporting countries. The goods upon which Japan is likely to demand special reciprocal treatment are, moreover, the classes of goods in which local industrial development is beginning in China, and in regard to which, therefore, protective tariffs are likely to be levied. The general point, however, was made clear by the Chinese that any discrimination of tariff treatment likely to be imposed upon foreign goods entering China would be discrimination on the basis of the product imported rather than discrimination against countries.

**Conditions of effective tariff autonomy**

To sum up, therefore, the conditions necessary for the successful exercise of tariff autonomy by China either on January 1, 1929, in terms of the Chinese circular letter to the legations, or at a later date, are chiefly three. Obviously the first and most important, as well as the most difficult, is the achievement of an effective, stable, central government which can have administrative unity and efficiency. The second is the preparation in detail of a national tariff law which can and will be applied uniformly throughout China and in a non-discriminatory fashion against the goods of all foreign nations. The third essential for complete tariff autonomy is the creation, training, and effective organization of a staff of Chinese officials. Even when these conditions are approximately fulfilled it would seem desirable, if not absolutely necessary, for an interim period to elapse during which the present tariff or some modification of it should be administered while the new administration was being perfected.

## V. THE ADMINISTRATION OF THE TARIFF[26]

**The Chinese maritime customs**

There is apparently no necessary relation in the minds of the Chinese leaders between the exercise of tariff autonomy and the maintenance of the existing administration by the Chinese maritime customs under the direction of a for-

[26] Bau, *op. cit.;* Hornbeck, pp. 466–67.

eign inspector-general. At the Washington Conference the Chinese delegation made it clear that they did not expect to disturb this administration, but the Chinese spokesmen in the Round Tables declared they did expect more Chinese officials to be placed in the service and trained for positions of responsibility.

The Inspector-General of Customs at the present time is a British subject but acts under the orders of a Chinese official. Sir Francis Aglen, who was inspector-general, was at first discharged and subsequently given a year's leave with the understanding that he would retire at the end of the year because early in 1927 he refused to follow the instructions of the Chinese authorities to collect the surtax of 2½ per cent tentatively authorized at the Washington Conference. The order for his dismissal from the service was issued by the Chinese government in Peking, which appointed Mr. Edwards, the present acting inspector-general, in his place. Mr. Edwards also refused to collect the tax, whereupon the Peking government, following the precedent of the Nationalist government at Hankow,[27] established another customs staff under Chinese control, immediately behind the maritime customs administration. The newly appointed customs officials collect the 2½ per cent while the regular customs administration collects the ordinary 5 per cent, which is largely hypothecated for the service of the debt. The revenue derived from the new taxes goes at present into the treasuries of the parties or military dictators in control of the region of collection, and a portion is appropriated for domestic loans.

**and the new nationalist customs service**

### VI. THE ABOLITION OF LIKIN[28]

Bound up with the question of tariff autonomy is the problem of *likin.* The powers, throughout their negotiations with China, have acted upon the assumption that China is a political entity. They have maintained this assumption, not only by the position they have consistently taken in demanding a uniform national tariff law, but also in the tacit assumption that within the state of China there should be free trade. In the original treaty of Nanking in 1842 the transit dues were recognized upon the moderate scale then in existence. After the imposition of the tax known as likin to meet the expenses of the Taiping Rebellion, the treaties of Tientsin in 1858 agreed to the commutation of these internal revenue charges on foreign goods by a single payment of 2½ per cent ad valorem.

**Increase of likin charges**

With the disorganization of government in recent years the variety and extent of likin charges have greatly increased. The collection of these revenues has necessarily fallen into the hands of the provincial authorities which are *de*

[27] The Hankow government collects a tax upon imports which is denominated a "consumption tax," but is in effect an import duty. The British government on December 18, 1926, strongly urged that the powers should authorize these collections unconditionally (see Whyte, p. 53).

[28] Bau, *op. cit.;* Hornbeck, p. 468.

*facto* in power in any region at any time. There has been some tendency for these authorities or some of them to refuse to honor the agreement under which likin is commuted by the payment of the 2½ per cent transit dues. There are recorded also various less direct ways of taxing the goods which have already paid import and transit tax.

Chinese and foreign merchants are agreed concerning the desirability of abolishing likin, but, owing to the absence of any strong central government and to other factors, such abolition is very difficult. In the only definite resolution adopted at the tariff conference on November 19, 1926, it was stated "the government of the Republic of China declares that likin shall be abolished simultaneously with the enforcement of the Chinese National Tariff Law, and further declares that the abolition of likin shall be effectively carried out by the first day of the first month of the eighteenth year of the Republic of China (January 1, 1929)."[29]

**Their connection with tariff autonomy**

There is a considerable measure of controversy as to whether tariff autonomy was meant to be conditional upon the abolition of likin. The Chinese view is that the resolution is simply a statement to show the conviction of the Chinese that likin is detrimental to their fiscal system and to industrial development and that they intend to abolish it. The declaration by the Peking government has been followed by a statement of the Nanking government that it would begin the abolition of likin on August 1, 1927. The whole problem, however, is regarded by the Chinese as a domestic question, since the payment of the 2½ per cent transit dues renders foreign goods not subject to likin charges.

The reply to this contention is that foreign powers are insistent upon the abolition of likin not only because in practice the immunity of foreign goods from payment is not always realized, but also because the likin revenue at the present time is one of the means by which provincial disunity is being perpetuated and even aggravated.

**The difficulty of abolition of likin**

The abolition of likin, on the other hand, becomes an increasingly difficult governmental operation. It is estimated that a million Chinese subsist directly and indirectly upon the collection of likin. There has been a great increase in the number of stations at which these internal revenue collections are made. The abolition of these stations would involve financial adjustments between the central government and provincial and local authorities which would be very difficult and would call for a high degree of administrative organization and authority. There is at the present time no government in China which has either the authority or the administrative ability to effect this abolition. The prospect of successful tariff autonomy simultaneous with the abolition of likin obviously depends therefore upon the establishment of an administrative unity which hardly seems possible by January 1, 1929.[30]

[29] Bau, *op. cit.*

[30] Bau, *op. cit.*

## TARIFF AUTONOMY IN CHINA

### 3. DOCUMENTS

The basic material for the Round Table discussions on the external political relations of China consisted mainly of four monographs, three of which were prepared with special reference to the needs of the conference.

Each member had a copy of the Report of the Commission on Extra-territoriality, published by the Department of State.

Dr. Mingchien Joshua Bau, professor of Political Science, Peking National Normal University and Peking National College of Law and Politics, prepared material upon the external political problems of China which will shortly be published in book form. The first three chapters, entitled "Tariff Autonomy and Its Exercise," "Extra-territoriality and Its Relinquishment," and "Concessions and Settlements and Their Transference to Chinese Rule," were printed as data papers for the conference. Dr. Bau has kindly allowed them to be reproduced as Sections 3, 4, and 5 of the second part of this volume.

Sir Frederick Whyte's *China and Foreign Powers* was written as a brief historical statement of British policy in China for the use of the members of the British group. After group discussions of the subject matter, the final draft was published just prior to the conference by the Oxford University Press on behalf of the Royal Institute of International Affairs.

Dr. Stanley K. Hornbeck's *China Today: Political* was published by the World Peace Foundation, 40 Mount Vernon Street, Boston, as Vol. X, No. 5 of its pamphlet series. It traverses the recent political history of China and gives an interpretation of the present situation, particularly in relation to American policy.

The three main studies available therefore were complementary. In addition valuable appendixes to each monograph contained practically all the recent official statements of policy which are necessary for an understanding of the international relationships with China. Documents, Section 6, of this volume contains some of the documents which were printed as appendixes to Dr. Bau's work. The three monographs used as a basis for discussion contain adequate references to original source materials which are, therefore, not specifically noted in the following summary.

The Japanese group at the conference also circulated translations of the official statements of Japanese policy in China, together with editorial comments thereon. These translations are reproduced in Documents, Sections 7 and 8 of this volume.

### REFERENCES TO DATA MATERIAL

1. Treaty relating to Chinese customs tariff (Washington) February 6, 1922 (text in Hornbeck, pp. 526–9).

2. Special Conference on the Chinese Customs Tariff (report in *China Year Book* [1926], chap. xxix, pp. 1106–46).

3. British Memorandum on China Policy, December 18, 1926 (text in Whyte, pp. 49–65).

4. Statement of Japanese policy by Shidehara, January 16, 1927 (text in Hornbeck, pp. 548–49).

5. Declaration of American policy of Kellogg, January 27, 1927 (text in Hornbeck, pp. 550–53).

6. Statement of Japanese policy by Tanaka, May 28, 1927 (Documents, Section 7, below).

7. Chinese statement by the Peking government, January 13, 1927 (text in Bau, Documents, Section 6, below).

8. Peking Conference Resolution on Tariff Autonomy, November 19, 1925 (text in Hornbeck, p. 464n.).

9. Hankow Agreement between China and Great Britain, February 19, 1927 (text in Whyte, pp. 65–73).

10. Customs tariff and maritime customs administration (Hornbeck, pp. 458–68).

11. Tariff autonomy and its exercise (Bau, Documents, Section 3, below).

12. The inspectorate of customs (Morse, *The Trade and Administration of China*, pp. 385–410).

## EXTRA-TERRITORIALITY IN CHINA

### 1. QUESTIONS FOR DISCUSSION

1. What, if any, statements in Parts I, II, III of the Extra-territoriality Commission's report are open to question?
2. What are the principal Chinese objections to the extra-territorial system?
3. What are the principal contentions of foreign governments or nationals in support of the continuance of the extra-territorial system?
4. What are the arguments for and against (*a*) the immediate abolition of extra-territorial rights, and (*b*) abolition by a progressive scheme?
5. What, if any, amendments should be made to the recommendations of the Commission on Extra-territoriality?
6. What express promises have the major foreign powers made with regard to extra-territorial rights?
7. Which of these promises can they carry out by unilateral action?
8. What further, if anything, might they do by unilateral action?
9. What can China, by unilateral action, do to attain the ends sought?
10. What, if any, forms of united action to the same ends should be undertaken?

### 2. SUMMARY OF ROUND-TABLE DISCUSSIONS

CHAIRMEN AND SECRETARIES

Round Table I
*Chairman:* KENZO TAKAYANAGI
*Secretary:* H. DUNCAN HALL

Round Table II
*Chairman:* SIR ARTHUR CURRIE
*Secretary:* KARL C. LEEBRICK

Round Table III
*Chairman:* WILLIAM H. KILPATRICK
*Secretary:* MALCOLM MACDONALD

Round Table IV
*Chairman:* GEORGE H. BLAKESLEE
*Secretary:* DANIEL J. FLEMING

#### I. THE ORIGIN OF EXTRA-TERRITORIALITY

The conception of law held in the minds of Occidental peoples is that of a body of rules, principles, and standards enforceable by the sovereign authority of a state throughout the territory over which that authority reigns, and applying with equal justice to all people resident in that territory. This conception is clearly connected with the rise of nation-states and of nationalism and democracy in Western Europe in the modern age. Law has not always been territorial in character. Nor has it always been formal and democratic in procedure. A great deal of medieval law was based upon the rights of persons and classes rather than upon general rules applying equally over a certain area. Justice was not always regarded as one and indivisible. Nor did there always exist formal machinery working by elaborate and recognized rules for the equal and impersonal dispensation of justice to all men of whatever degree. There was in the Middle Ages in Europe a great deal of justice dispensed by the personal fiat of king and feudal lord or village assembly. The rule of law is essentially a modern and Western-European, and to some extent a Christian, conception. As social life has grown more complex, codes of law have been built up for its regulation as the law merchant grew out of the trading contacts in the medieval fairs and provided a basis for the commercial law of all Western-European countries.

**Modern territorial law**

With the extension of commerce beyond Europe in the modern age, Occidental traders have come into contact with peoples whose social organization and legal conceptions are radically different from those which have developed in the West. It is a recognized principle of customary international law that the fiat of every sovereign state runs unchallenged within its own borders. But the differences of legal conceptions as between East and West were so fundamental and the dangers of misunderstanding leading to conflict so great that as trade developed the system grew up of European traders remaining subjects to their own law even while resident in other lands. The Chinese view of this arrangement is well illustrated by a Chinese statement quoted by Morse (*International Relations of the Chinese Empire, 1834–1860,* I, 111–12): "The barbarians are like beasts, and not to be ruled on the same principles as Chinese. Were one to attempt controlling them by the great maxims of reason, it would tend to nothing but the greatest confusion."

**different from eastern law**

This system which arose by mutual agreement in the first place and was not unwelcome to the Eastern countries has become known as extra-territoriality—the extension of jurisdiction by a state beyond its borders. It is different in origin and character from ex-territoriality—the exemption from jurisdiction of privileged persons, such as diplomats, or things, such as public vessels, physically within foreign territory. By its nature, however, it implies such exemption, and it is upon this consequential exemption from the jurisdiction of the state that most of the criticism of extra-territoriality in China at the present time has centered. As European commerce and industrial methods have penetrated the Eastern countries they have been accompanied by European education and social ideas. The existing local social and industrial organizations have been disturbed and the political systems have been radically altered. Nationalism, derived largely from European notions of sovereignty, has appeared,

**Extra-territoriality a compromise**

**which is now challenged**

and one of its first objectives has invariably been the abolition of the extra-territorial rights enjoyed by foreigners.

China is the only country in which the system remains in full effect, though elements of it are still to be found in Morocco and Egypt. Japan terminated extra-territorial rights by treaty negotiations in 1894. Turkey recently abolished them by unilateral action, later confirmed by treaty, and the system has been abandoned also in such countries as Siam and Persia.

### II. EXTRA-TERRITORIALITY IN CHINA

The practice of extra-territoriality in China began as a consequence of the Treaty of Nanking, 1842, to which reference was made in the preceding chapter. The principle was incorporated in the Regulations of Trade of 1843, which were worked out for the elaboration of the treaty and was given definition and precision in the China–United States treaty of 1844.[1] The treaties of Tientsin (1858) and later treaties further elaborated the privileges which have been extended on various later occasions.[2]

The present situation may be summarized as follows:[3]

**Extra-territorial rights**

1. Controversies in which no foreigners are involved are tried in Chinese courts according to Chinese law (cases before the mixed courts are an exception to this general rule).

2. Controversies between two or more nationals of the same treaty power are tried in the consular courts or other courts of that power, and the law applied is that of the power concerned.

3. Controversies between nationals of different treaty powers are determined, not by Chinese Courts, but by the authorities and the laws of the countries concerned, and according to agreement between these countries.

4. Controversies between nationals of non-treaty powers and nationals of treaty powers, wherein the latter are defendants, are determined according to arrangement between the powers concerned. In suits in which the non-treaty-power nationals are defendants, jurisdiction is in the Chinese courts.

5. Controversies in which all the parties are non-treaty-power nationals or in which non-treaty-power nationals appear as plaintiffs or complainants against Chinese defendants are settled in Chinese tribunals under Chinese law.

6. Controversies between Chinese and nationals of treaty powers are determined by the tribunals of the defendant, and the law applied is that of the country of the defendant.

7. Chinese police officials may arrest foreigners, but must turn over treaty-

[1] Bau, Documents, Section 4, below; Hornbeck, pp. 449, 493–4.

[2] Bau, *op. cit.;* Hornbeck, pp. 449, 496–97; Whyte, p. 5.

[3] Hornbeck, pp. 451–52; *Report of Commission on Extra-territoriality,* pp. 7–26.

power nationals to the proper authorities of their own nationality or of a country of which they are protégés.[4]

The abortive Mackay treaty between China and Great Britain in 1902, and the similar treaties with the United States and Japan in the following year and Sweden in 1908 contained definite statements that the powers would relinquish their extra-territorial rights when judicial reforms had been accomplished. The actual wording of the article in question is of some importance: "Article XII. China having expressed a strong desire to reform her judicial system and to bring it into accord with that of Western nations, Great Britain agrees to give every assistance to such reform, and she will also be prepared to relinquish her extraterritorial rights when she is satisfied that the state of the Chinese laws, the arrangement for their administration, and other considerations warrant her in so doing."[5]

**and their relinquishment**

In 1919 the Chinese representatives at Versailles presented an unsuccessful request to the Peace Conference for the termination of extra-territoriality.[6] However, she secured German recognition of the termination of her treaties by agreements of May 20, 1921.[7] By the Sino-Russian agreement of May 31, 1924, diplomatic relations between China and Russia were resumed upon the basis of the renunciation by Russia of extra-territorial privileges.[8]

### III. THE REPORT OF THE COMMISSION ON EXTRA-TERRITORIALITY

The Chinese delegation to the Washington conference in 1922 again submitted a claim for the abolition of extra-territoriality, and it was agreed by the nine powers concerned to appoint a commission of investigation "to inquire into the present practice of extra-territorial jurisdiction in China, and into the laws and the judicial system and the methods of judicial administration of China, with a view to reporting to the governments of the several powers before named their findings of fact in regard to these matters, and their recommendations as to such means as they may find suitable to improve the existing conditions of the administration of justice in China, and to assist and further the efforts of the Chinese government to effect such legislation and judicial reforms as would warrant the several powers in relinquishing, either progressively or otherwise, their respective rights of extra-territoriality."[9]

**The Commission on Extra-territoriality**

This Commission met in China in January, 1926, and after an investigation lasting for nine months presented a unanimous report. The report as published deals with the questions submitted to it under four heads: the present

[4] Hornbeck, pp. 451–52.

[5] Bau, *op. cit.;* Hornbeck, p. 509.

[6] Bau, *op. cit.;* Whyte, pp. 16–19, 46–47.

[7] Hornbeck, pp. 516–22.

[8] Bau, "Documents," Documents, Section 6, No. 11.

[9] Bau, *op. cit.;* Hornbeck, pp. 531–32; Whyte, pp. 23–27, 48–49.

practice of extra-territoriality in China, the laws and judicial system of China, the administration of justice in China, and finally, recommendations. The Chinese representative on the Commission signed the report with reservations concerning Parts I, II, and III.[10]

unfavorable to immediate abolition

The report is on the whole unfavorable to the Chinese claim for abolition. After a clear and critical description of the actual working of extra-territoriality and an examination of the Chinese objections to it, the report proceeds to similar examinations of the laws, judicial system, prison system, and judicial administration of China. The final recommendations of the Commission are summarized below.[11]

The Commissioners "are of the opinion that when these recommendations shall have been reasonably complied with, the several powers would be warranted in relinquishing" extra-territoriality.

The recommendations may be summarized as follows:

Recommendations of the Commission

1. The administration of justice should be protected from military interference.

2. The Chinese government should adopt a program for legal and judicial reform, including measures to remedy the criticisms advanced by the Commission; the codification of the civil and commercial law and revision of the criminal code, the establishment and maintenance of a uniform system of legislation, the extension of modern courts and prisons.

3. After the principal items of this program are carried out, the powers concerned might consider the abolition of extra-territoriality by a progressive scheme.

4. Pending this abolition, the powers should make certain modifications in the practice of extra-territoriality, including the use as far as practicable of Chinese law in the extra-territorial courts. The trial of mixed cases as a general rule before the modern Chinese courts, the reorganization of the special mixed courts to accord more with the modern Chinese judicial system, the correction of abuses arising from extension of extra-territorial powers to include certain Chinese persons and interests, and arrangements between the Chinese authorities and the powers for judicial assistance in such matters as the execution of judgments, summonses, and warrants.

An intelligent discussion of extra-territoriality obviously depends upon a clear perception of the facts, both in regard to judicial practice in the extra-territorial courts themselves, and to the state of Chinese law and justice outside the extra-territorial courts. A large part of the report of the Commission on Extra-territoriality is taken up with the survey of these facts. The first general criticism of Chinese law concerns the absence of any firm constitutional basis

[10] *Report*, p. 109.

[11] *Report*, pp. 107–9; also Hornbeck, pp. 544–47; and Bau, "Documents," Documents, Section 6, No. X.

for the law which is being used. This results, not only in an insecurity of the judiciary and constant encroachments by military leaders or their administrators into the sphere of the civil law, but also in great anomalies of legislation and in failure to fill the large gaps in existing legislation. It is natural that these gaps should be found mainly in those parts of the law which deal with matters such as commerce and which are regarded as particularly important from the point of view of the foreigners.[12]

**Lack of constitutional basis**

With regard to the judicial system, the Commission comments upon the control of the judiciary by administrative officials and the consequent lack of independent status. Outside of the modern courts the judicial machinery, consisting mainly of magistrates' courts, police tribunals, and military courts, is not of such a character as to command the confidence of foreigners. The Commission cites several important cases of military interference militating against the normal administration of justice which it regards as a most serious criticism which should be made against the judicial administration at the present time. Moreover, the laws which were studied by the Commission, though promulgated by the government at Peking, are not universally applied throughout China. Certain areas categorically refused to acknowledge these laws, and others have built up a subsidiary system of legislation. The most satisfactory courts in China are the so-called "modern courts," which number 139. This number was considered by the Commission to be inadequate. The number of trained judicial officials is also quite insufficient, and the provision made up to date for training further officials did not satisfy the Commission. The judiciary also appears to lack proper financial and administrative support. While the modern courts function satisfactorily as far as their power extends, there is only one such court to every 4,400,000 of the population. Most of the litigation of China is in the hands of magistrates' courts, but there is only one of them for every 300,000 people. The police and military tribunals were regarded by the Chinese government as outside the scope of the Commission's investigation.[13]

**Military interference**

**Laws not universally recognized**

**Number of courts inadequate**

### IV. THE CHINESE ATTITUDE

The first question which was faced in the Round-Table discussion was the correctness and adequacy of the picture which the Commission's report draws of the state of law and justice in China. It was agreed that the statements contained in the report were accurate, as far as they went; but the Chinese members and some others who are familiar with Chinese conditions pleaded that China had already made great strides in reform; that the number of courts which satisfy modern conditions is remarkably large considering the conditions under which they have been created; that the undertaking involved in modernizing the legal and judicial system of such a country as China was almost in-

**Reform has been substantial**

[12] *Report*, pp. 51–55.

[13] *Report*, pp. 79–83, 90–103.

comprehensibly difficult. The Chinese spokesmen represented that the leaders of modern China were working strenuously toward the reforms which the Commission set forth as desirable. They are doing this in the face of revolution, civil war, and internal conflict arising from differences of opinion concerning the development of the new political order.

**The worst abuses do not affect foreigners**

The Chinese themselves are suffering most from the present unsatisfactory state of the law. They claim that the foreigners are free from the worst abuses of the present system, even where they have given up or do not possess extra-territorial rights. Under the regulations of November 25, 1926, governing the trial of non-extra-territorial aliens, foreigners are free from the police tribunals, the magistrates' courts, and military courts.[14]

**Experience of Germans**

The position of the Germans and Russians since losing their extra-territorial privileges is a matter of some doubt. There has been some complaint, particularly from the Russians in Manchuria.[15] As the Chinese themselves have suffered from arbitrary taxation and government, the Russians, who are on much the same legal footing as the Chinese, have suffered also. It was maintained, however, that while these statements are correct, they represent abuses arising from an abnormal situation rather than a permanent condition. There has been a good deal of injustice, but the German and Russian traders have not, apparently, shared the recent experiences of Americans and Britishers. They have in many cases been able to continue their businesses when British and American traders were obliged to leave. The Germans in particular, it was maintained, are so satisfied on the whole that they make little complaint about the inconveniences.

**Chinese reluctance to Westernize their system**

The introduction of modern codes of law cuts across the old Chinese system and in many important respects is alien to Chinese principles of conduct and morality. There is some danger of attempting to force Western theories and practice upon the whole of China because of the position of a minority of alien residents in small sections of the country. The foreign residents in China are not, after all, very numerous. With the exception of a few thousand missionaries, most of them reside in treaty ports where they have access to the so-called "modern courts," which the British minister has recently recognized to be satisfactory according to Western standards. Many Chinese feel some reluctance to give up entirely their traditional methods of organization. The codes of law are admittedly incomplete and imperfect, even in Chinese eyes; but why should China have to revise her laws along Western lines and assume without question that those lines are the best for China as well as for the countries where they were originally developed? The Chinese recognize their duty to build up a satisfactory system of Chinese law, but not necessarily law designed primarily to suit foreigners. Nationals from many foreign countries are inter-

[14] Bau, "Documents," Documents, Section 6, No. XII.

[15] Hornbeck, p. 455.

ested in China, and the Chinese leaders are dismayed at the prospect of devising a "chop suey" legal system which may have some resemblance to the legal systems of each of these countries. The Chinese feel that the demand of the foreigners to have the same liberties as they have in their own countries is not entirely reasonable. Foreigners who wish to live and trade in China should, they feel, cast in their lot with the Chinese and accept what the Chinese have to offer.

The tradition of Chinese justice derived from the family organization on which the Chinese Empire has rested for thousands of years is based upon moral rather than legal principles. Arbitration is resorted to rather than appeal to authority. The Chinese method of settling disputes is by resort in the first place to the friendly arbitration of neighbors or elders. The gilds and the more recent chambers of commerce, for example, have in the past appointed their own courts from among their own membership. This principle of neighborly arbitration is, in the Chinese view, capable of wide extension. The provisions made under the foreign-controlled administration of the customs service for resort to arbitration in case of dispute was represented to be quite satisfactory and very popular with foreign merchants in China.

**Traditional use of arbitration in China**

On the other hand, it is clear that the very foundation of China's thought has been disturbed by the West, and many Chinese today desire to mold their politics and law upon European or American models. The simple administration of law in a village is difficult of application to such large and complicated issues as arise out of commercial and industrial contacts. China is changing. New interests have arisen which require codified law and courts upon the Western model. The provision of such courts is essential for the abolition of extraterritoriality; but, as the experience of Japan showed, this is a long and difficult task.[16]

**inadequate for modern commerce**

To sum up, therefore, there is at present a fundamental conflict between the more highly developed system of law of the industrialized Occident and the less highly developed system of China. In China there is not only an absence of provision for some of the most important problems of modern life, but there is also less regard for individual personality and immunities. Some Chinese are apt to take the position that if foreigners do not like the ways of China they have no need to come to China, and if they come they can always go away. But the Chinese themselves, or many of them, do not feel satisfied with their system and are anxious to improve it and to improve it along Western lines.

[16] The codification of Japanese law began as a result of Japan's contact with the Western powers. In 1872, in order to prepare for the abrogation of her extra-territorial treaties, she invited the assistance of a French jurist. The first draft of the laws was not published for ten years, and another ten years was necessary before the final codification took place and was promulgated in 1892. During this period also Japan steadily developed her police system, prisons, and judicial administration. The final abolition of extra-territoriality in Japan took place in 1899.

They want something better than the justice which at present prevails in China. It was argued in the Round Tables that the imposition of extra-territoriality by the foreigners and their persistent adherence to it have accelerated the effort of the Chinese people to get more highly developed legal and judicial systems of their own.

**World-tendency to uniformity of commercial law**

There is, moreover, a distinct tendency in the modern world, flowing naturally from the linking of the various countries more and more closely into one world complex of industry and trade, toward uniformity, especially of commercial law. If world-trade is to develop there must be an accentuation of this tendency toward uniformity. It was argued, therefore, that there should be adaptation and elaboration of the legal system of China sufficient for the conditions of modern life as they affect her commerce and contacts generally with the outside world. Foreigners who live in China must know where they stand. China will need in the future to look to foreign countries for capital and expert help, and will need first to get the confidence of those countries. She has nothing to gain in the modern world, but everything to lose, by antagonizing her neighbors.

### V. THE ARGUMENT AGAINST ABOLITION

**Security for foreign trade**

The provision of extra-territorial courts and the friction arising therefrom is extremely inconvenient to the foreign powers concerned. They have expressed their definite desire to abolish the system as soon as China is prepared and willing to protect the lives and liberty of the foreigners in her midst and to assume full responsibility for protecting property and trade. It is true that foreigners obtained their privileges in China by the use of force at a time when China was not ready to accord them. They not only insisted upon coming, in spite of opposition, but insisted and still insist upon laying down the conditions upon which they enter. While this is historically true, however, the facts of the present situation must be recognized. The foreigners are established in China, and they have developed certain businesses and established certain relationships which are of value to the Chinese as well as to themselves. These relationships necessitate the regulation of modern law. No business can continue today without the certainty and security which proceed from a proper legal and judicial system.

**essential for Chinese prosperity**

It was argued that the continued existence of foreign relationships with China, especially trading relationships, is necessary for the welfare of the Chinese people, who have gone too far along the road of international co-operation to be able to reverse their steps without great cost. The changed organization over large areas in China would suffer greatly, and is suffering today, from hindrances to trade and commerce. Many Chinese individuals, especially merchants, are directly involved in these relationships and are apprehensive of any sudden changes which might affect them detrimentally. They may often be prepared to pay the price of patriotism by submitting cheerfully to difficulties while their country is regaining the mastery of her own affairs; but they are anxious to reduce these difficulties of transition to the minimum.

It was agreed that on these and other grounds the dangers of premature abolition are very real. The revision of the Chinese legal system, promising as it is admitted to be as far as it has gone, has not yet been completed. The abolition of extra-territoriality and the exercise of judicial power by China before she is prepared might result in situations which would be more serious than those arising from the continuation of extra-territoriality.

The Round-Table argument on this point was very similar to the discussion which arose consequentially concerning the presence of foreign troops in Shanghai and other areas. The British memorandum of December 18, 1926, and the recent pronouncements of other foreign powers were admitted by the Chinese to contain concessions to Chinese sentiment and to represent a sincere desire for improvement of international relationships with China; but the Chinese people, it was maintained, are reluctant to take the protestations of the powers' friendship as sincere. They need to be convinced that the dispatch of troops almost simultaneously with the issue of specific statements was not a contradiction of words by deeds. The reply to this suspicion is that the troops were dispatched in order to prevent incidents in a time of disorganization which might have led, as they have led in the past, to more serious clashes between China and the powers, that the troops have been used with restraint and complete absence of provocative action, and that no foreign government would venture to fly in the face of public opinion at home by using them aggressively. The difficulty of convincing the Chinese that this attitude consistently represents the policy of the powers concerned is, however, very great, and is not lessened by what the Chinese regard as the provocative interpretation placed upon the presence of foreign troops by certain sections of the foreign nationals resident in China. The same argument was adduced against the continuance of extra-territorial privileges.

**Foreign troops in China**

**defended as protection against unfortunate incidents**

VI. CHINESE OBJECTIONS TO THE PRESENT SITUATION

The Chinese objections to extra-territoriality have often been stated.[17] The principal points relating to the present situation which were made in the Round-Table discussions by Chinese spokesmen were:

1. It is in derogation of China's sovereign rights.
2. There is a multiplicity of foreign courts and of foreign legal codes, giving rise to a widespread perplexity.
3. It is likely to be impossible to produce at a consular court the witnesses needed in the trial of a foreign defendant.
4. This tends to give the foreigner a sense of being outside the law, as the chances of his being convicted are slight.

**Chinese objections to extra-territoriality**

[17] See, e.g., *Report*, pp. 19–25; Hornbeck, pp. 452–53, footnote.

5. Foreigners under cover of extra-territoriality claim immunity from local taxes.

6. Chinese are found who register as foreign citizens in a foreign consulate and thereby secure immunity even when defying justice.

7. Whatever may have been the ground for creating the extra-territorial system in China, the need for it no longer exists.

8. So long as the system remains in force it tends to breed envy, dislike, and even hatred of the foreigner.

9. Under the present system the Chinese still feel uncertain of securing justice in certain foreign courts.

It was pointed out that the feeling in many parts of China at the present time in regard to the special privileges enjoyed by subjects of foreign states makes foreigners a target for criticism and more active expressions of resentment. There is a feeling on the part of some Chinese which inclines them to discriminate against those who have extra-territorial rights and in favor of those who have abandoned them. The Chinese insist, moreover, that the situation is not bounded by the technical niceties of international law. The suspicion is strong that technical and legal difficulties and criticisms are merely a screen behind which the foreigners tenaciously hold to privileges which have become irksome to the Chinese. They find it difficult to believe that the powers will do anything until they are forced by the active resentment of the Chinese people.

**Distrust of technicalities**

### VII. THE CONSTRUCTIVE PROPOSALS OF THE POWERS

The abuse of extra-territorial rights in certain cases was recognized by the report of the Commission on Extra-territoriality. Some of the recommendations of the Commission aim specifically at the reduction of these abuses. The attitude of the foreign powers chiefly concerned in this question would appear from official pronouncement to be clear and consistent. There is no marked disagreement between the attitude of the United States, Great Britain, and France. These powers have expressly stated on many occasions their recognition of China's right to be freed from extra-territoriality as soon as China is prepared to take the necessary steps for protection of life and property according to Western standards. The difficult conditions obtaining in China at the present time, particularly the lack of civil government to support the courts, prevent these promises from being carried into effect. The same situation prevents China from making more rapid progress toward fulfilment of the conditions which are regarded by the powers as necessary. Even after stable government has been established there will remain much to be done before the administration of Chinese justice is practically effective throughout China.

**Powers prepared for abolition**

The British government, in its memorandum of December 18, 1926, proposed that the Washington Treaty should declare their readiness to negotiate as soon as the Chinese themselves have constituted a government with authority to negotiate, and should state their intention pending the establishment of such a government to pursue a constructive policy in harmony with the spirit of the Washington Conference but developed and adapted to meet the altered circumstances of the present time.[18] In the same memorandum the powers were urged to agree to execute those recommendations of the report of the Commission on Extra-territoriality which can be carried into effect even under present conditions without great delay. Subsequently, on February 8, 1927, in a communication of the British government to the League of Nations, certain measures for treaty modification communicated to the Chinese authorities on January 27, 1927, were disclosed.[19] These measures were recognized as making considerable concessions to the Chinese. In announcing them the British government took a position which was in many respects in advance of the views of many British residents in China. The position taken by the United States and by Japan does not differ materially from that of Great Britain in this regard. Upon the basis of these pronouncements a progressive scheme for the abolition of extra-territorial privileges is possible as soon as the Chinese internal situation makes negotiation possible.

**Immediate preliminary steps**

### VIII. THE NEXT STEPS

The treaty powers are committed by repeated declarations to the complete abolition of extra-territoriality in China at the earliest possible moment. They have recognized the sincerity of the Chinese policy of judicial reform and taken note of the substantial progress already made in the face of great difficulties. They recognize, moreover, that prompt action on their part is highly desirable to convince the Chinese of the sincerity of their professions of friendship and good will and to assist in bringing order as quickly as possible out of a situation which is already bad and may possibly worsen rapidly. The immediate problem, therefore, is to find ways and means by which such action may be taken by the powers as may best promote stability in China and lead to the possibility of speedy abolition of extra-territoriality under conditions which will strengthen and not diminish international co-operation and good will.

**Further progress desirable**

In order to clarify the discussion, the Round-Table chairmen and secretaries acted upon a suggestion made in one of the Round Tables that a scheme should be drawn up containing the proposed steps which might be practicable in the immediate future. The statement reproduced below was therefore presented to the Round Tables as a basis for discussion.

1. A program capable of immediate execution prior to the establishment of a national government in China.

[18] Whyte, pp. 49–55.

[19] Whyte, pp. 61–64; Hornbeck, pp. 556–60; Bau, "Documents," Documents, Section 6, No. VI.

i) The powers should recognize the sincerity of the Chinese policy of judicial reform, and take note of the substantial progress made.

**An immediate program**

ii) The powers, while conscious of the element of risk involved in precipitate action, none the less should recognize that action is necessary.

iii) The powers should take immediate steps to rid the practice of extra-territoriality of all abuses that now surround it.

iv) The powers should put into operation without delay in their consular courts one or more of the codes of Chinese law already promulgated.

v) The powers should continue to develop this policy, along the lines of the measures proposed by the British government in the note handed to the Peking and Hankow governments on January 27, 1927; it being premised that these measures represent only the first steps in a deliberate policy designed to settle as many outstanding issues as possible during the period which must elapse before a stable government is established with which a new treaty can be made.

2. A program for adoption during a period of transition after a suitable national government has been established in China.

i) The complete relinquishment of extra-territoriality should be stipulated in a new treaty between China and the powers concerned, separately or collectively.

**More distant views**

ii) By an exchange of notes between China and the powers the following transitional system for the trial of foreigners should then be established:

(*a*) Foreigners should come exclusively under the jurisdiction of Chinese modern courts, which means exemption from magistrates', police, and military courts.

(*b*) Five special benches should be established in the existing courts at Peking, Shanghai, Hankow, Canton, and Chungking for the trial of foreigners.

(*c*) These modern courts and special benches should be courts of first instance for the trial of foreigners.

(*d*) There should be a court of appeal at Shanghai.

(*e*) There should also be a special bench for the consideration of such cases in the Supreme Court at Peking.

(*f*) Foreign lawyers subject to regulations should be admitted to practice in these courts.

(*g*) Interpreters should be attached to these courts.

(*h*) Certain foreign legal advisers should be appointed by the Chinese government to the before-mentioned special benches to help in matters of foreign jurisdiction, their function to be entirely advisory.

iii) The Chinese government, by a unilateral declaration, would make the following judicial guaranties:

(*a*) That no foreigner would be arrested without a proper judicial warrant, unless seized *flagranti delicto*.

(*b*) That the writ of habeas corpus should be applied.

(*c*) That publicity of trials and hearings should be observed.

**Their dependence upon Chinese unity**

It was pointed out immediately that underlying the whole discussion of the abolition of extra-territoriality there was an assumed and tacit hypothesis that at an early date there would emerge in China a government which would legislate for the whole of China and which could effectively administer its legislation. There was, however, considerable doubt in the minds of many members as to the soundness of this hypothesis. The optimism of the Chinese was not shared by all. It was made clear, in order to prevent misunderstanding, that considerable reservations existed in the minds of many members, not only concerning the immediate possibility of unified government in China, but also concerning the ultimate result of the civil war at present in progress. It was felt by some to be not only possible, but probable, that after a prolonged period of disorganization more than one government might emerge in China, and that the relations between these governments might range anywhere from complete independence to various forms of federalism.

**or local settlement**

With this explicit reservation in mind, the discussion of the detailed proposals was taken up. The schemes considered are broadly applicable to any form of stable government that may emerge in China. The suggestions made go beyond the strict letter of the official pronouncements of either Great Britain, the United States, or Japan. It was pointed out also that many other powers are concerned and that the practical problem is rendered considerably more difficult by the necessity of securing some approximation of uniformity of action by all the powers concerned.[20]

**First steps to reform**

The United States, however, has already adopted the recommendation of the Commission on Extra-territoriality (Section IV, subsection 1) "that the powers concerned should administer, so far as practicable, in their extra-territorial or consular courts such laws and regulations of China as they may deem it proper to adopt." This has been done by unilateral action, and it was urged that as a first step all the powers take similar unilateral action to meet such of the recommendations of the Extra-territoriality Commission as require unilateral action only, and specifically those which appear in Part IV, Section IV, Subsections 1, 2, and 3 of the *Report*. It was apparent that such action would be welcomed by Chinese opinion. The remedying of abuses connected with the extension of foreign citizenship to Chinese who are thereby enabled to shelter themselves under extra-territorial privileges would also be welcome to the Chi-

[20] A list of the treaties involved is given in the *Report of the Commission on Extra-territoriality*, pp. 113–14.

nese. The very difficult problem of the use of the foreign banks by Chinese militarists was raised in this connection. A further Chinese proposal was that foreigners employed in the civil service of the Chinese government should, in respect to charges relating to their official work, come under the jurisdiction of Chinese law and Chinese courts.

The section of the program suggested for adoption during a period of transition after a stable government has been established in China was not discussed in detail.

### 3. DOCUMENTS

The basic material for the Round Table discussions summarized here is described under chapter ii, dealing with tariff autonomy in China.

### REFERENCES TO DATA MATERIAL

1. *Report of Commission on Extra-territoriality in China,* Part IV, "Recommendations."

2. *China Yearbook, 1926,* chap. xxii, pp. 753–86, "Public Justice."

3. Bau, "Extra-territoriality and Its Relinquishment" (Documents, Section 4).

4. "Extra-territoriality in the China Treaties" (Hornbeck, pp. 449–558).

5. Morse, *Trade and Administration of China,* chap. vii, "Extra-territoriality."

## FOREIGN CONCESSIONS AND SETTLEMENTS IN CHINA

### 1. QUESTIONS FOR DISCUSSION

1. What are the main objections to the present system of municipal government in the International Settlement at Shanghai?
2. What are the principal contentions of the advocates of the existing régime?
3. Did the judicial inquiry settle the affair of May 30, 1925? If not, what steps should be taken to settle the matter?
4. What plan for the government of Shanghai will best meet the situation?
5. What are the principal objections to the continued existence of concessions, settlements, and leased areas?
6. What are the contentions in favor of their continuance?
7. What is the best procedure for restoring them to Chinese administration?

### 2. SUMMARY OF ROUND-TABLE DISCUSSIONS

CHAIRMEN AND SECRETARIES

Round Table I
*Chairman:* KENZO TAKAYANAGI
*Secretary:* H. DUNCAN HALL

Round Table II
*Chairman:* SIR ARTHUR CURRIE
*Secretary:* KARL C. LEEBRICK

Round Table III
*Chairman:* WILLIAM H. KILPATRICK
*Secretary:* MALCOLM MACDONALD

Round Table IV
*Chairman:* GEORGE H. BLAKESLEE
*Secretary:* DANIEL J. FLEMING

#### I. FOREIGN RESIDENTIAL AREAS IN CHINA

**The importance of Shanghai now**

The existence within the territorial jurisdiction of China of enclaves within which are exercised various forms and degrees of government by foreign consuls, municipal councils, or diplomats has within comparatively recent years become one of the chief points of irritation between China and the foreign powers concerned. The problem centers at Shanghai, which is the greatest trading port of China and the key to many forms of further development, political, economic, and social, in China. The foreign-controlled administration of Shanghai and its present occupation and temporary fortification by foreign troops also emphasize its importance in this connection. Both Chinese and foreign residents realize the urgency and importance of the problem it presents.

There are, however, a number of other areas of foreign residence in China within which municipal government is exercised in various ways by alien authorities. The occupation and control of these areas by foreign residents has developed since the period of trading contacts in the latter half of the nineteenth century. In some cases, particularly of certain Japanese colonies, the origin of foreign residence goes no farther back than the beginning of the twentieth century.[1] It is possible, if foreign trade with China should increase more rapidly, that other areas of foreign residence may develop and call for a still wider application of modern municipal government. Apart from the present somewhat tense situation in Shanghai, therefore, the relation of efficient municipal administration to Chinese sovereignty is likely to be an important problem in the future.

**and in the future**

**Foreign residential areas**

The origin of the practice of setting aside special areas for foreign residence is to be found in the Treaty of Nanking, 1842, which opened up the first five treaty ports to foreign trade. In the supplementary treaty of the following year certain areas within or adjacent to those ports were set aside for the use of the foreign traders. The number of open ports was increased by subsequent treaties and by voluntary action by the Chinese government, and is now forty-nine.[2] Generally speaking, the foreign residents, excepting most missionaries,[3] tend to live in definite areas within each port; but only in a minority of these ports are there one or more concessions or settlements under foreign municipal administration. The legal documents upon which such administration is based are different in every case.[4] The practice, and in some cases the boundaries, of foreign control have extended considerably as European and American and Japanese commerce has become greater in recent years. In some cases the basis of this control, and in practically every case its precise extent, depend largely upon custom, tacitly or expressly recognized by Chinese authorities, local or central. Beside the Chinese local and national authorities and the foreign residents, the foreign consular officials in local areas, the diplomatic corps at Peking, and eventually foreign governments, are involved in the present situation. The chief factor of change arises from the insistent challenge of Chinese nationalism, expressed partly through governmental action and partly through various forms of public opinion, to the practice, and in some instances the bases, of the municipal administration in these areas.

[1] Bau, "Concessions and Settlements and Their Transference to Chinese Rule" (Documents, Section 5); Hornbeck, p. 469, *China Official Yearbook, 1926,* pp. 594–608; Willoughby, *Foreign Rights and Interests in China* (1927 ed.), Vol. I, chaps. xvii–xxi.

[2] Hornbeck, p. 469.

[3] "The rights of foreigners to carry on trade and other pursuits, to hold land, etc., may be exercised, except by missionaries, only in the open ports" (Willoughby, *op. cit.,* p. 495). See for missionary rights, Willoughby, Vol. II, chap. xxviii.

[4] Willoughby, I, 501.

The main classes of foreign territorial jurisdiction in China may be distinguished as follows, arranged in order of the degree in which they may be held to derogate from China's sovereignty.[5]

Their main classes

1. Foreign residential areas in which some powers of municipal government have arisen without express legal authority based upon treaties or other explicit agreements, and where such administration could be taken over, amended, or abolished by the Chinese government if and when it was able and desired to do so.[6]

2. Settlements in the technical sense of the term, which has come to mean foreign residential areas where there are legal documents conferring some powers of local government upon the residents. The international settlements at Amoy and Shanghai come within this category, the latter being the more important both absolutely and in relation to the present situation.[7]

3. Concessions, in the strict sense of the term, meaning territory that has been formally leased to a foreign government which in consequence exercises various rights of municipal government. The authority in these concessions is usually vested in the foreign consul concerned, though there is often a municipal council with mainly advisory powers. The French concession at Shanghai and the five concessions at Tientsin come under this category, as did the recently surrendered British concessions at Hankow and Kiukiang.[8]

4. The legation quarter at Peking which is under the control of the diplomatic corps under conditions defined in the Boxer Protocol of 1901.[9]

5. Leased territories in which the government authority is completely transferred for a term of years, as at Tsingtao, Port Arthur, Kuangchouwan, Weihaiwei, and formerly at Kiauchau. The latter, which was leased to Germany in 1898, was captured by Japan in the Great War and was returned to China in December, 1922, as a result of negotiations during the Washington Conference. Weihaiwei was leased to Britain in 1898, but at the Washington Conference the latter agreed to negotiate for its surrender. A provisional agreement was reached by an Anglo-Chinese commission in 1924, but the British conditions were not acceptable to the Chinese government at that time and the agreement still awaits signature.[10]

In addition mention may be made of outright cessions of territory to foreign powers, such as those of Hongkong to Britain, Macao to Portugal, and Formosa to Japan. Here the transference of sovereignty is complete and presumably permanent.

[5] Willoughby, I, 504–8; Morse, *Trade and Administration of China,* chap. viii.

[6] Willoughby, I, 505.

[7] *Ibid.,* Vol. I, chap. xx.

[8] *Ibid.,* I, 504.

[9] Hornbeck, p. 473; Willoughby, I, 506–8.

[10] Willoughby, Vol. I, chaps. xvii–xviii.

Beside these main classes of territorial rights, foreign nations enjoy other rights and privileges for the benefit of their nationals in China connected with residence and trade and covering a wide range of concessions in the non-technical sense of the word. The privileges of extra-territoriality have been discussed on pages 80 ff., and the missionary privileges are mentioned on pages 106 ff. There are in addition numerous problems arising out of railway concessions,[11] rights of inland navigation,[12] spheres of interest,[13] mining rights,[14] wireless, cable, and telegraph agreements,[15] and similar privileges which are in their nature territorial. The complexity of these rights is very great, particularly since the legal bases for many well-established practices are obscure. As Chinese national sentiment rises, the tendency to examine these legal bases and to challenge customary practice is increasingly evident.

**Other territorial privileges**

### II. THE GROWTH OF SHANGHAI

The Round-Table discussions on this whole subject of concessions and settlements tended to concentrate upon the present situation in Shanghai. The problems there presented are immediate and urgent in their importance, both to China and to the foreign powers. In a sense the international settlement of Shanghai is the keystone of Western influence in China. Upon a satisfactory settlement of its exceedingly difficult and complicated problems depend in considerable measure the future relationships of China with the treaty powers.

Nowhere else are these problems so clear cut and attitudes so sharply defined. Shanghai, even more than Peking, is the stronghold of foreign influence, and especially of foreign commerce in China. The large colony of aliens in the International Settlement and the French concession represent to many Chinese leaders the most accessible, compact, articulate, and visible example of Western ideas and attitudes. The policies, decisions, and achievements of the municipal administration, the attitudes taken by the foreign newspapers, and the personal relationships of foreign nationals in Shanghai count in some ways for more than the governmental policies of the powers. They are nearer, more real, and more immediate in their importance. Moreover, these foreign colonies in China naturally exert powerful influence upon their respective governments. The views of their representative leaders have not always accorded with recent government policies, but the differences which have sometimes existed have not been readily apparent to the Chinese mind.

**The importance**

The Chinese city of Shanghai, which was opened to foreign trade by the Treaty of Nanking, was a city of approximately half a million inhabitants.[16] The Chinese officials with whom the agreement was subsequently negotiated

[11] *Ibid.*, chap. xv; Vol. II, chap. xvii.

[12] *Ibid.*, Vol. II, chap. xxxii.

[13] *Ibid.*, Vol. I, chaps. vi–xiv.

[14] *Ibid.*, Vol. II, chap. xxxv. [15] *Ibid.*, chap. xxxviii. [16] Hornbeck, pp. 469–73.

for the designation of an area of foreign residence set aside areas outside of the city walls consisting largely of mud flats and swamp. There were originally three separate foreign areas—British, American, and French—but in 1863 the two former were merged into what is now known as the International Settlement. The French concession retained its separate status and differs materially from the International Settlement in government.[17] Both are theoretically still under Chinese jurisdiction and sovereignty. Titles to land are registered with Chinese territorial authorities on the basis of perpetual leases, and the leaseholders pay land tax. Local jurisdiction and administration are delegated, but not surrendered, by the Chinese government to specially constituted courts and councils.[18] In the case of the French concession, however, the claim is made (but not admitted by the Chinese authorities) that it is a "concession" in the sense of being wholly outside of Chinese jurisdiction. The French consul exercises much greater power than his British or American colleagues, and is moreover directly responsible to the authorities of French Indo-China and thence to Paris.[19]

**and development of Shanghai**

With the growth of trade the foreign population of the International Settlement has increased until it now numbers 29,947, while in the French concession there are an additional 6,919 foreign residents.[20] At the same time the Chinese population, both of the foreign areas and of the native city and its adjacent districts, has increased rapidly until the whole aggregation forms one of the world's greatest cities.

The modern city and port has been built up, it is claimed, by the initiative, energy, and organizing capacity of British, American, French, and other foreign commercial interests. The modern streets and buildings reflect the efficiency of their builders. It must be remembered on the other hand that the wealth that has made this building possible has been gained from trade, which presupposes mutuality of benefit, so that it may be said that the Chinese have contributed co-operatively to the growth of Shanghai and have also gained from it.

**due to foreign initiative**

The actual form of municipal administration is discussed in the next section; but it is relevant to point out here that a million Chinese have been attracted by the better conditions of life under foreign administration to live in the International Settlement and the French concession. Among their number have been many political refugees. Chinese enterprises also have prospered in the foreign area and have come to contribute a large proportion of the municipal revenues. There has, in fact, been an increasing appreciation of the sanitation, security, and order provided by Western methods.

**Its Chinese population**

The actual extent of the area thus organized is a matter of some impor-

[17] Morse, *op. cit.*

[18] Bau, *op. cit.;* Willoughby, I, 497–500.

[19] Willoughby, I, 522.

[20] *China Yearbook, 1926,* p. 606.

tance. The pressure of growth has been such as to cause extension of boundaries which rest upon customary acceptance rather than upon legal regulations.[21] In this, as in almost every respect, consideration of the problem of Shanghai as it exists today and as it promises to develop in the near future is more practically important than insistence upon the strict historical letter of the law.

**and class conflict**

This problem was compared in the Round-Table discussions to that of Rome in the days of conflict between the patricians and the plebeians. There has developed in Shanghai a conflict between those who have until recently been the ruling caste in police and administrative affairs and the Chinese merchants, bankers, and workers who have become a vast majority of the population. In this conflict there is the added complication of race feeling.

Chinese speakers commented upon the effect which the psychological attitude of the foreign community has upon the Chinese people. The feeling of being unwelcome guests, of necessarily submitting to alien rule as a condition of residence in one of their own cities, even though it is admittedly foreign made, was represented as an important source of irritation. It was conceded on the other hand that there has been less racial discrimination and feeling than might have been expected under the peculiar circumstances, and that violent expressions of racialism, such as lynch law, have been conspicuously absent.

**The practical efficiency of foreign government**

It was conceded also that the foreign administration has not only provided a place of security and refuge for many Chinese, but is in itself an object-lesson of municipal efficiency.[22] Much of the discussion concerning the government of Shanghai proceeds at cross-purposes at this point. The characteristic British attitude in such a problem is pragmatical and matter of fact, estimating the situation not in terms of legal right or abstract justice but in terms of its practical bearing on human interests. The system works. The committee of business men who in their spare time administer or direct the administration of the International Settlement as a great modern city are concerned primarily in keeping the settlement running and in maintaining law and order. They are not interested in political theory as much as they are concerned with the cleanliness and fitness of Shanghai as a place in which to live.

**vis-a-vis with Chinese nationalism**

The Chinese objections, on the contrary, while not without their practical aspects, arise largely from the awakening sentiment of nationalism. For the most part they fall into three main groups: those which arise because the present form of municipal government impairs Chinese sovereignty, those which relate to the lack of Chinese representation on the municipal council, and those which arise from minor but irritating personal discriminations.[23] Examples of the first group of objections were adduced to show, as the incident of May 30, 1925, whatever its merits, clearly indicated: that sentiment may be-

[21] Willoughby, I, 523–54.

[22] Bau, *op. cit.*

[23] Bau, *op. cit.*

come an important practical fact. The second group of objections similarly tends to develop into the slogan of "no taxation without representation," and in this form is open to attack as being purely theoretical and out of relation to the facts of Chinese government. But behind the slogan is a growing demand for greater expenditure upon Chinese education in Shanghai and for similar very practical and important changes of administration. The third group of objections, exemplified by the discrimination shown or alleged to be shown in connection with municipal improvements, such as parks, is of importance not so much in itself as in the implication which it may be construed as bringing of racial inferiority. The triviality or even the truth of such discriminations is secondary to the feelings aroused by the annoyance or suspicion of such treatment.

The way to progress from such cross-purposes and misunderstandings appeared to lie in the dispassionate examination of the facts (including attitudes) concerned, the recognition that the modern growth of Shanghai presents a unique problem in municipal administration, and in the consideration of constructive suggestions toward the solution of that problem.

### III. THE MUNICIPAL ADMINISTRATION OF SHANGHAI

The growth of Shanghai in recent years has resulted in a problem of municipal administration that is extraordinarily difficult. Chinese methods of local government were not evolved to fit such conditions as have developed under the influence of modern commerce. The native sections of the city present a chaos of administrative difficulties. The French concession and the International Settlement immediately adjoining offer a striking contrast. The former is governed by the French consul with the aid of an advisory council; the latter by the Shanghai municipal council. The legal basis of this council and its relationship to the Chinese government on the one hand and to the foreign consuls and governments on the other are, therefore, important matters of history.

**The land regulations**

In setting aside the area for foreign residence in Shanghai, the Chinese agreed that land should be acquired by means of perpetual leases. The ultimate ownership remained in the hands of the Chinese government, and individual Chinese who owned land within the area retained their rights. In order to provide for the acquiring of leases, land regulations were issued in 1845 and have from time to time been amended and extended. The disturbed state of the country at the time of the Taiping Rebellion was responsible for the definite provision in 1854 of regulations for the municipal government of the settlement. The regulations upon which the municipal government has been established, however, were first promulgated in 1869. These regulations were approved by the diplomatic corps in Peking, but not submitted to, or approved by, the Chinese authorities. They omit the provision for Chinese representation which had been laid down in principle by a conference of the diplomatic body in Peking in

1864. The regulations were revised by the rate-payers in 1881 and approved by the diplomatic body in 1898, return being had at the same time to the earlier practice of submitting the regulations to the Chinese authorities for their approval.[24]

The administration is actually carried on by a municipal council of nine members elected annually by the rate-payers. In the annual meeting also the rate-payers may propose by-laws or amendments to the land regulations. These, before becoming valid, must receive the assent of the diplomatic body; but in practice regulations have been changed recently without this express approval.

**Status of municipal council**

The exact status of the municipal council appears to be unique. It has no parallel in history, with the possible exception of some of the "free cities" of the Middle Ages. Indeed, it was proposed at one period that it should be formed into such a free city. This idea has never been wholly dropped, and in practice the related principle that civil war and revolutionary disturbances must be kept outside the settlement has been successfully asserted.[25]

**Its relation to the British government**

The relationship of the municipal council to the Chinese authorities on the one hand and to the consuls and their governments on the other presents a unique situation. Normally, the council would appear to be responsible only to the rate-payers; but in times of emergency it has been in a position to call upon foreign governments for diplomatic or military support. For this reason the Chinese spokesmen in the Round Tables raised the question of responsibility and of consular jurisdiction. They asked whether the seeming independence of the municipal council was not really a screen for the imperialist purposes of the British and other governments while they were professing a certain sympathy with China's nationalist aspirations.

**one of virtual independence**

The British spokesmen's view of this matter disclosed a distinct difference between governmental policy and the local treaty-port view. It was contended that in actual fact the authority of the British government in Shanghai is very limited. Any change in the municipal system involves amendment of the land regulations. This can be done only by a long and intricate process in which the municipal council, the land-renters, the diplomatic body in Peking, and the Chinese government all play a part. Behind this most effective wire entanglement the municipal council holds a unique position among the municipal bodies of the world. It was represented as one of the greatest obstacles to the execution of the policy of the foreign powers in China that the public opinion of the British residents in Shanghai does not represent the general opinion in Britain or the official opinion of the British Foreign Office. The local British residents, however, are the representatives in the Chinese mind of British thought, and to a certain extent of the British government, and thus China tends to get an incomplete view of British policy.

In continuation of this point, the Chinese spokesmen asked for an explana-

[24] Willoughby, I, p. 513–19. [25] *Ibid.*, p. 515.

tion of the presence of foreign troops in Shanghai. The legal basis might be derived from the right to exercise police power, but the precise extent of this right is undefined. The practice of using rivers to bring gunboats inland also rests on rather indefinite treaty provisions. The Chinese asked, if the British and other governments were not responsible for the actions of the municipal council, why was a defense force sent to Shanghai at the cabled request of the municipal council for protection? The reply was made that it was to protect life and obviate clashes in a situation where no other method was deemed efficacious. In the same way the incident of May 30, 1925, was regarded as a matter to be settled with the governments rather than with the municipal council.

**except in crisis**

There was, however, little discussion of "incidents." It was generally agreed that they were not the real issue, but rather that it was best to discuss ways out of the situation in which such "incidents" arise. The presence of British and other troops in Shanghai was explained, not on the ground of legal right, but of practical necessity and wisdom. However undesirable as an infringement of Chinese sovereignty, it was considered necessary in the same way as the institution of the Chinese maritime customs had been necessary, to provide governmental service which China was unwilling or unable to provide. If the Chinese government in the past had been able, or at present was able, to give foreigners the necessary protection, it would not have been necessary to send a defense force to Shanghai. Its presence is an unusual remedy for an unusual situation.

The rendition of the so-called "mixed court" once again to Chinese jurisdiction was acknowledged to have been a definite and bold step toward meeting Chinese aspirations.[26]

**Proposals for Chinese representation**

Representation on the municipal council was the only other important issue discussed. Whatever the historical origin of the settlement, the fact must be faced that the Chinese residents at the present time greatly outnumber the foreigners in the International Settlement, contribute a large portion of the revenue, and feel entitled to ask for a share in controlling its expenditure. Since 1920 the Chinese Rate-payers Association has been in existence in Shanghai and has asked for representation on the council.[27] An advisory committe of five members was appointed, but the Chinese stated that it had met with the council only once, at the very beginning, for half an hour, and that subsequently it had submitted memoranda to the council without receiving acknowledgment.

Since the incident of May 30, 1925, the situation has changed on both sides. The annual meeting of foreign rate-payers in 1926 passed almost unanimously a resolution instructing the council to make representations to the powers with a view to securing the addition of three Chinese members at an early date. No final action has been taken on this resolution, though the diplo-

[26] Willoughby, Vol. I, chap. xxi.

[27] *Ibid.*, pp. 519–22.

matic body at Peking has approved it and the Senior Consul-General at Shanghai has so notified the Shanghai Chinese chamber of commerce.[28] In the meantime the Nationalist advance to the north encouraged the Chinese to demand at least equal representation with the foreign residents and ultimate transference of control to Chinese authority.[29] There the matter rests at the moment. By the force of obvious necessity the particular question of the administration of the International Settlement is beginning to be recognized as only part of the problem of devising an adequate government for the aggregation which is coming to be known as "Greater Shanghai." The remainder of the Round-Table discussion was placed in this setting.

### IV. GREATER SHANGHAI

**Administrative unity of the metropolitan area**

For any satisfactory solution of the problems of Shanghai it would appear to be necessary to regard the whole area as a unit for certain administrative purposes. Sanitation, preventive medicine, transportation, economical administration demand co-operative effort. The government of the foreign residential areas is part of a larger problem which needs to be studied as a whole.[30] The solution of the very vexed local problem would be simplified if it were regarded as a unit in a federal administration somewhat on the model of the London County Council.

**involves difficult constitutional problems**

This statement of a general principle was recognized to be merely a precondition of settlement. Detailed solution of such delicate problems as financial relationships and division of function between local and central authority demand the most exacting, expert, and impartial study over a prolonged period. It is obvious that the conceptions of democratic municipal administration which have been gradually developed in Europe and America cannot be transferred to China by a stroke of the pen or more or less casual discussion.

**which call for expert study**

The temper of the Chinese and foreign residents at the moment is likely to be such as to veto in advance as hopelessly impracticable any but the logically extreme positions on either side. Shanghai, however, has more than local significance and importance. Any scheme of government which could both safeguard the living conditions which foreigners regard as essential and at the same time provide a means of introducing modern efficient administration into China is worth consideration. Such a scheme, it was pointed out, need not necessarily eliminate the participation or even the dominance of foreign residents in such areas as the International Settlement, or involve the handing over of valuable property and intricate organization to popular election by an uneducated democracy.

[28] Willoughby, I, 521.

[29] Bau, *op. cit.;* also "Documents," No. III.

[30] Cf. statement on this point by General Sun Chuan-fang (Hornbeck, p. 471, footnote); also *China Yearbook, 1926,* pp. 1012–16.

The experience of Austria-Hungary after the war was cited as a case where a problem which had proved impossible of solution by the ordinary diplomatic and governmental methods yielded to analysis by an impartial expert commission. The solution suggested by that commission, on the basis of its analysis, was adopted and carried quickly into effect by co-operative international administration over a transitional period.

The primary necessity is for detached, expert study. Various suggested methods were put forward for accomplishing such a study, and it was believed that the experts could be found, and that governmental machinery would be adequate for such an investigation provided the necessary initiative and willingness to co-operate could be secured from a stable Chinese government as well as from the foreign powers.

### 3. DOCUMENTS

The basic material for the Round-Table discussions summarized here is described under chapter ii, dealing with tariff autonomy in China.

### REFERENCES TO DATA MATERIAL

1. Bau, "Concessions and Settlements and Their Transference to Chinese Rule" (Documents, Section 5).
2. "Concessions and Settlements" (Hornbeck, pp. 468–74).
3. Hankow Agreement, February 19, 1927 (Whyte, pp. 65–73).

## FOREIGN MISSIONS AND PACIFIC RELATIONS

### 1. QUESTIONS FOR DISCUSSION

*a*) In what ways are missions and missionaries helpful or harmful factors in Pacific relations?

*b*) How do the nationals in countries to which missionaries go evaluate the missionary enterprise?

*c*) Do those who hold certain religious beliefs possess the inherent right to propagate them?

( i) What criteria may be urged upon which choice of religion should be made?

( ii) What limitations, if any, should be placed upon them in reference to such matters as the use of inducements (educational, medical, etc.), interference with established social customs and practices, attitudes of platform and press?

*d*) How far should national considerations affect the conduct and activity of missionary work?

( i) How far should the missionary's national interests control?

( ii) How far should the national interests of the country to which he goes control?

(iii) What principles should guide action in regard to indemnities for loss of life or property by missionaries?

*e*) What limitations may a government rightly or wisely place upon the propagation of religion by aliens?

*f*) To what extent, if at all, should missionaries mix in politics?

*g*) What ethical standards should mark the contact of one religion with another in order to make for harmony and growth?

*h*) How can the missionary enterprise be used to better Pacific relations?

### 2. SUMMARY OF ROUND-TABLE DISCUSSIONS

CHAIRMEN AND SECRETARIES

Round Table I

*Chairman:* STEPHEN P. DUGGAN
*Secretary:* WILLIAM MAWSON

Round Table II

*Chairman:* T. Z. KOO
*Secretary:* MARY E. WOOLLEY

### 1. THE VARIETY OF MISSIONARY ENTERPRISE

Even preliminary examination of the effects of Christian missions upon international relationships brings into clear relief the great degree of variation in the objectives and methods as well as in the results of missionary enterprise. There are three main but not mutually exclusive causes for this variation. In the first place a great deal depends obviously upon the type of culture of the people to whom missions are sent. Methods that are worked out for a primitive people with a stone-age culture are not readily transferable to people with more developed civilizations. The same considerations must be borne in mind even within one national group. There must be considerable variation of appeal to different social and educational classes.

**Missions vary according to a) peoples**

**b) social classes**

More important than either of these causes at the present moment is the historical change of method and attitude that has been produced by the development of international relationships in the modern age and not less by the development of modernism in religion. The rise of national feeling in China has produced changing attitudes to missionary work both among the Chinese Christians and non-Christians, and among the missionaries in the field and in the home constituencies. These are linked in complicated ways with the religious differences and controversies which exist in the European and American missionary churches.[1]

**c) religious ideas**

*The relation of missions to Pacific depopulation.*[2]—In many ways the simplest and most satisfactory form of Christian missionary enterprise has been the extension at the same time of the higher form of religion and of the more developed material culture to primitive peoples such as were found in the islands of the Pacific. The missionaries brought great benefits to these peoples by assisting directly in the elimination of tribal wars, cannibalism, witchcraft, and similar practices, and by introducing them to the social heritage of European civilization as well as by protecting their rights and interests against the unscrupulous, or at least impetuous, approaches of other agencies of civilization. The example of New Zealand was cited as a clear case in which the native race recognizes its great debt to the early missionaries.

**The benefits Offset in part by lack of ethnological understanding**

On the other hand it may be argued that the depopulation of the Pacific islands supports the contention that the missionaries destroyed the social bases of native life. It has been said that the missionaries "taught the people to look up to Heaven, and while they were looking the land slipped away from under their feet." Religion, social life, economics, and politics are all bound together, and the missionary has not always been conscious of this fact when attacking what seemed to him obvious moral abuses. While much of our anthropological and ethnological knowledge has been the result of missionary study, it is true also that not all missionaries have been sympathetic with the native religions

**But responsibility of traders much heavier**

[1] Beach, *Missions as a Cultural Factor in the Pacific,* pp. 7–8.

[2] Beach, *op. cit.,* pp. 8–9.

and culture. The religious conceptions of the natives which the missionary may regard as superstitious are to them living realities. A change in beliefs revolutionizes their whole mental outlook. Conversion may free the native from the restraint of public opinion before the inner restraints of a Christian conscience are adequately developed. The social equilibrium of the group has often crumbled in consequence. The abandonment of religious rites and practices, even of a primitive kind, often reacts upon economic and social organization in unexpected and disastrous ways.

To place the blame for these undoubted consequences of European expansion in the Pacific solely upon the missionaries is, however, unjustified. The missionary is seldom alone in the field. He accompanies, and is sometimes preceded by, adventurers and traders who in the Pacific have often been of the most undesirable type. He therefore faces a people who are already in a state of profound upheaval because of their sudden contact with the less desirable elements of European life. Whatever his shortcomings and inadequacies, he must do what he can with a situation where the virus of change is already actively at work.

*Missions and the intelligentsia.*—The evangelical and democratic elements in Christian missions have directed attention not only to the more backward and childlike races, such as the Pacific islanders, but also to despised and depressed social classes within countries which possess a high degree of civilization.[3] In some cases the approach to these countries has been almost wholly by an appeal to such people. Such an approach has necessarily depended upon the material inducements, such as education, medical treatment, and improvement of social status in much greater degree than an approach to the more literate and intellectual classes would have called for. It has also encouraged a simplicity and even crudity of religious conceptions and presentation that has sometimes antagonized the intelligentsia and added to their distrust and resentment of the consequences of the Christian teaching.

**Evangelization of depressed classes**

**Often derived from simple theology of Christianity**

This type of missionary effort has had and still has a strong appeal to certain types of religious organization. It is responsible for the charges often made that the missionary, in order to get support for his own effort, misrepresented the people to whom he was sent, stressing the evil and neglecting the more desirable aspects of their culture. Such an attitude, even when produced by a genuine desire to help the country concerned, is essentially connected with the superiority complex which is anathema to the nationalist spirit of the Eastern countries at the present time. It is also connected subtly with the failure to distinguish between the essential religious message of Christianity and the elements of European culture which are not clearly distinguishable from it in the minds of some missionaries.

At the present time the spread of Christianity in this particular direction is

[3] Beach, p. 44.

ippines might take their rightful place as the oldest Christian community in the Orient.[9]

It is in China that the missionary movement is facing its fiercest criticism at the present time. This criticism comes from Europeans as well as Chinese, Christians as well as non-Christians. No movement which enters deeply into the life of the people can escape such criticism as crises like the present. Much of the conflicting criticism is due to the variety in the missionary movement of which mention was made earlier. The foreign trader is apt to blame the missionary for encouraging, if not causing, nationalism, at the same time as the nationalists are attacking the missionary for his close relationship with his home government and in particular for his reliance upon treaty provisions for special privileges and upon gunboats for protection. There is, obviously, a wide divergence of policy and opinion within the missionary group itself which adds to the double criticism which any neutral group inevitably receives in a period of strain and crisis.

**Nationalist criticism in China**

**a) Political meddling**

From the Chinese side, in addition to the general nationalist criticism concerning reliance upon treaty privileges,[10] there is the usual criticism directed against religious institutions and those connected with them of failure to live according to the high precepts they teach. This criticism is especially obvious where, as in China, the missionaries are aliens used to a considerably higher standard of living than obtains among their constituency. The logical conclusion to which this criticism may be pushed is that religion is not so much a way of life as a nationalization of present relationships. The only effective counter-argument is to be found in the extent of self-sacrifice practiced by religious exponents.[11] In this respect Communists claim to practice what the Christians preach.

**b) Insincerity**

The extent and power of the Communist opposition to Christian teaching in China is difficult to estimate; but it is clearly a significant factor in the present situation. Between the Communist, who regards all religion as an opiate, and the Christian missionary there is no common ground; but Communism itself in China, as elsewhere, has a psychological basis which is very similar to that of an aggressive religion. Communists tend to believe that they have been given the world-mission of saving the weaker nations from the domination of the imperialist powers. In pursuit of that mission they work with the zeal and self-sacrifice which is commonly associated with religious faith.

Probably the most serious obstacle to the spread of Christianity in China, however, comes from the traditional philosophic and rationalistic attitude of Chinese intellectual life.[12] Since the appeal of the missionary was, until recent-

[9] Beach, pp. 20–32.

[10] Hodgkin, Vol. VI; Hume, Vol. I, s.

[11] Hodgkin, Vol. IV.

[12] Hume, Vol. II; Hodgkin, Vol. V.

ly, primarily to the less intellectual classes of China, it has been difficult to measure the effect which his efforts have had upon the unconverted. There is some evidence to show that the tradition of rationalism in Chinese scholarship, reinforced by scientific scepticism or even materialism, has yielded little if at all to Christian teaching. The tendency to identify Christianity with foreign influence is a potent factor at the present time in reinforcing this resistance to Christian proselytizing. Aggressive anti-Christian movements are not native growths of the Christian spirit so much as temporary manifestations of racial and national estrangements. The traditional attitude of China is likely rather to be an easy tolerance against which aggressive Christianity may find it even more difficult to make definite headway.[13]

**c) Aggressive proselytizing**

The aggressive methods of Christian missions are in themselves an object of offense to many Eastern minds, as the following extract from a private letter written by a well-known Eastern philosopher and circulated during the Conference bears witness:

> Your western mind is too much obsessed with the idea of conquest and possession, your inveterate habit of proselytism is another form of it. Christ never preached himself or any dogma or doctrine—he preached the love of God. The object of a Christian should be like Christ—never to be like a coolie-recruiter trying to bring coolies to his master's tea-garden. Preaching your doctrine is no sacrifice at all—it is indulging in a luxury far more dangerous than all luxuries of material living. It breeds an illusion in your mind that you are doing your duty—that you are wiser and better than your fellow-beings. But the real preaching is in being perfect, which is through meekness and love and self-education.

**d) Confusion of religion and social theory**

Even among the Chinese Christians there is considerable criticism of missionary enterprise as it has been conducted in the past.[14] There is a clear tendency to distinguish between what are, for China, the essential and valuable elements of the Christian faith and what are in Chinese eyes mere encrustations of Western dogma embodying European conceptions of life. This tendency is welcome to many missionary leaders. One of them stated that in his view "The structure of missions seems to be crumbling, and I hope that a great deal more will crumble, in order that the débris of the old may be cleared for building anew. We see the probable failure of the institutional interpretation of Christianity. Only reliance on the spirit which is the heart of religion can lead on to success." In this distinction it is not likely that they will carry with them all the foreign missionaries. The Chinese Christian church, however, shares the nationalism which is prevalent in China, and the strains involved thereby contribute to the complications of international relationships in China today.

### 3. MISSIONS AND THE STATE[15]

The vexed problem of the reconciliation of religion and political loyalties is at least as old as the Roman Empire. The right to hold or propagate a reli-

[13] Beach, pp. 49–51. [14] Hume, I, 3; Hodgkin, Vols. III–VI. [15] Hodgkin, Vol. VI.

gious faith regardless of its effect upon the established government is not yet fully conceded in any country. In times of crisis this right may be challenged by state necessity, but normally toleration has been achieved and there is little persecution for religious belief. In one important respect, however, the problem lingers. There is general assent to religious freedom, including the right to teach and to set up institutions; but there is debatable ground in the conformity or nonconformity of those institutions to the general political system of the state. This institutional difficulty is perhaps most important in the region of education, which is so closely connected with training in citizenship. States tend to be jealous of institutions growing up which do not fully conform with national requirements.

**Religious freedom**

**and political citizenship**

The advent of modern missions coincidently with a quickening of nationalist ideas in the early nineteenth century added further complications to the relationship. This extraordinary outreach of missionary effort may well be regarded as the counterpart in the religious sphere of the sudden access of energy and assertion which spread European culture over the world. For the most part there was no direct connection between the increase of trading and the expansion of missions; but there were many indirect connections, and there may well have been more than coincidence in the fact that great world-movements of these types should have arisen together.

**Evangelical missions**

The penetration of missionaries into little-known lands has been a considerable factor in the extension of European domination over weaker peoples and the close contact of European states with such countries as Japan and China. The developed Western states have felt responsibility for their nationals working in other lands. Occasionally they have taken deliberate diplomatic advantage of their presence or of their wrongs. In China, particularly, the connection between missionaries and their governments has been close and at times questionable. There has been a distinct reaction from this position in recent years among many missionaries; but it must be remembered that a large part of the mission work in China rests upon specific treaty privileges gained as a result of war.[16] In the same way there are large institutions under foreign control built by moneys extracted from China in compensation for injury to mission work. At the present time, when the demand has arisen that all institutions shall conform to Chinese national requirements, these institutions may well be a source of irritation.

**and imperialism**

With most missionaries the time has gone by when they were willing to act as agents for their governments in such matters as securing maps, and many of them will not accept forced indemnities in the case of injury or damage to property. Opinion is, however, considerably divided on this point.[17] The position of the state must be considered also. A powerful government may not be willing to waive the right to defend its nationals and their property. The only logical

[16] Willoughby, *Foreign Rights and Interests in China,* Vol. II, chap. xxviii.

[17] Hodgkin, Vol. VI B.

The modern missionary attitude

position for missionaries to take up under such circumstances is to consider the naturalization of their individual status and of their mission property. The Y.M.C.A. in China and many other institutions have transferred or are transferring their property to Chinese hands with this object in view.[18]

Mission schools

The control of these institutions, and particularly schools and colleges, raises many difficult problems. Parties in China are sharply divided on the subject. Missionary opinion is equally divided. There are missionaries who feel that it would be a breach of faith with their home supporters and a betrayal of their trust to allow the Christian purpose of their institutions to be made secondary to general education. There are others who are content as long as opportunity is given for Christian teaching, even incidentally. There are fewer who would be willing that China should be helped educationally even if no specific Christian teaching were possible.[19]

Among the Chinese there are similar differences. Nominally there is liberty of religious teaching; but there is also a widespread demand that the missionary schools shall fit into the national system of education now projected, and even that a definite proportion of time shall be devoted to nationalist instruction. The criticism is inevitable that missionary schools have remained aloof, have not trained enough leaders for the needs of new China, and have not worked definitely enough toward the merging of their identity in Chinese institutions. The force of such criticism is obviously dependent upon divergent views as to the speed at which it is possible to attain these objects.

The attempt to register and control foreign schools is to be regarded primarily as an expression of nationalism, an assertion of sovereignty in an important sphere of jurisdiction, rather than an opposition to the methods and achievements of these schools in the past.

A passing phase

Japanese experience in just such a period of national assertion leads to the expectation that the present complication of the international situation arising from missionary activity in China may not be more than a passing phase. Much depends upon the interpretation placed upon it by the missionaries who are at present displaced. Since, generally speaking, their attitude is one of sympathy with Chinese aspirations, they are the less likely to embitter Chinese feelings. The general right to propagate religious ideas is not likely in normal times to be restricted in China unless anti-Christian Communism gets control. That the methods of propagation are felt by some missionaries themselves to need reconsideration is evidenced by the code of ethics presented for the consideration of the Round Tables.

[18] Hodgkin, Vol. VII; Hume, Vols. I s, III–IV; see also Warnshuis, *The Relationships of Protestant Mission Boards in America to the Churches in Japan, Korea, China, and the Philippine Islands, with Special Reference to Their Transfer and Control from America to the Orient.*

[19] Warnshuis, *op. cit.*, pp. 6–13.

#### 4. MISSIONS AS A FACTOR IN INTERNATIONAL RELATIONS[20]

The number of missionaries in such a country as China and the importance of their institutions are in themselves sufficient to indicate that missions must be regarded as an important factor in international relations. Not only do missionaries in China interpret an important aspect of the life of the countries from which they come, by their presence, their teaching, their writings, and their attitudes, but they perform a service not less important in their own countries. It is not an exaggeration to say that the addresses of returning missionaries, the study of missions in religious organizations, and the very wide circulation of mission textbooks, biographical and descriptive material, forms one of the most effective means for disseminating international information. The combined representations of mission boards organized powerfully on a nation-wide scale is likely to be as important in international affairs as the similar organizations for social reform are powerful in domestic affairs.

**Missionary propaganda**

A large part of the influence of foreign missions in international relations is therefore to be found in the home constituency. The missionaries, who are in any case likely to be above the average personality of the churches from which they come, have the advantage also of some degree of personal contact with the problems in the foreign field. The home constituency has a less direct contact, but wields considerable political power. The missionaries are constantly reinforced, moreover, with new arrivals, some of whom stay in the service for only a short period and find it difficult therefore to attain an adequate understanding of their task.

The original impulse of missionary work was to present a religious message to individuals, and this impulse still remains the chief purpose of missionary work. But in recent years the social implications of that work have become increasingly important, and it is upon those implications that the missionary is judged by outsiders, particularly by non-Christians. The difficult transition period through which China is passing concentrates attention upon the building up of social institutions adequate to meet the demands of a new situation. Few missionaries will consent to be silent concerning the character which those institutions should take. As uninvited guests, however, the expression of their opinion places them in a delicate position.

The ideal of the modern movement as presented to the Round Table represented the missionary rather as a servant than as a teacher, identifying himself with the needs and aspirations of the people to whom his service is offered rather than imposing upon them a stereotyped presentation of superior conceptions of life. It was further represented that he should go to learn as well as to teach, to give and take in friendship and common search, rather than to win over by all means open to him as many adherents to his way of thinking as possible.

**The ideal missionary**

[20] Hodgkin, Vols. III, VIII.

Cromwell's warning to the zealous Puritans to beware lest possibly they might be mistaken was quoted by a missionary leader in this connection.

The mutuality of the quest would be emphasized and extended to the sending as well as to the receiving countries if missionaries did not go only the one way, from the West to the East. It was suggested that, as a definite part of the missionary enterprise, leaders of Chinese thought, both Christian and non-Christian, should be invited to study and teach with the organized religions of the Western countries in order that a combined approach should be made to the understanding of religious conceptions. The study of even the most primitive religions, it was pointed out, has in the past thrown valuable comparative light upon the development of religious ideas.

**Mutuality of religious teaching**

The note upon which discussion ended, therefore, transferred a large part of the problem of foreign missions, particularly in their international aspect, from the so-called missionary countries to the countries from which the missionaries are sent. The aggressive impulse toward the extension of the Christian religion is the origin of the international situation which has developed, and the nature of this impulse can be best studied and influenced in the organizations from which it springs.

### 3. DOCUMENTS

The material for discussion concerning the relation of the foreign mission movement to international problems in the Pacific was contained in three studies printed as data papers for the conference. Dr. Harlan P. Beach, D.D., of the Yale Divinity School, prepared a study entitled: "Missions as a Cultural Factor in the Pacific," which was printed by the American group of the Institute. This study traversed the missionary activities in the South Seas, Hawaii, the Philippines, China, Japan, and Korea from the historical, statistical, and analytical viewpoints.

It was supplemented also by papers from Dr. A. L. Warnshuis, secretary of the International Missionary Council, entitled "The Relationships of Protestant Mission Boards in America to the Churches in Japan, Korea, China, and the Philippine Islands," and by Lester M. Wilson, Ph.D., of Teachers College, Columbia University, on "Summary of Legislation concerning Public Control of Private Schools and the Teaching of Religion in Public Schools in the United States."

Dr. Henry T. Hodgkin, secretary of the National Christian Council on China, and Dr. Edward H. Hume, former president of Yale-in-China, presented statements which are printed below (Documents, Sections 9 and 10), traversing the present criticisms and future policies of the missionary movement with special reference to China.

These papers were supplemented by mimeographed statements from Professor D. J. Fleming, Union Theological Seminary, New York, on "Suggestions for a Code of Ethics between Religions" (Documents, Section 11).

## POPULATION AND FOOD SUPPLY

### 1. QUESTIONS FOR DISCUSSION

*a*) The extraordinary increase in population during the last century, and its relation to:
  ( i) Expansion of agriculture on to the grass lands of the world.
  ( ii) Application of science to agriculture.
  (iii) Improvement of transportation facilities.
  (iv) Accumulation of capital.
  ( v) Natural increase, migration, and war.

*b*) The factors which influence the increase or decrease of population. Consideration of these phenomena involved the following questions:
  ( i) What is the bearing on international relations of:
    (*a*) Population and population trends?
    (*b*) Food needs and resources?
  ( ii) May a nation justifiably
    (*a*) Increase its population beyond its food resources, produced or purchased?
    (*b*) Close its undeveloped territory to other nationals with a view to maintaining a high standard of living?
  (iii) Is it moral for a state to encourage birth control, and does birth control show satisfactory results from the eugenic point of view?
  (iv) Does the international trade in foodstuffs show any sign of increasing?
  ( v) What is the natural increase of population in Japan, China, United States of America, Canada, Australia, New Zealand, other countries?

*c*) The means and results of increasing agricultural and pastoral production by:
  ( i) Expansion of crop areas.
  ( ii) Increase in yields per acre of crops and pastures.
  (iii) Shift of utilization of land from less productive to more productive crops.
  (iv) Shift from less productive to more productive classes of animals.
  ( v) Increase of animal products per unit of food consumption.
  (vi) Substitution of mechanical for animal power on farms.

*d*) Means, other than those set out in the preceding, by which the supply of human food can be increased.
  ( i) Substitution of vegetable for animal food.
  ( ii) Exchange of products between countries.
  (iii) Usage of fish and sea products.

## 2. SUMMARY OF ROUND-TABLE DISCUSSIONS

*Chairman:* JAMES D. DOLE
*Secretary:* WALTER NASH

### I. THE PROGRESS OF POPULATION IN THE NINETEENTH AND TWENTIETH CENTURIES

**The opening up of grass lands in the nineteenth century**

When Malthus wrote his famous essay a century and a quarter ago, predicting that in the Occidental world, as in the Oriental, population would soon press upon the food supply and be limited by famine and pestilence, only a small part of the vast prairies and steppes of Southern and Southeastern Russia had been broken for wheat; the Hungarian plain was still mostly a verdant pasture, divided into the large estates of nobles and cattle kings; the prairies and plains of Central and Western North America had not yet been crossed by white men, except a few fur traders; the pampas of Argentina were an unmapped wilderness; and only a fringe of land along the coast of Australia had been explored. Manchuria was the grazing and hunting domain of the Manchu princes, and scarcely an acre of grain was grown in Mongolia.

The utilization of these grass lands of the world for grain and meat production, supplemented by the use of animal manures and mineral fertilizer on some of the forest soils, and by the improvement of farm animals, has provided for an increase of population in Europe during the past century and a quarter since Malthus from not quite 200,000,000 to nearly 500,000,000, and in the United States and Canada from 6,000,000 to 125,000,000. This increase in population in Europe and North America has been due, not to increased fecundity, but to increased longevity, to medical advice, and a food supply vastly more diversified and costing twice as much to produce as the diet of a century ago. The influence, for example, of an abundant supply of pure milk for both infants and adults can scarcely be overestimated.

**made possible great population increases**

Even Asia has shared in the increase of population, despite the fact that it has had less arable grass land available; and, owing to deficiency of power and consequent inability to use modern agricultural machinery, has been less able to utilize those grass-land areas which it has. India, for example, owing largely to British peace, order, and sanitation, had about 60,000,000 more people in 1911 than in 1881, a gain of 2,000,000 a year, which is considerably more than the increase in the United States during the same period, and this increase is continuing;[1] while Java, under the benign rule of the Dutch, has increased from 3,000,000–4,000,000 inhabitants in the year 1800 to 35,000,000 today.[2] China probably gained over 100,000,000 people between 1800 and 1870, when

[1] The returns from the 1921 census show the much lower natural increase rate of 0.6 per cent annually, due to epidemics (including influenza) and war losses in the last decade.

[2] VanValkenberg, "Java, the Economic Geography of a Tropical Island," *Geographical Review* (October, 1925), p. 566.

the saturation point was apparently reached under the old régime;[3] and the people of Japan, since admitting Western civilization in 1854, have doubled in number.[4]

The population of the world as a whole increased from about 500,000,000 in the year 1700 A.D. to 600,000,000 in the year 1800; then to over 1,000,000,000 by 1850, to 1,500,000,000 in 1900, and to nearly 1,900,000,000 today. The population of the world has therefore trebled since the year 1800, and the increase in numbers during the first quarter of the twentieth century, despite the devastations of fratricidal war, was fully three times as great as during the entire eighteenth century. The population of the world is now increasing at the rate of nearly twenty millions a year, which gives an addition equivalent to the population of the United States every six years.

The ratio of this increase has varied in different parts of the earth, largely in relation to economic opportunity. There is today a wide variation between the density of population in different areas. China sustains a population of nearly four times as large as that of the United States, on an area in crops about one-half as large. In the United States there are about three acres of crops and nine acres of pasture and range land per inhabitant, whereas in China there is less than half an acre of crops and probably less pasture per person.

**Pressure of population is most acute in Japan**

In Japan, however, there is only a quarter of an acre of crop land per inhabitant, and practically no pasture. The ratio of crop land to population is lower in Japan than in any other country in the world equally self-sufficing. On fifteen million acres of crop land, an amount about equal to that in South Dakota or Oklahoma, Japan is producing most of the food required by sixty million people. Nowhere else is agriculture so intensive and so efficient in the utilization of land. The possibilities of production are more closely approached, probably, in Japan than in any other country of the world.[5]

Japan will be the first modern nation, self-governing and provided with the panoply of science, to face the issue between food supply and population in all its stark severity. If Japan solves this problem satisfactorily she will have shown the way which other nations will soon be grateful to follow, and will have made the greatest contribution which any nation can make to the welfare of the world.

Today we seem to be at another critical period in the history of the world, much like that existing in England when Malthus wrote his famous essay, but vaster in its significance. In Eastern Europe, in Western North America, in Argentina, in Australia, in China, and especially in Japan—in fact almost everywhere in the temperate zones—the rising waves of population are beating

[3] Chen-Heng Chen, "Changes in the Growth of China's Population in the Last 182 Years," *China Economic Journal,* Vol. I, No. 1 (January, 1927).

[4] Nasu, "The Population and Food Supply of Japan" (Documents, Section 15, below).

[5] Nasu, *op. cit.*

against the barriers of adverse physical conditions all along the shore line of settlement. Although it is possible to double the area in crops, the best land, the good land, even most of the land of fair quality, has already been brought into use.

How is the world, except possibly the United States and some of the British dominions, to avoid this impending pressure of population on resources? Will the twentieth century witness the agricultural exploitation of the tropics, like that of the grass lands of the temperate zones during the nineteenth? Or will the greatly increased use of fertilizers, the prevention of plant diseases, the more careful cultivation of crops permit the profitable utilization for crops of the poorer lands now in pasture or forest or lying idle, and also cause such an increase in the yield per acre of the lands already in cultivation, and in the efficiency of farm animals in transforming feed into food, as will meet the needs of the more numerous population for another century? Or will the decline in religious authority and the development of materialism diminish the birth-rate and possibly even induce eventual depopulation? Or will recurring wars keep the population comfortably within the limits set by the agricultural resources?

**but the problem is general**

These are questions that no one can answer at the present time, but they clearly indicate that the time is at hand when the leaders of the nations should take stock of the agricultural resources of the lands they should hold, and of the trend of population, and decide upon both a land policy and a population policy, lest large sections of the world's population sink into that condition of poverty, misery, and resignation which Malthus dreaded more than a century ago.

### 2. THE FACTORS THAT GOVERN THE GROWTH OF POPULATION

There is no evidence that any branch of the human race is inherently more fertile than any other. If different races multiply at different rates, the reason is, therefore, to be sought in external factors rather than in inherent differences of fecundity. Accordingly, it is necessary to inquire what these external factors may be, and this involves inquiry into the rate of increase of peoples. This rate is not constant throughout the history of a people. There has recently been an abrupt change in the rate of population increase. It was very moderate in the eighteenth century, but very rapid during the nineteenth.

**Cycles of population growth**

There appear to be cycles of population growth, in the earlier period of which the rate of increase is both cumulative and increasing to a maximum. After the maximum has been reached the opposite tendency slows up the rate of increase till population tends to become stationary unless some profound unforeseen social or other revolution changes the trend and starts a new cycle.

The most obvious reasons for the slowing of population growth are war, pestilence, and famine; but none of these is in fact of primary importance in its direct effects upon the numbers of the people. Such catastrophes affect but minor and purely temporary retardations of the onward march of population growth. Since 1914 no country has suffered more from war, famine, and pestilence than Russia; yet its population today is certainly larger by at least ten millions than it was at the outbreak of the great war. The other participants in that war returned within two years to their pre-war and pre-influenzal rates.

Nor does immigration or emigration greatly affect the growth of population, at least for a country of any considerable size. The chief causes that slow up the rate of population increase fall into one of two sets of factors. Either the means of subsistence may become so scarce that undernutrition, misery, wretchedness, and disease force a stationary state upon a population, or a high standard of living and general well-being may have a similar result. Which of these sets of factors will predominate depends mainly upon the standard of living of a people at the time when its population approaches the stationary stage.

**influenced mainly by social standards**

The analysis just developed does not preclude the possibility or probability of changed conditions starting a new cycle of population growth. In the nineteenth century conditions changed in Europe and North America by reason of the application of science to practical affairs. Various inventions, particularly the drilling of artesian wells, agricultural machinery, and improved transport, made possible the extension of agriculture to grass lands. These inventions increased the productivity of labor. Modern civilization is dependent upon the accomplishment of more work than human labor is capable of performing. This was brought about by the development of mechanical power, first from coal, then from petroleum and natural gas, and finally through hydro-electric power. The application of mechanical power made it possible for each man to produce a far greater surplus of foodstuffs than he could before. It liberated labor for other employment. The development of mechanical power is the basis of modern civilization.

**Modern productivity**

In the last analysis, therefore, it is into the exhaustion of our sources of power—coal, oil, natural gas—that we must look, as well as into the food supply, if we are to forecast population trends. It is upon the increasing use of mechanical power that every rise in standards of living depends. The United States with its high standard of living produces nearly one-half of the world's quota of coal, and over two-thirds of the total output of petroleum. It would require the work of three billion hard-working slaves to accomplish the work done in the United States by its mechanical resources. In short, under conditions of modern civilization any student of population must consider not merely the possibilities of increasing the food supply, but equally the available sources of mechanical energy.

**depends upon mechanical power**

Upon an increasing supply of available energy depends very largely the possibility of raising the world's general standard of living, and if the world's population is to reach a stable equilibrium without universal wretchedness and misery, it is imperative to raise the standards of living of the whole world to a high level before population is forced to become stationary.

The most important sources of energy at present are coal and petroleum, which differ in one important respect from food. Fresh food may grow each year where food grew the year before, but a ton of coal once mined or a barrel of petroleum once pumped up is gone forever and cannot be reproduced. Furthermore, food consumption increases directly as the population increases; but how much coal, oil, and iron a people can use, no man can now foresee. The consumption of coal, of iron, and oil has increased far more rapidly than the world's population. Since 1800, while the world's population increased two and one-half times, the world's coal production and pig-iron production increased nearly one hundred fold. The present rate of increase in the use of raw materials cannot go on very long without approaching exhaustion of some of them. If that point should be reached and science should not find a way out before the world's population becomes stationary, it will adversely affect the standard of living at which the stationary state is reached. It is possible that the advances of physical science may liberate new sources of energy which, like hydro-electric power, shall be perennially renewed by nature; but the prospect of discovering raw materials to take the place of diminishing stocks of iron and wood is less apparent at the present time.

**The sources of power are exhaustible**

**but new sources are possible**

### 3. THE POPULATION PROBLEM OF JAPAN

With the industrial development of Japan her population has doubled within the last sixty years. The standard of living has risen at the same time. But, her natural resources being very limited, Japan seems to have arrived at the saturation point in regard to population. No appreciable increase in agricultural land is to be expected in the future; the annual output of minerals is almost stationary; some of the manufacturing industries show signs of developing well; but, taken as a whole, the increase of national income is becoming inadequate to support the increasing population with the advancing standard of living. One of the most densely populated countries in the whole world, Japan is beginning to be troubled by her surplus population. The problem of unemployment is beginning to appear among her industrial workers; the Japanese peasants, who total one-half of her entire population and who cultivate on an average only two and a half acres of arable land per man, may be said to be in a state of chronic semi-employment by reason of their lack of land to cultivate.

**Japan's problem is urgent**

Japan has passed the stage of self-sufficiency. The rural population, despite its density and industry, which are limited only by the shortage of land available, is no longer able to supply all the food necessary for an urban population which has increased in less than three-quarters of a century from 30 per cent to 50 per cent of a total population which itself has doubled in the meantime. Until the close of the nineteenth century the home production of foodstuffs was adequate. The area of arable land was increased by 36 per cent and production was further increased by more intensive and scientific cultivation.

**Food production is inadequate**

The total amount of rice produced in Japan during the last forty-five years had increased from 150,000,000 to 300,000,000 bushels a year. The proportional increase of population during the same period of time, on the other hand, was not so great.

With increasing prosperity, however, the standard of living began to rise. The annual consumption of rice, the most important food staple in Japan, has increased from 3.5 bushels to 5.7 bushels per individual. Today 10 per cent of the annual consumption is imported from Korea and Formosa, and another 8 per cent from foreign countries, notwithstanding the utmost efforts to encourage the opening of new agricultural lands to improve the rice stock.

Japan's arable land area consists of some 15,000,000 acres, one-half of which is in the form of paddy (rice) fields. The population of Japan is approximately sixty millions. This means that there are four people to every acre. That is the highest ratio in the whole world, being more than three times that of Germany, four times that of France, and nearly twelve times that of the United States of America. The arable land available is estimated to be only some 16 per cent of the total of the land area, and it is very doubtful whether that percentage can be appreciably increased in the future. There is indeed some undeveloped land in Japan, but various reasons, such as barrenness of soil and poor irrigation and transportation facilities, make it impossible to use.

**and not capable of much increase**

Japan is a mountainous country, dotted with many volcanoes. Until recent years the arable land area was being augmented by some 100,000 acres of newly opened lands each year, but the tide has turned. Today, while nearly the same amount of newly opened agricultural land is added annually, a much greater amount of arable land is diverted to purposes other than agricultural. Favorably situated fertile lands are taken out of agriculture and used for the building of railroads, factories, shops, and residences. It is more than doubtful, therefore, whether the arable land area will be appreciably increased in the future. The crop yield per unit area may continue to increase, but too much cannot be expected of it, for even today Japanese agriculture is almost unrivaled in its degree of intensity. Thus Japan is being gradually driven to the necessity of importing a greater amount of foodstuffs each year.

It is true that a nation need not necessarily rely upon its own agriculture as an exclusive source of its food supply. In this age of international trade, foodstuffs can be brought from other countries, provided that exports are available with which to pay for them. Thus the question of food supply becomes a question of gainful employment as long as the food supply is abundant in the world as a whole and as long as international trade is undisturbed. The development of industry and trade within any country, however, is determined very much by the amount of its natural resources, together with its access to raw materials and markets. A country which is limited in these respects will be unable to develop its industry beyond a certain degree, and it will reach the sat-

**Industrial expansion is also limited**

uration point, in regard to its population, much sooner than a country with rich resources readily available.

Japan seems to have reached that point of saturation. Her industrial progress caused her population to grow to its present size; the education and general enlightenment of her people have caused wages, as well as the standard of living, to rise higher; the adoption of occidental civilization has made the aspiration for a better and richer life an established fact among her people. But because of limited natural resources both in agriculture and industry the expansion of national income has begun to retard. The population continues to increase and the standard of living to rise. Here lies the most vital question of present-day Japan in its most rudimentary form. Social unrest and various movements toward social reconstruction which have come to play such an important rôle in Japan today are mainly due to this disparity between population and gainful employment. The reaction on foreign policy is less evident, but just as real.

The remedies suggested may be grouped into four main classes: those connected with the reorganization of the internal economic system, those which depend upon an expansion of export industries, those which relate to emigration, and finally those which aim at slowing down the present increase in population either by birth control or by social developments having the same tendency.

While internal economic reorganization may solve problems of unemployment which occur as a result of defects in the economic order causing periodical cycles of depression, it is hardly adequate to cope with chronic underemployment arising from scanty resources.

The expansion of Japanese export industries is more hopeful as a line of solution, but there are grave difficulties in the way of securing the necessary raw materials and markets. The trend of world-economy is not as clearly toward international specialization and co-operation as it appeared to be in the middle of the nineteenth century. The example of Great Britain's dependence upon a world-market is not regarded by Japanese economists and business men as particularly reassuring. Japan is poor in raw materials, especially in certain basic minerals. For the extension of her industrialization she must depend also upon comparatively free access to wide markets. In almost every direction the existence of tariff barriers hems in her expanding industry. If China should begin to develop her own manufacturing industries at all rapidly, and particularly if she should bar access to her raw materials and place protective barriers around her developing industries, Japan's economic position will become quite precarious.

**by access to raw materials and markets**

**Emigration is not important**

Emigration might conceivably ease the population problem temporarily, if restrictive legislation did not bar the way in almost every direction. But the emigration of a million people annually is technically impossible. If the whole world were free to Japanese migrants, it is doubtful whether a number equal to

10 per cent of the annual increase in the population would emigrate. Moreover, historical experience does not support the contention that emigration can permanently relieve overpopulation.

While this may be logically true, it must at the same time be recognized that the existence of tariff and immigration barriers is a constant irritation to a proud people cooped up in a restricted area of inadequate resources. The question is bound to arise as to the sanction behind the frontier lines that have been drawn. Japan feels herself to be bottled up in a tiny island of the Far East. Other more favored nations can expand freely at the same time as their standard of living is raised. While other nations are expanding, ought the Japanese nation alone be forced to abide by its present limitations?

The Japanese, too, are multiplying. They have no wish to be numbered among the decaying nations of the world. It may be true to suggest that the aspirations of the Japanese race for a fuller expression of its national genius and spirit need not necessarily take the form of increasing numbers and wealth and power. The achievements of art and literature and religion may rank higher than material progress; but the suggestion that Japan should find expression along such lines does not come gracefully from Europeans and Americans, least of all from those who are already in possession of rich material resources to which the Japanese are denied access.

**except psychologically**

The last group of suggested remedies consists of those which aim at controlling the numbers of the population to accord with available resources. The practice of various forms of birth control is only one among several possible methods of achieving such control. Direct methods of contraception give rise to much-debated moral and religious problems which are of special importance in a country like Japan, where the family unit counts for more than it does in Western lands. From the purely scientific or eugenic point of view also the exercise of birth control is often regarded as questionable because of the tendency it has to limit the offspring of the most socially developed sections of the population. Moreover, birth control at best must lag a generation behind the actual problem which is urgent today.

**Birth control even if accepted**

The same argument is true of the related possibility that an increasing standard of living may result in checking the numbers and improving the quality of the population. Professor Yamasaki's diagrams reproduced in this volume indicate a distinct tendency to lowered birth-rates in the industrial, as compared with the agricultural, districts of Japan. But such a tendency operates effectively only in the long run of several generations.

In the meantime the development of higher standards of living, improved social organization, better sanitation, and the practice of preventive medicine operate to reduce death-rates and prolong the expectation of life. The great increase of European population since the industrial revolution is due to this pro-

**lags by a generation**

longation of life more than to any other single cause. Precisely the same factors are operating in Japan at the present time.

#### 4. THE PRESSURE OF POPULATION AND INTERNATIONAL RELATIONS

At the present moment the pressure of population in the Pacific area is greatest in Japan; but the problem does not concern Japan alone. In the first place it was clearly demonstrated in discussions that the prospect confronting Japan in the immediate future confronts every country somewhat more remotely. Even those countries where resources are still abundant, looking forward to the time when they may be more restricted, have claimed the right to regulate and control immigration so as to build up their populations according to their own desires. It is obvious, moreover, that in this era of world-industry and trade, Japan's problem is intimately bound up with the economic systems of other lands. Free access to raw materials and foodstuffs, and open markets for her manufactured goods, involve consideration of nationalist policies, tariff barriers, and similar protective devices. This is especially true of Japan's relations with her great neighbors in the Pacific.

**The problem is general**

**and tied up with trading systems**

It was emphasized, moreover, that the greatest trade in the world as it is organized today is between so-called "competitive" countries. The possibilities of co-operation, individual and international, have never been fully realized. The hesitancies and fears of narrow nationalisms paralyze these possibilities in greater degree than is commonly imagined. It is to the selfish interest of every country, though possibly not of every member of that country, to have her so-called "competitors" strong and able to trade. China exports annually goods to the value of rather less than two dollars per head of her population. Canada exports over one hundred dollars' worth per head, and other countries even more. It may not be possible to bring the economic organization of China rapidly up to these standards; but even a first approximation would materially affect the wealth of the world.

While such statements are true, and while it is clear also that civilization as it is understood today has been based upon the application of scientific thought to human affairs and particularly to human co-operation, it is not possible to ignore the political and psychological aspects of the problem presented by the relationship between the location of population and the distribution of resources and raw materials. The scientist tends to look upon the making of war and peace and treaties as minor episodes which do not in the long run very much affect the fate of mankind. The scale and intensity of modern warfare, however, result in social and spiritual losses which threaten to destroy civilization and do affect in marked degree the bases of economic and social organization and even the practice of science itself. The estrangements, hostile attitudes, and failures to co-operate involved in national conflicts which stop short of war

**It has important political aspects**

are probably even more costly. There is a very real and vital connection, therefore, between the politics and economics of international relations.

The problem of population in the Pacific at the present time is very real and may be the root of political as well as economic difficulties in the not distant future. It is intimately connected with the nationalism which the East has recently learned from Europe. It was forcibly argued that the present practice of nationalism tends to cut across the natural course of economic development. Economic activities pass across all boundaries and tend to unite people in the most distant lands; but the economic web is torn across by the political forces arising from national jealousies and suspicions. It is difficult in this age of scientific advance, and especially difficult in the Pacific, with its countless islands and vast regions still undeveloped or only partly developed, to become anxious about the ultimate problems of overpopulation. But it is obvious that the immediate problems arising from variant pressures of population in different Pacific areas are both important and urgent.

**upon which little information is available**

In view of this obvious fact the dearth of accurate information on the subject is surprising. Over large areas we are ignorant even of the bare numbers of the people, and nowhere has there been a full, accurate, and scientific analysis of the sources of population increase and their relation to available resources. There is a grave danger of the general ideas formulated by Malthus as a result of his first-hand investigations of a superficially similar situation over a century ago being applied to a modern problem containing quite different elements. There has been no comprehensive modern survey and analysis of the problem comparable with Malthus' investigation.

The Round-Table discussions revealed the general outlines of the specific problem in Japan, identified it as a world-problem, and indicated the necessity of gathering more definite detailed information concerning it. Such information must include the psychological and political factors involved; but the approach to the whole problem must be the approach of the scientist in search of facts, rather than the approach of the politician with solutions prepared in advance of the facts.

### 3. DOCUMENTS

The Round Table on "Population and Food Supply" held four sessions on July 21 and 22. The subject was discussed also in a forum of the whole conference on the evening of July 23.

The data material for these discussions consisted of the following papers, which were distributed to all members:

1. "The Problem of Population and Food Supply in Japan," by SHIROSHI NASU, professor of Agricultural Economics, Tokyo Imperial University (Documents, Section 12).

2. "A Note on the Geographical Distribution of the Density of Population, Birth-, and Death-Rates of Japan," by NAOMASA YAMASAKI, Institute of Geography, Tokyo Imperial University (Documents, Section 16).

3. "Japan's Fuel Supply," by PROFESSOR YOSHIKIYO OSHIMA, Tokyo Imperial University.

4. "Land Utilization in China," by O. E. BAKER, United States Department of Agriculture (address to the China group of the Council on Foreign Relations, New York). See Documents, Section 14.

5. "Some of China's Food and Mineral Resources," by O. S. LIEU and L. T. CHEN, Shanghai.

6. "Aspects of Australian Population," by G. L. WOOD, lecturer in Commerce, University of Melbourne.

7. "Resources and Possibilities of New Zealand—Food and Fuel," by WALTER NASH, secretary of the New Zealand Labor Party (prepared from plans worked out by the Canterbury branch of the Institute of Pacific Relations).

8. "A Graphic Summary of American Agriculture," by O. E. BAKER, Bureau of Agricultural Economics (separate from the *Yearbook of the Department of Agriculture* [1921], No. 878).

9. "The Factors That Govern Population Growth," by CARL L. ALSBERG, Stanford University (Documents, Section 12).

In addition to these data papers a series of statistical excerpts from yearbooks and similar sources, special articles, manuscript theses, and published books dealing with special aspects of the problem was tabled for reference.

Use was also made of about fifty wall maps and diagrams representing population and food-supply data from the United States, Japan, China, and New Zealand, loaned by Professor Nasu, Professor Yamasaki, Dr. Baker, and Mr. Walter Nash. A limited number of these diagrams is reproduced in this record.

## INDUSTRIALIZATION AND FOREIGN INVESTMENT

### 1. QUESTIONS FOR DISCUSSION

The subject involved consideration of the following main subjects:

*a*) The material conditions of industrialization:
  ( i) Raw materials.
  ( ii) Labor.
  (iii) Skill and management.
  (iv) Capital.

*b*) The extent of industrialization in various countries.

*c*) What will be the effect of industrialization upon the life of the workers in Pacific countries, and what steps will it be necessary to take in order to safeguard them?

*d*) How far is industrial development likely to be affected or limited by the scope of available markets?

*e*) What development of transport will be required to facilitate industrialization?

*f*) In what ways can capital be obtained for industrial development in Pacific countries having regard to:
  ( i) The bearing of loans on the economic and political conditions of debtor and creditor countries?
  ( ii) The effect of tariffs on investments?
  (iii) Public debt and taxation?
  (iv) The ratio of foreign and domestic capital?

### 2. SUMMARY OF ROUND-TABLE DISCUSSIONS

CHAIRMEN AND SECRETARIES

Round Table I
*Chairman:* SHIROSHI NASU
*Secretary:* MABEL CRATTY

Round Table II
*Chairman:* F. W. EGGLESTON
*Secretary:* JOHN A. RYAN

Round Table III
*Chairman:* SIR FREDERICK WHYTE
*Secretary:* G. L. WOOD

#### I. THE SPREAD OF INDUSTRIALISM

The extension of the industrial revolution to the Pacific countries is one of the significant facts of the present day. Already it has produced economic, social, and political effects of the first importance. It is likely to produce even greater effects, not only in the Pacific, but the world over, if the pace of industrial development should accelerate in the comparatively near future. Upon superficial examination there appear to be many favorable conditions for rapid industrialization. The slow advance of machine industry in European countries during the eighteenth and nineteenth centuries was due to the difficulty of building up a new technique and accumulating the capital necessary for large-scale production. The training of technical experts was not the least of the problems that faced industrial leaders in the early stages of the industrial revolution.

**The developing technique of industry**

At the present time, however, there are great resources of capital and large numbers of expert technicians who can be used to build up large-scale machine industry in a very brief period. The means of communication and of transference also are developed highly, so that expert knowledge and instrumental capital can easily be taken to promising areas. The same organization of international trade which spreads capital over a world-market is available to distribute the produce of the new industries.

Moreover, the perfection to which machine methods have been brought, both mechanically and psychologically, makes it possible to use modern organization under labor conditions which would have been hopeless in earlier periods. Where in the early days of mechanical power it was necessary for workmen to possess engineering skill, at the present time machines are repetitive, automatic, and practically fool-proof, needing only mechanical tendance. Engineering skill has been specialized, mechanized and concentrated until it is now much less necessary in the actual processes of manufacture.

**facilitates its extension**

Industrialism has in these ways developed the capacity to reproduce itself quickly in areas where conditions are favorable. The speed of reproduction has constantly increased as industrial methods have spread outward from Europe and the area of international intercourse has widened. Wherever geographical and political conditions are favorable, industrialism transforms the social structure rapidly and completely. It may even on occasion force political changes and leap over geographical limitations. The forces upon which modern industry is based are powerful to influence and reorient both the human, and in somewhat less degree the physical, bases of existing economic organization. Not even modern industry can fly in the face of natural forces; but those forces can be modified and rearranged so as to bring extraordinary results.

## 2. THE ECONOMIC POSITION OF THE UNITED STATES

**American capital accumulation**

It is with these facts in mind that the industrial development of the Pacific must be considered. The United States of America, with its economic and industrial system more highly developed than that of any other country in the world, illustrates the possibilities of industrial expansion in a very significant way. The rapidity with which industries developed after the frontier reached the Pacific Ocean until America became in the twentieth century the unchallenged leader in mechanical arts is in itself proof of the argument previously advanced. Under especially favorable conditions and aided by greatly improved human as well as mechanical technique, the industries of the United States have apparently reached the position where they are already seeking outlets beyond their domestic markets both for accelerated production and for accumulating capital. The extent of foreign investment is already large, the technique of foreign lending (hitherto undeveloped) is rapidly being improved and the habit of such investment is being formed. Unless the forces now in operation should be suddenly reversed it appears to be inevitable that both the foreign trade and the export of capital from America must assume larger proportions in the near future.

**provides a new dynamic**

This fact in itself is of great significance. Within recent years a waning and impoverished Europe has absorbed most of the available credit, but such a condition is not likely to last. The existence of such a powerful dynamic force as this export pressure of goods and of credit is new, at least in its magnitude. By its reactions upon the domestic policies alone of the United States it is likely to be a considerable factor. It is clear, moreover, that it is in the Pacific rather than in the Atlantic that the consequences of these policies are likely to be most important. Whenever and wherever the opportunity of industrialization offers, the existence in European countries and in the United States of the resources and technique of industrialization, probably in greater amount than in any previous period, is a new factor to be reckoned with.

### 3. CANADIAN MANUFACTURING DEVELOPMENT

**which has already affected Canada**

The industrialization of Canada has already proceeded rapidly, and its acceleration in recent years has been at least partly due to American capital and technique seizing its opportunity to enter the markets of the British Empire. The development has been specially rapid since 1900.[1] Between 1870 and 1924 the capital invested in manufactures rose from $78,000,000 to $3,500,000,000. Manufactured goods form practically the same proportion of Canada's exports as they do in the United States. Canada was recognized in the formation of the International Labor Organization to be one of the great industrial nations of the world, and the recent discoveries of mineral resources in northern Ontario have added considerably to her industrial potentialities.

### 4. AUSTRALIAN NATIONALISM

The British dominions in the South Pacific present a somewhat different situation, largely because of their isolation and the circumscribed extent of

[1] Canada adopted imperial preference in 1897; New Zealand and South Africa, in 1903; Australia, in 1908. The first preferential arrangements have been substantially increased by subsequent tariff revisions.

their domestic markets. Both New Zealand and Australia have, however, provided ready avenues for capital investment, mostly from Great Britain. Despite the strong British sentiment and definite practical inducements to continue borrowing solely from Britain, large Australian governmental loans have recently been floated on the American market.[2] There is no evidence available of the extent of private commercial borrowings, either from Britain or from the United States.

The policies of New Zealand and Australia in regard to industrial organization illustrate the tendency to divergent development on the part of these sister dominions. New Zealand, dominated politically by small farmers, maintains a comparatively low tariff with a substantial British preference. Her industrial development therefore, though increasing, has not yet reached the stage where it can take care of the home market, and still less is it in the exporting stage.[3]

**New Zealand has few manufactured exports**

Since the strong development of Australian nationalism coincident with federation, the Commonwealth on the other hand has raised high protective barriers to importation and aimed at industrial self-sufficiency. This tendency has been reinforced by remarkably powerful labor organization and by the building up within Australia of a legislative code for the protection and advancement of the standard of living of the workers so organized. The capital invested in manufacturing industries has risen from £80,000,000 in 1908 to £303,000,000 in 1925, while the total output has risen from £87,000,000 to £347,000,000 in the same period.[4] The usual concomitant of such factory development—an urban concentration of the population—is seen in a very marked degree in the growth of large cities, particularly of Sydney and Melbourne. Manufacturing industries in Australia are being rapidly built up to the saturation point of the local market, which, however, is growing rapidly both by natural increase and by immigration. The cost of this process is a matter of some domestic controversy, but there has been no effective challenge to the policy of economic nationalism pursued since federation.

**Australian industry is more developed**

The comparatively small extent of the local market at the present time causes high production costs which are accentuated by an elaborate labor code. This fact, together with the absence within Australia of resources of coal, mineral oil, or water-power comparable in extent and cheapness with those of Britain, the United States, or Canada, offer substantial hindrances to the development of Australia into a country of large industrial exports. The importance of Australia's industrial development, therefore, lies mainly in the check to imports into its own markets and the corresponding check to exports of food and raw materials.

**but export is difficult**

[2] Mills, *The Australian Public Debt.*

[3] Nash, *Industrialization in New Zealand.*

[4] Wood, *Australian Secondary Industries.* If these figures are corrected for the rise in general prices, the increase in both cases is almost exactly 100 per cent.

### 5. FOOD PRODUCTION IN HAWAII

The opposite situation is presented by the remarkable industrial development of the Hawaiian Islands, which is all the more noteworthy because of the potentialities of the other scattered islands in the Pacific Ocean. There are special factors in the Hawaiian development, such as the use of successive waves of immigrant labor, the organization of industry upon a large scale, a quite unusual reliance upon scientific research and direction, and, probably most important of all, the existence near at hand of the almost unlimited American market within which competitors are handicapped by high tariffs. The greatest industrial advance has occurred since the reciprocity treaty with the United States in 1876, and more definitely since annexation in 1898. In a small group of islands with a mixed population of 328,444 the production of the two main industries, sugar and pineapples, is valued at $100,000,000 annually. Practically the whole development of the sugar industry and much of the later pineapple industry, as well as the shipping and similar public utilities and commercial subsidiaries, have been developed by local capital. The extraordinary economic development of this small group of tropical islands is an indication of what may be done, perhaps with less ease, when the pressure of industrialized populations calls for the utilization of other islands in the Pacific.

**Hawaiian large-scale development**

### 6. INDUSTRIAL EXPANSION IN JAPAN

The outstanding and significant industrial development in the Pacific area within recent years has, however, been that of Japan. It is obviously impossible, within the limits of this summary, to attempt any adequate description or measurement of that development. Under the sympathetic direction of an effective government Japan has within half a century changed from a self-sufficient nation of farmers into a highly industrialized community dependent to an extent that is probably unique upon further industrial expansion and international co-operation. The pressure of her population upon limited agricultural resources has already been discussed. The cumulative increase of that population in the immediate future will necessitate an increasing measure of industrialization beyond that already achieved.

**Japanese development**

The stimulus to manufacture came to Japan in three successive periods of military necessity. During the Sino-Japanese war of 1894–95 the paid-up capital of Japanese corporations (including banks) more than trebled. The Russo-Japanese War, ten years later, caused further manufacturing expansion, and after another ten-year interval the European war of 1914–18 gave to the Japanese—as it did to American industry an unprecedented opportunity. Despite the subsequent depression, accentuated by the earthquake disaster, the war opportunity has raised Japan definitely to the position of a great exporting nation. At the same time she has established her position as a great shipping and

**especially since the war**

shipbuilding nation, and by her diplomacy as well as her military and naval equipment has ranked herself with the great powers.[5]

In consequence of these developments there has been a very great growth both in the total population of Japan and in the proportion of that total engaged in industrial pursuits. Great manufacturing cities have developed, trade-unionism has organized, and labor disputes have become a normal feature of Japanese social life. The political consequences of these developments are to be seen in the rapid formulation of a labor code and the tremendous experiment of manhood suffrage to be initiated in 1928.

has been accompanied by great social changes

Faced with these far-reaching social changes, the traditional order of society is already being adapted to the new situation. Such fundamental conceptions as those of the family, the relation between employer and employee, the social status of women, are in process of modification. The industrial workers, free from the age-old notions of obedience and loyalty, have demanded political as well as economic rights. The advantages of cheap labor have tended to disappear as the standard of living has risen. The costs of the protective policy have also become apparent and have issued in widespread discontent among the small farmers.[6] As such adventitious aids to industrialism as the exploitation of cheap labor and protective tariffs decrease in importance, Japanese industry is facing the stark realities of a national poverty of essential raw materials and limited access to markets.

and is now at a critical stage

The natural consequence of this situation is a tendency to seek revolutionary ways of escape. It does not seem likely, unless economic depression is unduly prolonged and severe, that revolutionary socialism will take deep root in the compact, homogeneous, and essentially co-operative and patriotic Japanese community; but intellectual interest has been aroused in such doctrines. There has, on the other hand, been a rapid and extensive development of economic co-operation, particularly in the rural industries and in those manufactures immediately connected with rural production. More than 14,000 co-operative societies claim a total of over three million members.

## 7. THE LIMITATION OF NATURAL RESOURCES

Poverty of raw materials

Japan has already come up against the two outstanding problems of industrialization in the Orient. Faced with the necessity to industrialize, possessing a stable, efficient government and resources of labor, capital, and organization that are adequate to the demands of a highly industrialized community, she lacks at present the two essential elements of success: access to abundant and cheap raw materials and easy entry to wide and wealthy markets. Since the

[5] Ishii, "A Brief Review of Japan's Industries," and "A Review of the Shipping Industry of Japan."

[6] There were in 1925 some 2,000 disputes involving 30,000 landowners and 134,000 tenant farmers, in addition to 293 labor disputes involving 41,000 workers.

lack of these elements is common to the whole group of Oriental countries and has been urged as reason for doubting the possibility of any considerable industrialization of the Far East, they are worthy of the fullest consideration.[7] Both are obviously interconnected, since upon some degree of industrialization bringing increased productive efficiency and therefore greater purchasing power will depend the capacity of the markets. Though the answer to both questions also must be found mainly in China, both are most clearly illustrated at the present time by the difficulties of the more developed Japanese industries.

The comparative poverty of Japanese resources in coal, mineral oil, iron, and other minerals is well known, and the pressure upon available agricultural resources is also becoming recognized. The lack of fuel may be counterbalanced by the development, which is already considerable, of hydro-electric energy and the efficient utilization by scientific processes of the low-grade coals of Korea and Manchuria. The lack of iron, however, forms a greater problem and is regarded by many expert students of the problem as offering an almost insuperable barrier to industrial development.

**prohibits the complete industrialization of Asia**

The basic importance of iron in an industrial civilization is obvious, and it appears to be clear, though final judgments regarding Chinese resources are hardly attainable at present, that the known reserves of ore are utterly inadequate to sustain production for the dense population of Eastern Asia at anything approaching the rate per capita already achieved in the United States.[8] But it may be queried whether such a comparison is legitimate or valuable at the present stage of development in China and Japan. The difficulties confronting industrial expansion in China are considered in another section of this chapter. Those difficulties are very great and extremely complicated. It is not likely that any very speedy solution for them can be found such as will make possible a rapid development of industrial production over the whole of China and its neighboring states.[9]

**but not of Japan**

There does not seem to be the same ground for doubting the prospect of immediate and considerable development in Japan, and, to a somewhat less extent, in certain of the coastal regions of China. The adequacy of the necessary mineral resources for this more limited industrial development in the Orient is less doubtful than their adequacy for complete industrialization.[10] It is to be remembered also that the resources of international trade may be employed to bring raw materials to the point of most economical manufacture. Italy's poverty in minerals has not prevented considerable manufacturing expansion in recent years. As shipping and transport generally develop in the Pacific it may be found more economical to bring iron to the available labor and power on the

[7] Bain, *Ores and Industry in the Far East,* especially chaps. ii–iv.

[8] Bain, *op. cit.*, chap. iii.

[9] Bain, chap. viii.

[10] Bain, chap. ix, especially pp. 210–16.

Asiatic seaboard, as it has in the past been brought to coal and industrial areas in Britain and the United States.

if she has access to Chinese reserves

For the present, however, the problem of Japanese industry is concerned rather with immediate access to the known and available iron-ore resources in certain parts of China. The 1915 attempt to make such access definite and sure by the use of military power is a matter of history. The insecurity of Japanese industry if for any reason the present trading access should be denied remains a prime factor in the Japanese concern with the Chinese political situation.

### 8. HINDRANCES TO FREE MARKETING

and to the Chinese market

The second present limitation to Japanese industrial expansion has somewhat the same relation to Chinese politics. The potential market offered by the Chinese population is already extremely important to Japanese manufacturers and may become vastly more important. The bearing of this fact upon the tariff situation in China has already been mentioned and does not need further emphasis. Japan, more than any other exporting country, depends upon this main outlet for her exports from her new manufacturing industries. The cotton industry provides a clear illustration, both of this necessity and of the potential competition, even in the absence of tariff protection, of native Chinese industry using cheap labor without legal regulation.

The situation of Japanese industry vis-à-vis China cannot, however, be considered apart from the trading situation elsewhere. Japanese spokesmen pointed out very clearly the cumulative repression of Japanese standards of living which is involved in the practically universal tariff barriers which shut out Japanese exports as restrictive legislation shuts out Japanese immigration. The lowering or adjustment of tariff barriers, or any development which has the same effect of increasing the market for Japanese exports, would tend immediately to relieve economic pressure in Japan, not necessarily at the expense of the importing countries.

### 9. THE BEGINNINGS OF INDUSTRIALISM IN CHINA[11]

Social disorganization limits Chinese development

The present extent and future possibilities of industrial development in China would seem to be much more limited than those of Japan. Apart from the limited supply of essential raw materials discussed previously, there are all the enormous difficulties which arise from unsettled government. The mere fact of severe foreign competition is in itself a severe handicap to the growth of native industries. At the present time the lack of any stable government in China prevents this handicap from being countered by the use of a protective tariff, and in addition gives decided advantages to the foreign competitors in such matters as security, taxation, and expert technical knowledge. Despite the unsettlement of revolution and civil war, the imports into China are steadily in-

[11] Bain, chap. viii.

creasing; but there is not much possibility, under such conditions, of rapid industrial progress. What factories exist seem to be passing under foreign control.

The lack of capital for any great industrial progress is discussed in a later section of this chapter. This lack emphasizes a further very important condition of industrialization: the necessity for improving the conditions of internal transport and of providing mechanical power in agriculture as well as in industry. In addition to these fundamental conditions other equally important factors such as the development of commercial, banking, and technical organizations, as well as the organization of labor along economic rather than political lines and its adaptation to industrial ideas are necessary.

It was agreed that, in theory, an extension of industrialization under controlled conditions would benefit the people of China, primarily because it would increase productive power and raise the standards of living. Under present circumstances, however, such controlled development appears unlikely. The present disturbed political condition operates as a check to immediate industrial expansion; but the spread of industrial ideas continues, and there is an obvious possibility of some measure of further elementary industrial development in certain of the coastal regions as soon as more stable political conditions are achieved. The social results of such changes may be considerably less desirable than the more thoroughgoing industrialization would be.

### 10. THE SOCIAL EFFECTS OF INDUSTRIALIZATION

Brief reference has already been made to the far-reaching changes in the social organization of Japan which have been set in motion by the advent of new industrial methods. Under a stable central government the most immediate problems, such as the factory conditions of labor, housing, wages, and the standard of living, have proved capable of some measure of control. It was pointed out in discussion also that by her active participation in the work of the League of Nations and the International Labor Office, Japan had been able to utilize the machinery of international co-operation to assist in solving such problems. The conventions agreed upon at successive International Labor Conferences have been put into active effect and have contributed materially to the rapid rise of standards of living in Japan.[12] At the same time it is clear that the most important ultimate effects of industrialization upon the psychology of the people are not amenable to government control. Sociological conceptions in Japan are going through a process of change as they did in England in the nineteenth century. The society which emerges will be vastly different from the Japan of sixty or even thirty years ago.

**and may aggravate its social consequences**

The lack of stable government in China makes it improbable that the beginnings of industrial production, confined even though they may be to small areas on the coastal rim, will be restrained and guided by social controls as they

[12] Ayusawa, "Industrial Conditions and Labor Legislation in Japan."

have been in Japan. The absence of such controls makes many students of Chinese conditions apprehensive of the immediate future.

Their apprehension is not so much because of the factory conditions, which are to be expected. Those who direct and control large-scale industry have for the most part learned the economic value of proper working, and even housing, conditions for their employees. They bring with them also standards of responsibility for the welfare of those employees which are generally new to such a country as China, and they are sensitive to the public opinion of their fellow-countrymen, both in China and at home, on these points. The conditions in the large-scale foreign factories are not likely therefore to give cause for complaint. The agitation for factory reform, on the contrary, owes much to the practical direction of foreign capitalists.

**Abuses are worst in small inefficient factories**

At the same time the absence of effective governmental control over the smaller and less efficient competing economic units tends to make the reform of factory conditions a slow and difficult process. Moreover, it has been the experience of other countries that the worst abuses of child and female labor, as well as low wages, long hours, and bad conditions of adult male labor, are worst in the small handicraft industries and rudimentary factories which find it difficult to struggle against the effective competition of machine industry.

**and home industry**

This fact is already being illustrated in China on a great scale. The industrialization of China may be a slow process, but its commercialization is much more rapid. The cheap, attractive imported manufactures penetrate area after area as transportation improves, with the result that groups of handicraft workers find their livelihood imperiled and cannot easily find alternative sources of income. This may happen in a variety of ways, as, for example, when modern steam shipping takes the place of a multitude of river boatmen. It is under such conditions that social and political disorganization is at its worst. The exploitation of family labor and the general deterioration of social standards occurs readily also in such stricken industries.

Mention has been made in another connection of the social consequences that arise from the crowding into cities as a result of modern commerce and industries. The problems of civil government, of overcrowding, public utilities, housing, and sanitation have proved difficult in countries where they have grown up slowly and under the aegis of responsible governments. They are likely to be more difficult still where government is lacking and where the problems arise with the rapidity that has marked their recent development in the Orient. Family, clan, and village relationships break up swiftly in the separatist atmosphere of city life. Social sanctions and responsibilities tend to disappear. There is no easier or better way to create a propertyless, irresponsible proletariat such as presents the most fertile opportunities for destructive anti-social propaganda.

### 11. THE EQUILIBRIUM OF WORLD-TRADE

The fear was expressed also in the Round Tables that rapid industrialization in the Orient would react unfavorably upon the economic interests of the countries which at present send their exports into China. The economists, however, were not greatly impressed with this argument. Their general faith in the benefits of mutual trade led them rather to emphasize the importance of the added productivity and purchasing power made available by industrialization and to deduce therefrom the probability of increased rather than diminished trade.[13]

**Increased purchasing power in China**

Important qualifications of this general proposition were, however, recognized. It is not at all impossible that groups of exporters may be affected adversely by any considerable development of native industry in what has been a great world-market. Though the total trade may be increased, it may be of different character involving some interests in loss and others in gain. Any change in economic equilibrium is bound to have such effects. The magnitude of such dislocations may even be great enough to affect seriously a whole industry. Both the British and Japanese cotton industries were cited as examples. Any very large development of home industry, whether factory or handicraft, would appreciably affect the Chinese market upon which Manchester, and still more, Osaka, have come to depend.

**may increase European trade unevenly**

One other possibility was faced: that by the imposition of higher import duties or similar handicaps to trading, the Chinese market might be restricted either involuntarily or by a deliberate effort to foster local manufacture. The cost of such a restriction would be heavy upon Chinese traders and consumers. The present disorganization has already cost them dearly. But in addition it has been a source of loss and apprehension to British and Japanese and other foreign exporters, and this loss would be greatly increased if ill-considered tariff changes or further disorganization should increase the artificial barriers to trade. It is essential to remember that loss inflicted upon foreigners in this way does not bring corresponding gains to the Chinese community. Sections of the community may profit from the disorganization, but there is a large net destruction of wealth, the cost of which is for the most part borne by those least able to bear it: the Chinese consumers.

**but may be hindered by nationalism**

### 12. FOREIGN INVESTMENTS IN THE PACIFIC

A separate Round Table spent three sessions in discussing the general aspects of foreign investments in the Pacific, with special relation to the situation in China. The chief result of these discussions was the realization of the almost complete lack of accurate information concerning the extent, nature, conditions, and effect of the investments actually in existence at the present time. There

[13] Hinton, "A Statement on the Effects of Industrial Development of the Orient on European Industries."

are few fields of importance in international relations where so much controversy has proceeded on such a slender basis of ascertained scientific fact. This is particularly true of the investment in non-governmental, commercial, and industrial enterprises. Generally speaking, there is available fairly accurate and accessible information concerning the extent of governmental borrowings. The conditions and legal obligations in respect to these borrowings, however, have been studied with greater care than their economic effects. There still remains a wide field for statistical and economic research in every country of the Pacific on this point. The research that is needed is both political and economic. There is no possibility of division between the purely political and purely economic aspects of the problem.

**Little information exists concerning foreign investments**

When one enters the field of commercial investments by private individuals and corporations there is an almost complete absence of accurate information from which intelligent discussion may proceed. The Round Table therefore made a definite recommendation that the Institute should regard the international transference of capital in the Pacific as a major field for its research activities.

Reference has already been made in this chapter to the changed position of the United States in regard to capital accumulation and export. With this must be considered the post-war position of Great Britain, concerning which more information is available, although its particular bearing upon Pacific problems remains to be investigated. The position of Canadian industrial development and its relation to American capital has also been touched upon, but the information does not at present exist for more than the merest general statement. In Australia and New Zealand the extent of governmental borrowing is accurately known and there has been a considerable amount of informed discussion concerning the effect which this borrowing may be expected to have both upon local development and upon economic conditions in the countries from which the capital is borrowed. The investigation of foreign investment through commercial, banking, shipping, and industrial enterprises remains to be undertaken. The same statement may be made of Japan, and in still greater degree of China. Nor can the Pacific islands be ignored in view of their potentialities as food-producing areas in the future. In the discussion which is summarized below, therefore, it must be premised that only cautious statement of generalities was possible in the absence of detailed factual information.

The chief interest in the discussion centered upon foreign investments in China. The view was advanced and disputed that China has offered in the past, and will offer in the near future, an attractive field in which foreign investors need be restrained by few scruples and little fear of governmental control. In the consideration of foreign investments in China an introductory contrast between the conditions in Hawaii and the Philippines was used to illustrate the importance of political factors. Within the last fifty years the Hawaiian Islands

**Hawaiian development contrasted with**

have achieved a position of great financial strength and independence. A remarkable development of production has been financed almost wholly from local accumulations of capital. In addition it was estimated that Hawaiian residents owned between twenty million and thirty-five million dollars' worth of securities in bonds and stocks of well-established companies in the United States. It was estimated that the surplus capital available for investment annually in Hawaii was as much as twenty-five to thirty million dollars. Some of this is invested already in the Philippines.

**the Philippines**

The position in the Philippines is very different. The governmental debt is considerably greater. Rates of interest are higher, the most favorable overdraft rate at present being 9 per cent, rising to 12 per cent. The banking capital available was regarded in the discussions as inadequate, and the commercial capital is also comparatively small. The view was expressed that in the Philippines as in Mexico, and in greater degree in China, political instability is a very large factor in the disturbance of industry resulting in high rates of interest and unprofitable business. Bankers have nothing to gain on the whole from such conditions, but the existence of high rates of interest inevitably creates a popular feeling of financial exploitation.

Arising from this point there was some discussion of the relation of economic investment to political control. In view of the political responsibility which may devolve upon the government by reason of investment in foreign countries, the State Department of the United States has informed bankers of its desire to be informed concerning projected loans and to be given the opportunity to interpose any objections. At the same time it expressly disclaims responsibility for indorsement of loans. There is no legal basis for this supervision, but the influence of the government has been sufficient for any objection to carry great weight. It has, however, been a very easy matter for misunderstandings to arise concerning this practice.

**Political considerations affect investment in China**

In China the connection between investment and international politics, particularly in relation to governmental loans, has been closer than in any other country. This is mainly due to the instability of the Chinese government. The statement was made that there was a scramble for foreign investment in China in the period just before the close of the nineteenth century. Some of the Chinese spokesmen repeated the suggestion, which has been commonly made in recent years, that the powers tried to create a régime under which they could exploit the riches of China. The chief means of doing so was by the building of railways and the securing of control over the spheres of interest tapped by the railways. To achieve these objects it was said that there was a rush of foreign capital into China.

The political aspects of this period have been the subject of considerable discussion. Strong attacks have been made both upon the political developments of the time and upon the political conditions which were attached to the loans. Even stronger criticism was made concerning later post-war unsecured loans which it was said were made for purely political, rather than economic, purposes. The Chinese objections were expressed to the international consortium as a means of subjecting China to the control of international financiers backed by the power of their governments. At the same time it was admitted that China badly needs foreign capital, though her leaders are very apprehensive of foreign control coming in with that capital. It was recognized also that the primary reason for the fear of foreign control lay in the absence of a stability of government in China.

which is relatively small

In traversing this general attitude it was pointed out that as a matter of fact the extent of foreign investment in China, and even of foreign trade in China, is remarkably small when allowance is made for the size of the country. China has a large territory inhabited by considerably more than four hundred million people. The total national debt of China is approximately twelve hundred million dollars gold, and of this total a considerable sum is held within China. The unsecured portion of the debt, mainly contracted in the most recent period, is approximately five hundred million dollars gold. These sums, while absolutely large, are small relatively to the size and potentialities of China. The national debt of Australia, with its six million people, is more than four times as large as that of China.[14] As a field for foreign investment and foreign trade Australia has been and still is overwhelmingly more important than China.

China's credit is low

China, in fact, has not offered an attractive field for foreign investments. The scramble of 1894–99 was not a great scramble on the part of foreign investors, but rather a political scramble in which governments were preparing a way for them to make investments. Those investments have for the most part never materialized. It was pointed out that bankers and their investing clients became more and more shy of fields of investment which involve or may in the future involve the intervention of their home governments to collect interest or to enforce special securities such as the hypothecation of particular sources of revenue for the service of the foreign debt. The experience of investors in such securities involving the necessity of political action has not in the past been particularly happy. In view of the many more attractive fields for investment, even the offer of high rates of interest is not sufficient to attract considerable sums of money.

During the past six years there has been practically a complete absence of foreign investments in China. By the end of 1925 practically all the unsecured and inadequately secured debts of China were in default. China's credit, and therefore China's borrowing power abroad, is practically zero. The price of many Chinese bonds is quoted today in the twenties. The result is that practically no foreign investor wishes to buy China's bonds or to make any new loans

[14] Mills, "The Australian Public Debt."

to China. The rehabilitation of Chinese credit, first by making satisfactory provision for the obligations at present outstanding, and secondly by providing adequately for the future service of the obligations which at present are not adequately secured, is necessary before there will be any willingness to invest further in loans either to the Chinese government or to Chinese industries.

The Consortium, which has often been represented as an attempt to fasten international financial control upon the Chinese people, may be interpreted from the point of view of the banker as the only possible means by which investors might be induced to place their capital at the disposal of China. The different national groups of bankers which formed the Consortium enlisted the co-operation of a great array of banking strength in each country. It was hoped by this strength that the investors might be induced to participate in Chinese loans. But as a matter of fact the Consortium has not functioned, and loans have not been made. Political conditions in China are such that there is no present prospect of foreign capital coming into China, except possibly under such conditions of international co-operation as were recently used for the financial rehabilitation of Austria and Hungary. The fear of a rush of international capital to exploit the virgin resources of the Chinese nation was regarded by the bankers and economists in the Round Table as a bogey. In their view it would be necessary, on the contrary, for China to go to considerable lengths in the improvement of her politics and administration before foreign investors could again be induced even to consider the possibility of co-operation in China.

**Financial reorganization**

On the other hand, the leaders of Young China feel that they have inherited a great many bad debts for which they are disinclined to undertake the responsibility. They are disposed, even at the risk of prolongation of their present difficulties, to fight shy of any form of international combination for loans. They do not have full confidence even in the League of Nations, and seem determined to deal with the powers as individuals and not as groups. They are anxious also to contract loans in the future only when these loans can be secured without political conditions. They recognize that this involves the necessity of reorganizing the financial administration of China. Of this, however, they are quite hopeful, and they point to the experience of the Cantonese government in 1925 both in the efficient collection of taxation and in the restoration of the market value of government securities. They place a considerable amount of faith also in the increasing willingness of the Chinese people to finance their own governmental necessities. By such means Young China hopes first to demonstrate that it can govern efficiently and that its own people have confidence in that efficiency and then to induce foreign investors to make loans to China for constructive purposes without attaching political strings to them. Such a program clearly commanded the approbation of those who were familiar with banking and economic experience in other countries.

Money for investment, they pointed out, demands these main essentials:

security and prompt payment, both of interest and of principal, when the period of the loan matures. These fundamental principles apply equally to government banking and finance. Both in commercial and public finance loans are made partly on security, but largely also upon confidence in the character of the borrower. Commercial banks often lend to young men starting in business because of the confidence they feel in the personal character, enterprise, and energy of the borrower. While the reputation of a borrowing government and its proved efficiency of administration is probably even more important because of the impersonal character of large international loans, yet it is not impossible that loans might be available for governments in whose stability and character investors had confidence, even though those governments were young and untried. The sympathy with which the political and economic difficulties of China are almost universally regarded at the present time makes such a possibility the more likely.

The best means of restoring it

### 3. DOCUMENTS

The source material for the three Round Tables which were concerned with economic development in the Pacific consisted both of prepared papers and of reference material.

The following data papers were distributed to members:

1. "A Statement on the Effects of the Industrial Development of the Orient on European Industries," by W. J. HINTON, professor of Political Economy, University of Hongkong (Documents, Section 14).

2. "China's Industrial Development," by D. K. LIEU, chief of Investigation Department, Chinese Government Bureau of Economic Information (Documents, Section 15).

3. "Some Practical Problems in Industry and Foreign Trade in China," by O. S. LIEU, managing director, Shanghai Cement Company.

4. "The Labor Movement in China," by CHEN TA, professor of Sociology, Tsing Hua College, Peking (Documents, Section 16).

5. "Child Workers in China," by MISS L. M. FRIEDLANDER, Wilson Research Student, University College of Wales, Aberystwith.

6. "A Brief Review of Japan's Industries," by AKIRA ISHII, formerly vice-president, Nippon Yusen Kaisha.

7. "A Review of the Shipping Industry of Japan," by AKIRA ISHII, formerly vice-president, Nippon Yusen Kaisha.

8. "The Financial Crisis in Japan," by JUNNOSUKE INOUYE, chairman, Japanese Council, Institute of Pacific Relations (Documents, Section 17).

9. "The Industrialization of Canada," by R. W. BROCK, Dean, University of British Columbia.

10. "Australian Secondary Industries," by G. L. WOOD, lecturer in Commerce, University of Melbourne.

11. "Human Resources and Occupations in New Zealand," by WALTER NASH, secretary, New Zealand Labor Party.

12. "Industrialization in New Zealand," by WALTER NASH, secretary, New Zealand Labor Party.

13. "The Rôle of the Banker in International Relations," by JEROME D. GREENE (Documents, Section 18).

14. "Some Political and Economic Effects of International Movements of Capital," by D. B. COPLAND, professor of Commerce, University of Melbourne.

15. "The Australian Public Debt," by R. C. MILLS, professor of Economics, University of Sydney.

In addition to these circulated papers, the following books were tabled for reference:

BAIN, *Ores and Industry in the Far East;* UYEHARA, *The Industry and Trade of Japan;* AYUSAWA, *Industrial Conditions and Labor Legislation in Japan;* REMER, *The Foreign Trade of China;* WILLOUGHBY, *Foreign Rights and Interests in China; The China Yearbook; The Canadian Yearbook; The Commonwealth Yearbook; The New Zealand Official Yearbook; Report of the Director of the International Labor Office to the 10th Session of the International Labor Office;* INTERNATIONAL ECONOMIC CONFERENCE, *Memorandum on Cotton.*

## IMMIGRATION AND EMIGRATION IN THE PACIFIC

The problems arising from immigration restriction and the treatment of resident aliens, together with the whole problem of racial contact, occupied the attention of the first conference of the Institute more than any other subject. There was in consequence a considerable amount of data material available for discussion at the second conference, a large part of which had been prepared in the meantime by the different national groups. This data material is listed at the close of the section.

### 1. QUESTIONS FOR DISCUSSION

*a*) What are the more significant causes of emigration in the Pacific area?
*b*) What are the outstanding causes of friction in the receiving countries?
*c*) What have been the principal methods hitherto of dealing with the problems thus arising?
*d*) What important problems arise in connection with each of the following in the several countries of the Pacific:
  ( i) admission of immigrants?
  ( ii) naturalization of immigrants?
  (iii) disabilities of immigrants, legal and extra-legal?
*e*) What problems specially arise in connection with the "second generation"?
*f*) What are the special problems of:
  ( i) foreign students?
  ( ii) foreign travelers?
*g*) What are the specific causes of dissatisfaction in connection with the foregoing problems and what is their order of importance?
*h*) What are the best methods of dealing with these several causes of dissatisfaction?

### 2. SUMMARY OF ROUND-TABLE DISCUSSIONS

CHAIRMEN AND SECRETARIES

Round Table I
  *Chairman:* ARCHBISHOP E. J. HANNA
  *Secretary:* ROY HIDEMICHI AKAGI

Round Table II
  *Chairman:* WILLIAM H. KILPATRICK
  *Secretary:* W. W. GOFORTH

Round Table III
  *Chairman:* HENRY T. HODGKIN
  *Secretary:* R. D. MCKENZIE

### I. THE NATURE AND EXTENT OF PACIFIC MIGRATION

*European mass migration in the nineteenth century.*—Modern experience in the problems arising out of human migration dates very largely from the development of steam shipping and the opening up of the continental plains by railways in the latter half of the nineteenth century. From the beginning of the machine age, indeed, there has been a progressive breaking down of the barriers to migration. Adam Smith's well-known saying that "man is of all baggage the most difficult to be transported" referred primarily to the difficulty of moving population from one part of England to another. While that difficulty still exists even in local areas, it has been very much lessened, not only by the development of mechanical facilities for transportation, but also by the changes in social organization and social sympathies which have resulted from the growth of modern industry.

**European migration**

The outflow of population from Europe in the latter part of the nineteenth century presents the phenomena of migration on a scale that is unique in human history. Such great open spaces as the United States and the British dominions were peopled rapidly at the same time as the population in Europe itself was more than doubled. The underlying reason for this remarkable outburst of racial energy is clearly the increased mastery which the new system of industry gave over natural resources and in the last resort over food.

In its later stages European mass migration was more definitely connected with improvements in the means of communication and transport. In certain cases the facilities for transportation became themselves an inciting cause of migration, as when the Atlantic shipping companies embarked upon extensive campaigns to encourage cheap travel or when railway companies attracted immigration as one means of drawing business to the railroad. Apart from the vested interest, the mere fact that communication and transport became easier and more certain was in itself a favoring condition for the encouragement of migration.

**depended on transportation facilities**

Only in isolated cases, however, such as that of Ireland, can the European emigration of the nineteenth century be regarded as due primarily to overpopulation relative to the resources of the countries concerned. Rather did it signify an increased economic power making it possible for individuals to seek even better economic or political or social opportunities in other lands at the same time as continuous improvement in economic conditions was taking place in their home country.

**and was not due to overpopulation**

*The origins of Asiatic emigration.*[1] The problems of migration in the Pacific are in many essential respects different from those which resulted from European immigration to the new lands which were mainly dominated by Anglo-Saxon forms of government. There has indeed always been a considerable measure of emigration from South China which is strictly comparable. The

**Cantonese emigration**

[1] Mears, *Resident Orientals on the Pacific Coast,* pp. 9–16.

provinces around Canton, from which most of the immigrants have gone to such developing regions as the Straits Settlements, have not been subject to the same pressure of population due to famines, floods, and similar disasters as have many other parts of China. The migration of their people was due very largely to the same causes—adventure, the desire for better conditions of life, and the attraction of former immigrants—which were powerful motives in drawing European immigrants to North America and the South Seas. They went also to communities where the social organization and prevailing culture was not unduly hostile to their admittance.

**Contract labor**

A large part of the Asiatic migration in the Pacific has, however, been of a very different type. Contract laborers have been introduced for economic reasons to work under the direction and control of Anglo-Saxon organizers of industry. The importance of this system of artificial encouragement to migration is not yet negligible. Contract labor, mainly Chinese, still exists in Samoa, New Guinea, and Nauru. The French government has recently decided to permit it in certain of the French South Sea Islands, and it is being asked for by the British planters in the New Hebrides.

Where such indentured laborers are not returned to the country of their origin, an alien community develops which tends to attract new members to itself from its homeland. In so doing it follows the same course of development as was followed by the European settlements.

**The influence of gold**

The development of isolated Chinese communities in many Pacific countries following the discovery of gold has had the same effect. The importance of gold discoveries in the history of Asiatic immigration into Australia and New Zealand, and equally into California and British Columbia, can hardly be overestimated. The Chinese settlements in the gold diggings were almost invariably unpopular, and after the first fever of the gold rushes had passed the tendency for these mining camps to expand into alien communities disturbing the economic and social homogeneity of the young countries was invariably a source of irritation.

**The new Pacific communities**

*The recent disturbance of economic equilibrium in Asia.*—Whatever the origin of these alien settlements, whether released contract labor or labor originally encouraged for developmental purposes, as with the Japanese who drifted to California from Hawaii, or mining camps, as with the Chinese almost everywhere, or free adventurous migration, the subsequent expansion, except in such areas as the Straits Settlements, has invariably caused resentment on the part of the Anglo-Saxon communities chiefly concerned. Unlike the American Indian or the Australian aborigine, the Asiatic immigrants were obviously not a vanishing race. On the contrary, they were remarkably efficient, economically and socially, and in some cases bade fair to outlive, outwork, and outbreed the dominant race. All the Pacific communities where this problem arose were young, struggling, sparsely settled regions in which the Asiatic immigration bulked large from a local viewpoint. When it became evident that, by natural increase and by immigration, the Asiatic settlers were rapidly multiplying and extending their economic activities, a demand always arose for restriction.[2]

While the competition of shipping companies never attained the same pitch as it did later in the Atlantic, the early efforts at regulation by limiting the number of immigrants per ship or per unit of tonnage is clear evidence of the beginning of that competition. There is evidence also of developing organization for the commercial encouragement of emigration from China, and, somewhat later, of governmental assistance and encouragement which has not wholly ceased in Japan. The activities of these commercial and semigovernmental agencies have been severely limited by the coincident imposition of restrictive legislation by the Anglo-Saxon communities. It is, however, a fair deduction, from the historical evidence available, that there were all the possibilities of a very large and cumulative movement of peoples across the Pacific.

**Feared mass immigration**

In the light of subsequent economic developments this deduction appears even more probable. As modernization has progressed, always accompanied by a rapid and cumulative increase of population, the inevitable tendency toward freer movement of peoples has appeared in the oriental countries. Increasing knowledge of other lands and peoples, the desire to travel and to take advantage of greater economic opportunities—all the motives that were behind the European mass migration of the late nineteenth century—have come into play. The mere disturbance of established traditional organization is responsible for shifts of population on a scale probably without historical parallel. Examples of this fact may be seen in the movements of population now taking place within Asia itself. There has apparently set in a steady stream of immigration from Korea to Japan; there are said to be a million Koreans, at least, in Manchuria, and the more recent movement of Chinese into Manchuria and Mongolia, mainly from Shantung, is estimated as high as from three to five hundred thousand annually. The immobilization of settlement in Asia has obviously been disturbed by political and economic change. It may reasonably be expected that this unsettlement will increase rather than decrease, and that an increasing population in every Asiatic country, freed from the traditional economic and social restraints, will become more and more a population on the move until a redistribution more suitable to modern conditions has been achieved. The experience of Europe shows that such a development may be quite consistent with the intensification of economic progress and the thickening of population in already densely settled areas.

**Migration has become an international problem**

*The international importance of migration.*—It is apparent, therefore, that the modern problems of migration are unique in many important respects. It was pointed out in the course of discussion that within very recent years the

[2] McKenzie, *Oriental Exclusion,* chap. i; Hall, *Asiatic Immigration into New Zealand: Its History and Legislation.*

Court of International Justice at The Hague instanced immigration as typifying questions which came solely within the jurisdiction of the states immediately concerned. Yet there was general assent to the statement made by the Round Table chairmen in summarizing the discussions on this subject, that "human migration under modern conditions of transportation and economic organization is believed to be one of the major international problems of the present day."

In elaboration of this statement it was pointed out that the present rapid means of transportation make it possible for large numbers of people to move rapidly from one part of the world to another. Then, too, the growth of industry has led to great differentiations in the standard of living. In earlier migrations, and even within the last century, the standards of living as between the European peasant and the Chinese peasant of the same period were approximately equal. Industrial development has in modern times made large differences in the standard of living as between different races and sections of the world. The growth of organized industry has also led to grave differences between the position of capitalists and laborers, the demand for labor in certain sections of the world being not only very great, but also being organized in ways which lead to rapid changes in the population. Probably most important of all is the extreme racial sensitiveness which has grown up comparatively recently with the growth of nationalism and the contact of race with race.[3]

## 2. THE CAUSES OF RACIAL FRICTION

The causes of racial friction

The resentment felt against the growing Asiatic communities in the new Anglo-Saxon settlements of the Pacific, and the fear that they would prove to be collecting points for an ever increasing volume of Asiatic immigration, trace back to a tangle which can in the strictest psychological sense be called a complex of causes. The importance of this little-understood and very intricate tangle arises largely from the emotional tone which provides its driving force. Investigation of its component elements proves to be extremely difficult in the light of present knowledge or lack of knowledge of many of the principal factors involved. Yet in view of the urgency of the problem there are few more important fields for human investigation. The profound social changes which are loosening the Asiatic peoples from their traditional moorings must be thought of in conjunction with the apprehensions of the Anglo-Saxon communities of the Pacific area which control the only accessible areas for emigration and in conjunction with the measures which they have already taken to make those areas inaccessible. Behind those measures lie little-understood psychological attitudes based upon what is popularly called instinct (which may or may not upon scientific investigation turn out rather to be prejudice) more than upon knowledge and understanding. It may be argued, furthermore, that

[3] Mears, pp. 16–24.

the most important results of restrictive measures and attitudes lie in the effect they have upon the psychology of the peoples excluded.[4]

The first Chinese immigrants, particularly, were said to lower the standard of living, drain wealth out of the country, introduce commercial methods and standards that were not compatible with current standards, and offer a real threat to the protection of specialized skilled labor by means of trade-union organization.

**are economic**

In the political sphere they were an alien community not interested in, or conformable to, democratic organization. They did not fit readily into the homogeneous nationalism which most of the communities concerned set in front of themselves as a democratic ideal. Moreover, they threatened to destroy the essential equality of status upon which democratic institutions rest. Their competition tended to drive out unskilled and skilled labor from the lower and middle ranks of society and to concentrate political power in the hands of economic oligarchies. The unfortunate phenomenon of the "poor white" in certain Anglo-Saxon communities was regarded as destructive of democracy.

**political**

The tendency for the Asiatic communities to remain apart and concentrated, living the cultural and social life of their homelands, was also a source of apprehension. Concentration itself magnified their importance, and the continued use of an alien language and alien customs was regarded as proof that they were not capable of assimilation. Resentment was heightened by the fact that for the most part the immigrants were coolie laborers, uneducated and illiterate, with apparently little desire or capacity for education. Ignorance of modern sanitation and hygiene, different moral conceptions and standards accentuated by the essentially masculine character of the immigrant communities, and the very strangeness of their habits and customs influenced the attitude of most Anglo-Saxons, not only toward the immigrants themselves, but also toward the countries from which they came. It is an unfortunate fact that much public opinion which influences policy in a democratic country is based upon conceptions of Chinese and Japanese in menial occupations in a strange land.

**cultural**

Behind and beneath a great deal of the social and cultural distrust and antagonism lies the fear of biological consequences arising from intermarriage.[5] There are widespread notions of heredity and interbreeding for which the observed scientific basis is as yet almost negligible. Even in the case of individuals who try to preserve an open mind concerning the consequences of interbreeding and are largely free from other aspects of race prejudice there generally remains a lurking doubtful fear.

**and biological**

Apart altogether from such a fear, the undoubted fact of the adverse social environment which in most communities at the present time surrounds the individual of mixed racial parentage reacts again as a check to miscegenation.

[4] Mears, pp. 24–58. [5] Mears, pp. 145–51.

When interbreeding has taken place it has often, though not invariably, been due to less desirable members of the races concerned ignoring social conventions. The children of such marriages have been handicapped from the beginning by poor heredity and have been doubly handicapped in a hostile environment where neither cultural group forms a sympathetic group in which they may develop. Unfortunate instances of individual failure to adapt to social necessities under such conditions are very frequently cited in proof of a general contention that the crossing of races is unnatural and produces undesirable results. Much evidence and more folklore concerning the results of animal breeding is used to support the contentions advanced, though practically all of it depends on unproved assumptions concerning human species and their physical analogies with the animal world.[6]

In much the same way there is a popular tendency to generalize from single instances, and even more from single races, to the whole racial problem. It appears to be clear, for example, that American experience with the negroes both before and after slavery has had a considerable influence upon the attitude of the American people to color problems generally.

**The economic causes are usually the dynamic**

All of these causes are subtly interconnected. Generally speaking, the economic factor acts as the inciting cause. The competition of the Japanese on California farms or in the Canadian fishing industry, or of the Chinese in retail business everywhere, provokes the active opposition of those who have suffered economic defeat, and the whole complex of racial prejudice is invoked in popular agitation. The fear of being swamped by mass immigration is responsible for most of the discriminatory legislation. When that fear is removed a quick improvement in feeling toward the immigrants is noted. This has apparently been the case in California. The reality of this improvement was questioned, but was testified to by Californians typical of various groups and by scientific investigation.[7] It was made clear, however, that any revival of the fear that effective exclusion might be endangered by legislation would revive the agitation in greater force than ever.

### 3. THE MAINTENANCE OF RACIAL PURITY

Like most other human problems, the control and direction of migration resolves itself in the last resort into biological terms. In racial intermixture, as in problems of human biology generally, the basis of accurately observed scientific fact is extremely small. For the most part individual opinions and national policies are based rather upon fear and prejudice than upon known fact.

The Anglo-Saxon communities in the Pacific have strenuously maintained

[6] Cf. Mears, p. 146.

[7] Mears, chap. xvii, especially pp. 390–92.

policies of immigration restriction, or even exclusion, based upon the assumption that racial purity is a desirable ideal. It is true that the scientific definition of this ideal is difficult, but in practice it has proved comparatively simple to approximate to the ideal, especially in Australia and New Zealand, where the patriotic connection with Great Britain, itself a country of emigration, simplifies the issue. The doubt was raised as to whether in the course of the twentieth century such a separatist ideal will continue to be practicable or whether the progress of communication and transport will result in the blending of the races of the Pacific as of the Mediterranean in an earlier period.

**Race fusion is feared**

Such an idea is most unwelcome to public opinion in the Anglo-Saxon communities. They are decidedly adverse to any racial blending such as that which has occurred in various parts of South America. Nor is this aversion wholly on the Anglo-Saxon side. Both the Japanese and the Chinese are proud races with a long social heritage which they are not always willing to share.

Apart, however, from the ultimate solution of the problem, which is at present not a matter of any practical interest, it was argued and seemed to be generally agreed that the magnitude and suddenness of the problem warranted measures of control. It is true that there has been considerable blending of racial types in Europe in historical times, and that some of the mixed races, such as the British, have proved to be extremely vigorous. It is also true that China has successfully absorbed many foreign elements into her population. But these elements have been absorbed in comparatively small numbers over long periods of time. There is no historical instance of the absorption of masses of immigration of alien culture in a brief time. On the other hand, the recent experience of Australia and New Zealand, as well as the United States, was cited to show the difficulty of absorbing even immigration from countries of similar culture which came in large volume in short periods of time.

**on the scale now possible**

The biological evidence of racial crossing that is available is too confused by environmental conditions and has been the subject of too little scientific investigation as yet to throw much light on the problem. There has been a great deal of intermarriage between Maoris and Whites in New Zealand, between Polynesians and Chinese in various Pacific islands, and among the many races of the Hawaiian Islands. There seems to be little evidence of physical or mental degeneration as a result of these crosses, but the evidence awaits much fuller analysis before any final conclusions can be drawn from it.

**Evidence is scanty**

The factors of environment are at least equally important with those of heredity, and it is in the differing social environments that the explanation is to be found for most of the divergent opinions held on this subject. It was stated, for example, that the chief problem confronting the Eurasian in his mental and social development was the lack of social tradition and background. Torn between two cultures and recognized by neither, he has not yet built up a characteristic culture for himself.

The factor of numbers must also be considered. The mass of a problem may alter its character. Blending that may be possible on a small scale under favorable conditions in Hawaii or New Zealand may have little except theoretical relevance to the large problem. In particular, while it may establish certain elementary biological facts, such as that physical deterioration is not an inevitable result of racial crossing, it is difficult to establish the probability of similar results being achieved under different social circumstances. Apart from the vexed question of the transmission of acquired qualities, there have to be considered all the subtle and important influences, both of physical and mental, of prenatal and post-natal, environment. The social and biological factors in the problem are in fact inextricably connected. There was a tendency to argue that both the physical and cultural results of racial mixture were good or were bad. It is at least clear that the physical or biological results cannot be considered apart from the reaction upon them of the social environment.

**and confined to special environments**

On the other hand, it was argued, cultural interchange may readily take place and is now taking place without free migration and intermarriage. The blending of cultures which in the past has been fruitful of human progress can go on without the blending of racial stocks. In view of the present lack of knowledge and of the widespread apprehensions that exist, the maintenance, at any rate for the present, of barriers to migration may be defended as preservative of peace and racial good will. Mass migration between the Pacific countries is not a solution of the problem of international relations in the Pacific. While this appears to be generally agreed, much depends upon the actual restrictions to migration and upon the manner in which they are imposed. The psychological results of their imposition on both sides warrant careful investigation.

**Cultural interchange not dependent on race fusion**

### 4. THE CONTROL OF MIGRATION[8]

The deliberate restrictions to increasing freedom of migration have resulted from both governmental and non-governmental action in countries both of immigration and of emigration. The extra-legal restrictions ranging from social boycott to violent action in the receiving countries have generally been the cause of legislation which has minimized, though it has not always eliminated, the non-governmental restrictions. It may be argued that the effort to arrive at a solution of the problem by governmental action is in itself a social advance.

Governmental control of migration has been most important in the receiving countries, though Japan particularly, among the countries of emigration, has co-operated actively by such means of restriction as the various "gentlemen's agreements" into which she has entered. The use of governmental machinery obviously raises the question into the sphere of international relations. The argument was advanced that restriction affected only individuals, and that it was not the Japanese or Chinese nation which was excluded, e.g., from the

[8] Mears, chap. v; McKenzie, *passim*.

United States, but merely Japanese and Chinese. This argument was not accepted by the oriental members of the Round Table.

Governmental action ranges from more or less rigid inspection through the collection of various forms of taxation and the application of tests of literacy to the administration of quota systems and of complete exclusion subject to stated exemptions. The variety of this action was discussed in the 1925 conference of the Institute and is further detailed in the memorandum submitted to the recent conference by the International Labor Office.[9]

**Present legislation is effective**

The general effectiveness of this legislation and administrative procedure which has been developed was accepted. For the present it is adequate to prevent any possibility of mass migration from Asia to America or Australia and New Zealand. In that prevention the leaders of Japan and China have acquiesced as a measure of practical statesmanship.

Certain problems arise, however, out of the manner of the legislation and methods of its administration. The latter are traversed as far as their most important field, the western coast of the United States, is concerned, by Professor McKenzie's study entitled *Oriental Exclusion*. The only important point added in the course of discussion concerned the status of American women who have forfeited their nationality by marrying Orientals, and who, if they are divorced, cannot regain their American nationality.

### 5. THE TREATMENT OF RESIDENT ALIENS

The treatment of resident aliens is intimately connected with the administration of exclusion laws.[10] The actual situation in the western states of America is discussed in detail in the study made by Professor Mears, entitled *Resident Orientals on the Pacific Coast*. It was urged in discussion that in so far as exclusion has been effective in removing the fear of mass immigration, the time was ripe for considering the removal of discriminatory legislation against the limited number of aliens who are actually resident in America. The virtual absence of such legislation in other countries practicing exclusion was urged in support of the argument.

In the case of those Orientals who were born in China or Japan, naturalization is impossible by virtue of the law of 1790, which would be extremely difficult to alter at this date.[11] Their children born on American soil, however, are American citizens, and as such entitled to the privileges of education and opportunity enjoyed by every other citizen of the United States. The removal of social prejudice against them, and particularly the opportunity of marriage, presents a difficult problem. The oriental communities of the Pacific coast are dominantly masculine; they do not intermarry with the white community, and cannot bring in wives from Japan or China.[12]

**Resident aliens therefore present less difficulty**

[9] Documents, Section 22.

[10] Mears, *passim*, especially chaps. vi–viii.

[11] Mears, chap. iv.

[12] McKenzie, chap. vii.

In part the problem arises from concentration. The geographical dispersion of these colonies in course of time will tend to lessen local prejudice and to facilitate education and social intercourse. At present social intercourse is considerably interfered with by fear of intermarriage.

The interracial commissions which operate in other parts of the United States were evidenced as means for promoting better relationships. The strongest advocates of exclusion tended to agree that, provided the exclusion issue was regarded as settled, progress along the line of adjustment with the aliens now resident was likely to be facilitated.

### 6. THE AMERICAN IMMIGRATION ACT OF 1924

While there is reason to expect more rapid progress under these conditions, it was made clear that the Exclusion Act of 1924 is by no means a closed issue as far as Japan is concerned. Japanese members of the Round Tables pointed out that the Act was neither forgotten nor regarded as unimportant in Japan. No active steps were likely to be taken by the Japanese concerning it, but they awaited action on the part of the United States and would not regard the matter as settled until some action was taken.

**The Japanese view of the American Act of 1924**

The fact of exclusion is accepted; the manner of exclusion rankles. From the Japanese point of view the situation will not be satisfactory until the discriminatory principles of the Act of 1924 are eliminated. The placing of Japan upon the same quota basis as other countries, the revival of the Gentlemen's Agreement, or any kind of treaty agreement which places the Japanese upon an equality with other races, would satisfy Japanese opinion. The Japanese do not feel that the particular method adopted should be suggested by them. It is a matter in which America has the next move.

Organized labor in Japan agrees with this viewpoint, as the following statement by a labor member of the Japanese group made in the Round Table will indicate:

> In the Japanese mind it is a question of sentiment. The Japanese do not think they are an inferior race. It is true that the conditions of Japanese labor today may be low, when compared with those in other advanced countries like America, but this is principally the result of environment. If Japanese laborers are placed in America then they will attain an advanced condition of labor; if they are placed in Australia they will rise to a position occupied by the Australian laborers. Therefore the Japanese laborers very much regret the environment in which they are placed. From this point of view especially they very much regret that the question of discrimination should have arisen from the fraternal labor organizations in other countries. We believe that a country with a high standard of labor conditions should help a country with a lower standard of labor, instead of discriminating or restricting against it.
>
> This is exactly the principle which organized labor in Japan is trying to carry out with regard to Korean laborers. The Korean laborer's condition is lower than

that of Japanese laborers, so that what organized labor in Japan is trying to do is to help the Korean laborers to raise their standard.

Moreover, Korean laborers in Japan are actually taken into the trade-unions, and in this way organized labor is trying to better Korean laborers' conditions in Japan.

Even if the quota basis is recognized and adopted, it will not help the problem of overpopulation in Japan, but it will mitigate the insulted sentiment in Japan. Although the American people may regard the issue as a closed affair, the Japanese cannot think so in sentiment. Therefore, in this respect it is a question of taking more advanced steps in solving the questions between American and Japanese organized labor.

We do not object to the freedom of restriction in dealing with domestic problems, but if this right is misused it is going to disturb international peace and understanding. International problems should be dealt with from the point of view of mutual respect and mutual understanding and mutual assistance. If the emigration problem is met from this point of view, it will be solved very satisfactorily.

American members of the Round Tables pointed out that any attempt at the present time to repeal the Act of 1924 or revise it in any serious way would probably fail. If such an attempt were made under pressure or encouragement from foreign sources its failure would be quite certain. The resentment felt against the diplomatic correspondence at the time of the passing of the Act, and particularly against the interpretation of the language used by the Japanese Ambassador as equivalent to a threat, was recalled as an example of the effect of outside interference upon legislation.

The self-restraint of the Japanese people at the present time in regard to a matter upon which they feel deeply was regarded by many members as the most hopeful feature of the whole situation.

**The American view**

The complication of the present quota system and the probability of changes in it were given as further reasons for the unwisdom of suggesting at the present time that Orientals should be brought under the general law. The whole question of immigration is under criticism and may possibly be reviewed in the near future. The bringing of Japanese immigrants under the quota system would not cause any very great increase in the numbers of Japanese coming into the United States; but it would still leave the difficult situation that immigrants were being admitted who, under the law of 1790 as at present interpreted, were incapable of naturalization. It would also open the way for China and other Asiatic countries to come under the quota, and the numbers admissible from China would be much greater on the present basis than those from Japan. If in the future the basis for calculating the quota should be changed, the whole question might be reopened. There is, therefore, a reluctance to reconsider the legislation on the part of those who were largely responsible for its passing in 1924.

The suggestion has been made that a conference or commission to examine the whole question should be summoned on the precedent of the conferences held in South Africa to consider the somewhat similar East Indian problem. It was felt, however, that the time was probably not yet ripe for such a step. Failure would entail disappointment and set back the possibility of solution almost indefinitely. Time to promote better understanding of attitudes and interests on both sides and to allow the bitterness of controversy to die down was felt to be essential. The acquiescence of Japanese members and others with this suggestion does not constitute a willingness to regard the matter as finally settled. The present legislation keeps open an irritant wound, the ultimate healing of which is necessary for international good will in the Pacific.

### 7. THE QUESTION OF SOVEREIGNTY

**Sovereignty**

In the problems of migration, as in all international relations, the question of sovereignty arises. The restraint of individual liberty in order to allow for the development of the greater liberty within organized society is a commonplace of political evolution. In the nineteenth century the rights of nation states were emphasized; but as the society of nations begins to develop, the obligations of those states one to another are emerging to modify their individual rights. The conception of sovereignty is changing. It is being recognized that unless war is to be accepted as normal and inevitable, some lessening of state sovereignty must be expected, some yielding of absolute liberty in order to enjoy the larger good.

**and domestic jurisdiction**

There is general recognition of the theoretical truth of this idea; but its application to particular problems such as the unlimited right of a state to control its own immigration policies clearly illustrates the difficulty of working it out in practice. Questions reserved for "domestic jurisdiction" are the remnants of what a comparatively short time ago was unlimited state sovereignty. By the gradual development of international law, the multiplication of treaty agreements, and, more recently, the development of international institutions, there have gradually emerged limiting conditions to the freedom of state action. There is a clear tendency, moreover, for questions to pass from the sphere of purely domestic interest and jurisdiction into the sphere of international agreement.

The Covenant of the League of Nations provided (Article XV) that although disputes threatening a rupture must be submitted to the Council, the latter cannot consider purely domestic questions. Article XI of the Covenant, however, provides that "any war or threat of war, whether immediately affecting any of the members of the League or not, is hereby declared a matter of concern to the whole League, and the League shall take any action that may be deemed wise and effectual to safeguard the peace of nations." This article may easily prove to be a very important means by which domestic questions may gradually be transferred to the international sphere.

In paragraph 2 of Article XI it is "declared to be the friendly right of each member of the League to bring . . . . any circumstance whatever affecting international relations which threatens to disturb international peace or the good understanding between nations upon which peace depends" before the League.

**are modified by international development**

During the discussion of the Geneva Protocol the applicability of Article XI was especially noticed by the Japanese delegation, and they insisted upon an amendment that even though a question were decided under the Protocol to be a domestic question, it still might be considered by the Council of the League under Article XI.

In the British Commonwealth the vexed question of Indian emigration has been the subject of the various dominions to legislate for the control of sovereign competency in matters of immigration and the treatment of resident aliens. Recent imperial conferences have been faced with this question, which involves the status of India within the British Commonwealth. In many respects the issues raised are comparable with those of the wider problems of immigration. Stress has been laid rather upon the better treatment of Indians resident in the dominions and upon the methods of immigration restriction than upon the right of unrestricted entry. Considerable progress has been made toward agreement. The sovereign right of the dominions to control the composition of their populations is conceded; but even in the difficult case of South Africa, by conference, discussion, and compromise some measure of agreement has been reached which in the meantime satisfies both parties.

**The example of the British Commonwealth**

It was suggested that the experience of the British countries might point the way to similar development in the more difficult and wider international sphere.

On the other hand, it was emphatically stated that in many countries at the present time public opinion was such that there would be strong opposition to any development that tended in the direction of handing over migration questions to international discussion or control in any form. Young developing countries, such, for example, as Australia and New Zealand, are apt to feel that the quality of their population is the greatest of all questions they have to consider. They would be reluctant to yield any measure of control over that question to any outside body. The history of Indian immigration has tended to show, however, that the methods of control may properly be the subject of conference and mutual agreement.

### 3. DOCUMENTS

The American group of the Institute published two research studies which were undertaken in order to provide information asked for at the previous conference. The first of these studies was by Professor Eliot G. Mears, of Stanford University, entitled *Resident Orientals on the American Pacific Coast: Their Legal and Economic Status.* It is a comprehensive and detailed statement of the position of Orientals as stated in treaty rights and constitutional guaranties, in regard to naturalization, personal relations, property rights, and occupational status, and includes also a review of the various occupations into which Orientals enter and the social circumstances under which they live.

The second research study was made by Professor R. D. McKenzie, of the University of Washington, and is entitled *Oriental Exclusion: The Effect of American Immigration Laws, Regulations, and Judicial Decisions upon the Chinese and Japanese on the American Pacific Coast.* It includes a brief history and analysis of the exclusion movement in the United States and traverses the effect of that legislation and its administration upon various classes of oriental immigrants, such as laborers, merchants, students, etc.

Both of these studies may be obtained from the secretary of the American Group, Institute of Pacific Relations, 129 East 52nd Street, New York City.

The American group also circulated official reprints of the following documents:

1. "*Treaty, Laws, and Rules Governing the Admission of Chinese* (rules of October 1, 1926), issued by the United States Department of Labor, Bureau of Immigration.

2. *Immigration Laws and Rules of March 1, 1927,* issued by the United States Department of Labor, Bureau of Immigration.

3. *Admission of Aliens into the United States (No. 926, General Instructions Consular, Diplomatic Serial No. 273),* issued by the Department of State.

A compilation of the immigration laws of Australia, Canada, New Zealand, and Japan reproduced from photostats of the laws of those countries was criticized as misleading because it had not been edited so as to show the effect of codifications and amendments. It was therefore withdrawn at the request of members from some of the countries concerned.

A preliminary psychological study of opinions and attitudes in typical American groups regarding oriental peoples and questions was carried out by Goodwin B. Watson, Ph.D., of Teachers' College, Columbia University, and issued for the confidential use of conference members. In its present incomplete form it is not available for general publication.

A study made by Roy Hidemichi Akagi, Ph.D., on behalf of the Japanese Students' Christian Association in North America, entitled *The Second Generation Problem: Some Suggestions toward Its Solution,* was issued to all members.

A manuscript copy of a thesis prepared at the University of Toronto by L. T. Cheng on "The Oriental Immigration Problem of Canada" was tabled for reference.

In addition the following data papers were made available:

1. "Legislative Aspects of Asiatic Migration," prepared by the International Labor Office, League of Nations (Documents, Section 22).

2. "The International Labor Organization and Its Contacts with the Countries and Problems of the Pacific," by WILLIAM CALDWELL, International Labor Office, Geneva.

3. "The Superiority of Race: Some Considerations in Approaching the Study of Racial Difference," by ELLSWORTH FARIS, Department of Sociology, University of Chicago.

4. "Some Reasons for the Importance Attached by Americans to the Standard of Living," by A. L. DEAN, director of Research, University of Hawaii.

5. "The Japanese Race from an Anthropological Point of View," by AKIRA MATSUMURA, assistant professor of Anthropology, Imperial University, Tokyo.

6. "Statistics of Japanese Abroad," prepared by the Japanese group.

7. "Australian Immigration Laws and Their Working," by A. H. CHARTERIS, professor of International Law, University of Sydney, Australia (Documents, Section 24).

8. "Effect of Migration on the Economic Condition of Laborers in the Lands to which Migrants Go: Differences in Standards of Living as a Barrier to Immigration," by G. L. WOOD, lecturer in Commerce, University of Melbourne.

9. "The Resources of Australia," by GRIFFITH TAYLOR, professor of Geography, University of Sydney (Documents, Section 25).

10. "Asiatic Immigration into New Zealand: Its History and Legislation," by T. D. H. HALL.

11. "The Chinese Immigrant in New Zealand," by WILLIAM MAWSON.

12. "The Education and the Economic Outlook for the Boys of Hawaii," by ROMANZO ADAMS, professor of Sociology, University of Hawaii.

13. "The Social Status of the Japanese in Hawaii," by TASUKA HARADA, professor of Japanese, University of Hawaii.

14. "The Second-Generation Oriental in America," by WILLIAM C. SMITH, University of Hawaii, formerly assistant professor of Sociology, University of Southern California.

15. "The Outstanding Cultural Assets of the Chinese People: The Chinese Point of View of the So-Called Material Civilization of the West," by SOPHIA CHEN ZEN, formerly professor of History, National University, Peking.

## DIPLOMATIC RELATIONS IN THE PACIFIC

### 1. QUESTIONS FOR DISCUSSION

*a*) What use has been made of the following devices in the international settlements in the post-war years:
  - ( i) Conference?
  - ( ii) Conciliation?
  - (iii) Arbitration?
  - (iv) Judicial settlement?

*b*) How far does machinery of this character exist in the Pacific?

*c*) What are the advantages, the defects, and limitations of this machinery?

*d*) Is it possible to treat the Pacific as a regional area with respect to:
  - ( i) The development of international co-operation?
  - ( ii) The adjustment of international disputes?

*e*) Disarmament (specifically excluding discussion of matters at present under negotiation between governments):
  - ( i) Definition.
  - ( ii) Relation to police problems, security, peace-time industries.
  - (iii) What is the pertinent machinery for dealing with the problems as thus defined?
  - (iv) Is there a regional problem in the Pacific?

*f*) What is the significance of the Treaties of Locarno?
  - ( i) On what principles are they based?
  - ( ii) Can they be extended?
  - (iii) What is meant by the "outlawry of war"?
  - (iv) What is the effect upon diplomacy of the "renunciation of war as an instrument of policy"?

*g*) The League of Nations in the Pacific.

### 2. SUMMARY OF ROUND-TABLE DISCUSSIONS

*Chairman:* R. L. Wilbur
*Secretary:* Persia Campbell

#### I. THE NEW DIPLOMACY

Underlying the whole of the Conference discussions and the work particularly of the round tables and forum on "Diplomatic Relations in the Pacific" is the assumption that it is important to educate public opinion concerning international problems and relations. The Institute of Pacific Relations is an experiment in this form of adult education. While its field and its methods differ from other bodies formed for the study of international problems, it has arisen, like many other institutes and councils, from a realization in recent times of the changed nature of international relationships.

Much of the machinery for the adjustment of international disputes necessarily retains the diplomatic character which it took on during the nineteenth century. This is particularly true in the Pacific. There is, however, a growing feeling that something more is needed than diplomatic machinery, the chief purpose of which is an adjustment of disputes. The increasing interdependence of national units in the modern world has forced the realization that we need international machinery rather for the constructive purpose of fostering and directing international co-operation.

The development of transport and communication in the last half-century has brought increasing possibilities of international contact. The building of the great continental railways at the same time as steam shipping turned the oceans into channels rather than barriers of communication has already wrought a transformation in our economic life, comparable in importance and far wider in its scope than the earlier economic revolution which resulted from the development of machine industry in Western Europe. It is a commonplace that the improvement of political organization particularly by the more effective dovetailing of local and central governments and by the breaking down of despotism and oligarchy followed quickly upon the industrial revolution. This is seen most clearly perhaps in the history of Great Britain during the nineteenth century. The advent of democratic forms of parliamentary government, the building up of an effective civil service, and the evolution of local government correlated with the new national administration are essentially products of the new conditions brought about by machine industry. These political developments, however, lagged considerably behind economic change, and this lag was the cause of much social stress and conflict.

**The industrial revolution changed domestic politics**

The political consequences of the new economic revolution are predominantly international in character. It was inevitable that the first clear realization of those consequences should occur in Europe. The war of 1914–18 clearly proved the inadequacy of the existing machinery for international co-operation to stand the strain of the new developments. The consciousness of this inadequacy and the widespread determination in Europe to build more adequate and more constructive machinery is the chief element in the so-called "new diplomacy."

The new diplomacy must be viewed therefore against the background of the modern world. It is essentially a product of democratic institutions, of universal education, and of improved methods of communication. While much that was valuable in the technique of diplomatic methods is still used, it tends to be used against the background of a much more interested, alert, and enlightened public opinion. In an age when it is possible for tens of thousands of people over a wide area comprehending many national units to listen to the dis-

**and is changing international politics**

cussions of international problems by responsible statesmen, there is obviously much less room for hole-and-corner secret diplomacy. The use of private conference as a part of the technique of discussions is not disputed; but it is clear that a more powerful public opinion than ever before, and, moreover, a public opinion that is tending to become international in outlook and interest, is a factor to be reckoned with.

It is clear also that responsible statesmen in every country are sensitive to the existence of this public opinion and that their activities have been notably affected by it. The methods of diplomatic negotiation have undergone a remarkable development in the period since the war. While use is still made of the old methods of diplomatic exchange, there has been an increasing use of various conference methods for important and difficult problems. In the use of such conference methods the realization of public interest and sentiment has often been an appreciable factor in the settlement. There are many types of conference capable of being used, varying in power from a conference of experts empowered by governments to explore definite problems and make recommendations, to conferences of plenipotentiaries invested with full power to make executive decisions which shall be binding on their governments. In many instances, such as the economic and financial conferences promoted by the League of Nations, expert discussion, by merely clarifying the issues without committing responsible governments in any way, has produced a situation in which agreed facts are recognized and solution follows almost automatically.

**along democratic lines**

In addition to official conferences there have been also increasing numbers of non-official conferences for the discussion of international problems. These are both a symptom and a cause of the quickened public interest in international affairs. In so far as they maintain a detached and dispassionate scientific attitude to the problems under consideration, they have a value in the education of the public opinion which is regarded as the important new element in international relationships.

The parallel which may be observed between the political transformation of the nation states following the industrial revolution of the eighteenth and early nineteenth centuries, and the political changes which are in process of development in the international sphere at the present time, would not be complete without some reference to the beginnings of an international civil service. The functions of government in democratic states have depended for their efficiency upon the evolution of competent public officials. Constructive international co-operation awaits the development of similar permanent expert services.

**involving an international civil service**

To many students of international relations this is the chief importance and value of the League of Nations. The beginnings, not only of international legislation, but also of international administration and an international judiciary, already promise success in the evolution of institutions adequate to discharge the main functions of government in the international sphere. The reconciliation of these functions with the established functions of national government is a problem similar to, but enormously more difficult than, the reconciliation of local and national governments which was largely achieved in the nineteenth century. It is enormously complicated also by the emotional associations which have come largely from a century (or less) of universal education based in great part upon the necessity of developing citizenship on a basis of national loyalties.

Without permanent institutions of an international character for the interpretation and administration of international law and treaty agreements, and still more for the fostering of new methods of international co-operation, we are reduced to the state of nature, "where every man is enemy to every man," a state more dangerous than ever in the modern world. It was long ago pointed out that the life of man under such conditions is likely to be "nasty, poor, brutish, and short." With the development of modern communications it is beginning to be realized that Hobbes's apophthegm is applicable to nations as well as to individuals.

The diplomacy of intrigue, based largely upon the idea of war as a means, and perhaps the only ultimate means, for the settlement of international disputes is faced with the alternative of a new diplomacy of discussion, based upon the idea of mutual co-operation. The development of this alternative depends, however, not only upon the invention of new machinery for international government, but also upon the development of public opinion to provide the power to work that machinery.

### 2. DIPLOMATIC RELATIONS IN THE PACIFIC

*Inadequate means for international co-operation.*—One of the chief difficulties which international problems in the Pacific area offer at the present time is the comparatively undeveloped nature of the machinery which exists for international co-operation. This was clearly pointed out in the speech with which the Chairman of the Institute of Pacific Relations summed up the impressions left by the Conference.[1] He said:

**Inadequacy of machinery in the Pacific**

> In the first place, the most outstanding thing to me is the inadequacy of our international machinery. In the Pacific when we approach the problem of China with our present machinery for the settlement of international disputes it reminds me of a lot of old men gathered around a modern office building trying to hem in a conflagration with buckets full of water. We are simply behind the needs of the times. Instead of prompt emergency measures we have the long, slow process of diplomacy; we have inadequate procedure; but we have had a glimpse at least of the possibility of some advance which might be made in this field of international association. It seems to me that this is our great problem: how to get these contacts established and build up

[1] Closing address by President Ray Lyman Wilbur, *Institute News-Bulletin* (October, 1927).

the machinery for co-operating so that things can be done; and in this field, while there are many factors involved, anyone who can present a good idea can be of the greatest service. I am satisfied that those who are working on this problem will take anything that can be used.

The next thing that seems to me striking is the growth of community feeling in the Pacific in spite of the distance. Unconsciously we are beginning to feel that the Pacific is part of a great community of nations, a great arena around which nations are finding mutual interests.

The third thing I have been impressed by is that too much of the thinking that has been done about the Pacific in much of our literature and in many of our diplomatic and government circles belongs on the "retired list." It is out of date. It needs fresh points of view and new men, not to repeat in the Pacific the tragedies of the Atlantic.

*The disparity of social ideas between East and West.*—It was pointed out in discussion that several factors contributed to the weakness of the international machinery at present available in the Pacific. This weakness is probably greater than exists in any other world-area. In part it is due to the very great divergence of social organization and governmental machinery between East and West. Even in a country like Japan, which has so largely been modernized on European models, there still exist great barriers to understanding.

**is due to social causes**

Many of these difficulties take shape around the problem of language. No better exposition of this particular problem could be asked than the following statement made in the Forum on Diplomatic Relations by a member of the Japanese group:

I would like to speak on the problem of language, not only as a medium of expression, but as a medium of understanding between the peoples of different countries. As a member of the Round Table on "Diplomatic Relations in the Pacific," I hope it will not be altogether inappropriate for me to speak here on this problem, which, to my mind, has a much greater significance than we might think at first sight.

**such as language**

With all due respect to what is to be said in favor of the possibilities of conference as a machinery for diplomatic and international relations, I have always felt, and am still feeling even in this present conference, the tremendous difficulties arising from the difference of languages.

Speaking, for a moment, only about a purely unofficial conference, like this one of our Institute, having a rather broad and undefined field of activities, the difficulties seem almost too great—so great that it makes us almost suspect the wisdom of having only one language as the official one of the conference. I think all of the members from my country would agree with me in saying that we might have been able to participate a little more intelligently and intelligibly were it not for the difficulties of the language, and that, what is more important, we might have secured for members of our group perhaps better and stronger men had it not been for the same difficulty.

It is not my intention, however, to speak to you about this obvious matter. I have come during the course of this conference to think of a plain and simple fact, which has some bearings on this question of the language at the Conference, and which also has a rather important connection with the problem of China, and especially with her relations to Japan. Had it not been for this fact, I would not have brought up this question of language at all.

Undoubtedly we are exceedingly fortunate to meet here at this Conference not a few of the competent and brilliant leaders of the Young China. Nothing is more important, in a conference like this, than the attitude of mind of the members and their correct interpretation of the ideas and ideals of the people of their respective countries. And all these aims have been achieved for China wonderfully well, with remarkable skill and command of language, by her able representatives. We shall always be grateful for what they have done here.

There is, however, the other side of the shield. Are there not in China today still hundreds of millions of her common people who do not speak English, who do not understand Anglo-American ideas, and therefore are not able to follow their leaders and live up to the standards set by their leaders who have been educated in America or England? To make the situation more complicated, there are in China today, side by side with the able leaders with the Anglo-American training, a number of progressive leaders in different fields of activity who have been educated in Japan and therefore speak Japanese, and negotiate with the Japanese in either the Chinese or Japanese language. Some of them do not speak English, and consequently are sometimes unduly neglected in the eyes of English-speaking foreign correspondents, and incidentally, of the Western countries in general. Let me add, although it seems not necessary to a gathering like this, that, when I speak of the leaders trained in Japan, I do not mean Chang Tso-lin and men of his type. Chiang Kai Shek, himself, is one of those leaders.

The existence in China, roughly speaking, of these two sets of leaders, one communicating with Japanese leaders in the Chinese or Japanese language, and the other coming in contact with the rest of the powers through the medium of English is a plain fact; but this fact should not be overlooked, for it sometimes implies a great deal more than the simple difference in the medium of expression; it involves two sets of philosophies and perhaps two different lines of approach to their national problems.

The National Chinese Movement seems to Japanese to be incorrectly appraised if judged according to those institutions which are almost solely products of Occidental history, e.g., representative government. It takes generations to get this so that it is an adequate instrument. The New China must draw something from its *own* past; and Japan is conscious of this element in the situation, and sometimes questions the extent to which the application of Western formulae in the language and forms of a democratic state is applicable in the immediate future to China. This question is not to be misunderstood as implying a lack of sympathy with the splendid effort being made to "modernize" China's system of government. But Japanese contacts with China offer us a more balanced view, we feel, of the process of Chinese transformation than is likely to be got by those who rely only on the medium of a language used in the democratic West.

The phenomena of China as seen by us are diverse. We are inclined to think that they are often unduly simplified by our Western friends to correspond with their preconceived ideas. What is needed is the objective point of view which takes account of all the elements and faces them with a desire both to establish the truth of facts and to try to better them. In both regards the Japanese, whether men of science or responsible statesmen, are animated with a common purpose, one which is based upon the fundamental sympathy with the strivings of the Chinese people for self-expression and their orientation into a community of nations where full equality prevails in terms of a common appreciation of international justice.

This statement draws attention, it will be remarked, not only to the language difficulty, but also to the very different social organization as between East and West. It was difficult enough for Europe to establish diplomatic relations with Old China. It is doubly difficult to do so in this transitional period before Young China has learned to govern itself. The breakdown of organized government in China obviously contributes to the difficulty of diplomatic negotiation.

**and to less contact in the past**

In addition, the network of treaties providing for international co-operation is very much thinner in the Pacific than in the Atlantic.[2] This fact was construed as an advantage in many ways, since less account must be taken of past commitments in considering new international arrangements. Even allowing for the diplomatic *impasse* presented by the relations of China with the treaty powers, there is infinitely less heritage of past disagreement and controversy than exists in Europe.

**Neither the League of Nations**

*The Washington Conference treaties.*—The further complication was recognized in the Round Tables that such international machinery as does exist at present functions with far less effectiveness in the Pacific than in any other area of world-politics. Neither Russia nor the United States is a member of the League of Nations or of the Permanent Court of International Justice, while China's membership is more nominal than real at the present time. The League of Nations has not functioned in practice as a superstate, but rather as a co-ordinating body recognizing and working through the sovereignty of its states. Under its aegis there has grown up a network of treaties in Europe providing means for the settlement of disputes between European states. Its activity in the Pacific has been greatly crippled by the inability to work through an effective government in China, and also by the fact that two great Pacific powers, Russia and the United States, remain outside of its organization. This fact bears also upon the possibility of developing treaty arrangements in the Pacific similar to those of Europe.

The conference on the limitation of armaments held at Washington in 1922 formulated treaties which provide the basis for international co-operation within the Pacific, but the provisions of the Washington treaties, which at present offer the only alternative to the regular diplomatic machinery for the settlement

[2] Duncan Hall, "Analysis of the Existing International Machinery for the Settlement of International Disputes in the Pacific."

of disputes, are very vague and limited. The operation of the Four Power Pact providing for conciliation procedure is limited to the insular possessions and insular dominions of the contracting parties and does not apply to disputes arising on the mainlands of the United States, Canada, or the principal Japanese islands. Article VII of the Nine Power Treaty concerning China provides that disputes arising out of the operations of that treaty shall be dealt with by conciliatory procedure not dissimilar from that of the Four Power Pact.[3] Disputes arising on the Chinese mainland are therefore partially provided for. The treaty between the four great Pacific powers also excludes all disputes relating to matters of domestic jurisdiction, even where such disputes concern insular possessions or insular dominions. The Four Power Pact must be read together with the other Washington treaties, and particularly with the provisions in the naval treaty regarding the maintenance of the status quo of naval bases and fortifications in the Pacific. Much of its value is derived from these latter provisions. The treaty, however, provides only for a joint conference to which matters in dispute shall be referred for consideration and adjustment. As a whole it is exceedingly vague and limited and unlikely to give an adequate sense of security to the parties involved.

**nor the Washington treaties**

It must be remembered also that the psychological value of the Washington treaties was considerably undermined by subsequent developments, and particularly the passing of the American Immigration Restriction Act in 1924 and by the revived naval competition.

It was unfortunate that the Washington Conference did not provide more definite machinery for continuing negotiations. A number of disputes have arisen with regard to China and also with regard to technical matters, such as the elevation of guns, cruiser competition, etc., for which no conference machinery was available and which had therefore to be taken up through the ordinary diplomatic channels.

**provide adequate machinery at present**

Certain specific conferences to discuss problems relating to China were definitely provided for and have been convened, albeit after considerable delay, due largely to the intervention of the old diplomacy. This long delay is generally recognized to have contributed materially to the fact that when the conferences did convene conditions had so far worsened that their deliberations were for the most part inconclusive. The virtual failure of the conferences on tariff and extra-territoriality was not due to defects in the conference method so much as to the circumstances under which the conferences were called, and particularly to the long intervening delay.[4]

It was made clear also that leaders of Chinese opinion have no objection to the peaceful conference method of negotiation. They do distrust and resent conferences where China is in a minority of one confronting a solid *bloc* of treaty

[3] Hornbeck, *China Today*, pp. 523–25.

[4] See above, chaps. i and ii.

powers whose unanimous agreement is necessary for any decision. Chinese statesmen tend to look rather toward bilateral conferences on a basis of equality.

*The League of Nations in the Pacific.*—In much the same way Young China, after her Shantung experience at Versailles, distrusts the League of Nations and is not willing to admit its complete disinterestedness. It was, however, pointed out that within the League at the present time there are a great many active, disinterested small countries from the leaders of which China might reasonably expect sympathetic understanding. The technique which is being developed at Geneva in such matters as the dissection of problems, the obtaining of legal opinions from the Permanent Court of International Justice, and the methods of conference and discussion is beginning to take on a definite form and produce results. This technique and the existence also of a highly trained and internationally minded secretariat in touch with expert knowledge in practically every country of the world makes the League more and more valuable as an instrument for the achievement of international co-operation.[5] In the present suspicious temper of Young China, however, and in the light of China's past experiences of international co-operation, the reluctance of her leaders to submit their nationalist demands to any such body is readily understandable.

**The League is handicapped in China**

**and also by the abstention of Russia**

International discussion in the Pacific is further complicated by the abstention of Russia and the United States from membership in the League and by the firm determination of other Pacific powers that no diplomatic machinery shall be allowed to develop in the Pacific which undermines the League's competency.

**and the United States**

The position of the United States was very clearly and sympathetically stated. It was made clear that the factors which have operated against her entry into active membership of the League and its associated organs are derived from deep historical causes. The people of the United States are probably more consciously pacific than the people of most other countries, and the realization of that fact enters into all American governmental policies. There is little or no hostility to the principle of international co-operation, but on the contrary a great deal of sympathy and active interest in it. There is, however, a deeply rooted distrust of European diplomacy and disinclination to become involved in European intrigues. This distrust and disinclination strike a ready if less articulate response in the British Dominions, and to some extent also in Great Britain itself.

**whose foreign policy is regional**

It was urged that the foreign policies of the United States are regional in character. The traditional antagonism to European interference in the affairs of North and South America and the correlative reluctance to become involved in European affairs are still very strong. Successive governments have, however, developed a policy of co-operation with, and encouragement of, those activities of the League of Nations which are definitely world-wide in character

[5] See "Notes on Certain Aspects of the Work of the League of Nations of Interest to the Pacific Countries" (Documents, Section 28).

and not dominated by European necessities. It was stated as the view of a powerful section of the public opinion of the United States that more real gain to the cause of the League would accrue from this disinterested and detached co-operation than from complete identification. The United States was represented as playing the rôle of a friendly critic or co-operative "opposition" in the political sense.[6]

In criticism of this point of view, which was recognized as widespread and powerful in the United States, it was contended by other American spokesmen that the position of the United States was less effective outside the League, and that many of the League's alleged weaknesses, such as its preoccupation with Europe, were largely due to the abstention of America from active participation. It was maintained that the significance of the Dawes plan was not that it came, but that it came so late. It was urged that if the United States had been a member of the League, this financial settlement might have taken place several years earlier and Europe might have been spared the financial disasters to which it was in fact subjected.

Furthermore, it was argued that the failure of the United States to join the League was partly responsible for the present situation in China. The delay in holding the Tariff Conference was due to the protracted refusal of France to ratify the Washington treaties, and this was represented as being due in part to American abstention from the League. France wished to use her ratifying of the treaties as a bargaining point in her effort to get some form of security agreement from the United States. If the United States had entered the League originally, as the French were led to expect, it might be argued that this reason for holding up the Washington treaties would not have existed.

Such different interpretations of historical events among Americans themselves, however, do not greatly affect the present problem beyond demonstrating, if further demonstration were needed, the close connection that necessarily exists between international policies in apparently separate regions and controversies. There is no possibility of isolating the Pacific as a region for specific agreement out of relation to general international affairs. It seems clear, however, from the sustained action of successive governments, that the people of the United States have a definite interest in international co-operation, and that the objection to entangling alliances refers specifically to Europe and its old system of family diplomacy. There is neither historical background nor widespread sentiment against either co-operation in world-wide policies or definite engagements in the Pacific.

It was argued that the people of the United States had come to America originally to get away from Europe. This is largely true of the later waves of immigration as well as of those early settlers who founded the traditions of the republic. America has, in this sense at least, consistently turned its back upon

[6] Cf. Blakeslee, *The Recent Foreign Policy of the United States.*

European diplomacy and its face toward the Pacific. The counter-argument was obvious that in the Pacific of the present day America is again face to face with Europe, but that the meeting has been due to different approaches on both sides. In the modern world with its economic unity and ever developing communications, national or regional isolation becomes less and less possible. The profound significance of this elementary fact is inescapable.

The question therefore arose of the reconciliation of the interests and commitments into which the United States has already entered in the Pacific region with the developing rudiments of world-organization. The view was emphatically expressed that those Pacific countries (and even more the European countries which have important Pacific interests) which are members of the League regard their obligations under the Covenant as binding and prior to any other specific agreements that might be entered into in any region. Any form of international co-operation which may develop in the Pacific must of necessity, therefore, be consonant with that attitude.

**Regional agreement in the Pacific**

This does not, however, preclude the possibility of regional agreements. Indeed, it was felt that such developments in the Pacific, not necessarily within the League as it is constituted at present, might contribute largely to the separation of the essential world aspects of international co-operation from the more definitely European commitments which the present League inherits from the circumstances of its origin. It was stated that the objections of American opinion to such regional agreements as may develop in the Pacific, and also to sympathetic co-operation in general problems of world-interest, would be far less than were the objections to American entry into the League of Nations. It is not possible, however, in view of the expressed attitude of many of the other powers concerned, even if it were possible in face of the economic and political facts, to regard the Washington machinery as an alternative exclusive of the League and of European diplomacy. The Pacific needs its Locarno; but it needs also that its Locarno shall be in harmony and constructive relationship with the developing organs of international government at Geneva. The concluding discussions of the Round Table are therefore to be read in relation to this general situation.

### 3. A CONSTRUCTIVE PROPOSAL

The Round Table had before it a definite constructive proposal in the shape of a draft treaty drawn up by Professors Shotwell and Chamberlain, of Columbia University. This draft was originally prepared in response to a declaration by M. Briand that France would welcome a specific engagement with the United States providing for the settlement of international differences without recourse to war. The chief significance of the treaty as tentatively drafted for public discussion lies in its adaptation of the Locarno agreements for the renunciation of war as an instrument of policy. Its text is derived almost entirely from the text of existing treaties, and represents what, in the authors' view, are "the possibilities of an American Locarno." This text, together with explanatory comment by Professor Shotwell, is printed below (Documents, Section 23).

The primary purpose for which the draft was made was to elicit public discussion and criticism in view of the possibility of action by the United States in response to M. Briand's speech. With the exception of some five or six newspapers (some of them, however, such as the *Chicago Tribune*, the *Washington Post*, and the *New York Evening Post*, being influential and important), the response within the United States has been favorable. It was claimed that sufficient indication had been given that the general principles of the draft were not unwelcome to American public opinion. These general principles were defined as the renunciation of aggressive war as an instrument of policy, the definition of aggression, and agreement not to support nations which are aggressive under this definition, which is taken from Article 5 of the Locarno Pact.

**The Locarno principles**

In the second part of the draft, arbitration and conciliation are envisaged as the alternative to settlement by war; but the draft is not framed as a treaty for compulsory arbitration or conciliation. It does state that in every case the provisions of Part I (dealing with the renunciation of war) shall apply; but it is not mandatory in determining the alternative procedure to war. In this respect it is consistent with the new spirit of post-war diplomacy. It emphasizes the possibilities of constructive co-operation and negotiation in advance of the crisis. It looks toward the directing of political issues to political bodies for their solution, rather than to the arbitrament of war.

The Round Table was asked to consider the applicability of the draft, not so much as between the United States and France, but rather as a basis for an American Locarno, a general agreement with other countries, perhaps in the Pacific area. The authors attempted to draft the treaty with reference to American opinion and history and recent diplomatic development. They sought to give due consideration to the position of a great power which stands outside the League of Nations, and at the same time include nothing inconsistent with the obligations to the League of any power which may agree to negotiate it. It was urged that, on the contrary, it opens up the possibility of such a regional agreement consistent with a world-league as was discussed in the previous section.

**considered in relation to the Pacific**

The first point raised in discussion concerned the necessity of any such agreement. It was suggested that preoccupation with the possibilities of war and the necessity of erecting safeguards against war was a major cause of the psychology which often ended in war. The activity of pacifists, it was suggested, might be just as mischievous as the professional activities of militarists in this connection. The possibility of war in the Pacific within the immediate future was scouted, and the wisdom of directing attention to the possibility was therefore questioned.

In opposition to this view the experience of 1914 was recalled and it was urged that in the absence of well-established and trusted means of international understanding war was always possible. Moreover, the very unlikelihood of immediate war creates a situation favorable to the establishment of such machinery under conditions which enable it to function constructively and become firmly established before the strain of crisis comes to test it. One of the merits claimed for the proposed draft was that it would tend to assist the development of co-operative negotiatory machinery in a time of comparative quiescence. The draft was claimed to be rather a peace insurance scheme than a scheme for the prevention of war.

Three definite points of criticism were made by a Japanese critic:

It will be noted that these criticisms of the treaty were solely to the point that it should be extended to cover the Monroe Doctrine on the one hand and be made much more effective, generally, by strengthening the provisions for arbitration.

**Japanese criticism**

1. With regard to arbitration, Article 7 contains a proviso to the effect that differences which affect the vital interests, the independence, or the honor of the two contracting states, and at the same time do not concern the interest of a third party, should not be subject to arbitration. This sort of proviso has not been an unusual characteristic of arbitration treaties, but, as it has often been pointed out, this would take the teeth out of the treaty. Who is to decide whether or not a controversy involves "vital interests"? Not an organ over and above the contracting parties, but one of the contracting parties. There is danger that, under the pretext of "vital interests" many cases may be taken out of the application of this article.

2. With regard to domestic jurisdiction, Article 6 says: "The High Contracting Parties agree to submit disputes arising between them to arbitration, judicial settlement or conciliation as set forth in the following articles of this treaty, provided that the dispute does not concern a matter which under international law is solely within the domestic jurisdiction of one of the High Contracting Parties; nevertheless in every case the provisions of Part I shall apply." I support the last portion of this Article, namely, the provision that in every case involving the domestic jurisdiction of one of the High Contracting Parties no appeal to arms is to be allowed. My doubt is in connection with the second part of this Article, namely, the exclusion of disputes concerning domestic jurisdiction from arbitration, judicial settlement, or conciliation. In the present era of international solidarity many international disputes arise, even concerning points which may, under international law, be considered to rest within domestic jurisdiction. Moreover, what is meant by domestic jurisdiction in international law is by no means clear. Under such circumstances the lack of an independent organ to determine whether or not a certain question belongs to the domestic jurisdiction of one of the parties will be a serious defect. For one of the contracting parties may at its will avoid judicial or quasi-judicial examination, under the pretext that the point is within its domestic jurisdiction.

3. Article 2 proposes an exception to the principle concerning the outlawry of war in the case of the so-called Monroe Doctrine. In effect it proposes that in disputes which involve this doctrine the United States be left free to resort to war. On this point I am inclined to think that America does not go far enough toward the set-

tlement of international disputes by arbitration, judicial settlement, or conciliation. It is true that there is a proviso that the United States will use its best endeavors to secure the submission to arbitration or conciliation of a dispute between an American and a non-American power, but this is a unilateral declaration which in no way binds the United States to an agreement that she will not resort to arms. I fully realize that perhaps this sort of provision may be necessary in order to get the United States to sign such a treaty, but I am afraid that on the other hand such a provision in the treaty would be rather unfavorably received by the Japanese people. They would also fear that the Monroe Doctrine—which is not a rule of international law but a policy, unilateral in its character, supported by the strength and power of the United States alone—may, through such a recognition in treaties, be elevated into the realm of accepted international law. Thinking of Japan's position in the Orient, they will also feel that while the position of the United States in the Western Hemisphere would be safeguarded by such an exception, the position of Japan would not. It would strike them as being altogether too unilateral in its nature.

All three points of criticism, it will be noted, assumed that the treaty as drafted did not go far enough. This was more clearly indicated by the speaker quoted previously. He said:

I am in full sympathy with the idea of the complete renunciation of war as a means toward settling international disputes, which is so clearly set forth in Article 1 of the present draft treaty for permanent peace. This idea was first recognized in the Covenant of the League of Nations, and again in the Geneva protocol of 1924 and the Locarno treaties of 1925. The draft treaty under our consideration at present would apply the same principle to international disputes that may rise in the Pacific area. It is the embodiment of this idea in the draft, and the endeavor to make it practicable, of which I wish to express my heartiest appreciation and support.

Japan's foreign policy has undergone a great change in recent years. In the primary stage of the diplomatic relationships between Japan and the Western powers, the one central idea which governed the foreign policy of Japan was national safety. Japan feared that her own national integrity might suffer the same fate that had befallen that of her neighboring powers. But times have changed. So far as we can see there is today no strong military or naval power trying to invade her territory. Her national security is now assured, and she is on her way to international co-operation.

**concerned the inadequacy of the draft**

This new orientation of Japanese diplomacy is partly due to the desire on the part of Japan to promote the natural development of her people, and partly due to the humanistic and liberal trend of thought among our thinking people. Thus we have been, and still are, faithfully supporting the League of Nations. We have sent the ablest men of our country to Geneva to help in the growth of the League of Nations, which aims at a peaceable and just ordering of international society through international co-operation. We highly regret that America is not a member of the League, and that the League is often accused of being a league of European nations and not a league of the entire world. We highly regret that, because of the failure of America to enter the League, international frictions which may arise in the Pacific cannot be properly dealt with by this international organization.

There is, however, very little prospect of the United States entering the League in the near future, and we must take this fact, however unpleasant it may be, into consideration, and devise some means whereby we may avoid a recourse to war by any Pacific power. We need a treaty which is more comprehensive than the Four-Power Treaty. It is in this regard that the present draft treaty has a peculiar value. If this sort of treaty prevents the United States from entering the League of Nations for a long time to come, I fear that Japan will hesitate a great deal before she accepts such a treaty. On the contrary, however, if the draft serves as a stepping-stone to the entry of the United States into the League, I think that Japan will support it.

Coming to the draft itself, I heartily support Article 1 and Article 3. I realize that, from an American standpoint, the assumption of such a duty on the part of the United States is historically a great forward step, although the duty of neutrality as set forth in Article 3 does not seem to go far enough. I am also in favor of Article 4 and Article 5, which provide for a progressive codification of international law and a progressive reduction of armament. If there is any criticism to be made in regard to this draft it is not that the plan is too idealistic but that it does not go far enough.

**which reflects American opinion**

On the other hand, it was argued by American members that if the treaty were to be construed as an indirect step toward getting the United States into the League, such an interpretation would be fatal to any favorable action by the Senate. It was claimed, however, that, as the criticism had shown, the draft treaty could not be regarded in such a light. It was rather an attempt to place the United States in a more logical position to co-operate with the League, as it has in fact been doing without undertaking all the responsibilities of League membership, some of which are objectionable to American public opinion. Discussion made it clear that the public opinion of other countries besides America must be considered. As an instrument of educational discussion the draft treaty was designed to bring the issues of such a possible agreement into clear relief. The actual scope of any such agreement must obviously depend upon governmental negotiation and action.

### 4. THE PROBLEM OF DISARMAMENT

**Regional disarmament**

During the discussion of the suggested bilateral draft treaty of permanent peace the point was made that the possibility of regional disarmament was involved in any such agreement. It was strongly urged that the effectiveness of international co-operation, whether through the League of Nations or outside its machinery, depended ultimately upon the success achieved in promoting disarmament.

In a brief statement presented to the Round Table it was argued that regional disarmament was both necessary and within practical possibilities in the Pacific.[7] The size of the ocean and the wide distances separating the various countries were stated as reasons for regarding a regional agreement as possible both in military and in naval armaments. The question plainly resolves itself

[7] Eggleston, "Memorandum on Naval Disarmament in the Pacific."

largely into one of naval bases, since the effectiveness of a naval force is dependent upon bases near at hand. It was suggested, therefore, that the time was ripe to consider an extension of the Washington agreement.

The limitations of any such disarmament agreement were clearly stated. Apart from the fact that agreement can be made effective only in relation to such armaments as require construction over a long period, there is little possibility, in the present state of opinion, of extending the agreement far enough back into the economic life of the countries concerned to make practical the elimination of competition in the substitute and auxiliary forces and in their subsidiary services. On the other hand, the psychological effect of any steps taken toward disarmament is a factor in the education of public opinion.

Moreover, the limited agreement which may be reached at a single conference requires interpretation and adaptation if it is to be effectively administered. Attention was directed therefore to the necessity in the Pacific of providing machinery for international co-operation out of which continuous negotiation for armament limitation might grow as a by-product. It was urged that a single conference, dealing necessarily with only a fraction of the settlement required, may have the bad psychological effect of giving the impression of complete settlement. For effective disarmament, a continuous body accumulating technical expertness and taking up the complicated problems in detail is equally necessary with the continuous pressure of public opinion, or "moral disarmament."

**needs permanent machinery**

5. INTERNATIONAL RELATIONS IN MANCHURIA[8]

The clash of interests and policies in Manchuria attracted the attention of the Round Table as indicating a source of potential misunderstanding and conflict. The position of the various powers was therefore discussed particularly in relation to the railway development now in progress and to its economic and political implications.

The problem of Manchuria is a problem between China, Russia, and Japan which in the first instance is a problem of control of railroads. In 1896 China granted Russia the privilege of extending its trans-Siberian railroad across Manchuria in order to have a direct route to a Russian seaport. Two years later permission was given to extend that line down from Harbin to Dairen (also named Dalny by the Russians, and Talienwan by the Chinese). After the Boxer Rebellion Russia secured an agreement that she would not have to evacuate Manchuria, the whole of which had been occupied. Out of this situation arose the Russo-Japanese War.

After this war in 1905 the Manchurian railroad system was divided, Japan having the section from Changchun down to Dairen, which is now known as the South Manchurian Railway, one-half of the stock being owned by the Jap-

[8] The treatment of this subject is largely based upon the statement made by Professor George H. Blakeslee to the Conference Forum on July 26.

anese government. North of Changchun to Harbin and east and west through Manchuria is the Chinese Eastern Railway, which is under the control of Russia. There are in Manchuria other railroads actually constructed and still more in contemplation. These are sometimes referred to as Japanese lines, but as a matter of fact they are Chinese lines built in co-operation with the South Manchurian Railway.

**The Chinese Eastern Railway**

Each of the three powers interested in Manchuria—China, Russia and Japan—has railroad claims, policies, and interests and ambitions which conflict with those of the other powers. Concerning the Chinese Eastern Railway there is a clash between Russia and China. Three years ago, by the Russo-Chinese agreement of 1924, it was definitely stipulated that the Chinese Eastern Railway should be operated on a basis of absolute equality between Russia and China. Since the manager of the railway, however, is Russian, Russia has succeeded in controlling its administration. The terms of the agreement of 1924 provided that there should be a board of ten directors, five representing the Soviet government and five the Chinese government, and that one of the five appointed by the Chinese should be president. The general manager should be a Russian, and the directors should have a quorum of seven present at any meeting with a vote of six members to be effective. The Russians have stayed away from the meetings, so that it has been impossible to get a quorum to transact business, and therefore the actual authority over the railway has remained in the hands of the Russian general manager.

**is a source of friction between China and Russia**

That situation has led to a series of incidents causing acute friction between the Russian and Chinese governments. For example, in January, 1926, when Marshal Chang Tso-Lin wished to move some of his troops over the railway, he was told by the Russian manager that he would have to pay cash in advance for their transportation. Chang Tso-Lin promptly arrested the Russian manager. Thereupon the Soviet government sent an ultimatum to China demanding his release and intimating that if he should not be released within a certain number of hours, troops would be sent to Manchuria to effect the release. Since that time China has gradually taken back certain of the administrative agencies of the railway. She has taken over most of the shipping which formerly was operated on the rivers by the railway company, has taken over the schools in the railroad zone, and also the telegraphs. It is stated that the Chinese intend to continue the process until the railway comes completely under Chinese control. There is therefore almost a head-on collision between Russia and China over the administration of the Chinese railway.

In addition there is a clash of viewpoints between Russia and Japan relating to the building of the railroads through Central Manchuria. They are legally not Japanese lines, but Chinese. Only one of them, that from Changchun to Kirin, appears to be operated by the South Manchurian Railway Company. In general the South Manchurian Railway Company advances the capital necessary to build the lines and acts as purchasing agent. Sometimes it builds lines under contract, and usually after the roads have been built and transferred to Chinese administration two or three prominent positions are reserved for skilled Japanese railroad administrators.

**Competing Japanese lines**

The most important of these lines is the one which was opened to traffic in 1926, running north to Tsitsihar. It was built under arrangements similar to those described preceding, and Russia formally and vigorously protested against the building of the line on the ground that it interfered with the Russian interests. In general it may be said that Russia regards Central and Northern Manchuria as constituting a Russian sphere of interest. This view is based ultimately upon the treaties between Russia and Japan in 1907, 1910, and 1916. It is to be remembered also that in the period of railway competition in China, the competing governments established among themselves the tacit principle of not allowing any parallel or competing lines. The interpretation of competition has included lines coming within a hundred or two hundred miles, or connecting with or crossing an existing line.

In 1907, and more specifically in 1910, there was an agreement between Japan and Russia dividing Manchuria between them for railroad-building and similar purposes. Northern and Central Manchuria were to be a Russian sphere, and Southern Manchuria a Japanese sphere. The Russians, however, are not now in a position legally to maintain any protest on the basis of the old secret provisions of treaties which have been disowned by the Soviet government. Japan, in co-operation with China, is now carrying on a system of railroad expansion in a zone which Russia regards as closed. There is a line running up to the Chinese Eastern Railway to Tsitsihar. Another line north of Harbin has been constructed for about fifty miles. The plan is to extend it to Aigun on the Amur River. A whole new system is thus developing in Northern Manchuria.

**are being built throughout Manchuria**

Another line has been built and is being operated by the South Manchurian Railway from Changchun to Kirin. In all probability it will connect with the Japanese line from the Korean seacoast to the Korean-Manchurian border, and if that plan is carried out there will be a railway under a measure of Japanese control running from a Korean seaport direct to Changchun. Furthermore, there are plans for the extension of the railroad from Changchun to Taonan. The route is now being surveyed by Chinese engineers, and when completed will make a new railroad across Manchuria, made up of different links which, when united, will make a line east and west about 150 miles south of the Chinese Eastern Railway and in competition with it, and under Chinese-Japanese control. Whenever these lines are built Russia protests.

The outstanding feature, perhaps, of this whole expansion in Central and Northern Manchuria is that the new railroad lines are built on the standard railroad guage, 4 feet 8½ inches, while the Russian lines are built on the broad gauge of 5 feet. All of these lines, therefore, are feeders for the South Man-

**on standard gauge**

churian Railway, which is a standard-guage line. They are not direct feeders to the Chinese Eastern Railway. Moreover, the fact is to be remembered that in case of military necessity it is a comparatively simple matter to adapt a broad guage to a standard track by moving in one rail, whereas it is difficult to build the new track necessary for the reverse process. The situation is therefore that there is a direct clash of policy between Russia and Japan over this railroad expansion in central Manchuria.

There is also a difference of policy between Japan and China. The Japanese government recently made an official protest against the building by the Chinese of a railroad from Mukden through Hailung to Kirin, on the ground that it infringed one of their earlier concessions. This fact shows that the railroad problem in Manchuria is three-cornered, and not simply a problem between Russia and Japan. The greatest difference between Japan and China, however, relates to the territory in the southern strip of the peninsula in which Dairen is situated. In 1898 this territory was leased by China to Russia for twenty-five years, but the lease was transferred to Japan in 1905, after the Russo-Japanese war. It would therefore have expired in 1923, but in the so-called "Twenty-one Demands" made by Japan in 1915 it was definitely stipulated that this lease should be extended from twenty-five to ninety-nine years. If the treaty made by Japan with China as a consequence of these demands is regarded as valid, the Japanese have a legal lease which will not terminate until 1997. The Chinese, however, regard the treaty extension of the lease as invalid and of no effect.

**The lease of Dairen**

There is, then, a vigorous clash of interests and policies between each of these three powers in Manchuria. In their economic aspect the differences appear to be of much the same character as those which existed between American railways fifty years ago. Apart from political influences, there is no reason to doubt that they might be settled by compromise and on a commercial and business-like basis. It is, however, very evident to students of the Far East that the present situation in Manchuria is very much like the situation that existed there before the Russo-Japanese war. It is therefore an acute example of the difficult complication of economic development by political and strategic interests, and as such it gives cause for considerable apprehension to those who are concerned with the maintenance and development of peace and international co-operation in the Pacific. It also presents a clear and urgent case of international conflict for the settlement of which the existing international machinery is utterly inadequate. The only medium for negotiation concerning this problem is to be found at present in the same diplomatic machinery that functioned at the time of the previous conflict.

## 3. DOCUMENTS

The Round Table for the discussion of diplomatic relations between the Pacific countries was set up as as result of a request received from the Australian National Council of the Institute that opportunity be given for the discussion of disarmament problems.

The following data papers were circulated as a basis for discussions:

1. "Naval Disarmament in the Pacific," by HON. F. W. EGGLESTON, chairman, Australian group.

2. "Japan's Internal Problems and Her Relationships with China, Russia, America, and the British Commonwealth," by YUSUKE TSURUMI (Documents, Section 24).

3. "Analysis of the Existing Machinery for Settling International Disputes in the Pacific," by H. DUNCAN HALL, professor of Political Science, Syracuse University.

4. "Draft Treaty of Permanent Peace between the United States of America and . . . .," by PROFESSOR J. T. SHOTWELL, director of the Division of Economics and History of the Carnegie Endowment, and PROFESSOR J. P. CHAMBERLAIN, of Columbia University (Documents, Section 27).

5. "Notes on Certain Aspects of the Work of the League of Nations of Interest to the Pacific Countries," prepared unofficially by members of the League secretariat (Documents, Section 28).

6. "The Imperial Conference and Dominion Status: A Canadian View," by P. E. CORBETT, professor of Roman Law, McGill University, Montreal.

7. "The British Empire and the League of Nations," by P. E. CORBETT, professor of Roman Law, McGill University, Montreal.

## INTERNATIONAL EDUCATION AND COMMUNICATION

### 1. QUESTIONS FOR DISCUSSION

ROUND TABLE I

*a*) To what extent should the curriculum provide opportunity for instruction in international affairs:
  ( i) In the elementary schools?
  ( ii) In the secondary schools?
  (iii) In the institutions of higher learning?

*b*) Do textbooks give adequate recognition of the international point of view?

*c*) How can exchanges of students and teachers be developed and made more effective?

*d*) In what other ways may students be given opportunity to extend their knowledge of other countries?

ROUND TABLE II

*a*) What specially effective methods for educating adults on Pacific conditions and problems have been used by organizations in each country?

*b*) What suggestive lessons can be derived from failures in the same field?

*c*) How can the press best be made a constructive factor in international education and the undesirable aspects of its influence be reduced?

*d*) How can radio be most effectively used for international education?

*e*) What plans for traveling seminars and pilgrimages on international affairs could profitably be developed or extended in the Pacific area?

### 2. SUMMARY OF ROUND-TABLE DISCUSSIONS

CHAIRMEN AND SECRETARIES

Round Table I
  *Chairman:* Ada Comstock
  *Secretary:* C. H. Currey

Round Table II
  *Chairman:* Soichi Saito
  *Secretary:* Galen M. Fisher

Round Table III
  *Chairman:* Henry S. Pritchett
  *Secretary:* John Nelson

I. INTERNATIONAL TRAINING IN SCHOOLS

One of the greatest of the many educational problems confronting every country at the present time is the difficulty of combining a realization of the new international structure within which modern society functions with the traditional knowledge and philosophy which in every country are important for economic efficiency and for national development. All countries, whether old or new, have to restate their history, their philosophy, their whole outlook on life in such terms as will harmonize with the new world that has been produced by the scientific and economic developments of the last generation. The problem is particularly acute in such a country as China, and has been well stated in a passage which was quoted from Professor Hu Shih's *The Development of the Logical Method in Ancient China:*

**Education for world-citizenship**

> How can we best assimilate modern civilisation in such a manner as to make it congenial and congruous and continuous with the civilisation of our own making? This larger problem presents itself in every phase of the great conflict between the old civilisation and the new. In art, in literature, in politics, and in social life in general the underlying problem, as far as I can see, will depend solely on the foresight and the sense of historical continuity of the intellectual leaders of New China, and on the tact and skill with which they can successfully connect the best in modern civilisation with the best in our own civilisation. When the philosophies of Ancient China are re-interpreted in terms of modern philosophy, and when modern philosophy is interpreted in terms of the native systems of China, then, and not until then, can Chinese philosophers and students of philosophy truly feel at ease with the new methods and instrumentalities of speculation and research.

It was suggested that in every country there are groups of people, mainly obscure teachers and writers, working to restate the civilizations of their countries in such a form as will bring their future citizens to understand their relation to the new world that has developed. The extent to which such a restatement can be made effective in the actual practice of the education of the mass of the people will influence very greatly the possibilities of international good will in the new generation.

A great deal depends upon the conception which is held of the purpose of education. If it is confined to the transmission from one generation to another of technical equipment, whether literary or manual, sufficient to provide for further economic development both individual and national, there is likely to be little scope for the practice of international education. Instruction which is formal and purely intellectual also offers less scope than education interpreted in a broader sense which allows for aesthetic and emotional training.

**based on national citizenship**

The objections which might be raised to such extensions of educational activity as lessening the economic efficiency of instruction were met by arguments similar to those which are commonly used to defend the teaching of citizenship. It was contended that the course of events in the next generation may prove that the ability to live in peaceful and constructive co-operation both within the modern state organization and internationally may be the *sine qua non* of civilized existence. Economic efficiency, it was contended, is not as a matter of fact likely to be decreased by broad generalized education aiming at individual development along lines suited to modern conditions of life. On the other hand, civilization may perish in international conflict.

**is possible at early ages**

Experience in lands as remote as Japan and Wales was cited to show the possibility, even in the elementary schools, of teaching international attitudes consonant with the finest patriotism. The gift of "friendship dolls" by American to Japanese children was cited as an example of good teaching and effective stimulation of international interest through intellectual as well as emotional processes. The evocation of such emotional attitudes in impressionable childhood is likely to be an obvious factor in international relations in the future. Such attitudes, of one kind or another, are inevitably developed, often from chance impressions or even from sheer ignorance. The responsibility of teachers in such matters is very clear. The difficulties of right education where emotional attitudes are concerned are, however, very much greater than the problems involved in instruction. It was pointed out that the use of pictures, photographs, cinema films, or similar methods descriptive of ways of life widely different from those of the children to whom they are shown might lead under certain circumstances to misunderstanding.

### 2. UNIVERSITIES AND COLLEGES

**and easier in universities**

While in the direct sense the influence of higher institutions of learning is less widely diffused than that of the elementary schools, it must be remembered that the teachers are trained, and many of the texts or sources of texts produced, in universities. The opportunity for international exchange and understanding in the university world is considerably greater and is increasing. In every country for which information was available there was reported a stimulation of international interest among university students.

This often takes concrete form, as in the International Relations Clubs established in more than a hundred American universities since 1919. The Carnegie Endowment for International Peace sends small selected libraries to these clubs, to be set aside in an "International Mind Alcove" of the university libraries. Assistance is also given by providing expert lectures. A great deal is being achieved also by the international exchange of professors and students which is probably greater now than at any time since the Middle Ages. Well-endowed foundations are extremely interested in the promotion of such exchanges. In 1925, for example, the Carnegie Endowment invited a hundred American professors to go to Geneva to witness the Assembly of the League of Nations.

**Exchange of students and teachers**

The exchange between East and West is, however, very one-sided. Students come in great numbers from Oriental countries to America and Europe. Professors and lecturers go freely also from Western institutions to the Far East. But there is little movement of students from Europe and America to study in Japanese and Chinese universities, and few Oriental scholars visit the

West in a teaching capacity. Occidentals will not take time to learn the difficult Oriental languages, but take it for granted that Oriental scholars will learn theirs. In the same way there are still very few endowed chairs or other provisions for the teaching of Oriental history and civilization in Europe, America, or Australia. Educated Chinese and Japanese know far more about Occidental countries than scholars in those countries know of China and Japan.

In the United States at the present time there are at least ten thousand foreign students. Among them are twenty-five hundred Chinese, about a thousand Japanese, almost the same number of Filipinos, over twelve hundred from Latin America, and a hundred from India. These students stay one to four years, learning in a very intimate way the civilization of the West. Upon their reception depends to a very large extent the psychological attitude they take up toward Western culture. The influence of returned students in China is an obvious illustration of this point.

**is at present one-sided**

The number of Chinese students in Japanese universities is much larger than the corresponding number even in America. It was estimated as between four and six thousand. Japanese-trained students are becoming more and more prominent in political and judicial life in China. Chinese spokesmen reported a general feeling that students returned from Japanese universities without the good will that most returned students feel for the countries in which they were trained, and attributed this largely to the different social reception they received. It was stated on the other hand that this relationship was improving.

The recent establishment of the Sun-yat-sen University in Moscow provides a center in which several hundred Chinese students, largely from military academies, are trained in Russian military methods and propaganda.

### 3. ORGANIZATIONS FOR ADULT EDUCATION

**Associations for adult education in international affairs**

The agencies for adult education in the technical sense of the word are a product of very recent times. The number and range of such agencies has increased very rapidly. In so far as they aim at specific vocational or general cultural education, their relationship to international problems is much the same as that of the universities and colleges, except that their students are often more directly interested in social problems.

There are in most countries also a growing number of educational organizations of various types aiming specifically at the improvement of international relationships either by some particular means, such as the League of Nations, or by the spread of general information. The institutions vary considerably in aims and effectiveness; some, like the Royal Institute of International Affairs in Great Britain and the Council on Foreign Relations in America, rely on research and private expert discussion. Others, like the Foreign Policy Association of America and the League of Nations Unions in various countries, aim at a wider public. While in almost every case their discussions and publications

are multiplying

naturally and necessarily take account of the problems which interest their constituent members in each particular country, yet in so far as they insist upon accurate facts they are a real force in international understanding. The various conferences and institutes which are promoted for discussion of international problems are also a considerable factor in adult education, particularly in America. International federations of various organizations holding periodic international congresses were also mentioned as contributing factors in international understanding. Such bodies as the Federation of University Women have rapidly improved their international organization and made effective arrangements for university exchanges and traveling fellowships.

### 4. THE PRESS AND PROPAGANDA

The press depends on public support

The influence of the daily and periodical press was a subject too vast and too intricate for adequate discussion in the brief period available. The importance of this influence was recognized as greater than almost any other agency of adult education, and the more so because it is continuously growing. The technique of journalism has altered considerably with the spread of universal democratic education. Journalists in the Round Table interpreted what is often spoken of as a decline in editorial influence as rather a growth in reader intelligence. The inevitable pressure exerted by a wide reading constituency toward the provision of accurate, uncolored news was represented as an economic factor of considerably greater weight than advertisement. The growth and experience of news-gathering agencies was cited in support of this contention. It follows that in so far as success in journalism comes from catering to the reading public, responsible journalists are very sensitive to opinions and demands expressed by the individuals or groups who make up that public. The first difficulty with the press is obviously to claim its attention for news that has not hitherto been deemed important or of general interest.

and co-operation

It was forcibly argued that mere negative criticism was futile. It is easy to condemn the press and complain of its inadequacies. There is a large and increasing number of people interested in international affairs. If in every country those people who are interested would take pains to let their newspapers know they want information on this subject the papers would quickly respond. The accuracy of the information which is printed is even more important than its volume. Newspapers are sensitive to the problem and are quickly influenced by systematic campaigns of correction or restatement, such as some economic and religious groups maintain. In this respect also, it was maintained, journalists would welcome and respond to constructive, co-operative criticism.

Consideration of such steps led naturally to a discussion of the relation between news and propaganda. It was made clear that journalists, from their experience, are very shy of material written impersonally and objectively. They know that their readers for the most part demand human interest and action.

Biased propaganda

The working journalist is more likely therefore to interpret material than to accept it as contributed. Much of this material is necessarily propaganda in the sense of representing interested views or facts as they appear from certain angles. It was argued that there was a definite place for propaganda of this type, provided the field was open for criticism and rebuttal. As a matter of actual fact, everyone practices propaganda of this type. Unfortunately, however, recent experience, particularly during the war, has invested both the word and the practice with unscrupulous associations. Propaganda to most minds, therefore, connotes a disregard for accuracy, fairness, and just statement whenever such a disregard is likely to be effective in making a case. The constructive methods of dealing with this problem also were stressed. The best way of dealing with biased reports is to have adequate information from responsible sources. It would be a great gain also if the sources of this information were made clear. Particularly in those countries which are committed to democratic government, frankness and honesty in dealing with a responsible press are essential.

is least effective where adequate news is available

It was suggested that investigation should be made into the methods of collection, organization, and distribution of news in the Pacific. The source of news upon which the public opinion is formed which influences important international policies should be responsible and as far as possible open to public knowledge and criticism. The news-gathering agencies carry heavy responsibility in such connections. There is, however, little possibility of continuous critical observation. In the long run everything depends upon the actual observer and recorder of the news, and upon his training, technique, and opportunities of observation. In certain cases much may depend upon the environment in which he works from day to day. Examples were cited where influential papers received biased news of international importance from local sources with local prejudices.

### 5. NEW AVENUES OF COMMUNICATION

Throughout the discussion it was apparent that international relations at the present time depend in extraordinary degree upon the recent improvements in means of communication. In the economic sphere the development of steam shipping and continental railways has turned the whole world into one great market. Economic unity or interdependence is likely to precede political co-operation; but the great increase of international communication is very significant of changing relationships. It was argued that the chief characteristic of modern diplomacy is that it must be carried on against a much more important background of public opinion. The unmistakable post-war trend of public interest in international problems is recognized by responsible statesmen and reflected in their attitudes and actions.

It is therefore of considerable importance that easy and cheap communication should be established between individuals as well as organizations in various countries. The growth of international commerce works in this direction;

**This depends on cheap communications**

but it has not yet proved itself to be sufficiently powerful to prevent international conflict. The multiplication of personal connections is also a hopeful development. Cheap universal postage, the reduction of travel costs, and radio communication were instanced as factors in promoting international understanding. Like all forms of education, they are capable of misuse; but the cure for the dangers arising from inadequate knowledge is generally recognized now to be a more adequate knowledge.

Apart from official and commercial intercommunication, attention was drawn to several by-products of telegraphic communication. The chatter of operators on the circuit results in a limited but important spread of international understanding. When the Japanese earthquake disaster was made known, the radio operators in a world-wide organization contributed a day's pay throughout the service for immediate relief. Of even greater importance is the increasing and already important chatter of the amateurs. Many thousand amateur operators talk nightly to their fellows in nearly every country of the world. Examples were cited of messages concerning the Institute of Pacific Relations transmitted from New Zealand to New York and reported also as being heard clearly in England; and of messages from Tomsk, in Siberia, being relayed to America through New Zealand amateur stations.

**The possibilities of radio**

A strong plea was made for the freeing of the radio amateurs from restrictions by which they are now handicapped in certain countries, and for the continued reservation to their use of a comparatively narrow wave-band covering a few meters. The possibilities of long-distance communication by low-powered stations using short wave lengths has been demonstrated by amateur experimentation in the face of expert neglect and disbelief, and there still remain great possibilities of scientific as well as practical advance. The voluntary, co-operative, and continuous experimentation being carried on by thousands of amateurs every night in every country would seem too valuable to be hindered or interfered with by governmental restrictions or commercial monopoly. There is, however, some apprehension lest governmental and commercial services may step down into the field of short-wave transmission, which they have previously neglected and which the amateurs have proved valuable, in such a way as to crowd out amateur experiment.

**depend largely upon amateur experiment**

The possibilities of amateur radio from the international point of view are potentially unlimited, the more so when cognizance is taken of the experiments in wireless telephony now in progress almost everywhere. Broadcasting is widely recognized as a powerful means of adult education. It has so far been expensive and has depended largely upon high-powered, long-wave transmission. The recent use of the cheaper, low-wave transmission brings appreciably nearer the more universal use of broadcasting and also the possibilities of more extensive international use of broadcasting facilities over long distances.

Apart from broadcasting, the possibilities of long-distance international telephony may now be envisaged. Commercial telephony between London and New York is an established fact; but in addition there are numberless experiments going on between amateurs with simple but apparently effective equipment. Conversations between Australia and America, New Zealand and Texas, and over similar long distances offer some indication of what possibilities the future may hold.

### 6. THE RADIO CONTROVERSY IN CHINA

**The radio problem in China**

Arising from the consideration of the possibilities of international radio communication, some discussion took place concerning the problem presented by the diplomatic aspects of the controversy between Japan and the United States regarding radio concessions in China. An outline of the main facts of this controversy, together with an authoritative presentation of the American point of view, was contained in a paper prepared for presentation to the conference.[1] A statement traversing this presentation was made by the Japanese group at the conference;[2] but in the absence of adequate preparation no effective discussion was possible of the difficult problems involved. In part the problem is one of the relationship between government control and the transmission of news of international importance. The whole question of national or international control of news bristles with difficulties which are particularly acute at the present time in China.

**involves difficult international problems**

The policy of Japan and the United States toward the Open Door in China also requires consideration in the light of the technical aspects of the effort to establish a monopolistic control over an important means of communication. It has been stated that this radio controversy presents the outstanding diplomatic difference between the United States and Japan at the present time. The fact that three separate radio contracts irreconcilable with each other were entered into within a brief period by different departments of the Chinese government at Peking is, moreover, a clear illustration of the international complications resulting from lack of a stable government in China.

**and accentuates the Chinese problem**

Pending settlement of the controversy, China lacks effective radio communication with the outside world, and this in itself is a matter of great importance. The cable and radio communications between the British dominions, resulting in cheap and voluminous communication, was cited as much superior to the arrangements existing at present between other Pacific countries.[3] The necessity for constructive suggestions was evident in order to break the present deadlock in China. The prospect of an official conference between American

[1] Manton Davis, "The Radio Situation with Reference to the United States, China, and Japan" (Documents, Section 25).

[2] Ishii, "China's Radio Communication Problem" (Documents, Section 26).

[3] "Australia's Communications with Other Pacific Countries."

and Japanese experts aiming at amicable solution of an extraordinarily difficult technical and diplomatic problem was regarded as a hopeful development in the conference method of the new diplomacy.

## 3. DOCUMENTS

The discussions on education and communications were taken up by three Round Tables, one of which considered the subject from the point of view of the schools and colleges, while another considered institutions and processes of adult education. In addition the subject was considered in an evening forum of the whole Conference. The third Round Table discussed "Communications in the Pacific," and its discussion was continued by a smaller group presided over by Professor George Grafton Wilson.

A preliminary study of textbooks in use in different Pacific countries, prepared by the local Hawaiian group of the Institute, was circulated, but members from some of the countries concerned objected to it as incomplete and inaccurate, and it was therefore withdrawn.

Attention was drawn also to the section dealing with the work of the Committee on Intellectual Co-operation in the memorandum prepared by members of the League of Nations secretariat entitled "Notes on Certain Aspects of the Work of the League of Nations of Interest to the Pacific Countries" (Documents, Section 24).

The following data papers were used for general circulation:

1. "Public Opinion and International Relations," by IVY L. LEE.

2. "Communications," by WALTER S. ROGERS (a paper presented at the Conference on American Relations in China, Johns Hopkins University, Baltimore, September, 1925, prefaced by a memorandum from the United States Navy Department, dated June 20, 1927).

3. "Communications," by WILLIAM J. PAPE, vice-president of the Associated Press.

4. "The United Press," by KARL A. BICKEL, president, The United Press.

5. "The Radio Situation with Reference to the United States, China, and Japan," by MANTON DAVIS, Radio Corporation of America (Documents, Section 29).

6. "China's Radio Communication Problem," by AKIRA ISHII (Documents, Section 30).

7. "Australia's Communications with Other Pacific Countries," by the Deputy Postmaster-General of Australia.

8. "Communication on the Pacific: Its Part in Peace and Commerce: The Present Conditions," V. S. MCCLATCHY (reprinted from *San Francisco Business*, May 11, 1927).

The following books and publications were tabled for reference:

*Preparatory Documents for the Conference of Press Experts* (Geneva, 1927); TIMOTHY TINGFANG LEW, *China in American School Textbooks;* WALTER LIPPMAN, *Public Opinion;* F. A. MARVIN, *The Evolution of World Peace,* pp. 179–91; C. K. WEBSTER, *The Teaching of World-Citizenship;* G. D. DAVIES, *International Education in the Schools of Wales and Monmouthshire; World Wireless Message of the Children of Wales; Declaration concerning the Schools of Britain and the Peace of the World; Scheme for a First Course in General History.*

# THE PACIFIC MANDATES

## 1. QUESTIONS FOR DISCUSSION

*a*) How far are the mandatory powers fulfilling their obligations?

*b*) How far is the League of Nations' supervision of the mandatory system effective?

*c*) What are the dissatisfactions, if any:

( i) of the mandatory powers?

( ii) of the natives?

(iii) of the non-mandatory powers?

(iv) of the European populations in the islands?

*d*) Are the natural resources of the territories being satisfactorily developed?

## 2. SUMMARY OF ROUND-TABLE DISCUSSION

*Chairman:* L. T. Chen

*Secretary:* Marion J. Hunter

Within the wide Pacific Ocean there are thousands of scattered islands inhabited by native peoples who, before the advent of European traders, lived in a stage of development approximating the Stone Age. Most of these islands have been claimed as territorial possessions by one or another of the great powers, but this claim has for the most part been based rather upon strategy than upon effective economic utilization. The example of certain islands, however, notably Hawaii, indicates the importance which may attach to the Pacific islands as future sources of tropical raw materials and foodstuffs.

**The Pacific mandates**

The partial exploitation of the islands for the sake of these tropical products, and indeed the mere contact of the more backward peoples with aggressive civilization, has already resulted in a considerable diminution of their population. The great problem presented by the Pacific islands lies in the reconciliation of the welfare of the island peoples with the development of the island resources for the benefit of industrialized peoples elsewhere.

The existence of four separate mandatory groups within the Pacific area is a significant experiment looking toward this reconciliation. The main facts regarding the mandated territories of Micronesia, Western Samoa, New Guinea, and Nauru were summarized in data papers presented to the Round Table.[1] The international machinery by which their government is supervised is de-

[1] Yamasaki, "Micronesia and Micronesians"; Eggleston, "The Mandates of New Guinea and Nauru" and "The Mandated Territory of Western Samoa," by the New Zealand group.

scribed in the statement prepared for the Conference by members of the League of Nations secretariat.[2]

The mandatory territories were formerly German possessions, captured by allied forces in the early stages of the European war. They were allocated by the Supreme Council of the Allies during the preliminary discussions which preceded the treaty of Versailles. This allocation was later confirmed by the League of Nations, which issued to the various powers concerned mandates to govern the territories, "as a sacred trust of civilization." Japan received the mandate for the former German possessions in Micronesia; Australia received the mandate for German New Guinea directly as a member of the League. The mandate for Western Samoa was received by New Zealand through the British Foreign Office, and is therefore administered by New Zealand on behalf of the British Empire. The mandate for Nauru was given to the British Empire and is at present administered by Australia.

**are administered nationally**

In each case the mandatory power assumes complete national responsibility for the government of the territory intrusted to its care; but the treaty of Versailles set up, as a part of the League of Nations machinery having separate constitutional authority, a Permanent Mandates Commission, which has power to supervise the government of all mandatory territories. The Permanent Mandates Commission receives annual reports concerning each territory. It has power also to call for any further information either written or oral. Upon the basis of the information received it reports to the Council of the League of Nations. The Commission as such has no executive authority whatever. It has power merely to draw up recommendations to the Council of the League. The ultimate check, therefore, upon the administration by the mandatory powers lies in the public opinion focussed by the publicity given to the discussions at Geneva. None of the mandatory powers has refused to supply information which has been asked for, and as far as the Pacific mandates have been concerned, the Commission has expressed general satisfaction with the existing administration.

**under international supervision**

All of the mandatory powers, however, objected to the recent proposals which were made to give access to the Commission by petitioners and to issue a new and more detailed questionnaire as a basis for future annual reports. The general attitude of the mandatory powers was that they should be given opportunity to develop consistent policies of administration over a sufficiently long term of years without undue interference. They were willing to provide any information concerning those policies, but they objected to dissatisfied petitioners being allowed to approach the Permanent Mandates Commission except through the proper official channels provided by the mandatory governments themselves.

It is difficult for those not familiar with conditions in the mandatory terri-

[2] See Documents, Section 28.

tories to realize fully the difficulties involved in the transformation of native life within the last century.[3] The introduction of metal tools was cited as an innovation which has enabled the native to provide for his needs in a fraction of the time previously needed. The new leisure resulting from this situation is a source of danger. The introduction of European ideas of individual property has also caused a tremendous revolution of thought involving the whole social and religious, as well as economic, life of the native people. Many investigators regard these social and psychological factors as more important in the depopulation of the Pacific than the introduction of diseases.

**Economic and social changes**

A significant difference in this respect, however, is to be seen in the contrast between Polynesia and Melanesia at the present time. It was vigorously asserted on behalf of the Polynesian race, in New Zealand, Samoa and other South Sea islands, that the adaptation to modern life was successfully under way. The Polynesian population is increasing, notably in Samoa, and the Polynesian has a very hopeful outlook toward the future. It is not possible, therefore, to write off the native races as likely to disappear within a brief period of time. On the other hand, the progress made in Samoa toward political self-government and also toward economic progress has been extremely encouraging under the mandatory administration. At the present time there are bound to be growing pains in this development.

**need gradual adaptation**

Some considerable discussion took place in the Round Tables concerning the difficulty of ascertaining the grievances and dissatisfactions of the native peoples. The native is naturally reticent in the presence of foreigners, especially as any grievances which he has are likely to be intimately connected with his social and religious life. He is inhibited also from free expression by the difficulty of language. The use of interpreters is not always a satisfactory medium for expression. Moreover, the foreigner must have a considerable knowledge of native life if he is to comprehend the full significance of native statements. It was felt, therefore, that in the administration of the mandated territories fuller use should be made of administrators with anthropological training and experience. The chief danger which was felt to be ahead of the territories lies in this direction. The good will, both of the mandatory governments and of the directly responsible administrators, is manifest. The Australian government of Papua has been recognized as owing its undoubted success to the anthropological experience and training possessed by its administration under Sir Hubert Murray. The Australian universities have also been encouraged recently to develop departments of anthropology with the especial purpose of training administrators and investigators. New Zealand possesses almost a century of experience in dealing with the Maoris, but has made little use of scientific anthropological training in the administration of its mandate.

**Anthropological understanding is necessary for successful administration**

In the course of Round-Table discussions of this point it appeared to be

[3] Tennent, "Samoa and the South Sea Islands as a Problem of the Pacific."

generally agreed that it would be impolitic and probably impracticable to make the League of Nations an alternative court of appeal for factional grievances, but that an administration sympathetic with the best interests of the natives and able to enter into an understanding of the native attitude and point of view offered the best guaranty for the safeguarding of native interests. With such a safeguard it was felt that the natives might reasonably be expected to increase in numbers and make rapid progress toward self-government at the same time as the economic development of the resources of the island was steadily pushed forward. It is probable that by the use of more effective imported labor, economic development might be considerably hastened; but the expressed intention of the mandatory powers as well as the implication of their mandatory responsibilities are quite definitely supported by the public opinion of the countries concerned in placing economic development as subordinate to the welfare of the native peoples.

### 3. DOCUMENTS

The following papers were circulated in order to provide source material for the discussions on the mandated territories in the Pacific.

1. "Notes on Certain Aspects of the Work of the League of Nations of Interest to the Pacific Countries," prepared unofficially by members of the League secretariat (Documents, Section 28).

2. "The International Labor Organization and Labor Problems in Mandated Territories," by WILLIAM CALDWELL, International Labor Office, Geneva.

3. "Micronesia and Micronesians," by PROFESSOR NAOMASA YAMASAKI, Imperial University of Tokyo.

4. "Samoa and Other South Sea Islands as a Problem of the Pacific," by HUGH C. TENNENT.

5. "The Mandated Territory of Western Samoa," prepared by the New Zealand group.

6. "Memorandum on American Samoa," by A. C. ELKINTON.

7. "The Mandates of New Guinea and Nauru," by HON. F. W. EGGLESTON, chairman of the Australian Group.

## THE FUTURE OF THE INSTITUTE

At the request of the Secretariat, the entire forenoon of the last day of the Conference was devoted to Round-Table discussions of the future of the Institute, together with matters pertaining to the conduct and preparation of the Conference. It was recognized that the presence of Institute leaders from each of the constituent national groups offered an invaluable opportunity for the funding of points of view and opinion upon the Institute itself, its aims, functions, philosophy, and future program.

The following questions for discussion were submitted:

1. What is the inclusive aim of this Institute? What should be its functions in the attainment of this aim? How do these several functions make for this aim? Wherein does this Institute differ from the Williamstown Institute, the Pan-Pacific Union, the Royal Institute of International Affairs, and the various peace foundations?

2. What should be the place and function of the several kinds (and degrees) of research activities in the work of the Institute?

3. What kind and degree of publicity is desirable (*a*) in connection with the work of the Conference? (*b*) in connection with the other functions of the Institute? What, if any, publications should the Institute conduct?

4. What are the best means of intergroup communication?

5. In what typical ways may individual members of this Conference further the work of the Institute in their respective countries after adjournment?

6. What should be the size and character of the national group representations at the next conference?

7. What suggestions can be made for improving the procedure of the Conference?

8. What principles should govern the Institute in the inclusion of new political or racial units?

### SUMMARY OF ROUND-TABLE DISCUSSIONS

1. *What is the inclusive aim of this Institute? What should be its functions in the attainment of this aim? How do these several functions make for this aim? Wherein does this Institute differ from the Williamstown Institute, the Pan-Pacific Union, the Royal Institute of International Affairs, and the various peace foundations?*

*Member from Japan:* I believe that there are three main aims of this Institute: first, study; second, spread of information; third, personal contacts.

*Member from United States:* It seems to me that there are two functions of this Institute. One has to do with public opinion and the other with facts in the more material sense. We could say with respect to public opinion that we have the object of first discovering and then educating public opinion in the Pacific countries. With respect to facts we have first to discover, then to compile, facts with respect to Pacific countries. That leaves four rather distinct methods which we have in view: discussion, publicity, research, information.

We have discussion which centers around the Conference, whose main aim is to discover what public opinion is on current problems.

Publicity means the dissemination of the results of such discussion to a broader public. We certainly wish to reach a broader public than is assembled at the Conference.

Then we have research, the discovering of facts and the relation between them. That involves the setting in motion of long-time projects for assembling data and squeezing all the principles one can out of them.

Finally, the information necessary for intelligent discussion must be compiled and made available.

*Member from China:* Not only should the members of the Conference study the facts, but we ought also to try to impart to others the definite results we get, not to put over any special object, but to create what may be called an international mind. We ought to carry on a sort of educational campaign for the general public so that it can be impartial and dispassionate on controversial issues. Try to educate people to live as citizens of the world.

*Member from United States:* I would like to stress the fact that it is the interplay of ideas and attitudes by the different nationals in the Institute which is one of its unique contributions to the adjustment of difficulties in the Pacific.

*Member from China:* The main difference, so far as I know, between this Institute and all other organizations exists not so much in the general sentiment of helpfulness but rather in the method. All the other organizations sooner or later in their discussions seem to gravitate to certain general policies on the issues between nations. The best thing here that I find is that this Institute as a whole does not encourage anybody to come to the Conference to attack or to defend any given policy. Its conclusions tend to be purely spiritual and intellectual. This Institute will have, at least in the intellectual sphere, all over the world, a larger influence because of this character. It seems to me much more objective and less capable of being suspected of any propaganda used in the sense of having something to put over. I do not think that this Institute has anything to put over.

*Member from United States:* There are four different ways of considering this Institute.

The first is to consider the Institute a fact-finding organization. Stress research between the conferences, and during the conferences emphasize the assembling of facts.

Second, make the Institute an agency for unofficial diplomacy. That would mean the bringing together of men who have a considerable knowledge of the problems of the Pacific, including those who are in a position to exert considerable influence upon their home governments. These men would consider the outstanding issues such as extra-territoriality and immigration, reach some solution, and then attempt to induce their home governments to adopt it.

Third, regard the Institute as an organization for adult education. From this point of view the aim is to bring to the Conference, not so much experts or those who are in close touch with their governments, as men and women who will represent a cross-section of their home people, and then to educate them in the issues of the Pacific.

Fourth, some combination of the three aims already mentioned.

*Member from New Zealand:* I think, personally, that the main object of this Institute should be fact-finding. It should be a fact-finding organization. I do not think that this can be denied in any way. Unofficial diplomacy, I think, would clash with fact-finding. If we have unofficial diplomacy in the Institute, the members will be on guard so as to avoid conflict. This will to a certain extent make the Conference dependent upon the attitude of the members of certain groups, such as Great Britain and China, and Japan and California. I cannot see how diplomacy can be dealt with as one of the objects of the Institute. It will come into conflict with the fact-finding object.

*Member from Japan:* This second session of the Institute has given an impression, so far as our group is concerned, of an emphasis placed on nationalism. Before we came here our group had several discussions in which we expected that we would discover from each other the differences of personal opinion at the Institute. Upon arrival, I must confess that an atmosphere was created which put more emphasis on group opinion. I want to avoid that tendency. It is rather dangerous.

*Member from China:* I want to be very frank. After coming here I have not only learned a good deal, but I am very much impressed by the Institute. Our little encounters with the British have given us the British point of view, and will help us to understand British attitudes. It certainly has helped materially in understanding the other side of the case. Our understanding will gradually be reflected, and, I hope, will be accepted by the people in China.

In my opinion the supreme value of the Conference lies in the spiritual manner. Here we come in contact with representatives of all nationalities. I begin to feel that the world is not limited to China. The world is a far larger thing. I find that all people are really friendly. The mere discovery of that spiritual atmosphere in this Institute in my opinion constitutes its supreme value. The whole world is lovable. We are by circumstance, residing in certain quarters of the earth, and bringing here people from all parts of the world makes a new start in the world's history. Nationalism governs the world. We begin to see that we are not only citizens of one nation, but citizens of the world. We feel that our responsibility and duty is not limited to our own people, but extends to other people also. As to the other technical functions, the Chairman has already said it is an Institution which is endeavoring to render a very great service.

*Member from Great Britain:* The Royal Institute of International Affairs is concerned with the study of international difficulties. It follows two main lines. One is meetings in which papers are read and discussion follows. The most fruitful of its activities is the small group meeting together in a round table and discussing particular matters. These meetings are secret and no notes are taken.

*Member from United States:* Does the Royal Institute have any research program?

*Member from Great Britain:* Its research work is carried on through different groups.

*Member from Australia:* It carries on a private information service for the benefit of the members. The report on foreign affairs is drawn by the Empire Parliamentary Association, which is composed of a number of autonomous groups. This information service is conducted in London and is circulated to all members of the various parts of the Empire. It is a summary of developments regarding public affairs. It is confidential, but all the material is open to the public.

*Member from Great Britain:* There is nothing official about the Royal Institute. We have a membership of 1,200 in the British branch. It is supported by subscription or donations. The headquarters building was given by a Canadian.

*Member from United States:* The Williamstown Institute of Politics has the following characteristics: (1) It is not international in membership. (2) There are no interim activities, either research, education, or publicity. (3) The courses of lectures are mainly given by foreign experts. (4) Its round-table leaders, who are appointed months in advance, take a prominent part in the discussions. (5) It deals with the problems of the whole world, not primarily with those of the Pacific. (6) It seeks the fullest publicity and gets it. (7) Its annual session continues four weeks. (8) It is supported by one or two very large gifts. Quite a large tuition fee is charged, which covers the cost of keeping the college open, but does not pay the fees of the speakers and experts. (9) Membership is by personal application and invitation.

*Member from Australia:* There are two differentiating features about the Williamstown Institute: its national character and the fact that it is an autocracy, controlled by two able men.

*Member from United States:* Are there any similar institutions in Australia, Japan, China, or Canada?

*Member from Great Britain:* I do not think so. There are summer schools in the English universities which pay a great deal of attention to foreign affairs. There is nothing corresponding to the institutes in America.

*Member from United States:* The Pan-Pacific Union has an inclusive program and considerable publicity. It gets up all sorts of gatherings of Pacific leaders—educational, commercial, scientific. It is semigovernmental.

It emphasizes points of agreement rather than the differences among Pacific nations.

Except for Japan, its work is centered in the Honolulu office.

Mr. Ford supplies the impetus, gets the people together, and leaves them to do the work. The Pacific Science Congress grew out of his great promotive ability, but is now independent.

*Member from United States:* The Council on Foreign Relations in New York is a society similar to the Royal Institute of International Affairs in London. It issues a magazine on foreign affairs, the best magazine on international affairs published in the United States, if not in the world. It exerts a great influence upon the public and upon intelligent people in the United States. The Council holds round tables throughout the year. The whole winter is devoted to them. The desire at these round tables is to secure facts. The Council has also dinners for its own members, who are usually men of distinction or experts on foreign affairs and research in New York.

*Member from China:* In China we have an organization something like the Council on Foreign Relations. It is still in its infant stage. Last year the professors especially interested in political and social science gathered together and organized what is known as the National Association on Chinese Foreign Relations. This organization has now a rather selected membership of about eighty members, mainly teachers in Peking. We have monthly dinners, and at these dinners we discuss the problems of China in relation to other countries, chiefly diplomatic problems. Sometimes we take up economic and political problems. At the time when I left Peking they were planning to publish a magazine in Chinese. We give public lectures for the student bodies in Peking, and also for the outside public, and in this way we attempt to educate the public.

*Member from Great Britain:* Most of us know the Institute through the Conference. I have written down five things which the Institute might do through conferences: (1) create a clearing-house for different ideas, and opportunities for personal contact; (2) make a definition of problems; (3) find what agreements can be assumed; (4) discover gaps in the knowledge of Pacific problems, thus indicating lines of research; (5) Discover lines of advance in solving problems or definite states of disagreement, with reasons therefor.

*Member from Great Britain:* May we not keep in our heads the distinction of what the Institute may do and what the individual members may do? There is nothing to prevent the members from going back and trying to help their countries. The function of the Institute is to give these people the proper knowledge to do this.

*Member from Japan:* When there is a program to be discussed, it should not be entirely political. It should go deeper into the sociological basis of the problems of the Pacific. If we discuss only the political side of questions, this will become merely a diplomatic meeting.

*Member of Secretariat:* I wonder if we have a real understanding of the Institute. The Conference is over, and we are going to prepare for another one. Underlying the principles of the Conference is the question, What is this Institute driving at, and by what means are we going to attain that end?

There are two different conceptions of what we are doing. The first is, the Institute as a project for getting the facts. The other, the Institute as a project for getting the facts and then presenting these facts to the people.

*Member from Great Britain:* What are the facts? This is the first question. In my view, it is essential that this Conference should concentrate on enabling us to get a better knowledge of the facts than we could have without it; but I also hold it is the function of this Institute to deal with the meaning of the facts. The next question is whether this Institute is going to take the function of saying "This is the right meaning of the facts, and it is up to us to get the people to believe this." The members must get at the facts and the meaning of the facts. But if we are going any farther, we are going toward ruin. If we try to insist that these are the right things we are headed for disaster.

*Member from Great Britain:* Do you mean that the Institute should not publish these facts, or that it should not publish them for a specific purpose in diplomacy?

*Member from Great Britain:* A Conference member makes a speech on Russia, giving his point of view. The address is printed and made public, without the discussion that followed. All of that is invaluable to the public and helps them to make up their minds. But the moment the Institute starts making up the mind of the people, it starts trouble. Take the cancellation of the Chinese treaties. We are all free to put our own conclusions in front of the people, and the Institute can print what we have said; but the moment the Institute goes about preaching that the Chinese treaties should be abolished, it starts difficulties. We must be a body that includes every point of view. A body must be devoted to research or it must be devoted to propaganda.

*Member from United States:* Taking the definition of publicity of the member from Great Britain, his statement is unanswerable. But there are certain situations that must be considered as to the sort of publicity which must be carried on. We have to act one way in one country, and another way in another. Our friend from England is living in a country where everyone, because of his contact with the rest of the world, is interested in international relations. The United States is so large that fifty or sixty million people have never seen the ocean. A vast number of them are not interested in international relations. They resent the idea of international relations and they think that by not being interested in them and by resenting them hard enough they can make them cease to exist. There is a great deal of propaganda needed to stir up these people into taking an interest in these matters. This means that aggressive efforts to penetrate through the barrier of disinterest must be made. Therefore I think that we should organize definite propaganda that will not be inconsistent with the point of view of the member from Great Britain.

*Member from United States:* Am I right in quoting the member from Great Britain as agreeing on three things: first, finding the facts; second, interpreting the facts; and third, the most careful avoidance, as an Institute, of offering any solutions? In some countries the handing out of information seems to be synonomous with the handing out of conclusions. Does the member from Great Britain see any reason why the American group should not interpret as well as carry on studies, and also try to get less informed groups to take up the studies of these questions? Would it not be justified in providing material for studies, propagating no solutions, but propagating the kind of study it thinks essential? Is there any reason why the American group should not aid the groups that are making these studies?

*Member from Great Britain:* Provided we leave them free to decide what to do with our information.

2. *What should be the place and function of the several kinds of research activities in the work of the Institute?*

*Member of Secretariat:* I believe the problem which confronts the Institute in its research work is the problem of combining scientific thoroughness with practical utility.

With that object in view the research program of the Institute will demand very close co-ordination among the different national councils and the secretaries. A great many of the research problems which are undertaken will emerge from this Conference.

There are a great many bodies in the field already doing research on Pacific relations. This Institute has not the personnel, money, or equipment to embark on a research program of its own. Its work must be more vicarious than direct. It will endeavor to stimulate and initiate projects and in general mobilize the research resources of all the Pacific countries. It must depend on national councils and those they enlist in each country for actual conduct of research projects.

*Member from United States:* Should we engage in pure research? Or should we concentrate on research pertaining to pressing world problems?

*Member from United States:* Research ought to be distinguished from information. The efforts of the research department of this Institute should be directed especially toward the discovery of the long term tendencies in the Pacific area and the isolation and measurement of the most fundamental factors involved. Research should aim to bring the best scientific resources which any of the countries have to the study of the problems. It should be science in the most technical sense of that term. If we do not stimulate that kind of scientific investigation of Pacific problems, I do not know who will. It is my hope that the interest of the research committees will be to stimulate the long-term investigations which may not seem to have any immediate application to practical problems.

I think we also need information which does bear on immediate practical problems; but I should say in order to assure ourselves of getting the long-term studies it would be better to have their supervision under a different department of the Institute from the information service. The national councils should be merely advisory in relation to research. They should suggest to the central organization here at Honolulu the researches which they think are desirable, if they are of international character.

If there are researches which a particular national group wishes to undertake which are not international in character, it might undertake or stimulate them without consulting the central organization at all, but in general the Institute research should clear through the central office.

Preliminary consideration of a problem may show that the research has already been done. If in an oriental language, translations may be the thing required; in other cases, a bibliography.

I should like to see two secretaries, one for research and one for information. The duties of the research secretary would be to carry on correspondence with research workers of various countries. The information secretary would have to be in close contact with the political situation, and see that informational papers are prepared when needed. These two types of activity would be quite different, and by keeping them separated their balance would be maintained.

*Member from United States:* One of the most pressing problems for research at the present time is that of population and food supply. It conditions the life of all nations. This has immediate as well as long-term aspects.

*Member from Hawaii:* We should carry on research work, the need for which has been exposed by our meeting here.

*Member from United States:* The research secretary might compile a list of important subjects of the Pacific area requiring research. Such a list could be used by many professors in giving their graduate students topics for study.

*Member from Canada:* The research problems should be outlined in advance, so that the members of each national group will know in advance more about the Conference and be able to conduct research between conferences. If that is done, when the Conference gathers every two years, there will be a series of pertinent facts worked up and laid before the members of the Institute attending. There should be a certain number of scientific members who could amplify and explain those facts with reference to particular problems. At the same time there should be business men and men of affairs in attendance to share in the discussion of these facts. Such knowledge should be spread as individual members think desirable when they return to their own countries. This plan offers a mechanism for combining the two aims, research and education.

*Member from United States:* I would like to say a few words about the relation between the American group and the Social Science Research Council. The latter is made up of representatives of most of the learned societies. Due to the interest of the American group of this Institute of Pacific Relations in carrying on research in Pacific problems, the Social Science Research Council, last summer at its annual meeting, agreed to reorganize one of its committees to consider research in international relations. This committee will receive research projects from the American group, and if it approves of them, will recommend that they be carried out, which means that the necessary financial support will probably be provided by some of the large foundations in America. The situation now is that the American group has a research committee as well as the Social Science Research Council, and Dr. Shotwell is chairman of both.

3. *What kind and degree of publicity is desirable (a) in connection with the work of the Conference? (b) in connection with the other functions of the Institute?* What, if any, publications should the Institute conduct?

*Member from Canada:* A prominent magazine refused an article about the Institute because the daily press did not give sufficient emphasis to the proceedings day by day to create a public appetite, and the magazine thought for this reason the public was not interested in what was going on.

We need both frank discussion and a frank chronicle.

The policy of secrecy gives the public the impression that something sinister is being done behind closed doors. It gives the impression that we are disguised, unofficial diplomats. It is unreasonable to think that the press cannot be fair in interpreting the remarks of the "pundits."

If a policy of successive secrecy is followed it will cripple the Secretariat and lead the press to violent criticism of the Institute or to a determination to break through and interpret it its own way.

*Member from Canada:* We want to disseminate an interest in foreign affairs. Does this require many news items about the work of the Institute? We surely do not need to boom the Institute.

*Member from Canada:* If we follow a wise procedure we can get the co-operation of the newspapers in interpreting what we have said and discussed here.

*Member from New Zealand:* Does the member from Canada mean we should invite the press to sit in at round tables like this one?

*Member from Canada:* No. Our round tables had better remain private. The forums, however, should always be open, and every member should accept the responsibility for what he says, knowing that publicity is permitted.

*Member from United States:* This would necessitate a change of such programs as those of the first week of the present Institute, where discussions at round tables were summarized in reports to forum. This may limit those who speak at round tables because they will have no assurance that what they have said in the morning may not become publicly reported in the evening forum.

*Member from Canada:* It will probably be necessary to impersonalize the reports brought to forum each evening so that the names of persons speaking in the round tables need not be given.

*Member from United States:* If it is reported that there was a consensus of opinion from a given round table, everyone knowing who were at that forum, then even an impersonal report is likely to lead to difficulties.

*Member from Canada:* There is far more danger from secret meetings than from meetings where reporters are admitted under wise control.

*Member from United States:* One great danger is the independence of the headline writer, who reads between lines and features items as he pleases.

*Member from Japan:* We have said a good deal about the disadvantages of publicity. We need now to consider whether it is advantageous or not.

*Member from Canada:* The Secretary must know what the policy of the Institute is going to be. Over four hundred papers in the United States, Canada, New Zealand, and Australia have been releasing publicity stories about the Institute already. How can their co-operation be retained if we court publicity before and after our Institute meetings and then shut down on it at the actual gatherings?

*Member from China:* We must either have more publicity or shut it out altogether. The kind of publicity we have had this time doesn't satisfy anybody. As regards this year's discussion, I personally do not see anything about which we could not have taken the press men into our confidence. Two years ago when we took the press men into our confidence we had pretty good results.

I do not remember any serious mishap. I think we did better two years ago than we have done this year. Publicity after the Institute is most important in China. It is important to let the people know there is such a movement working for international understanding. Hitherto China has thought that this sort of activity was confined to religious bodies; but if it is known as an undertaking of men of affairs, it will have a distinct influence upon the thinking of the general public. At a time when China's mind tends to extreme nationalism, information of this kind giving new facts on internationalism would be very wholesome.

*Member from Great Britain:* We need two types of forum: one thoroughly open, and one a continuation of private round tables.

*Member from United States:* No organization in the world has all of its sessions public. If we have a larger proportion of open sessions the needs of the press and public will probably be satisfied.

*Member from United States:* I shall be interested to know whether at the next conference an attempt is to be made to combine the forums and public meetings. This has been a weak point of this Conference. If our evening meetings could be public, giving to the press and the public freely the opportunity to attend, it would take away some of the ill feeling about exclusion. Our evening meetings did not equal our forums of two years ago.

*Member from United States:* It seems to me very important that the policy for publicity should be determined long in advance of the meeting, and that everyone who comes to the Conference knows beforehand what is to be public and what is not. There was some confusion between the Institute members and the press. If the press knows what our policy of publicity is to be, there will be no confusion.

*Member from Australia:* The Harris Institute holds a public lecture in the afternoon, and the public and press is not admitted to the evening meetings. It is impossible to have frank and free discussions if we have meetings open to the public and the press.

*Member from United States:* The point just raised by the member from Australia is very important. The newspaper feels it necessary to pick out any possible point in an article or speech that may have the least bit of a pungent character and make it the headline for that particular speech, which sometimes is very distorted. You will have to make up your minds to run that risk, and at any public conference the members must assume full responsibility for whatever they may say. We can always be protected at the round tables, where we can speak freely on any subject.

*Member from Great Britain:* Are you speaking of American publications or newspapers?

*Member from United States:* I am speaking of the press of the world. There is no distinction. You must bear in mind that a newspaper is printed to be interesting, and to make it interesting they must put in the headlines those things that arouse curiosity and interest.

*Member from Japan:* What was the working of publicity at this Conference? Were the newspaper men not allowed? Did you furnish them what was necessary?

*Member from United States:* They were given a censored statement of what had happened. Any publication of the secret meetings would have been a violation of confidence. The open meetings were attended by the press, and they were at liberty to write what they wished. . . . . I would invite leading newspaper men to attend all meetings, and let them judge what is best to put before the public. A number in this Institute are rather handicapped with the language, and may sometimes even misinterpret themselves. You cannot expect those people to talk freely if they are going to run the risk of having their remarks published in the newspapers. The newspapers, I am certain, will not quarrel with those who desire closed meetings.

*Member from United States:* The subjects discussed in round table would be far too technical for the average reporter. It is very important that this Institute be reported accurately. Prepared speeches and open forums should be thought of as press matter. When a man talks from a manuscript he is perfectly willing to commit himself there. He may no doubt be treading on delicate ground, but when questions are put to him, he may not be able immediately to assemble his thoughts and say just what he actually wishes, and in such a situation a reporter is not altogether welcomed. Nevertheless this Institute is making a tremendous mistake in not allowing the fullest opportunity for the press to report its workings. I am certain that the daily newspapers are prepared to carry out the views of this Institute without giving out any discreet matters discussed at these meetings.

*Member from United States:* All things in America are important in respect to the amount of space they are given in the newspapers. One of our problems is to get men of real significance to come here. If they don't think the thing is important, they won't come.

Another important matter is the furnishing of foreign editors with material that will help them in their knowledge of international affairs. The last point is, How shall we protect ourselves against the belief that we are a propaganda body?

*Member from United States:* The American group would like to stimulate a conscientious study of these problems, rather than to get the press to speak of the Institute as a body that is handing out decisions and solutions. It proposes to get as many other organizations to study these problems as possible, without mentioning the Institute.

4. *What are the best means of intergroup communication?*

*Member from Hawaii:* Is it desirable to continue the monthly bulletin sent out recently from the central office?

*Member from Australia:* Most of the members seem to think the best work of the Institute will be done through its regular publications. A good deal depends on the quality and size of the *News Bulletin* and whether it is to be developed.

*Member of Secretariat:* Do we want to maintain communication between the groups and what is the most practical means of communication? Does it consist of sending letters from one group to another? Do we favor a more formal type of publication? We in Honolulu realize the immense importance of intergroup communication after the Conference is over. Here we are very far from our groups, and we are left in the middle of the Pacific Ocean to carry on. We cannot carry on unless there is a desire for contact and a means of maintaining that contact.

*Member from China:* Couldn't the secretary of each group inform the Secretariat when a member of that group is traveling?

*Member from Japan:* It would be helpful for the nationals interested in the different countries if they could, between sessions of the Conference, secure information from other institute councils of their activities. I am not particular how often the news organ is published, whether quarterly or bimonthly. I should think the result of the research activities would better be put in the form of a monograph or pamphlet than in a regular periodical, and let news be distributed by periodical publication.

*Member from New Zealand:* I think, in addition to the monthly news bulletins, that we should have certain information on the Institute, which should be distributed.

*Member from United States:* A solid quarterly would entail a very heavy financial burden. Better continue to publish the *News Bulletin* and improve it, but defer the proposed quarterly for two or three years, and meanwhile send out multigraphed articles of merit to all the national councils for insertion in leading reviews and papers.

*Member from United States:* With regard to the character of the periodical to be published by the Institute, I am inclined to believe that it should be a journal to give information about the Institute itself. It seems to me a little ambitious to try at this time to inaugurate a new journal of a character of which the Institute would be proud.

*Member from Australia:* We should have a membership fee for helping finance the Institute and paying for data papers.

*Member from United States:* It is better publicity to sell your material than to give it away. People are much more likely to read it if they pay for it than if it is given to them free.

*Member of the Secretariat:* In this field the Secretariat considers its function as that of distributing material for the Institute. The aim of the Secretariat is to provide machinery for the activities of the Institute, a process by which the Institute may carry out its policy of creating understanding. We are not interested in what uses are made of this material after it is sent out. We believe that the information which is provided will build up a public opinion which will in due time improve international relations. Our task is mechanical. When we receive material from any group and it bears the approval of that group, we will send it out. In this field our success will depend entirely on the co-operation of the different groups. The Australian group has already begun very fine co-operation, but they are the only group that has as yet managed to do so.

5. *In what typical ways may individual members of this Conference further the work of the Institute in their respective countries after adjournment?*

*Member from Philippine Islands:* Courses in schools might be given, co-operating with the aims of the Institute. Members of the Institute might influence school faculties in this direction.

*Member from Great Britain:* I agree with the last speaker. There is a fundamental lack of facilities for study of the Orient in the Occident. Those of us who have any influence in universities should try to get extensive studies started in the universities in these subjects.

*Member from United States:* We can encourage the exchange of Institute professors from one country to another, as in the case of Professor Hall, from Sydney to Syracuse.

*Member from Australia:* We should arrange to write articles and publish them.

*Member from Canada:* What the Canadian group has in mind is to organize units in the larger cities of Canada, to be devoted to the study of Pacific problems. Should there be men capable of presenting the Pacific point of view traveling through the country, we will see that an opportunity is given them to speak in conferences and groups, such as the Canadian clubs.

I shall report to my immediate principals the results of this Conference and give them an impression of the Institute.

I shall further put myself in touch with some of the gentlemen connected with external affairs at Ottawa, and report what I have learned. They have to deal with problems of the Pacific, and if I can convey to them some of my impressions it may be of service.

*Member from Japan:* I think I can give talks to various groups with which I am connected both in and out of the university, and write articles about this Conference. Also we will endeavor to get experts to come to our regular group meetings in Tokyo to discuss the problems of the Pacific.

*Member from Japan:* I might add one thing: the co-ordination of the different international organizations in Japan.

*Member from United States:* The American group is now studying just how to connect up the existing organizations in various parts of the country. Insofar as it can be worked out, the Institute will have to try to get a few branches organized to study foreign affairs and bring the problems of the Pacific to the attention of the people.

*Member from China:* I think our work could be divided into two or three main lines: (1) We will have to reorganize the material that has been furnished during this Institute and put it in a form that can be used by our groups in China in our own language. (2) Circulate the ideas of the Conference among student groups, schools and colleges, and business men. (3) Try to feed this material into the local press. (4) In the next few years try to establish five or six local units.

*Member from New Zealand:* In New Zealand we should call conferences of our branches in the four main centers of the Dominion and give them full particulars of the work which has been done. We should organize regional conferences, have public meetings to explain the work of the Institute, and also contribute articles to the press.

*Member from United States:* Our own views will not be all that the public wishes. I think that the important thing for the members here to do is to hand on to those members who could not be present all that was said here; but we should use discretion when giving such material to the public.

*Member from Australia:* In reporting what has been going on here we should not quote anybody or quote the views of any particular group. I would report my conclusions of the findings as such and such, but I would not give them as the considered opinions of the whole Institute.

*Member from United States:* We should never say, in writing or speaking about the Institute, that the Institute agreed on this or that. We should go no farther than to give the opinions expressed or the facts presented. It should be remembered that the whole purpose of the Institute is to get away from making decisions.

*Member from United States:* How can we spread the work of the Institute at home and describe its character without quoting anything that was said here in confidence?

*Member from United States:* In my experience of reporting the Conference two years ago we had to work hard to inform the public, because they were not interested. I had difficulty in defining the name of the Institute. We should find effective ways of educating the public on the questions which have become commonplace to us.

*Member from China:* The members of our group feel that they want publicity for the Conference just as far as possible in China.

*Member from United States:* A number of people reasonably well informed have come together here to meet and talk with various nationalities. Each of us might become what I may term a "missionary" to his own country to attempt to give to our nationals somewhat of an international mind. It seems to me that we would lose one of the very prime purposes of our coming together if we could not influence the public of our countries to a better understanding of those questions that we have had the opportunity to discuss here with members of other nationalities.

6. *What should be the size and character of the national group representations at the next Conference?*

*Member from United States:* The Institute membership is made up of three classes: (1) Authorities or experts. These are men of technical training who should act as a ready reference library for the use of this Institute. They should not monopolize the discussions. (2) Representatives of the political, social, and commercial activities. They have been rather inarticulate this year, which is unfortunate. In the last analysis it is they who have to solve the problem. We need the practical common sense of men and women of affairs. The most vital thing is, not how we get into certain situations, but how to get out of them. We must establish the right balance between men of technical knowledge and men of affairs. (3) The interpreting class. They are in the main a responsible class of trained craftsmen. It is upon their help after the Institute adjourns that we shall have to rely to secure lively interest in the various communities.

*Member from United States:* The present Conference is too big. We would get better results if the total membership were about one-half of what it is this year. The United States delegation is altogether too large. One-half of that number would be entirely enough.

*Member from China:* Perhaps we should not be too arbitrary. Since there are more Americans interested in foreign relations than the other groups in the Pacific, why should there not be more represented than in other groups?

*Member from United States:* The proportion of the Caucasion group should be more nearly related to the numbers in the oriental group.

*Member from Japan:* Fifteen Americans would not be sufficient to represent all groups in that country. If we should meet in Japan, Japanese delegates would naturally preponderate.

*Member from Great Britain:* The character of the group is more important than the size. The average character of the groups should be very high. Concentrate on this type of representative. It is natural that the United States should have a larger representation than Great Britain.

*Member from Japan:* The number should correspond to the type of problems discussed. One type of problem requires many experts. At this Conference we have discussed far too many problems, and therefore have needed an undue number of experts.

*Member from China:* In the future we should concentrate on one or two fields, such as political and cultural, and not spread out. This will make it possible to get better participants.

*Member from United States:* The education of some of the young people in our countries is an important matter. The British delegation has brought several of the student type. Should not other countries follow this policy?

*Member from Great Britain:* I have tried to classify the representatives here, and find that academic members form 37 per cent of the whole. I think the business men and politicians are not represented enough.

*Member from United States:* Every effort was made to increase the number of business men and men of affairs, but it was very difficult to get them even to visualize it. They have no idea of the significance of international affairs in business.

*Member from Australia:* We should leave this matter very elastic. It would be ridiculous to have as many representatives from Australia, Canada, etc., as from the United States.

*Member from Hawaii:* There should be enough members in each national group to furnish one representative to each round table. We are here for contacts and information and discussion, and we should have enough from each country to carry that out.

*Member from New Zealand:* I suggest that the council in each country consider the various interest groups in allocating its quota.

Agriculture should be represented, as well as manufacturing, commerce, public service, education, and labor. Steps should be taken to insure representation at least of each of these various groups.

*Member from United States:* There are a very large number of organizations in the United States that are deeply interested in international affairs, far more so than in any other country in the world. We had to have such things as missions and commercial interests represented.

*Member from United States:* Each national council must first know what the program is to be before it can intelligently build up its delegation.

*Member from Hawaii:* Are we not making a mistake in not inviting a large number of young men as visitors, who will later do the things we want done?

*Member from Canada:* I should suggest we have editors as observers.

*Member from China:* I would not like to see the Conference very much larger.

*Member from United States:* How do the Chinese and Japanese feel about the size of the groups?

*Member from Japan:* We have no objection to a large American group.

*Member from China:* Certain considerations must be given for the size of the American group. There are certain great interests to represent. A good portion of the financing of the Institute comes from American organizations.

*Member from Australia:* I think that the round tables were a little too large. I think it may be quite possible that smaller groups would get at our viewpoints better.

*Member from United States:* The academic man predominates because he is an expert in some specific field and he usually knows more about the problems of his specific job than anybody else. We need experts as a foundation for this Institute to provide the facts. I do not think that the academic men gave particularly academic expressions. Yesterday I listened to Mr. Mears at the Round Table on Immigration, and he stated very distinct facts to our Japanese friends, things that they should take home. But I myself think there are too many professors here.

*Member from United States:* It has been very interesting to me to note that frequently in these round tables when we have got into a conflict of opinion or into a haze, it was the outcome of a remark by an expert.

*Member from Great Britain:* From my point of view the most important part of the Conference has been the informal expression of opinion. I should not like to see the membership of the groups enlarged. It might make round-table discussions impossible.

*Member from United States:* In regard to size and character of the national group representations at the next Conference, the aim of the American group was to combine in one company of people a great many different elements. A third of the delegates might be regarded as experts in their particular line. We also made sure the delegates were representative of the different geographical areas of the United States. Third, we made sure they were representative of the different sections of population. Fourth, we tried to get people who would on their return be able to introduce better study programs into the universities, public bodies, and private organizations. We were weakest in representatives of the business men and labor organizations.

7. *What suggestions can be made for improving the procedure of the Conference?*

*Member from Japan:* We ought to concentrate on a few topics and not spread out as we have done. This would be of service both in choosing members and in the effective discussion at round tables.

*Member from United States:* It would be well to reduce the outside entertainments and receptions so that members would have more time in the afternoons for informal conferences, for recreation, and, for intimate acquaintance.

*Member from Canada:* I think that for succeeding conferences we need to define the function of the round table very clearly. It should develop its methods of collecting points of view on any given topic. Consideration should also be given to the topics of the round table. Should there be just one topic under discussion, or more than one? The university man, expert, or research man should keep his information on hand, and use it only when called for. In this way we could get farther and save a great deal of time in developing the points of view. This involves expert leadership of round tables. Courtesy has dominated the choice of leaders for round tables. I think the round table is so important that it ought to be led on a different basis than has been done this year. Leaders should bring out from the round tables material to be discussed in the forum.

*Member of Secretariat:* What do the members feel about the value of data papers and printed pamphlets?

*Member from United States:* They should be given to us long enough in advance of the Conference to study in preparation for the round-table discussions.

*Member from United States:* Had we been advised two months ago just what topics were to be discussed, we might have come with some particular data. If it is left until we arrive here, it is impossible to get posted on the program subjects.

*Member from United States:* The local committee drew up a program on the basis of correspondence and visitation by the Secretariat which it believed would be acceptable to the members of the Institute. They circulated it among the different groups four months ago with requests for criticism. Only one group sent in criticisms. Now it developed that when the groups came here, they found that they were not in perfect agreement with the local committee's program. They wished quite a different program, and proceeded to draw up a new one.

*Member from Japan:* I, for one, was sorry to see that the program was changed. Those who have the handicap of the language must be taken into consideration. We prepared for the Conference on the basis of the program that was circulated and which we accepted. We need some preparation. We must have more time to read the papers, so that I hope this will be taken into consideration before the next conference. Then the secretaries of the groups should get together and study beforehand some of the common problems. They should get acquainted with the personnel. I think in this Conference there was not sufficient time given to get acquainted. We must have more time to get together. I would suggest that one day a week should be set aside for this. This year we had to study even on Sunday.

*Member from United States:* Do you favor an extension of time of the Institute?

*Member from Japan:* Yes. Some are fortunate in being able to stay here three weeks, but some cannot stay as long.

*Member from Australia:* The date of the meeting is not altogether convenient for the Australian group. It comes in the winter, when the universities are in session. Business men cannot come at that time either. We must get away from here on the first steamer offering.

*Member from Great Britain:* I should say this Conference would be better if divided up into six round tables instead of four.

*Member from Japan:* I think we should not aim at solving too many problems at one conference. In that case we would have difficulty in getting the best people.

*Member from Canada:* The program ought to be made up ahead of time. It should be flexible, but the general ideas should be written down. The program this year showed lack of balance.

*Member from Great Britain:* Everybody should know in advance on what main lines this Conference is going to proceed. The Secretariat should confer with the national groups on this matter.

*Member from United States:* I want to put in a plea for a general public meeting. If some of the statements of Sir Frederick Whyte and Dr. Yui had been made public, it would have been far better for all concerned. I also suggest that the forums come in the morning, when we are not all tired and sleepy.

*Member from Great Britain:* The forum gives you the opportunity to have the members of the Conference together and to obtain a certain amount of information to be used in the discussion of the problems. I think the idea of giving information in round-table discussion is deadly. If the forum is to come after the round table, you must avoid the feeling that the question has been discussed.

*Member from United States:* We don't want people to tell us what to think in order that we may then be able to think.

*Member from Great Britain:* I think that this Institute would almost double its usefulness if we could have another week together now. I believe in three weeks' time we could do far more toward our end than we have done in a fortnight's time. Personally, I cannot keep up with the pace that we have been going. I think if we had a little more time to get together it would be of more benefit.

8. *What principles should govern the Institute in the inclusion of new political or racial units?*

*Member from Japan:* Should representatives from the states of Central and South America, and U.S.S.R. be invited to the Conference? What about Fiji, Samoa, and Borneo?

*Member of Central Committee:* An invitation was sent to the University of Mexico and also to the National Academy of Science in Russia, as well as to Dutch East Indies. None of these accepted.

*Member from Japan:* Shall we add Latin and Slav mentalities to these three types we already have present, namely, Chinese, Japanese, and Anglo-Saxon?

*Member from Great Britain:* I have felt very much the absence of Russia. Many things have been said which I would like very much to have had Russia answer or explain.

*Member from China:* With regard to Russia, we ought to give attention to grouping in terms of thought-life. One distinct factor that is missing here is Russia's viewpoint. It represents a new approach to life. I think next time we ought to get a representation from Russia; we shall not be able to get a comprehensive viewpoint otherwise.

*Member from United States:* The South American countries are apt to feel that they are left out of our problems, and it would be a help to them if they were included. At least Mexico, Chili, and Peru ought to be invited.

*Member from Great Britain:* We should include the main racial units that are in the Pacific: French, Latin-Americans, Dutch East Indies, and Russia. Were they all invited to attend this Institute?

*Member of Pacific Council:* We tried to get someone from Java, but they were not interested.

I hope Russia will be here with us next year.

We tried to get someone from Mexico, but had no response. The people in South America do not think of the Pacific. They think of relations with Europe rather than with the Pacific countries.

*Member from United States:* It seems to me we should make contact with some institution in Paris interested not only in Indo-China, but also in the French Pacific islands. If France, Netherlands, or Latin America were admitted, then of course we would have a further language question.

In that connection I should like to raise the question whether the Institute as a whole ought not to make a special appropriation to assist the oriental groups in bringing interpreters with them, if some of their able representatives did not speak English.

*Member from United States:* I do not think that those in South America are sufficiently interested in what is going on in the Pacific.

*Member from United States:* And yet they come more or less in contact with the Orient.

*Member from United States:* I think that the Institute would be well advised that it should not increase its representation at all. You will increase very largely not only the people who speak but the questions discussed, and I doubt if it will be possible to invite Russia. You will inevitably bring in another group of skilled diplomats. In my opinion it would not be advisable to include Russia.

*Member from United States:* I do not think that we can profitably discuss the problem of Manchuria without having the voice of Russia here.

*Member from United States:* Is there any danger that a Russian group would merely represent an agitating government attitude?

*Member from China:* Russia is now throwing out a tremendous challenge to the existing orders of life. How can we discuss these matters if we do not have her ideas fully represented?

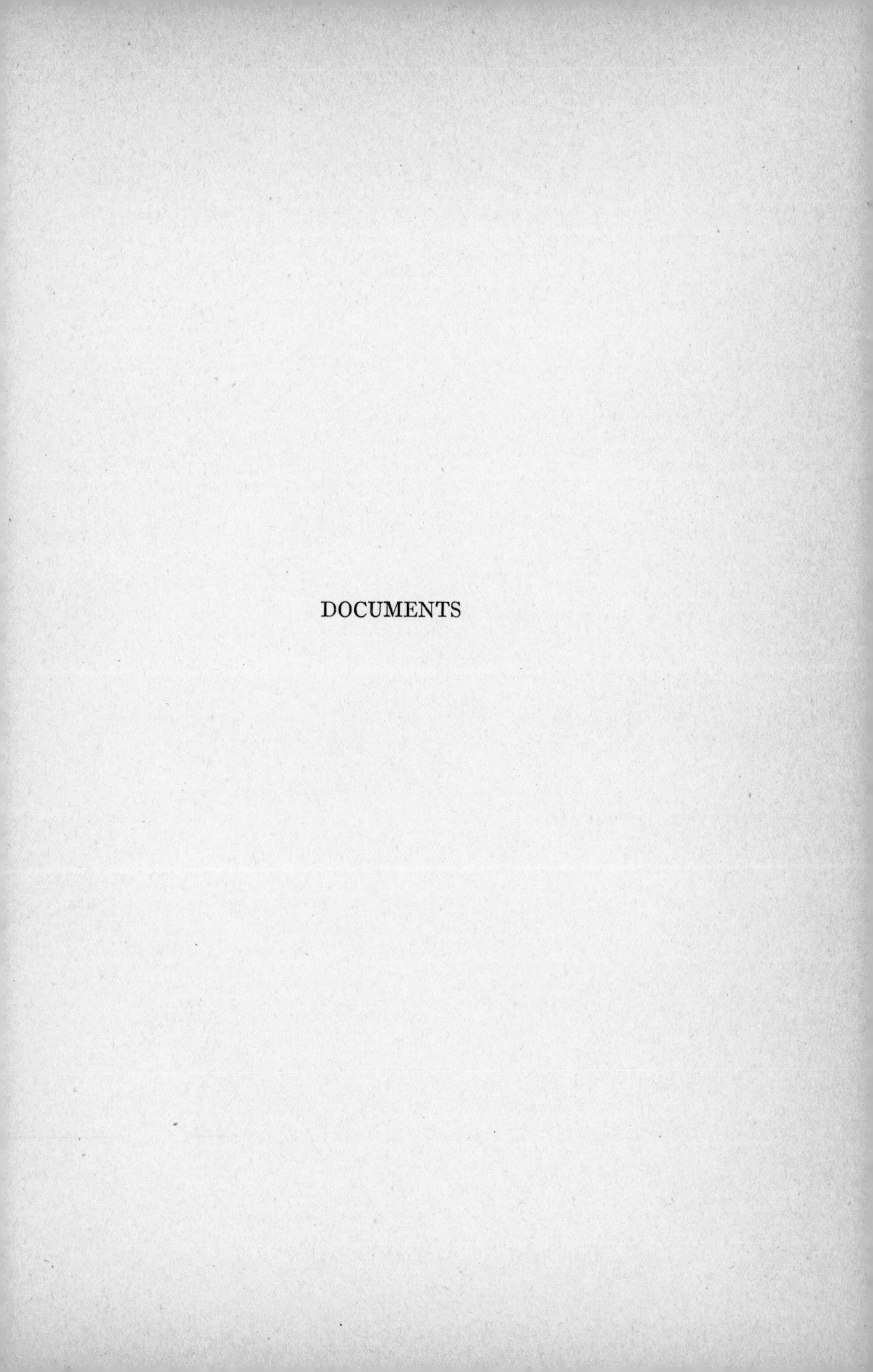

DOCUMENTS

# SECTION 1

# THE GEOGRAPHY OF THE PACIFIC

HERBERT E. GREGORY
Director, Bishop Museum, Honolulu

### I. TOPOGRAPHIC RELATIONS

The Pacific Ocean is a huge affair: it is long and wide and deep. From Bering Sea to Wilkes Land on the Antarctic Circle the distance is 9,300 miles, and along the equator the distance is 10,000 miles—two-fifths of the circumference of the earth—and more than three times the width of the Atlantic. These great stretches of water form the axes of an area comprising more than 55,000,000 square miles—the area of the United States is about 3,000,000 square miles. The Pacific is nearly twice the size of the Atlantic and greater in area than all the continents and islands combined. The volume of Pacific water is incomprehensibly great. If all the lands above sea-level—plains, plateaus, and mountain systems—were piled into the Pacific they would sink to the bottom and be submerged at a depth of about 12,000 feet. If the water were drained from the Pacific the descent from the present shore line to the floor of the deepest valley would be greater than the present ascent to the loftiest Himalayan peak.

In a geological sense this vast water-filled basin comprises two parts: (1) The Pacific continental border and associated continental islands; (2) oceanic islands which have no genetic relation to continental masses. The line separating these two parts extends from New Zealand past the Kermadecs, Tonga, and Samoa, and continues northward in an undetermined position. West of this line the islands, shoals, and intervening spaces have been structurally parts of larger land masses. They have been submerged and emerged, connected and disconnected, in various combinations at several periods during geologic time. They occupy a region of general crustal unrest.

East of this changing border of an Australian-Asiatic continent and extending nearly to the American shores is the true Pacific depression, a submerged region of plateaus and intervening broad valleys from which rise mountain masses with relatively small areal bases. The general arrangement is a floor at profound depth from which rise volcanic masses as individual mounds or combined to form ridges or long, narrow submarine highlands. Most of these peaks and ridges terminate below sea-level and are revealed only by soundings; some of them terminate above sea-level and stand as islands. But they are true oceanic islands; they have never been parts of the continents of Asia, Australia, and America. They are all volcanic masses with outer slopes descending steeply to great depths. Some of them retain their original form; others are much eroded, and still others have been worn down to submarine platforms on which grow coral reefs.

Unlike the western Pacific, the eastern Pacific has experienced relatively few changes. Its present depth and position of islands are essentially those of past geologic times. The evidence shows that most Polynesian oceanic islands have experienced uplift and subsidence at different times, at different rates, in different amounts, at different places. So far as known, the extreme range in oscillation is something like 1,200 feet, so that islands now separated by less than 500 feet of water may have been nearly or quite joined, but islands now separated by as much as 1,000 feet probably were not joined, and parts of the sea floor at greater depth doubtless have never felt the air. There is no geographic evidence for greatly enlarged islands, vanished archipelagoes, or "lost Pacific continents."

Associated with this twofold division of the Pacific and structurally dependent on it are equally great differences in the topography of the lands which form the eastern and western Pacific borders. Along the coast of the Americas the sea meets the land abruptly; deep water lies immediately off shore; coastal islands are rare and of little importance. Except for the artificial break at Panama the coast from Chiloe Island to Vancouver Island is a wall essentially continuous for nearly 7,000 miles. The Asiatic coast, in contrast, is fringed by closely spaced islands extending from Kamchatka through the Kurile, Japanese, and Nansei islands to Taiwan, thence through the Philippines, the Tulour Islands, and the Moluccas to Papua, Thursday Island, and down the Australian coast to Tasmania.

As compared with those bordering the Atlantic, the lands bordering the Pacific are difficult of access from the sea. The Atlantic is bordered by plains; the Pacific, by mountain ranges. Although the Pacific is nearly twice the size of the Atlantic, the amount of bordering land drained into the Pacific is only about one-fourth that drained into the Atlantic. Of North-American Pacific rivers only the Yukon, the Columbia, and the Colorado hold first rank. The rivers of Central America and South America contributary to the Pacific are small affairs chiefly of local interest. On the long line of coast from Cape Horn to Bering Sea only two indentations provide the requisites for a good harbor: protection for many ships and easy access to a productive back country. The great Pacific rivers of Asia, the Amur, the Hwang-ho, and the Yangtze-Kiang pile their waters into practically inclosed seas. The Australian rivers entering the Pacific are short and of small volume.

The distribution of land around the Pacific has still another bearing: it marks out feasible routes of plant, animal and human migration across and into the Pacific. At the north the land connections are close. Bering Strait is but 36 miles wide, and in past geological time may have been narrower and even closed. At many times its waters have been coated with continuous sheets of ice. Also the Commander Islands and the long chain of Aleutian Islands stand as a series of stepping stones between Asia and America. That these two northern routes are feasible and were many times used is demonstrated by the close affinities of the plant life, animal life, and human life of Siberia and Alaska. In fact it is probable that these north Pacific routes were used by the original ancestors of the native inhabitants of the whole Western Hemisphere. On the Asiatic coast the distribution of land favors migration, not only along the continental border, but along and among the islands which form the outer boundary of Okhotsk Sea, Japan Sea, Yellow Sea, and China Sea.

For the Pacific as a whole perhaps the most significant feature of land distribution is the extension of Asia southeastward through the Malay Peninsula and on through Sumatra, Java, Celebes, Ceram, Papua—five big islands associated with many small islands in such manner as to form nearly continuous land. And beyond Papua as far as Fiji the ocean is packed with islands. In essence this great region of Indonesia and Melanesia is a suburb of Asia. In age and composition its rocks are those of the continent; its animals and plants predominantly are those which now live or once lived on the larger land mass.

Human beings like those of the Asiatic continent have been living in this suburb doubtless since this form of animal life has been in existence. The earliest trace of human beings on earth is the fossil remains of a manlike creature which lived in Java some 600,000 years ago. It may well be that in Indo-China and adjoining islands originated the first groups of human beings that hunted animals, caught fish, cooked food, and built shelters, and that their descendants migrated to Malaya and Indonesia before Western Asia, Europe, and Africa were known. Even Australia, hanging pendant on the Java-Papua chain, offers no special difficulties of access from the north. At the present time the narrow Torres Strait is full of islands, and during the early days of human migration it is probable that Papua, Australia, and Tasmania were united. It seems not unlikely that before the last glacial period an explorer from southeast Asia, after a succession of short trips on logs or rafts, could reach Papua and proceed thence overland to Tasmania.

But the oceanic islands offered no facilities for migration. They mark out no route from anywhere to anywhere. They are small, wide spaced, irregularly distributed, and for plants and man to reach them involves exceptional conditions. Few of the plants and still fewer of the animals common to Asia and the Americas are found in the Polynesian islands, and it is doubtful if human beings saw them before Rome had extended her empire into Syria, Germania, Gaul, and Britain. But even these scattered islands are much more closely related to Asia than to America. Their plant and animal affinities are predominately Asiatic. The Pacific islands are associated with Asia in the same way that Great Britain, Iceland, Spitzbergen, and Nova Zembla are associated with Europe, and the West Indies with South America. In a geographic sense the Pacific is an Asiatic ocean. The remoteness of its connection with the Americas is an outstanding geographic feature.

### 2. CLIMATIC CONDITIONS

As a geographic factor in Pacific history climate ranks with topography. Not that temperature and humidity and winds determine the places where men may live; the human race has amply demonstrated its ability to work and to think, to raise families, and to provide necessities and comforts in all climates. Only the dog and the mosquito vie with man in their capacity for successful adjustment. The influence of climate arises from the fact that most important food plants give large yields only in climates which permit a relatively long growing season. Hence the wealth of the world's vegetation and the bulk of the world's population are found in the Tropics and along the tropical edges of the temperate zones.

For the Pacific region as a whole some of the fundamental climatic features are:

the difference in climate in the same latitudes on opposite sides of the ocean; the preponderant influence of the water as compared with land; the exceptional regularity of the wind system in the eastern and extreme southern Pacific; the presence of monsoons; and the essential uniformity of climate throughout Melanesia, Polynesia, and Micronesia. In the Pacific, readings on the thermometer have little significance; the character of the wind, the altitude above sea, and the nearness to the sea have much more meaning.

North of Latitude 50° the Asiatic side of the Pacific is much less hospitable than the American side. In northern Sakhalin only tiny fields of rape and barley grow, and those in particularly favorable places. In Kamchatka ordinary agriculture is not practiced. In corresponding latitudes, British Columbia and southern Alaska boast of their agricultural possibilities and of their delightful climate. The Japanese island of Hokkaido, which has the latitude position of Southern Oregon, has the climate of British Columbia or Massachusetts. The islands of Hondo and Kyushu, on which most of the Japanese live, correspond in latitude to northern and to southern California, but have the climate of Washington and Oregon.

As the air over oceans never becomes so warm or so cold as air over land, the islands of the Pacific and much of the bordering coast are characterized by moderate temperatures and absence of sudden great changes. No part of the Pacific border from Sakhalin to Tasmania or from Alaska to southern Chile experiences the abrupt change from heat to cold, from wet to dry, common to the interior of continents. For all the oceanic and continental islands within the vast area between the Americas and the Philippines or Sumatra the mean annual temperature varies little from 70°; the difference between the warmest and the coldest month being about 10.° Humidity rather than the heat is the disagreeable feature of such islands as Papua, just as almost continuous cloudiness rather than cold makes the climate of the Aleutian Islands unattractive.

The prevailing winds of the Pacific, like those of other parts of the earth, are in general "westerlies" between latitudes 28° and 60° on both sides of the equator and southeast or northeast trade winds between latitudes 28° N. and 28° south. The westerlies in the North Pacific lie outside the region of inhabited oceanic islands, but they strongly affect the coasts of North America. Likewise in the South Pacific the westerlies, the "roaring forties" of sailor lore, lie beyond most inhabited lands. But in the South Island of New Zealand days without strong west winds are rare.

Over the inhabited Pacific as a whole the trade winds prevail. They characterize the climate of Polynesia, Melanesia, and Micronesia, and of two-thirds of Australia. Some islands have no other winds. Farther west in Idonesia and Southeast Asia the trades are interrupted or even replaced by monsoons. The most significant effect of trade winds is the uneven distribution of rainfall. Blowing across low islands, no rain is dropped, and many atolls and reefs lack the fresh water necessary to support life. Where the trade winds cross high islands or high edges of continents rain is dropped in abundance on the windward side but is deficient on the leeward side. Thus islands in the trade-wind belt, like Hawaii, the Marquesas, and Fiji, have a "wet side" and a "dry side." On continental areas this feature is emphasized. In the belt of the northeast trades, the gulf coast of Mexico is flooded with rain while Lower California has little. In the southeast trades the Amazon Valley and the Queensland coast are soaked, while on the Peruvian-Chilean coast the amount of rainfall is measured in fractions of an inch, and in West Australia the mining centers are supplied with water drawn from the end of a pipe 350 miles long. The Dutch merchant explorers made maps and wrote books about Australia a century before Captain Cook entered the Pacific. But their descriptions concern the northern, western, and southern coasts, which they found "barren" and of doubtful value for settlement. Captain Cook, sailing from New Zealand, found rich southeastern Australia. It may be that Australia is English rather than Dutch because of the happy circumstances which brought Cook to the windward side instead of the lee side of a land mass in the trade-wind belt. Throughout the whole trade-wind belt the rainfall of islands and continental borders is such that deserts are associated with areas too rainy for agricultural use.

### 3. SOIL

Soil, like climate and topography, is a prominent geographic factor. The composition, texture, and extent of soil, combined with climate, determines the areas suitable for high-grade agriculture, and therefore has much to do with the distribution and density of the human population. The defects of climate can be remedied by irrigation and hothouse treatment and the defects of soil by artificial fertilization, but these processes are only supplementary aids to original favorable conditions. Irrigation does not reclaim deserts; it makes parts of them useful. In the United States the area possible to irrigate compared with that needing irrigation is a plow furrow in a twenty-acre lot. Both large-scale irrigation and extensive fertilization are beyond the reach of primitive man; they are features of highly developed civilization.

For the Pacific region, the soils of continental areas, including the islands of Indonesia and Melanesia, which were once parts of the Asiatic continent, are of all known varieties. The choicest soils are the flood plains and valley sides of rivers, and the greatest flood plains support the greatest population. In an agricultural sense California is the San Joaquin and Sacramento valleys; agriculture in Japan, Australia, and New Zealand is primarily in the valleys heading in the mountains not far from the coast. In Manchuria 12,000,000 people live on the flood plains of the Liao and Singora rivers, and in China a population equal to that of the United States makes its home on the deltaic plain of the Hwang Ho and the Yangtze-Kiang.

The Pacific oceanic islands have but two kinds of soil: decomposed basalt (lava) and decomposed limestone, formed of ground-up and weathered organisms associated with coral reefs. The lava soils correspond to those of the wheat belt of Washington and Idaho; the limestone soils resemble those of Kentucky and Tennessee.

### 4. FLORA AND FAUNA

The native fauna and flora of the Pacific region is interesting in itself but its chief geographic interest lies in the abundance and character of the plants and animals suitable as food for the first settlers. In this respect the Pacific coasts of North America and of Asia were peculiarly favored. Wild cereals, fruits, and nuts were abundant; also wild animals suitable for food. Likewise Papua, Australia, Indonesia, the Philippines, and most of Melanesia were supplied with native foods in quantities ample for considerable populations. But the indigenous flora of Polynesia includes little suitable for food, and the native land fauna lacks almost everything.

### 5. THE FIRST MIGRATIONS

In a broad sense this outline of distribution of land, of climate, soil, and food supply is believed to picture the Pacific before the coming of man. Guided and perhaps controlled by these geographic factors, groups of human beings have made their way into and beyond the Pacific Ocean. Individuals, families, and tribes have followed each other in successive waves from some area in Southeast Asia northward to Bering Sea and to America; eastward to Samoa, Hawaii, Mangareva, and to remote Easter Island, and southward to Tasmania and New Zealand. Traditional and historical records for any part of the Pacific prior to about 500 B.C. are vague and confusing; but there is little doubt that some migrations had occurred before the Glacial Age, and it is highly probable that for the past 10,000 years all the Pacific borders, and all the islands of Malaya, Indonesia, and parts of Melanesia and of Micronesia have been occupied by man. Granting sufficient time, the settlement of those parts of the Pacific region offered no great difficulties. Except for short sea routes between near-lying islands, there was land to walk on and food to be had along the way.

But the settlement of eastern Micronesia and of all Polynesia was quite another undertaking. The obstacles seem unsurmountable. On a possible route from the Philippines to Hawaii via Caroline and Marshall islands, the spacing of feasible landing places, roughly, is 400 miles, 300 miles, 210 miles, 60, 70, 50, 80, 120, 130, 240, 420, 110, 1,900 miles. Along the southern route to Tahiti, through Melanesia, the landings east of the New Hebrides are spaced at 480, 90, 270, 300, 480, 180, 490 miles. Proceeding on this route to the Marquesas involves stretches of water 500 miles wide, and if the route diverges at Rarotonga the distances are even greater. Easter Island lies 2,500 miles from Rapa across a barren sea. The route from Samoa to Hawaii is 2,200 miles, with a practical stopping-place at 1,000 miles. From Tahiti to Hawaii the distance is 2,400 miles with possible stopping-places at 500 miles and 1,000 miles. The nearest landing place to Hawaii is more than 800 miles away. To reach these islands at all when the means of transport was an outrigger canoe and when even the existence of the islands was unknown seems beyond the range of human possibilities.

Even for modern navigators the finding of an uncharted island in the Pacific is no slight task. Magellan (1519–20) sailed across the Pacific, finding only two little islands in a distance of 9,000 miles. In a cruise from South America, Loyasa (1525–27) seems to have passed through Polynesia and Melanesia without seeing any islands at all. In 1590 (?) Mendano de Negra sailed from Peru to Solomon Islands (7,000 miles), sighting only one island en route. On a second two-years' voyage planned as an island-hunting expedition he found the Marquesas, and, 5,000 miles farther on, the Santa Cruz Islands. Continuing from Santa Cruz to the Philippines (4,000 miles), his pilot, Quiros, saw one other island. New Caledonia, a high mountainous island 250 miles long, was seen by Europeans only after about twenty expeditions had traversed that general region. Ships had been going back and forth across the northern Pacific for 200 years before any part of the 1,100-mile-long Hawaiian chain was made known to Europeans, and the smaller islands northwest of Niihau were first sighted by foreigners one at a time during the period 1786–1859. In coming north from Atiu to Kauai, Captain Cook visited Christmas Island but did not see Suvarov, Manuhiki, Starbuck, Malden, and Fanning islands, which lay almost directly in his course. After 250 years of navigation, only about half the Polynesian islands had been visited by Europeans or Americans. Though lying near the path of sailing ships, the most important of the Caroline Islands—Truk, Ponape, and Kusaie—probably were not visited by white men until the first quarter of the nineteenth century, 300 years after Magellan had sailed along their edge. For many islands the first landing dates from 1800 to 1860, and the first account of some islands was given to the world after 1875. The latest edition of hydrographic charts shows the location of islands which probably do not exist, and in the large expanse of so far poorly charted sea doubtless other islands remain to be found.

And after the islands had been found the task of the Polynesian pioneers was not finished. They found the natural conditions in their new home favorable for small groups living under primitive conditions, but unfavorable for a large population and for the development of social and political life. They could support themselves by fishing, hunting birds, and gathering roots and seeds. But the food supply was markedly deficient in kind and amount. The islands were less well supplied with food plants than any other part of the world except the Arctics, and in no other part of the world were there originally so few animals useful to man. Sea food was the one abundant article of diet. Polynesia lacked the rice, coconut, breadfruit, taro, and yams of the Asiatic region and the corn, potato, and fruits of the American continents. It also lacked cattle, swine, sheep, deer, and other wild animals so abundant elsewhere.

But these pioneers seemed determined to make Polynesia a home for themselves and their children. They introduced from islands farther west the coconut, the taro, the breadfruit, bananas, and sweet potatoes and the paper mulberry for making cloth, and with only wood and stone tools and implements, felled trees, built boats and houses, made terraced fields and irrigation ditches, and walled fish ponds. It is worthy of note that all Polynesian islands now known had been permanently settled or settled and abandoned by these agriculturists before the coming of Europeans. Even such tiny volcanic masses as Necker and Nihoa islands were occupied. When Europeans came to the Pacific the most desirable valleys and shores were thickly settled, and the indigenous edible plants and animals had been largely replaced by introduced foods. In view of the difficulties of settlement it need occasion no surprise to find that Polynesia was the last part of the Pacific, and probably the last large area on the earth's surface, to be colonized.

That some islands east and north of Fiji were visited by a few stray humans as early as 1,000 B.C. is not an unreasonable assumption, though unsupported by evidence, but researches of the past decade make it increasingly clear that Polynesian civilization developed since the beginning of the Christian Era. And it is interesting to note that the migratory waves into Polynesia during the eleventh, twelfth, and thirteenth centuries are coincident with the movements which brought the Huns into Europe, the Moslems to India, and spread the Empire of Kublai Khan over most of

Asia. It may be that these migrations and others of that period in Europe, Africa, and South America had a common cause.

### 6. DISTRIBUTION OF POPULATION

From the days of first settlement the Pacific populations along the Asiatic border have been increasing slowly and intermittently in the region north of the Japan Sea, rapidly and consistently along the coastal belt from Hondo to Malaya and in Indonesia. Most of the increase probably is natural; it has been little affected by immigration or emigration. On the North American borders, also in Australia and New Zealand, the increase is largely the result of immigration. In Polynesia, Melanesia, and Micronesia there has been a large net decrease.

The migration of alien races to the Pacific produced different results in different places. In Indonesia the native population was little affected. They were capable agriculturists who, under European leadership, continued to produce all they needed for themselves and then produced more for the use of their peaceable conquerors. In the Philippines 250 years of Spanish occupation made few fundamental changes. A few thousand soldiers, officials, and priests could neither kill off nor absorb 10,000,000 natives. In Australia, North America, and South America the natives were variously disposed of as incumbrances on desirable lands. In New Zealand the English recognized their equals and took them into partnership. The other Pacific islands were treated by the immigrants as areas for religious and commercial exploitation, with little regard for the natives.

The results of natural increase and migrations, the wiping out and building up of races during the past 300 years, have brought about the following situation: on the Asiatic coast the islands of Hondo and Kyushu in Japan, Korea, all of southeastern China, Indo-China, and Malaya have about all the people that the geographic conditions permit; but the island of Hokkaido, and all eastern Siberia, Manchuria, and perhaps Mongolia are underpopulated; of the Indonesian islands, Java, the size of England or of New York State, with the population of England and nearly four times the population of New York, including all its cities, seems amply supplied, but Borneo and the Celebes are not; Borneo, four and a half times the size of England or Java, has one-eighteenth of their population, and Celebes one and a half times their size, only one-thirteenth of their population. Papua, in the latitude of Java, Ceylon, and Venezuela, is twice the size of New Zealand and considerably larger than Japan or California; the population is only about twice that of Hawaii. The population of some hundreds of smaller islands in Polynesia, Melanesia, and Micronesia ranges from one to three a square mile, and many islands formerly settled no longer are inhabited.

The Pacific coast states of North America and South America, also Australia, are obviously underpopulated; all of them are advertising for settlers. There is no question but that large areas of sparsely settled land lie within and around the Pacific; but naturally not all parts are capable of supporting the dense populations of India or Holland. Australia is the size of the United States, but the comparison ends with about that statement. Four-fifths of the continent promises little. The humidity and rainfall of Papua and Borneo are unfavorable for the full utilization of its enormous resources, and the extreme ruggedness of central New Caledonia limits the extent of agricultural development. But the proportion of arable and grazing land on those islands and on the larger islands of Indonesia is fully that of Japan, and an additional 50,000,000 people would still leave them much less crowded than is Java.

If topography, climate, and soil measure the possible degree of settlement, all the Pacific islands will witness much increased population, for their commercial possibilities are great. That the cultivation of sugar-cane and pineapples and rubber in the Pacific islands is profitable needs no further demonstration, even though carried on in but a few places. But it is not so commonly known that the experimental plants of corn and cotton show remarkable yields in Melanesian islands and that large areas suitable for rice are available. The cultivation of sago, sisal, cocoa, coffee, tobacco, sweet potato, and vanilla is still in the hands of amateurs. California gets its bananas through New Orleans. Canned fish from Washington and Alaska find ready sale throughout Polynesia. Copra is the only export of many islands, but it is handled in such an unbusinesslike manner that the industry is considered speculative, and this in the face of an unsatisfied demand for vegetable oils. Fortunately, crops in Pacific islands do not compete for space. Coconuts grow best on land otherwise of little use. Sugar-cane lands are not fruit lands, and grazing lands are not adapted for agriculture.

Hawaii has shown what can be done with Pacific tropical islands. The territory has a population of 328,000, and the annual value of its agricultural exports exceeds $100,000,000. This is twice the population of any other island group in Polynesia, Melanesia, and Micronesia, and five times the value of agricultural exports from all the hundreds of islands in those regions, but nobody thinks the limit has been reached in either population or agricultural production. The cattle ranches at Haleakala and Kohala are large and profitable. But Hawaii has no geographic advantages not possessed by the Marquesas, Tahiti, Fiji, New Hebrides, New Caledonia, the Marianas, and many other island groups. The difference is that Hawaii has been intelligently developed; the others have not. Money has been poured into agricultural experiments and into studies of transportation and marketing. In a few other islands the same procedure has been followed in a half-hearted way, but in most Pacific islands commerce rests on hope that small inducements will lead the natives to bring in something which may be sold at a profit. Many Pacific islands have witnessed a decline in agriculture and industry during the past three hundred years. The native plantations of taro, breadfruit, and sweet potatoes, are overgrown with jungle, and the fish ponds are filled with mud.

Though discovered, mapped, and tentatively settled by the Dutch, Australia was annexed by England on the theory of "non-use." If this principle still holds in international law, much of Australia and most of the French and English Pacific islands are still available for any nation which cares to annex and develop them.

But can the white man live in the tropics? Can bananas grow in Norway? Can polar bears live in Samoa? As a matter of fact, some millions of white men do live there—in the West Indies, Central America, Brazil, Queensland, and Hawaii—and probably most white men could live there if they wanted to. It is an interesting question in physiology, but geographically has little meaning. With the development of natural resources in mind, the question is rather, Can the human race thrive in the tropics? The answer is easy. About half of the human race now live there, and from the tropics have come a goodly share of the world's inventions, literature, art, and religious thought. The essence of agricultural practice is to place a plant in its most congenial environment; perhaps the solution of some race problems lies in that same direction.

For the Pacific there is sufficient variety of geographic environment to provide favorable conditions for people of different tastes and occupations, and it seems not unlikely that if all the Pacific lands were available for all Pacific people, the population could be so distributed as to obviate overcrowding for many generations to come.

The progressive depopulation of the Pacific islands presents an important problem. Tropical agriculture, stock-raising, fishing, and mining, call for laborers. Progress is prohibited unless the working population is increased. "White-collar men" seem to come of themselves, but field labor must be supplied. Reinforcements must come, either by safeguarding and developing the native races or by bringing in alien races. At present the native labor is being replaced by Asiatic immigration—Japanese, Chinese, Malay, Hindu. The approximate figures are these:

POLYNESIA

| | | |
|---|---|---|
| Natives, 1870 | 690,000 | |
| Natives, 1920 | 200,000 | |
| Whites, 1920 | 37,000 | (exclusive of New Zealand) |
| Asiatics, 1920 | 145,000 | |

Thus in 50 years the native population of Polynesia has decreased about 70 per cent. At present the Asiatics about equal the natives and greatly outnumber the whites, except in New Zealand. The total white population of Polynesia, excluding New Zealand and Hawaii, is only about 2,000.

MELANESIA

| | |
|---|---|
| Natives, 1870 | 3,060,000 |
| Natives, 1920 | 1,020,000 |
| Whites, 1920 | 28,000 |
| Asiatics, 1920 | 66,000 |

Thus the native population of Melanesia has decreased 66 per cent in 50 years. At present the Asiatics outnumber the whites more than two to one.

MICRONESIA

| | |
|---|---|
| Natives, 1870 | 273,000 |
| Natives, 1920 | 91,000 |
| Whites, 1920 | 360 |
| Asiatics, 1920 | 13,000 |

Thus, during 50 years the native population decreased about 65 per cent. In 1925 there were only 66 whites among the total population of 56,293 individuals.

Indonesia tells another story. In 50 years its native population *increased* about 35 per cent. These increasing millions of Indonesians and Asiatics occupy territory immediately adjoining the relatively empty Australia. But even here there are more than six times as many Asiatics as whites.

The Chinese hold a strong position in Samoa, the Society Islands, and the Marquesas. It seems not unlikely that the Indo-Chinese in New Calendonia, the Hindus in Fiji, and the Japanese in Hawaii will determine the future cultural tone of those islands. If the native population continues to decrease and the Asiatics continue to fill their places, the Pacific islands are destined to become racially, as well as geographically, an appendix to Asia. This tendency may be economically desirable—perhaps it is inevitable. But I sometimes wonder if the failure to make much of native labor is the result of intelligent vision or of a demand for immediate profits.

The Pacific is fairly bristling with geographic problems, but food and population stand first in order of importance. That the unoccupied lands will be occupied and the vast potential resources developed goes without saying. Historically the settlement of desirable new lands has been accompanied by national and racial friction. For the Pacific, it is my belief that a knowledge of the geographic facts and their intelligent interpretation will go far toward warding off this misfortune.

## SECTION 2

## RACES OF THE PACIFIC

P. H. BUCK (Te Rangihiroa)
Formerly Director of Maori Hygiene

Professor Gregory has dealt with the geography of the Pacific. He has pointed out the various land connections that existed and the chains of closely studded islands that formed possible routes from Asia to North America across the Behring Straits and from Asia to Australia and out into the Pacific as far as the Fiji Group.

If we accept the theory that man originated in Central Asia and was driven out by climatic changes, we can imagine various waves of people spreading out from a common center. The weakest and the most primitive were the first to go. Though at present the oldest geological traces of man are to be found in southern Britain and Southwestern Europe, we are concerned in the ethnic waves that passed to the East.

One of the most primitive races of man, the Tasmanians, passed from the continent of Asia at its southeastern corner, along the chain of large islands to Australia, and finally halted in its wanderings on what is now the island of Tasmania, to the south of Victoria. Another primitive race, the Australian aboriginal, followed the same route from Asia and peopled the island continent of Australia. Yet another primitive people, the Negrittos, are found in the Andaman Islands and in isolated groups in the forest fastnesses by the wayside in the Malay Peninsula, some of the islands of Indonesia and in New Guinea.

Oceanic negroids appear in the Pacific area in two divisions: the Papuans of New Guinea and the Melanesians in the large island groups that lie to the east of New Guinea. The Melanesians occupy the groups known as Melanesia, the Black Islands. They are a black or dark-skinned race with negroid physical characteristics and woolly hair. Owing, as Dr. Gregory has pointed out, to the easy water stages between the island masses, they reached as far as the Fijis. There they halted. The open Pacific lay before them and formed a barrier to further progress toward the east.

In the large islands of Indonesia, besides remnants of the Negrittos and Papuans, we have the advent of two other racial elements. One of these was of Mongoloid origin and is now known as the Malays. They are short-headed. The other element, which are long-headed, were termed Indonesians by the anthropologists who first described them. The races of Indonesia consist of various blends of Negritto, Papuan, Malayan, and Indonesian.

The Pacific coast of Asia is peopled by the great Mongoloid division of mankind who have absorbed various racial elements in the course of time. Japan was peopled by the Ainu, of Caucasian stock. The Mongoloid waves which subsequently occupied Japan absorbed to a large extent the original inhabitants. The Japanese thus have Caucasian blood in their veins.

The two Americas were peopled by Mongoloid waves which crossed from Asia by the Behring Straits route referred to by Dr. Gregory. They extended throughout the length and breadth of the land. As is to be expected, the most primitive type was pushed down to the most remote part, the southern point of Tierra del Fuego.

Here briefly we have the human setting of the Pacific land boundaries before the advent of Western civilization. The early peoples who framed the Pacific were, practically speaking, pedestrians. With the exception of the Melanesians, who crossed ocean ditches, they *walked* to their destinations.

The last part to be settled by man was the true Pacific, the many remote isles set in the vast expanse of ocean known as Polynesia. The reason is not far to seek. Pedestrians could not get there. These islands awaited the coming of a race that could not only invent or adopt a form of ocean transport, but that had the courage to venture out on unknown depths and across vast expanses of speckless sea.

The race with the necessary initiative and courage was bred from a Caucasian wave that, instead of following the main route of their stock into Europe, were deflected to the East. The Proto-Polynesians somewhere about Southeast Asia or Indonesia came in contact with people of Mongoloid stock. The resulting Polynesian thus inherits physical characteristics in varying degree from his Caucasian and Mongoloid ancestors. When he left the Asiatic continent he became a seafarer. He invented or utilized the single-outrigger canoe to serve as transport in the great adventure that lay before him.

Somewhere about the beginning of the Christian Era he tackled the problem of the Pacific as it then existed. There were two routes open to him; the southern route along the north coast of New Guinea or the northern route through Micronesia. Micronesia consists of the groups of small islands that lie north of the New Guinea area and includes the Marianas, Carolines, and Marshall Islands. As over 90 per cent of the native population of these islands are Polynesians, it seems likely that the northern route was the one followed.

With an empirical knowledge of the stars, winds, currents and seasons, obtained no doubt by many trials and losses, the Polynesian migrators set out to conquer the Pacific. The Samoan group was reached and formed a distributing center to the surrounding islands. The Fijis were reached, and tradition abounds with struggles against a black-skinned race.

From Samoa exploring expeditions were made to the east and the Society group was reached and settled. Tahiti and Raiatea in this group formed another distributing center. From here successive waves passed to the east through the Tuamotu, Marquesas, and Austral groups, and on as far as Easter Island. Expeditions sailed to the north and colonized the Hawaii group. New Zealand in the southwest was discovered in the tenth century, and the famous, "Fleet," made the final settlement in the fourteenth century.

The foregoing is a brief outline of the colonization of Polynesia where a tract of ocean roughly 4,000 miles by 5,000 was explored by a Stone Age people in outrigger canoes dubbed out with stone adzes. To modern man, accustomed to the luxury of ocean liners, it is difficult to stress sufficiently the wonder and glory of this achievement. The Phoenicians, who bear the palm of ancient navigation, had metals, and their voyages were mostly conducted in the land-locked Mediterranean. The Vikings hugged the coast of Europe. Both Phoenician and Viking had metals. In the seventh century European navigation had gone a few miles down the African coast. At the same period Hui-terangiora, in his canoe, "Te Ivi-o-atea," had sailed to the region south of Rapa in the Austral group and seen bull kelp, icebergs, sea lions, and "a sea covered with white material like arrow-root."

The romance of the bare recital given lies in the traditional narratives handed down by different branches of the race. The Polynesians had no written language, but their traditional lore was orally learnt in special courses of instruction given by learned men to the sons of chiefs and priests. Pride of race and family prestige rendered a knowledge of ancient lore an absolute necessity. Thus there are rich fields of information still available in the islands of Polynesia.

Many voyages were undertaken for the pure love of adventure. After discovery and settlement, voyages were still made to keep up a connection with the nearer home lands. Thus voyages were often made between Hawaii and Tahiti in the Society group, a distance of over 2,000 miles. The canoes set out from the channel between Kahoolawe and Maui and sailed south by keeping Hokupa, the north star, behind them. When TePiko-o-Wakea, the mid-point of space, was reached, Hoku-pa sank into the sea behind. They were in the region of the Equator. The star Newe was then taken as the southern guiding star, and finally Tahiti was reached. On returning, they took the starboard tack against the southeast trades, and thus had the wind abeam. After crossing the line, the north star was picked up again. The problem, however, was that as they had got to the East by taking the starboard tack, how were they to find Hawaii, which lay to the west? They solved the problem as the masters of sailing vessels did centuries after before accurate chronometers enabled them to take a correct longitude. They sailed on until the north star was judged to be the same height above the horizon as it was when observed in Hawaii. Then they turned west and sailed down on the same latitude. Originally, the height of the star must have been judged by eye. Some far-seeing navigator, however, invented a primitive sextant out of a calabash. The top of the calabash was cut off with a level rim in the form of a bowl. Some distance below the rim four holes at right angles were bored through on the same level. To make an observation, the calabash was filled with water to the level of the lower edge of the holes. The eye was applied to one of the holes, and the observer glanced upward over the edge of rim above the opposite hole. The instrument had to be held level or the water spilled through one of the holes. When the north star could be seen on the edge of the far rim of the calabash the bow of the canoe was turned to the west and the canoe sailed down to Hawaii. Admiral Rodman, of the United States Navy, obtained one of these calabashes and had the angle between the water-level and the line from the hole to the far rim measured. The angle was 19 degrees, and Hawaii is on the 19th degree of latitude, north. Thus, as the Admiral said, they had an instrument of mathematical accuracy. The picture of a brown-skinned Polynesian navigator in an outrigger canoe which has sailed 2,000 miles, taking a shot at the north star through a hole in a calabash, must surely intrigue the imagination and arouse our admiration.

New Zealand was discovered by Kupe in the tenth century. He returned to Tahiti, and not only told the tale of his discovery but gave the sailing directions by which it might be reached from Tahiti. The right season of the year was that known as Tatau-uru-ora, which roughly corresponds with November. The date was the Orongonui, which is the twenty-eighth of the Maori lunar month. The bow of the canoe was to be directed a little to the left of the setting sun. These sailing directions have since been checked by civilized man on a modern chart. The southeast trades are steadiest in November and December. In this season, if a course is set from Tahiti of about a point to the left of the setting sun, the vessel will make New Zealand somewhere on the long stretch of coast that lies between the north and east Capes of the North Island. The historic "Fleet" in the fourteenth century made its landfall on this stretch of coast at Whangaparaoa, near Cape Runaway, by following Kupe's directions that had been orally handed down for four centuries. Red is the color of chieftainship. The scarlet blossoms of the Christmas trees (*Metrosideroo tomentosa*) that bloom throughout December along the coast line gave them a chiefly welcome to their new home.

The colonizing canoes sailed down to New Zealand on the port tack with the southeast trade abeam. In addition to sail, paddles were used. Crews were selected from men who were "stout of shoulder to bear the strain of the deep-sea paddle." Chants used on the voyage have been handed down and preserved in tribal narrative. Such a one is that which comes down from the Aotea canoe that made the voyage to New Zealand in 1350 A.D.

> Aotea is the canoe,
> Turi is the chief,
> Te Roku-o-whiti is the paddle!
> Behold my paddle!
> It is laid by the canoe-side,
> Held close to the canoe-side.
> Now it is raised on high—the paddle!
> Poised for the plunge—the paddle!
> Now we leap forward!
>
> Behold my paddle, Te Roku-o-whiti.
> See how it flies and flashes,
> It quivers like a bird's wing
> This paddle of mine.
> Ah the outward lift and the dashing,
> The quick thrust in and the backward sweep,
> The swishing, the swirling eddies,
> The foaming white wake
> And the spray which flies from my paddle!

The interesting feature of the voyages is the psychology of the navigators. They had no fear of the sea. The sea gave them food. It was their friend. There must also have developed the idea that there were always islands to be found in the Pacific. To this was added the spirit of pure adventure. Thus, when a voyager was lost, the disaster was regarded as due to his own fault in not judging the season or reading the stars aright. The discovery of a new island gave *kudos* to the discoverer. It was metaphorically alluded to as a fish that had been fished up out of the depths of the unknown. To every race has been given the love of home. The small island of Aitutaki in the Cook group is, according to myth, tied to the bottom of the sea by a vine. The idea of the fish and the knotted vine is thus brought out in the following incantation.

Within the circle of the sea,
It holds a fish of note,
It holds a porpoise,
It holds a whale,
It holds a fish which reaches to the heavens,
It holds a fish o'er which the rainbow arches,
Held in the immensity of ocean.
It is my land!

The incidents described give some small idea of the spirit of the Polynesian race. They were the super-Vikings of the Pacific. They were making long sea voyages when Europe dared not lose sight of land. I have dealt at greater length with this people because the Institute is meeting on an island set in the Pacific, an island discovered and settled by a branch of the Polynesian race.

The Polynesian, after his first contact with Western culture, passed through a period of trial and darkness. Some of the branches will never see the rising of the sun of race prosperity. Others will. I understand that the object of this Institute is to help all races of the Pacific, whether great or small, to pass through the darkness of ignorance and prejudice that ends in war to the light of a better mutual understanding and respect that will end in an abiding peace. We can thus share in the hope expressed by the tattooed Maori sentinel as he stood in the watch tower of his cliff-girt fort when he awaited the coming of the dawn that would end his vigil and sang into the gloom of night:

Oh soldiers of the Fort
Arise lest ye go down to death.
High up, high up, the thundering surf
On Harihari's cliffs resounds,
And loud the wailing sea
Beats on the Mokau coast.
But here am I, on guard,
Watching, seeking, peering,
As on those rugged rocks
The sea-hawk sits
And watches for his prey.

Soon will the Sun
Rise flaming o'er the world!

## SECTION 3

## TARIFF AUTONOMY AND ITS EXERCISE

MINGCHIEN JOSHUA BAU, M.A., Ph.D.
Professor of Political Science, Peking National Normal University and
Peking National College of Law and Politics

The first outstanding issue between China and the interested powers is tariff autonomy.

In international law, as an attribute of sovereignty, every state is free to regulate its own tariff rates on exports and imports and to administer customs in accordance with its own legislation. And this right is presumed to be inherent in the sovereignty of a state, regardless of its standing or power.

China, however, is the leading exception to this general practice. She is the only great state of the world that does not enjoy the liberty of regulating and administering her own tariff.

The origin of the tariff restrictions dates back to the Opium War of 1839–42. Prior to 1842 China enjoyed autonomy in arranging her own tariff matters. However, after the deplorable war, when China was defeated, England denied her tariff autonomy and imposed upon her a uniform tariff rate. Article X of the Treaty of Nanking, August 29, 1842, stipulated:

> His Majesty the Emperor of China agrees to establish at all the ports which are, by Article II of this treaty, to be thrown open for the resort of British merchants, a fair and regular tariff of export and import customs and other dues, which tariff shall be publicly notified and promulgated for general information. And the Emperor further engages that when British merchandise shall have once paid at any of the said ports the regulated customs and dues, agreeable to the tariff to be hereafter fixed, such merchandise may be conveyed by Chinese merchants to any province or city in the interior of the Empire of China, on paying a further amount as transit duties, which shall not exceed ——— per cent on the tariff value of such goods.[1]

In pursuance of this provision, in the supplementary treaty of October 8, 1843, the tariff of import and export duties was agreed to be 5 per cent ad valorem except in some instances when the rate went up as high as 10 per cent.[2] In the subsequent American treaty of July 3, 1844,[3] and the French treaty of October 24, 1844,[4] there was attached in each case a tariff of duties. By the conclusion of other treaties and the operation of the most-favored-nation clauses, the privilege of the tariff convention, except as otherwise specifically and expressly stipulated, was extended to the other powers that entered into treaty relations with China.

[1] Hertslet's *China Treaties,* I, No. 1, 10, footnote.

[2] *State Papers,* XXXI, 132, 141 ff.

[3] *State Papers,* XXXII, 791 ff.

[4] Hertslet's *China Treaties,* I, No. 1, 10.

Tracing the origin of her servitude in tariff matters, it is evident that China did not relinquish her tariff autonomy of her own accord, but was deprived of it, against her will, by England, who took advantage of her unfortunate defeat in a crusade against the black drug and in consequence of the sheer ignorance of the Chinese government authorities relative to the importance and necessity of tariff autonomy in national life.

Coming to the foreign administration of the Chinese maritime customs, the origin was found in the Taiping Rebellion, when, in 1853, the Chinese city of Shanghai, being captured by the rebels, and the Chinese customs closed, the foreign consuls collected the duties for a while. Finding, however, the work irksome, on June 29, 1854, the British, American, and French consuls entered into an agreement with the Shanghai Taotai for the establishment of a board of foreign inspectors.[5] In the agreement containing rules of trade,[6] November 8, 1858, it was stipulated that the Chinese High Commissioner of Customs could of his own choice appoint a foreign subject to assist him in the administration of the customs. On February 18, 1898, Great Britain secured from the Chinese government the pledge that, while British trade predominated, the inspector-general of the Chinese maritime customs should be a British subject.[7] In the final protocol for the settlement of the Boxer trouble, September 7, 1901,[8] the revenues of the Chinese maritime customs were pledged as the first security for the indemnity of four hundred fifty million Haikwan taels, to be paid in thirty-nine years, the amortization to finish by the end of 1940, and, because of the postponement for five years granted by the powers for China's entrance into the Great War, by the end of 1945.

From this study of the origin of the foreign administration of the Chinese maritime customs it is seen that the first institution of a board of foreign inspectors was a mere *modus operandi* to meet the exigency of the Taiping rebellion, that the subsequent appointment of a foreign inspector-general was a voluntary concession and measure of expediency on the part of the Chinese government, that the declaration that a British subject should be appointed inspector-general while the British trade predominated was obtained in that memorable year, 1898, as part of the frightful international scramble for concessions, and that the pledging of the revenues of the maritime customs as first security for the Boxer indemnity stabilized the foreign control of the maritime customs probably for the period of the service of the loan. And it is also to be here mentioned that the efficient and honest administration under the foreign supervision has contributed not in a small way toward the credit standing of the Chinese government in domestic and foreign loan obligations.

Chinese objections to the tariff system are well known. Unilateral or non-reciprocal, the tariff as fixed imposes restrictions on China and offers no concession or compensation of a same kind in return. Unscientific taxing all alike at 5 per cent ad valorem, it does not differentiate between raw materials and manufactured goods, nor distinguish luxuries from necessities. Rigid and inflexible, it does not permit increase or decrease as the needs of revenue require, resulting occasionally in shortage of rev-

[5] Morse, *The Trade and Administration of China*, p. 367.

[6] Hertslet, I, No. 7, 39–40.

[7] MacMurray, 1898/2.

[8] MacMurray, 1901/3.

enue. Further, it does not permit the application of a protective tariff for the bringing up of infant industries and the encouragement of vital industries necessary for economic self-sufficiency of a state in time of war. Again, it necessitates the existence and practice of an inland transit tax known as likin, which tends to destroy Chinese domestic commerce and deter the growth of Chinese industry. Above all, in so far as the tariff rate cannot be altered without the consent of the powers—nay, what is worse, the unanimous consent of the powers enjoying, or that may enjoy, save otherwise expressly stipulated, the most favored nation treatment—to that extent is China's sovereignty impaired.

In view of these serious objections China has been incessantly asking for a raise of tariff rates, and, what is more important, a recovery of tariff autonomy. As early as 1902 and 1903, in the Mackay treaty of September 5, 1902,[9] in the American treaty of October 8, 1903[10] and in the Japanese treaty under the same date,[11] China obtained consent for an increase of the import tariff to 12½ per cent and of export duty to 7½ per cent ad valorem upon the condition of, and in recompense for, the abolition of likin. The condition, however, that all powers enjoying, or who may enjoy, the most favored nation treatment should enter the same engagement rendered the provisions non-effective.

At the Paris Peace Conference, China, having joined the Allies in the Great War, put in the claim for the execution of the aforesaid provisions and the recovery of tariff autonomy.[12] The victorious powers regarded the claim as outside of the province of the Peace Conference, though China was enabled to recover her tariff autonomy as regards Germany, Austria, and Hungary.

At the Washington Conference China again entered her claims in regard to the tariff. She asked first for the immediate raise of the import rate to 12½ per cent—a rate, as it has been seen, stipulated in the commercial treaties of 1902 and 1903; second, for the grant of the right of differentiating rates within a maximum, as for example between luxuries and necessities; and, third and lastly, for the complete restoration of tariff autonomy after a designated period. The first two requests were rejected, largely in view of the lack of a stable and effective government and the prevalence of militarism and chaos; but the third, or last, was granted. Accordingly, the Nine Power Treaty, February 6, 1922, relating to the Chinese customs tariff, was concluded.[13] An immediate revision of the customs schedule of duties on imports to make rates of duties equivalent to 5 per cent effective was authorized, the revised tariff to become effective as soon as possible, without awaiting ratification, but not earlier than two months after the publication by the revision commission.[14] A special conference was to be convened in China composed of the representatives of the powers,

[9] Hertslet, I, No. 28, 174.

[10] Hertslet, I, No. 100, 566, 568, Art. 4.

[11] Hertslet, I, No. 66, 384, Art. I.

[12] *The Shantung Question and Other Claims, as Officially Presented to the Peace Conference at Paris by the Chinese Peace Commission,* pp. 88–89.

[13] *Report of Conference on the Limitation of Armament* (February 6, 1922), pp. 1630–39.

[14] *Conference on the Limitation of Armament, Department of State,* p. 1634.

signatory and adhering, to prepare the way for the abolition of likin and the fulfilment of the other conditions laid down in the commercial treaties of 1902 and 1903 with Great Britain, America, and Japan, with a view to levying the surtaxes provided therein (Art. II). Pending, however, the fulfilment of these objects and as interim measures the special conference should consider the levying of a uniform surtax on dutiable imports not exceeding 2½ per cent ad valorem, excepting in certain cases of luxuries on which a greater surtax might be imposed, not to exceed 5 per cent ad valorem (Art. III). Meanwhile, in order to retain the confidence of the powers, China on her part made the promise not to effect any change which might disturb the present administration of the Chinese maritime customs,[15] though qualified with the statement that it could not reasonably be construed to preclude China's legitimate aspirations gradually to make this important branch of the Chinese government more national in character. On the other hand, in order to obviate misconstruction, China reserved the right to bring up the question of tariff autonomy on all appropriate occasions in the future.[16]

In pursuance of the Nine Power Treaty relating to Chinese customs tariff, the Tariff Revision Commission duly met at Shanghai in 1922[17] and published a new revised tariff schedule.[18] The Nine Power Treaty relating to Chinese customs tariff becoming effective because of the belated settlement of the gold franc question which caused France to withhold the ratification of the Washington treaties relating to Chinese matters on August 5, 1925,[19] China issued invitations to the powers to attend a special tariff conference at Peking on October 26, 1925.[20] The scope of the conference as stipulated in the aforesaid treaty was limited to the preparation of the way for the speedy abolition of likin and for the fulfilment of other conditions laid down in the commercial treaties of 1902 and 1903 with Great Britain, America, and Japan and to the consideration, prior to the abolition of likin and the fulfilment of the aforesaid conditions, of the application of interim provisions and the authorization of the levying of a surtax on dutiable imports at a uniform rate of 2½ per cent ad valorem, except in cases of certain articles of luxury whereon the surtax should not exceed 5 per cent ad valorem.[21] The Chinese government, however, proposed, in the invitation to the special conference, to broaden the scope so as to include the discussion on the complete restoration of China's tariff autonomy.

[15] Senate Document 126, p. 770, 31st Meeting, Committee on Pacific and Far-Eastern Questions, February 3, 1922, 3 P.M.; p. 174, 6th Plenary Session, February 4, 1922, 67th Congress, 2d Session.

[16] Senate Document 126, p. 183, Sixth Plenary Session, February 4, 1922, 67th Congress, 2d Session; pp. 185, 597.

[17] Cf. Clarruce S. K. Chow, "Revision of the Chinese Treaty Tariff in 1922," *Chinese Social and Political Science Review,* January, 1923.

[18] *China Yearbook, 1925,* pp. 460–67.

[19] J. V. A. MacMurray to Waichaopu, August 10, 1925, *Far-Eastern Times,* August 13, 1925.

[20] Text of invitation, *Peking Daily News,* August 20, 1925.

[21] Arts. II and III, Nine Power Treaty relating to Chinese customs tariff, February 6, 1922.

In connection with the said treaty, it may be recalled that on January 5, 1922, at the 17th meeting of the Committee on Pacific and Far Eastern Questions of the Washington Conference, the Chinese Delegation, in giving their assent thereto, declared that it was their intention to bring up again the question of the restoration to China of her tariff autonomy for consideration on all appropriate occasions in the future. In pursuance of the above declaration, the Chinese Government propose that the said question be also brought up at the forthcoming Conference and expects that some arrangement will be made to remove the tariff restrictions hitherto imposed upon China.[22]

On October 26, 1925, the conference met in its first plenary session, thirteen powers being present: China, America, Belgium, Denmark, France, Great Britain, Italy, Japan, the Netherlands, Norway, Portugal, Spain, and Sweden.

At the first plenary session the Chinese delegates asked for the recognition of China's tariff autonomy:

1. The participating Powers formally declare to the Government of the Republic of China their respect for its tariff autonomy and agree to the removal of all the tariff restrictions contained in existing treaties.

2. The Government of the Republic of China agrees to the abolition of Likin simultaneously with the enforcement of the Chinese National Tariff Law which shall take effect not later than the first day of January in the 18th year of the Republic of China (1929).

3. Previous to the enforcement of the Chinese National Tariff Law, an interim surtax of 5% on ordinary goods, 30% on Grade A luxuries (namely, wine and tobacco) and 20% on Grade B luxuries shall be levied, in addition to the present customs tariff of 5% ad valorem.

4. The collection of the above-mentioned interim surtaxes shall begin three months from the date of signature.

5. The decisions relative to the above four articles shall be carried into effect from the date of signature.[23]

It is manifest, from a close study of these proposals, that the Chinese government refused to regard the abolition of likin as a condition or prerequisite to the enforcement of the surtaxes stipulated in the commercial treaty of 1902 and 1903 with Great Britain, America, and Japan, or to the complete restoration of China's tariff autonomy, and instead made declaration that likin would be abolished at the same time with the enforcement of China's national tariff law, that is, on January 1, 1929. It is also evident that the Chinese government broke the bounds of the interim surtaxes in asking, instead of 2½ per cent, 5 per cent on ordinary goods, and instead of 5 per cent on luxuries, 30 per cent on wine and tobacco and 20 per cent on the other articles of luxury. It is further observed that, taking lesson from the obstacle placed by the French withholding the ratification of the Washington treaties practically for three and a half years from February 6, 1922, to August 5, 1925, the Chinese government asked for the immediate collection of the before-mentioned interim surtaxes three months from the date of signature, and the putting into force of those articles likewise from date of signature, without awaiting ratification.[24]

[22] Text of invitation, *Peking Daily News,* August 20, 1925.

[23] "Proposals Relating to Tariff Questions Submitted to the Special Tariff Conference, October 26, 1925, by the Chinese Delegation," *Peking Daily News,* October 27, 1925.

[24] For the Chinese proposals, November 21, 1925, on the abolition of likin and the expenditure of revenues from surtaxes, see *Peking Morning Post* (in Chinese), November 22,

In the second session of the committee on tariff autonomy, November 2, 1925, in response to the aforesaid Chinese proposals, the proposals made therein by the leading powers in relation to China should be noted. The British delegation made the following statement:[25]

The British Delegation, recognizing the inherent right of all independent and sovereign states to tariff autonomy and considering that the fulfilment of the provisions of the Treaty of Washington of February 6th, 1922, will constitute a step towards the attainment by China of such autonomy, formally declare that in addition to the carrying out of the terms of that treaty they are willing to submit to the ratification of their Governments such further measures as may be devised and agreed upon at this Conference with a view to ensuring within a reasonable period the full realization of China's claim to complete liberty of action in matters relating to her tariff.

It is to be observed that the British delegation took the position that if the other powers at the conference should agree on any measures relative to China's recovery of tariff autonomy, the British delegation would be glad to submit such measures to the ratification of their government.

The statement of the American delegation, in part, follows:

We affirm the principle of respect for China's tariff autonomy and are prepared to negotiate a new treaty that shall give effect to that principle and which shall make provision for the removal of tariff restrictions contained in existing treaties and for putting into effect of the Chinese National Tariff Law.

To carry out the provisions of the Washington treaty and at the same time proceed with the larger programme contemplated, we suggest:

1. That the Powers, other than China, authorize the levying of a surtax of 2½ per cent to be effective on all goods on February 1, 1926, and that there be prepared immediately a schedule of luxuries upon which a rate of 5 per cent shall be authorized to be effective not later than July 1, 1926. The increased revenues thus derived shall be held by the Customs Administration subject to such disposition as may be agreed upon in this conference.
2. That provision shall be made for the levying of the full amount of the surtaxes at the land frontiers.
3. That a new treaty be made which shall provide:
   i) Three months after the treaty here concluded shall come into force the Chinese shall be at liberty, as an interim revenue, and until tariff autonomy shall become effective, to impose a new and uniformly enforced schedule of duties at rates from 5 per cent (the present rate) to 12½ per cent on imports and from 5 per cent (the present rate) to 7½ per cent on exports.
   ii) That from the same date, the rates of duty levied at all land frontiers shall be same as those levied at the maritime frontiers.

---

1925; for the Chinese proposals, December 10, 1925, regarding the valuation of commodities, and the Chinese declaration regarding the levying of duties and taxes on foreigners residing in China, and the Chinese declarations regarding the abolition of the export duties and coast-trade duty of native goods not destined for exportation to foreign countries, see "Press Communique, 5th Meeting of Committee II on Provisional Measures," *Peking Daily News,* December 11, 1925.

[25] Sir Ronald Macleay, on behalf of the British delegation, made the statement, *Far-Eastern Times,* November 4, 1925.

iii) That the increase of the customs revenues derived from putting into effect these provisions shall be accumulated by the Customs Administration and applied for the purposes hereafter specified.

iv) That Likin and related internal taxes which may be agreed upon shall be abolished.

v) That for the purpose of abolishing Likin, funds from the Customs revenues shall be apportioned among the provinces in lieu of Likin.

vi) That if Likin be collected anywhere in violation of agreements entered into for its abolition, the taxpayer shall be entitled to a refund from the Customs Administration of the full amount which he paid as Likin.

vii) That the increase in the customs revenues derived from the increase in rates of duty shall be devoted to the following purposes:
(*a*) Compensation to the provinces in lieu of Likin;
(*b*) Payment of rebate charges;
(*c*) Refunding of the unsecured debts;
(*d*) Administrative expenses of the Central Government.

viii) That, subject to the fulfilment of the provisions of Articles 4, 5, 6, and 7 above, the present treaty restrictions on the Chinese tariff shall cease to be effective and the Chinese National Tariff Laws shall come into force on January 1, 1929, as suggested by the Chinese Delegation.

ix) That an effort be made to devise a plan whereby it may be reasonably expected that this treaty will go into force at an early date after signature.

x) That if proposed by a majority of the contracting Powers before January 1, 1928, there shall convene on May 1, 1928, a Conference of the representatives of the contracting Powers, for the purpose of deciding whether Likin has been abolished and of negotiating any further agreements that may need to be arrived at with regard to subject matter of this treaty.[26]

Notwithstanding the complicated character of the statement, the American delegation, in essence, made the proposal that the United States of America would be ready to permit the coming into force of China's exercise of tariff autonomy on January 1, 1929, on condition that China should abolish likin, and the application of the interim surtaxes to compensation to the provinces in lieu of likin, payment of rebate charges, refunding of the unsecured debts, and administrative expenses of the Central Government; and that on the proposal of the majority of the contracting powers before January 1, 1928, another conference should be convened on May 1, 1928, to determine whether China had fulfilled the condition of the abolition of likin.

The statement of the Japanese delegation, in part, reads as follows:

1. The Contracting Powers, other than China, hereby solemnly declare their recognition of the principle that, as an inherent right of a sovereign state, China is to enjoy full autonomy with respect to customs tariff.

2. China shall recover the exercise of the tariff autonomy in the manner indicated in the following paragraphs.

3. China shall establish immediately a national tariff law with a schedule appertaining thereto, to be put in force within a period of three years and upon the abolition of Likin by China as declared by her.

4. During the interim period mentioned in the preceding paragraph China may levy

[26] Mr. John V. A. MacMurray, on behalf of the American Delegation, made the statement, *Far-Eastern Times,* November 4, 1925.

on articles of import a surtax as authorized in paragraph 2 of Article 3 of the Washington Treaty.

5. During the same interim period, China, on the one hand, and the Contracting Powers on the other, shall conclude severally treaties, which may incorporate reciprocal conventional tariffs to be applied on certain special articles if so desired by both parties. The new treaties so concluded shall continue in force for a certain definite period.

6. The national tariff law mentioned in paragraph 3 shall become operative, so far as the treaty Powers are concerned, simultaneously with the enforcement of the treaties above mentioned.

7. The new treaties to be concluded shall supersede all existing treaties between China and the other contracting Powers, in matters relating to customs tariff.[27]

It is to be observed that the interim surtaxes sanctioned by Japan do not exceed what the Washington Treaty stipulated, namely 2½ per cent on ordinary dutiable imports, excepting in cases of certain articles of luxury, whereon the surtax shall not exceed 5 per cent ad valorem; and that while Japan, on the one hand, is ready to grant tariff autonomy by January 1, 1929, upon the abolition of likin, on the other hand she desires to enter into a reciprocal conventional tariff arrangement with China to be applied on certain articles. That is to say, while on the one hand she gives tariff autonomy, on the other hand she ties the hands of China again on certain articles of trade in which she is most interested.

The one concrete and outstanding accomplishment of the Special Conference was the adoption of the Committee on Provisional Measures of the Conference on November 19, 1925, of the resolution recognizing China's exercise of tariff autonomy on January 1, 1929:

The Delegates of the Powers assembled at this Conference resolved to adopt the following article relating to tariff autonomy with a view to incorporating it together with other matters, to be hereafter agreed upon in a treaty which is to be signed at this Conference:

The Contracting Powers other than China hereby recognize China's right to enjoy tariff autonomy; agree to remove the tariff restrictions which are contained in existing treaties between themselves respectively and China; and consent to the going into effect of the Chinese National Tariff Law on January 1, 1929.

The Government of the Republic of China declares that Likin shall be abolished simultaneously with the enforcement of the Chinese National Tariff Law; and further declares that the abolition of Likin shall be effectively carried out by the first day of the first month of the eighteenth year of the Republic of China (January 1, 1929).[28]

The significance of this resolution cannot be overestimated. In the commercial treaties of 1902 and 1903 with Great Britain, America, and Japan, wherein the abolition of likin was made a specific condition, not of tariff autonomy, but of the increase of import tariff to 12½ per cent ad valorem, and the export tariff to 7½ per cent ad valorem, in the present resolution, the abolition of likin was not made a condition for the exercise of tariff autonomy, not to say for the increase of tariff rates. What it

[27] Dr. Kioki's statement, November 2, 1925, second session of the Committee on Tariff Autonomy, *Far-Eastern Times,* November 4, 1925.

[28] Official Bulletin, Special Tariff Conference, Committee II, fourth meeting at Chu Jen Tang, on Thursday, November 19, 1925, at 10 A.M., *Peking Daily News,* November 20, 1925.

amounts to here is a pledge of honor solemnly undertaken by China that, simultaneously with the enforcement of tariff autonomy, she would carry out the abolition of likin.

On account of civil war, change of administration, and departure of some of the Chinese delegates from Peking, the Conference adjourned on July 3, 1926, *sine die,* the delegates of the foreign powers, however, stating: "They expressed the unanimous and earnest desire to proceed with the work of the conference at the earliest possible moment when the delegates of the Chinese Government are in a position to resume discussion with the foreign delegates of the problems before the Conference."[29] After the breaking up of the Conference, certain actions on the part of China deserve our close observation. Beginning from October 11, 1926, the Nationalist government at Canton collected the 2½ per cent surtax as sanctioned at the Washington Conference; and since then, wherever the influence of the Nationalist government reached, the Washington surtaxes have been collected,[30] without regard to the conditions laid down in the Nine Power Treaty, February 6, 1922, relating to Chinese tariff matters or the unanimous protest of the diplomatic corps at Peking.[31] The British memorandum of December 18, 1926, advocating an immediate and unconditional grant of the Washington surtaxes, the Peking government also decided, beginning from February 1, 1927, to collect the Washington surtaxes,[32] and, what is more, to put into effect the full exercise of tariff autonomy on January 1, 1929. To this effect the Chinese government delivered on January 13, 1927, a circular note to the legations in Peking.[33]

With the announcement of China's determination to put into effect a Chinese national tariff law on January 1, 1929, without the completion of the special tariff conference, a great problem arises between China and the twelve powers attending the aforesaid conference, that is, What will the powers concerned do when, on January 1, 1929, China shall actually exercise tariff autonomy, with or without the abolition of likin?

Respecting tariff autonomy, the various powers seem to be well disposed toward China.

Much of the problem therefore hinges on whether China can abolish likin by that date. If China could do so, probably with the exception of Japan, who might wish to seek the enforcement of a reciprocal conventional tariff arrangement before the application of the Chinese national tariff law, and of the United States, who might insist on the formality of completing the mode of procedure as laid down at the

[29] Communique issued Netherlands legation on behalf of the delegates, July 3, 1925, *Hsun Tien Shih Pao,* July 5, 1925.

[30] *Shun Tien Shih Pao,* October 9, 1926.

[31] *Shun Tien Shih Pao,* November 5, 1926.

[32] Cabinet Decision, January 12, 1927, *Shun Tien Shih Pao* (in Chinese), January 13, 1927.

[33] See Appendix. Dr. V. K. Wellington Koo to heads of the missions or legations, Peking, January 13, 1927, also cf. *Far-Eastern Times,* January 15, 1927; also the three presidential mandates, relating to the enforcement of Washington surtaxes and the exercise of tariff autonomy, January 12, 1927, *Far-Eastern Times,* January 14, 1927.

Washington Conference, there is practically no question but that the powers would let the measure come into force. Circumstances, however, seem to indicate that, by January 1, 1929, it would virtually be impossible for China to effect the abolition of likin. Likin, or the inland transit tax, is a provincial revenue collected and expended by the provincial authorities, now generally known as *tuchuns, tupans,* war lords, or what not. If the Central Government should be in full control of these provincial satraps, the abolition of likin might be effected with no great difficulty and delay. Now, as it is well known, because of civil war and the breakdown of the central authority and the assumption of power by these *tuchuns,* or *tupans,* who virtually regard themselves as uncrowned kings of their realms, the abolition of likin has become a concomitant question with the assertion of the central authority, the abolition of *tuchuns,* and the unification of China. Added to this are the attendant obstacles of finding a substitute of revenue to replace likin and a livelihood for those thousands of Chinese now subsisting on the collection of likin. Such being the significance and magnitude of the question; and as it is not within the province of this treatise to deal with the problem of the unification of China or the other attendant questions, suffice it to state within limits of safety and moderation that it is virtually impossible for China to effect the abolition of likin within such a short period as contemplated by the exercise of tariff autonomy on January 1, 1929. And what might be possible for China to do by that date would probably be the issuance of a presidential mandate ordering the abolition of likin, and make that as a pious starting-point for a gradual extirpation of this destroyer of Chinese domestic trade and industry.

It being impossible for China to carry out the pledge of honor to abolish likin by January 1, 1929, the question arises, Will China assert her tariff autonomy by that date without the simultaneous execution of the pledge? From the circular notice of China dated January 13, 1927, declaring her intention and decision to put into effect the Chinese national law by January 1, 1929, it is reasonable to believe that China would in all probability proceed to assert her tariff autonomy by that date.[34]

[34] It is to be noted that while tariff hitherto has been only a question in international relationships, after the advent of tariff autonomy it will become a predominant issue in Chinese domestic politics, as between protectionists and freetraders, which might divide the present political parties or even the nation.

## SECTION 4

## EXTRA-TERRITORIALITY AND ITS RELINQUISHMENT

MINGCHIEN JOSHUA BAU, M.A., Ph.D.
Professor of Political Science, Peking National Normal University and Peking National College of Law and Politics

The second outstanding issue between China and the interested powers is extra-territoriality.

By extra-territoriality is meant exemption from the operation of territorial law. It is a fundamental principle in international law that the territorial sovereign exercises supreme power over all the people, native or alien, residing within the limits of his territory. With the concession of extra-territoriality, however, the supreme power of the territorial sovereign is limited or impaired to the extent that aliens enjoying the privilege are exempted from the jurisdiction of his tribunals.

The origin of extra-territoriality in China, like that of tariff restrictions, dates back to the days of the Opium War (1839–42). In the Treaty of Nanking in 1842 there was no specific mention of the grant of extra-territoriality, but in the subsequent general regulations governing the British trade at the five ports of Canton, Amoy, Foochow, Ningpo, and Shanghai, concluded on October 8, 1843, extra-territoriality of a unilateral kind was granted for the first time.[1] The *modus vivendi* as provided gratified the desire of the foreigner for exemption from the operation of the Chinese law and subjection to the laws of his own country and obviated a good deal of friction between the Chinese and foreigners.

Since then, following the precedent set by Great Britain, the other treaty powers have at various times secured the same privilege. Today there are yet sixteen states enjoying the right of extra-territoriality, namely, the United States of America, Belgium, Brazil, Great Britain, Denmark, France, Italy, Japan, Mexico, the Netherlands, Norway, Peru, Portugal, Spain, Sweden, and Switzerland.[2]

It will be useful to review briefly the practice of extra-territoriality in China. As a rule, it follows the person of the national. It exempts foreign nationals enjoying the privilege, not only from the judicial process of local tribunals, but also from liability of search. In general, all consuls of the treaty powers are authorized to exercise extra-territorial jurisdiction in courts known as consular courts.[3] The laws applied in

[1] *State Papers*, XXX, 398 ff.; *Questions for Readjustment Submitted by China to the Paris Peace Conference*, App. I, p. 35; Article 13, Supplementary Treaty of Commerce, October 8, 1843, abrogated by Article I of the treaty of June 26, 1858.

[2] *Report of the Commission on Extra-territoriality in China*, Appendix I, "List of Extra-territorial Powers and Pertinent Treaty Clauses," pp. 113–14.

[3] Cf. Willoughby, *Foreign Rights and Interests in China*, revised and enlarged ed., chaps. xxii–xxvii.

these extra-territorial courts are the laws of the nations exercising extra-territorial jurisdiction, save in rights of realty, which are determined according to *lex situs,* and save also probably in local laws and municipal ordinances of the Chinese government. The tribunals that have jurisdiction over mixed cases between a Chinese defendant and a foreign plaintiff have been commonly known as mixed courts, a foreign assessor being usually permitted to attend trials in such courts.

Under aegis of extra-territoriality, and sometimes in defiance of China's sovereignty, unwarranted practices have been committed by the treaty powers, such as the foreign post-offices and radio stations established by the powers, police boxes or stations established by Japan in Manchuria, and the maintenance of foreign troops in China, some duly authorized by treaty stipulations, such as the legation guards at Peking and the Allied guards on the Peking-Mukden Railway,[4] and some unauthorized by law or treaty.

Chinese objections to extra-territoriality are too well known to need reiteration. Extra-territorial jurisdiction constitutes a derogation and an infringement of Chinese sovereignty. Consular judges are sometimes found unsatisfactory in view of the lack, in many instances, of legal and judicial training. The combination of consular and judicial functions violates the modern principles of the separation of administrative and judicial functions, thereby not infrequently maladministering justice in favor of foreign nationals. Multiplicity of courts and diversity of laws give rise to evils of judicial uncertainty and disparity of judgment and punishment. The consular, or extra-territorial, courts lack control over plaintiffs and witnesses that are not of the defendant's nationality, the jurisdiction being personal. The difficulty in obtaining evidence for crimes committed in the interior and the remoteness of some of the extra-territorial courts from the scene of the crime renders any immediate, efficient, and fair administration of justice well nigh impossible. The immunity of foreigners from the operation of Chinese regulations relating to traffic, taxation, and the press often constitutes a source of friction between foreigners and Chinese authorities. The irregular extension of protection by the extra-territorial powers to Chinese, Chinese firms, and individuals by permitting registration at their consulates often removes those persons and their business interests fom the jurisdiction of Chinese law and courts. Foreign premises, being not subject to search and entry by Chinese judicial or other authorities, extra-territorial nationals often give protection to Chinese citizens on their premises, and Chinese criminals thus protected cannot be arrested without due consent of the consular authorities concerned. The shooting by the Japanese mill authority of the Chinese labor representative, the ignoring by the police authorities of the appeal of Chinese laborers for redress and justice and the shooting at an unarmed crowd upon the order of the British police inspector in the famous incident of Shanghai, May 30, 1925, were all done under the aegis, not only of the foreign settlement, but especially of extra-territoriality.

Foreign objections to extra-territoriality are none the less serious. Foreigners involved in a lawsuit in the interior of China cannot adjudicate the matter on the spot, but must bear burdensome delay, expense, and other inconveniences in extricating themselves from the clutches of their own law. Appeals from the judgments of

[4] Articles 7 and 9, final protocol of September 7, 1901, MacMurray, 1901–3.

foreign courts cannot be passed to the Chinese superior or supreme court, but must be taken to courts beyond the territorial limits of China, which is not only unfair to Chinese, but sometimes very inconvenient for foreigners. Multiplicity of courts and diversity of laws being the inevitable consequences of the practice of extra-territorial courts, foreigners, no less than Chinese, suffer from judicial uncertainty and disparity of judgment and punishment. The existence of extra-territoriality and the absence of extradition arrangements often render it impossible for the foreign powers to bring to justice persons who move beyond the reach of the jurisdiction of the foreign courts in China. What is more, it being the policy of China not to open up her entire territory to foreign trade and commerce until the abolition of the system of extra-territoriality, foreigners, with the exception of missionaries and those engaged in philanthropic work, are not accorded the right to unlimited travel, trade, and residence in all parts of China, but are generally confined only to treaty or open ports.

The movement for the relinquishment of extra-territoriality has become a decided policy of China. As early as 1902, China made a move in this direction and secured consent to abolish this special right, upon the successful judicial reform to be undertaken by China, from Great Britain in the treaty of September 5, 1902,[5] and subsequently from the United States of America in the treaty of October 8, 1903,[6] from Japan in the treaty of the same date,[7] and from Sweden in the treaty of July 2, 1908.[8] At the Paris Peace Conference, 1919, China submitted her request *inter alia* for the abrogation of extra-territoriality,[9] which was not regarded with favor. However, in consequence of the Allied victory in the Great War, 1914–18, she succeeded in recovering extra-territoriality from Austria-Hungary, Germany,[10] and subsequently Russia.[11]

At the Washington Conference, 1921–22, China again submitted her claim.[12]

In response to China's claim respecting radio stations, the powers represented at the Conference decided that those legitimately maintained in China should limit their uses only to official messages, save in the case of the interruption of commercial radio stations or in accordance with the terms of the concessions, but that those stations illegitimately established in China should be handed over to the Chinese government with due compensation.[13] As regards the foreign post-offices, the four powers maintaining postal stations in China, to wit, the United States of America, France, Great

[5] Hertslet, I, No. 28, 182, Article XII.

[6] Hertslet, I, No. 100, 575, Article XV.

[7] Hertslet, I, No. 66, 386–87, Article XI.

[8] MacMurray, 1908/11, Article 10.

[9] *Questions for Readjustment, Submitted by China to the Paris Peace Conference*, p. 17.

[10] "Sino-German Agreement, May 20, 1921, Article III," *Chinese Social and Political Science Review*, October, 1924. Also see German declaration, Mr. von Borch to Dr. W. W. Yen, May 20, 1921.

[11] "The Sino-Russian Agreement, May 31, 1924, Article XII," *Chinese Social and Political Science Review*, July, 1924.

[12] Senate Document 126, 67–2, pp. 475, 499, 504, 528, 503, 601, 505, 519, 548, 732, 480, 502, 572, etc.

[13] *Ibid.*, Fifth Plenary Session (February 1, 1922), p. 123.

Britain, and Japan, agreed to withdraw the same not later than January 1, 1923, save from the leased territories, or as otherwise specifically provided by treaty, on condition that China should maintain an efficient postal administration and contemplate no change in the present postal administration so far as the status of the foreign (French) co-director was concerned.[14]

With reference to foreign armed forces, including police and railway guards, maintained in China without the authority of any treaty or agreement, the powers other than China expressed their willingness to withdraw such armed forces as soon as China could assume the protection of the lives and property of foreigners, and resolved to instruct their diplomatic representatives at Peking, whenever China should so request, to associate themselves with three representatives of China to conduct collectively a full and impartial inquiry relating thereto.[15]

With respect to extra-territorial jurisdiction, the powers represented at the Washington Conference, other than China, willing to relinquish it as soon as judicial reforms of China should warrant so doing, authorized the establishment of an international commission consisting of one representative from each of the powers signatory or acceding to make necessary inquiries relating thereto, and asked that China should appoint a representative to sit as a member of the commission and afford facility for the successful accomplishment of its task.[16]

In pursuance of this decision of the Washington Conference, the International Commission on Extra-territoriality in China met in Peking on January 12, 1926. The representatives of thirteen powers were present—to wit, the United States of America, Belgium, British Empire, China, France, Denmark, Italy, Japan, the Netherlands, Norway, Portugal, Spain, and Sweden—of which Denmark, Norway, Spain, and Sweden were the powers that acceded to the Washington Resolution. On September 16, 1926, the Commission rendered a joint report.[17]

The report[18] consists of four main parts. Part I presents the Commission's findings of fact regarding the present practice of extra-territoriality in China. Part II treats of the laws and judicial and prison systems of China. Part III relates to the administration of justice in China. Part IV consists entirely of recommendations to China, as well as to the extra-territorial powers, with a view to correcting certain abuses in the practice of extra-territoriality.

In general, the report is unfavorable to China's claim for the abolition of extra-territoriality. It virtually states that, as far as her claim for the relinquishment of extra-territorial jurisdiction is concerned, China is as yet found wanting. To put it in a more courteous way, as the Commission did, it renders the opinion that when the recommendations of the Commission shall have been reasonably complied with, the

[14] *Ibid.*, p. 115.

[15] *Ibid.*, p. 116.

[16] *Ibid.*, p. 98, Fourth Plenary Session, December 10, 1921.

[17] The Chinese delegate, Dr. Wang Chung-hui, in signing the report, made the statement: "By signing this report, my approval of all the statements contained in Parts I, II, and III is not to be implied."

[18] *Report of the Commission on Extra-territoriality in China,* September 16, 1926. Department of State, Government Printing Office.

several powers would be warranted in relinquishing their respective rights of extraterritoriality.

It may well profit us to review the leading criticisms of the Commisison with regard to Chinese law and judicial administration.

First, Chinese laws lack constitutional basis of adoption and promulgation. Since the institution of the Republic, three constitutions have so far been declared in force, namely, the Provisional Constitution, the Constitutional Compact of 1914, and the Constitution of 1923; but all three have been set aside one after another. The last-mentioned constitution was put aside by a provisional government established in October–November, 1924, and since then no single constitution has been recognized as the one in force. In view of the lack of an effective constitution and indefinite closing of the parliament, Chinese laws have not had legal sanction under the constitution, but rest on executive mandates of the President and administrative ordinances of the Ministry of Justice. "From the juridical point of view, the laws appear to be regulations applied with the force of law by the courts, but subject to change and rescission at any time by their creator, the President and the Ministry of Justice."[19]

Second, the magistrates' courts are pronounced to be very unsatisfactory. Under the Manchus, the administration of justice was intrusted to the magistrates of districts, who combined in themselves the legislative, administrative, and judicial functions. With the advent of the Republic, in spite of the establishment of modern courts, which as yet number only some 150, the magistrates' courts still continue to be by far the most predominant local courts of first instance, numbering some 1,800.[20] According to Chinese law, wherever no modern court or judicial office has been established, the magistrates of the localities have full civil and criminal jurisdiction within their districts. In such courts right of counsel is denied, although it may be very necessary. Detention in civil cases is permitted. The magistrate can inflict a penalty up to sixty dollars and pass sentences of detention up to thirty days, against which redress is to be had only by an appeal to a superior administrative authority or to the administrative court at Peking. Since the larger portion of litigation falls within the jurisdiction of these magistrates' courts, the need of reform in this direction can be appreciated.

Third, the police laws and tribunals are also found to be unsatisfactory. The police may arrest persons in cases *flagrantis delicti* under certain specified circumstances without requiring either an expeditious trial or the release of the accused on bail pending a hearing. They may sentence a person to thirty days' detention, or sixty days' in the metropolitan area. For cases within their jurisdiction, no judicial appeal to a higher court is possible, but the appeal is to a higher administrative authority and finally to the administrative court. Further, given the authority to exercise the power of investigation coextensive with that of procurator, they can exercise the power, as long as they please, before turning a case over to the procurator for investigation and prosecution. They can exercise absolute discretion in the admission, or exclusion, of relatives, friends, and the public, during trial and detention. They can

[19] *Report, op. cit.*, p. 32.

[20] *Report, op. cit.*, p. 68.

thus arrest persons and conduct examinations and trials without any reference to the law courts.

Fourth, the power given to military authorities and courts is excessive. Civilians who commit offenses against the military and naval codes are to be subject to them. Not infrequently civilians have thus been put to death without ordinary due process of law. On the other hand, civilians having complaints against the military must bring them to the military and naval courts. Thus by the inclusion of civilians in the jurisdiction of the military and by the exemption of the military from the jurisdiction of the civil courts the power of the military over the civilian has been unduly increased. In such military and naval courts the trial is, moreover, conducted *in camera;* legal counsel is not permitted; appeal is not sanctioned; and corporal punishment up to 600 blows of bamboo is applied. Cases adjudicated in times of emergency are not subject to a reconsideration by the ordinary courts after the withdrawal of martial law. Injuries suffered by civilians during the period of martial law cannot be redressed after the repeal of martial law save by an appeal to the military court.

Having seen the leading criticisms of the Chinese law and judicial administration made by the Commission, let us now consider whether these criticisms warrant further retention of extra-territorial jurisdiction. While the report is of inestimable value, not only as a contribution to the knowledge of the world relating to extra-territoriality in China, but also as a collateral aid to the Chinese in their struggle for a political and judicial régime that will guarantee the security of life, liberty, and property, we are nevertheless driven to a conclusion that is diametrically different from that reached in the report.

First, the lack of a certain and definite constitutional basis of law, though constituting a very regrettable feature of Chinese jurisprudence today, is but a passing phase in the great and spectacular birth of Chinese democracy. While England, the birthplace of modern constitutional government, did not produce a real and definite workable constitutional system of government for several centuries, while the United States of America was fortunate enough not to be menaced by civil war until some seventy years after the success of the Revolution, the Chinese Republic has yet had only less than two decades to evolve a constitutional régime, which is a very short time in comparison with long periods of constitutional struggle and evolution as found in the history of England and the United States of America; and, what is worse, she is unfortunate enough to have civil war coming close on the heels of the Revolution—a situation whose immensity of difficulty and magnitude of significance can only be appreciated by the realization of the need of a Washington and a Lincoln combined. It is, therefore, practically safe to expect confidently that, given reasonable time, the Chinese Republic will be able to evolve a constitutional democracy successfully and place the law and judicial administration on a sound and definite constitutional foundation. Besides, the existence of a written constitution has not been always necessary for the operation of a government or the administration of justice. The British government is operated in accordance with the principles and ways of an unwritten constitution. The Manchu government had existed for many years without a written constitution. And yet peace and order was maintained and reasonable measure of life, liberty, and property was obtained.

Second, the grave dissatisfaction felt over the operation and jurisdiction of the magistrates' courts does not justify a further retention of extra-territorial rights. These courts exist mainly as a legacy of the Manchus, and partly as a very unsatisfactory substitute for the want and insufficiency of modern courts. They will undoubtedly be removed, or abolished, as soon as sufficient modern courts or judicial offices can be established. Further, foreigners that have surrendered extra-territorial rights, and, in fact, all non-extra-territorial foreigners, are exempt from the jurisdiction of these "magistrates' courts," but are subject to that of modern courts exclusively. According to the law relating to procedure in cases involving non-extra-territorial nationals, promulgated by mandate of the President on May 23, 1919, and amended on October 20, 1920, cases involving non-extra-territorial nationals fall within the jurisdiction of the modern courts, and, in case of the absence of modern courts in the district, they are to be transferred to the nearest modern district court.[21] Criminal cases, after a preliminary adjudgment by the district magistrate, are likewise remitted to the pertinent modern court and procuratorate.[22] The modern courts of China having been found on the whole satisfactory,[23] and non-extra-territorial nationals being by law removed from the jurisdiction of magistrates' courts, the further retention of extra-territorial rights on this score is rather untenable.

Third, the objection to the excessive power vested in the police, though commanding the full sympathy of the Chinese, does not nevertheless justify a refusal to surrender the extra-territorial rights. The Germans, who surrendered the extra-territorial right, have been exempted from police jurisdiction.[24] Such being already the practice, all extra-territorial powers that may surrender the extra-territorial jurisdiction can, by invocation and demand, obtain the similar privilege of exemption. In fact, according to the revised regulations governing the trial of non-extra-territorial nationals in civil and criminal cases, promulgated on November 25, 1926,[25] police offenses are specifically exempted from police tribunals.

Fourth, the objection to military interference in the administration of law and courts is likewise very sound, as far as the suffering of the Chinese at the hands of military despotism and terrorism is concerned; but when used as a reason for the further retention of extra-territorial rights, it is not well grounded. It is true that there has been a good deal of interference in the administration of justice by military authorities as shown by the cases of summary execution of civilians without due process of law;[26] but it is even more true that such military interference occurred only in the cases of Chinese civilians who participated in politics and military matters, and that such military interference in cases having no relation to politics or military

[21] *Report, op. cit.*, pp. 44–45.

[22] "Revised Regulations Governing the Trial of Non-extra-territorial Nationals in Civil and Criminal Cases, November 25, 1926, Articles 2 and 4," *Public Document Supplement, Chinese Social and Political Science Review,* January, 1927.

[23] *Report, op. cit.*, pp. 80, 100.

[24] *Report, op. cit.*, p. 83.

[25] *Supplement, Chinese Social and Political Review* (January, 1927), Article 2.

[26] *Report, op. cit.*, pp. 92–97.

matters is practically unheard of and unknown. To put it in another way, while life, liberty, and property of Chinese civilians who participated in politics and military factions have been insecure and arbitrarily dealt with, or even destroyed by military interference in the administration of justice, life, liberty, and property of the millions of Chinese civilians not participating in politics and military factions have been, on the whole, secure and immune from military interference in the administration of jus-

TABLE I

NUMBER OF FOREIGNERS AND FOREIGN FIRMS IN CHINA ENJOYING EXTRA-TERRITORIAL RIGHTS*

| Nationality | Persons | Firms |
|---|---|---|
| 1. American | 9,844 | 482 |
| 2. Belgian | 549 | 25 |
| 3. Brazilian | 1 | 0 |
| 4. British | 15,247 | 718 |
| 5. Danish | 626 | 45 |
| 6. Dutch | 469 | 35 |
| 7. French | 2,576 | 176 |
| 8. Italian | 783 | 46 |
| 9. Japanese | 218,351 | 4,708 |
| 10. Mexican | 12 | 1 |
| 11. Norwegian | 575 | 16 |
| 12. Peruvian | 0 | 0 |
| 13. Portuguese | 3,739 | 174 |
| 14. Spanish | 216 | 16 |
| 15. Swedish | 489 | 6 |
| 16. Swiss | 429 | 25 |
| | 254,006 | 6,473 |

| | Percentage |
|---|---|
| 1. Japanese | 87.4 |
| 2. British | 6.0 |
| 3. American | 3.8 |
| 4. Portuguese | 1.4 |
| 5. French | 1.2 |
| 6. Other nationalities | 1.6 |
| | 100.0 |

* Customs Report, *The Foreign Trade of China* (1925), p. 219.

tice. Foreigners living in China, being supposed not to participate in politics and military factions, and, in fact, being all engaged in peaceful pursuits of education, trade, industry, and residence, the danger from military interference in the administration of justice is very small. What is more, in accordance with the revised regulations governing the trial of non-extra-territorial nationals in civil and criminal cases, promulgated on November 25, 1926, not only police offenses, but also criminal, naval, and military offenses or other special crimes, stipulated in the criminal laws, of the non-extra-territorial nationals are exempt not only from the jurisdiction of police tribunals, but also from that of military courts: "When non-extraterritorial nationals are guilty of police offences, or criminal offences of the navy or army or other special crimes stipulated in the criminal laws, they shall be dealt with by the ordinary courts in accordance with the common procedure" (Article II).

Fifth, the sole argument advanced by the powers in refusing, as yet, to surrender the extra-territorial rights is that life, liberty, and property of foreigners in China are not yet safe under the Chinese administration of justice. While it is true that life, liberty, and property of both Chinese and foreigners are not absolutely secure in China, it is nevertheless to be stated that, in international law, what foreigners can expect from a territorial sovereign is the same treatment as meted out to his own people; that they have no right to expect the same security of life, liberty, and property as accorded them in their own lands; and that by choosing to come to a strange

TABLE II

NUMBER OF FOREIGNERS AND FOREIGN FIRMS IN CHINA NOT ENJOYING EXTRA-TERRITORIALITY RIGHTS

| Nationality | Persons | Firms |
|---|---|---|
| 1. Austrian | 193 | 8 |
| 2. Czechoslovakian | 156 | 6 |
| 3. Finnish | 2 | 0 |
| 4. German | 3,050 | 518 |
| 5. Hungarian | 1 | 0 |
| 6. Russian | 79,785 | 932 |
| 7. Others | 48 | 6 |
| | 83,235 | 1,270 |

land, they have to cast their lot and take the same chances with the people of the state in question. Viewing the matter in this light, foreigners in China cannot claim the same security of life, liberty, and property as they enjoy in their own lands, but, on the contrary, they should be satisfied with the lot and condition of the Chinese. What is more, in accordance with the revised regulations governing the trial of cases involving non-extra-territorial nations, these foreigners coming under the jurisdiction of the Chinese law courts, in comparison with the Chinese, are already accorded a superior and favored status, or position, before law, being exempt, as we have seen, from magistrates' courts, police authority, and military tribunals, and subject exclusively only to modern courts with specially trained judges and procurators.

Sixth and finally, the Chinese modern courts and prisons have been found, as we have seen, by the International Commission on Extra-territoriality in China to be satisfactory. The Germans, Austrians, and Russians who came under the jurisdiction of Chinese law and courts have found their new status and condition of life satisfactory. Save for a few exceptional cases of irregularity or dissatisfaction, which are unavoidable under a condition of chaos and civil war, the aliens that surrendered extra-territoriality have testified well for the protection of life, liberty, and property accorded by the Chinese authorities. Not only this, they have found the new status more convenient and advantageous than the old in some ways. For, whereas formerly they could not settle their legal cases readily, they can now resort to the nearest Chinese modern courts. While formerly they could not go to the interior of China other than the open ports, they can now, with the protection of the Chinese government, reside and trade in the interior of China, a right denied the extra-territorial aliens.

In view, therefore, of the exemption of non-extra-territorial nationals from the jurisdiction of the magistrates' courts, police authority, and military courts, it can be safely concluded that the leading objections raised in the Report of the Commission on Extra-territoriality in China do not warrant any further retention of extra-territoriality in China, and that inasmuch as the non-extra-territorial nationals are placed exclusively under the jurisdiction of modern Chinese courts and care of modern prisons and detention houses, all of which have been found satisfactory,[27] and that the experience of the Germans, Austrians and Russians have found the new conditions of life satisfactory and beneficial, an immediate and full relinquishment of extra-territorial rights can consequently be predicted.

[27] *Report, op. cit.*, pp. 80, 100, 86, 103.

## SECTION 5

# CONCESSIONS AND SETTLEMENTS—AND THEIR TRANSFERENCE TO CHINESE RULE

MINGCHIEN JOSHUA BAU, M.A., Ph.D.

Professor of Political Science, Peking National Normal University and Peking National College of Law and Politics

The third outstanding issue between China and the powers is the foreign concessions and settlements.

By concessions we mean those areas set apart for foreign residence, leased severally to the foreign powers, for which an annual land tax or rent is paid to the Chinese government and wherein foreigners obtain titles to their pieces of land from the powers concerned through their respective consular authorities.

By settlements are meant those areas set apart for foreign residence, whose land titles still remain upon the registrars of the Chinese land office, and wherein foreigners cannot obtain fee simple titles to land, but may acquire perpetual leases.

The origin of concessions and settlements dates back to the opening to foreign trade and residence of the five ports at Canton, Amoy, Foochow, Ningpo, and Shanghai in 1842 through the Treaty of Nanking, and to the setting aside of certain reserve areas for foreign residence and trade in these five ports as provided in the Supplementary Treaty of 1843 (Article VII).[1]

The origin of local self-government in the concessions and settlements dates back to the land regulations made by the treaty powers with the consent of Chinese authorities, which constitute the charters for municipal home rule. For example, the land regulations of 1845 governing the Shanghai settlement were made with the concurrence of the Chinese authority and conferred upon foreign renters the right of municipal self-government.

The local government in the concessions and settlements varies from the rule by the consuls of the treaty powers concerned as sole administrators to the government by a municipal council elected by the rate-payers residing therein. For instance, in the Japanese, Belgian, and Italian concessions of Tientsin, the consul is the sole administrator.[2] In the international settlement of Shanghai, the local government is vested in a municipal council composed of not more than nine, and not less than five, members elected annually by a popular vote of the foreign renters and rate-payers.[3] The charter of municipal home rule is the Land Regulations, first granted in 1845 and subsequently thrice revised in 1854, 1866, and 1881 by the foreign land-renters and

[1] *State Papers,* XXXI, 132 ff.

[2] Morse, *The Trade and Administration of China,* p. 217.

[3] *State Papers,* IX (1898), 970 ff.; Hertslet, II, No. 130, 664 ff.; *Land Regulations and By-Laws for the Foreign Settlement of Shanghai, 1923* (Shanghai: Kelly & Walsh).

the powers concerned, with practically no express consent of the Chinese authorities, but with tacit acceptance after the revision had been completed and presented as a *fait accompli.*[4]

The legal status of concessions and settlements has become quite definite and clear. Though under the municipal control of consul or council, the area is still Chinese territory, over which Chinese sovereignty remains unsurrendered. What foreigners acquire therein is the delegated power of municipal home rule. Exercising the unsurrendered jurisdiction, the Chinese government exacts from the powers an annual land tax on the concessions and collects land tax from foreigners holding real estate in the settlements. Again, as an exercise of sovereignty, she maintains her judicial tribunals in the concessions and settlements; in the case of foreigners, delegating the power to the consul by the grant of extra-territorial jurisdiction; in the case of Chinese, establishing mixed courts for the trial of cases in which Chinese are defendants. Further, as an incident to sovereignty, she reserves the power to declare the neutrality of these concessions and settlements in time of war, allowing, however, the right of self-defense in case of a hostile attack. Moreover, as territorial sovereign, she can take whatever measures regarding the concessions and settlements in time of war as are necessary for her own safety, such as the closure of the ports. Besides, because of the unsurrendered sovereignty, the Chinese residing in the concession and settlements are still under obligation to render allegiance to the Chinese government and pay taxes accordingly. Finally, the grant being by lease or voluntary reservation, there is the implied condition or obligation on the part of foreigners to use the settlements or concessions only under the condition of quiet enjoyment, the territorial sovereign reserving the right to abate nuisance or impose due restraint. Thus, the self-governing municipalities in the concessions and settlements possess only the powers of the purely local, corporate, and municipal functions, to attend to police, sanitation, roads, and other local and administrative functions of municipal government. That is to say, they do not enjoy any inherent right of local self-government, but derive their privileges from the Chinese government through the proper authorities of the powers concerned, in the form of treaty stipulations or land regulations, subject, like any right of extra-territoriality, to the negotiation and modification of China and the foreign powers concerned.

Recent developments in relation to the concessions and settlements should be observed. Upon the severance of diplomatic relations with Germany on March 14, 1917, the Chinese government took over the administration of the German concessions in Tientsin and Hankow.[5] In the Treaty of Peace between the Allied and Associated Powers and Germany, June 28, 1919, China obtained the retrocession of the German concessions at Hankow and Tientsin (Article 132).[6] Simultaneously with the declaration of war on Germany and Austria-Hungary on August 14, 1917, the

[4] Cf. Kotenev, *Shanghai: Its Mixed Court and Council.*

[5] For the "Rules of Procedure Governing the Assumption of Control of the German Concessions," communicated by the Ministry of Interior to the Ministry of Foreign Affairs, March 28, 1917, see MacMurray, 1917/7.

[6] MacMurray, 1919/1.

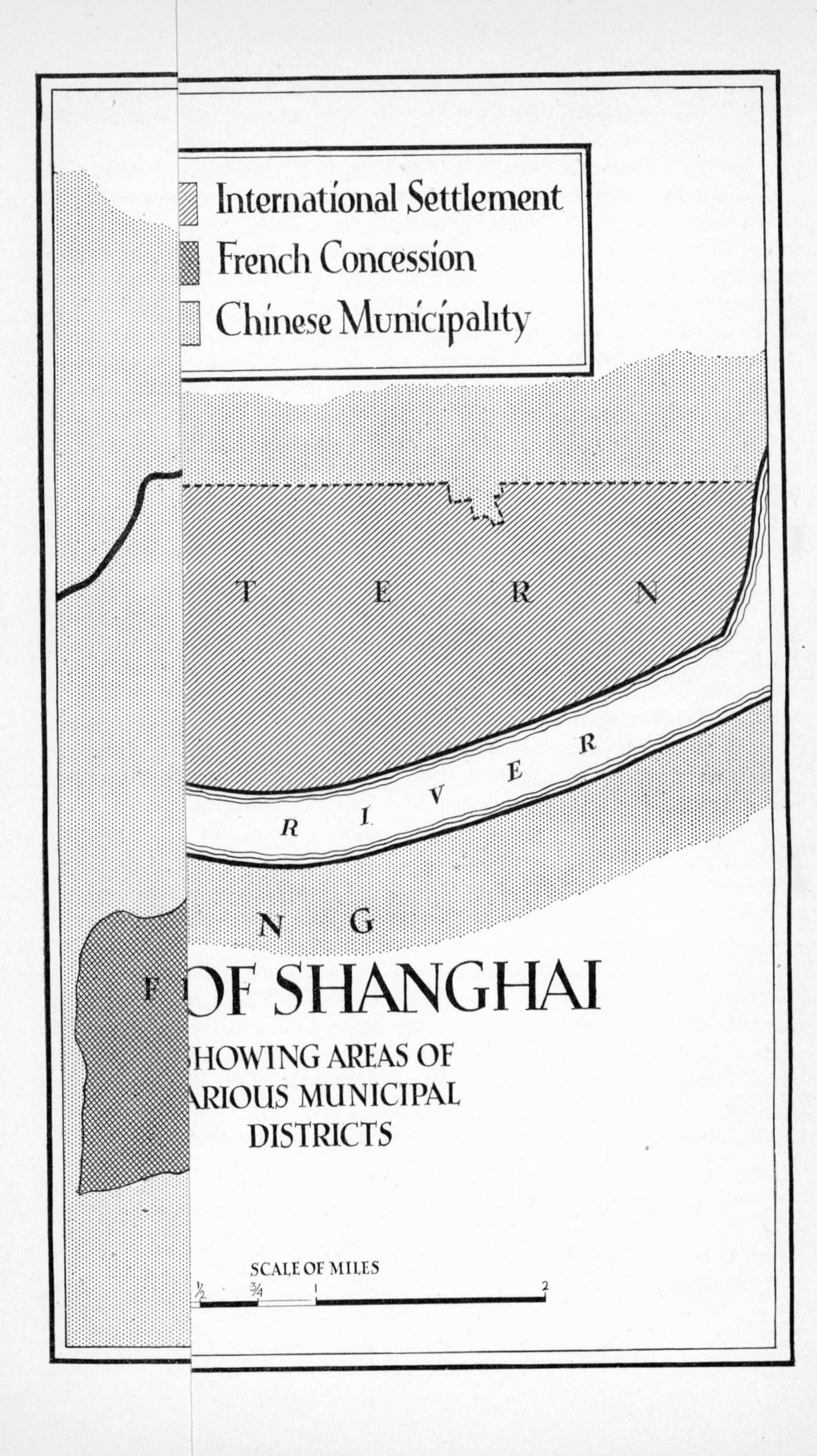
International Settlement
French Concession
Chinese Municipality
T E R N
R I V E R
N G
F
OF SHANGHAI
SHOWING AREAS OF
ARIOUS MUNICIPAL
DISTRICTS
SCALE OF MILES
½
¾
1
2

Chinese government also took over the Austrian concession at Tientsin.[7] Further, as China terminated all relations with the old Czaristic régime of Russia by the Presidential Mandate of September 23, 1920,[8] the Chinese government likewise took over the control of the Russian concessions at Tientsin and Hankow. In the Agreement on General Principles for the Settlement of the Questions between the Republic of China and the Union of Soviet Socialist Republics, May 31, 1924, China obtained the retrocession of Russian concessions in China (Article X). On February 19, 1927, the Nationalist government of the South recovered the British concession at Hankow,[9] and, on the next day, the British concession at Kiukiang.[10]

It will be interesting here to list the concessions and settlements retroceded and outstanding (by June 13, 1927).

CONCESSIONS AND SETTLEMENTS RETROCEDED

1. Ex-German concession at Tientsin (1917).
2. Ex-German concession at Hankow (1917).
3. Ex-Austrian-Hungarian concession at Tientsin (1917).
4. Ex-Russian concession at Tientsin (1924).
5. Ex-Russian concession at Hankow (1924).
6. Ex-British concession at Hankow (1927).
7. Ex-British concession at Kiukiang (1927).

CONCESSIONS AND SETTLEMENTS STILL OUTSTANDING AS BY TREATY STIPULATIONS

Shanghai:
1. International settlement (1843).
2. French concession (1849).

Amoy:
1. Kulangsoo international settlement[11] (1902).

Canton:
1. British concession } commonly known as Shameen Settlement (1861).
2. French concession }

Hankow:
1. French concession.
2. Japanese concession (1898).

Chunking:
1. Japanese concession (1901).

[7] MacMurray, 1917/7.

[8] *Millard's Review* (October 9, 1920), pp. 281–82.

[9] *Shun Tien Shih Pao,* February 22, 1927, Owen O'Malley to Chen Yu-Jen, February 19, 1927; also see *Chinese Social and Political Science Review,* April, 1927.

[10] Agreement Relative to the British Concession at Kiukiang, Owen O'Malley to Chen Yu-Jen, February 20, 1927, *Shun Tien Shih Pao,* February 24, 1927; also see *Chinese Social and Political Science Review,* April, 1927.

[11] *Illustrated Maps of the Provinces of the Republic of China* (in Chinese), published by the New Asia Geographical Society, Wuchang.

Chinkiang:

1. British concession (1861).

Hangchow:

1. Japanese concession (1895).

Soochow:

1. Japanese concession (1895).

Tientsin:

1. British concession (1861); retrocession pending.
2. French concession (1861).
3. Japanese concession.
4. Belgian concession; retrocession pending.
5. Italian concession.

Newchwang:

1. British concession (1861).

Shasi:

1. Japanese settlement (1898).[12]

Yinkow:

1. Japanese settlement (1905).[13]

Antung:

1. Japanese concession.

Foochow:

1. Japanese concession.

The benefits derived from the concessions and settlements are of significance. Situated at the very door of China, they have often served to the Chinese as real object lessons in municipal government. Protected by foreign forces, they have fostered Chinese trade and industry, and, in times of trouble and disorder, become the fortresses of Chinese life, liberty, and property. Despite these advantages there is nevertheless a growing sentiment against their further continuance and existence.

First, the existence and practice of concessions and settlements impair and obstruct the exercise of Chinese sovereignty over these areas. The Chinese residing therein cannot be arrested except with the consent of the consul, or, in the case of the International Settlement of Shanghai, of the senior consul. Chinese troops are not permitted to pass through these areas. In the case of the International Settlement of Shanghai, the municipal council can make by-laws freely with only the approval of the consuls and ministers of the foreign powers concerned and the rate-payers in special meetings assembled, but without the check and concurrence of the Chinese authorities, either local or central, thus interpreting the limits of the land regulations at their own pleasure and expanding them to such an extent that they have virtually succeeded in converting the municipality into a foreign free state situated on Chinese soil, and thereby obstructing the exercise of the sovereign powers of the Chinese government in matters of taxation, protection, arrest, and other matters of administration. "This assertion of exclusive authority and the power has made each concession

[12] MacMurray, 1896/6.

[13] MacMurray, 1905/18.

virtually *un petit état dans l'état,* to the impairment of China's rights as a territorial sovereignty."[14]

Second, in recent years, these concessions and settlements have become the harbor of safety for political refugees or opponents of the government. In consequence, these political opponents or refugees resided therein and plotted against the existing government virtually under its own nose. The feeling is therefore growing that as long as these special foreign areas exist, there will be no end to the civil war in China, and that to save China from the prolonged torture of civil war the complete recovery of these areas is indispensable.

Third, while the Chinese constitute the bulk of the inhabitants and contribute by far the largest share of the revenues of these municipalities, the Chinese are on the whole denied the right of representation in the municipal council. As an eloquent illustration, in the International Settlement of Shanghai, while the foreign population residing therein in 1924, numbering 21,656, constituted merely 2½ per cent of the total population, the Chinese population residing within the limits of the International Settlement numbered in 1924, 827,932,[15] constituted 97½ per cent of the International Settlement population, and paid the bulk, or at least the major portion, of the municipal revenue;[16] yet it was nevertheless denied the franchise, with no right to vote or to be voted and no privilege of municipal representation, excepting the five members of the Chinese Advisory Committee,[17] whose function it was to offer opinion and advice without any executive or legislative authority. In spite of the belated resolution passed by the annual meeting of the rate-payers held on April 14, 1926,[18] to admit three Chinese members into the municipal council of Shanghai, the concession falling far short of the demands made by the Chinese representatives in 1925, the Chinese dissatisfaction in this respect is still very considerable and tense.

Fourth, the abuse of municipal and police powers by the authorities of the concessions and settlements has rendered further retention of these areas by the foreign powers concerned very irksome and odious to the Chinese. Illustrations from the Shanghai affair of May 30, 1925, will suffice to convince us of this truth. The Japanese cotton mills located within the limits of the International Settlement of Shanghai, enjoying the special protection of extra-territoriality and the foreign settlement,

[14] *The Shantung Question and Other Claims, Submitted by the Chinese Delegation to the Paris Peace Conference,* published by the Chinese National Welfare Society, p. 84.

[15] *Report of Shanghai Municipal Council* (1924), p. 122.

[16] While foreign householders paid an assessed rental of rateable foreign houses in 1924, $1,655,133.54, which quite measure up to the amount paid by Chinese householders, namely $1,723,839.73, of the total revenue of 1924—$8,430,391.73—derived from land tax, general municipal rate, special rate, wharfage dues, license fees, rent of municipal properties, revenue from public and municipal undertakings and so forth, the Chinese residing therein, constituting, as we have seen, 97½ of the total settlement population, the proportion paid by the Chinese, it is moderately estimated, must exceed that by the foreign population, if it does not actually constitute the bulk or at least the major portion of the municipal revenue.

[17] A resolution sanction by the foreign rate-payers on April 7, 1920.

[18] *China Yearbook, 1926,* p. 1016.

could with impunity commit the inhumanity of the employment of child labor, serious brutality to children and women, and the murder of the Chinese labor martyr, Ku Cheng-hung. Upon the appeal of the laborers and students, the Shanghai municipal authorities upheld wrong and suppressed justice by setting free the Japanese accused and muzzling Chinese pleas for redress. When the tide of indignation had gone beyond the control of the police by normal methods—that is, when the students held demonstrations, distributed handbills, and harrangued crowds, and came to the Louza police station with the support of a mob to ask for the release of the students arrested, the police, under the order of the British inspector, fired on the unarmed crowd, resulting in many casualties.

In consequence of these serious objections, the restitution of these concessions and settlements has for a long time become the national aspiration of the Chinese. At the Paris Peace Conference, 1919, the Chinese government submitted the claim for the restoration of these special foreign areas.[19] The request, however, was ignored.

At the Washington Conference, thinking that Chinese public sentiment was not so strongly opposed to the foreign concessions and settlements as to the Shantung decision rendered at the Paris Peace Conference and other questions, the Chinese delegation deliberately omitted the mention of the subject in order not to complicate the other issues. In consequence the powers took no action in regard to this subject.

With the advent, however, of the Shanghai affair of May 30, 1925, the tide of sentiment was entirely and radically changed. What were once felt to be the fortresses of Chinese life, liberty, and property now became engines of atrocity and inhumanity. What was once regarded as a boon now became a bane. Among the thirteen points, therefore, submitted in connection with the Shanghai affair, besides the rendition of the mixed court, municipal franchise was demanded.[20]

*a*) The Chinese may participate in the municipal council and ratepayers' meetings. The ratepayers' representation in the council shall be proportioned to the amount of the rate payable and paid to the municipal revenue and the qualifications for franchise (of the Chinese) shall be similar to those of the foreigners.

*b*) For the purpose of the franchise, distinction shall be made as to whether the property is privately owned or owned as agent for another person. The rights of franchise shall be exercised by the private owner of property and where property is owned by an agent, the actual owner of such property shall exercise the franchise.

The nature of the demand is very sweeping. The bulk of the revenue in the International Settlement of Shanghai being paid by the Chinese and a large portion of the settlement property being owned by the Chinese under the protection and registration of foreign names, the franchise, if granted literally, will sweep away the foreigner or international control and turn it into an overwhelming control of the municipal council by the Chinese.

China rejecting judicial inquiry as a mode of settlement, the case of the Shanghai affair is yet unsettled, and so is the question of Chinese enfranchisement. Though it has been reported that on April 14, 1926, as we have seen, at the annual meeting

[19] *The Shantung Question and Other Claims, op. cit.*, pp. 83–86.

[20] Waichaopu to Diplomatic Body, June 25, 1925, *Peking Daily News,* June 25, 1925.

of the rate-payers, a resolution providing for the election of three Chinese members in the municipal council was passed, the concession falling far short of the Chinese demand, the Chinese desire in this regard remains ungratified.

The mode of restoration or transference to Chinese rule now remains to be considered. It does not seem wise for the foreign powers concerned to restore the concessions and settlements to the Chinese government without providing the adequate representation of the Chinese on the municipal council or legislature, for this mode of transfer will smother the Chinese aspirations for democracy and local home rule. The best mode of restoration or transfer is rather to make these semi-independent city-government centers of municipal home rule, or cradles of Chinese republican democracy, with a small admission of foreign co-operation and assistance. It being accepted as a fundamental principle, in the science of constitutional government, that local self-government is the cornerstone or foundation of a true and great democracy, such advanced and important centers of Chinese and foreign residence and trade should be made the starting-points or roots of Chinese republican and constitutional democracy.

To this end, and respecting the International Settlement of Shanghai, a scheme for its transference to Chinese rule is herewith submitted:[21]

1. That the Chinese residing within the limits of the International Settlement of Shanghai, with the requisite qualifications of rate-payers and councillors, similar to those of the foreign, shall be given all the rights of enfranchisement.

2. The Chinese shall have the right to lease, or own, or acquire use of land in any form, in the International Settlement of Shanghai, under the same conditions as foreigners.

3. That the membership of the municipal council shall be expanded from nine to twenty-one, elected, as before, annually; eleven to be elected by the Chinese rate-payers and ten by the foreign rate-payers; but one foreign member shall retire annually and a Chinese take his place, until at the end of ten years the whole membership shall be elected by the qualified rate-payers.

The twenty-one elected members shall elect six more out of the other qualified rate-payers to make a total membership of twenty-seven, the proportion of the Chinese and foreign co-opted members being similar, in each case, to the ratio of nationalities of the members in the council.

4. A mayor shall be elected by the first elected twenty-one members of the council, who shall hold office for a year but shall be eligible for re-election, and who shall devote his whole time during the tenure of his office to the administration of the municipality, and receive a compensation determined by the council and approved by the rate-payers, but which shall not be increased nor reduced during tenure of office.

[21] In response to a kind request of Dr. W. W. Yen, formerly premier of China, who was then one of the three plenipotentiary commissioners for the negotiation and settlement of the Shanghai affair of May 30, 1925, to work out a scheme for the reorganization of the municipality of the Shanghai International Settlement as basis for discussion with the representatives of the powers, the writer submitted in the fall of 1925 a study or memorandum containing this scheme of reorganization, which has been, however, somewhat modified to suit the progress of events and conditions in China.

5. The police shall be reorganized so as to include a Chinese chief superintendent, and other Chinese inspectors, and to bring about a gradual nationalization of the force.

6. The Chinese government shall have full authority to exercise rights of sovereignty within the limits of the International Settlement of Shanghai, consistent with the terms of the grant of municipal home rule.

7. No amendment of land regulations or municipal charter shall be made without the express consent of the Chinese government.

8. By-laws made in pursuance of land regulations or municipal charter in conflict with provincial or national laws shall be invalid, through repeal by provincial legislature or judicial review by competent courts.

9. Chinese special areas, Nantau, Chapei, Kiangwan, and Woosung, shall be amalgamated with the International Settlement and the French concession of Shanghai into one municipality under a charter of municipal home rule as before prescribed.

Such a scheme of reorganization does not entail a complete retrocession of the Settlement to the Chinese government, as was done in the case of the other concessions already restored, but it stipulates a gradual and progressive conversion of the municipal home rule from one under foreign control to one under Chinese control, "of the people, by the people, and for the people." It provides that at the outset the Chinese representation on the municipal council should occupy only one-half of the seats. In the course of ten years, one foreign member on the council retiring and one Chinese acceding to his place every year, the composition and complexion of the representation on the council will gradually change from a foreign-dominated to a Chinese-dominated chamber of legislature and body of executive. The co-option of more members, other than those elected, was provided to give room and opportunity to those men of integrity and occupation who would not care to run the gauntlet of election and who yet are very desirable elements for municipal representation. The requirement of the elected mayor to devote his whole time to the work of the office and to receive a stipulated salary not increasable nor reducible during his tenure of office makes possible for him to have devotion to service, independence of action, initiative of leadership, and courage of conviction. The nationalization of the police under the Chinese chief superintendent and other Chinese inspectors gives the Chinese the kernel of political power in the municipality. The consolidation of the Chinese special areas, Nantau, Chapei, Kiangwan, and Woosung, with the International Settlement and the French concession into one municipality will unify the municipal administration of Shanghai. Thus the scheme aims to make the city government of Shanghai a great cornerstone of Chinese democracy and home rule.

# SECTION 6

# DOCUMENTS RELATING TO THE CHINESE QUESTION

COMPILED BY MINGCHIEN JOSHUA BAU

Professor of Political Science, Normal University, Peking, and Peking National College of Law and Politics

## I. RUSSIAN DECLARATION OF 1919 AND 1920

The first declaration, namely, the one of July 25, 1919, was originally sent to the Chinese government by wireless, Russia being at the time isolated from other countries by the intervention and blockade of imperialistic states, in which intervention the Chinese government, too, took, among others, an active part. This declaration was published in the official governmental organ in Moscow in its issue of August 20, 1919. Then later it was sent through different channels, by mail, to the ministry of foreign affairs in Peking, though the Chinese government denies having received it—which is quite conceivable.

When, in 1920, General Chang Su-lin was in Moscow, a new declaration was handed to him, and at the same time he was given a correct copy of the first declaration, the one of 1919.

### AN UNAUTHORIZED TEXT

The text of the latter was recently published in the *Peking Leader*. All the other texts used by the papers, and sometimes by official quarters, are but a falsification and have no force.

Representations to this effect were more than once made to the Chinese government. Unfortunately, however, official Chinese institutions have hitherto preferred using a text which had never been signed by Mr. Karakhan and cannot have the significance of an official document. It would be right if the Chinese diplomacy would use the original authentic documents, instead of inexact translations of cables supposed to have been received at Peking. This may be the more advisable that the question is about a document which was ignored and was not recognized at Peking for several years after its issuance. And again, this particular persistence in her own mistake is especially difficult to understand since the Soviet government, by whom this document was issued, gives an explanation, pointing out the precise text, which was published in the governmental organ soon after the document itself was issued.

As regards the Declaration of 1920, it is being quoted quite exactly by the papers and in this instance both the government and the press are indeed handling a precise text. It is the same declaration which was originally handed to General Chang Su-lin in Moscow in 1920.

### CHINA'S REPLY

With regard to the answer given to this latter declaration by the Chinese government, it should first of all be noted that this so-called answer was given two years after the declaration, and within the next few days we shall make a special statement in this reference.

The following is a translation of the Russian text published in the *Izvestia,* the official organ of the All-Russian Central Executive Committee, in its issue of August 20, 1919, No. 988.

### DECLARATION OF THE COUNCIL OF PEOPLE'S COMMISSARIES TO THE CHINESE PEOPLE AND THE GOVERNMENTS OF SOUTH AND NORTH CHINA

On this day when the Soviet Army, having defeated the army of the counter-revolutionary despot, Koltchak, supported by foreign bayonets and foreign gold, is making a triumphant entry into Siberia, where it is marching to unite with the revolutionary people of Siberia, the Council of People's Commissaries sends the following brotherly message to all the peoples of China:

It is not in order to commit acts of violence, to enslave or conquer that Soviet Russia and the Soviet Red Army are now, after a struggle of two years and unprecedented efforts, marching over Ural to the East. Every Siberia peasant and worker knows this by this time. We carry to the peoples their emancipation from the yoke of foreign bayonets and foreign gold, which are strangling the oppressed peoples of the East and—foremost among them—the people of China. It is not only to our toiling classes that we are bringing help, but also to the people of China and we once again recall to it what we had told it since the first days of the Great October Revolution of 1917, but what had possibly been concealed from it by a corrupt American-European-Japanese press.

Immediately after seizing the power in October, 1917, the Workers' and Peasants' Government made an appeal to the peoples of the world, proposing to them to establish a real lasting peace.

This peace should have been based on the renunciation of all seizures of alien land, of bringing by force of alien nationalities into the fold of another people, and of all contributions. Every people, great or small, whenever it lives and whether it had hitherto had independent life—or had been included against its own will into the make-up of another State—must enjoy full liberty in its inner life, and no Government must keep it by force within its boundaries.

Then the Workers' Peasants' Government declared null and void all the secret treaties signed with Japan, China, and the former Allies—treaties through which, by violence and bribery, the Tsar's Government, together with its allies, had fettered the nations of the East and, especially, the people of China, to the interests of Russian capitalists, Russian landlords, and Russian generals. The Soviet Government had already then proposed to the Chinese Government to enter into negotiations on the cancellation of the treaty of 1896, the Peking Protocol of 1901, and all the agreements with Japan from 1901 to 1916, and the handing over to the Chinese people of all that had been taken away from it by the Tsar's Government either on its own account or in common accord with the Japanese and the Allies. Negotiations on this question were proceeding till March, 1918, but the Allies jumped unexpectedly at the throat of the Peking Government, showering gold upon the Peking mandarins and the

Chinese press and forced the Chinese Government to give up all relations with the Russian Workers' and Peasants' Government. Without waiting for the Chinese Eastern Railway being turned over to the Chinese people, Japan and the Allies seized this line themselves, made an irruption into Siberia, and even compelled the Chinese troops to lend them a hand in this criminal and unprecedented brigandage, while the people of China, the Chinese workers and peasants, could not even know the truth why this onslaught was made on Manchuria and Siberia by the American, European, and Japanese depredators.

Today we are calling again to the Chinese people and wish to open their eyes.

The Soviet Government has renounced all the conquests made by the Tsarist Government, which had taken away from China, Manchuria, and other parts of the country. Let the peoples themselves who live in these areas decide within the limits of which state they want to remain and which country they wish to make their home.

The Soviet Government forsakes its share of the Boxer Indemnity, and this it is obliged to repeat for the third time because, according to information having reached us, in spite of our renunciation, this portion of the indemnity is still being raised by the Allies with a view to satisfying the fancies of the former Tsarist ambassador to Peking and former Tsarist consuls in China. All of these Tsar's lackeys have long since lost their powers, but they nevertheless remain where they were and continue, with the help of Japan and the Allies, to deceive the Chinese people. The people of China must know this and must drive them out of the country as cheats and deceivers.

The Soviet Government annuls all special privileges, all the factories of the Russian merchants on Chinese soil. No Russian official, priest, or missionary shall interfere in Chinese affairs, and if he is guilty of a criminal offense, he shall be tried in all justice in local courts. There must be no other power, no other courts but the power and courts of the Chinese people.

Besides these main points, the Soviet Government is ready to come to an agreement with Chinese people, in the persons of its duly authorized representatives, also on all other questions, and thus once for all do away with acts of violence and injustice committed on China by former Russian Governments in common with Japan and the Allies.

The Soviet Government is fully aware that the Allies and Japan will do all in their power so that this time again the voice of the Russian workers and peasants might not reach the Chinese people, telling it that in order to give back the Chinese people all that has been seized from them, it is necessary first to do away with brigands installed in Manchuria and Siberia. Therefore, its message to the Chinese people the Soviet Government sends with its Red Army, which is going over Ural to the east to help the Siberian peasants and workers in their fight for liberation from bandit Kolchak and his ally, Japan.

If the people of China wish to become free, like the Russian people, and be spared the lot prepared for them by the Allies at Versailles, which would make of China a second Korea or a second India, let it understand that its only ally and brother in its struggle for national freedom are the Russian workers and peasants and their Red Army.

The Soviet Government makes a proposal to the people of China, in the person of its Government, to enter without delay into official relations with us and send its representatives to meet our army.

[*Signed*] L. KARAKHAN
Acting People's Commissary for Foreign Affairs

Moscow, July 25, 1919

The following is a translation of the Russian note of September 27, 1920:

*To the Ministry of Foreign Affairs of the Chinese Republic:*

More than a year ago, on July 25, 1919, the People's Commissariat of Foreign Affairs of the Russian Socialist Federative Soviet Republic issued a declaration to the Chinese people and the governments of North and South China, wherein the Russian Government, renouncing all the former Tsarist treaties concluded with China, and returning to the Chinese people all that had been seized from it by force and robbed by the Tsar's Government and the Russian bourgeoisie, proposed to the Chinese Government to enter upon official negotiations with a view to establishing friendly relations.

We have now had information conveyed to us to the effect that this declaration has been received by the Chinese Government, and that the various layers and organizations of the people of China are voicing their sincere desire that the Chinese Government should start negotiations with us with a view to establishing friendly relations between China and Russia.

The Government of the Chinese Republic has delegated to Moscow a Military and Diplomatic Mission, headed by General Chang Su-lin; we welcome most gladly the arrival of the Chinese Mission to Moscow, hoping that through direct negotiations with your Representatives we shall establish a mutual understanding of the common interests uniting China and Russia. We are satisfied that there do not exist any such questions between the Russian and Chinese peoples as could not be solved to the common advantage of both of them. We are aware that the enemies of the Russian and Chinese peoples are trying hard to prevent our friendship and our closer rapprochement, for they understand that the friendship of two great peoples and their reciprocal help will so much strengthen China that no foreigners will then be able to put such fetters on and rob the Chinese people as is being done today.

Unfortunately, however, there is something standing in the way of an early establishment of friendly relations between China and Russia. Your mission, which could perfectly well ascertain our sincere and friendly attitude toward China, has not up till now received the proper instructions which could empower it to enter upon the path of settling formal friendly relations between the two peoples.

Whereas, it expresses its regret at the rapprochement being delayed, and important political and commercial interests of both States failing to materialize, the People's Commissariat of Foreign Affairs, prompted by its desire to be helpful and to speed up the establishment of friendship between the two peoples, declares that it will unswervingly abide by those principles which were laid down in the Declaration of the Russian Soviet Government of July 25, 1919, basing on them the friendly agreement between China and Russia.

In development of the principles contained in that Declaration, the People's

Commissariat of Foreign Affairs deems necessary, for the benefit of both Republics, to propose to the Ministry of Foreign Affairs of the Chinese Republic the following main points of agreement:

ARTICLE I

The Government of the Russian Socialist Federative Soviet Republic declares null and void all the treaties concluded with China by the former governments of Russia, renounces all seizures of Chinese territory and all Russian concessions in China, and restores to China, without any compensation and for ever, all that had been predatorily seized from her by the Tsar's Government and the Russian bourgeoisie.

ARTICLE II

The Governments of both Republics shall take all the necessary measures for immediately establishing regular trade and economic relations. A special treaty to this effect shall be subsequently concluded on the principle of the clause of the most favored nation, applying to both contracting parties.

ARTICLE III

The Chinese Government pledges itself: (1) not to proffer any aid to Russian counter-revolutionary individuals, groups or organizations, nor to allow their activities in Chinese territory; (2) to disarm, intern and hand over to the Government of the Russian Socialist Federative Soviet Republic all the detachments and organizations to be found in Chinese territory at the time of the signing of this Treaty, which are fighting against the R.S.F.S.R. or States allied with her, and to give over to the Government of the R.S.F.S.R. all their arms, supplies and property; (3) the Government of the Russian Socialist Federative Soviet Republic takes upon itself the same obligations with regard to persons or organizations carrying on a rebel struggle against the Republic of China.

ARTICLE IV

All the Russian citizens residing in China shall be subject to all the laws and regulations acting in the territory of the Chinese Republic and shall not enjoy any rights of extraterritoriality. The Chinese citizens residing in Russia shall be subject to all the laws and regulations acting in the territory of the Russian Socialist Federative Soviet Republic.

ARTICLE V

The Government of the Chinese Republic pledges itself, immediately upon the signing of the present treaty, to sever connections with persons styling themselves as diplomatic and consular representatives of the Russian State without having any powers from the Government of the Russian Socialist Federative Soviet Republic, and to deport such persons from China. To hand over to the Russian State, in the person of the Government of the Russian Socialist Federative Soviet Republic, the buildings of the Embassy and consulates and other property and archives of the same, situated in Chinese territory and belonging to Russia.

ARTICLE VI

The Government of the Russian Socialist Federative Soviet Republic renounces any compensation paid out by China as indemnity for the Boxer rising, provided that under no circumstances shall the Government of the Chinese Republic pay any money out of this indemnity to the former Russian consuls or to any other persons or Russian organizations putting up illegal claims thereto.

ARTICLE VII

Following immediately upon the signing of the present Treaty there shall be mutually established diplomatic and consular representatives of the Republic of China and the Russian Socialist Federative Soviet Republic.

ARTICLE VIII

The Russian and the Chinese Governments agree to sign a special treaty on the way of working the Chinese Eastern Railway with regard to the needs of the Russian Socialist Federative Soviet Republic, and in the conclusion of the treaty there shall take part, besides China and Russia, also the Far Eastern Republic.

The above points of agreement the People's Commissariat of Foreign Affairs advances as the main clauses, which can be discussed in a friendly way with your representatives and amendments made which the Chinese Government shall deem necessary for common benefit.

The relation between the two great peoples are not exhausted by the agreement as stated above, and representatives of both States will have to settle subsequently trade, frontier, railway, customs and other questions, embodying them in special treaties.

All measures will be taken on our part with a view to establishing closest and sincere friendship between both parties, and we hope that on the part of the Chinese Government there will also be made an equally sincere and prompt proposition, thus making it possible to proceed at an earliest date to the conclusion of a friendly treaty.

[*Signed*] L. KARAKHAN
Acting People's Commissary for Foreign Affairs

MOSCOW, September 27, 1920

## SINO-RUSSIAN AGREEMENTS, MAY 31, 1924

Agreements between the Republic of China and the Union of Soviet Socialist Republics (and Annexes), signed at Peking, May 31, 1924:

### I. AGREEMENT ON GENERAL PRINCIPLES FOR THE SETTLEMENT OF THE QUESTIONS BETWEEN THE REPUBLIC OF CHINA AND THE UNION OF SOVIET SOCIALIST REPUBLICS

The Republic of China and the Union of Soviet Socialist Republics, desiring to re-establish normal relations with each other, have agreed to conclude an agreement on general principles for the settlement of the questions between the two countries, and have to that end named as their plenipotentiaries, that is to say:

His Excellency the President of the Republic of China: Vi Kyuin Wellington Koo.

The Government of the Union of Soviet Socialist Republics: Lev Mikhailovitch Karakhan.

Who, having communicated to each other their respective full powers, found to be in good and due form, have agreed upon the following Articles:

ARTICLE I

Immediately upon the signing of the present Agreement, the normal diplomatic and consular relations between the two contracting parties shall be re-established.

The Government of the Republic of China agrees to take the necessary steps to transfer to the Government of the Union of Soviet Socialist Republics the Legation and Consular buildings formerly belonging to the Tsarist Government.

ARTICLE II

The Governments of the two Contracting Parties agree to hold, within one month after the signing of the present Agreement, a conference which shall include and carry out detailed arrangements relative to the questions in accordance with the principles as provided in the following Articles.

Such detailed arrangements shall be completed as soon as possible and, in any case, not later than six months from the date of the opening of the Conference as provided in the preceding paragraph.

ARTICLE III

The Governments of the two Contracting Parties agree to annul at the Conference as provided in the preceding Article, all Conventions, Treaties, Agreements, Protocols, Contracts, etc., concluded between the Government of China and the Tsarist Government and to replace them with new treaties, agreements, etc., on the basis of equality, reciprocity and justice, as well as the spirit of the Declarations of the Soviet Government of the years of 1919 and 1920.

ARTICLE IV

The Government of the Union of Soviet Socialist Republics, in accordance with its policy and Declarations of 1919 and 1920, declares that all Treaties, Agreements, etc., concluded between the former Tsarist Government and any third party or parties affecting the sovereign rights or interests of China, are null and void.

The Governments of both Contracting Parties declare that in future neither Government will conclude any treaties or agreements which prejudice the sovereign rights or interests of either Contracting Party.

ARTICLE V

The Government of the Union of Soviet Socialist Republics recognizes that Outer Mongolia is an integral part of the Republic of China and respects China's sovereignty therein.

The Government of the Union of Soviet Socialist Republics declares that as soon as the questions for the withdrawal of all the troops of the Union of Soviet Socialist Republics from Outer Mongolia—namely, as to the time-limit of the withdrawal of such troops and the measures to be adopted in the interests of the safety of the frontiers—are agreed upon at the Conference as provided in Article II of the present Agreement, it will effect the complete withdrawal of all the troops of the Union of Soviet Socialist Republics from Outer Mongolia.

ARTICLE VI

The Governments of the two Contracting Parties mutually pledge themselves not to permit, within their respective territories, the existence and/or activities of any organizations or groups whose aim is to struggle by acts of violence against the Governments of either Contracting Party.

The Governments of the two Contracting Parties further pledge themselves not to engage in propaganda directed against the political and social systems of either Contracting Party.

ARTICLE VII

The Governments of the two Contracting Parties agree to redemarcate their national boundaries at the Conference as provided in Article II of the present Agreement, and pending such redemarcation, to maintain the present boundaries.

ARTICLE VIII

The Governments of the two Contracting Parties agree to regulate at the aforementioned Conference the questions relating to the navigation of rivers, lakes and other bodies of water which are common to their respective frontiers, on the basis of equality and reciprocity.

ARTICLE IX

The Governments of the two Contracting Parties agree to settle at the aforementioned Conference the question of the Chinese Eastern Railway in conformity with the principles as hereinafter provided:

1. The Governments of the two Contracting Parties declare that the Chinese Eastern Railway is a purely commercial enterprise.

The Governments of the two Contracting Parties mutually declare that with the exception of matters pertaining to the business operations which are under the direct control of the Chinese Eastern Railway, all other matters affecting the rights of the National and the Local Governments of the Republic of China—such as judicial matters, matters relating to civil administration, military administration, police, municipal government, taxation, and landed property (with the exception of lands required by the said Railway) shall be administered by the Chinese authorities.

2. The Government of the Union of Soviet Socialist Republics agrees to the redemption by the Government of the Republic of China, with Chinese capital, of the Chinese Eastern Railway, as well as all appurtenant properties and to the transfer to China of all shares and bonds of the said Railway.

3. The Governments of the two Contracting Parties shall settle at the Conference as provided in Article II of the present Agreement, the amount and conditions governing the redemption as well as the procedure for the transfer of the Chinese Eastern Railway.

4. The Government of the Union of Soviet Socialist Republics agrees to be responsible for the entire claims of the shareholders, bondholders and creditors of the Chinese Eastern Railway incurred prior to the Resolution of March 9, 1917.

5. The Governments of the two Contracting Parties mutually agree that the future of the Chinese Eastern Railway shall be determined by the Republic of China

and the Union of Soviet Socialist Republics to the exclusion of any third party or parties.

6. The Governments of the two Contracting Parties agree to draw up an arrangement for the provisional management of the Chinese Eastern Railway pending the settlement of the question as provided under Section (3) of the present Article.

7. Until the various questions relating to the Chinese Eastern Railway are settled at the Conference as provided in Article II of the present Agreement, the rights of the two Governments arising out of the Contract of August 27, September 8, 1896, for the construction and operation of the Chinese Eastern Railway, which do not conflict with the present agreement and the Agreement for the Provisional Management of the said Railway and which do not prejudice China's rights of sovereignty, shall be maintained.

ARTICLE X

The Government of the Union of Soviet Socialist Republics agrees to renounce the special rights and privileges relating to all concessions in any part of China acquired by the Tsarist Government under various Conventions, Treaties, Agreements, etc.

ARTICLE XI

The Government of the Union of Soviet Socialist Republics agrees to renounce the Russian portion of the Boxer Indemnity.

ARTICLE XII

The Government of the Union of Soviet Socialist Republics agrees to relinquish the rights of extra-territoriality and consular jurisdiction.

ARTICLE XIII

The Governments of the two Contracting Parties agree to draw up simultaneously with the conclusion of a Commercial Treaty at the Conference as provided in ARTICLE II of the present Agreement, a Customs Tariff for the two Contracting Parties in accordance with the principles of equality and reciprocity.

ARTICLE XIV

The Governments of the two Contracting Parties agree to discuss at the aforementioned Conference the questions relating to the claims for the compensation of losses.

ARTICLE XV

The present Agreement shall come into effect from the date of signature.

In witness whereof the respective Plenipotentiaries have signed the present Agreement in duplicate in the English language and have affixed thereto their seals.

Done at the city of Peking this Thirty-first Day of the Fifth Month of the Thirteenth Year of the Republic of China, which is, the Thirty-first day of May, One Thousand Nine Hundred and Twenty-four.

[*Seal*] V. K. WELLINGTON KOO
[*Seal*] L. M. KARAKHAN

## II. AGREEMENT FOR THE PROVISIONAL MANAGEMENT OF CHINESE EASTERN RAILWAY

The Republic of China and the Union of Soviet Socialist Republics mutually recognizing that, inasmuch as the Chinese Eastern Railway was built with capital furnished by the Russian Government and constructed entirely within Chinese territory, the said railway is a purely commercial enterprise and that, excepting for matters appertaining to its own business operations, all other matters which affect the rights of the Chinese National and Local Governments shall be administered by the Chinese Authorities, have agreed to conclude an Agreement for the Provisional Management of the Railway with a view to carrying on jointly the management of the said Railway until its final settlement at the Conference as provided in Article II of the Agreement on General Principles for the Settlement of the Questions between the Republic of China and the Union of Soviet Socialist Republics of May 31, 1924, and have to that end named as their Plenipotentiaries, that is to say:

His Excellency the President of the Republic of China: Vi Kyuin Wellington Koo,

The Government of the Union of Soviet Socialist Republics: Lev Mikhailovitch Karakhan,

Who having communicated to each other their respective full powers, found to be in good and due form, have agreed upon the following articles:

ARTICLE I

The Railway shall establish, for discussion and decision of all matters relative to the Chinese Eastern Railway, a Board of Directors to be composed of ten persons of whom five shall be appointed by the Government of the Republic of China and five by the Government of the Union of Soviet Socialist Republics.

The Government of the Republic of China shall appoint one of the Chinese Directors as President of the Board of Directors, who shall also be the Director-General.

The Government of the Union of Soviet Socialist Republics shall appoint one of the Russian Directors as Vice-President of the Board of Directors, who shall also be the Assistant Director-General.

Seven persons shall constitute a quorum, and all decisions of the Board of Directors shall have the consent of not less than six persons before they can be carried out.

The Director-General and Assistant Director-General shall jointly manage the affairs of the Board of Directors and they shall both sign all the documents of the Board.

In the absence of either the Director-General or the Assistant Director General, their respective Governments may appoint another Director to officiate as the Director-General or the Assistant Director-General (in the case of the Director-General, by one of the Chinese Directors, and in that of the Assistant Director-General, by one of the Russian Directors).

ARTICLE II

The Railway shall establish a Board of Auditors to be composed of five persons, namely, two Chinese Auditors, who shall be appointed by the Government of the Republic of China, and three Russian Auditors who shall be appointed by the Government of the Union of Soviet Socialist Republics.

The Chairman of the Board of Auditors shall be elected from among the Chinese Auditors.

ARTICLE III

The Railway shall have a Manager, who shall be a national of the Union of Soviet Socialist Republics, and two Assistant Managers, one to be a national of the Republic of China and the other to be a national of the Union of Soviet Socialist Republics.

The said officers shall be appointed by the Board of Directors and such appointments shall be confirmed by their respective governments.

The rights and duties of the Manager and the Assistant Managers shall be defined by the Board of Directors.

ARTICLE IV

The Chiefs and Assistant Chiefs of the various departments of the Railway shall be appointed by the Board of Directors.

If the Chief of Department is a national of the Republic of China, the Assistant Chief of Department shall be a national of the Union of Soviet Socialist Republics, and if the Chief of Department is a national of the Union of Soviet Socialist Republics, the Assistant Chief of Department shall be a national of the Republic of China.

ARTICLE V

The employment of persons in the various departments of the Railway shall be in accordance with the principle of equal representation between the nationals of the Republic of China and those of the Union of Soviet Socialist Republics.

ARTICLE VI

With the exception of the estimates and budget, as provided in Article VII of the present Agreement, all other matters on which the Board of Directors cannot reach an agreement shall be referred for settlement to the Governments of the Contracting Parties.

ARTICLE VII

The Board of Directors shall present the estimates and budget of the Railway to a joint meeting of the Board of Directors and the Board of Auditors for consideration and approval.

ARTICLE VIII

All the net profits of the Railway shall be held by the Board of Directors and shall not be used pending a final settlement of the question of the present railway.

ARTICLE IX

The Board of Directors shall revise as soon as possible the statutes of the Chinese Eastern Railway Company, approved on December 4, 1896, by the Tsarist Government, in accordance with the present Agreement and the Agreement on General Principles for the Settlement of the Questions between the Republic of China and the Union of Soviet Socialist Republics of May 31, 1924, and in any case, not later than six months from the date of the constitution of the Board of Directors. Pending their revision, the aforesaid statutes, insofar as they do not conflict with the present Agreement on General Principles for the Settlement of the Questions between the Republic of China and the Union of Soviet Socialist Republics and do not prejudice the rights of sovereignty of the Republic of China, shall continue to be observed.

ARTICLE X

The present Agreement shall cease to have effect as soon as the question of the Chinese Eastern Railway is finally settled at the Conference as provided in Article II of the Agreement on General Principles for the Settlement of the Questions between the Republic of China and the Union of Soviet Socialist Republics of May 31, 1924.

ARTICLE XI

The present Agreement shall come into effect from the date of signature.

In witness whereof, the respective Plenipotentiaries have signed the present agreement in duplicate and have affixed thereto their seals.

Done at the city of Peking, etc., etc.

## DECLARATION I

The Government of the Republic of China and the Government of the U.S.S.R. declare that immediately after the signing of the Agreement on General Principles between the Republic of China and the U.S.S.R. of May 31, 1924, they will reciprocally hand over to each other all the real estate and movable property owned by China and the former Tsarist Government and found in their respective territories. For this purpose each Government will furnish the other with a list of the property to be so transferred.

In faith whereof, the respective Plenipotentiaries of the Governments of the two Contracting Parties have signed the present Declaration in duplicate in the English language and have affixed thereto their seals.

Done at the city of Peking, etc.

## DECLARATION II

The Government of the Republic of China and the Government of the U.S.S.R. hereby declare that it is understood that with regard to the buildings and landed property of the Russian Orthodox Mission, belonging as it does to the Government of the U.S.S.R., the question of the transfer or other suitable disposal of the same will be jointly determined at the Conference provided in Article II of the Agreement on General Principles in accordance with the internal laws and regulations existing in China regarding property-holding in the inland. As regards the buildings and property of the Russian Orthodox Mission, belonging as it does to the Government of the U.S.S.R. at Peking and Patachu, the Chinese Government will take steps to immediately transfer same as soon as the Government of the U.S.S.R. will designate a Chinese person or organization in accordance with the laws and regulations existing in China regarding property-holding in the inland.

Meanwhile the Government of the Republic of China will at once take measures with a view to guarding all the said buildings and property and clearing them from all the persons now living there.

It is further understood that this expression of understanding has the same force and validity as a general declaration embodied in the said Agreement on General Principles.

In faith whereof, etc., etc.

### DECLARATION III

The Government of the Republic of China and the Government of the U.S.S.R. jointly declare that it is understood that with reference to Article IV of the Agreement on General Principles, the Government of the Republic of China will not and does not recognize as valid any treaty agreement, etc., concluded between Russia since the Tsarist régime and any third party or parties, affecting the sovereign rights and interests of the Republic of China. It is further understood that this expression of understanding has the same force and validity as a general declaration, etc., etc.

### DECLARATION IV

The Government of the Republic of China and the Government of the U.S.S.R. jointly declare that it is understood that the Government of the Republic of China will not transfer either in part or in whole to any third Power or any foreign organization the special rights and privileges renounced by the Government of the U.S.S.R. in Article X of the Agreement on General Principles. It is further understood that this expression of understanding has the same force, etc., etc.

### DECLARATION V

The Government of the Republic of China and the Government of the U.S.S.R. jointly declare that it is understood that with reference to Article XI of the Agreement on General Principles:

1. The Russian share of the Boxer indemnity which the Government of the U.S.S.R. renounces will, after the satisfaction of all prior obligations secured thereon, be entirely appropriated to create a fund for the promotion of education among the Chinese people.

2. A special Commission will be established to administer and allocate the said fund. This Commission will consist of three persons, two of whom will be appointed by the Government of the U.S.S.R. Decisions of the said Commission will be taken by unanimous vote.

3. The said fund will be designated as it accrues from time to time in a bank to be designated by the said Commission.

It is further understood, etc.

### DECLARATION VI

The Government of the Republic of China and the Government of the U.S.S.R. agree that they will establish equitable provisions at the Conference as provided in Article II of the Agreement of the U.S.S.R. by the relinquishment of the rights of extra-territoriality and consular jurisdiction under Article XII of the aforementioned

Agreement, it being understood, however, that the nationals of the Government of the U.S.S.R. shall be entirely amenable to Chinese Jurisdiction.

In faith whereof, etc., etc.

DECLARATION VII

The Government of the Republic of China and the Government of the U.S.S.R., having signed the Agreement on General Principles, hereby agree, in explanation of Article V of the Agreement for the Provisional Management of the Chinese Eastern Railway, which provides for the principle of equal representation in the filling of posts by citizens of the Republic of China and those of the U.S.S.R., that the application of this principle is not to be understood to mean that the present employees of Russian nationality shall be dismissed for the sole purpose of enforcing the said principle. It is further understood that access to all posts is equally open to citizens of both Contracting Parties, that no special preference shall be shown to either nationality, and that the posts shall be filled in accordance with the ability and technical as well as educational qualifications of the applicant.

In faith whereof, etc., etc.

PEKING, May 31, 1924

*Mr. L. M. Karakhan,*

*Extraordinary Plenipotentiary Representative of the Union of Soviet Socialist Republics to the Republic of China, Peking*

DEAR MR. KARAKHAN: On behalf of my Government, I have the honour to declare that, an Agreement on General Principles for the Settlement of the Questions between the Republic of China and the U.S.S.R. having been signed between us today, the Government of the Republic of China will, in the interests of friendship between the Republic of China and the U.S.S.R., discontinue the services of all the subjects of the former Russian Empire now employed in the Chinese army and police force, as they constitute by their presence or activities a menace to the safety of the U.S.S.R. If you will furnish my Government with a list of such persons the authorities concerned will be instructed to adopt the necessary action.

I have the honour to remain, etc.

[*Signed*] V. K. WELLINGTON KOO
Minister for Foreign Affairs of the Republic of China

PEKING, May 31, 1924

DEAR DR. KOO: I have the honour to acknowledge the receipt of the following note from you under this date:

[Here follows the text of Dr. Koo's note, given above.]

In reply I beg to state on behalf of my Government, that I have taken note of the same and that I agree to the propositions contained therein.

I have the honour to be

Very truly yours,

L. M. KARAKHAN
Extraordinary Plenipotentiary, etc., etc.

## III. RECOMMENDATIONS OF THE COMMISSION ON EXTRA-TERRITORIALITY IN CHINA, SEPTEMBER 16, 1926

The commissioners, having completed their investigations and having made their findings of fact as set forth in Parts I, II, and III of this report, now make the following recommendations:

The commissioners are of the opinion that, when these recommendations shall have been reasonably complied with, the several powers would be warranted in relinquishing their respective rights of extra-territoriality.

It is understood that, upon the relinquishment of extra-territoriality, the nationals of the powers concerned will enjoy freedom of residence and trade and civil rights in all parts of China in accordance with the general practice in intercourse among nations and upon a fair and equitable basis.

### RECOMMENDATIONS

I

The administration of justice with respect to the civilian population in China must be entrusted to a judiciary which shall be effectively protected against any unwarranted interference by the executive or other branches of the Government, whether civil or military.

II

The Chinese Government should adopt the following program for the improvement of the existing legal, judicial and prison systems of China:

1. It should consider Parts II and III of this report relating to the laws and to the judicial, police and prison systems, with a view to making such amendments and taking such action as may be necessary to meet the observations there made.

2. It should complete and put into force the following laws:
   (1) Civil code.
   (2) Commercial code (including negotiable instruments, law, maritime law and insurance law).
   (3) Revised criminal code.
   (4) Banking law.
   (5) Bankruptcy law.
   (6) Patent law.
   (7) Land expropriation law.
   (8) Law concerning notaries public.

3. It should establish and maintain a uniform system for the regular enactment, promulgation and recission of laws, so that there may be no uncertainty as to the laws of China.

4. It should extend the system of modern courts, modern prisons and modern detention-houses with a view to the elimination of the magistrates' courts and of the old-style prisons and detention-houses.

5. It should make adequate financial provision for the maintenance of courts, detention-houses and prisons and their personnel.

III

It is suggested that, prior to the reasonable compliance with all the recommendations above mentioned but after the principal items thereof have been carried out, the Powers concerned, if so desired by the Chinese Government, might consider the abolition of extra-territoriality according to such progressive scheme (whether geographical, partial or otherwise) as may be agreed upon.

IV

Pending the abolition of extra-territoriality, the Governments of the Powers concerned should consider Part I of this report with a view to meeting the observations there made and, with the co-operation of the Chinese Government wherever necessary, should make certain modifications in the existing systems and practice of extra-territoriality as follows:

1. Application of Chinese laws:

The Powers concerned should administer, so far as practicable, in their extra-territorial or consular courts such laws and regulations of China as they may deem it proper to adopt.

2. Mixed cases and mixed courts:

As a general rule mixed cases between nationals of the Powers concerned as plaintiffs and persons under Chinese jurisdiction as defendants should be tried before the modern Chinese courts (Shen P'an T'ing) without the presence of a foreign assessor to watch the proceedings or otherwise participate. With regard to the existing special mixed courts, their organization and procedure should, as far as the special conditions in the settlements and concessions warrant, be brought more into accord with the organization and procedure of the modern Chinese judicial system. Lawyers who are nationals of extra-territorial powers and who are qualified to appear before the extra-territorial or consular courts should be permitted, subject to the laws and regulations governing Chinese lawyers, to represent clients, foreign or Chinese, in all mixed cases. No examination should be required as a qualification for practice in such cases.

3. Nationals of extra-territorial Powers:

*a*) The extra-territorial Powers should correct certain abuses which have arisen through the extension of foreign protection to Chinese as well as to business and shipping interests the actual ownership of which is wholly or mainly Chinese.

*b*) The extra-territorial Powers which do not now require compulsory periodical registration of their nationals in China should make provision for such registration at definite intervals.

4. Judicial assistance:

Necessary arrangements should be made in regard to judicial assistance (including commissions rogatoires) between the Chinese authorities and the authorities of the extra-territorial Powers and between the authorities of the extra-territorial Powers themselves, e.g.:

*a*) All agreements between foreigners and persons under Chinese jurisdiction which provide for the settlement of civil matters by arbitration should be recognized, and the awards made in pursuance thereof should be enforced, by the extra-territorial or consular courts in the case of persons under their jurisdiction and by the Chinese courts in the case of persons under their jurisdiction, except when in the opinion of the competent court, the decision is contrary to public order or good morals.

*b*) Satisfactory arrangements should be made between the Chinese Government and the Powers concerned for the prompt execution of judgments, summonses and warrants of arrest or search, concerning persons under Chinese jurisdiction, duly issued by the Chinese courts and certified by the competent Chinese authorities and vice versa.

5. Taxation:

Pending the abolition of extra-territoriality, the nationals of the Powers concerned should be required to pay such taxes as may be prescribed in laws and regulations duly promulgated by the competent authorities of the Chinese Government and recognized by the Powers concerned as applicable to their nationals.

SIGNED IN THE CITY OF PEKING, September 16, 1926

## IV. REVISED REGULATIONS GOVERNING THE TRIAL OF NON-EXTRA-TERRITORIAL NATIONALS IN CIVIL AND CRIMINAL CASES

(PROMULGATED ON NOVEMBER 25, 1926)

ARTICLE I

These regulations are applicable in the trial of the following cases: (1) When non-extra-territorial nationals are the accused in criminal cases; (2) In civil cases between non-extra-territorial nationals and Chinese; (3) In civil cases among nationals of non-extra-territorial nations; (4) In civil cases when non-extra-territorial nationals are the defendants and nationals of other nations are the plaintiffs.

ARTICLE II

When non-extra-territorial nationals are guilty of police offenses, or criminal offenses of the navy or army or other special crimes stipulated in the criminal laws, they shall be dealt with by the ordinary law courts in accordance with the common procedure.

ARTICLE III

The High Court or High Procurate or the Judicial Department of the Tutung's Yamen shall determine and notify the court concerned by order beforehand in regard to the question of jurisdiction, according to local conditions and circumstances. A report thereof shall be submitted to the Ministry of Justice.

In case there be inconvenience in the transference of the case to a court remotely situated, or when there are special conditions which render the transference impossible, the authorities responsible shall render a report and apply to the Ministry of Justice for instructions.

ARTICLE IV

In districts without ordinary law courts when non-extra-territorial nationals are involved in criminal cases, the district magistrate shall adjudge the case promptly and then send the whole case together with a detailed statement of the judgment given and all documents to the court having jurisdiction over it and at the same time submit a report to the High Procuratorate or the Judicial Department of the Tutung's Yamen for future reference.

ARTICLE V

Non-extra-territorial nationals to be put under custody or imprisoned on account of criminal cases shall be accommodated in modern prisons, or in suitable quarters if there are no modern prisons.

ARTICLE VI

The regulations governing civil or criminal law suits and articles provided by other law and ordinances shall be applicable in regard to the procedure not provided for in these regulations.

ARTICLE VII

Defects in the present regulations may be revised at any time by the Ministry of Justice who shall apply to the President of the Republic for the issuance of instructional mandates executing same.

ARTICLE VIII

The present regulations shall be effective from the day of promulgation.

## SECTION 7

# OFFICIAL STATEMENTS ON CHINA BY THE JAPANESE GOVERNMENT[1]

### I. STATEMENT ISSUED BY THE DEPARTMENT OF FOREIGN AFFAIRS ON MAY 28, 1927

Taking into consideration the fact that, owing to the present commotion in China, in which we remember especially the incidents that occurred in Nanking, Hankow, and other places arising from the imperfect protective measures taken by the Chinese authorities, the lives and property of our nationals resident there were subjected to grave danger and injury and this country even suffered an indignity, it is not improbable that under the present circumstances similar unfortunate incidents may occur in North China, where disturbance is imminent. The disturbances are now feared to spread towards Tsinan, and we felt profound anxiety about the safety of the lives and property of Japanese residents there. They number as many as two thousand, and as the district is situated inland far from the coast, it is impossible to protect them with naval forces, as in the case of those in the Yangtze Valley. In order to prevent the recurrence of unhappy events, therefore, the Japanese government is compelled to protect the lives and property of its nationals with military forces. In view of the fact, however, that arrangements for the dispatch of troops to effect such protection naturally require a considerable space of time, while the situation of warfare changes every minute, it is decided to dispatch immediately as an emergency measure a force of about two thousand men to Tsingtao from the Japanese garrison in Manchuria.

This protection of our residents by military strength is a matter of pure and urgent necessity demanded for the self-defense and security of our nationals, and by no means implies any unfriendly intention toward China and her people, nor is it intended to interfere with the strategic operations of any of the northern and southern troops and hinder their military movements.

The Japanese government, therefore, declares that, although it despatches troops as an unavoidable measure of self-defense as before stated, it has no intention whatever of keeping them for a prolonged period, and the troops will be wholly withdrawn immediately the fear of danger to our residents in that region ceases to exist.

### II. TRANSLATION OF STATEMENT OF BARON TANAKA, PRIME MINISTER AND FOREIGN MINISTER, GIVEN TO THE PRESS, APRIL 22, 1927

I have now formed the Cabinet at the Imperial command and it is a great pleasure to me to make the following statement on the occasion of the assumption of my duties.

The statement I made as President of the Rikkon-Seiyukai before the general meeting of the party on April 16 regarding the administration of domestic and foreign affairs embodies the general policies of my Government, and it is superfluous

[1] Translated by the Japanese group at the Conference.

now to reiterate it in detail. The chief aim of my Government is to clear up the atmosphere of unrest prevailing in our economic circles at the present time, invigorate our national spirit, and, on the basis of a fundamental policy of industrialization of the country, carry into effect the renovation of administrative methods, the improvement of education, the decentralization of administration, the development of agrarian districts, the enforcement of social policies, and the maintenance of the sanctity of judicial power. With reference to our foreign policy, the problem of the utmost importance and urgency to Japan and the Far East is the situation in China. We have long entertained profound sympathy with the legitimate aspirations of the Chinese people and are determined to help them to attain their end, taking into careful consideration the situation at home and abroad. But I consider that such aspirations should be attained in due order and by appropriate means, and I am convinced that it is not the true desire of the Chinese people to disregard such considerations and leave the commotion in China to grow more intense. Moreover, I think that, if the legitimate aspirations of the Chinese people are fulfilled, they will have no wish to endanger the present relations between China and the Powers. It seems that the Powers which have important relations with China are not averse to accede to the legitimate demands of the Chinese people. I have then no doubt that there is a way to satisfy their demands without causing any grave situation in the relations between China and the Powers, and I earnestly hope, therefore, that the Chinese people will give serious attention to this consideration. In the matter of Communist activity in China, Japan can hardly remain indifferent, as she is vitally concerned with the preservation of peace in the Orient generally and is so placed as to be directly and most deeply affected by the results of such activity. It is also a matter of extreme importance from the general viewpoint of the peace of the world and the happiness of mankind in general, and, Japan is ready to co-operate with the Powers, after taking into consideration the character of the particular problems involved, the appropriate time, and the proposed measures to be taken. I am confident that this stand which we take will be well understood by our friendly neighbor Russia.

Lastly, I believe that our legitimate economic development will undoubtedly be welcomed by the Powers with which we are in relations of friendliness and intimacy, and I am firmly resolved to co-operate with all nations for the maintenance of peace and order in the world and for the promotion of the weal of mankind.

## SECTION 8

## TREND OF JAPANESE EDITORIAL COMMENT ON PROBLEMS OF CHINA[1]

### I. EDITORIAL COMMENTS ON PREMIER TANAKA'S POLICY TOWARD CHINA

The *Tokyo Asahi*, the *Osaka Asahi*, the *Jiji Shimpo*, the *Tokyo Nichinichi*, and the *Osaka Mainichi*, commenting upon the policy of the Tanaka Cabinet toward China, all consistently warn against a positive policy and wish for maintenance of a more cautious attitude toward China.

*Tokyo Asahi:* Although there are some regrettable points in the Shidehara diplomacy, in regard to the protection of Japanese subjects in China as well as its views on the China situation, the fundamental policy of non-interference in domestic affairs is quite necessary even today. No one can foretell the future of China; nevertheless it is advisable to let Chinese themselves settle their own internal affairs. It is vital that we should foresee their future development. As every word and action of Premier Tanaka is being closely watched by the Chinese, we hope the present administration will be extremely cautious in executing its policy toward China.

*Osaka Asahi:* Absolute non-interference in internal affairs, protection of our subjects in China, and removal of unreasonable pressure upon the interests of Japan are three important conditions in connection with the policy of Japan toward China.

We should not be dragged into such an unwise and rigid policy of other powers. That non-interference in another country's domestic affairs and self-protection can stand side by side was explained by our former minister of foreign affairs, Baron Shidehara. The only defect of our former administration was the lack of adequate defense to meet emergencies. The present administration should lay special emphasis on this point in view of the unsettled present condition of China.

*Jiji Shimpo:* To comprehend the real motive of the Chinese people and to interpret the interests of Japan is vital in formulating a new policy with due sympathy for the present conditions of China. The new administration should not be hasty because of immediate uprisings. We sincerely hope that the new administration will not adopt any radical change in its policy toward China, neither resort to any rigid policy, as we are sure that is not the real purpose of the administration.

*Tokyo Nichinichi:* It is generally recognized that the declaration of Premier Tanaka's foreign policy contains some military color. We appreciate this difficulty and sincerely hope for profound caution in dealing with foreign powers, making it impossible to apply the extreme feature of Baron Tanaka's foreign policy. Some say that the Tanaka administration is bent on an extreme reactionary policy, but both Baron Tanaka himself and the Seiyukai can not ignore the trend of the times nor the tendency of public opinion. As it is inconsistent with his former views, we believe that there will be no radical change in the foreign policy of the present administration.

[1] Translated by the Japanese group at the Conference.

Furthermore, we hope most earnestly that the new administration will formulate a new policy toward China and Russia, in view of recent happenings, whereby we offer moral support instead of a joint expedition. Such a policy must be clearly stated at the special session of the diet.

*Mainichi:* Contrasting some of the statements of Baron Tanaka prior to his acceptancy of the premiership with the conditions today, people are somewhat uneasy. Should the Seiyukai administration join other powers in an expedition to China in realizing an aggressive policy a serious situation would result. We can't be too severe in our criticism of the Seiyukai, which cannot gain much by such an unwise policy. Before such a policy is put into application it needs careful consideration, and we hope for a complete reversion of such a policy in conformity with the desire of the people.

*Chugai:* Premier Tanaka's policy toward China seems quite sound, particularly when it is compared with his earlier views. Under the present circumstances of China there is no benefit to us in any positive policy. On the contrary, such a policy will lead us into a delicate position. This is the point to which the Tanaka administration should give most careful consideration. However, we must avoid danger to our national honor or interests by the overinsistence of non-interference.

*Yamato Shinbun:* It is improbable that there should be a basic change in our foreign policy simply because of the change of administration. The reason why the former cabinet did not resort to arms is because of the intimate economic relations between the two countries. Consequently to resort to arms is unthinkable, regardless of the change of administration. It is needless to say that as long as China remains out of order and irresponsible, however, we should take some reasonable measures.

## II. THE SHANTUNG EXPEDITION

All the leading papers in Japan took a very cautious attitude toward the Shantung Expedition. Before it was decided to send the expedition, the *Jiji, Tokyo Asahi, Osaki Asahi, Hochi, Tokyo Nichinichi, Osaka Mainichi,* and others carried an editorial to the effect that this was only as a last resort in a special emergency and should be limited only to the protection of life and property of our residents in China. The government should declare this purpose clearly, and not overstep this limitation.

The *Tokyo Asahi* and the *Osaka Mainichi* advised the government to take diplomatic instead of military measures in persuading the northern and southern parties to take the necessary steps to come into closer touch with each other, and this in their opinion was not interference.

*Hochi* and *Osaka Asahi:* Rather than send such a force it would be better to withdraw the residents of Peking to Tientsin, and those in Tsinan to Tsingtao.

It was decided on May 28 to send the expedition, and on the thirtieth all of the papers came out with a warning to the government that this was a very serious matter, as well as of great responsibility, so every precaution should be taken to give the Chinese to understand that it was for protection alone.

*Jiji:* The foreign and war departments should see to it that this was done in a fair and cautious manner, and when their presence was no longer needed the soldiers should be withdrawn at once.

*Tokyo Asahi:* The expedition was to be limited absolutely to protection to resident Japanese only (observe strict neutrality toward the Chinese forces), and not in the slightest measure show sympathy for either side. Nor should this be used as a pretext for sending more troops.

*Osaka Asahi:* The responsibility of our government has become greater because of this expedition.

*Hochi:* The government seems to have been rather hasty in this action, although we can understand that the sole object was to protect its citizens. There must have been many other measures to which it might have resorted, and to resort to arms is a very unwise expedient.

*Tokyo Nichinichi:* In order that the army may have no need of entering farther than Tsingtao, let the government recommend a truce between the North and the South. Because Japan is liable to be misunderstood, every precaution should be taken that our purpose is clear. We of course understand that the Chinese are afraid that we are going to intervene against the southern troops, but we should make them understand that our fears are more about what the northern forces might do.

*Chugai:* The government should be on its guard against playing into the hands of the northern forces by this expedition, which may have an influence on the whole Chinese situation.

### III. RECENT COMMENT

After the forces were dispatched there was a cessation of military activity in China, so there is now more of an attempt to solve the situation by diplomatic measures, and so most of the papers urge the government to withdraw the troops, there being no more need.

*Tokyo Asahi:* Why was there any need of sending troops to China in the first place? And as we look at the situation now there is far less need, so they should be returned at once.

*Tokyo Nichinichi* and *Osaka Mainichi:* In regard to the expedition, it seems we were not able, nor was there any need, to protect our residents in Tsinan. On the other hand there is no doubt that we have lost much by the misunderstanding we have aroused, so according to the original purpose and consideration of present conditions the troops should be sent back at once.

*Jiji:* Since there has been a cessation of hostilities there is no more need of a force for protection and the army should be withdrawn. If the unsettled conditions of Tsinan continue, the government should withdraw both residents and troops. These troops should under no consideration prolong their stay indefinitely.

*Hochi:* In regard to the expedition, the government should preserve the principle of non-intervention and absolute neutrality to all factions.

*Yamato:* The fall of Chang Tso Ling is only a question of time, and there is no doubt but that the southern government will be recognized, so the government of Japan will be wiser to turn its support to this southern side.

## SECTION 9

## MEMORANDUM ON MISSIONS

HENRY T. HODGKIN
Secretary, National Christian Council of China

The following memorandum deals almost exclusively with the point of view of the Protestant missionary movement, as the writer is not sufficiently in touch with the Roman Catholic movement to be able to speak on it with any authority. Further, the detailed references and the general point of view are broadly those which have been gained through experience of the missionary movement in China, although the writer has had some opportunities of studying it in Japan, Korea, India, and elsewhere. This memorandum is simply to be regarded as a personal expression and in no sense representing the point of view of the National Christian Council, of which the writer happens to be a secretary.

### I. THE PURPOSE OF THE MISSIONARY MOVEMENT

The conception which has given birth to the missionary movement is the conviction that the Christian Gospel contains a revelation of God through the person of Jesus Christ, that this revelation is valuable for all times and for all people, and that it is of importance for the lives of individuals and for human society that this revelation be known and understood and that all that is involved in it should be accepted and made the basis of individual and social life. In the early days of the modern missionary movement stress was placed to a very large extent upon the message of individual salvation, and there was a tendency in certain quarters to an overemphasis upon this aspect of the Christian Gospel, leading to the idea that the Christian religion was almost exclusively concerned with the rescue of individuals from evil in this world and the next, whatever happened to human society. More recently, while this aspect has not been forgotten, the tendency of the missionary movement has been to emphasize the relation of the individual to the community and the importance of applying the principles of Christianity in the common life so that society may be improved and, to use the Christian terminology, the Kingdom of God may come on earth. This changing emphasis has produced a new orientation on the part of the missionary movement toward public questions. It has been accompanied by an increasing emphasis upon the educational side of the missionary movement and it has led to a fairly general recognition by missionaries that political, social, international, and other fields of human endeavor fall rightly within their consideration and activities.

This development in the missionary movement corresponds to a similar change in the Christian churches in the countries which have sent out missionaries. While it does not affect all sections of the movement in the same way, its influence is felt everywhere, some responding to the change and others reacting against it.

While this change should be noted and recognized as a factor involving the missions in peculiar difficulties at the present time, it must not be assumed that the charges made of missionary work as a direct agent of governments are thereby established. It cannot be too emphatically stated that the missionary movement as a whole does not exist to further political or commercial aims of foreign powers in China or elsewhere. Some of the reasons leading to this view will be examined later, but it is not possible to absolve all missionaries or missions from having been led into such association. The outstanding fact, however, is that the movement as a whole represents a single-hearted desire to pass on to other peoples the benefits of the Christian gospel. Its educational work is not deliberately designed to put over one cultural point of view upon peoples brought up under another, but rather it desires to contribute to intellectual development and emancipation as an integral part of the Christian Gospel. Its medical work is not an attempt to wean people away by kindness from allegiance to the traditions and ideals of their own past, but rather the natural expression of the Christian spirit of pity and love. Its organization of churches is not an elaborate system for Westernizing the East or for creating a number of persons who will be more Western than Eastern in outlook and loyalty (running-dogs of foreigners), but rather an honest effort to make permanent the fellowship of Christian persons so that it may be more deeply rooted in the lands which have only recently heard the Christian message.

That the missionary movement has come under suspicion recently because of such a supposed connection between political, commercial, and missionary purposes is a fact which must be examined into later in this memorandum. The writer is not prepared to acquit the missionary body of all blame in the matter, although much the larger causes may be found elsewhere. But under this section the one point to make clear is that in purpose and in essence there is no such connection; that the missionary movement takes its stand upon a purely altruistic platform; that the funds for its work are contributed by persons whose aim in so doing is to please God and to serve his great family on earth; and that in so far as the missionary may become the instrument of unjustifiable cultural, political, economic advance (or exploitation), this is adventitious and in general a complication of, or departure from, his main purpose.

## II. THE WORK OF MISSIONS

It is manifestly impossible in such a memorandum as this to give even any adequate summary of missionary operations. The facts are sufficiently well known in broad outline and are available in works of reference so far as details are concerned. The stages of missionary work may be indicated as follows:

*a*) Pioneer work, when the initiation, management, and actual work is entirely in the hands of foreigners who, as time goes on, employ suitable agents from the country concerned to help them in their efforts.

*b*) The coming of the infant churches, when small groups are gathered who have embraced the Christian faith, who need much shepherding by the foreigner and are unwilling or unable to stand alone. In this period there is little self-consciousness in the Christian group, and they are not only content but eager for foreign guidance and help at every point. In this stage educational work begins to assume a somewhat difference aspect, as being not simply a means of expressing the spirit of the Christian Gospel, but as also a necessary means toward building up the churches and leading them toward self-control and fuller self-expression.

*c*) The transition from mission to church control, when the churches have found themselves in greater or less degree and are able to assume increasingly heavy responsibilities in matters of finance, organization, and extension. This period may be a very long one, particularly where the second period has been unduly prolonged and where the missions have not prepared the churches for their larger responsibilities. It may also be a very difficult stage if the missions hold their control longer than seems meet to the churches or if the external circumstances introduce an element of strain.

*d*) Full control by the church, when the missionary, so far as he is still at work, is the servant of the church and accepts his appointment in the same way as pastors and teachers who are native to the country. This is the recognized aim of mission work. The problems of missionary development today are largely those created by the different views as to the methods and the rate at which progress should be made to this desired end. In different sections of the Pacific area mission work will be found in all of the stages referred to. The relation to political issues will vary according to the stage reached, as will be shown later.

It is evident that a movement which aims to produce such profound changes in human life and in society must, from the nature of the case, have far-reaching consequences in every realm of human interest. In the early days Christianity was a disturbing element, and it was said of the Christian missionaries that they had "turned the world upside down." It was the effect of Christianity upon social institutions that led to such bitter persecution. Where slavery, polygamy, idol or state-worship, tyranny of every kind, war, the traffic in human beings, and other great evils come up for criticism if not for unflinching opposition, and where these practices are deeply imbedded in the social order, there cannot fail to be disturbances affecting the whole of society. That Christian missions have produced such effects is obvious, and they may be more open to criticism for having produced them too seldom and too slightly than for having been excessive as "disturbers of the peace." Broadly speaking, Christianity has erred by being acquiescent in relation to existing evils and accepting compromises with the *status quo* far more often than it has erred by excessive zeal for reforms. In fact the usual criticism of the Christian church in the East today is that it is not Christian enough, far more often than that its passion for the Christian way of life has been too manifest. Thus the current attacks upon the missionary movement are not mainly those which we might expect by a contemplation of Christian ethics and church history. This will be made clear in what follows.

### III. THE MISSIONARY MOVEMENT AND INTERRACIAL RELATIONS

As has been shown, the missionary movement rests upon assumption that the Christian Gospel is of value—indeed of permanent value to the whole world. It is not the purpose of this memorandum to argue this point. It will be conceded by most that true Christianity has a value, not for one race alone, but for all. As to how that value should be made available for races that have hitherto not received it may be a matter for fair discussion. It is, however, contended that those persons who hold the conviction that Christianity is unique and in some sense essential for the well-being of humanity should not be debarred from expressing that view so long as it be done in ways that do not offend the good sense of the peoples to whom they go. It is generally recognized that there should be freedom for the spreading of ideas which are not actually subversive of human welfare, and even in regard to the latter there is a strong conviction that in the main they had better, in a general way, be allowed to kill themselves against the common sense of humanity rather than be suppressed by an enlightened minority.

On this ground the claim of the missionary movement to toleration would seem to be a fair one, and it should be evident that a similar claim can be sustained for, say, Buddhism or Islam. The Christian missionary should not claim what he will not concede to another, and the missionary enterprise should be prepared to stand or fall as it meets on even terms at the bar of humanity those other systems of thought and modes of living which have claimed or do claim the allegiance of men.

It cannot be denied that missionaries have at times departed from this principle and have claimed or received special privileges. In fact, the association of the missionary with the idea of special privileges is one of the chief points of attack at the present moment in China. Before dealing with the question, however, it may be well to raise certain deeper issues.

It is easy to see that persons who are possessed with a strong conviction that the truth which they know and try to follow is of value to others who do not know it may assume an attitude of superiority in dealing with those others. In recent years the sensitiveness of the non-Christian peoples in their contacts with Western nations has undoubtedly increased, and this had led to a feeling among the more educated and sensitive peoples of the East that the missionary movement in essence was an expression of racial superiority. That missionaries have in a number of cases fallen into this false and un-Christian attitude can hardly be denied. Nevertheless the Christian message is so deeply rooted in the conception of the personality of Jesus, which is so truly that of a humble man between whom and others we find no such barrier, that the danger alluded to has perhaps not been as much felt as might be expected from the nature of the case. In many missionaries the characteristics of their Master have been so shown as to save them from this taint of racial superiority. It must, however, be admitted that the very idea of bringing to a people a message which is felt to be superior to anything which they have received from their own past creates a difficult situation. The modern missionary movement is, generally speaking, alive to the value of many of the traditions, philosophies, and religious conceptions which have molded the peoples of the East, and the attempt to establish the superiority of Christianity by setting a light value upon these may be said to be discredited by all modern missionary leaders. The deeper resentment against missions may fairly be said to arise from an attitude of racial superiority assumed (often quite unconsciously) by individual missionaries. This may be a matter of heredity and upbringing which even the nature of the Christian Gospel has failed to eradicate. But it may also actually be fostered in persons who have imperfectly understood and entered into the spirit of Christ by the very nature of the work in which they are engaged.

Certain assumptions have not infrequently been made by missionaries and the supporters of missions which foster this same attitude and which should be brought out clearly in any consideration of the subject. The following may be specified:

1. *That Western civilization is superior to the civilization of the East because it is Christian.*—It may be fairly said that this assumption until recently was very prevalent in the missionary movement. The products of modern science and of many other influences which have molded Western civilization were too readily assumed to be evidences of the superiority of Christianity. Until recently it was assumed that modern machinery and inventions were necessarily a boon to any nation. The increase of wealth, the higher standard of living among the people, the better sanitary conditions, and the many other aspects of Western civilization were freely quoted as evidences of the value of Christianity. This assumption undoubtedly helped the Christian missionary at a certain period of his work and gave him a certain prestige. This was true until the assumption began to be challenged and educated men from the East began to doubt the value of many aspects of Western civilization as it was revealed through closer acquaintanceship, especially during the Great War. It may be said that the missionary movement no longer seeks to claim the whole of Western civilization as an evidence of the value of the Christian faith, and what was an asset has in certain respects become a liability.

2. *That religious toleration should be maintained by superior force if necessary.*—This assumption led, among other things, to the so-called "toleration clauses" for missionaries in China; and until the last ten or fifteen years it was generally regarded as a helpful thing that the Christian movement in China had grown up under the protection of these clauses which rested ultimately upon the fact that Western nations had at their disposal stronger military forces than China. Again it may be said that religious toleration secured in this way did give an opportunity for the Christian church in China to grow up when it might, in the early stages, have been crushed by local opposition. These clauses further made it possible for missionaries to travel and reside in centers not open for foreign residence generally, and thus to create centers of Christian activity in which the foreign missionary resided and where foreign capital was invested.

This assumption is challenged from the point of view of those who believe that, while religious toleration is in itself good, it is not good that it should be maintained by coercion, especially if that is exercised by foreign powers who, in many of their relationships with the nation concerned, have shown themselves far less than disinterested. In regard to this assumption there is a growing feeling among missionaries that the criticism on this second ground is valid, and that the Christian movement loses rather than gains through the kind of support indicated. That is to say, in this particular again, that which was previously regarded by almost all missionaries and by most Chinese Christians as an asset is coming to appear to very many as a liability.

3. *That people ought to be and would be glad to have good done to them.*—It may fairly be said that in the Victorian era there was scarcely a question in the minds of the people as to whether those who seemed to be less fortunate would be, or at

least ought to be, glad to receive the help of those who regarded themselves as more fortunate. A great deal of the philanthrophy of that era seems, in the light of the present attitude, to have been tinged with the spirit of patronage, which may be regarded as the doing of good in a superior way. Very often those who patronize have no conception that the person whom they desire to help may be rather hindered than helped by that type of assistance, and that it may legitimately be resented. It cannot be denied that missionary work was largely carried on upon this assumption. It seemed perfectly obvious to convinced Christians that they had something supremely good to offer and that those to whom they went with their message, with their education, with their medical help, etc., would be the better for receiving such help and would therefore, at any rate in the long run, be glad to have it. This underlying assumption is today very widely questioned even by those who are confident that the Christian Gospel and outlook on life contain positive goods which peoples who have not received them would be the better for receiving. The resentment on the part of peoples who regard the whole missionary movement as an unjustified assumption of superiority has made itself felt reflexly in the movement as a whole and in many of its leaders. The effort is being made increasingly to come alongside the people to whom the Christian message is presented, and rather to give them the opportunity of discovering its value than so to insist upon its value as to awaken a resistance.

### IV. THE MISSIONARY AND COMMERCIAL ENTERPRISE

The missionary movement is frequently regarded as a part of the commercial approach of foreign peoples to China (or other nations). This view is supported by the fact that the trader and the missionary have frequently entered a country at about the same time, the missionary sometimes availing himself of the facilities offered to traders (as in the case of Robert Morrison and many others), and the business man in other cases using an opening made through the action of missionaries. When a foreign nation is little known this confusion between various aspects of its approach is easily accounted for.

A further cause of confusion is the fact that the scale of missionary living is on a much higher level, in the great majority of cases, than that of the mass of the people among whom he works. Large sums of money are expended in medical and educational work. Chinese servants, teachers, catechists, etc., are employed on a large scale. Western capitalism seems to be behind the whole movement. It is felt to be but another expression of "this great rich country" which comes with her resources and her skill to trade with a poorer people.

The identification of missionary and trader matters but little where trade is carried on in a sound way and where there is no element of exploitation or no sense of there being such on the part of the people of the country concerned. Recently, however, great emphasis has been placed upon the idea of exploitation. What precisely this means and how far the charge can be made good against Western peoples trading in the Pacific area it is not for this paper to discuss. But it may be pointed out that traffic in alcohol and opium can scarcely be regarded in any other light, that forced labor and slavery are certainly examples of exploitation on any showing, and that the employment of persons of a supposed lower civilization or state of culture on terms that could not be offered to others is open to severe criticism. All these aspects of the commercial contact of the white races with others have been or are known. To identify the missionary movement with them is completely to misunderstand it. Missionaries have repeatedly protested against these and similar evils. The anti-opium and anti-alcoholic movements have been largely inspired and promoted by missionaries and their supporters. The same is true of movements against forced labor and slavery. Recently investigation of child labor, efforts to improve labor conditions, and other similar services have been inaugurated by missionaries. Not all missionaries have supported such efforts; but it would be fair to say that they would never have commenced, or, if started, would soon have languished, had it not been for missionary activity. In fact the missionary has time and again been the subject of bitter criticism by the trader because of his supposed or actual influence in limiting profits through attacking what he believes to be illegitimate practices in trade.

The more drastic criticism of the capitalistic system today by various socialistic or communistic movements has carried the discussion of these questions to a further point. Missions, in a certain sense, do rest upon the capitalistic system. Among missionary givers are large capitalists, and certain enterprises are well known to owe their existence to gifts from persons of great wealth who have come under criticism for the way in which that wealth was obtained. It is believed by many that the missionary movement is hampered in taking a bold Christian line in regard to the capitalistic system or certain evils connected with it because of the dependence of the enterprise on such givers. It can scarcely be questioned that there is an element of truth in this suggestion, though it would be difficult to maintain it in any large way. Many missionaries are still to be found who will not allow any such connection to hamper their freedom of expression. Some are earnestly seeking for ways whereby they may be more free to deliver their social message, for example, by living more simply or by earning their own living while carrying on missionary work. Such are, however, a small minority. The fundamental critics of the capitalistic system cannot fail to regard the missionary movement as a whole as a dangerous factor, or at least as giving them no assistance in their effort to alter the existing social order.

Two smaller items should be referred to here: (1) There are certain missionaries who have started industrial enterprises in connection with the missions (or in rare cases as personal concerns). This is much less frequent round the Pacific Basin than in Africa and India. Such efforts are often felt to be a very valuable part of missionary effort, training hand and eye, fitting people to earn an honest living, developing character through industry, and so forth. In Africa these efforts are a very important factor in the development of the country and an integral part of mission education. It is almost impossible to make clear to the average person wherein lies the difference between such efforts and ordinary trading, and there are some cases where there has been virtually no difference and where the missionary has used these methods for supporting a school, giving scholarships to deserving children (not even, in some cases, excluding his own!). It must be frankly admitted that these pieces of work give some real ground for the identification of missions with the commercial enterprise; and it may, in passing, be remarked that the greatest possible care should be exercised to give no just cause for criticism.

2. There are certain cases where chambers of commerce have supported missionary work and grants have been made by business concerns out of their trading profits, rather than by individuals. This plan, which has not been at all widely followed, is open to the objection that the missionary enterprise is regarded by big business as a means whereby its aims can be furthered, and that argument has been used both by missionaries and by business men. At the same time the movement (if it can be so called) is a welcome sign that the altruistic ends of missions are more generally recognized and respected by business men, and it is true that, in the main, the subventions made have been used as the fulfilment of a moral obligation toward the people of the country where the trader works. Many high-minded men have supported this movement without any thought to increasing profits, and have been glad to pay, as it were, a tax from the profits of the firm much as similar gifts are often made to hospitals in the West. Nevertheless the practice needs to be watched.

### V. THE MISSIONARY AND THE CULTURES OF THE EAST

From the nature of the case the missionary movement raises far-reaching questions affecting the culture and social life of the peoples to whom it comes. Take an institution like polygamy, which is closely connected with the family system and the urgent need for the raising up of male descendants in countries where ancestor worship is practiced. The Christian missionary, generally speaking, has not found it possible to acquiesce in this custom, and he thus appears as one who is interested in destroying the social system and bringing in something which is distinctive of Western culture. It is intensely difficult to divide the religious interest from social and cultural questions; in fact it is not possible in many cases to do so. Nevertheless the missionary has not always been as careful to avoid this confusion as in the light of events, he may well wish he had been. To him the whole social system he represents and the cultural ideas he has imbibed from childhood are part of one whole. They are the warp, as it were, of which his religion is the woof. It is no wonder that he has carried his culture with him in ways not always essential to the carrying of his religious message.

This cultural and social effect of missions has been studied in a very thorough way in recent years, especially in Dennis' monumental work[1] and in many special studies. Missions have expressed this aspect of their work largely through their schools and colleges and hospitals, and also in specific attack upon social customs which are felt to be degrading or immoral. How far a country is justified in excluding a religious faith which is felt to be subversive of existing social customs is a subject for discussion which arises at this point and which cannot be dealt with in this memorandum. But granting the right of a country to exclude certain specific teachings (as witness the laws of the United States and other countries in regard to polygamists) it may be urged that, on the whole, the deepest convictions of mankind have agreed, in all countries, that the Christian way of life is, per se, of value to society.

The missionary, however, needs to study the culture and social customs of the country to which he goes in order that he may not challenge or destroy what is not essentially hurtful or contrary to the principles of Christianity. By failing to make

[1] *Christian Missions and Social Progress.*

such a study the missionary in the past has not infrequently identified his prejudice with his real task; he has waged war against a custom which seems to an unsympathetic mind to be idolatrous or immoral, but which on closer examination may appear to be harmless. Some missionaries feel, for example, that the reverence to Confucius by making three bows is not in any true sense an act of worship, and that the opposition to this practice has been an instance of prejudice and lack of sympathy rather than a genuine expression of Christianity.

Recently in China the whole missionary movement has been attacked as a piece of "cultural exploitation." This phrase seems to mean that Westerners have deliberately tried to denationalize Chinese, to substitute Western for Chinese culture, to bring China in a very subtle way under the spell of Western ideas and thus under Western political influence, and, in short, that China's most precious possessions in her own great past were being insidiously attacked under the name of bringing her good news. This claim cannot, in the writer's opinion, be made good; but there is just enough ground for it to cause the missionary to examine his work very carefully to recognize that he has given some ground for the charge, and to see that in his work in the future he discriminates more carefully between the essence of his faith and its accessories.

The following specific questions should be referred to under this head:

1. *The teaching of Chinese classics in mission schools.*—There has not been, generally speaking, as much attention to this subject in mission schools as on general grounds would be desirable. This is due in part to the lack of intimate knowledge of the subject by missionaries administering such schools, to the difficulty of securing first-rate teachers within the available subventions, to the methods of teaching which have often been used in classical teaching, and to the fact that students in mission schools come largely for English language and modern subjects and do not take the classical education so seriously. At the same time a more persistent recognition of the fact that the new China must draw her life-ideals in large part from her own past and that Christianity is a fulfilment rather than a destruction of that past would mean a far deeper determination than has generally been present to overcome the difficulties. Where there is such a determination ways can usually be found.

2. *Registration of mission schools.*—On general principles most missionaries now agree that mission schools should be registered with the government. Missions have, however, in most cases been slow, and probably too slow, in reaching this conclusion and acting upon it. At the present time the demand for registration is very urgent. It is due to a resentment against the idea of a system of education within China controlled and financed by foreigners (a thought stimulated by the recent Educational Commission, 1922, which, though of great value in many ways, left a fear in the minds of many Chinese), to the rising nationalist movement and the recognition of education as a prime factor in producing national unity, and to the prevalent anti-foreign bias which calls for what is termed the "restoration of educational rights."

The difficulties in the way of registration are considerable, including the problem of securing suitable Christian Chinese to manage the schools, the doubt as to whether the requirements will tend to eliminate effective Christian teaching, and the fear of party (Kuo Ming Tang) interference and management. By patient effort on both sides it seems likely that these and other difficulties will be met. Some demands made very insistently now may be modified, and some missionary attitudes may be changed. It seems clear that only as the schools register will they be able to make the kind of contribution to China that will be free from the suspicion at any rate of "cultural exploitation." It may well be, however, that some will be justified in going rather slowly in this direction until the mind of China is expressed in a clearer and more nearly final way on some of the issues raised.

3. *The study of Chinese culture and present-day thinking by missionaries.*—A great advance in this matter has been made in recent years through the establishment of schools of study in China and in England and America, as well as on the continent of Europe. But in the writer's view not nearly enough has been done. Far more thorough work along both the lines indicated is needed, not simply for the few missionaries who do special types of work, but for all. The unconscious attitudes must be corrected, a real appreciation of the deeper sides of Chinese life must be seen in the missionary if he is to avoid the errors referred to previously. China is sensitive—perhaps hypersensitive—on this point today. It is for the missionary organizations to see that they send out men and women who are sensitized so that they will take impressions quickly, who are eager to learn as well as to teach and who are on the lookout to avoid giving needless offense.

4. *The clearer differentiation between the essential and the adventitious in the Christian message.*—It will be obvious that the dangers referred to before will be observed if the missionary sees clearly exactly what it is that he has to give to the East. Study of this point is needed, not only in preparation for coming out, but during the whole period of missionary work. Help should be given to younger missionaries and candidates. There may be some who would be better eliminated because they are unable to shake off certain assumptions and attitudes that are not essential to Christian effort.

## VI. THE MISSIONARY AND POLITICAL ISSUES

The missionary has been regarded, not only as partner in the commercial advance of the West and as an insidious enemy of Eastern culture and social habits, but also as a part of the political aggression of Europe and America. This view also draws support from certain facts which have, in the writer's view, been given an undue prominence and have indeed helped to create a false impression. Nevertheless, there are grounds for fair criticism and it will be our purpose here to consider these as well as the questions on which misunderstandings exist.

A. The position of the missionary has been secured in certain countries through treaties which have given to the missionary a place of special privilege. As such treaties are under discussion in China in a marked way at the present time, it may be well to concentrate attention on this case. Here again it is impossible in the compass of this memorandum to give a full statement of the case, which is admirably dealt with in various public documents and books. The salient point must be enough.

The rights of missionaries are of three kinds: (*a*) Those shared by all foreigners in any country, such as the right to appeal to his own consul, and such guaranties as are normally given by any civilized country to the citizens of other countries resident in their territory; (*b*) the special rights granted by treaty to citizens of the "treaty powers," including the right to have any case against him tried by his own country's representative according to its procedure, exemption from taxation, and so forth; (*c*) the special rights granted by treaty to the missionary as such, which include the right to reside and hold property in cities not open to other foreigners, and the right to propagate his religion.

In regard only to the second and third group is there any dispute, and since the second will be dealt with in other ways, the third only need be mentioned here in any detail.

It should be remembered always that these privileges were sought and obtained largely by missionaries, that they are solely for the benefit of missionaries and Chinese Christians, and that the rights have been enjoyed to the full during a considerable period of time. This consideration should at the same time make clear why the missionary movement is involved today in the criticism of the whole structure of the treaties, and also absolve the missionary of today from the charge of unjustifiable "interference in politics." The treaties being under criticism, the missionary who has a special place in them cannot simply stand aside as if the whole matter were no concern of his. If these clauses are not his concern, whose are they! It may further be urged that since missionaries form no small part of the foreign community in China they have as much right as any other foreigners to express their view in regard to the second class of rights, it always being clear that an equal right is granted to other foreign residents. This much needs to be said because the missionary has been severely challenged in regard to this matter in recent discussions. A further point, which may not be as readily conceded, but which seems to the writer equally cogent, is that any true view of religion implies the attempt to moralize all human relationships, and where grave moral issues are raised by political arrangements, the forces of religion are culpable if they remain silent.

It scarcely seems necessary to discuss how far it was wise or right in the early days of China's relation to foreign powers for missionaries to claim and receive special privileges either for themselves or for their converts. The Christian conscience has a way of discovering with ever increasing clearness what is involved in the Christian ethic. Today there is a very large body of missionaries and mission supporters who are not only prepared to give up these special privileges, but who are eager to see the whole treaty system altered so that any privileges they may have in the future be only such as are accorded freely by the Chinese people and government. Chinese Christians, broadly speaking, share the general view in the country that the time has come for treaty revision or abrogation. Since the missionary movement in China has largely passed from the first and second into the third stage, it becomes the missionary to be very sensitive to this opinion. It means that Chinese Christians generally would rather take certain risks of persecution in the unsettled times and throw themselves on the reasonableness of their fellow-countrymen than take shelter behind the foreign powers whose treaties have hitherto been the guaranty of their protection.

It is true that a good many missionaries still believe that the clauses are wise and right and that to disturb the *status quo* while China is in so unsettled a state is neither safe nor is it the best thing for China herself. While differing from this opinion, the writer wishes to express respect for those who hold it because he believes it to be based upon a deep love of China and a profound conviction in regard to what is in the interest of the Kingdom of God.

At the same time it is necessary to point out that a very large body of missionary opinion has been voiced in a contrary direction. A full statement of the opinion expressed during the last two years is appended to this memorandum. This will show that an overwhelming majority of expressed opinion from missionary and Christian circles tends in the same direction with certain variations in detail. The National Christian Council of China in October, 1926, after a very careful scrutiny of this material, passed the following resolution which may be said fairly to represent the bulk of this opinion:

*Resolved,* That, while the National Christian Council is not in a position to speak officially for the organizations which have combined to bring it into existence, yet, after studying closely all the recorded actions of these organizations, we, collectively and as individuals, place on record our conviction:

1. That the Christian church and Christian missions should preach the Gospel and perform Christian service in China upon the basis of religious liberty freely accorded by the Republic of China, and that all provisions in the treaties with foreign countries for special privileges for the churches or missions should be removed.

2. That the present treaties between China and foreign powers should be revised on a basis of freedom and equality.

3. That we are glad of the steps already taken towards this end by the governments concerned, and trust that they may persist in their efforts till satisfactory results have been achieved.

4. That whatever were the historical circumstances which led to the present state of affairs, its speedy remedy is now the joint responsibility of Chinese and foreigners and that in this task we need the spirit of persistent forbearance, understanding, and love on both sides.

The Council therefore calls Christians in China of whatever nationality or occupation to a more fearless following of Christ, whatever the cost, and to co-operation in bringing his spirit into our international relationships.

From the foregoing it will be seen that there has been a decided change in missionary opinion in recent years and that there is now a strong conviction in many quarters that the political status of the missionary should not be one of special privilege in China and that he should be ready to accept such provisions as China may freely accord to him in the prosecution of his peaceful avocation.

More recently the British government has taken the initiative in regard to this question in the memorandum handed to the Chinese government (North and South) at the end of January, 1927, as follows: "His Majesty's Government are prepared to accept the principle that British missionaries should no longer claim the right to purchase land in the interior, that Chinese converts should look to Chinese law and not to the Treaties for protection; and that missionaries' educational and medical institutions will conform to Chinese laws and regulations applying to similar Chinese institution."

B. The relation to treaties is not the only question which arises in this connection. Another ground for identifying the missionary with the political activities of his country has been found in the indemnities which have been sought and secured in respect of missionaries who have lost their lives and mission property that has been destroyed. The assumption of foreign powers in dealing with China has been that such losses must be made good in kind. It is doubtful whether the western powers would be prepared to accept any such claim made upon them by China, and indeed the United States in 1881 definitely repudiated any obligation, although on one occasion at any rate a grant was made as an act of grace. That foreign powers make such a claim in China is felt to be a sign of that assumption of superiority now so deeply resented by Chinese. The claim is not made by all missionary societies, and some even refuse any indemnity offered either for loss of life or property. There have, however, been enough cases where the claims have been made and the indemnities accepted to cause a conviction that missions generally share the attitude and are virtually a part of the governmental organization of the states from which the missionaries come.

This conviction is all the deeper because of cases where the death of the missionary has been made the pretext for a definite aggressive move, as in the seizure of Kiaochow by Germany after the murder of two German missionaries. The exaction of the Boxer Indemnity and the large amounts accepted by missions in North China on account of their losses at that time is another case in point. Many missionaries today feel that harm was done to the whole movement by the acceptance of such money and the investment of it in splendid buildings which are a constant witness to China of the close relationship between the missionary enterprise and the political activities of governments.

A considerable and probably an increasing body of missionaries now feel that all indemnities, whether for life or propetry, should be refused; more are opposed to making any claim, while not unwilling to accept anything that is offered by Chinese authorities. Others regard the making of a claim as the simple assertion of a human right, and the failure to do so as tantamount to acquiescence in evil. The number who would accept any money payment in respect of the death of a missionary is probably not large, though it is impossible to make any estimate. This question is likely to arise again in an acute form in view of the considerable property losses incurred during the recent unsettlement. It would be highly desirable if a common policy based on a clear sense of what is right should be accepted by the missions. In seeking to reach any such agreement Chinese Christian opinion would, of course, be given very great weight.

C. The period of the European war was unfortunate from the point of view of the position of missionaries in China. At that time not a few missionaries went home or stayed at home to enter the fighting forces, to engage as chaplains, Y.M.C.A. workers, and officers to the Chinese labor corps. Many missionaries took a strongly nationalist viewpoint and did not hesitate to express themselves. Some undertook some definite propaganda for their own countries. When the question of China coming into the war was being discussed a good deal of pressure was brought upon her to come in and missionaries were not slow to express an opinion. The treatment accorded to German missions in Hong Kong and other incidents which may have been quite inevitable all served to deepen the sense of a close relationship between the missionary movement and the political activities of governments. It is not intended to pick out any for criticism—it is simply necessary to record the fact.

D. A similar situation has developed in recent months. Fearing some danger to missionaries in the interior in the event of disturbance at Shanghai or elsewhere, governmental authorities have used the strongest possible pressure short of actual injunctions to get missionaries to withdraw from their stations. It has been almost impossible to resist this pressure, and very few have done so. The writer is not prepared to criticize the governments for giving this advice. The fact, however, remains that the general withdrawal of missionaries at a time when the situation did not seem, in many local centers, to call for any such action has again suggested to the Chinese mind that the missionary is simply a part of the state machine and is ready, when the choice has to be made, to accept its advice in stead of remaining at the post of duty. The writer believes that most missionaries could not do other than follow this advice, while expressing his keen appreciation of the fact that a few were prepared to face all that was involved in rejecting the advice given—yet it is these latter who have demonstrated to China that there is a spirit in the missionary movement independent of the governments and that missionaries recognize a higher duty than obedience to a secular authority. With the many who felt compelled to leave we can only express sympathy in what was often a position of the most acute pain and distress.

E. The position accorded to Roman Catholic missionaries as being of official status, but refused by Protestants, must also be referred to. This led in times past to a very grave confusion in regard to the issue we are considering. Further, the fact that many Chinese turned to missionaries in law cases for their support and advice must be remembered as a serious item in the charge against missions. Recently a large number of such cases have been examined, and it was found that the vast majority were those of Roman Catholic missionaries. No doubt in many cases such interference was prompted by a real desire to right a wrong, and doubtless many wrongs were righted. But, in the light of events, it is likely that far the largest proportion of missionaries would agree that such action, however high the motive, has done harm rather than good, and that any such interference in the local administration of justice is unwarrantable even when a palpable injustice is being committed.

The missionary movement in its developing life has thus touched upon the political field at many points, of which some only are mentioned here. Other aspects have been more prominent in other fields. Recalling the four stages mentioned earlier, it may be urged that in the first and second stages there is justification for some kind of political protection if sought and given in the right way. The movement meets with unreasoning prejudice and may at least claim to be given a fair hearing, much as Paul claimed his rights as a Roman citizen. The early converts are often few and weak, and if they meet with persecution based on mere prejudice and superstition they may, not unnaturally, be ready to avail themselves of special privileges where they can be gained in a legitimate way. Whether the the treaties between China and Western powers can be so regarded is no doubt open to question. But at the time when these rights were claimed and accepted little if any objection was felt on such grounds, and the Chinese Christians have until recently been only too glad to avail themselves of the protection secured through the treaties.

In the third stage the time comes when the rights of the churches established through missionary effort must be increasingly recognized and the initiative begins to pass from the missionary to the Chinese and other nationals. At this point the missionary should recognize the natural desire of the churches to make their own position clear, and hence the withdrawal of the missionary's claim to special privilege has become an obvious corollary of his whole aim and method in carrying on the work. This stage in China is being reached or has been reached at the time when national consciousness is deeply stirred in regard to the whole question of the treaties. It is clear that this environment indicates a more definite and rapid break with the past than might have otherwise seemed necessary.

In the fourth stage, which is already reached in certain advanced groups, the question of any relation between the missionary and politics could scarcely arise. The Christian church will act according to the convictions which it holds, and the place of the missionary is simply as a member of that church and not as a separate individual or as belonging to a separate group. He will certainly not wish to claim special privileges, and he should be more than ever careful not to complicate the issue by any action that tends to make the missionaries a specialized and distinct group of persons. He will still, of course, have to consider his position and his duty as a citizen of the country from which he comes. Some missionaries, realizing this problem as a peculiarly difficult one in the later stages of missionary work, have considered the advisability of changing their nationality. This question is too intricate to be more than alluded to in this memorandum.

### VII. PRESENT TENDENCIES IN THE MISSIONARY MOVEMENT

A few words may perhaps be added to draw attention to certain tendencies in modern missions which have a distinct bearing on international and interracial contacts. It cannot be maintained that these are universal and universally accepted as satisfactory, but it cannot be denied that they are marked tendencies and that a comparison of the movement now with its aspect fifty years ago would fully demonstrate this general line of development.

*a*) There is a growing readiness to confess the faults of Western civilization, to admit frankly that it is not fully Christian, and to approach the Far East, not simply critical of its civilization, but in the belief that West and East together can discover and work out the Christian ethic for our common life more adequately than either country could do alone.

*b*) There is a very strong desire to withdraw as soon as possible from the predominant place in the Christian movement. This is shown by the many schemes which have been adopted or are now under discussion for giving the control of the Christian movement to Chinese, the missionary accepting his place under direction from the proper Chinese authorities and making his contribution rather as a servant of the Chinese church than as pioneer, director, or administrator. Almost every department of missionary work in China shows marked advances in this matter during the last ten years.

*c*) There is a strong movement toward the elimination of special privileges which have been granted to missionaries and to Chinese Christians under the treaties. This does not mean that missionaries and missionary societies would not be glad to continue the work which they are doing in different parts of China, but many believe that it would be better that some of this work should in the meantime be closed rather than that it should rest upon privileges which have been secured through the treaties now criticized.

*d*) There is increasing emphasis upon the constructive rather than the destructive elements in the Christian message. Undoubtedly the Christian message does involve the destruction of evils and superstitions. The whole trend of the missionary movement, however, now is to leave the destructive forces to work themselves out, and to emphasize the personality of Jesus Christ and the simple, essential features of his life and teaching as set forth in the New Testament. This tendency is coupled with a greater readiness to learn from those to whom the Christian message is brought and a much more general recognition of the value of other religious systems. A higher standard of missionary training is being demanded from year to year, although not all missionary societies are moving in this direction.

*e*) Greater stress is being laid upon the social and international implications of the Christian Gospel. The missionary movement still bases its work on the conception of an individual change of heart, the introduction of new motives and a fresh dynamic into the spirit of the individual who comes under the Christian influence; but it is much more freely recognized than formerly that it is incumbent upon the Christian church to study the social problems of the day, to realize the fact that the individual is to a large extent the creature of his environment, and that it is the bounden duty of Christians to study that environment with thoroughness and sympathy and to do their utmost to remold it in accordance with Christian principles. So far as China is concerned, this latter movement seems to correspond to the tendency of Chinese Christians who are not in the main of the introspective or mystical type, but rather tend to judge the Christian faith by its practical results in the common life.

## VIII. THE VALUE OF MISSIONS IN RELATION TO THE SOLUTION OF RACE QUESTIONS

In the foregoing sections an effort has been made to deal candidly and as fully as space permitted with various aspects of the missionary movement which have come up for criticism as proving a hindrance rather than a help toward improving race contacts in the world of today. While laying emphasis on the central purpose of missions, the writer has not hesitated to face the inherent difficulty of the missionary in fulfilling that purpose, nor has he desired to hide or minimize his failure to do so in many cases. Nevertheless he would not be true to his own convictions if the memorandum were to close on the note of defense or merely of explanation. To the writer's mind the missionary movement has, in the main, been a factor making for better understanding and good will, and he believes this is more true today than ever in spite of certain matters to which much attention has been turned. This contention is based upon the following grounds.

*a*) The missionary movement has put into many lands a multitude of men and women of good will who, whatever their faults, have rendered and are rendering unselfish service of a very high grade and are showing by life even more than by word that racial barriers can be overcome and that there is a basis on which the deepest fellowship can be achieved between persons of varying points of view. These lives are the biggest asset of the missionary movement. When many foreigners are frankly concerned chiefly with profit-making or with securing a political and economic advantage for their country, here is this large body of foreigners who in the main put these things on one side and work for pure love to interpret the highest things which the West has to offer to the East.

*b*) The actual work done in schools, colleges, hospitals, asylums, churches, etc., has created numberless points of mutual understanding, has broken down prejudices, has produced men and women in the countries concerned who have the international spirit and groups wherein race and nation come to take a relatively smaller place as men work together for a still higher unity—the one family under heaven.

*c*) The missionary has, on the whole, acted as a wholesome check upon other aspects of racial contacts inspired by less worthy ideals. Traders who have been guilty of exploitation have been challenged as in the opium traffic and other similar evils. A watchful eye has been kept upon those aspects of the situation which tend to produce friction, and not infrequently there have been missionaries who have fearlessly exposed the same.

*d*) On the whole the missionary has sought to interpret the East to the West. Unfortunately there have been some who have put the worse elements of eastern life under the limelight and have thus tended to create a false sense of superiority and so vitiate race contacts. But by translation of classical writings and a sympathetic study of the life of other peoples missionaries have also done much to lay a foundation for a better mutual understanding.

*e*) The essential message of the Christian missionary is one of reconciliation. Where that message has gripped men it has done its own work. The incomparable figure of Jesus Christ has won the allegiance of many millions in the East and West alike. He is universal, however national many of his followers may be. There is something in Christianity which breaks through the failure of individual Christians be they diplomats, traders, or missionaries. This something is in essence a healing power to our many discords. It is this which ultimately justifies the missionary movement.

## SECTION 10

# FACING THE FUTURE OF THE MISSIONARY MOVEMENT

EDWARD H. HUME, M.D., LL.D.
Formerly President of Yale in China

### I. THE PRESENT SITUATION

1. *Missions are being challenged.*—The missionary movement is being vigorously challenged today in many quarters. Not only are men and women in Western lands raising basic questions as to the inherent right of individuals or groups to propagate such religious beliefs as they may hold, and as to the limitations, if any, that should be placed upon those who desire to propagate their religious beliefs: but not a few of our Oriental friends have started to state frankly their criticisms of missions; witness recent magazine articles with such titles as: "An Oriental Looks at Christian Missions,"[1] or "China and Christianity,"[2] and many others.

2. *Some underlying factors.*—In studying the criticisms before us, which deal, admittedly, with the less happy phenomena of the missionary movement, two considerations must be borne in mind. The first is that missions grew up during a period of history when war was still trusted as the most decisive thing in existence. "Submit the dispute," men said, "to the arbitrament of arms." This warlike spirit in politics, never more potent in history than during the past three centuries, was often paralleled by an aggressive mood in religion, the two influences interacting to increase the desire for mastery. The second is that those who went as missionaries were conscious of being sent, *missi.* They carried an unusually developed sense of commission and felt that this put upon them a responsibility to achieve something and an equally great responsibility to report what they had achieved. This led, in many cases, to undue emphasis on statistics, particularly with regard to records of conversion.

3. *The Oriental criticizes frankly.*—The Oriental has been conscious for decades that his status was held to be inferior by many of the Westerners who came to propagate their religion. Today the extreme critics have become vocal to a degree. Some of their complaints are as follows:

1. The missionary is apt to regard himself as a superior being. Not only does he think of his message as incomparable, but his attitude is often one of disdain. He still claims far too many of the positions of administrative control in church, school, and hospital.

2. The missionary is often unsympathetic. He does not share deeply enough in the suffering, the griefs, and the disappointments of the people among whom he labors. He often complains about things that affect his own well-being without appreciating fully how much more those suffer in whose midst he works.

[1] Cornelius, in *Harper's Magazine,* March, 1927.

[2] Hu Shih, in *Forum,* July, 1927.

3. The missionary, whether as teacher or preacher, frequently overlooks the significance of Oriental cultures and religions. He compares these unfavorably with his own. He brings his Scriptures, his classics, his textbooks, his maps, his methods in church or college, and assumes that these will be acceptable. Important as they are, adapting them to local environments is essential.

4. The missionary does not sufficiently trust the people among whom he works. He acts as if they were financially irresponsible; what is more as if they would never become able to manage their own finances in church and educational work.

5. The missionary commonly hesitates to intrust authority of any sort even to those whom he has trained. He is, therefore, likely to find himself, in such countries as China, suddenly confronted with a situation where he must surrender authority. Because men and women have not been taught the use of power, he fears disintegration for the work he has wrought so faithfully.

6. The missionary has too often related himself unwisely to the political situation. Sometimes, with friendly intent, he has defended those involved in legal difficulties, while at other times he has withheld sympathy from national movements that sought to establish or to regain a country's rightful independence.

7. The missionary board, back of the missionary, has in many instances thought of itself as permanently in control of the activities of those it has sent out. It has hesitated to transfer authority into the hands of local organizations in the Orient.

8. The organization which the missionary has built up is likely to prove far too complex for the Orient. Many of its buildings are too extensive and too costly; its institutional plans and administrative machinery are often too cumbersome to be easily naturalized.

9. The missionary organization is in a great many cases entirely too Western in its atmosphere. It has been created by Westerners who have not understood the East and who have not learned to adjust their own systems to an Eastern environment.

10. The missionary organization appears to be intimately related to the politics of Western lands. Each transfer of property must be registered at a consulate; every missionary's movements must be controlled by Western consular officials; in times of trouble the consul is expected to demand protection or indemnity. The common people are apt to gain the impression of an intimate connection between missions and governments.

11. The missionary movement as a whole appears to be dependent, in many instances, upon gunpowder and armed force. Many are pointing out that this seems quite foreign to the spirit of Jesus as illustrated in the Sermon on the Mount.

Now it is undoubtedly true that such criticisms as these emanate from a minority in the Orient. By far the larger part of those in touch with missions are genuinely friendly to the missionaries in their midst and deeply appreciative of the constructive work they have done. At times of national unheaval, however, as in the case of China today, criticism is apt to burst out with unusual violence. During the storm of a political revolution, with excitement running high, even the man on the street, ordinarily so friendly, may begin to find fault with missionaries for the inconsistencies in their lives. The communist, finding opportunity to proclaim his doctrines, is apt to call out that religion is nothing but an opiate for the soul, while the materialist asserts that science is displacing religion, which men now believe, he says, to be little more than a superstition, well enough adapted to simple folks in uneducated and uncultured social groups. At such a time, too, the nationalist may insist that the missionary teacher is restraining his pupils or his employes from participation in current patriotic movements. Such a sudden breaking loose of a storm of complaint is not to be wondered at. In the political sphere the insistence on "self-determination" is becoming widespread, leading to much unrestrained abuse and conflict. The issues are serious and require thoughtful study.

4. *The Occidental reflects.*—Hitherto many Western Christians had taken missions for granted. They had become accustomed to maps of the world in which the Orient was represented in solid black and the Occident as wholly white, with a few white rays penetrating the darkened areas and beginning to dispel the universal blackness. Many are beginning to reflect on the phenomena now taking place, and realize that:

1. The missionary movement has developed during, and been an accompaniment of, the great era of colonial expansion on the part of Western powers.

2. It has been an outgrowth of, and often an expression of, the idea of the church militant.

3. It has often carried a very dogmatic, creedally formulated message.

4. Some of the missionaries of this era have been true iconoclasts, not only literally breaking down idols, but also attacking with violence whatever they regarded as a sign of religious opposition.

5. The missionary movement has built up in the West a vocabulary of antithesis. We were Christians; those of the Orient were heathen.

6. There has been rejoicing, both private and public, in the political openings that have made it possible for Christianity to enter one land after another, even when the entrance of missionaries into a given area has been practically forced. When missionaries suffered persecution or even death, our political agents usually demanded heavy indemnities.

7. The West has, in general, been quite unaware of the spiritual values in other religions, and too often unappreciative of their quest for eternal truth.

8. Our missionaries have had far too little intimate fellowship with the people of the countries among whom they have worked. Too often they have isolated themselves. Too often they have been so busy proclaiming their own message that they have failed to hear the desires and complaints, and in particular, to discover the deeper spiritual feelings that those about them would have liked to express.

9. The missionary attitude has been too often that of "doing for" instead of "working with."

Now as the West thus reflects, it appreciates that such states of mind, such outward conduct and attitudes, while often regrettable, were a product of the period. We ourselves, as well as our missionaries, were part and parcel of our medieval conception of life. We lived in a military age; we had cultivated an attitude of superiority. When our missionaries went to the Orient, they were not apt to shed these elements derived from their environment.

On the other hand, unless there had been deep conviction with regard to their message, our missionaries would not have cared to give their lives to an extraordinarily difficult task. Unless our early missionaries had been possessed by a unique devotion, they would not have dared to face the perils incident to their endeavor. It was the union of conviction and of devotion that enabled these pioneer workers to stand firm under the difficult conditions they faced during this war-trusting period, which, we now begin to hope, is coming to an end.

5. *A changing spirit.*—Certain clear signs are to be seen that a new day is at hand.

1. The spirit of science is compelling us to be tolerant, to listen to the other man's opinion, to test our own work in the laboratory, and to cultivate a spirit of humility in the presence of the eternal facts of the universe.

2. Realizing that religion is the quest of the soul for God, we have begun to discover the significance of the spiritual search in Buddhism, in Hinduism, and in other oriental religions.

3. We are recalling that Jesus was an oriental figure and that the traits of character he emphasized in the Sermon on the Mount were, many of them, more readily understood by the Oriental than by the Occidental. The man from India, China, and Japan may, therefore, find in Jesus much that had never been understood by the West.

4. We are recognizing that if Jesus is to influence the Orient he must become naturalized there. He can scarcely come close to the oriental mind if he continues to be regarded as a foreigner.

5. We are beginning to see that the work of missions is likely to consist more largely in interpreting the life and message and sacrifice and spirit of the Founder of the Christian religion, rather than merely in philanthropic activities, however significant these may be. Thoughtful persons throughout the Orient record their deep appreciation of the educational and medical contribution made by Western missions. Without them the revolutionary changes in the social structure now so conspicuous everywhere would scarcely have come about in the way they have. And yet, as to the future, the Orient is likely to call for effective interpreters of the religious spirit, rather than for technical skill only.

6. We are discovering that the missionary boards in the Occident and the various church constituencies that support them must be awakened to a new attitude of confidence in the Orient, of determination to minimize denominationalism, and of willingness to pledge aid in men and money to indigenous bodies that stand ready to take up the work brought into being by missionaries.

### II. POSSIBLE OUTCOME OF THE PRESENT SITUATION

1. *Christianity may cease to be a force in the Orient.*—The record of the Nestorian missionary approach to China in the seventh century, followed by its total disappearance within a couple of hundred years, due in large measure to religious compromise, indicates the possibility of failure in a religious movement. The Franciscans who came in the thirteenth century, led by John of Monte Corvino, failed, similarly, to leave a mark in China. The ultra-foreign character of their work was undoubtedly

their undoing. A third and a very promising missionary movement in China was started by the Jesuits late in the sixteenth century, but it, too, after 140 years of progress, encountered proscription and faced possible extermination. The Emperor had been offended; there were controversies between contending orders; and the prospect that Christianity might again disappear was very real.

The crisis facing the missionary movement in China today is of a different sort, but even more basic and perplexing. Some of the reasons for this crisis grow out of causes indicated in the earlier paragraphs of this statement. In China, as elsewhere, Christianity may lose all vital influence unless the missionary movement of the new day revises its program and methods.

In those countries where a strong nationalism has arisen it is not unnatural that political leaders should view with concern, if not with suspicion, the presence in their midst of foreigners who advocate methods devised in other lands and adapted to different civilizations. The primary question today is as to whether the missionary movement is really making it possible for the message of Christianity to become naturalized. If so, it will endure.

2. *Materialism may become widespread.*—The disappearance of Christianity from one land or another may be followed by a setting up, even though for but a limited time, of materialism as a dominant philosophy. In Russia, governmental authorities would like to see religion banished. The continued observance of religious forms in that land and the widespread clinging to worship at the shrines everywhere gives evidence of the way in which the religious instinct is basic in the human soul. Of late, apostles of modern materialism have visited the Orient and proclaimed their gospel. They have had wide hearing and have made a lasting impression in many quarters by their assertion that the West is materialistic and that it cares little today for Christianity.

3. *Loss of religious co-operation.*—More serious even than that Christianity should appear to have lost its influence in this land or that, and more serious even that it should be replaced by materialism, is the danger that the West may lose the opportunity to co-operate with the Orient in the spiritual realm. China, for example, has reached a stage where she is unwilling to have her soul saved for her by the West. What a calamity if the West should lose the opportunity to work alongside of her in spheres other than mechanical and commercial! Living alone religiously, China might become so chauvinistic in her inner religious attitude as to prevent the normal growth of her spiritual being. No country can afford to give up the sense that others are working with her in the realm of religion as in that of politics, of commerce, and of science.

### III. AN APPROACH TO A NEW PHILOSOPHY OF MISSIONS

1. Whatever our conclusions as to the ethics of religious propagation in countries other than our own, and whatever we find as to the desire for religious interchange between East and West, four requirements stand out as fundamental in formulating a new philosophy of missions.

*a*) We must have a new interpretation of Christianity and of its founder. Clearly neither Western nor Eastern peoples are likely to be interested much longer in Christian dogma, or even in medical and educational work merely, important though these philanthropic activities may be. The Orient is asking today for a frank statement about, and an honest interpretation of, the person, the teaching and the spirit of Jesus. The Oriental will himself be able increasingly to establish and conduct the schools he needs and to administer the hospitals he needs. From the West he is sure to desire something deeper. It is more than probable that the early Buddhist missionaries from India to China secured their foothold by the humble life they lived and the sincerity with which they taught the truths of their master. Clearly enough, their religious message had no accompaniments of militarism, of commerce, or of modern science.

*b*) We must seek a new understanding of the spiritual values in oriental religions. They, too, are engaged in a quest. They, too, are attempts to find a way of life. Theirs is an honest search for eternal truth. Theirs are earnest endeavors to find God. The founder of the Christian religion must have had this in his consciousness when he said: "I came not to destroy but to fulfil."

We need to understand a great deal more about the major religious emphases in China and India. In China, for example, to select three of the major words in its religious vocabulary—*hsiao, ho, jen*—the first lays emphasis on the filial relationship; the second, on spiritual harmony; the third, on what we may call, for lack of a better term, humanity. The Christian character *jen,* humanity, is that of a man beside two horizontal strokes, the upper representing heaven and the lower our earthly existence. Humanity is the thing that links the eternal with the temporal.

*c*) We must secure, as representatives of Christianity in the Orient, men who have accepted the new conception of Christianity, who are willing to seek a new understanding of the Oriental religions, and who seek to bring these two into harmony. They must approach the Orient as humble students of religion, and must remain students all their lives. They must share consciously with their oriental brothers in a co-operative search for eternal truth. They must be unassuming, co-operative fellow-workers in a spiritual task, working in genuine fellowship, sharing with their oriental colleagues in success and failure, joy and sorrow. They must seek no office, desire no authority, but must join, rather, with those of other religious faiths, both in seeking fuller understandings of religious truth and in seeking to spiritualize the entire social order.

*d*) There must be messengers from the Orient who bring a religious message to the West. They must not only give us an understanding of religion as the Oriental sees it, but must be men who will enlarge and enrich our conceptions of Christianity.

2. For some this new approach to a philosophy of religion will be an easy achievement. They have already lived in the atmosphere of understanding and appreciation. For many in Western lands, however, a process of education will be needed so that they may better understand this enlarged view of life, and, grasping it, throw their influence in the direction of establishing it. They must be willing to think of all religious endeavor as a common task, providing, when needed, financial support for the day's work without hesitancy. Where confidence exists in those who lead a movement, material support cannot be withheld. Their emphasis must be, not so much on the word "devolution" as on the thought of recognition that India and China must naturally take leadership and control in the field of religion.

### IV. SOME OF THE STEPS IN THE PROCESS

Given the new philosophy of missions just hinted at, men and women from different lands will meet and outline a program of procedure with such emphasis on method as is congenial to their setting. A few simple steps suggest themselves:

1. Not organization, but fellowship, is required. Men and women whose attitude transcends narrow nationalism must be set free to move about in Occident and Orient to develop a sense of comradeship. Their task will not be to create bodies with officers and by-laws, but rather to help citizens of different nations to meet each other and to understand each other's religious approach.

2. Administrative organization must be simplified. Fewer officers and more co-operating workers, less machinery and more of the spirit of the common task, will be called for.

3. The new spirit and the new attitude that unite those thus engaged in religious activities will have to find statement in the simplest terms, so that others may understand something of the process and of the goal.

4. So far as possible, the activities hitherto conducted by Westerners will secure Oriental leadership. If committees are formed for church or school or orphanage, Westerners may or may not be asked to serve thereon. Their services must be at the disposal of the oriental leaders who need their aid as counsellors or professional workers.

5. Unadapted and unadaptable Westerners will naturally drop out of the picture. Those who lack pliability of temperament and buoyancy of spirit will not understand how to share in this new endeavor.

6. Mission boards in the Occident and missions in the Orient will come more and more to put their property, as they put their personnel, at the disposal of indigenous bodies. Initiative and leadership, which have hitherto been repressed, will be given all possible encouragement, and the material goods which the West has been able to bring together will be at the service of the common task.

7. Mission boards in the Occident will soon discover that their largest function will be to act as co-operating groups who offer financial and professional aid and who provide, above all, an understanding personnel for the task in the Orient.

The foregoing statement records an attempt to think through a few of the aspects of the present situation, facing frankly the criticisms of the missionary movement, and reflecting on their significance and on certain present dangers. It records a conviction that the new day needs a new philosophy for missions, as for other activities of human life. If religion is a universal human instinct its origin in the human soul is the same in the Orient as in the Occident. The Occident needs to learn the lesson that the religious horizons of the human race are not broadened by dominance and assertiveness so much as by a dedication of men as brothers to a spiritual quest. Missions reconstructed on this understanding of their task are likely to find permanent welcome from the Orient.

## SECTION 11

## SUGGESTIONS FOR A CODE OF ETHICS FOR THE RELATIONS BETWEEN RELIGIONS

D. J. FLEMING
Professor of Missions in Union Theological Seminary, New York City

Just as practitioners of law or medicine have their codes of ethics, so should religionists have standards of behavior between themselves. Such standards, if widely recognized, would not only lessen the occasions of intergroup strife, but would make for a surer approach to the frontiers of conceptions of human behavior.

It must be acknowledged that no such code exists, nor does man possess enough systematized ethical experience to formulate an adequate code. Its development must be experimental and experiential. Our immediate objective, therefore, is no absolute set of standards, but an ongoing, developmental process, looking toward the formulation of ever truer insights.

The following points attempt to focus ethical judgment on several of the more conspicuous abuses and ideals in the contact of religion with religion, and are intended to serve only as a starting-point for discussion.

I. Ethical criteria:

*a*) The ethical criteria governing choice among values, creeds, and customs is not for this day primarily authority, nor the welfare of any creed, but the widest possible welfare of humanity as judged by experience extensive in range and time.

*b*) The ethical criteria governing objective in the touch of one religion on another is that the relation shall result in the best growth in all respects of the adherents. Among other things, therefore, the objective will include:

(1) The ability and the disposition on the part of the adherents to make increasingly discriminating, efficient decisions for themselves.

(2) The conception that no man has the right to preach his doctrine unless he is willing to receive and learn as well as to give, i.e., unless he maintains a humble and teachable spirit with respect to his own religion as well as others.

(3) The forwarding of better relations and understandings between adherents of different religions, so that all religions may have the fullest freedom to develop the best that is in them, on the basis of mutual understanding and respect.

(4) The development of alert, creative men and women, of discriminating minds, appreciative in an intelligent way of the best and finest in all life, even though they may not come to agree with the religion of their teacher. This objective will exclude as unfair:

(*a*) Attempting in uneducative ways, or by ways that do not honor personality, to undermine or overwhelm the faith of the uneducated or of those unskilled in argument among the adherents of another religion.

(*b*) Fixing the religious decision of an adherent of another faith without helping or encouraging him to make a choice, so as to prevent his making a free choice when he has grown older or more experienced, as a particular instance of failure to respect personality.

*c*) The ethical criteria governing reciprocal spirit is that when the adherents of one religion make an aggressive approach to the adherents of another religion, the former should seek to conduct themselves as they would wish the adherents of the latter to approach them and their people.

II. Tolerance:

*a*) The loose principle of universal tolerance is not ethically sound. Beliefs and practices may embody explicit or inexplicit evils. Hence critical examination is necessary on the basis of the criteria before stated. One should not be tolerant of what has proved inimical to the welfare of humanity judged by tested experience over a range of time.

*b*) Religious toleration, whether by individuals or groups, when thus justified, should not be maintained by external coercion (cf. treaty provision of religious liberty in China).

III. Individual choice:

In conformity with criterion *a*, individuals should have the right voluntarily to change their religious adherence.

IV. Propagation:

In conformity with the given criteria, systematic effort to propagate by solid methods any opinion, creed, or practice which is sincerely believed to make for the enrichment of life, or to share those values felt by anyone to flow from his religion, should be recognized as proper. Some indication as to what is meant by solid methods is given by the following:

*a*) Expressing contempt for another religion, the abuse and misrepresentation of it, or intentionally setting a light value on its attainment is wrong.

*b*) The use of material, medical, educational, and economic means, not to secure converts, but as advantages which can be secured only on condition that the people in question listen to the giver's message, is questionable.

*c*) The use of material, medical, educational, and economic means in such association with a religious message as to act as attractions, but so as to leave listening to the message effectually optional, is permissible.

*d*) Dependence on the example and fruitage arising from one's religion (e.g., the disinterested relief of human sorrow, suffering, and need, and all noble, joyous, and unselfish living) with the definite concern that others, seeing this as the natural expression of one's religious life, may be drawn to one's source of life and power, or for no other reason than that such kind of life is deemed by one to be highest, is proper.

*e*) Special privileges in behalf of the aggressive adherents of any religion should consist only of those freely granted by the people to whom they go, and not wrung from them by the superior physical force of governments (cf. China).

*f*) Indemnities for losses of life and property suffered by the aggressive adherents of any religion may be received when freely offered as a voluntary expression of the sense of human justice, but should not be claimed or forcibly collected.

V. Conversion:

The right of conversion, if properly conducted, from one religion to another should be granted.

*a*) The use of physical force, persecution, threats of loss, veiled coercion, or undue pressure to secure conversion is unethical.

*b*) The use of political, social, educational, and economic inducements to conversion in such a way as to amount in practice to bribes is to be deprecated.

*c*) Detaching a person from one or more of the groups to which he belongs (family, caste, clan, tribe, village, religious body) under the motivation of merely increasing the numbers under one's religious label is unworthy (i.e., proselytization in its worse sense). Such detachment of a minor without the consent of the parents is also unworthy.

VI. Change in group customs:

*a*) The inspiration and insights of religions may rightfully be brought to bear upon all situations which involve moral issues in the degree that the religions moralize human relationships in accordance with I*a*, preceding.

*b*) Aggressive adherents of any religion when crossing cultural boundaries should not fail to make a discriminating study of the culture and social customs of the group to which they go, since unwisely or unnecessarily to challenge or destroy local mores and ethical standards is wrong. They should realize that the adoption of a new faith frequently leads to the loss of elements of indigenous culture dependent upon the old faith, and hence they should accept responsibility for such destruction and provide new outlets where possible for old values. Consideration should be given to the possibility of maintaining continuity of belief essential to the preservation of morale by incorporating elements of value from the old faith in the new.

*c*) The aggressive adherents of any religion should, in general, place main emphasis upon constructive phases of their faith, building first before destroying.

*d*) Aggressive religionists should temper their activities by a realization of the fact that sudden changes in social custom, organization, or belief are likely to work more harm than good where they are unduly subversive of established social controls.

*e*) The expression by converts of contempt for the seniors of their community as upholders of the old faith should be discouraged, for the effect on morality and social life is very great.

## SECTION 12

# THE FACTORS THAT GOVERN POPULATION GROWTH

CARL L. ALSBERG
Director, Food Research Institute, Stanford University

I shall state my points categorically without proofs, since there is no time for more than this. The discussion which is to follow should clarify any matter concerning which any of you have doubts.

My first point is that there is no evidence that any branch of the human race is inherently more fertile than any other. If different races multiply at different rates, the reason is, therefore, to be sought in external factors rather than in inherent differences of fecundity. Accordingly, it is necessary to inquire what these external factors may be, and this involves inquiry into the rate of increase of peoples. Dr. Baker has told you that this rate is not constant throughout the history of a people. He has shown you that recently there has been an abrupt change in the rate of population increase. It was very moderate in the eighteenth century, but very rapid during the nineteenth. This shows that there are definite periods or cycles in population growth. Let us first consider the rate of population growth in a given cycle.

In the earlier years of any given cycle the population increases faster each year than it did the preceding year until a maximum rate of increase is reached. Thereafter, in the later years of the cycle, the population increases less fast each year than it did the preceding year, until finally there comes a year when there is no increase at all. The population has then become stationary. All this is illustrated by the chart upon the wall, presenting graphically the population growth of the United States. It indicates that in its present cycle the maximum rate of increase of the population of the United States came about 1914. Since that time the rate of increase has begun to slow up and the indications are that some time around the year 2000 the population will have become stationary at something under two hundred millions, unless some profound unforeseen social or other revolutions take place to change the present trend and start a new cycle.

If the statements I have just made are sound, certain questions come to mind at once. Why should there be cycles of growth in a people's history? Why should population's growth slow up?

Let us take the last question first. The most obvious reasons for the slowing of population growth would, one might suppose, be war, pestilence, and famine. As a matter of fact, these catastrophes effect but a minor and purely temporary retardation of the onward march of population growth. Surely since 1914 no country has suffered more from war, famine, and pestilence than Russia; yet its population today is certainly larger by at least ten millions than it was at the outbreak of the great war. The other participants in that war returned within two years to their pre-war and pre-influenzal rates. The war caused but a momentary hestitation in the steady onward march of population growth.

One might next suppose that immigration into a country or emigration out of a country would greatly affect the growth of population. Such, however, is not usually the case, at least for a country with any considerable population. When any country has a population which is absolutely as large as that of the United States, any normal amount of immigration will not seemingly alter the course of population growth. This curious fact was pointed out by Benjamin Franklin in 1751. I quote: "The importation of foreigners into a country that has as many inhabitants as the present employment and provisions for subsistence will bear will be in the end no increase of people. . . . . Nor is it necessary to bring foreigners to fill up any occasional vacancy in a country; for such a vacancy (if the laws are good) will soon be filled by natural generation."

What, then, are the causes that slow up the rate of population increase, if they are not war, pestilence, or famine? Unfortunately it is easier to say what does not cause it than to say what does. In a general way one may say that two sets of factors are involved. Either the means of subsistence may become so scarce that undernutrition, misery, wretchedness, and disease force a stationary state upon a population, or a high standard of living and general well-being may have a similar result. The indications in the light of present-day knowledge are that which of these factors will predominate depends upon the standard of living of a people at the time when its population approaches the stationary stage. And this is an important consideration that we shall have to discuss in greater detail a little later.

I do not wish to give you the impression that nothing can effect the rate at which populations trend toward a stationary state. As Dr. Baker has told you, and as I have pointed out, there may be rather abrupt changes starting a new cycle of population growth. What I have just been saying applies to any given cycle only. It does not preclude the beginning of a new cycle.

Let us next consider what are the factors that start a new cycle. Dr. Baker pointed out that in the nineteenth century it was the extension of agriculture to grass lands. He told you this was possible because of the invention of well-drilling and agricultural machinery and of railways. In other words, it was due to the application of science to practical affairs; but let us delve into this matter a little further. These inventions increase the productivity of labor. Modern civilization is dependent upon the accomplishment of more work than human labor is capable of performing. This was brought about by the development of mechanical power, first from coal, then from petroleum and natural gas, and finally through hydro-electric power. To spade an acre by hand requires more than fourteen days of labor. A 16-inch sulky plow, drawn by three horses can cover more than 3.01 acres per day in the spring and 2.5 acres in the fall. A tractor pulling three 14-inch plows will cover over 8.6 acres in spring plowing and over 8.01 in fall plowing. The application of mechanical power made it possible for each man to produce a far greater surplus of foodstuffs than he could before. It liberated labor for other employment. The development of mechanical power is the basis of modern civilization.

In the last analysis, therefore, it is into the exhaustion of our sources of power—

coal, oil, natural gas—that we must look, as well as into the food supply, if we are to forecast population trend. It is upon the increasing use of mechanical power that every rise in standards of living depends. The United States with its high standard of living produces nearly one-half of the world's quota of coal, and over two-thirds of the total output of petroleum. It would require the work of three billion hard-working slaves to accomplish the work done in the United States by its mechanical resources.

In short, under conditions of modern civilization any student of population must consider not merely the possibilities of increasing the food supply, but quite as much the available sources of mechanical energy. Dr. Baker has considered the possibilities of the former. Let us now give some attention to the latter, for it is important to know which is likely to become insufficient earlier, food or mechanical energy. The question is really of vital importance.

Upon an increasing supply of available energy depends very largely the possibility of raising the world's general standard of living; but, as we have seen, it is imperative to raise the standards of living of the whole world to a high level before population has to become stationary, if the world's population is to reach a stable equilibrium without universal wretchedness and misery.

Now, coal and petroleum differ in one important respect from food. Fresh food may grow each year where food grew the year before, but a ton of coal once mined or a barrel of petroleum once pumped up is gone forever and cannot be reproduced. Furthermore, food consumption increases directly as the population increases. Not so coal or oil consumption. Man can only fill his belly about so full; but how much coal, oil, and iron he can use no man can now foresee. And so we see that the consumption of coal, of iron, and of oil has increased far more rapidly than the world's population. Since 1800, while the world's population was increasing two and one-half times, the world's coal production and pig-iron production was increasing nearly one hundred fold. The present rate of increase in the use of raw materials cannot go on very long without approaching exhaustion of some of them. If that point should be reached and science should not find a way out before the world's population becomes stationary, it will adversely affect the standard of living at which the stationary state is reached.

You have very probably been asking yourself, What has all this to do with Pacific relations? It has everything to do with them; for in one way or another it is economic pressure, resulting from population pressure, that has caused most major conflicts in the world. If all the world had the same standard of living, if no nation were under serious economic pressure, if all populations were stationary at the same high standard of living, there would be nothing to gain by war by conquest or by exploitation.

Only if and when we reach this state does there seem to be much chance for universal peace. That is, I suppose, a utopian dream, but no man is wise enough to say what is and what is not utopian. Therefore it would be good policy for the peoples of the earth at least to strive to raise the level of those with low standards of living; for what seems to me most important is that all should reach equilibrium at the same high level.

## SECTION 13

# THE PROGRESS OF POPULATION

O. E. BAKER
Agricultural Economist, U.S. Department of Agriculture

The spread of agriculture during the past century across the virgin and fertile prairies of the United States and Canada, Argentina and Australia, Russia and Siberia, Manchuria and portions of Mongolia, is a romantic and fascinating story, but its profound significance has not been fully apprehended. Hundreds of books have been written about the Industrial Revolution in Western Europe and Eastern North America which ushered in our modern civilization and has been considered its basis; but scarcely a volume has described the agricultural revolution in Eastern Europe and Western North America which transformed the grass lands into grain lands and supplied the food and fibers that made the Industrial Revolution possible.

Prior to the nineteenth century agricultural settlement in Europe and North America, in Japan and Eastern Asia, had been confined by geographic conditions largely to originally forested lands. The forests supplied fuel and building material, and the ever running streams that are found in forest areas provided drink for man and beast. Most of the grass lands of these continents were grazing grounds for nomads—Hungarians, and Tartars in Southeastern Europe, Indians and later cattle and sheepmen in Western North America, Manchus and Mongols in Eastern Asia. The lack of wood and water prevented the utilization of these grass lands for agriculture, and the establishment of civilization. When Malthus wrote his famous essay a century and a quarter ago, predicting that in the occidental world, as in the oriental, population would soon press upon the food supply, and be limited by famine and pestilence, only a small part of the vast prairies and steppes of Southern and Southeastern Russia had been broken for wheat; the Hungarian plain was still mostly a verdant pasture, divided into the large estates of nobles and cattle kings; the prairies and plains of Central and Western North America had not yet been crossed by white men, except a few fur traders; the pampas of Argentina were an unmapped wilderness; and only a fringe of land along the coast of Australia had been explored. Manchuria was the grazing and hunting domain of the Manchu princes, and scarcely an acre of grain was grown in Mongolia.

Three great inventions account in large measure for the agricultural development of these grass lands and the marvelous and unprecedented increase in population and wealth which has followed: (1) the invention of well-drilling appliances, (2) the development of grain-harvesting and threshing machinery, and (3) the invention of the steam locomotive and construction of railways. Wells gave water to the trackless wastes; grain-harvesting machinery enabled one man to do the work of five, releasing the other four for work in urban industries; and the railroads brought wood and coal to the settlers and provided cheap and rapid transportation to market for their grain and other products.

### THE INCREASE IN POPULATION

The utilization of these grass lands of the world for grain and meat production, supplemented by the use of animal manures and mineral fertilizer on some of the forest soils, and by the improvement of farm animals, has provided for an increase of population in Europe during the past century and a quarter since Malthus from nearly 200,000,000 to nearly 500,000,000 and in the United States and Canada from 6,000,000 to 125,000,000. This increase in population in Europe and North America has been owing, not to increased fecundity, but to increased longevity, to medical advice, and a food supply vastly more diversified and costing twice as much to produce as the diet of a century ago. The influence, for example, of an abundant supply of pure milk for both infants and adults can scarcely be overestimated. Had the death-rates at the beginning of the nineteenth century continued, a rapid depopulation would have taken place in two-thirds of Europe and in both the United States and Canada during the past 30 years.

Even Asia has shared in the increase of population, despite the fact that it has less arable grass land available, and, owing to deficiency of power and consequent inability to use modern agricultural machinery, has been less able to utilize those grass-land areas which it has. India, for example, owing largely to British peace, order, and sanitation, had about 60,000,000 more people in 1911 than in 1881, a gain of 2,000,000 a year, which is considerably more than the increase in the United States during these years, and this increase is continuing;[1] while Java, under the benign rule of the Dutch, has increased from three or four million inhabitants in the year 1800 to 35,000,000 today.[2] China probably gained over 100,000,000 people between 1800 and 1870, when the saturation point was reached, apparently, under the old régime;[3] and the people of Japan, since admitting Western civilization in 1854, have doubled in number.[4]

The population of the world as a whole increased from about 500,000,000 in the year 1700 A.D., to 600,000,000 in the year 1800, then to over 1,000,000,000 by 1850, to 1,500,000,000 in 1900, and to nearly 1,900,000,000 today (see Table I). The population of the world has trebled since the year 1800, and the increase in numbers during the first quarter of the twentieth century, despite the devastations of fratricidal war, was fully three times as great as during the entire eighteenth century. The population of the world is now increasing at the rate of nearly 20,000,000 a year, which is an addition equivalent to the population of the United States every 6 years.

[1] The returns from the census of 1921 have since become available. Only a slight increase is shown for the preceding decade, owing to epidemics of disease, especially influenza, and to war losses. But at present the natural increase rate is about 0.6 per cent a year.

[2] S. H. Van Valkenberg, "Java, the Economic Geography of a Tropic Island," *Geographical Review* (October, 1925), p. 566.

[3] Chang-heng Chen, *Chinese Economic Journal,* January, 1927.

[4] *Encyclopedia Britannica* (old series), article "Japan."

THE INCREASE OF POPULATION IN THE UNITED STATES AND CANADA

The growth of population in the United States and Canada, therefore, is not unique, but merely a part of a world-wide development resulting largely from the occupation of the grass lands of the world, the progress of science, and the increase of capital. However, the rate of increase of population in these North American nations has been at an unusually rapid rate, in large part because of the late discovery of America by European races and the exploitation of a virgin and almost unoccupied continent by means of modern transportation facilities and agricultural and industrial machinery.

TABLE I

ESTIMATE OF THE WORLD'S POPULATION, 1685–1924*

| Year | Authority | Estimate (Millions) | Year | Authority | Estimate (Millions) | Year | Authority | Estimate (Millions) |
|---|---|---|---|---|---|---|---|---|
| 1685... | Riccioli | 500 | 1845... | Michelot | 1,009 | 1886... | Levasseur | 1,483 |
| 1740... | Nic. Struyck | 500 | 1854... | v. Reden | 1,135 | 1891... | Havenstein | 1,467 |
| 1804... | Malte-Brun | 640 | 1868... | Kolb | 1,270 | 1896... | *Statesman's Yearbook* | 1,493 |
| 1810... | *Almanach de Gotha* | 682 | 1870... | F. Behn | 1,359 | 1903... | Jaraschek | 1,512 |
| 1816... | A. Balbi | 704 | 1874... | Behm & Wagner | 1,391 | 1906... | Jaraschek | 1,538 |
| 1822... | Reichard | 732 | 1878... | Levasseur | 1,439 | 1910... | *Annuaire Statistique* | |
| 1828... | L. Bergius | 847 | 1883... | Behm & Wagner | 1,433 | 1913... | Knibbs | 1,632 |
| 1833... | Stein | 872 | | | | 1914... | Knibbs | 1,649 |
| | | | | | | 1924... | *Int. Yearbook of Agric. Statistics* | 1,853 |

* These estimates of the world's population are given by S. H. Knibbs, "The Mathematical Theory of Population, of Its Character and Fluctuations, and of the Factors Which Influence Them," Appendix H, *Census of Commonwealth of Australia, 1917*, except those for 1924, which are from the *International Yearbook of Agricultural Statistics*.

One hundred and fifty years ago, when the United States declared its independence, there were about 2,500,000 people scattered along the Atlantic coast from Georgia to Maine. A quarter-century later, by the year 1800, population had more than doubled; in a half-century, by the year 1825, it had quadrupled; and by 1850 it was nine times as large as in 1775. Up until the Civil War Malthus' statement that given plenty of food and normal freedom from disease population tends to increase in geometrical ratio, held true. But in the next quarter-century a decline occurred in the rate of increase, a greater decline than can be explained by the influence of the Civil War. Population had not doubled by 1875, and between 1875 and 1900 it increased only 73 per cent. From 1900 to 1926 the increase in population has been about 50 per cent,[5] and it is now increasing at the arithmetical ratio of about 1,600,000 each year. This growth of the American nation from 2,500,000 to over 115,000,000 people

[5] Press statement of United States Census Bureau, January, 1925, and *Fourteenth Census* (1920), I, 20–21.

during the 150 years since the Declaration of Independence, with the accompanying increase in wealth and culture, is probably the most extraordinary development in human history.

But the rate of increase is decreasing. Both birth-rates and death-rates are falling. But death-rates cannot go much lower. Dublin and Lotka have shown that after the present natural increase rate in the United States is corrected for the abnormal age grouping of the population, the natural increase would be reduced to one-half, or to about 5 per thousand. It appears not improbable that the population of the United States will reach a stationary stage of 200,000,000 near the year 2000 A.D. Automobiles and other worldly interests are only too successfully competing with children as objects worthy of sacrifice.

The trend of population in Canada, though the figures are much smaller, shows a similar but less regular rate of increase. The population in the year 1800 was about 400,000; in 1825 it had doubled; in 1850 it was nearly six times as great as in 1800; and by 1875 it had almost doubled again. But between 1875 and 1900 it increased only about 35 per cent. From 1900 to 1925, however, owing principally to the settlement of the prairie provinces, the increase was about 75 per cent. I do not know whether any studies have been made for Canada similar to those of Dublin and Lotka for the United States.

### POPULATION IN THE ORIENT

It is interesting in this connection to compare the trend of population in the United States during the past century with that of China during the century preceding. If the data presented by Chang-heng Chen in last January's issue of the *Chinese Economic Journal*, based on official reports, may be accepted, the population of China in the year 1750 was only about 25,000,000 greater than that which the United States will reach about the year 1950, and was increasing at about the same rate as the increase in the United States today. This rate of increase continued with greater or less uniformity for a century. About the year 1850 the increase was much less rapid, the saturation point under the existing social and technical régime having been nearly reached; and since about 1870 there has been, apparently, no increase in the population of China. China is now sustaining nearly four times as large a population as that of the United States on about one-half as large an area in crops. In the United States there are about 3 acres of crops and 9 acres of pasture and range land per person, whereas in China there is less than a half-acre of crops and probably even less pasture per person.

However, in Japan there is only a quarter-acre of crops per person and practically no pasture. The ratio of crop land to population is lower in Japan than in any other country of the world equally self-sufficing. On 15,000,000 acres of crop land, an amount about equal to that in South Dakota or Oklahoma, Japan is producing most of the food required by 60,000,000 people. Nowhere else is agriculture so intensive and so efficient in the utilization of land. The possibilities of production are more closely approached, probably, in Japan than in any other country of the world.

Japan will be the first modern nation, self-governing and provided with the panoply of science, to face the issue between food supply and population in all its stark severity. If Japan solves this problem satisfactorily, as I believe she will, she will have shown the way which other nations will soon be grateful to follow, and will have made the greatest contribution which any nation can make to the welfare of the world.

### THE LIMITATION OF THE LAND

Neither science nor invention, capitalism nor individual initiative, which appear to have been the great forces that have promoted this increase in population, can expand the arable area of earth appreciably, nor raise the crop yields per acre beyond a certain point; and after all is said, the conclusion is as clear as at the beginning: that the land and the food it produces sets the limit to population.[6] Only a small proportion of the surface of the earth is arable. A third of the United States and of Southern Asia, almost one-half of Africa, and fully four-fifths of Australia are unsuited for crop production because of deficient rainfall; three-fourths or more of Canada and of Siberia, because of deficient temperature. Of the 52,000,000 square miles of land on the earth's surface outside the polar ice caps, about 10,000,000 square miles have climatic conditions too cold for crop production; 17,000,000 square miles more are too dry for crops, leaving 25,000,000 not too cold or too dry. About 11,000,000 square miles more of this area that has sufficient temperature and moisture are too rough and mountainous for production of crops, and of the remaining 14,000,000 square miles, probably 3,000,000 square miles have unfavorable soils. There is left, therefore, only about 10,000,000 square miles, or one-fifth of the land surface of the earth, possessing physical conditions suitable for crops. Of these 10,000,000 square miles, about 4,000,000 square miles are crops at present.

Recalling that this potentially arable land yet unused is mostly poor land, it appears that unless the acre-yield of the crops is increased, the population of the world cannot be more than doubled and maintain the present standard of living with reference to agricultural products. If crop yields could be doubled, by the use of fertilizers and manures, as they have been during the past century in the humid-climate and industrially developed countries of Northwestern Europe, the population of the earth could be quadrupled, that is, approach 8,000,000,000 of people. This is the limit set by Professor Penck, of the University of Berlin. But as much of this potential crop land of the world has a semi-arid climate, where the limiting factor on crop production is water, and not soil fertility, this estimate I believe is too optimistic. The

[6] Recent experiments indicate that a food prepared largely from yeast, containing 55 per cent protein and high in vitamines especially, can be manufactured for less than 10 cents a pound, or for one-half the present wholesale price of meat. The yeast plants utilize over 90 per cent of the nitrogen supplied in the form of ammonium sulphate (as compared with less than 10 per cent for most crops), a large per cent of the phosphate, supplied as ground phosphate rock, and provide one and three-fourths pounds of protein food for each pound of molasses or sugar supplied. Moreover, the yeast crop can be grown in 13 hours, instead of 13 or more weeks for most field crops; and ten men in a yeast factory equipped with large tanks, pumps, and other machinery can produce as much protein as 1,000 farmers raising live stock. This vegetable protein is an excellent food; but whether it can be made sufficiently palatable to be used in large quantities by the American people remains to be determined. However, as the food energy required by the yeast plant must be obtained from sugar or starch, the principal effect of the extensive preparation of such food would be to transfer the land requirement to this extent from the temperate zones to the tropics.

limit upon the world's population, if it remains dependent upon agricultural production, must be placed probably not beyond three times that of the present population.

If the population of the world should double again during the next century as it has during the past century, this saturation point is only about 150 years ahead of us; and meanwhile the advance of crop production onto poorer lands will mean in many countries, especially those lacking in capital, a lowering of the standards of living.

Today we seem to be, therefore, at another critical period in the history of the world, much like that existing in England when Malthus wrote his famous essay, but vaster in its significance. In Eastern Europe, in Western North America, in Argentina, in Australia, in China, and especially in Japan—in fact, almost everywhere in the temperate zones—the rising waves of population are beating against the barriers of adverse physical conditions all along the shore line of settlement. Although it is possible to double the area in crops, the best land, the good land, even most of the land of fair quality has already been brought into use. There is rising before the eyes of intelligent men today the same vision that rose before the eyes of Malthus: a vision of human misery and degradation for most of the world like that existing among some of the peoples of the Orient for centuries past.

How is the world, except possibly, the United States and some of the British dominions, to avoid this impending disaster? Will the twentieth century witness the agricultural exploitation of the tropics, like that of the grass lands of the temperate zones during the nineteenth? Or will the greatly increased use of fertilizers, the prevention of plant diseases, the more careful cultivation of crops, permit the profitable utilization for crops of the poorer lands now in pasture or forest or lying idle, and also cause such an increase in the yield per acre of the lands already in cultivation, and in the efficiency of farm animals in transforming feed into food, as will meet the needs of the more numerous population for another century? Or will the decline in religious authority and development of materialism diminish the birth-rate, possibly even induce depopulation eventually, as it did, apparently, in the ancient Roman Empire and may yet accomplish in the United States? Or will recurring wars keep the population comfortably within the limits set by the agricultural resources?

These are questions that no one can answer; but they clearly indicate that the time is at hand when the leaders of the nations should take stock of the agricultural resources of the lands they hold and of the trend of population, and decide upon both a land policy and a population policy, lest most of the world sink into that condition of poverty, misery, and resignation which Malthus foresaw more than a century ago.

## SECTION 14

## LAND UTILIZATION IN CHINA

O. E. BAKER
Agricultural Economist, United States Department of Agriculture

I have never been in China. But in the past two or three years I have become interested in agricultural conditions and land utilization in the Far East, partly because we are preparing an agricultural atlas of the world and have had to study such statistical data as exist relative to the land and the agriculture of these countries, and partly because the population of the United States during the twentieth century is trending onward at much the same rate, apparently, that China's population was increasing during the eighteenth century. As a picture of conditions that may exist in our country two or three centuries hence, unless some new factor or group of factors interrupts the trend of population, the present agricultural situation in China is interesting.

In 1749 China's population was apparently about 177,000,000, which is some 60,000,000 more than our own at present.[1] From 1749 to 1759 China gained 17,000,000 people, according to the official figures, which is about the same number that the United States seems likely to gain between 1920 and 1930. From 1759 to 1771, China increased about 20,000,000 people in the 12 years. Then, apparently, more complete census returns were achieved, or else new provinces were included, for in 1775 the return is over 50,000,000 higher. From 1780 to 1790 the increase was 24,000,000; then population seemingly remained stationary for a decade, but by 1820 was around 350,000,000, a gain of 50,000,000 or more during the preceding 30 years, which is about the same increase per year as in the United States at present. Only 15 years later, in 1835, a population of 400,000,000 was reached, according to the Chinese statistics, and by 1850 the population had risen to 429,000,000, an increase of 25,000,000 during the preceding 15 years. Since 1850 the population of China has remained more or less stationary and was estimated by the Chinese post-office in 1923 (undoubtedly the most reliable estimate) at 438,000,000 for China proper and Manchuria. The increase in population in Manchuria more than accounts for this 13,000,000 gain since 1850.

The population of China, in other words, appears to have reached a saturation point under the old economic and technical régime; the struggle for existence has become a very real thing; and war, famine, disease, and the other factors which Malthus included under the terms "misery" and "vice" are keeping the population within the limits set by the natural and technical resources.

Although we may place our hopes in the minds of men, and even more in the social and economic ambitions of women, and trust that our country, at least, may es-

[1] Chang-heng Chen, "Changes in Growth of China's Population in the Last 182 Years," *Chinese Economic Journal* (January, 1927), pp. 62–63.

cape this fate which has befallen China and which seems to be facing nearly all other countries of the world except France and some of the British dominions, it seems worth while, nevertheless, for China's sake if not for our own, to consider the present conditions in that country, especially with reference to the utilization of the land, and inquire whether the development of modern agricultural and industrial technique could ameliorate the situation. Our interest in Chinese agriculture is justified, not only from the humanitarian and scientific standpoints, but also because the adoption of modern agricultural technique by Chinese farmers would have very important economic consequences for the people of the United States.

May I note in this connection that I am speaking this evening as a university professor, that I have not submitted a memorandum or manuscript for approval by the United States Department of Agriculture, and that the Department is in no wise responsible for what I may say. However, I surmise that if authority to speak were requested, the Department would approve most, if not all, of my conclusions. It is because I have been temporarily a university professor that I am able to exhibit the cultivated land, crop, and farm animal maps before you. These are based on data, by *hsiens,* published in *Statistical Tables of Agriculture and Commerce, 1918,* Department of Agriculture and Commerce, Peking, 1922, which I have been able to edit while teaching in Clark University this spring. The *hsiens* were located and the maps dotted by two students in the School of Geography, Mr. La Fleur and Mr. Foscue, assisted in the translation of the Chinese language by Mr. Cheng and Miss Huang, also students in the School of Geography. The climatic maps were prepared by Mr. Koppe and Mr. Banks, two other students in the school.

## LAND AREA

The total area of the eighteen provinces of China proper is about 981,000,000 acres, or a little over one-half that of the United States. If Manchuria be added, where the Chinese share the government to some extent with both the Russians and the Japanese, the total area becomes 1,214,000,000 acres, or nearly two-thirds that of the United States; and if Mongolia and Sin Kiang (commonly called Chinese Turkestan) be included—both are vast deserts mostly—the total area is increased to 2,441,000,000 acres, which is an area nearly a third larger than that of the United States. Half of the area of the Chinese Republic, thus defined, it will be noted, is included in China proper and Manchuria, and half in Mongolia and Sin Kiang. Thibet is omitted because the Chinese appear to have lost control over that country.

## LAND RESOURCES

As in the United States, the eastern portion of this vast Chinese Republic, especially the southeastern portion, is humid, while the western and northwestern is arid, more arid than our western states. Climatic records are few in China, and in the northwestern provinces and Mongolia are lacking almost entirely; nevertheless, with the aid of observations concerning the native vegetation, it does appear possible to estimate the area having sufficient rainfall for crop production within an error of 10, or possibly, 15 per cent. This area is estimated roughly at 1,300,000,000 acres, or slightly over one-half of the entire area of the Chinese Empire, excluding Thibet. In the

United States only one-fourth of the land area is too dry for crop production. The proportion of the land too dry for crop production in the entire Chinese Empire (excluding Thibet) is therefore about twice as great as in the United States.

TABLE I*

CHINA AND DEPENDENCIES. PRELIMINARY ESTIMATE OF AREA OF CULTIVATED LAND IN 1918, NUMBER OF FARMS, 1918, AND TOTAL POPULATION, 1923 (POST-OFFICE ESTIMATE)

| Province or District | Cultivated Land (Acres) | Number of Farms (Families) | Cultivated Land per Farm (Acres) | Population | Population per Farm | Cultivated Land per Capita |
|---|---|---|---|---|---|---|
| Capital district | 2,446,000 | 635,000 | 3.85 | 34,187,000 | 7.2 | 0.47 |
| Chihli | 13,625,000 | 3,983,000 | 4.20 | | | |
| Shantung | 15,983,000 | 5,350,000 | 2.98 | 30,803,000 | 5.8 | 0.52 |
| Honan | 16,700,000 | 5,325,000 | 3.14 | 30,832,000 | 5.8 | 0.54 |
| Shansi | 7,353,000 | 1,530,000 | 4.82 | 11,081,000 | 7.3 | 0.66 |
| Shensi | 5,333,000 | 1,308,000 | 3.62 | 9,466,000 | 7.3 | 0.56 |
| Kansu | 3,000,000 | 854,000 | 3.48 | 5,928,000 | 7.0 | 0.51 |
| Kiangsu | 13,833,000 | 4,542,000 | 3.03 | 33,786,000 | 7.4 | 0.41 |
| Anhwei | 6,833,000 | 2,873,000 | 2.38 | 19,833,000 | 7.0 | 0.34 |
| Chekiang | 5,531,000 | 3,340,000 | 1.67 | 22,044,000 | 6.6 | 0.27 |
| Kiangsi | 6,383,000 | 3,800,000 | 1.68 | 24,467,000 | 6.4 | 0.26 |
| Hupeh | 7,500,000 | 3,636,000 | 2.07 | 27,167,000 | 7.5 | 0.28 |
| Hunan | 1,666,000 | 3,831,000 | 1.59 | 28,444,000 | 7.4 | 0.25 |
| Szechwan | 20,833,000 | 6,038,000 | 3.45 | 49,783,000 | 8.2 | 0.42 |
| Fukien | 2,960.000 | 1,621,000 | 1.82 | 13,158,000 | 8.1 | 0.22 |
| Kwangtung | 8,734,000 | 5,310,000 | 1.68 | 37,168,000 | 7.0 | 0.24 |
| Kwangsi | 2,951,000 | 1,771,000 | 1.67 | 12,258,000 | 7.0 | 0.24 |
| Kweichow | 2,716,000 | 1,482,000 | 1.67 | 11,115,000 | 7.5 | 0.24 |
| Yunnan | 1,916,000 | 1,300,000 | 1.47 | 9,839,000 | 7.6 | 0.20 |
| China proper | 151,016,000 | 58,531,000 | 2.58 | 414,012,000 | 7.1 | 0.365 |
| Fengtien | 7,631,000 | 1,736,000 | 4.40 | 12,487,583 | 7.4 | 0.61 |
| Kirin | 7,480,000 | 589,000 | 12.68 | 5,511,406 | 9.3 | 1.41 |
| Heilungkiang | 6,478,000 | 336,000 | 19.30 | 4,000,000 | 11.9 | 1.62 |
| Manchuria | 21,589,000 | 2,661,000 | 8.11 | 22,083,000 | 8.2 | 0.98 |
| Jehol | 2,714,000 | 620,000 | 2.73 | ...... | ...... | ...... |
| Charhar | 944,000 | 116,000 | 8.13 | ...... | ...... | ...... |
| Suiyuan | 913,000 | 67,000? | 13.67 | ...... | ...... | ...... |
| Mongolia (inner) | 4,571,000 | 803,000 | 4.45 | ...... | ...... | ...... |
| Sin Kiang | 2,004,000 | 460,000 | 4.36 | 2,491,000 | 5.4 | 0.8 |
| China and dependencies | 179,180,000 | 62,455,000 | 2.85 | 442,046,000 | 7.1 | 0.4 |

* Based mostly on *Statistical Tables of Agriculture and Commerce, 1918*, Department of Agriculture and Commerce, Peking, 1922.

This lower proportion of humid and subhumid and semiarid land in the Chinese Empire than in the United States is owing primarily to the east-west trend of the Himalaya Mountains and several low ranges which extend eastward from the Thibetan Plateau more than halfway across China proper. These mountains cause the precipitation on their slopes of much of the moisture in the winds blowing northward in the warm season from the Indian Ocean and the South Sea; whereas in North America the broad open Mississippi Valley permits the moisture-bearing winds from the Gulf of Mexico to blow unimpeded across the central states and on into Canada. As a consequence the lines of equal annual rainfall trend north and south across the plains region in Central North America, whereas in Southeastern Asia they trend from the southwest toward the northeast.

The land in the Chinese Republic too dry for crop production, located mostly in Mongolia and Sin Kiang, like that in the United States, is used to a large extent for grazing live stock, principally cattle, horses, sheep, and goats. Much of this area, however, is too dry even for grazing—probably of larger proportion than in the United States, where less than 10 per cent is too arid for the grazing of sheep.

Over 90 per cent of the area in the Chinese Republic having sufficient rainfall for crop production is included in the eighteen provinces of China proper and Manchuria. The area in inner Mongolia having sufficient moisture for crops is estimated at 64,000,000 acres, or 100,000 square miles, but this is only a guess, and probably an optimistic one. In Sin Kiang (Chinese Turkestan) the present area under cultivation is about 2,000,000 acres, mostly non-irrigated, according to the Chinese statistics. The few climatic records in this province show an almost rainless climate, but these records are from irrigated districts. We have allowed (not estimated, for the data do not exist on which to base an estimate) 34,000,000 acres of potentially arable land in this province. The total cultivated areas outside of China proper and Manchuria, therefore, is probably not in excess of 100,000,000 acres, or less than 8 per cent of the total arable area of the Republic.

The other climatic condition that limits crop production is temperature. China has a more southerly location than the United States, the center of area, and of population also, lying in about latitude 30, as compared with latitude 40 for these centers in the United States. As a consequence there is only a very small proportion of the area having sufficient rainfall for crop production in China that does not also receive sufficient heat. This land in China too cold for crop production is practically restricted to the mountain peaks and high arid plateaus. The area of these high-altitude lands too cold for crops which is located within the regions having sufficient rainfall probably does not exceed 5 per cent of the total area in these regions. This may be compared with 9 per cent for the United States. Subtracting this 5 per cent from the 1,300,000,000 acres having sufficient moisture for crop production, there remain, roughly, 1,235,000,000 acres having both moisture and temperature conditions that permit the production of crops.

The third physical limitation upon the area of land available for crop production is that of land relief, or topography—the lay of the land. As only a few small areas have been topographically surveyed in China, it is necessary to assume that in an area as large as the humid and subhumid portions of China, nearly all of which land was originally covered with forest, the proportion of the land too mountainous or rough for crop production would be similar to the proportion in the humid forested area of the United States. Of the 750,000,000 acres originally covered with forest in the United States, about 300,000,000 acres are too hilly or rough to use for crops, or 40 per cent. This is nearly twice the proportion for the United States as a whole, since all of the hilly land in the East and much of the mountainous land of the West was originally clothed with forest, whereas the level and rolling areas of the central and western states were mostly clothed with grass or with desert shrubs. But in view of the fact that China proper contains many mountainous areas, and, like the Eastern United States, has mostly a humid climate where erosion is more rapid than in sub-humid to arid climates, it seems fitting to apply this much higher figure to determine the proportion of the area of China not tillable, than the 20 per cent figure for the United States as a whole. Reducing the 1,235,000,000 acres of land in the Chinese Republic climatically suitable for crop production by 40 per cent, there remains 740,000,000 acres as a rough estimate of the area in China climatically and topographically available for crop production.

The fourth physical factor limiting the area of land suitable for crops is the soil. The control of this factor over crop production is not as rigid as that of temperature, which can be altered only by constructing greenhouses or using heat in other ways, or that of moisture, which can be overcome in small part by irrigation or drainage, nor even that of topography, which in China is modified over large areas by terracing the hillsides. Soil conditions can be and are more readily ameliorated by man than these other physical conditions; consequently it is difficult to say to what extent they would set a limit to crop production, especially in a country like China, where labor is abundant and cheap, and the use of fertilizing materials is common practice. However, all forms of amelioration of these physical conditions are expensive, even the modification of soils by the use of fertilizers; and undoubtedly in China, as in the United States, it would not pay to build a rice field on a sand dune, nor, perhaps, to attempt to use a sandy flat for any agricultural purpose.

If it may be assumed that the Chinese farmers are no more likely to use very sandy land, or sterile clays, than the farmers of the United States, and that the proportion of such soils in two such large and otherwise similar areas is similar, this figure of 740,000,000 acres of land climatically and topographically suitable for crop production must be further reduced by 5 per cent to allow for unproductive soils, or to about 700,000,000 acres.

To recapitulate: Nearly half of the 2,400,000,000 acres of land in the Chinese Republic (excluding Thibet) is too arid for crop production. About 5 per cent of the remaining half (53 per cent) which receives sufficient rainfall is too cold. Probably 40 per cent of the remaining 48 per cent climatically suitable is too mountainous or rough, while 5 per cent of the remainder is probably too sandy. This leaves only about 29 per cent of the land area of the Chinese Republic physically available for the production of crops. In the United States the corresponding proportion is 51 per cent.

China has, therefore, about 28 per cent less land physically available for crops than the United States, i.e., about 700,000,000 acres as compared with about 975,000,000 acres. But as China has a population 280 per cent greater, the area of land on which it is physically possible to grow crops is at present 1.6 acres per person in China and 8.3 acres in the United States. In other words, the United States now has five times as large an acreage of potential crop land per capita as China.

### LAND UTILIZATION

As nearly as can be estimated on the basis of existing data, the area of cultivated land in China and its dependencies is about 180,000,000 acres. This figure is obtained after editing the agricultural returns by *hsiens,* which correspond to counties in the United States, as published in a Volume entitled *Statistical Tables of Agriculture and Commerce, 1918,* already referred to.[2] I have edited the *hsien* figures in this Chinese publication in much the same way that our Bureau of Census edits the results of the tabulation of returns by our own census enumerators. The Chinese have been honest in publishing in this statistical volume the most obvious errors, sometimes indicated by a question mark, and after a study of the Chinese statistics I am of the opinion that they are not much worse than the first crude tabulation of our agricultural census returns from the southern states. The number of *hsiens* whose figures are inconsistent or obviously wrong are relatively few, and by checking the agricultural data against the estimates of the population made by the Chinese post-office, I believe the error in this estimate of cultivated land in any province has been brought within 25 per cent, and for China as a whole, within 10 per cent.

After thus correcting the most obvious errors in the statistical data, necessarily in a rough and hasty manner for lack of time, I was pleased to find in the 1926 *China Yearbook* an estimate of 180,000,000 acres for the area of cultivated land in China proper and Manchuria.

In 1919 there were about 354,000,000 acres of land in harvested crops in the United States, to which should be added at least 13,000,000 acres of crop failures, and as much more summer fallow. In 1919 there were, therefore, about 380,000,000 acres of cultivated land in the United States, or over twice the acreage in China of the previous year. The area of cultivated land per capita of the total population of the United States was in that year 3.6 acres, whereas in China it was about 0.4 acre. In other words, there is about nine times as much cultivated land per person in the United States as in China.

### PROPORTION OF POTENTIAL CROP LAND IN CROPS AT PRESENT

This contrast is not so striking, however, as the fact that the proportion of the physically cultivable land in the United States which is cultivated is nearly 39 per cent, whereas in China the proportion is only about 26 per cent. Why should China, an old country with the severe pressure of population on land resources indicated by this figure of four-tenths acre of cultivated land per person, nevertheless cultivate a much smaller proportion of its cultivable land than the United States, which is only now emerging from the pioneer period of development and in which the pressure of population on the land is lighter than in almost any other country in the world? One would expect that in China almost every hillside would be terraced to its top, all land it was possible to irrigate would be irrigated, all land it was possible to drain would be drained, and that long since settlers would have pressed out upon the subhumid prairies of Manchuria and the semiarid plains of inner Mongolia, instead of having just

[2] The volumes for the years 1919 and 1920 are also available in the United States Department of Agriculture library, but the data for these later years are less complete, owing to the political situation in the southern and southwestern provinces.

started to do so, almost timidly, during the past quarter-century. Why do large tracts of tillable land lie untouched, as I am told, in the neighborhood of many cities, sometimes even within the city walls, as at Nanking? To this seemingly anomalous situation in China let us now devote our attention primarily. The answer to this question is to be found, I believe, principally in two words: "machinery," and its corollary, "power."

### POWER ON FARMS IN THE UNITED STATES

In the United States progress in agriculture, perhaps fully as much as in manufacturing and mining, has been dependent upon the development of machinery and of power to operate it. The plowing of a 40-acre field, 6 inches deep, involves the movement of 50,000 tons of earth, and the distance traveled using a single 12-inch plow is fully 330 miles. At 2 miles an hour, this would require 165 hours, or over 16 days of 10 hours each. But think how much more laborious the effort and how much longer time would be required if this 40-acre field had to be spaded by hand, or perhaps we should say "by foot." Obviously it would be beyond the capacity of one or even several men in a single season.

The average area of cultivated land per farm in Southern China, where rice is the important crop and is usually followed the same season by some other crop, is 1⅔ acres. But in Northern China, where wheat, millet, and the sorghums are dominant and only a part of the land grows a second crop the same season, less labor per acre is required and the farms are twice as large, averaging about 3⅓ acres of cultivated land per farm. The average area of cultivated land per farm for all China, including Manchuria, where the farms are still larger, is 3.1 acres. Probably this is about as large an area on the average as a farmer and his son, or hired man, can comfortably cultivate by using hand tools. In the United States the average acreage of crops per farm, including the small negro-tenant cotton farms of the South, is 57 acres, which is eighteen times the average acreage of cultivated land per farm in China. This eighteen-fold greater acreage of crops per farm in the United States than in China is made possible by the use of machinery and of power adapted to its operation.

The horse power available on the farms in the United States in 1924, two-fifths supplied by horses and mules and three-fifths by mechanical engines, was about 52,360,000.[3] This was 58 per cent greater than the horse power available in all the factories of the United States. On the other hand, the amount of labor employed in agriculture, including the labor of farmers and their families, was 17 per cent less than that employed in manufacturing. The average horse power per man available in agriculture is nearly 6¼, whereas in manufacturing it is only 3¼.

Neither of these figures includes the power developed by the laborers themselves. In manufacturing this is almost insignificant; the employees in most industries merely watch and guide the machines, or help to administer the organization. But in agriculture muscular labor is still significant; perhaps one-third as much energy is

[3] C. D. Kinsman and others, "An Appraisal of Power Used on Farms in the United States," *U. S. Department of Agriculture Bulletin 1348*, p. 6, corrected by 1925 census data that became available later. The power developed by automobile other than trucks is excluded in this estimate.

expended as would be if no machinery existed. If a man's physical strength may be considered to equal one-sixth that of a horse, we should add to the 52,360,000 horse-power available on farms about 500,000 more horse-power of human labor, which

TABLE II*

CHINA AND DEPENDENCIES. PRELIMINARY ESTIMATE OF ACREAGE OF RICE, WHEAT, MILLETS, AND SORGHUMS, 1918

| Province or District | Rice | | Wheat | | Sorghums and Millets | |
|---|---|---|---|---|---|---|
| | Acres | Percentage of Cult. Land | Acres | Percentage of Cult. Land | Acres | Percentage of Cult. Land |
| Capital district | 8,000 | ....... | 363,000 | 15 | 966,000 | 39 |
| Chihli | 238,000 | 17 | 2,842,000 | 21 | 5,340,000 | 40 |
| Shantung | 253,000 | 2 | 6,028,000 | 37 | 5,255,000 | 33 |
| Honan | 1,260,000 | 8 | 5,961,000 | 26 | 5,833,000 | 35 |
| Shansi | 827,000 | 11 | 2,159,000 | 29? | 1,833,000 | 25 |
| Shensi | 340,000 | 6 | 2,473,000 | 46 | 362,000 | 7 |
| Kansu | 73,000 | 2 | 1,500,000 | 50 | 367,000 | 12 |
| Kiangsu | 5,000,000 | 36 | 4,061,000 | 29 | 2,114,000 | 15 |
| Anhwei | 3,500,000 | 51 | 1,645,000 | 24 | 603,000 | 9 |
| Chekiang | 3,817,000 | 69 | 650,000 | 11 | 116,000 | 2 |
| Kiangsi | 4,650,000 | 70 | 250,000 | 4 | 19,000 | ....... |
| Hupeh | 4,750,000 | 64 | 900,000 | 12 | 594,000 | 8 |
| Hunan | 4,396,000 | 71 | 608,000 | 5 | est. 40,000 | 1 |
| Szechwan | 6,981,000 | 34 | 4,166,000 | 20 | 2,100,000 | 10 |
| Fukien | 2,100,000 | 70 | 287,000 | 10 | 5,000 | ....... |
| Kwangtung | 6,200,000 | 70 | ............. | 0 | Little | ....... |
| Kwangsi | 2,097,000 | 69 | 100,000 | 4 | Little | ....... |
| Kweichow | 1,852,000 | 68 | 125,000 | 5 | 50,000 | 2 |
| Yunnan | 1,230,000 | 64 | 200,000 | 10 | 100,000 | 5 |
| China proper | 49,572,000 | 32.8 | 34,318,000 | 22.7 | 26,697,000 | 17.7 |
| Fengtien | 180,000 | 2 | 221,000 | 3? | 4,465,000 | 58 |
| Kirin | 169,000 | 1 | 1,048,000 | 14 | 2,414,000 | 32 |
| Heilungkiang | 8,000 | ....... | 1,153,000 | 18 | 2,025,000 | 31 |
| Manchuria | 357,000 | 1.7 | 2,422,000 | 11.2 | 8,904,000 | 41.2 |
| Jehol | 3,000 | ....... | 103,000 | 4 | 2,226,000 | 83 |
| Charhar | 90,000 | 10 | 612,000 | 65 | 174,000 | 18 |
| Suiyuan | ? | ....... | 159,000 | 18 | 416,000 | 46 |
| Mongolia (inner) | 93,000 | ....... | 874,000 | 19.1 | 2,816,000 | 61.6 |
| Sinkiang | 88,000 | 4.4 | 801,000 | 40.0 | 72,000 | 3.6 |
| China and dependencies | 50,110,000 | 28.0 | 38,415,000 | 21.6 | 37,489,000 | 21.0 |

* Based mostly on *Statistical Tables of Agriculture and Commerce, 1918*, Peking, 1922.

would raise the total to nearly 53,000,000. Were the farmers and farm laborers in the United States dependent for power solely upon their own muscles they could develop less than 3 per cent of the power available to them on farms at present.

Let us compare this power available to the average farmer and farm laborer in the United States with that available to the farmers and farm laborers in China.

### POWER ON FARMS IN CHINA

The principal sources of power on farms in China are men, cattle, and horses. There are over 60,000,000 farm families in China, almost ten times as many as in the United States. Let us assume that these farm families average two farm workers, the farmer and a son or a hired man. This was the case in the United States until recent years, but now there are only about one and three-fourths workers per farm. Let us further assume that these 120,000,000 farm workers exert their full muscular strength

TABLE III*

NUMBER OF LIVE STOCK IN CHINA, 1918

| Province or District | Horses | Mules and Asses | Cattle | Swine | Sheep | Poultry |
|---|---|---|---|---|---|---|
| Capital district | 25,459 | 74,618 | 31,210 | 152,014 | 56,335 | 1,138,000 |
| Chihli | 311,181 | 514,407 | 516,711 | 2,995,591 | 1,032,800 | 8,058,000 |
| Shantung | 184,795 | 937,506 | 974,726 | 2,145,203 | 788,493 | 16,672,000 |
| Honan | 263,704 | 670,510 | 945,160 | 1,230,683 | 1,016,261 | 12,005,000 |
| Shansi | 97,058 | 314,983 | 304,330 | 391,853 | 3,335,401 | 2,321,000 |
| Shensi | 191,915 | 179,995 | 519,363 | 845,953 | 1,000,389 | 2,610,000 |
| Kansu | 236,620 | 383,116 | 455,841 | 529,410 | 5,235,065 | 2,770,000 |
| Kiangsu | 39,274 | 268,523 | 1,209,411 | 4,868,897 | 865,432 | 33,555,000 |
| Anhwei | 127,380 | 472,492 | 1,345,726 | 4,926,986 | 888,689 | 31,595,000 |
| Chekiang | 1,406 | 5,368 | 577,184 | 1,942,192 | 743,888 | 18,702,000 |
| Kiangsi | 30,675 | 7,411 | 1,409,083 | 3,372,642 | 94,755 | 18,778,000 |
| Hupeh | 154,619 | 142,352 | 1,604,544 | 4,868,910 | 874,716 | 23,870,000 |
| Hunan | 40,000 | 9,000 | 1,450,000 | 4,000,000 | 702,948 | 23,000,000 |
| Szechwan | 280,000 | 230,000 | 3,600,000 | 10,000,000 | 2,780,987 | 45,000,000 |
| Fukien | 8,804 | 2,027 | 370,547 | 1,828,137 | 367,891 | 12,882,000 |
| Kwangtung | 5,000 | 1,000 | 1,700,000 | 5,000,000 | 385,463 | 40,000,000 |
| Kwangsi | 5,000 | 1,000 | 600,000 | 1,800,000 | 311,722 | 13,000,000 |
| Kweichow | 30,000 | 7,000 | 600,000 | 1,600,000 | 77,874 | 9,000,000 |
| Yunnan | 40,000 | 20,000 | 500,000 | 1,100,000 | 1,006,140 | 8,000,000 |
| China proper | 2,110,279 | 4,241,308 | 18,713,836 | 53,598,471 | 21,564,849 | 323,156,000 |
| Fengtien | 808,734 | 343,543 | 475,239 | 4,574,610 | 611,674 | 8,458,000 |
| Kirin | 616,742 | 113,695 | 506,557 | 1,401,553 | 219,839 | 4,535,000 |
| Heilung Kiang | 764,775 | 70,619 | 259,623 | 1,074,839 | 235,884 | 2,817,000 |
| Manchuria | 2,190,251 | 527,857 | 1,241,419 | 7,051,002 | 1,067,397 | 15,810,000 |
| Jehol | 160,136 | 124,321 | 182,759 | 394,969 | 582,642 | 2,016,000 |
| Charhar | 51,710 | 12,753 | 104,528 | 207,043 | 552,125 | 458,000 |
| Suiyuan | 61,606 | 28,290 | 104,407 | 90,300 | 498,786 | 167,000 |
| Mongolia (inner) | 273,452 | 165,364 | 391,694 | 392,312 | 1,633,553 | 2,641,000 |
| Sinkiang | 166,218 | 305,253 | 508,291 | 23,477 | 4,324,818 | 3,080,000 |
| China and dependencies | 4,702,200 | 5,239,782 | 20,355,240 | 61,365,262 | 28,590,617 | 344,687,000 |

* From *Statistical Tables of Agriculture and Commerce, 1918*, Division of Statistics, Department of Agriculture and Commerce, Peking, 1922; except that estimates were necessary for Hunan, Szechwan, Kwangtung, Kwangsi, Kweichow, and Yunnan. Sheep data for these provinces are from *Chinese Economic Monthly*, November, 1924.

in their work. As a man's power is about one-sixth that of a horse, the power developed by these 120,000,000 men is equivalent, perhaps, to that of 20,000,000 horses.

The average number of horses, mules, and asses in China and dependencies in 1914 and 1915, for which years data are available for all China, was about 9,700,000, and the number of cattle, 22,000,000, which apparently includes water buffalo, if the statistical data given in the 1918 report previously referred to may be accepted for live stock without editing, which I have been unable to do.

These figures indicate that China has nearly two-fifths as many horses, mules, and asses, and one-third as many cattle, as the census reports on farms in the United States. Let us assume that all these horses, mules, and asses in China are used to develop power on farms, although the Chinese statistical reports indicate that the figures include all horses, mules, and asses in each province, many of which are probably used for transportation. And let us further assume that each cow or steer, ox, or calf, develops as much power as a horse, certainly an overestimate. Adding the 20,000,000 horse-power potentially available in the farmers and farm laborers themselves to the 9,700,000 horses, mules, and asses, and the 22,000,000 cattle, an estimate is reached of nearly 52,000,000 horse-power available for agricultural production in China and dependencies. This is a maximum estimate. Undoubtedly half the horses and mules and probably three-fourths the cattle in China are used for power on farms. These proportions indicate a minimium horse-power available on Chinese farms of 36,-000, 000.

### POWER PER ACRE AND PER MAN IN CHINA

It appears, therefore, that China has between 70 and 100 per cent as much available power on farms as that in the United States. This power available for the production of crops needs to be considered from two standpoints: (1) that of the land, or the amount of power available per acre, and (2) that of the man, or the amount of power available per person employed in agriculture. Dividing the 180,-000,000 acres of cultivated land by 40,000,000 horse-power (an average of the maximum and minimum estimate), it appears that the average area of cultivated land per horse-power in China is about 4 acres. In the United States it is about 7 acres. In other words, the farmers of China have available nearly twice as much power per acre as the farmers in the United States.

Moreover, it seems likely that a larger proportion of this available power is utilized in China, because nearly half of it consists of human labor, which undoubtedly is kept employed most of the year, owing in part to the warmer climate. In the United States the power available is mostly that of horses, mules, and tractors, which are in use a surprisingly small proportion of the year. In view of this more continuous use of power in China, it is not unlikely that four times as much power is applied to the average acre of crop land as in the United States.

Let us now view the matter from the standpoint of the man or the amount of power available per farm. Dividing the 44,000,000 horse-power by the 62,000,000 farms, we have an average of less than three-fourths of a horse-power per farm. In the United States the average is over 8 horse-power per farm, or fully ten times as much.

Apparently land is scarce in China compared with the United States, and men are cheap, for the Chinese apply probably four times as much power to the acre of crop land as we do in the United States, while we put ten times as much power in the hands of each farmer. But we will recall that the proportion of the cultivable land in China which is cultivated is only about 26 per cent, whereas in the United States it is nearly 39 per cent. With almost as much power available as in the United States, why should the Chinese leave 520,000,000 acres, more or less, of their tillable land untilled, an amount which is nearly three-fourths of their tillable area?

### INFLUENCE OF LIMITED POWER PER MAN ON LAND UTILIZATION

This concentration of power in China on the best land seems to be owing primarily to the character of the power available and to the use of hand tools rather than of modern machinery. About half of this power available on farms in China is human labor, whereas in the United States human labor probably does not constitute over 3 per cent of the total. Human labor without the use of agricultural machinery and a relatively large amount of power cannot produce enough food on poor land to maintain a family. The man with the spade and the hoe cannot dig up and cultivate more acres of poor land than of good land. Even if he has a horse or mule, which perhaps one-tenth of the farmers of China have, or an ox, which perhaps three-tenths more of the farmers possess, he can plow at most only a few acres. For the Chinese farmers who depend on their own muscles solely for power—and these constitute, according to the statistics, over half the farmers of China—two acres per farm or one acre per man in the rice regions and twice as much in the wheat and millet regions seems to be the average amount of land that can be spaded and cultivated by the farmer and his son or hired man in the period of time permitted by the progress of the seasons.[4] These 2–4-acre farms must support five to six people. These five or six people will eat 10–14 bushels of wheat, or equivalent other food, per person yearly, which is 50–80 bushels of wheat or equivalent per family. As the average acre yield of wheat in all China is apparently less than 12 bushels, it undoubtedly does not exceed 8 bushels on the semiarid or less fertile soils. This is about the acre yield on such soils in the United States. It would require, therefore, 8–10 acres of these lands to grow enough wheat to feed a family, which is twice the average acreage per farm in the wheat-growing regions. Even on the better land it is obvious that to produce enough food for a family to live on the farmer must either grow another crop on the land the same year, which many farmers do, or else cultivate a larger acreage by means of horses, mules, or cattle.

Most of the horses and mules in China, it will be noted, are in the wheat- and millet-growing regions of Northern China, where the land yields only one-third to one-half as much food per acre as in the rice-growing regions of Southern China. The less productive crop per acre requires the cultivation of a larger acreage per farm and utilization of more power.

The acreage of cultivated land is, in general, less dense in Southern China than Northern China. This may be owing in part to a smaller proportion of tillable land; but it is also doubtless owing in part to the fewer work animals and the opportunity which the rice crop affords of concentrating human labor on the best lands. Obviously the man who is dependent on his own muscles and can therefore handle only 2 or 3 acres, must cultivate the more fertile land in order to obtain enough food for himself and family to live on, and must, if possible, grow the most productive crop, which is rice. Not being able to increase the acreage, he must increase the yield per acre by every means. He must irrigate wherever possible—one-third of the cultivated land of China is irrigated, as compared with less than 6 per cent in the United States. He must fertilize every plant, because every plant is precious.

It is principally the small quantity of power available per man, particularly for plowing the land, I believe, that restricts the utilization of the land in China to about one-fourth of the potentially arable area.

[4] Records of time required in spading gardens, kept by Department of Agriculture employees, indicate that it would require about 15 days to spade up an acre of land.

The ability to utilize low-grade land for crops which the farmers of the United States possess because of their command of power is best illustrated perhaps by the semiarid portion of the Great Plains region. Here, where the yield per acre is low, the cost of production is kept low by the use of the most efficient machinery. In western Kansas there are about 140 acres of crops per farm; in eastern Washington, nearly 200 acres. Although the land may yield only 7 or 8 bushels of wheat per acre, the production per farm is 1,000 bushels of wheat or more. Compare this with the 30–50 bushels of wheat and millet which the Chinese farmer could produce by hand tools alone in the semiarid northwestern provinces of China, not more than half enough to sustain a family.

This dependence on machinery and power in regions of deficient moisture is as true with reference to cotton as to wheat. Farmers are "sledding" their cotton in the Texas Panhandle, thus gathering ten to twenty times as much per man as could be picked by hand, just as they harvest their wheat with a binder or combine. They cannot afford to pick the cotton crop by hand unless it is high in price. Despite low prices, the production of both cotton and wheat continues to expand in this Great Plains region, while the acreage of all crops contracts in the mountainous portions of the eastern states because the plains land is well adapted, and the mountain land is poorly adapted, to the use of machinery.

It is significant that the vast steppes of Southeastern Russia and Manchuria, as well as the grassy plains of Argentina and of the United States and Canada, awaited the development of agricultural machinery during the latter decades of the nineteenth century before they were plowed up and planted to crops.

### THE POSSIBILITY OF POWER FARMING IN CHINA

The existence of these 500,000,000 acres, more or less, of uncultivated tillable land in China, an area approximately equal to that in the United States, and fully two and one-half times as great as the cultivated land in China, is a challenge to all those who are interested in the welfare of China. It is my opinion that much of this land located not over 30 miles from a railroad, especially the subhumid to semiarid land in the northwestern provinces, could be profitably plowed and seeded to wheat by using machinery such as is used in our own wheat-growing regions. Whether tractors or horses would prove the cheaper source of power could be determined by a few season's experience on an experimental farm, or, perhaps, even on the basis of existing information. The utilization of unused land would afford employment for a few Chinese, and could not occasion complaint that machinery was displacing human labor, such as would arise if machinery were used on the rice lands of Southern China, or the lands in Northeastern China already growing wheat.

The fact that the United States exports wheat to China almost every year, and many years exports rice also, suggests, however, that modern machinery could economically be utilized on the best rice and wheat lands. But the displacement of human labor that would result from the extensive use of modern farm machinery on the cultivated lands of China would have such serious economic and social consequences that it should be undertaken only with the utmost caution. Unless industry developed in the cities with sufficient rapidity to absorb the surplus rural population that would result, as industry is doing in the United States at present, the replacement of men by machines in the agriculture of China would probably mean the starvation of millions.

The expansion of industry in China, like the expansion of agriculture, is dependent, it would seem, upon the further development of power. The increase of power in China is, apparently, in turn dependent primarily upon the consumption of coal. Whether a rapid increase in consumption of coal can be economically secured by the exploitation of China's own supply, or must be dependent in large part upon imports, or whether neither domestic production or importation of coal is likely to increase very rapidly, and the consequent expansion of industry in China to the American or European magnitude is economically impossible, I am incompetent even to possess an opinion upon.

This is a subject upon which our chairman, I understand, can speak with as much authority as anyone. But I can state, perhaps with as much authority as anyone need possess, that under the conditions existing in China, notably with the best land already utilized for crops, agricultural production cannot increase as rapidly as population might increase if it were not restricted by the food supply. Let us devote a few minutes to this subject of agricultural production in relation to population in China.

### AGRICULTURAL PRODUCTION AND POPULATION

Although the yield per acre of rice in China is, apparently, about 40 per cent higher than in the United States, the acre-yields of the other cereals are so much lower, if we have converted the Chinese units of measure into English units correctly, that the average acreage yield of all the cereals for which comparison can be made—principally rice, wheat, corn, barley, and the grain sorghums—is, according to the official data, which in part is confirmed by unofficial data I have received, about 20 per cent lower in China than in the United States (see Table IV). With only two-thirds as much of the tillable land actually tilled in China as in the United States, and with the acre-yield of the cereals (which include over three-fourths of the cultivated land in China and nearly one-half in the United States), possibly 20 per cent lower in China than in the United States, is it not possible that agricultural production in China may increase more rapidly than population, and the standard of living, therefore, be raised? To this question the future will probably answer "No," unless the volume of manufactured products increases more rapidly than the volume of agricultural products.

Agricultural production is not capable of a rapidity of expansion comparable with that in manufacturing. Agriculture is based on the land, and good land is limited in extent. Land, moreover, normally can be cleared, reclaimed, or otherwise prepared for crop production only slowly. In the United States, for instance, the most rapid increase in agricultural production was probably during the two decades 1869–89, when agriculture expanded onto the very fertile prairie lands of the Upper Mississippi Valley, probably the largest area of land of high fertility in the world. The increase in agricultural production during these twenty years was over 100 per cent, or at the rate of 4–5 per cent a year. After the best land had been brought into use, about the year 1900, agricultural production increased less rapidly, about 11 per cent between 1899 and 1909, 13 per cent between 1909 and 1919, and about 5 per cent during the 5-year period 1919–24, or from 1 per cent a year between 1899 and 1909 to nearly 3 per cent a year between 1919 and 1924. During the past few years, for the first time since 1900, agricultural production increased more rapidly than population: 14.8 per cent as compared with 8.7 per cent increase in population during the 5-year period. This more rapid increase in agricultural production since the World

TABLE IV

CHINA AND UNITED STATES. PRINCIPAL CEREAL CROPS COMPARED (PRELIMINARY ESTIMATES)

| Crop | Acreage | Production | Yield per Acre |
|---|---|---|---|
| Rice: | | | |
| China (average of 1916–18)...... | 50,000,000 | 87,500,000,000 lb. | 1,750 lb., or 139 per cent of |
| United States (7-year average, 1914–20)................... | 981,000 | 1,295,000,000 lb. (Brown rice assumed for China and calculated for the U.S.) | 1,262 lb. |
| Wheat: | | | |
| China (average, 1914–18)........ | 50,700,000 | 543,000,000 bu. | 10.8 bu., or 75 per cent of |
| United States (average, 1914–20). | 58,205,000 | 845,000,000 bu. | 14.5 bu. |
| Corn: | | | |
| China (average, 1914–17)........ | 8,000,000 | 94,000,000 bu. | 11.75 bu., or 44 per cent of |
| United States (average, 1914–20). | 105,000,000 | 2,832,000,000 bu. | 27.0 bu. |
| Barley: | | | |
| China (average, 1914–18)........ | 10,730,000 | 172,000,000 bu. | 16.0 bu., or 63 per cent of |
| United States (average, 1914–20). | 7,920,000 | 202,000,000 bu. | 25.4 bu. |
| Grain sorghum: | | | |
| China (2- and 4-year averages)... | 19,000,000 | 238,000,000 | 12.5 bu., or 63 per cent of |
| United States (average, 1914–20). | 4,911,000 | 98,500,000 | 20.0 bu. |
| Total of these five cereals:* | | | |
| China................. .. | 138,000,000 | 2,505,000,000 | 18.1 bu., or 80 per cent of |
| United States............. | 177,000,000 | 4,000,000,000 | 22.5 bu. |

These five cereals include 77 per cent of the cultivated land in China and 48 per cent in the United States.

War is the principal cause of the present depression in agriculture, and, being caused by very exceptional conditions, is certainly transient.

But these increases in agricultural production are small compared with the increases in manufactured products. From 1899 to 1909 the physical volume of manufactured products increased 59 per cent, according to the recently completed index tables compiled from the census returns by Day and Thomas. From 1909 to 1919 the increase was only 36 per cent; but in the four years from 1919 to 1923 the increase was 22 per cent, and all of this increase occurred between 1921 and 1923. Manufactured products, in other words, are increasing from 3.5 to 11 per cent a year, or at an average rate during the past quarter-century about four times that of agricultural production.

Agricultural production per capita of the total population in the United States decreased 8 per cent between 1899 and 1909, and has scarcely held steady since 1909, whereas the per capita production of manufactured products has nearly doubled since 1899. The increasing income per person in the United States and rise in general welfare is obviously to be attributed primarily to the increase of manufactured products, rather than of agricultural products.

If agricultural production in the United States during the past quarter-century has increased less rapidly than population, except during the few years since the World War, despite all the advance in scientific knowledge and the development of a vast organization for dissemination of this knowledge and promotion of agriculture, how can agricultural production in China be expected to increase as rapidly as population might increase if it were not restrained by poverty and disease?

The principal hope for improvement in the general welfare of the Chinese people is to be found in the rapid expansion of manufacturing, so rapid that it will be greater than the increase in population. If manufacturing can be expanded so rapidly as to attract labor from the farms more rapidly than men can be born and raised on the farms, thus encouraging greater efficiency in agriculture, as well as manufacturing, China will have solved its population problem. Whether or no such an expansion of urban industry in China is possible, I have no knowledge; but there are several here this evening, I understand, competent to express an opinion.

## SECTION 15

# THE PROBLEM OF POPULATION AND FOOD SUPPLY IN JAPAN

DR. SHIROSHI NASU
Professor of Rural Economics, Imperial University of Tokyo

This paper treats of the conditions in Japan proper, Formosa and Korea being excluded because of different prevailing conditions.

### I

For about 300 years, down to the time of the Meiji Restoration (1868), the population of Japan remained practically stationary, fluctuating between 28,000,000 and 33,000,000. The nation at that time was adhering strictly to its policy of isolation; and being economically self-supporting, the whole population subsisted on the native food supply.[1] The factors tending to prevent the increase of population at that period were the then prevailing politico-economic system of society, the limited productive power of national economy, and some restrictive practices of the people. Thus, by way of further explanation, the more important of the before-mentioned factors were as follows: (1) Under the feudal division of social classes, freedom of employment and change of dwelling, as well as the disposal of land, were restricted, and this resulted in delaying the development of new agricultural land. (2) The question of the balance of power among the feudal lords, as well as other political considerations, caused the ruling class to be somewhat indifferent to the matter of land development. (3) Frequent calamities and famines exacted a heavy toll of human lives. (4) The hardships of daily existence tended to make marriage difficult and birth control a common practice, especially among the agricultural class. (5) With a low standard of living and a very meager knowledge of sanitation, it was to be expected that the death-rate, especially infant mortality, would be very high.

### II

The Meiji Restoration marked the change from the feudal system to a centralized modern government, and with this change most of the before-mentioned conditions disappeared. We can see that with the abolition of the feudal division of social classes, freedom of employment and dwelling came to be universally recognized, and at the same time there occurred a movement similar to the abolition of serfdom (*Bauerenbefreiung*) which took place in Europe during the first half of the nineteenth

[1] It is true that some trade with foreign countries was carried on through the port of Nagasaki, but it was not enough to impair the self-supporting character of national economy. Its significance lay primarily in serving as an evidence of early contact with other cultures.

century. As a result the farming districts and their peoples were released from the many shackles which had for so long restricted their freedom.

With the removal of the isolation policy, the stimulus of foreign commerce caused a sudden expansion of the nation's newly liberated productive power in agriculture, industries, and trade. Another stimulus of equal importance was the development of communication facilities within the country. The individualistic system of law, i.e., the law modeled after occidental law which was gradually introduced thereafter, . . . . replaced customary law, which had regulated the communal life of pre-Restoration days; and while it is true that today the newly adopted law is, apparently, not entirely without some evils, it cannot be doubted that during the transition period it hastened the development of enterprises and served thus to increase the nation's productive power. At any rate, the nation's productive power has progressed with phenomenal rapidity since the beginning of the Meiji era. It was for this reason that the legal ban against certain methods of preventing increases in population which had been widely practiced during the Tokugawa régime was accepted by the people without having to suffer much hardship. Both medical science and the knowledge of sanitation made rapid strides, so that within the sixty-year period since the Restoration, the population has jumped from 32,000,000 to 60,000,000. This last figure represents the population of Japan proper alone.

## III

The problem of food supply arising from the increasing population was answered chiefly by an accompanying increase in the output of agricultural products within the country. Two factors contributed to effect this increase in production: one was the marked increase in farming area, resulting from the adoption of the policy to encourage cultivation of new lands; the other was the increase in the production per unit of area made possible by the improvements in methods of cultivation.

In 1880 (the 13th year of Meiji) the total area under cultivation was:

| | Cho* |
|---|---|
| Rice fields (paddies) | 2,620,000 |
| Uplands | 1,850,000 |
| Total area tilled | 4,470,000 |

* 1 cho equals 2.45 acres.

But in 1925 the figures had changed to:

| | Cho |
|---|---|
| Rice fields | 3,090,000 |
| Uplands | 3,010,000 |
| Total area | 6,100,000 |

The increase during this 45-year period is shown in Table I.

These figures would probably not be extraordinary from the standpoint of a newly opened country like America. But for Japan, whose agricultural activities began over 2,000 years ago, to have increased its tilled acreage within half a century by more than one-third of the total area is a fact worthy of special note.

Population per Thousand
Hectare of Total
Area of
Each Country
Population per Thousand
Hectare of Arable
Land of
Each Country
Poland
France
Rumania
Jugoslavia
Bulgaria
Irish
Free State
Spain
Lithuania
Dependencies
of India

more recently we have been importing not only some 4,000,000 koku[2] from Formosa and Korea, but as much more from foreign countries. Also from 3,000,000–5,000,000 koku of wheat is being imported annually at present. In addition, eggs, dairy products, and meat are imported in considerable quantities. This trend of affairs will likely continue at an ever increasing rate. Thus it can be seen that the twentieth century, while it brought industrial development, has made of Japan a food-importing nation.

The fact that Japan, with an area equal to only one-twentieth of that of the United States, is able to support a population of over 60,000,000, or over one-half of that

TABLE IV

ARABLE LAND AND POPULATION COMPARED, 1924

| Countries | Area (Unit, 10,000 h.)* | Population (Unit, 10,000) | Population (per 100 h.) |
|---|---|---|---|
| United States | 13,820 | 11,200 | 79.6 |
| British India | 12,210 | 31,880 | 260.9 |
| Russia | 9,900 | 9,590 | 96.9 |
| Canada | 2,750 | 920 | 33.4 |
| France | 2,290 | 3,918 | 171.1 |
| Argentine | 2,130 | 950 | 44.7 |
| Germany | 2,020 | 6,260 | 309.6 |
| Poland | 1,830 | ? | ? |
| Spain | 1,600 | 2,170 | 135.7 |
| Italy | 1,320 | 3,960 | 299.4 |
| Roumania | 1,170 | ? | ? |
| Australia | 870 | 564 | 64.8 |
| Brazil | 760 | 3,060 | 398.5 |
| Japan | 620 | 5,900 | 950.4 |
| Czechoslovakia | 590 | 1,360 | 230.4 |
| Great Britain | 570 | 4,370 | 761.4 |
| Hungary | 540 | 820 | 149.8 |
| Sweden | 380 | 600 | 158.5 |
| Egypt | 340 | 1,552 | 408.4 |
| Denmark | 260 | 330 | 128.7 |
| Chili | 190 | ? | ? |
| Belgium | 120 | 770 | 629.1 |
| Holland | 90 | 720 | 779.7 |
| New Zealand | 74 | 130 | 170.7 |
| China | ? | 44,490 | ? |
| Mexico | ? | 1,420 | ? |

* h. (hectare) = 2.471 acres.

of the United States, can be attributed to many factors, but not the least of these is the fact that agriculture, as carried on in Japan, is extremely intensive. More than half of the population makes its livelihood from plots of land so tiny as to tax the credulity of Americans or Europeans. There are in Japan about 5,500,000 farmers who, on the average, cultivate only 1 cho (2.45 acres) of land, and these constitute 53 per cent of the total number of households. So were it not for the most intensive method of cultivation, the present Japanese population could hardly have been supported even with her recent development in industry. Table IV shows the number

[2] The figure for 1925 was nearly 7,000,000 koku.

of people per 100 hectares of cultivated land in the various countries, and you can easily see that Japan leads the world in that respect.

But Japan has just about reached the point where the returns on her agricultural efforts will begin to decrease irrespective of any added endeavors she may make to increase her production. In so saying, however, I do not imply that this new predicament is in any way a result of the "law of diminishing returns." It is said that this law has begun to be felt by American farmers during recent years, but in Japan its effect was felt long ago. Heretofore we have unceasingly tried to ward off its deterrent effects with science and improved technique, an effort which, of course, must be continued in the future. But what I refer to as the barrier to further progress of Japanese agriculture is the fact that the trend toward increasing farm area which has

TABLE V

| Year | Newly Added Land (Cho) | Lost to Other Uses (Cho) | Net Gain (Cho) |
|---|---|---|---|
| 1918 | 79,000 | 29,000 | 50,000 |
| 1919 | 70,000 | 20,000 | 50,000 |
| 1920 | 54,000 | 25,000 | 29,000 |
| 1921 | 50,000 | 35,000 | 15,000 |
| 1922 | 44,000 | 41,000 | 3,000 |
| 1923 | 33,000 | 50,000 | −17,000 |
| 1924 | 33,000 | 51,000 | −18,000 |
| 1925 | 33,000 | 44,000 | −11,000 |

continued since the opening years of the Meiji era is now definitely stopped. Little by little agriculture is losing the more fertile land, gaining in place much poorer land. As you may already know, the present cultivated area of Japan is only 15.6 per cent of the country's total land area. But to effect any appreciable increase is extremely difficult because Japan is a mountainous country, much of it being of barren, volcanic nature. According to the 1920 report of the Department of Agriculture and Commerce of Japan,[3] there was in 1919 some 1,700,000 cho still to be developed in the future. Some 300,000 of that land has already been opened up, so that there remains only 1,400,000 cho which can still be utilized hereafter in expanding the farming area. If this remaining 1,400,000 cho is completely developed it should increase the present cultivated area by one-fourth, but it is very doubtful whether this increase will actually be realized or not. Notwithstanding the addition of 300,000 cho since 1920, the total area under cultivation did not increase so much, because during the same period more than two-thirds of that area was used for other than agricultural purposes. The amount of land newly added to and lost from the agricultural domain between 1918 and 1925 is shown in Table V.

It can be seen from the figures given that the annual increase in tilled area, which had been around 40,000 cho, began to fall after the termination of the World War, and after 1923 the area of land newly developed became less than the farming land

[3] *Kochikakucho-kairyo Jigyo Yoran (Catalogue of Land Utilization and Development Enterprise)*, February, 1920, p. 20.

changed to non-arable land, with the result that the total cultivated area of the country began to decrease. Moreover, the lands newly added were such as had been left untouched because of unfitness from the standpoint of fertility, water convenience, and transportation, while on the other hand most of the lands which were lost by being devoted to such as town sites, roads, and railroad beds were excellent both as to fertility and location. We can hardly hope for any improvement in the natural attributes of agricultural land in Japan; all we can do is to supplement the natural shortcomings by our efforts in the field of technical development.

## V

Excepting an economic phenomenon of self-sufficiency which might obtain in an isolated nation, the size of population that can be supported within a nation cannot be determined solely by the amount of food produced therein. This is clearly illustrated by Great Britain, which imports the major portion of her food supply. But importation of food from other countries entails a payment in return. And this will necessitate—except in the case of an opulent nation which can meet such payments with the interest on its foreign loans—either the exportation of its own products in return or payment with the service of its merchant marine or other undertakings. Of course, as a temporary measure a debt could be incurred to make the payment, but it is neither a common practice nor a policy to be long continued. So in the final analysis the size of population which a nation can support will be determined by the condition of the people's gainful employment.

Opportunities for gainful employment, however, are governed in the long run by the extent of a nation's natural resources and economic status. Therefore a country poorly endowed by nature becomes easily saturated with her population. I wish to state at this point that I do not believe with Malthus that population is limited by the productive power of agricultural lands alone, but rather that this limitation is fixed by the combined producing power of agriculture, industry, and commerce. Advancement in the technique of production permits the accommodation of a larger population, while an elevation in the standard of living produces a contrary effect; the resultant of these two tendencies will indicate the direction of the fluctuation of population. But it goes without saying that the actual problem cannot be solved by this alone, for there is a very intimate relation between the degree of utilization of the existing natural resources and the prevailing social economic system. That is to say that natural resources, even though they may be the means of providing the people with the necessities of life, will often be left undeveloped unless such development can interest or prove profitable to its owner or some other capitalists. Therefore an enterprise which would naturally be undertaken if considered from the standpoint of the rentability of both the capital and labor combined is now very often not promoted, thus depriving the people of the opportunity of getting work. In case of unprofitable business, the manager of a factory may reduce the output and dismiss many employees, while the poor people are not provided with the product; or rich, aristocratic people might keep vast tracts of land as their pleasure grounds and deer forests, as in some European countries, while the nation wants to open it for the purpose of agricultural production. In those cases we cannot be said to have developed the natural resource to its utmost limit. Moreover, if the technique of production is improved, a fewer number of laborers can produce greater volume and a greater part of the capital would be expended for machinery than for labor. So it follows that as the technique of production continues to improve the problem of unemployment will necessarily rise from time to time, just as Karl Marx has contended. And the people who thus lose employment, not having sufficient purchasing power, will become an impeding force to the growth of production. These unemployed are also an added burden to society and would appear to be surplus population.

Here I would like to define as surplus population the coming into existence of such population as cannot be supported according to the standard of living then obtaining. It is a concept arising from the combination of productive power, population, and the standard of living. Even though there should be an increase in population, if productive power exceeds that in growth and the resulting products are so well apportioned as to raise the standard of living, then there results no excessive population. On the contrary, surplus population will come into being even though the population decreases if the productive power becomes so contracted as to necessitate a drop to a lower standard of living.

In this sense, surplus population of a modern industrial nation can be considered from two standpoints: (1) as a problem of natural resources versus population, (2) as a problem inherent to the capitalistic system of national economy.

## VI

We have now come to the very core of the population and food-supply problem of Japan. The attention of the entire world, especially of the Pacific countries, is now focused upon the growth of Japanese population. And the problem of surplus population is compelling some thinkers of Japan to base our immigration policy upon the right of national existence and international justice.

If a surplus population can be said to exist in Japan, to which of the two classes just enumerated does it belong? Some Japanese Marxists contend that the existence of the surplus population is wholly attributable to the capitalistic system. They believe that by advancing the Marxian principle they completely negate the Malthusian theory. But I cannot agree with them. To be sure, the utilization of natural resources in Japan probably has not reached the maximum point; but it is also true that it has come very close to the limit of the utilization attainable with the present store of scientific knowledge. If, just as there is no absolutely perfect man in the world, we cannot hope for an absolutely thorough utilization of natural resources, then Japan's problem of surplus population more properly belongs to the first of the two conditions, namely, a problem of population versus natural resources. Granting that the system of private ownership is to some extent an obstacle to the 100 per cent utilization of our natural resources, it would be assuming a biased position to argue therefrom that the first condition exerts no influence. On the contrary, the first condition is most important in our case, although I admit that, with the solving of the second question, Japan's capacity for supporting her population may become somewhat increased. But at this last point Japan must go hand in hand with other nations, and even when it goes successfully we cannot expect too much of it. A few years' increasing population would be quite sufficient to cover any remaining waste land in Japan with necessary human labor, despite the fact that some people think there is a considerable undeveloped district in Hokkaido. My contention, therefore, is that there is at the bottom of Japan's population question a fundamental problem which cannot be solved, however much the economic system may be changed or modified. More than a half of Japan's population is engaged in almost profitless, small-scale farming; and the fact that not only the hillsides, but in some places even the mountain summits, are being tilled is the most eloquent evidence of the utmost exertion which the Japanese are devoting to the development of their natural resources.

At this point let us survey the trend of increase in the Japanese population. I stated that the population has doubled itself during the past 60 years. This trend is

TABLE VI

| Period | Births per 1,000 | Deaths per 1,000 | Increase per 1,000 |
|---|---|---|---|
| 1874–78............ | 25.3 | 18.4 | 6.9 |
| 1879–83............ | 25.2 | 18.3 | 6.9 |
| 1884–88............ | 27.4 | 20.9 | 6.5 |
| 1889–93............ | 28.6 | 21.2 | 7.5 |
| 1894–98............ | 30.2 | 20.5 | 9.7 |
| 1899–1903.......... | 32.2 | 20.5 | 11.7 |
| 1904–08............ | 31.2 | 20.5 | 10.7 |
| 1909–13............ | 33.7 | 20.5 | 13.4 |
| 1914–18............ | 32.6 | 22.0 | 10.6 |
| 1919–23............ | 34.4 | 23.2 | 11.2 |
| 1924............... | 33.8 | 21.2 | 12.6 |
| 1925............... | 34.9 | 20.3 | 14.7 |
| 1926............... | 34.7 | 19.2 | 15.5 |

still not on the wane. By comparing the increase with the birth-rate and death-rate we obtain the figures in Table VI.

According to Table VI we note that the rates of both the births and deaths are increasing, whereas in most European countries both indicate a contrary tendency, as shown in Table VII.

The rate of increase resulting from the excess of births in Japan now exceeds that of England, is about equal to that of Germany and Italy just before the war, or to that of Canada, Australia, and Holland at present. Upon the basis of these figures it cannot be said that the Japanese race has yet passed the peak of its capacity to multiply. And if the death-rate is to be curtailed the rate of increase would become even greater, as shown in the case of 1926, when the death-rate was exceptionally low, resulting in the increase of population by nearly a million. Of course that would be true only under the assumption that other circumstances are such as to guarantee the existence of the increased population. The marriage age in Japan has recently shown a tendency to retard, and the birth-control movement is not only being talked about more freely, but is coming to be practiced in some circles. These facts may have some effect upon the vital statistics of the future. But as yet their influence is not sufficient to change the general trend. It is interesting to note in the following marriage statistics a downward trend in the last few years.

| Year | Cases of Marriage per 1,000 of Population |
|---|---|
| 1920 | 9.76 |
| 1921 | 9.14 |
| 1922 | 8.95 |
| 1923 | 8.77 |
| 1924 | 8.68 |
| 1925 | 8.73 |

As compared with 8.77 marriages per 1,000 of population in Japan in 1923, it is interesting to see the following figures for the various European countries for the same year:

| | |
|---|---|
| Belgium | 10.5 |
| Germany | 9.4 |
| France | 9.0 |
| Austria | 8.6 |
| Italy | 8.4 |
| England and Wales | 7.7 |

The population of Japan has shown a steady increase since the beginning of the Meiji era, with no present indications of ceasing, and the standard of living has kept pace with the population by steadily rising. Such being the case, it is an indisputable fact that Japan proper has had to this day no surplus population in the sense that the increased population has threatened the standard of living. We can deduce therefrom that the concept of surplus population which has so frequently been alleged to exist in Japan must have been based upon a comparison with other countries which have vast territories, abundant natural resources, and sparse population. If it were not so, then we can interpret it only as a warning against the apparently foreseen evils of unemployment and lowering of the standard of living in the future.

## VII

But it would now appear that the state of affairs foreseen for so long has at last arrived. The problem of surplus population is beginning to reveal itself in concrete form, and not as a concept based upon comparison with other countries. Japan seems to have come to a turning-point in her history. The real significance of the recent social unrest in Japan, i.e., the social movement among tenants and industrial laborers which has become very significant of late, can be understood only in the light of all these facts as a background. This social unrest is the revelation, either conscious or unconscious, of the desire to expand the productive power of the national economy which has just about come to a standstill, and incidentally, as an expression of the mass instinct for living, to find therein the only way to self-preservation.

Of course this unrest cannot be said to be entirely free from the influences of the various currents of thought in the wider world, such as, for instance, Marxian doctrines or the theories of Henry George, nor can it be denied that it is partly due to peoples ever becoming keener to the idea of social justice and more and more democratic; but it appears to me that the real driving power behind the social movements which have gained momentum so suddenly in recent years is the disparity between Japanese population and the opportunities for employment. The natural resources have been utilized almost to the utmost extent possible under the existing economic régime, and it will be will-nigh impossible to support any added population; therefore the fundamental motive behind the social movement is to reconstruct the present economic system so as to be able to improve the utilization of natural resources, to

TABLE VII

BIRTH- AND DEATH-RATES OF VARIOUS COUNTRIES COMPARED

| | 1861–70 | 1871–80 | 1881–90 | 1891–1900 | 1901–10 |
|---|---|---|---|---|---|
| | 1. ANNUAL BIRTH-RATE PER 1,000 OF POPULATION | | | | |
| Japan | ............ | 25.1 | 28.1 | 29.8 | 32.9 |
| England and Wales | ............ | 25.5 | 32.5 | 30.0 | 27.2 |
| Germany | ............ | 39.1 | 36.8 | 36.1 | 33.4 |
| France | ............ | 25.4 | 23.9 | 22.1 | 20.7 |
| Italy | ............ | 36.9 | 37.8 | 35.3 | 32.5 |
| European Russia | ............ | 49.5 | 47.2 | 47.1 | 47.0 |
| Holland | ............ | 36.4 | 34.2 | 32.5 | 30.7 |
| Belgium | ............ | 32.7 | 30.2 | 28.9 | 26.7 |
| | 2. ANNUAL DEATH-RATE PER 1,000 OF POPULATION | | | | |
| Japan | 12.2 | 19.6 | 20.8 | 20.5 | 23.5 |
| England and Wales | 22.4 | 21.5 | 19.2 | 18.4 | 15.8 |
| Germany | 26.9 | 27.1 | 25.1 | 22.2 | 18.7 |
| France | 23.6 | 23.7 | 22.1 | 22.1 | 19.4 |
| Italy | ............ | 30.0 | 27.3 | 24.7 | 21.5 |
| European Russia | ............ | 35.7 | 33.2 | 34.3 | 31.4 |
| Belgium | 23.7 | 22.9 | 20.6 | 19.4 | 17.0 |
| Austria | 30.8 | 31.5 | 29.5 | 26.6 | 23.3 |
| | 3. ANNUAL RATE OF EXCESS OF BIRTH | | | | |
| Japan | ............ | 5.5 | 7.3 | 9.3 | 9.4 |
| England and Wales | ............ | 4.0 | 13.3 | 11.6 | 11.4 |
| Germany | ............ | 12.0 | 11.7 | 13.9 | 14.7 |
| France | ............ | 1.7 | 1.8 | 0.0 | 1.3 |
| Italy | ............ | 6.9 | 10.5 | 10.5 | 11.0 |
| European Russia | ............ | 13.8 | 14.0 | 12.8 | 15.6 |

raise the efficiency of labor, and to effect a more equitable division of wealth. It aims to remove every artificial barrier relating to the utilization of natural resources, and also to reduce to a minimum the unemployment which is the creation of our modern capitalistic system. It is for this reason that the political parties which attached themselves to the *bourgeois* class and contributed to the capitalistic development of the country thus far have suddenly fallen into people's disfavor. Their mission is ended, and there awaits for them either the fate of gradual decay or complete reorganization. So the two major political parties, Seiyukai and Rikken-Minseito, which began to fear for their future because of the formation of the proletarian parties,

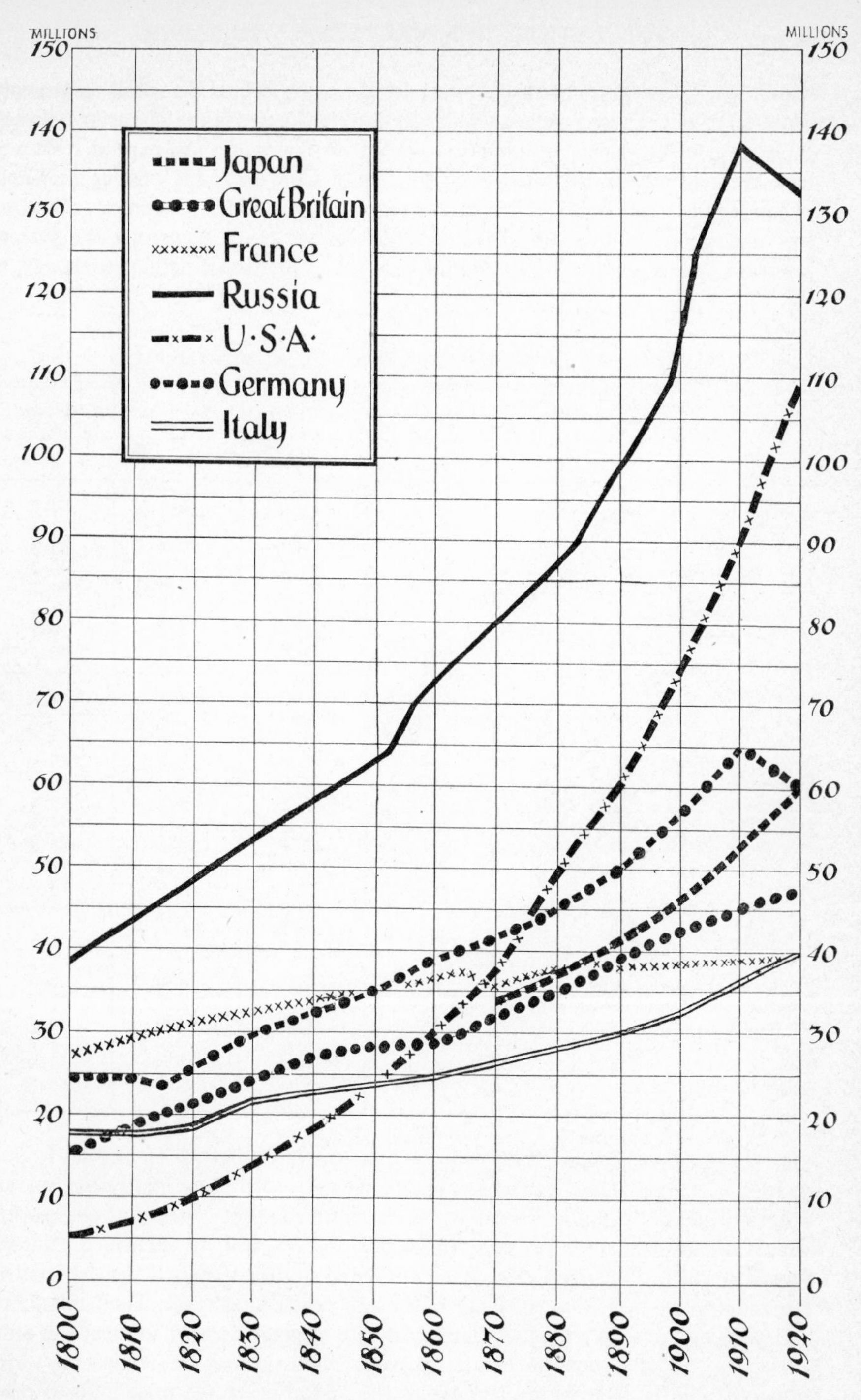


DIAGRAM SHOWING GROWTH OF POPULATION IN VARIOUS COUNTRIES DURING THE NINETEENTH CENTURY (PREPARED BY S. NASU)

have added to their new platforms many elements of social policy in order to regain popularity. Some of them are even trying to court the favor of the radical elements among university students.

But returning to the principal argument, What proof have we that a surplus population now exists in Japan? I think that this evidence lies in the fact that while the agricultural area has ceased to expand and industry and commerce are already coming to a standstill, the growing trend of population still continues unchecked. Or, stating it in another way, the proof lies in the loss of balance between the rate of increase of national production and that of population, which fact is giving rise to the problem of unemployment everywhere. The situation is particularly acute in the farming districts because the outlet to the cities is now very narrow. I have already stated that the area of agricultural land has begun to decrease, and that its capacity to support the population appears to have reached the limit. It may be that with improved farming methods and the use of better machinery the time may come when even the present agricultural population will be found to be more than necessary. Now as to commerce and industry, their phenomenal development since the beginning of the Meiji era cannot be attributed to the abundance of natural resources in Japan, but rather to protective policies of the government and the cheaper cost of production. And this cheaper cost of production was not due to advanced technique of high efficiency, but to low wages and the laborers' low standard of living. Protective policy, moreover, frequently boosted prices,[4] thus lowering still further the standard of living of the people who were existing on a meager income. The expansion of Japan's commerce and industry was made possible, not because the nation possessed great natural resources or high productive efficiency, but rather because of a premise that much of her population, especially the laboring class, was content to eke out a bare existence. Therefore when this premise disappears it will naturally follow that the expanding tendency of commerce and industry will be checked. Now expansion of commerce and industry will necessarily increase the nation's wealth, and this increased wealth in turn will necessarily raise the standard of living of a certain circle which gradually will spread; therefore it follows that the foregoing premise gives rise to a condition which will be its own undoing. This difficulty can be avoided only by those nations which are rich in natural resources, have vast colonial possessions to be exploited, or are always in the vanguard of technical advancement. But Japan is not one of these favored nations. The World War had brought more extensive rights for the laboring class, higher wages,[5] and an elevation of the general standard of living; therefore when the abnormal prosperity of war time passed, the commerce and industry of the country was confronted with a grave crisis. Japan was still struggling in the throes of this acute situation when the earthquake wiped out 7,000,000,000 yen of the nation's wealth at one stroke.

The menace of unemployment has spread gradually from the agricultural and laboring class to the white-collared class. It is a significant fact that as the educated class began to feel the pinch of this problem, the social movement also began to gain

[4] High-priced sugar is an example. Tobacco manufactured under government monopoly is another.

[5] Now Japanese workers get nearly the same wages as European workers.

more sympathy and support from these intelligentsia. The standard of living is today still becoming higher; and this, I am afraid, may be due to the fact that Japan is consuming the portion which should serve as the capital for further production. If that is true, the present state of affairs cannot long continue without some radical change. What might be done is to prevent further rise in the standard of living, or perhaps even to lower it, or, that being unfeasible, to check the growth of population. But when all these methods are inadvisable or insufficient, then the solution will necessarily have to be sought through the channel of emigration of the surplus population. In view of the fact that as a civilized people the material condition of the majority of the Japanese still leaves much to be desired, it would be unreasonable to demand the acceptance of a lower standard, and the appeals for economy so frequently heard from statesmen and moralists can have application only to the wealthy class. If it should happen to influence the masses, it would only be to the extent of slightly slowing up the rise in the standard of living. Therefore the final solution of the problem must lie in one of the following three situations: (1) A change in the system or technique of production, (2) decrease in the rate of increase of population, and (3) emigration. But all these three are accompanied with many difficulties.

In thus stating at length the acute predicament in which we find ourselves today, I do not propose to indulge in idle pessimism. We must see facts as they are, however painful it may prove. Even just to grope about for a solution to the difficulty is far better, in my opinion, than to idle away the time in dancing above the volcano. Japan is now being tested; and our courage should mount higher as the difficulties increase. Bearing in mind the lesson of our proverb to the effect that though man may fail seven times he will succeed the eighth, let us apply the indomitable courage that was stirred up by the earthquake to the solution of this vital question of national life and death. For the nation which remains inactive and supine in such a situation, death is the only fate. Neither the present world-situation nor Japan's position in the Orient will permit her decline. We believe that the Japanese not only have the same right to existence as other nationals, but are destined to make a great contribution to world-civilization.

## VIII

I have set forth the relation between the population problem and economic development of Japan, and have explained how the surplus population is becoming an imminent menace. I shall now examine the bearing all this has upon the problem of food supply. If, in this age of extensive international trade, it is not necessary for a nation to depend solely on its own agriculture for food, then the food question becomes a problem of employment and not of agriculture. There are actually many who advocate the policy of solving the population problem by developing commerce and industry even at the sacrifice of agricultural interests. But we must not overlook the importance of native food production, whether from the standpoint of national defense or in the light of the trend of the world's economic progress. Even in times of peace, maintenance of agriculture is of utmost importance because, as the agricultural nations become industrialized, their population increases, and at the same time their ability to export food and raw materials declines; moreover, as such industrialized nations curtail their importation of industrial products, to that extent is the ability of the hitherto exporting nation to purchase agricultural products abroad lessened. It is for this reason that Great Britain has been taking such urgent steps to encourage her agriculture in recent years; she further has in mind the alleviation of the unemployment situation that has been created by overindustrialization, and the desire to place the national economy upon a more solid foundation.

Now, the amount of food necessary in Japan can be determined by the size of population and the consumption per individual. Growth of population, on the other hand, can be determined by the combined capacity to produce and to purchase food, while the amount of consumption is related to the degree of prosperity. And it is because all these factors are simultaneously subject to change that nobody can exactly foretell the future need of food supply; all we can do is to make conjectures.

Some scholars maintain that peoples, like natural organisms, have a limit as to the growth possible within the territory which they occupy, and when that limit is passed the rate of growth begins to decline and finally ceases altogether. In Japan there are some authorities, like Dr. Inagaki, who support this view upon the basis of statistical study. Dr. Inagaki has devised a formula for making the curve of increase in population, according to which Japan's maximum capacity is 104,000,000, and the 100,000,000 mark will be reached 276 years hence. His formula and the results of his computation are as follows:

DR. INAGAKI'S FORMULA FOR GUESSING FUTURE POPULATION

$y$ . . . . population at a certain date in the future.
$y_0$ . . . . population at a certain fixed date in the past.
$x$ . . . . years between $y$ and $y_0$.
$r$ . . . . ratio of annual increase of population.

Now, Malthus' formula was as follows,

$$y=y_0(1+r)^x \quad \ldots \ldots \quad (1)$$

but Dr. Inagaki believes this $r$ not to be a fixed number, but a function of population, that is, a number which will change according to the growth of population. Therefore $y^c$ being the population which changes,

$$r=ay^c \quad \ldots \ldots \quad (2)$$
$$a=A-By^c \quad \ldots \ldots \quad (3)$$

From (1), (2), and (3),

$$y=y_0(1+Ay^c-By^{2c})^x \quad \ldots \ldots \quad \text{Inagaki's formula}$$

$A$ and $B$ must be calculated from the census figures.

$$A=\frac{\Sigma ry^{2c}\Sigma y^{3c}-\Sigma ry^c\Sigma y^{c4}}{(\Sigma y^{3c})^2-\Sigma y^{2c}\Sigma y^{4c}}$$

$$B=\frac{\Sigma ry^{2c}\Sigma y^{2c}-\Sigma ry^c\Sigma y^{3c}}{(\Sigma y^{3c})^2-\Sigma y^{2c}\Sigma y^{4c}}$$

$^c$ must be also calculated in the method of approaching gradually, and these $A$, $B$, $c$ differ according to the nation.

In case of Japan, Dr. Inagaki arrived at the following results after elaborate calculations:

$$C=1$$
$$A=0.0000474155$$
$$B=0.00000000045556$$

If we take 1925 as the basic year, $y_0=59,920,000$

$$y=5992(1+0.0000474155y-0.00000000045556y^2)^x$$

But the theory that the life and death of a people is subject to the same regularity as an animate organism has not yet emerged from the stage of a mere hypothesis; in truth, the number of people that can be supported in a given area is largely determined by its socio-economic organization, state of its productive technique, and

TABLE VIII

| Year | Population | Ratio of Average Annual Increase between That Year and 1925 (Percentage) |
|---|---|---|
| 1928 | 62,000,000 | 11.89 |
| 1932 | 65,000,000 | 11.57 |
| 1939 | 70,000,000 | 10.87 |
| 1948 | 75,000,000 | 9.94 |
| 1958 | 80,000,000 | 8.78 |
| 1973 | 85,000,000 | 7.39 |
| 1996 | 90,000,000 | 5.77 |
| 2043 | 95,000,000 | 3.93 |
| 2201 | 100,000,000 | 1.86 |
| ........ | 104,080,000 | 0.0 |

the conditions governing its international trade. That is the reason why the population of Japan at one time remained stationary for three centuries, and at another time doubled itself within half a century. Dr. Inagaki's formula cannot explain these situations. We may even assume the norm to be theoretically applicable to the increase of population under certain conditions, but when these conditions change, the norm alone will not tell you exactly the actual fluctuation of population; the latter will be more dependent upon the extent to which that norm is applicable under a given socio-economic situation. When advancement in arts and science causes a sudden increase in the economic efficiency of a nation, the maximum limit of its capacity to support its population will be greatly raised; and no one can determine the maximum point above which it may not climb. Such being the case, Dr. Inagaki's theory amounts to nothing more than a statement of a tendency for the growth of population to be checked when the increase of population of a given country has exceeded a certain point. Therefore our belief is that, if the expansion of industry stops, the growth of population will likely stop short of even 100,000,000, when a sudden development in the machinery of production may cause the population to exceed 150,000,000, or even

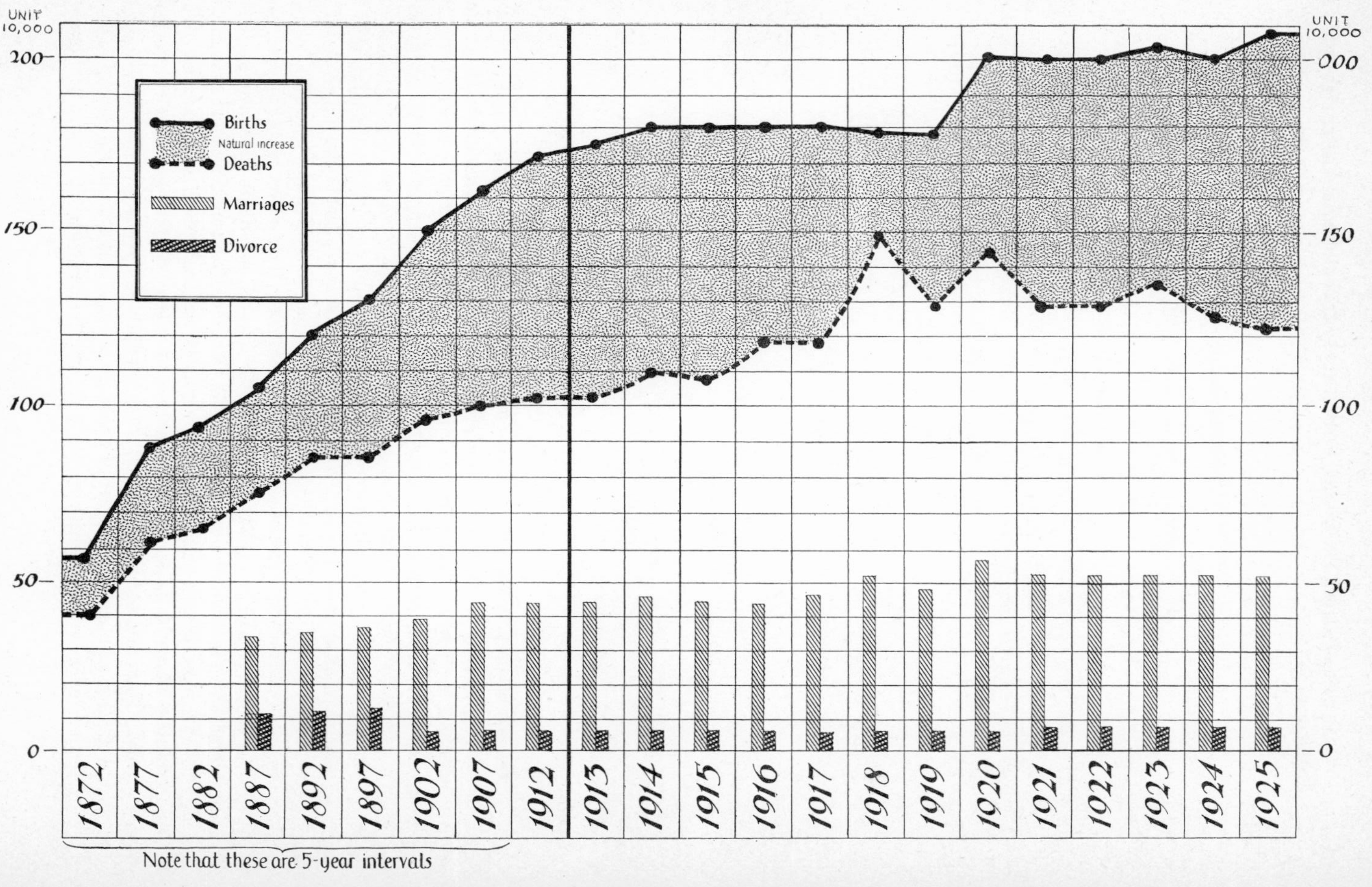


DIAGRAM SHOWING GROWTH OF POPULATION IN JAPAN, 1872–1925

200,000,000. By basing the computation upon the increase of population from 1909 to 1913, we obtain 14.17 per cent as the rate of future increase. Assuming this rate to continue unchanged, we obtain the following table of population:

POPULATION OF JAPAN (CALCULATED)

| Year | Population |
|---|---|
| 1917 | 56,032,000 |
| 1927 | 64,501,000 |
| 1937 | 74,246,000 |
| 1947 | 85,464,000 |
| 1957 | 98,376,000 |
| 1967 | 113,239,000 |
| 2017 | 228,839,000 |

$$\text{Ratio of increase} = \sqrt[5]{\frac{\text{Population of 1913}}{\text{Population of 1908}}} - 1 = 14.17 \text{ per cent}$$

This calculation is based upon the assumption that population increases indefinitely at an unchanging rate; but it need hardly be stated that this assumption is even more doubtful than Dr. Inagaki's formula. As a matter of fact the growth of Japanese population since the date of the foregoing computation is different from the figures given in the table. I am inclined to believe that the future fluctuations of our population will be more in accordance with Dr. Inagaki's deductions, though I can hardly agree with his maximum figure, or the time.

## IX

So much for conjectures as to the future changes in population. Taking up the question of food consumption, we think that the increase in the nation's wealth will raise its standard of living, which in turn will effect a change in the food consumption of the individual. But since man's capacity for food has a definite physiological limit, the amount of food per individual cannot exceed that limit. In the term "food" should be included, not only the food actually consumed, but also any that may be wasted; the proportion of waste varies greatly with the wealth of the individual. According to Volume XLII of *Ryoshoku-Kenkiu* (*Food Research*), edited by Dr. Inagaki, the Americans are supposed to waste 25 per cent of their food as uneaten remnant of their meals, and the Japanese about 7.5 per cent. Another important fact is that, as civilization tends to change, the kinds of food consumed will change. For example, a starch-containing food of given calories may come to be replaced by a protein food of the same caloric value. In the case of cereals, wheat has to a great extent taken the place of rye in the Occident; so in Japan rice has gradually replaced barley. From this it naturally follows that the consumption per individual of any single article of food will vary with the rise in the standard of living. The actual situation in Japan in regard to rice is as follows:

| Time | Annual Consumption per Individual (in Koku) |
|---|---|
| 50 years ago | 0.7 (3.5 bu.) |
| 20 years ago | 1.0 (5.0 bu.) |
| Today | 1.14 (5.7 bu.) |

Barley, on the contrary, has shown a steady decline in the consumption per individual. Now if we study the changes in the consumption of various agricultural products per individual and apply it to the estimated future population, we can roughly estimate the amount of each food that will be needed. But it is also possible to ignore the matter of future population and estimate the future demand upon the premise that the past fluctuations in demand for food will continue in the future somewhat as before. Dr. Ando, of the Governmental Agricultural Experiment Station

TABLE IX

FUTURE DEMAND FOR STAPLES

| Year | Rice (Koku) | Wheat | Barley (Naked) | Barley |
|---|---|---|---|---|
| 1927 | 6,908,000 | 1,017,000 | 659,000 | 807,000 |
| 1937 | 7,890,000 | 1,409,000 | 538,000 | 645,000 |
| 1947 | 9,011,000 | 1,737,000 | 429,000 | 518,000 |
| 1952 | 9,629,000 | 1,877,000 | 384,000 | 463,000 |
| 1957 | 10,292,000 | 1,994,000 | 341,000 | 409,000 |

in Tokio, used the latter method in computing the future demand for the staple cereals shown in Table IX.

As compared with Table IX, the following tables estimate the future demand for rice on the assumption that the rate of consumption per individual will remain unchanged:

A. FUTURE POPULATION COMPUTED AT THE FIXED RATIO OF 14.17

| Year | Amount (koku) |
|---|---|
| 1937 | 8,460,000 |
| 1948 | 9,740,000 |
| 1957 | 11,220,000 |

B. FUTURE POPULATION COMPUTED BY DR. INAGAKI'S THEORY

| Year | Amount (koku) |
|---|---|
| 1939 | 7,980,000 |
| 1948 | 8,550,000 |
| 1958 | 9,120,000 |

According to the two foregoing tables the future demand for rice as shown in Table IX is less than that shown in Table A, but more than that shown in Table B. That is to say that barring a great change in the rate of increase of population or in the consumption of rice, Dr. Ando's estimate can be taken as showing the probable future demand for cereals. Or, proceeding upon the assumption of Dr. Inagaki's theory that the rate of increase of population will decrease, the demand for cereals for the next twenty years will not vary greatly from the figure obtained by Dr. Ando's assumption.

In the tables just given all but the important foods of Japan have been omitted. Of course meat is also a necessary food, but its use in Japan, as shown in Table X, is so limited as to be in no way comparable with vegetable foods. Moreover, since the greater part of animal food is fish—and it is not as yet a difficult matter to increase the supply of fish in Japan—I have omitted its study. The reader will doubtless be able to see that the problem of food supply in Japan is primarily a problem of cereals.

TABLE X

RATIO OF MEAT AND VEGETABLE FOODS TO THE AGGREGATE OF FOOD CONSUMED, PER INDIVIDUAL

| | AMERICA | | JAPAN | |
|---|---|---|---|---|
| | Dry Weight (Percentage) | Calory (Percentage) | Dry Weight (Percentage) | Calory (Percentage) |
| *Animal foods:* | | | | |
| Milk | 13.3 | 14.5 | 0.086 | 0.098 |
| Eggs | 1.0 | 1.5 | 0.157 | 0.240 |
| Meat, etc. | 7.4 | 10.8 | 0.305 | 0.470 |
| Fish | 0.3 | 0.4 | 1.618 | 2.029 |
| Total | 22.0 | 27.2 | 2.166 | 2.827 |
| *Vegetable foods:* | | | | |
| Bread | 39.8 | 38.6 | (Rice) 52.36 | 53.24 |
| Vegetables | 10.1 | 7.3 | 14.64 | 11.07 |
| Fruits | 3.8 | 2.8 | 0.87 | 0.69 |
| Sugar | 14.4 | 14.1 | 2.40 | 3.32 |
| Miscellaneous | 9.9 | 10.0 | 27.57 | 28.85 |
| Total | 78.0 | 72.8 | 97.83 | 97.16 |

TABLE XI

| | American (Grams) | Japanese (Grams) |
|---|---|---|
| Milk | 127.4 | 0.54 |
| Eggs | 9.7 | 1.00 |
| Meat, etc. | 70.4 | 1.94 |
| Fish | 3.2 | 10.28 |
| Total | 210.7 | 13.76 |
| Bread | 380.0 | (Rice) 332.66 |
| Vegetables | 96.5 | 93.05 |
| Fruits | 35.9 | 5.55 |
| Sugar | 137.5 | 15.22 |
| Miscellaneous | 94.9 | 177.55 |
| Total | 744.9 | 635.39 |

According to Table X, Americans derive 73 per cent of their calories from vegetable foods, and the Japanese, 97. Of the latter amount, according to Dr. Ando, the Japanese derive about 50 per cent from rice and 15 per cent from wheat, from which fact it can be seen how important a rôle those two cereals have in the food situation in Japan. Dr. Inagaki's computation of the dry weight of the daily consumption of food by Japanese and Americans is given in Table XI.

Table XI shows that the amount of food consumed by the Japanese is only 66.5 per cent of that consumed by Americans; but upon the basis of bodily weights of the two peoples the ratio ought to be about 81 per cent (weight of American, 64 kilograms; of Japanese, 52 kilograms), while the ratio would be 87 per cent if the comparison is based upon the area of body surface. In Table XII Dr. Inagaki has made allowances of 25 per cent and 7.5 per cent for the food wasted by Americans and Japanese respectively, and computed the food calories actually consumed by the two peoples, and showed the Japanese as consuming 82 per cent of the amount consumed by Americans—both by weight and calory.

Thus we are able to see the importance of rice and wheat, especially the former, to Japan, and also that the demand for them will increase greatly in the future. How to meet this future demand is the grave problem confronting Japanese statesmen and

TABLE XII

TABLE OF ACTUAL DAILY CONSUMPTION OF FOOD

| | Americans | | Japanese | |
|---|---|---|---|---|
| | Dry Weight (Grams) | Calory | Dry Weight (Grams) | Calory |
| *Animal foods:* | | | | |
| Milk | 95.6 | 436.1 | 0.5 | 2.3 |
| Eggs | 7.3 | 44.2 | 0.9 | 5.6 |
| Meat, etc. | 52.8 | 325.3 | 1.8 | 11.1 |
| Fish | 2.4 | 12.0 | 9.5 | 47.7 |
| Total | 158.1 | 817.6 | 12.7 | 66.7 |
| *Vegetable foods:* | | | | |
| Bread | 285.0 | 1026.6 | (Rice) 307.7 | 1251.4 |
| Vegetables | 72.4 | 218.8 | 86.1 | 260.1 |
| Fruits | 26.9 | 84.7 | 5.1 | 16.2 |
| Sugar | 103.1 | 422.8 | 16.3 | 78.1 |
| Miscellaneous | 71.2 | 300.5 | 162.0 | 678.0 |
| Total | 558.6 | 2053.4 | 577.2 | 2283.8 |
| Grand total | 716.7 | 2871.0 | 589.9 | 2350.5 |

agricultural experts. The rate of annual increase in rice production for the last 35 years was 13.4 per cent, as compared with 12.3 per cent rate of increase for population. So although the rate of increase in rice production slightly exceeded the rate of increase of population, consumption of rice per individual increased by 18.7 per cent, so that in the twentieth century Japan was forced into the position of a rice-importing nation. Even though the consumption per individual does not increase hereafter, the demand for rice is bound to increase as population increases. At the present time Japan, in order to make up for the shortage of native rice, imports some 5,000,000 koku from Korea, 2,000,000 koku from Formosa, and between 2,000,000 and 5,000,000 koku from foreign countries. Consumption of rice will increase at least by 10,000,000 koku in 10 years, 20,000,000 koku in 20 years, and 30,000,000 koku in 30 years; and how to meet this increasing demand is the question.

## X

Many projects have recently been undertaken with the aim of solving this problem. The first plan is to invest 350,000,000 yen in Korea within the next 10 years to increase the irrigated area by 350,000 cho, thus adding 200,000 cho of paddy fields, and to effect various improvements in agriculture with the ultimate aim of increasing the yield by 8,200,000 koku, of which amount 5,000,000 koku would be available for shipment to Japan proper in addition to an equal amount which Korea ships to Japan today. The second plan is to increase the rice-growing area of Formosa by 130,000 cho between now and 1948, so as to add 3,000,000 koku to the 2,000,000 koku which is being imported from there today. The third plan calls for expanding the rice-growing area in Japan proper and increasing the yield per unit of area. Some authorities are of the opinion that, by utilizing the land in Japan proper to the maximum limit, about 1,200,000 cho can be added to the present rice-growing area, and that the yield per unit of area can be increased 25 per cent by improving the methods of cultivation and by the selection of better seed rice. If such a growth can be effected the increased yield would amount to 28,000,000 koku. This, added to 8,000,000 koku's increasing shipment from Korea and Formosa, will make the total increase of 36,000,000 koku. So at least for the next 30 years Japan will be relieved of its rice problem, even to the extent of eliminating the present importation from foreign countries. And in the case of wheat, Dr. Ando states that if lands now devoted to barley and naked barley be utilized for wheat growing and the yield per unit of area be increased, the total annual yield of wheat would reach 20,000,000 koku within 30 years, and thus easily meet the national demand.

The statements and figures set forth up to this point would seem to indicate that so far as cereals are concerned Japan will be self-supporting, at least for the time being. But the problem is far from being so simple. In the first place it is doubtful if the project in Korea can produce the anticipated surplus of rice. The present annual consumption of rice per individual in Korea is 0.7 koku, but we may expect this figure to rise with the standard of living—say, to 0.8 koku within 10 years—and assuming the increase in Korean population in the next 10 years to be 2,500,000, the increased consumption in Korea 10 years hence will be 4,000,000 koku annually, thus leaving only 4,200,000 koku to be shipped to Japan. If the increase in population and consumption continues at the same rate for the following ten-year period, Korea will probably have no surplus to send to Japan proper unless the same kind of undertaking be continued upon a larger scale. The plans regarding Formosa may be consummated, but the success of the plans for the expansion of rice-growing area and increasing yield per unit area in Japan proper is at best problematical; I, at least, have serious misgivings.

A further point to be considered is whether, granting the realization of the plans to be feasible, it would be a paying proposition. Man cannot subsist on cereals alone, and to procure many other necessary things capital and labor must be wisely expended. If undue expenditure is made to increase the production of cereals so that the cost far exceeds the cost of that in other countries, the people of such a country would incur great expense in maintaining a bare existence. Nominal increase in wages not only does not add to the happiness of the laborers' lot, but tends to curtail the exporting power. And as the price of industrial products rises, the purchasing power of the agricultural products will drop, thus working greatly to the detriment of the farmer. Such a nation will become economically isolated to a degree because neither agriculture nor industry will be able to exist without a protective tariff. But if a nation poorly endowed with worldly goods and with a population far exceeding the opportunities for employment becomes thus isolated, a lower standard of living and untold miseries will follow as an inevitable consequence.

Might not Japan be led into such an unfortunate predicament by her extreme self-supporting policy as regards food supply? As a matter of fact the present production cost of rice is around 37 yen per koku, or from 50 per cent to 100 per cent higher than the cost of production in China or America,[6] and I have grave doubt as to the ultimate success of a plan for increasing the production of rice without giving due consideration to the cost of production. Here, it would seem, is an urgent need for finding some means of lowering the cost of rice production and at the same time preserving the happiness of the farming class.

To raise the price of food unduly is to invite the decline of commerce and industry, with the added danger of creating unemployment in those fields. Japan's agriculture today can give employment to only 50 per cent of its population. We must not forget that Japan's population problem is mainly a problem of employment. And at the same time it would be dangerous for Japan to import so much food as to suppress her own agriculture, thus increasing unemployment among her agricultural class. The efficiency of Japanese labor still being low as compared with western countries, the problems of commerce and industry became increasingly acute as wages increased,[7] so that it is now with great difficulty that they (industry and commerce) can properly absorb even one-half of the annual increase in population. A decline in the price of food may cause a drop in the cost of production, but the resulting slight expansion in commerce and industry will not be sufficient to absorb the several millions of unemployed from the agricultural class. In short, Japan cannot lean for support upon agriculture exclusively, nor upon commerce or industry alone; on the other hand, however, she finds no little difficulty in developing these three fields simultaneously. This is probably due to the fact that population and the standard of living have exceeded the territory and present productive power of the country. Here we are beginning to feel the effects of the surplus population discussed previously in this paper.

## XI

In such a situation how can we give employment to the greatest number and foster in them a hope for a higher standard of living? To my mind the way lies in developing to the maximum extent the productive power of the land and people, and to such portion of the population as still remains a surplus element, notwithstanding declining birth-rate, open up the way to emigration. To give employment to the greatest possible number it will be necessary to continue the intensive agricultural methods; but an undue investment of capital in agriculture should be guarded against. It is important to bear in mind at this point that the degree of self-sufficiency can be raised without causing an excessive rise in food prices by varying the kinds of food consumed; for example, by increasing the consumption of potato and fish in such a manner that the standard of living is not lowered. Assuming the yield of potato per "cho"

[6] The cost of production of 1 koku (5 bushels) of rice is roughly estimated to be around 25 yen in California, and 15 yen in China.

[7] The average annual income of workers in 663 factories was 1,738 yen for the year 1925, and that of miners in 85 mines 1,779 yen.

to be 2,500 kwan, or approximately 60 koku, it would be possible to produce 30,-000,000 koku from 500,000 cho. Moreover, the Japanese derive only 11 per cent of their protein food from animal foods, while Americans and Europeans get 45 per cent of their protein from that source; so it would seem that the Japanese could increase the percentage of their animal protein, notwithstanding the differences in climate and physique which make a vegetable diet more suitable. Stock-raising, however, does not give much promise of development because it requires so much land. But there is yet much room for increase in the use of fish as food.

Indeed, the consumption of fish as food is increasing very rapidly as Table XIII shows.

TABLE XIII

| Year | Amount of Fish Used as Food (Million Kwan)* | Annual Consumption per Individual (Kwan) |
|---|---|---|
| 1916 | 198 | 3.56 |
| 1917 | 192 | 3.42 |
| 1918 | 130 | 2.29 |
| 1919 | 128 | 2.24 |
| 1920 | 211 | 3.64 |
| 1921 | 208 | 3.55 |
| 1922 | 259 | 4.35 |
| 1923 | 274 | 4.54 |
| 1924 | 329 | 5.39 |
| 1925 | 394 | 6.40 |

* 1 kwan = 8.28 lb.

Japan may be able to support 100,000,000 as far as food alone is concerned if the use of rice, potatoes, and fish are properly combined. Greater use of aquatic products is desirable as a means toward sustaining more population.

In order to increase the productive capacity of a nation it is necessary to exercise a rather thorough social regulation of the use of land. Any artificial obstacle to the development of land—whether it be for agriculture, forests, mines, or hydro-electric plants—must be eliminated. Socialization of land is desirable for many reasons. For instance, an unduly high rental of agricultural land will raise the price of agricultural products and consequently hamper the growth of commerce and industry. Such being the case, it becomes desirable from the standpoint of national economy to force down the rental to some degree; such a step would benefit the agricultural entrepreneur by increasing his profits and hastening the increase of land utilization.

National productive efficiency can be increased through technical and industrial education and proper socio-economic organization. Here is a world which has on one hand many idle rich, on the other hand an industrious class which must struggle even for the very chance to work; a world in which speculation brings far greater returns than honest labor. Any society so constituted cannot possibly foster the proper attitude toward labor. No wonder that our productive efficiency is very often curtailed by labor disputes, idleness, indifference, and frequent unemployment. We must direct present society toward the point of maximum productiveness which is compatible with social justice and stability. At the same time we must eliminate the condition of semi-idleness that now prevails in government offices and private firms as a result of employing more men than are actually needed. This change can be accomplished only by promoting technical education and by enabling the people to engage in truly productive labor which shall give due compensation in wages and social recognition. Another important prerequisite is the equitable international distribution of the raw materials and fuels which are scarce in Japan.

Such portion of the population as cannot be supported without lowering the present standard of living, notwithstanding the utmost efforts to improve methods of production and to eliminate the various defects in the existing economic system, shall be placed in the category of surplus population with the view of promoting their emigration. But the number of Japanese who have emigrated during a period of over half a century is very small; being as follows: Asia, 264,000; Europe, 3,000; North America, 157,000; South America, 64,000; Oceania, 137,000—to the total of 625,000. Besides these about 400,000, 180,000, and 200,000 have migrated to Korea, Formosa, and Saghalien respectively. The emigration of a mere 10,000 or 20,000 per year can hardly be seriously considered as providing the solution to our population problem; and even if the rate of emigration was allowed to increase hereafter, it probably could not find an outlet for even 10 per cent of the annual increase of nearly a million.

Such being the case, even with the combined measures of improving technique of production and economic system and of promoting emigration, it will be extremely difficult properly to dispose of the annual increase of population and to maintain the present standard of living. It appears to me that the increase in population will necessarily be checked. Japan is now a nation of excessive births and excessive deaths. A curtailment of both rates with a possible drop in the increase of population is a condition which should not cause alarm. In this modern age a nation should stress creative power instead of mere size of population; quality rather than quantity. But that is not to say that we would welcome the contraction of the size of population without good reason or in a way which would be interpreted as an evidence of national debility. To have an opportunity of growing is vital to a nation as well as to an individual.

Japan today is making a desperate effort to solve this problem. The increase in population is adding impetus to the democratization of Japanese society and the socialization of her economics. It is, furthermore, forcing the reorganization of the capitalistic economic system and the abandonment of the imperialistic policy. These two things which made possible the growth of Japanese population are now being forced out of existence, as it were, by the child of their own creation. We see revealed in the difficult situation of modern Japan both an image of the world's pains and the way of human progress. Those who would interpret the increase of Japanese population as an evidence of an aggressive policy do so only to reveal their ignorance of the conditions in modern Japan. What modern Japan is asking for is a peaceful existence and development procured through a more just socio-economic system and a more just international relation. Japan's progress toward the goal will be blocked by extreme selfishness, unwarranted international suspicion, conceited nationalism, and unscrupulous monopolization of huge wealth and resources. Our earnest desire is that the Japanese, in their efforts to solve the problems confronting them today, should not only display such an attitude as to command the respect of other nations, but should work in unison with other peoples to contribute to the progress of the world.

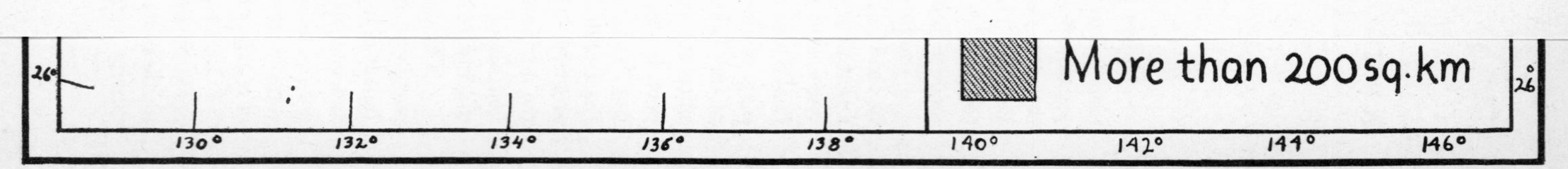


MAP OF JAPAN SHOWING DENSITY OF POPULATION IN 1925 BY PREFECTURES (PREPARED BY PROFESSOR N. YAMASAKI)

SECTION 16

# A NOTE ON THE GEOGRAPHICAL DISTRIBUTION OF THE DENSITY OF POPULATION, BIRTH- AND DEATH-RATES OF JAPAN

NAOMASA YAMASAKI
Professor of Geography, Imperial University of Tokyo

## DENSITY

*Japan proper.*—In spite of being very mountainous and with undeveloped flat plains, Japan is much favored by a temperate climate and abundant precipitations, so Japan proper is densely populated, 157 per square kilometer, and it ranks as one of the most dense countries in the world, coming next to Belgium, Holland, and Great Britain. The geographical distribution of the density is very much diversified in the topographic divisions of the country, according to their physical nature as well as the mode of propagation of civilization since ancient times.

In Honshu, or the main island, there are two large centers of great density, namely, the Kinki district in the west and the Kwanto district in the east. The former was a seat of imperial residences, such as Nara, Kyoto, etc., for more than two thousand years, and also of the commercial cities and ports, Sakai in the Middle Ages and Osaka and Kobe in recent times. On the other hand the Kwanto district is a delta plain of the largest area in Japan. It has Tokyo in its center, which was the capital of the Tokugawa shogunate for three centuries and is the metropolis of the empire since the era of Meiji Restoration in 1868. Yokohama, the greatest foreign trade port, is situated also on the coast of this district. Between these, along an old highway, Tokai or the East Sea district forms a most populous belt. These well-developed coast plains with their sunny oceanic climate have made agricultural and industrial progress. They are also famous for their tea. Another center of dense population is in the northern part of Kyushu. Not only is it well known for its fertile plains with flourishing agriculture, but also there has enjoyed a remarkable development of manufacturing industry in recent years, because here are the richest coal fields of Japan.

The districts along the calm water of the Inland Sea, or Setouchi, have been well populated since the dawn of the history of the empire. The ancestors of the present Japanese migrated from their home in Kyushu along the coast of this sea by water and land until they settled in the Kinki district. All these districts here mentioned are populated with a density more than the mean density of Japan proper, or, in round numbers, over 150 per square kilometer, and the most of them have more than, or nearly, 200, a number rarely met with in the rest of the world.

Less populated is the northeastern district of the country. No prefectures to the north of 37° N. exceed the mean density. The density decreases distinctly in the northernmost districts, where it becomes one-half and even one-third of the mean density. This is due chiefly to the fact that the northern winters are more severe and

it is far distant from the intellectual and economic centers of the country. Famine, or at least shortage of crops, in Japan is especially noticeable in these districts owing to the frequent occurrence of abnormal climate. The mountain districts of Central Japan, some prefectures along the Sea of Japan in West Japan, and two more on the Pacific coast in the islands of Shikoku and Kyushu are also under the mean density.

*Hokkaido.*—The Hokkaido was the home of the Ainu until half a century ago, when Japanese immigrants began to arrive. Industrial development in various directions, especially in agriculture and fisheries, attracted many people to this island, and now there are about two and a half millions, among whom the natives number only 0.6 per cent. That number is gradually decreasing, from 18.347 in 1914 to 15.461 in 1924, notwithstanding the fact that the Ainu are especially protected by reservation

TOWNS

| Population | Number of Towns |
|---|---|
| Under 500 | 82 |
| 501– 1,000 | 266 |
| 1,001– 2,000 | 2,279 |
| 2,001– 5,000 | 7,050 |
| 5,001– 10,000 | 1,733 |
| 10,001– 20,000 | 392 |
| 20,001– 25,000 }<br>25,001– 30,000 } | 78 |
| 30,001– 40,000 | 36 |
| 40,001– 50,000 | 31 |
| 50,001–100,000 | 51 |
| Above 100,000 | 21 |
| | 12,019 |

laws. The density is 28 for all of Hokkaido. When we exclude Chishima, or the Kuriles, most of which are exceedingly sparsely inhabited islands, the density of the main island is 32. This figure is quite small when compared with that of other parts of the country. The prefectural authorities are endeavoring to promote inner colonization, and the number of immigrants annually has varied between 56,315 and 91,465 during the past eleven years ending in 1924, or the actual increase varies between 12,469 and 70,010.

*Karafuto.*—Karafuto or the southern half of the island Saghalin is the least populated region of Japan, owing to very severe winters and recent occupation. It measures only 4.2 of density. Before it was ceded to Japan in 1905 there were scarcely 2,000 natives and some Russians. The latter left the island gradually and were replaced by Japanese farmers, fishermen, and others who numbered a total of 150,650 in 1924.

*Formosa.*—This is a well settled island with a density of 111. Most of the inhabitants are of Chinese origin (94 per cent of the total population) and live chiefly as farmers in the western fertile plain. The central mountains and eastern coast zone are the home of the aborigines of Malayan descent, the number being estimated at 100,594 with a density of 2.5. Japanese increased in number from 164,335 in 1910 to 183,722 in 1925, but constitute, however, only 4.6 per cent of the total population.

*Korea.*—The mean density of population in Korea is 82, nearly equal to that of northernmost Honshu. Well populated is the southern half or the peninsular part of

## SECTION 17

## A STATEMENT ON THE EFFECTS OF THE INDUSTRIAL DEVELOPMENT OF THE ORIENT ON EUROPEAN INDUSTRIES

W. J. HINTON, M.A.
Department of Political Economy, University of Hongkong

The subject allotted to the British members of the Conference is limited to the effects of the industrial development of the Orient on European industries, and does not include any account of the present extent of industrialization, which will be dealt with by our Japanese and Chinese colleagues. But it has been necessary to form some idea of the history of this process in order to approach the subject of the effects on the trade of Europe, and through that trade on European industry. Thus this statement falls into two parts: the first dealing in a general way with the history of the industrial development of the Orient regarded particularly from the point of view of its past effects on trade, and the second with such recent effects on European trade as are described in the material at our disposition. The reactions of these trading effects on industry are more difficult to trace.

For the first part there are valuable studies by Japanese and American authors, viz., *The Industry and Trade of Japan,* by S. Uyehara, M.Sc., published London, 1926; and *The Foreign Trade of China* by Professor C. F. Remer, Ph.D. The most comprehensive treatment of all the problems involved in the industrialization of the Orient, as far as we know, is in Dr. J. B. Condliffe's articles on "The Industrial Revolution in the Far East," in the *Economic Record* for November, 1926, and May, 1927. There is also a work of Professor Harold M. Vinacke, entitled, *Problems of Industrial Development in China,* published in 1926 by Princeton University Press, but this is too general in form and not sufficiently recent in material to be of great use for our present purpose.

For the second part of this statement, in addition to the foregoing works, a most useful document is a memorandum on cotton, presented to the International Economic Conference at Geneva this year. The corresponding memoranda on other industries were not available to us up to the moment of sailing from England, but as the effects of the industrialization of India, Japan, and China are felt above all in this industry, the omission is not fatal. The *Survey of Overseas Markets,* published in London last year by the Balfour Committee on Industry and Trade, together with the annual reports of the Department of Overseas Trade on which it is based, will be found useful, and for China the "Reports and Abstracts of Statistics," being Part I of the *Foreign Trade of China,* published by the Chinese Maritime Customs, together with the *Analysis of Imports and Exports,* are useful for purposes of reference and to bring the work of Remer up to date. It does not appear from the program that India is included in the scope of this inquiry, but some account should be taken of that subcontinent, as it forms part of the complex of international trade to which China and Japan also belong, and is much affected, especially as regards the cotton trade, by the competition of both Japan and China. We are not aware of any recent work on the industrialization of India parallel to those of Uyehara, Vinacke, and Remer, but some useful information may be obtained from the *Statement Exhibiting the Material and Moral Progress and Condition of India,* which also contains a list of sources for those who wish to go further into the matter. As it lies outside the Pacific, India is only introduced in this statement where necessary to understand the course of international trade.

We would like to forestall criticism of this statement in certain respects. As already indicated, it is incomplete in respect of India, and of strictly contemporary conditions in China and Japan. These defects can be remedied at or after the Conference, for the Chinese and Japanese delegates will deal with contemporary conditions in their countries, and material exists for an Indian study.

But there is a more fundamental criticism. The subject set for us has not been covered, and only a preliminary exploration has been undertaken. Our excuse must be the almost boundless magnitude of the task, apart from the shortness of the notice at which the statement was prepared. Assuming that, in spite of the political and economic disunion of Europe, that continent is a significant unit for this investigation, then the inquiry should follow through three phases.

1. A study of the history and present extent of the industrialization of the Orient.

2. A further study of the effects of that industrialization on the oriental-European trade. Here the difficulty will be to disentangle the effects of Industrialization from those due to other causes both in Europe and America.

3. A final study of the connection of the changes in trade, so disentangled, with changes in European industry, classified by industry and by country. Here also the difficulty will be to distinguish between effects traceable to the oriental developments and those due to other not necessarily dissimilar causes.

Thus stated, it is clear that the answer to the question put to us would require several researches of the first magnitude and great difficulty, which it might or might not prove worth while to undertake. Viewed in this light, our statement is no more than a somewhat fragmentary statement of the history of the effects of oriental industrialization on oriental foreign trade, some recent changes in the distribution of that trade by continents, some effects of the oriental industrialization on the cotton industry in Great Britain, where a causal connection is generally admitted to exist, and some considerations which emerge, but are not worthy to be called conclusions, in view of the explanatory and tentative character of our inquiry.

For those who have no time to read the whole of this statement, Part II and the section entitled "Considerations which Emerge" will probably suffice. It is on these considerations, in our opinion, that discussion can most usefully be concentrated.

The British Deputation has also been favored by a memorandum by J. S. M. Ward, M.A., F.S.S., etc., head of the Intelligence Department of the Federation of British Industries, founded on the latest annual reports of the Department of Overseas Trade on India, China, and Japan, respectively, and I take this opportunity of acknowledging my indebtedness both to that memorandum and to the officers of the Department of Overseas Trade, and to Professor L. D. Stamp, of the London School of Economics.

### I. THE INDUSTRIAL DEVELOPMENT OF THE ORIENT

As by "the Orient" we are to understand the Far East, excluding India, so by industrial development we are to understand certain phases which are conceived as more significant than the rest, on account of the history of similar developments in Europe and America. These developments in the Western lands are called the Industrial Revolution, and consisted, as we all know, of a change in the technique and organization of certain industries, especially transport, mining, metallurgy, and textiles. The change consisted in a continually increasing employment of inanimate sources of energy in those and later in other industries. Accompanying these technical changes were changes in the organization of those engaged in the industries, in the direction of an increased specialization of function and subdivision of labor. From these changes resulted wider social changes, a breaking down of the older productive groupings, and a period of individualism, followed, as it seems by a recrystallization of society into new forms of association. This process in its more general form we shall call industrialization, and the result, industrialism, or industrial capitalism. The process and the system alike vary from time to time and place to place, as feudalism varied in Medieval Europe, but the similarities are obvious and recognizable enough. It is the appearance of industrial capitalism in the Far East with which we are now concerned.

Before we proceed to description it may be useful to lay down a few general propositions which will serve as guides. The possibility and progress of industrialization depend on certain factors, two of which are essential prerequisites, and two determinants of the rate at which the process takes place. The prerequisites are a rationalistic, as distinct from a traditional, habit of mind in a considerable part of the population, and especially in its traditional leaders. An intellectual revolution must begin before the industrial revolution can commence. The second prerequisite is a centralized government in the area concerned, which can guarantee life and property and enforce a reasonably uniform code of law and a reasonably uniform and stable currency, permitting of the accumulation of capital. Granted these conditions, the rate at which the transformation will take place depends mainly upon the rate at which the transport system can be extended, and upon the development of a modern banking and financing system of sufficient elasticity to fit the growing system and aid its growth. Lest we should be accused of unnecessary refinement of analysis, it may be as well to point out that it is probably the presence of these factors in and about the treaty ports of China, and the absence of some or all of them elsewhere in China, which have determined the localization of most of the successful examples of industrialization in or near the treaty ports.

#### INDUSTRIAL DEVELOPMENT OF JAPAN

Japan is a much smaller country than China or India, and her social structure on its political side allows her to satisfy the prerequisites of industrialization more rapidly than either of the two subcontinents, China and India. She had a hereditary ruling class and a culture consciously derived from a foreign model, that of China. The few leaders who perceived the material superiority of the new Western model over the old Chinese model were able to effect a change in the government which gave them effective control while strengthening the national sentiment by the rehabilitation of the ancient national symbolic figure, the Mikado. With the necessary population ready to work for wages, it was only a question of time and capital to acquire and put into effect the new technique. And first attention was paid to transportation. The coasting trade was developed, beginning in 1870, and of course, as in China, the foreign shipowner played a great part. However, in 1885 the Nippon Yusen Kaisha

TABLE I

INCREASE OF TONNAGE OF SHIPS

| Years | Steamships | Sailing Ships | Total |
|---|---|---|---|
| 1873 | 26,000 | 8,000 | 34,000 |
| 1894 (Japanese-Chinese War) | 96,500 | 45,000 | 141,500 |
| 1904 (Japanese-Russian War) | 797,000 | 327,000 | 1,124,000 |
| 1913 | 1,528,000 | 828,000 | 2,356,000 |
| 1922 | 3,241,300 | 961,000 | 4,202,300 |

TABLE II

TONNAGE AND NATIONALITY OF SHIPS WITH CARGOES THAT ENTERED JAPAN (1,000 TONS)

| | 1893 | 1903 | 1913 | 1918 | 1921 |
|---|---|---|---|---|---|
| Japan | 318 | 5,131 | 12,530 | 14,361 | 19,305 |
| Great Britain | 1,258 | 4,127 | 7,228 | 1,348 | 4,900 |
| France | 59 | 213 | 412 | 59 | 329 |
| Netherlands | 10 | 172 | 180 | 719 | 515 |
| Russia | 58 | 355 | 723 | 521 | 30 |
| Germany | 268 | 1,268 | 1,679 | ........ | ........ |
| U.S.A. | 87 | 961 | 1,331 | 383 | 2,528 |
| Total (including others) | 2,214 | 13,419 | 24,659 | 17,772 | 27,931 |
| Japan's percentage | 14.4 | 38.2 | 50.8 | 80.8 | 69.1 |

managed its first ocean voyage (to Bombay, significantly enough). Japanese shipping received a great impulse after each of her wars, a fact not unconnected with the consistent and very expensive support and control of this industry by the Japenese government. During the great war Japanese ships appeared on all the oceans of the world, and an enormous expansion of tonnage took place. In spite of the acute shipping depression which followed the war, and especially the competition of British and United States ships on the Pacific routes, Japan remains the third-greatest shipping power, and could carry all her trade in her own bottoms and provide for all her military transportation in the event of war. Since the recovery of her full sovereign rights which resulted from the successful termination of the first stage of her transformation in 1894, she has been able to reserve her coasting trade to her own ships, an example which China will no doubt follow at the first opportunity. Tables I and II show the growth of the Japanese merchant marine.

The railway development was equally striking, and a marked contrast to the state of comparatively arrested development in this form of transport in China since the revolution. Table III shows the growth of the railways.

This expansion of the means of communication was accompanied and made possible by a corresponding expansion of the financial mechanism. The currency was unified soon after the Restoration, and after some preliminary troubles with inconvertible paper issued both by the government and the national banks, a strong central bank, the Bank of Japan was established in 1882, which after 1884 had a monopoly of issue and kept its notes at par. The victory over China brought an indemnity which was utilized to base the currency on a gold exchange standard, and the Yokohama Bank, founded at about this time, provided the facilities for a growing foreign trade. It would take us too far from our theme to trace this development in detail.

TABLE III

GROWTH OF THE RAILWAYS OF JAPAN (EXCLUDING FORMOSA AND KOREA)

| Year | Private (Miles) | State (Miles) | Total (Miles) |
|---|---|---|---|
| 1872 | 18 | ............ | 18 |
| 1877 | 64 | ............ | 64 |
| 1883 | 181 | 63 | 244 |
| 1887 | 324 | 317 | 641 |
| 1893 | 557 | 1,322 | 1,879 |
| 1897 | 661 | 2,288 | 2,949 |
| 1903 | 1,226 | 3,010 | 4,236 |
| *1907 | 4,453 | 445 | 4,896 |
| 1912 | 5,217 | 767 | 5,984 |
| 1917 | 5,999 | 1,834 | 7,833 |
| 1922 | 6,722 | 2,150 | 8,872 |

* The sharp increase in mileage of state railways in 1907 is due to nationalization of part of the existing private lines. In the table we have not included the Korean and Manchuria systems, though they are in reality part of the Japanese economic system. The Korean railways are about 1,200 miles, and the South Manchurian, 680 miles. There are also 480 miles of railway in Formosa.

The expansion of the means of transport, communication, and finance was accompanied by an expansion in the foreign trade, which falls into well-marked periods, both in regard to the rate of increase of the trade, and also in regard to its character and distribution. It is these changes which affected European industry. We must therefore study them in some detail.

Table IV shows the exports and imports of Japan divided into three periods corresponding with the three stages through which the industry and trade of the country have passed.

In reading Table IV, account must be taken of the changes in price level, the most important, of course, being subsequent to 1914. Thus in 1920, when prices were at their highest, being about 259 per cent of the price level of 1913, the total nominal values were over three times the pre-war trade, but corrected for price only about

132 per cent of that figure. The 1924 imports were, of course, connected with replacement after the earthquake of the previous year.

The first period of foreign trade extends from 1868 to about 1885, at which date the trade began to increase rapidly and change in character. The period ends with the Sino-Japanese War, after which Japan secured the restoration of her full liberty of action by the removal of treaty restrictions similar to those of which China is now complaining.

In this first period, up to say 1900 or thereabouts, the trade of Japan was a trade in raw materials, particularly raw silks, against manufactured goods. Raw silk, indeed, still remains the staple export to this day, being 39 per cent of the exports in

TABLE IV

EXPORTS AND IMPORTS OF JAPAN*

| Years (Average) | Exports (Yen) | Imports (Yen) |
|---|---|---|
| (1) 1868–72 | 15,799,600 | 22,661,400 |
| 1873–77 | 22,124,400 | 26,585,400 |
| 1878–82 | 30,267,000 | 32,618,000 |
| 1883–87 | 42,113,600 | 32,768,800 |
| 1888–93 | 77,118,000 | 72,466,000 |
| (2) 1894–98 | 139,200,000 | 223,040,000 |
| 1899–1903 | 243,880,000 | 270,406,000 |
| 1904–8 | 377,040,800 | 441,879,200 |
| 1909–13 | 495,683,000 | 544,132,800 |
| (3) 1914–16 | 808,895,000 | 628,203,700 |
| 1917–19 | 1,887,992,300 | 1,625,904,300 |
| 1920–23 | 1,571,607,500 | 1,956,924,700 |
| 1924—— | 1,807,233,000 | 2,453,390,000 |

* Uyehara, p. 50, see also pp. 52 and 53. Figures are not given for 1925 and 1926, but the report of the British Department of Overseas Trade for 1926 shows a further increase in imports and exports.

1925. Such manufactures as were exported were the surplus products of domestic industries, simple in character and small in amount. This stage may be compared with a similar condition in China before the revolution.

It was at this time that the European and American traders in Japan enjoyed a position similar to that which they have (but can hardly be said to enjoy) in China, today.

The second period was begun by the application of a protective tariff, Japan having regained control of her customs, and steel, machinery, shipbuilding, and chemical industries were developed by the government, to be handed over later to private control. This tariff, as usual in tariff history, was raised again in 1911, and the Russo-Japanese War, falling in this period, gave a great impulse to all industries, including textiles. The cotton-textile industry did not become of national importance until 1896, but by 1899 it had an export of 30,000,000 yen, consisting almost entirely of coarse-count yarns. In this second period the Japanese textile industry was passing through the stage in which the Chinese industry is today.

By 1905 exports of cotton piece goods amounted to 16,000,000 yen out of a total cotton export of 49,000,000, and there was a tendency to spin somewhat finer counts.[1]

Apart from the loss of the Japanese market in coarse counts, the European and American spinners and weavers had thus to face Japanese competition in China, though to be sure they had already lost a great deal of that market to India, for the coarse counts of yarn.

Up to the great war, Japanese industry was not very diversified. The cotton-textile industry, as in other countries, had been one of the first to feel the tendency to industrialization. Like the countries of continenal Europe at an earlier time, and like India, it had begun its competition in the market for low counts, forcing England to concentrate on the finer counts and the better qualities of piece goods. There were many miscellaneous and fairly simple manufactures depending on cheap sweated labor, of which matches are an example, and there were the heavy iron and steel and shipbuilding and engineering industries but recently escaped from government tutelage. But the war cut off the supply of all kinds of manufactures formerly derived by the East from Europe, and Japanese-manufactured goods, in spite of considerable inferiority, were in keen demand all over the East, and indeed the world. The variety of Japanese industries increased very rapidly, and the existing industries underwent a sudden and not altogether healthy expansion, the extension of plant being in advance of the improvement in technique and efficiency. In this expansion, which we have traced in shipping, the cotton industry took a full share, as may be seen from Table V.

TABLE V

General Growth of the Cotton-Spinning Industry in Japan between the Years of 1903 and 1925*

| Year | Capital | | | | | No. of Spindles (Thousands) | | | | |
|---|---|---|---|---|---|---|---|---|---|---|
| | No. of Companies | No. of Mills | Authorized (1,000 Yen) | Paid up (1,000 Yen) | Reserve Funds (1,000 Yen) | Ring | Mule | Total | Doublings Spindles | No. of Looms |
| 1903 | 51 | ..... | 38,555 | 34,029 | 5,123 | 1,295 | 86 | 1,381 | 127 | 5,043 |
| 1913 | 44 | 152 | 113,036 | 86,444 | 33,803 | 2,365 | 49 | 2,414 | 321 | 24,224 |
| 1918 | 43 | 177 | 192,877 | 138,494 | 92,426 | 3,176 | 52 | 3,227 | 385 | 40,391 |
| 1919 | 54 | 190 | 221,927 | 165,758 | 139,073 | 3,436 | 52 | 3,488 | 411 | 44,401 |
| 1920 | 56 | 198 | 394,327 | 276,535 | 165,697 | 3,761 | 52 | 3,813 | 466 | 50,583 |
| 1921 | 61 | 217 | 429,577 | 295,648 | 182,040 | 4,117 | 45 | 4,161 | 538 | 54,994 |
| 1922 | 64 | 235 | 462,107 | 317,148 | 202,774 | 4,472 | 45 | 4,517 | 602 | 60,765 |
| 1923 | 60 | 228 | 463,977 | 323,787 | 211,298 | 4,184 | 14 | 4,198 | 501 | 61,421 |
| 1924 | 56 | 232 | 512,362 | 349,821 | 212,872 | 4,845 | 25 | 4,870 | 677 | 64,235 |
| 1925 | 54 | 230 | 509,213 | 351,805 | 221,778 | 5,152 | 34 | 5,186 | 752 | 68,160 |

* Cunningham, *op. cit.*, p. 8.

[1] *Report on the Cotton-Spinning and Weaving Industry in Japan, 1925–26*, by W. B. Cunningham, His Britannic Majesty's Consul, Osaka, p. 7.

In this third period, since 1914, Japan came of age in the economic world, and that fact is represented in the composition of her exports and imports. Apart from raw silk, which is less a raw material than a very special type of partly finished goods, the exports show an increase (reckoned in percentage of the total) in wholly finished articles, and a decrease in the proportion of exports of "food and drink" and "raw materials and unfinished articles."

Table VI is the statement of these variations as given by Uyehara.

TABLE VI

PERCENTAGE OF EXPORT TRADE

| | 1912–14 (Average) | 1915–18 (Average) | 1919–22 (Average) | 1923 |
|---|---|---|---|---|
| 1. Food and drink | 10.3 | 10.5 | 6.9 | 6.3 |
| 2. Raw materials and unfinished articles | 30.8 | 28.2 | 18.4 | 14.8 |
| 3. Raw silk | 28.6 | 21.6 | 30.9 | 39.2 |
| 4. Wholly finished articles | 29.1 | 37.1 | 42.4 | 37.4 |
| 5. Miscellaneous | 1.2 | 2.6 | 1.5 | 2.3 |

TABLE VII

JAPANESE EXPORTS OF COTTON YARN AND COTTON PIECE GOODS TO ASIA AND ELSEWHERE (IN METRIC TONS)

| Destination | Cotton Yarn | | | Cotton Piece Goods | | |
|---|---|---|---|---|---|---|
| | 1911 | 1924 | 1925 | 1911 | 1924 | 1925 |
| Asia | 47,183 | 44,588 | 51,799 | 10,271 | 61,124 | ......... |
| China | 46,303 | 29,715 | 35,536 | 9,567 | 36,007 | ......... |
| India | 326 | 14,551 | 15,691 | 63 | 14,273 | ......... |
| Other Asiatic countries | 554 | 323 | 572 | 541 | 10,844 | ......... |
| Elsewhere | 9 | 4,076 | 4,145 | 637 | 5,370 | ......... |
| Total | 47,192 | 48,665 | 55,944 | 10,908 | 66,494 | 104,239 |

Japan is thus ceasing to be predominantly an exporter of raw materials and unfinished articles, apart from silk, and is increasing her exports of wholly finished goods. It should be remembered that cotton yarns are included in the heading "Unfinished Articles," and this item is decreasing in *relative* importance, owing to Indian and Chinese competition and the development of weaving at home. This statement is borne out by Table VII, taken from the *Memorandum on Cotton for the World Economic Conference.*

Uyehara divides the other manufactured goods for export into three groups as in Table VIII.

Of these, Group 1 shows the trade resulting from the new industries called into existence by the great war; Group 2, highly mechanized industries, not so new in their origin, and Group 3, goods requiring more hand labor. Table IX shows the changes in value and percentage of total exports before the war, at the end of the war, and in the post-war depression.

It should be remembered that wholesale prices in 1918 were about 196 per cent of those in 1913, and in 1923 about 199 per cent. Thus, if we revalue the exports under Group 3 for 1923, we get a figure of some 40,500,000 yen to compare with the

TABLE VIII

VALUE OF MAIN MANUFACTURED GOODS FOR EXPORT, EXCLUDING TEXTILE GOODS (YEN 1,000)

| Article | 1913 | 1919 | 1920 | 1921 | 1922 | 1923 | 1924 |
|---|---|---|---|---|---|---|---|
| *Group 1:* | | | | | | | |
| Insulated electric wire | 251 | 8,411 | 8,043 | 3,273 | 7,816 | 1,609 | 1,365 |
| Iron manufactured goods | 699 | 25,001 | 21,069 | 9,112 | 10,321 | 11,409 | 13,119 |
| Machinery | ....... | 16,722 | 16,710 | 12,883 | 14,425 | 9,202 | 10,362 |
| Watches and clocks | 993 | 1,831 | 1,359 | 950 | 1,422 | 1,296 | ....... |
| *Group 2:* | | | | | | | |
| Oil and wax | 9,991 | 35,450 | 32,534 | 7,889 | 12,478 | 10,921 | ....... |
| Hosiery | 9,013 | 39,070 | 36,043 | 12,891 | 17,666 | 21,205 | 22,015 |
| Paper | ....... | 25,402 | 23,124 | 18,939 | 16,127 | 15,167 | 15,560 |
| Cement | 655 | 6,544 | 10,059 | 7,078 | 3,907 | 2,009 | 2,364 |
| Glass and glass manufactures | 3,318 | 19,680 | 23,238 | 9,797 | 10,308 | 10,118 | 13,972 |
| Rubber tires | ....... | 7,114 | 8,018 | 4,478 | 5,999 | 3,899 | 3,233 |
| Dyes and coating and filling matters | 497 | 9,278 | 8,796 | 6,168 | 5,628 | 3,982 | ...... |
| *Group 3:* | | | | | | | |
| Matches | 11,864 | 32,968 | 28,454 | 16,239 | 15,562 | 10,649 | 9,212 |
| Hats | 5,619 | 8,579 | 6,817 | 3,456 | 5,555 | 3,941 | 4,816 |
| Buttons | 3,311 | 10,285 | 9,982 | 4,136 | 6,400 | 7,268 | 8,955 |
| China and porcelain | 6,637 | 22,629 | 31,452 | 20,791 | 21,210 | 23,460 | 25,427 |
| Toys | 2,489 | 13,001 | 21,189 | 7,003 | 7,414 | 7,140 | 8,292 |

TABLE IX

EXPORTS OF MANUFACTURED GOODS (EXCLUDING TEXTILES)

| All Goods which Come under: | Value (Yen 1,000) | P.C.* | Value (Yen 1,000) | P.C. | Value (Yen 1,000) | P.C. |
|---|---|---|---|---|---|---|
| Group 1 | 10,032 | 1.69 | 159,250 | 8.12 | 34,930 | 2.13 |
| Group 2 | 42,791 | 7.24 | 161,325 | 8.22 | 94,294 | 5.76 |
| Group 3 | 63,021 | 10.66 | 117,130 | 5.98 | 80,905 | 4.93 |

* P.C. = Percentage of the total value of exports.

63,000,000 yen of exports in this group in 1913, and even the 1918 exports are only the equivalent of some 60,000,000 at pre-war prices. It is clear that in 1923 Japan had gained little real ground in manufactures other than textiles. In Group 1 there was an increase at pre-war values of about 75,000,000; in Group 2, an increase of 4,000,000, and in Group 3, a loss of 23,500,000. We may tentatively draw the conclusion that in the trades depending on cheap sweated labor Japan is losing her advantage (which, as a matter of fact, has passed to China). In the newer industries she had (in 1923) lost the greater part of gains which in 1918 had been worth 55,000,000 yen even in pre-war values, and in the older machine industries she was doing little more than holding her own. It is unfortunate that Mr. Uyehara chooses the earthquake year, but there are other reasons to suppose that it is particularly in the field of textile manufactures that the Japanese competition is felt. We shall perhaps be justified in confining our later study of the effects on European industries of the industrialization of Japan mainly on cotton textiles.

Turning now to imports, we see changes corresponding to those in the exports; that is to say, an increase in the proportions of the imports of food and raw material and a decrease in those of manufactured goods. For raw cotton Table X is of interest as showing the growth of the cotton-textile industry over a long period.

TABLE X

IMPORT OF RAW COTTON

| Years (Average) | Quantity (Picul)* | Value (Yen) |
|---|---|---|
| 1888–92 | 666,428 | 6,755,943 |
| 1903–07 | 3,521,918 | 90,373,027 |
| 1908–12 | 4,498,658 | 140,878,540 |
| 1913–17 | 7,121,191 | 215,390,908 |
| 1918–22 | 8,010,479 | 552,175,350 |
| 1923 | 8,769,700 | 513,172,438 |
| 1924 | ............... | 604,530,000 |

* Picul = 132.28 lb.

The greater part of these imports came from China and India. Of other imports we may note those of cotton and woolen manufactured goods, and imports of machinery and iron and steel goods.

It is clear from Table XI that the import of cotton goods has become stationary if measured in value, and we judge it must be decreasing if measured in quantity. The woolen goods trade is more satisfactory to the chief exporter, Britain. To some extent its increase may be regarded as an instance of the tendency to which we shall refer in our conclusion, for loss of trade in one direction to be compensated by increased purchases of the commodity in which the country losing the trade still maintains an advantage. Japan still has to import textile and some other machinery.

To sum up, the foreign trade of Japan shows that she has passed through the stages of being an exporter of raw material and goods manufactured by simple hand processes, while importing Western manufactures and the apparatus of Western transport. She has also passed through the next stage in which some simple machine textile industries are added and the home demand for the coarser counts of yarn satisfied by home industry. A development of this phase was her entry into competition in the great neutral market of China, where her coarser yarns and rougher piece goods competed with Indian textiles, and with the latter drove the European goods of the same grade out of the market. This phase ended at the outbreak of the great war, and she was hurried into a further development of miscellaneous engineering and general industries, some of which have been able to survive the post-war readjustments, though others have had to close down. The textile industries underwent expansion with the rest, but meantime China had entered, in certain regions, on the second phase of development, and Japan found herself faced with severe competition in her own grades of production by Chinese textiles in the Chinese market. Her remedy has been to set up factories in China and to attempt to move into the finer grades of spinning and weaving in the Japanese mills. At present she is in danger of being pinched between the Chinese competition in the coarser grades, and the European and American competition in the finer qualities. There are conditions affecting the efficiency of her labor which make it doubtful if she can rapidly move into these

TABLE XI

IMPORTS

| Years | Cotton and Woolen Manufactured Goods | |
|---|---|---|
| | Cotton Goods (Yen) | Woolen Goods (Yen) |
| 1912 | 10,083,000 | 12,444,000 |
| 1919 | 7,000,000 | 12,301,000 |
| 1920 | 15,024,000 | 31,270,000 |
| 1921 | 8,752,000 | 31,083,000 |
| 1922 | 13,569,000 | 49,953,000 |
| 1923 | 7,483,000 | 46,600,000 |
| 1924 | 12,036,000 | 61,818,000 |
| | Machinery and Iron and Steel Goods | |
| | Machinery (Yen) | Iron and Steel Goods (Yen) |
| 1913 | 36,762,000 | 58,349,000 |
| 1919 | 89,222,000 | 251,038,000 |
| 1920 | 110,571,000 | 279,222,000 |
| 1921 | 119,882,000 | 157,680,000 |
| 1922 | 114,371,000 | 167,430,000 |
| 1923 | 102,241,000 | 131,083,000 |
| 1924 | 138,660,000 | 216,798,000 |

higher grades. Meantime she is increasing her production of piece goods and pushing them in the Indian market, where there is every reason to believe that she will meet resistance by a protective duty if her competition increases in severity. She must also contemplate a similar possibility in China.

The effects of these changes on the trade with Europe are discussed in Part II. It is now necessary to consider the process of industrialization in China.

### INDUSTRIAL DEVELOPMENT OF CHINA

The prerequisites of industrialization in China have never been fully satisfied in all parts of the country. The rationalistic or scientific habit of mind, as distinct from the traditional, did not triumph amongst the ruling class until they were on the verge of collapse, and then only in a few persons. That collapse took place, and since the revolution, or at any rate since the monarchistic movement and death of Yuan Shih Kai, there has been no continuous and effective central government. This would not have been of great importance had there been any reasonable continuity in the provincial government; but with the exception of Shansi this has not been so. The modern habit of mind has meanwhile continued to spread among the intellectual leaders of the nation, and this has given rise to a sense of frustration and exasperation which would be largely dissipated if a powerful government could secure an outlet for these abilities and energies in the economic and political development of the country.

In the meantime the prerequisites—good government and the modern outlook—have been satisfied in the treaty ports more nearly than anywhere else in China, and

TABLE XII

APPROXIMATE TONNAGE OF SHIPPING ENTERED AND CLEARED
(IN MILLION TONS)

| Year | British | Japanese | Chinese* | Others | Total |
|---|---|---|---|---|---|
| 1870........ | 3 | .......... | 0% | 4 | 7 |
| 1880........ | 10 | .......... | 5=31% | 1 | 16 |
| 1890........ | 16 | .......... | 6=24% | 3 | 25 |
| 1900........ | 23 | .......... | 8=20% | 10 | 41 |
| (1905)....... | (35) | (6) | (16)=22% | (16) | (73) |
| 1910........ | 34 | 19 | 20=22% | 16 | 89 |
| (1915)....... | (38) | (24) | (24)=26% | (50) | (91) |
| 1920........ | 40 | 28 | 28=26% | 8 | 104 |
| (1925)....... | (43) | (35) | (33)=25% | (17) | (128) |

* Includes junks entered and cleared.

it is among the Chinese of the larger of these ports, and particularly Shanghai, that industrialization has gone farthest. From this, as from many other points of view, China may be divided into three regions, the treaty ports, their hinterlands served by rivers and railways, and the interior, largely untouched by modern commerce and quite untouched by modern industry. So far, then, as industrialization has taken place, it has done so by the action of Chinese, Japanese, Europeans, and Americans, for the most part in or near the centers of foreign jurisdiction.

Then there is the factor of finance. The failure of the Chinese governments to grapple with the question of the currency is important in this connection. While it would be inaccurate to state that industrial development is impossible in the welter of all kinds of money, which makes up the currency of China today, no one can doubt the necessity for unification if China is to follow the footsteps of Japan. The presence of stable monetary systems for the larger denomination—at least under the guidance of the foreign banks in the ports—has had something to do with the localization of industry there. Also the important development of Chinese joint stock banking in those ports since the European war is an important and encouraging factor. Given the desired improvement in political conditions, it is probable that these banks could and would provide for the very rapid expansion of the financial facilities necessary for the industrialization of China.

The remaining one of the four factors is transportation. Here again there is arrested development. Shipping has increased, but the railways in 1927 show little real growth compared with 1915, and on the whole are much less effectively run. It is not easy to find a measure of the growth of shipping exactly parallel to that given for Japan, but Table XII taken from the Chinese Maritime Customs returns, shows approximately the growth of shipping since 1870, and the percentages beside the Chinese tonnage show how little relative progress the Chinese mercantile marine has made.

We may contrast with this the progress of shipping in Japan over the same period, and note that whereas in 1893 Japan's share of some 2,200,000 tons of ships with cargo entering Japan was 14.4 per cent, in 1918 it was 80.8 per cent of an entry of 17,800,000 tons, and in 1921, 69.1 per cent of the larger total of 27,900,000 tons. However, it is clear that though the Chinese have not succeeded in getting their shipping into their own hands, they have been plentifully supplied with water transport by other nations.

It was the foreigners who pressed for the rapid construction of railways, but there was very little work undertaken before the Sino-Japanese war. Between 1895 and 1915 something like 6,000 miles of railway were built. In 1899 there were about 800 miles, and development proceeded rapidly after the Boxer troubles. The effects of the spread of the railways is described in *Chinese Maritime Customs Returns of Trade and Trade Reports, 1899,* p. 1, quoted by Remer. Where railways extend "districts suddenly commence to hum with life and activity, and there springs up a flourishing trade which was formerly undreamed of." There have been many schemes, but little construction since the Revolution, and the mileage in 1923, the last year for which figures are available, is about 7,000 miles in operation. There is said to be about the same mileage under construction or contract, but one must not jump to the conclusion that this mileage is being constructed, or will be constructed, in the near future.

The situation in China, therefore, seems to be that the general industrialization of the country is arrested at the moment by the lack of a strong and enlightened central government, or a number of strong and enlightened provincial governments. How long this state of affairs will continue is for the political experts to say. If we could assume that problem solved, then the rate of the expansion of the railway system would probably become the limiting factor.

As in the case of Japan, it is possible to trace in the foreign trade of China the changes which have already been wrought by such industrialization as has taken place, and the reaction upon China of the industrialization of India and Japan. For this purpose Remer divides the period at 1885, 1896, and 1913.

The characteristics of these periods are as follows: In the period from, say, 1871 to 1885 there was very little change in the volume or silver value of the trade of China. On the export side it was a trade in a few special commodities, of which tea and silk were by far the most important. On the import side there were cotton goods, woolens, and metals, but the demand for the cotton goods showed no signs of increasing. The whole trade was sluggish, as the Chinese did not feel any strong want for the Western products and the exporters were interested only in silk and tea. The extension of water transport was only at its beginnings in the interior.

From 1885 to 1898 important changes showed themselves. The volume and value of the trade increased steadily, imports increasing more rapidly than exports. This period is marked by a great increase in the demand for cotton manufactures, both yarn and piece goods. The demand for yarn increased more rapidly than for piece goods. The export of raw cotton to Japan begins about 1878, and the cotton thus exported came back in part as yarn.

Even in the first period the competition of India and Japan in the sea trade had begun to show in the export statistics, and in this second period Japanese competition in silk begins to be marked. The silk industry also seems to show the first signs of industrialization, for at the end of the period steam filature silk appears in the returns. The first railway to operate was built in 1888 from Tientsin to Tongshan, and by the year 1895 had been extended to Shanhaikuan. But it remains true that for all practical purposes there was no industrialization in China at the end of this period, with the important exception of the steamship. Export was still concentrated on a few commodities. In the imports cotton manufactures and opium predominated, the former steadily growing in comparison with the latter.

At this time there was strong competition for the trade in cotton goods, Great Britain, the United States, India, and Japan being involved. In the lower counts the Asiatic countries were most successful. Indian yarn came in in quantity after 1876; Japanese imports into China of cotton yarn show a similar sudden increase in 1898. This Indian and Japanese yarn took the place, very largely, of the old handspun yarn, and did not compete directly with the finer British yarns. In coarse cotton goods the Americans were affected more than the British, who were able to retreat to the safer ground of the finer qualities, where their competitors for the time were unable to follow them. On the whole it seems that the trade with Japan was an increasing proportion of the whole, while that of the United States grew less rapidly than the total trade. The share of Britain and British India is difficult to determine, as it passed through Hongkong and no statistics of its distribution thence were kept; but as the share of Hongkong increased, it seems reasonable to suppose that the British and Indian share at least did not decrease. In shipping, as we have seen, the British were easily supreme.

The next period is from 1895 or 1898 to 1913. This is the period of railway expansion and the battle of the concessions. At the beginning there were 800 miles of railway, and at the end, some 6,000. It was also the period in which, after a reaction in the Boxer troubles, the active elements of the Chinese people came to recognize definitely the superiority, in material matters at least, of the Western civilization. Japan and America were the chief schoolmasters of young China, and the "scientific" habit of thought had a wide extension in this period. There was also a central government which, in spite of its obvious defects, did govern. Consequently, by the end of the period the stage was set for the second act in the drama of industrialization.

This was a period of great growth in the international trade of the world, and in this movement of expansion Japan and India took a share. But the rate of increase of the foreign trade of China remained practically unaltered, so that relatively she was left behind. Fluctuations were more considerable during this period than the preceding.

In the Chinese market during this period, 1895–1913, there was a growth of national rivalry among the foreign merchants and agents in whose hands the trade still lay, and there were interesting changes in the organization of the European and American firms which we have no time to follow out.[2] One important feature was the increasing penetration of the foreign firm's representatives into the interior, and their development of an export trade in a variety of new products, of which the soya bean is the best-known example. Small mills and factories for standardizing and preparing these products began to spring up at the treaty ports. There was also some foreign activity in stimulating demand for certain foreign products along the lines opened by the railways. The situation is thus described by Remer:

> Industrial development slowly followed the development of trade, bringing with it slowly rising wages. In 1913 China was a great agricultural country into which improved transportation had carried along a few lines and to a small extent the consequences of contact with the commercial and the industrial organization which is characteristic of the West. The commercial organization of China has been more adaptable in the face of new developments than the industrial organization, so that the penetration of what for want of a better term we may call modern commerce has been more rapid than has been the penetration of modern industry.

The export trade at that time began to extend to a larger number of commodities, and the relative importance of tea and silk declined still farther. This is in the main a normal and healthy sign, showing that the economic development of the country had fairly begun, and in the following period this change from what might be called the export of luxury raw materials and drugs to a general export of all kinds of necessary raw materials was carried still further. The competition of Japan and India continued to be felt by China in the silk and tea trades, but as usual, some kind of stability was reached on the basis of specialization. Thus the American tea and silk market fell to Japan, the English tea market to India, and the Russian to China. The European silk market was divided with Japan.

In the import trade the place of cotton manufactures became still more important, rising to 182,400,000 Haikwan Taels in 1913, or 32 per cent of the total imports. Up to 1904 the imports of yarn and cloth increased at about the same rate, that of the yarn being the greater. But from 1904 to the end of the period, and, one may add, into the next period, the imports of yarn were less than those of cloth. The cause was the development of native cotton spinning in China, though figures of the production are not available. This was the period of Indian and Japanese competition in the yarn market, and after varying fortunes the imports from these two countries of this commodity were about equal in 1913.

In passing, we should mention the trade in kerosene oil which dates from the preceding period and grew steadily with the growth of foreign trade. It concerned America at first, but in 1889 Russian oil, and in 1895 Sumatran oil, appear.

In 1898 the imports were American oil 48,000,000, Russian oil 37,000,000, and Sumatran oil 14,000,000 gallons. The total imports in 1913 were 184,000,000 gallons,

[2] See Reimer, pp. 128–31.

value 25,400,000 taels, being 4.5 per cent of the value of all imports. This trade is important because, like the trade in tobacco, it has been developed by large-selling monopolies who have been able to perfect a system of distribution which has done much to open the interior to trade and extend the hinterlands of the treaty ports. Both trades are also interesting as affording the outstanding examples both of Anglo-American combination and Anglo-American rivalry.

The import of iron and mild steel seems to have increased evenly, but by the end of the period the competition of the native industry at Hanyang was beginning to be felt. Naturally, there was a considerable import of railway plant and material in connection with the expansion of the railways, and imports of machinery increased from 1,500,000 taels in 1899 to 7,000,000 taels in 1913. Of the other trade which might throw light on the extent of industrialization, that in coal, imports reached

TABLE XIII

COTTON MILLS IN CHINA

| Year | Number of Mills | Number of Spindles | Number of Looms |
|---|---|---|---|
| 1896 | 12 | 417,000 | 2,100 |
| 1909 | ? | 800,000 | ? |
| 1910 | ? | 812,300 | ? |
| 1911 | ? | 832,300 | ? |
| 1912 | ? | 832,300 | ? |
| 1913 | 31 | 870,800 | 3,152 |
| 1915 | 31 | 1,008,986 | 4,564 |

about 1,500,000 tons in 1903 and remained at about that figure, while exports increased with the development of Chinese mines until at the end of the period they equaled the imports.

Still speaking of the period 1895–1913, we may note the main features of the distribution of this trade among the nations, regarded from the point of view of the shares in the trade. Great Britain and France increased their trade at the same rate as the total increased, or nearly so. We had 11.7 per cent in 1899 and 11.4 per cent in 1913. The figures for France were 5.8 per cent in 1905 and 5.3 in 1913. In each case there is also the indirect trade of these countries through Hongkong, the exact amount of which cannot be determined.

India and the United States lost ground relatively, India falling from 7.8 per cent to 5.5 per cent during the period, and the United States from 9.5 per cent to 7.6 per cent. Japan, Russia, and Germany were securing an increasing proportion of the trade, the percentages being: Japan, 11.5–19.7 per cent; Russia, 4.8–6.7 per cent; Germany, from 3.1 per cent in 1905 to 4.5 per cent in 1913.

As Remer points out,[3] it is very difficult to estimate the exact extent of industrial development in China at this time, just before the outbreak of the European war, as exact statistics are not forthcoming. Remer's estimate is, for the whole of China, "no more than from six to eight hundred establishments of a modern sort at

[3] *Foreign Trade of China*, p. 166.

the end of 1913." Table XIII, prepared by the same authority, is of particular interest, as it shows the growth of the cotton-textile industry. The total number of spindles did not exceed one million until 1915 in China. The same point in development was reached in India in 1876, and in Japan in 1898. The dates are significant as showing the lateness of China's development.

The advance by Japan in the cotton trade at this period in China was at the expense of India and the United States more than of England. Great Britain was supreme in the Chinese market for the finer grades of cotton goods up to 1914, and she was first in the imports of plain fabrics. American imports showed remarkable fluctuations, but lost ground relatively to Japan.

In addition to the textiles, the *China Yearbook* mentions 40 flour mills, many of them Russian affairs in Northern Manchuria; 25 soap and candle factories, 18 glass factories, 34 oil mills, 16 shipbuilding and engineering establishments, 20 cigarette factories; about twenty cities had match factories, and 35 electric light and power; there were 13 paper mills, numerous printing works, one iron and steel plant, and a small number of mines and smelting establishments.[4]

We may therefore say that at the beginning of the great war China was in approximately the position of Japan in 1900, referred to previously, and her political relations with the foreign powers were not dissimilar. Her failure to proceed from that point as Japan did is due to the comparative failure of her political revolution, a question outside the scope of this present inquiry.

In the remaining period, 1914–21, the economic life of China, like its political life, is closely connected with that of Japan. During the war the foreign trade declined, but from 1919 to 1921 there was a real boom and a great increase in the trade, which continued up to 1924, but received a check in the following year, the last for which the customs figures are available. The export of food products, raw materials, especially vegetable oils, and, during the war, of metals, increased at the expense of the former staple exports. Imports were checked by the European war, up to 1918, though there was a steady growth in imports of what might be called Western luxuries, such as cigarettes. The cotton imports fell in relative importance. They were 40 per cent of all imports in 1905; in 1914 they were 31.3 per cent, and in 1921, 23.1 per cent. The boom was largely a price boom, and the quantities of cotton piece goods and cotton yarn continued to decline. This tendency referred to by Remer, is also illustrated in Table XIV.

The decreased imports of cotton yarn reflect the growth of cotton spinning in China. The imports of cotton piece goods came in increasing part from Japan. In 1914 Great Britain sent more piece goods into China than did Japan. In 1917 and on to 1921 Japan had taken and maintained the lead. The boycott of 1925 intensified this tendency. Here are the figures for the export of cotton piece goods from England to China in 1913, and again in 1924 and 1925, in metric tons.[5]

| 1913 | 1924 | 1925 |
|---|---|---|
| 59,395 | 24,623 | 14,907 |

[4] Quoted in Remer, 167, p. 10.

[5] *Memorandum on Cotton* (International Economic Conference, 1927), p. 71.

It may be of interest to quote Remer's estimate of the degree of industrialization in 1921, the latest date for which he gives information.

There were in China in 1915 thirty-one cotton mills with one million spindles and 4,500 looms. It may be estimated that in 1921 the number of mills was between 60 and 70, the number of spindles about two million, and the number of looms about 14,000. About fifty of these mills were under Chinese ownership and control. There were about 40 flour mills in China in 1913. In 1921 there were at least 125. There were between 400 and 600 factories using power-driven machinery in China in 1913; a list for 1921 would probably show more than 2,000. In 1921 Shanghai, Dairen, Hankow, Tientsin, Canton, and Hongkong were really industrial centers of importance, and there were many industrial establishments in other cities, such as Tsingtau, Hangchow, Wusih, and Nantungchow. Finally, there was in 1921 an export of factory products which was valued at about four million Haikwan Taels, and which included cotton piece goods, cotton yarn, candles, cement, matches, paper and soap.[6]

TABLE XIV

TRADE IN COTTON YARN AND COTTON PIECE GOODS, CHINA* (METRIC TONS)

| Average | Cotton Yarn | | | Cotton Piece Goods | | |
|---|---|---|---|---|---|---|
| | Import | Export | Balance | Import | Export | Balance |
| 1909–13 | 141.626 | 1.110 | 140.516 | 141.890 | 2.575 | 139.355 |
| 1913 | 163.080 | .888 | 162.192 | 183.531 | 2.889 | 180.642 |
| 1923 | 46.085 | 6.046 | 40.039 | 118.276 | 9.588 | 108.686 |
| 1924 | 34.066 | 9.501 | 24.565 | 139.551 | 12.252 | 127.299 |

* *Memorandum on Cotton* (International Economic Conference, 1927), p. 69.

These exports of Chinese factory products have grown since that date, as shown by the following table, taken from the customs reports:

CHINESE FACTORY PRODUCTS EXPORTED TO FOREIGN COUNTRIES

| Year | Value of Exports in Haikuan Taels |
|---|---|
| 1921 | 3,724,813 |
| 1922 | 5,091,302 |
| 1923 | 12,145,616 |
| 1924 | 18,810,291 |
| 1925 | 15,378,913 |

These figures make it evident that in spite of political troubles the China of the treaty ports at least has entered on a rapid phase of industrialization, the details of which we shall hear from our Chinese colleagues.

## II. SOME EFFECTS OF THE INDUSTRIALIZATION OF THE ORIENT ON THE DISTRIBUTION OF TRADE BY CONTINENTS ON THE COTTON TRADE OF THE UNITED KINGDOM

It is clear that the effects of the industrialization of the Orient on European industry must operate through the changes produced in international trade. These

[6] Remer, *The Foreign Trade of China,* p. 203.

changes can be traced in some industries and in some countries, but in the absence of detailed statistics of production, such as we may soon hope to have as a result of the recent World Economic Conference at Geneva, we cannot hope to show in detail the changes which have resulted in European industry during the past few years as a result of changes in the distribution of the trade of China and Japan. In any case, even with full figures, the disentanglement of the effects of such changes from similar effects produced by like changes in other parts of the world would involve a research of the first magnitude. For the industrialization of the East, intensified and accelerated by the World War, is only one phase of a similar movement in other parts of the world.

TABLE XV

CHINESE FOREIGN TRADE FROM 1921 COMPARED WITH THE PRE-WAR YEAR 1913 (UNIT, 1,000,000 TAELS)

| | 1913 | 1921 | 1922 | 1923 | 1924 | 1925 |
|---|---|---|---|---|---|---|
| | IMPORTS | | | | | |
| Asia | 374.97 | 532.61 | 572.78 | 571.58 | 590.27 | 624.62 |
| Europe | 154.81 | 195.39 | 203.66 | 188.12 | 229.14 | 174.44 |
| America | 37.28 | 187.60 | 177.40 | 164.78 | 206.53 | 149.72 |
| Others | .70 | 17.25 | 21.19 | 24.15 | 13.16 | 16.31 |
| Total | 567.76 | 932.85 | 975.03 | 948.63 | 1039.10 | 965.09 |
| Index No. wholesale prices | 100 | 150 | 146 | 156 | 154 | 159 |
| | EXPORTS | | | | | |
| Asia | 243.91 | 402.56 | 425.71 | 486.90 | 504.97 | 445.84 |
| Europe | 104.72 | 76.53 | 105.28 | 117.41 | 138.82 | 156.22 |
| America | 38.30 | 90.69 | 98.85 | 128.80 | 101.86 | 144.49 |
| Others | .59 | 31.48 | 25.05 | 24.81 | 26.13 | 29.80 |
| Total | 387.52 | 601.26 | 654.89 | 751.92 | 771.78 | 776.35 |
| Index No. prices | 100 | 150 | 146 | 156 | 154 | 159 |

Some light is thrown on the question, however, by tracing the changes in the geographical distribution of the trade of China and Japan, especially during the period of readjustment following the crisis of 1921, in comparison with the position in the pre-war year, 1913.

Tables XV–XXII show the values of the import and export trade of China and Japan with Europe, Asia, America, and the rest. They also show the percentage of the total trade which went to each of these divisions, and in one of the tables an attempt is made to reduce the growth in the trade free of the effects of the gigantic price inflation of the period. The price indexes are those given in the *International Statistical Yearbook,* and they are given below the values in the tables.[7]

[7] The tables for Japan are based on the table in Uyehara, pp. 74, 75, the totals being made by us and percentages roughly calculated. For China we have used the figures in the annual reports of the Department of Overseas Trade, which are drawn from the reports of

Tables XV and XVI show the growth in the value of the foreign trade of the two countries; Table XVII shows the result of revaluing these figures at the level of the prices of 1913.

TABLE XVI

JAPANESE FOREIGN TRADE FROM 1921 COMPARED WITH THE PRE-WAR YEAR 1913 (UNIT, 1,000,000 YEN)

| | 1913 | 1921 | 1922 | 1923 | 1924 |
|---|---|---|---|---|---|
| | | | IMPORTS | | |
| Asia | 348.055 | 664.599 | 736.088 | 819.631 | 995.368 |
| Europe | 208.297 | 266.412 | 382.306 | 421.880 | 531.880 |
| America | 127.021 | 586.868 | 619.836 | 566.106 | 718.972 |
| Others | 22.222 | 51.617 | 92.987 | 120.477 | 137.976 |
| Total | 705.595 | 1569.496 | 1831.217 | 1929.094 | 2384.196 |
| Index No. prices | 100 | 200 | 196 | 199 | 207 |
| | | | EXPORTS | | |
| Asia | 275.928 | 614.891 | 672.146 | 587.125 | 750.737 |
| Europe | 140.024 | 74.004 | 145.515 | 87.602 | 167.939 |
| America | 190.986 | 512.374 | 752.942 | 686.583 | 770.120 |
| Others | 15.496 | 39.348 | 20.227 | 64.840 | 82.454 |
| Total | 622.434 | 1240.617 | 1590.880 | 1426.150 | 1771.250 |
| Index No. prices | 100 | 200 | 196 | 199 | 207 |

TABLE XVII

JAPAN'S IMPORT AND EXPORT TRADE REVALUED AS AT 1913 PRICES, TOTAL TRADE (MILLION YEN)

| | 1913 | 1921 | 1922 | 1923 | 1924 |
|---|---|---|---|---|---|
| Imports | 706 | 780 | 910 | 970 | 1150 |
| Exports | 622 | 620 | 810 | 720 | 850 |

Thus we see there has been a real advance in the volume as distinct from the inflated values of Japan's foreign trade as a whole. But the trade of Japan with Europe does not show the same expansion; as can be seen in Table XVIII.

It is interesting to notice the erratic variations in the exports of Japan to Europe, and the slow recovery of her imports from Europe to about their pre-war values. Compare with this the corresponding figures for China.

---

the Maritime Customs. Here also it has been necessary to rearrange the items and roughly calculate the percentages. There is no reason to doubt the substantial accuracy of the tables, but they should be checked and recalculated, as most of them were constructed under difficulties while traveling, when the likelihood of accidental errors is much increased.

From Tables XIX–XXII it would appear that in China and Japan, as elsewhere in the world, the real growth of international trade has been somewhat slow since the catastrophe of the war and the subsequent boom and crisis. For the world as a whole the volume of goods to be carried by sea has even now (1927) hardly increased at all in comparison with 1913 figures, and the increase in the corrected value of world-trade in 1925 over 1913 is given by the *Report of the World Conference* as only 5 per cent, while in 1923 the world's trade had not reached the pre-war level. Judged

TABLE XVIII

JAPAN'S TRADE WITH EUROPE REVALUED AS AT 1913 PRICES, (MILLION YEN)

| | 1913 | 1921 | 1922 | 1923 | 1924 |
|---|---|---|---|---|---|
| Imports......... | 208 | 134 | 195 | 212 | 257 |
| Exports......... | 140 | 37 | 74 | 44 | 81 |

TABLE XIX

CHINA'S IMPORT AND EXPORT TRADE REVALUED AS AT 1913 PRICES, TOTAL TRADE (MILLION TAELS)

| | 1913 | 1921 | 1922 | 1923 | 1924 | 1925 |
|---|---|---|---|---|---|---|
| Imports........... | 568 | 610 | 615 | 610 | 680 | 610 |
| Exports........... | 387 | 400 | 447 | 482 | 500 | 490 |

TABLE XX

CHINA'S TRADE WITH EUROPE REVALUED AS AT 1913 PRICES (MILLION TAELS)

| | 1913 | 1921 | 1922 | 1923 | 1924 | 1925 |
|---|---|---|---|---|---|---|
| Imports........... | 155 | 130 | 140 | 120 | 150 | 105 |
| Exports............ | 105 | 50 | 72 | 74 | 90 | 98 |

by this standard the export trade of China has done well to increase by 25 per cent, but the import shows only 4 per cent. But the European component in the Chinese trade is 3 per cent below pre-war levels in imports and 7 per cent below in exports.

From these and some other considerations it seems clear that the share of Europe in the trade of China and Japan since 1913 has diminished relatively and perhaps absolutely. It remains to consider whether this decrease is connected with the process of industrialization, and if so, how.

On this point the most recent reports of the British Committee on Industry and Trade, and the memorandum on cotton prepared for Geneva are quite explicit.

"Taking the world as a whole, the widespread development of home manufactures to meet needs formerly supplied by imported goods is by general consent one of the outstanding features of the post-war economic situation, and this is perhaps the most important factor tending either to limit the volume or to modify the character of British Export Trade." The survey goes on to cite among other cases China, India, and Japan, with special reference to the cotton trade.

TABLE XXI

PERCENTAGE SHARES OF JAPANESE FOREIGN TRADE

| | 1913 | 1921 | 1922 | 1923 | 1924 |
|---|---|---|---|---|---|
| | A. IMPORTS | | | | |
| Asia | 49 | 42.5 | 40.2 | 42.3 | 42 |
| Europe | 29.5 | 17 | 20.7 | 22 | 22.4 |
| America | 18 | 37 | 34 | 29.5 | 30 |
| Others | 3.5 | 3.5 | 5.1 | 6.1 | 5.8 |
| | B. EXPORTS | | | | |
| Asia | 45 | 49.5 | 42.3 | 41 | 43 |
| Europe | 22.5 | 6 | 9.2 | 6.2 | 9.5 |
| America | 30.5 | 41.5 | 47.4 | 48 | 43.5 |
| Others | 2.0 | 3.0 | 1.2 | 4.6 | 4.0 |

TABLE XXII

PERCENTAGE SHARES OF CHINESE FOREIGN TRADE

| | 1913 | 1921 | 1922 | 1923 | 1924 | 1925 |
|---|---|---|---|---|---|---|
| | A. IMPORTS | | | | | |
| Asia | 66 | 57 | 58.7 | 60.3 | 56.8 | 64.7 |
| Europe | 27.25 | 21 | 20.8 | 19.8 | 22 | 18 |
| America | 6.6 | 20 | 18.2 | 17.3 | 19.8 | 15.5 |
| Others | .12 | 1.8 | 2.2 | 2.5 | 1.3 | 1.7 |
| | B. EXPORTS | | | | | |
| Others | .1 | 5.2 | 3.8 | 3.3 | 3.4 | 3.8 |
| America | 9.8 | 15.0 | 15.0 | 17.0 | 13.2 | 18.5 |
| Europe | 27 | 12.7 | 16.3 | 15.6 | 18 | 20.3 |
| Asia | 63 | 66.7 | 65 | 64.8 | 65.4 | 57.4 |

We may therefore pass on to consider that trade as affording the best example of the effects on an European industry of the competition of local manufactures in the Far East. In doing so it is convenient, and in accordance with the facts, to consider India, China, Japan, and the East Indies as one economic region, entered at the western end by the filaments of European trade, and at the eastern by those of American trade, and having a much slighter connection with the Australian and New Zealand, South African, and South American regions. Within that region the textile products of Japan, India, and China compete, especially in the coarser qualities; and they also compete in certain goods on the margin with England and America. From the European (not the British) point of view, it makes little difference whether European trade is lost within this region to Indian, Chinese, or to Japanese competition. From this and many other economic points of view the area is one.

To quote now the memorandum on cotton: "The shift in the consumption of cotton and in the production of yarn and cloth from the exporting countries of Europe to the great consuming markets in Asia has carried with it a reduction of world-trade in cotton goods . . . . the volume of the recorded trade in yarn has fallen by 23 per cent, and the trade in cotton piece goods by about 5 per cent. This loss has fallen mainly on the United Kingdom." Figures quoted in that work show that on

TABLE XXIII

BALANCES OF YARN AND PIECE GOODS EXPORTED BY CERTAIN COUNTRIES (IN THOUSANDS OF METRIC TONS)

| | 1913 | 1925 |
|---|---|---|
| | YARN | |
| United Kingdom | 90.1† | 82.1† |
| China | 162.2* | 24.6‡* |
| India | 70.4† | 6.5* |
| Japan | 46.9† | 55.3†§ |
| | PIECE GOODS | |
| United Kingdom | 576.1† | 376.5† |
| China | 180.6* | 127.3‡* |
| India | 249.4* | 116* |
| Japan | 2.5† | 103.2†§ |

* Export balance.
† Import balance.
‡ Figures for 1924.
§ Average, 1909–11.

an average in 1923–25 we exported only 76.5 per cent of the quantity of yarn exported by us in 1909–11. As an illustration of the severity of competition within the eastern area, India's exports for the same period for cotton yarn fell to only 18.9 per cent of her earlier figures, and Japan to 96.8 per cent. The explanation of the change is the rise of the Chinese spinning industry. France, Italy, and Belgium, however, increased their exports in the same period, though not necessarily in Far Eastern markets.

As a further illustration of the changes in trade, in piece goods the United Kingdom has only 68.8 per cent of her former trade, while Japan has 814.5 per cent, and the United States, Italy, France, and India all show increases. The changes are summarized in Table XXIII, showing the relative positions of these countries as exporters:

The losses in exports both of yarn and piece goods by the United Kingdom should be noted, also the change of India from the export to the import of yarn, and the great decline in the imports of yarn by China, and finally the remarkable increase in the piece goods exports of Japan. It must be remembered, however, that the figures for quantities exaggerate the actual loss of trade by Great Britain, as the losses have been mainly in the cheaper grades of goods, so that the loss in values is not so great.

It would, of course, be an error to attribute all the foregoing loss to the industrialization of the East, even in the cotton trade, but it is probably true that the present severe depression in the cotton industry in Lancashire is mainly due, apart from errors of finance, to the industrialization of the East. The situation, however, seems to have become stable, and the decline has been checked for the last four years. "The question with which Lancashire is now struggling is how to adjust an industry with heavy capital charges to a smaller production and at the same time maintain an export trade which depends on being able to compete in the world-markets with newer industries employing cheaper labor in eastern countries. The competition is mainly with the industries within the importing market itself."

We have taken the most striking instance of an industry directly affected by the industrialization of the Orient. The connection cannot be so definitely traced in other industries, and little is to be gained at the moment by attempting to do so. It must not be supposed that the losses due to the industrialization of the East really effect a great curtailment of British foreign trade as a whole. Our trade is well distributed; exports to the whole area of British India, the East Indies, French Indo-China, Siam, China, and Japan amounted to only about 22.5 per cent of our total exports in 1913, and of this India took 13.38 per cent. In 1923 the figures show China, Japan, and India taking 17.6 per cent as against 19 per cent in 1913. In other parts of the world we have made gains which offset our losses in cotton in the East, and we have increased our share of the world's trade since 1913 the figures for 1923 being: imports, 16.81 per cent, exports, 14.03 per cent of the world's international trade. In the same year the United States with two and a half times our population and thirty-two and a half times our area had imports, 14.54 per cent, exports 16.88 per cent. Her trade, however, was growing more rapidly than that of the United Kingdom.

### III. SOME CONSIDERATIONS WHICH EMERGE

Even a cursory examination of the foregoing descriptive material shows why it is necessary to write "considerations" where we would have wished to write "conclusions." Apart from the fact that this actual investigation, by unavoidable circumstances, was assigned only a short time before the delegation left England, the scope of the inquiry and the nature of the material make a conclusive descriptive study a prolonged and difficult task calling for the co-operation of a number of workers.

Our statement of the considerations which seemed to us of importance was prepared before we had the advantage of consulting the extremely valuable articles on the industrial revolution in the Far East by Dr. Condliffe in the *Economic Record*, especially that for May, 1927.

These should be read with our own statement of considerations, and we are happy to note a general convergence in point of view.

The separation between political and economic factors, always dangerous, is really misleading here. The future industrialization of the Orient and the effects on the world in general and of Europe in particular depend upon political factors. To take the most obvious instances, the industrialization of China waits on the development of security and a modern code and judicial administration. Its effects on international trade will be profoundly modified by tariff autonomy and the use made of that power. In considering those political questions, it is idle and misleading to ignore the economic interests involved on either side. It is earnestly to be hoped that some agreement will soon be reached on the political question, for, until it is reached, economic forecasting is really impossible and economic development difficult.

Assuming a settlement of these political questions, it appears that in China the limiting factors to the rate of industrialization for the immediate future will be transportation and finance. In this conclusion we have also assumed that the resources of China in coal and iron are sufficient to support a modern economy for herself and Japan, and that she can easily raise or import enough food. It is an assumption which should be closely examined, for it is by no means obviously true, and we understand that a contrary opinion is held in some well-informed quarters.

As the industrialization of the Orient is proceeding at present, it seems to be part of a world-wide change. Within the thin filaments of the nineteenth century world-economy based on territorial specialization in manufactures against raw materials and food, there are growing up new systems of trade complexes. The United States itself was one of the first of these to form. Such a complex is growing up on the Asiatic littoral from Persia to Japan. The chief components are India, China, and Japan, and the system as a whole is penetrated by trading connections with Europe, North America, and to a less degree with Australia and New Zealand. Within this system there is a growing national differentiation. Japan, free and powerful, is most advanced industrially. India is moving rapidly toward dominion status in the British Commonwealth of Nations, and already has fiscal freedom. China is more backward at present in all these aspects, but universally admitted to be on the threshold of development.

The growth of this system and its components has been marked in each part by changes in the foreign trade, in which trade Europe has hitherto played a very large part. This modification falls into three phases in its fullest development in Japan, but India and China are following the same general cycle of change.

In the first phase there is a slow increase in the quantity of exports, resulting from the penetration of persons and ideas along lines of communication. At the same time a demand slowly arises for certain of the coarser and simpler products of more advanced industrial countries, alongside of an earlier demand for a few luxuries or curiosities. Coarse cotton yarns afford the best example of this; they replace local spinning and often increase local handweaving for the time being. Later in this phase there is an increase in the importation of coarse woven goods. The value and volume of trade in this is not as great as in the later phases.

The second phase shows an increase in the variety of the imports and the beginning of simple textile machine industries to supply the home market and take advantage of the lower level of real wages in the less developed countries. Those parts of the area, in this case India and Japan, who move first into this stage develop an export trade to the less advanced parts. The European industries concerned have to avoid this competition by specializing on higher grades, and in new kinds of imports to meet new wants, the latter being made effective by the increased purchasing power of the Eastern peoples affected. A trade also develops in production goods, of which textile machinery is the best example. The fundamental heavy industries begin to be developed, usually under government encouragement.

In the third stage there is a diversification of industry in the Eastern country, which begins to manufacture miscellaneous articles the use of which it has learned from the West. Its advantage in labor costs is reduced in this phase, as the standard of living in the industrialized area grows faster than the efficiency of the labor increases. In this period the foreign trade continues to increase in amount, in value, and in variety; but its distribution between continents or political units changes, especially where the Eastern country has a policy of protection, as it will normally have. It is this third phase in which Japan finds herself today, while China is still in the second phase.

At the moment the industries of Europe are probably more affected by the inheritance of the post-war period of inflation and intensified nationalism than by the industrialization of the Orient. European industry has failed to keep pace with the remarkable developments in the United States, mainly because of the tariffs and administrative hindrances to trade which constitutes that heritage. Even in the Orient, if British trade in India is taken as typical, industrialization is not the only cause of the decline of trade. According to the survey of overseas markets, three-fifths of the loss may be attributed to diminished consumption, a quarter to increased local production, and about one-seventh to increased foreign competition. It is therefore impossible to say that the present check to European industries as a whole is the result of the industrialization of the Orient.

But in the Lancashire cotton industry it is possible to trace a direct connection between the industrialization of the Orient and the comparative stagnation of the industry, though even here factors of finance and organization must not be overlooked. And it appears probable that the compensation for losses here may have to be sought in other industries, though the resources of specialization in certain types of textile are not exhausted.

As to the relative shares of the European continents and the American continent in the growing trade of the Orient, the question is not of prime importance in the absence of any political unit corresponding to these geographical expressions. But it would appear likely, though we have not sufficient basis for a statistical forecast, that the larger share will go to America in the Pacific, though Europe should do better in the Indian Ocean. If there were any prospect of an economic United States of Europe the outlook would be changed. It seems likely, too, that the trade of this industrialized area in the Orient with Australia and New Zealand will increase relatively rapidly.

However the trade of the North Pacific and Indian Ocean littoral states may be divided between the economic systems in touch with it on the East, West, and South, there will most probably be an enormous extension of that trade both within the area and with the outside world. Increasing specialization resulting from competition must be expected both within the group and in the outer systems. We must also expect political tensions arising out of these relations, for we are witnessing a growth of nationalist feeling concurrently with this development of the monsoon lands and the East Indies. Whether that system will be self-sufficient in the main or not it is probably too soon to say.

It will not be necessary to remind this Conference that the reality behind the exciting struggles of national producing organizations is not so much the tension of competition in the market as the extension of the area and volume of the market and the gross increase of the wealth of the system as a whole. But it is necessary to rid our minds of all unconscious bias caused by the employment of the symbolism and vocabulary of warfare in these essentially different activities of international trade. If economic conditions are conceived in terms of war they are apt to cause wars, even if they are only tariff wars.

It is very possible that new nations will show the same short-sighted jealousy on the shores of the Pacific as the older models have shown in the Mediterranean and Atlantic basins. In its eagerness to secure all the possible gain for itself, each nation may forget that the gross increase in wealth depends more on half-conscious co-operation than on overconscious rivalry. It may confound the economic interpreters of history by yielding to a strange longing to go to war with its best customers.

Let us each make it clear through our proper channels of influence that the industrial and commercial development of the Orient does not involve any necessary loss for any nation, in Europe or elsewhere.

## SECTION 18

# CHINA'S INDUSTRIAL DEVELOPMENT

D. K. LIEU, F.R.S.A.
Bureau of Economic Research, Peking

Manufacturing industries in China may be classified according to their size and nature into three different kinds: (1) workshop industry, (2) cottage industry, and (3) modern factories. The first is the same as a workshop in medieval Europe, with its master-workman, journeyman, and apprentices. In some cases, however, it may have grown to such size that it is more like a modern factory than a medieval workshop, yet for one reason or another, it cannot be very well classified under (3). There may be more than one hundred workmen in one establishment, yet the shop is owned and operated by a master-workman, with no capitalistic proprietor nor manager who has not served apprenticeship in the trade himself. In some instances there may be such a proprietor, but the management is in the hands of a master-workman who has full power in running the business, without consultation with the proprietor, and who shares as much as a half of the profits. The proprietor and the master-workman are really partners, the former being a sleeping partner. Besides, the shop has no expensive labor-saving machinery, but the most important part of the manufacturing process involves special manual skill. Also, there is no power plant, although electric power may be rented from a local company. Under such conditions the shop has certainly outgrown the size of the medieval establishment and may have a few departments each with a score or more workmen, yet the mere size of it will not put it in the same category as modern factories.

By cottage industry is meant such manufacturing as is carried on in the homes of the workers. Members of the same family are usually engaged in the same trade, although sometimes the husband may be employed in a factory or workshop while the wife and children carry on the cottage industry themselves, such as the making of lace, hair nets, or knitted goods. The number of workers in such a manufacturing unit is necessarily small, generally smaller than that in a workshop, yet sometimes relatives and friends may gather under one roof to work together, thus converting the home into something like a small workship. The raw materials are often obtained from factories or commission merchants, who pay for the work at piece rate and dispose of the products when finished. In such cases the workers are really employees of these factories or merchants, though the work is carried on in their own homes. Match factories, for instance, usually have the match boxes made in the workers' homes, with material supplied by the factories, and this arrangement saves floor space in the factories and is convenient to both parties where the work needs no supervision. In other cases the cottage manufacturers also produce on their own account and dispose of the products at market places to retail shops or along the streets. All peddlers of toys and other simple products are of this class.

From the considerations in the first paragraph we may define a modern factory as an industrial establishment which is not owned or managed by a master-workman, but which has expensive modern machinery with, perhaps, a modern power plant. Many people may not agree to this definition, and I am not unaware of the fact that factories are often classified according to the number of workmen in them. In fact, the provisional Chinese factory regulations of March 29, 1923, also define a factory as an industrial establishment employing more than one hundred laborers. Still, for the purpose of the present article, and perhaps for Chinese economic studies in general, the distinction based on the nature of the management and the utilization of machinery is more useful, as workshops so classified have more features in common with each other than with modern factories. Concerning machinery, it may even be convenient to draw the line arbitrarily at $10,000 yuan (Chinese silver dollar) as the minimum cost of the plant of a modern factory, because many small workshops organized along old-fashioned lines are now equipped with modern lathes and presses, but they do not exceed a few thousand dollars altogether. Good illustrations of modern factories in China are steam filatures, cotton mills, and the so-called machine flour mills (as distinguished from old-fashioned mills which grind flour with millstones operated by mules or electricity).

## CHINESE HANDICRAFT INDUSTRY

Some concrete instances illustrating the conditions in these three kinds of manufacturing units will show the industrial development of China more clearly than any number of general statements. The fur and leather business of Hsuanhwa may first be described as an example of the workshop industry. There were over sixty shops in the business in that locality at the time of investigation by this Bureau (September, 1925), employing about 5,600 men. The largest had 140 laborers; five others had more than a hundred, but the majority of the comparatively large firms employed between 40 and 80. Although the business had long been established in Hsuanhwa, the laborers are mostly natives of another district. They are engaged only for a part of the year, from seven to nine months. Those who scrape the skin—an important part of the manufacturing process—need have the highest skill and are paid the highest wages; those who cut the skin into the proper sizes come next; and those who comb the fur, last. The scraping is done with a brush made of the stems of *kaoliang* (sorghum). While wet, the inside of the skin is covered with fine sand so that whatever flesh remains on it takes on the sand and becomes stiff, when it can be easily scraped off with a spade-like knife. The fur is cleaned with an iron comb, and then beaten with a slender cane to remove dust and particles of earth. Drying is done in the sunshine, and soaking process is carried on in a wooden vessel, 3½ feet high and from 4 to 5½ feet in diameter. In it is a paste made of ingredients mixed with the hand, and when the skins have been soaked for a fixed number of days in the paste, they are taken out, each piece being taken by two men who shake it until no particle of the paste remains on the fur. All other work is also done by hand, with the help of simple hand tools. The largest demand is for fur rugs, which comes mostly from foreign exporters. The foreign firms of Shanghai began to buy them as early as 1882, and Tientsin merchants appeared in the market in 1891. Even in the latter year the number of furriers in Hsuanhwa did not exceed ten. Then it suddenly increased to over twenty some two years later, and over fifty in 1915. The trade received a set-back during the great war, the number falling to thirty in 1916 and 1917. In 1920 recovery began, and in 1922 there were forty-three shops producing coarse furs, including rugs, valued at $490,000, and sixty-one shops produced $1,600,000 worth of fur in the year following. Divided by 5,600, it meant an average annual production of $285 per laborer.

Another workshop industry which is of even greater importance is porcelain manufacturing in Kingtehchen, Kiangsi. No one today can tell exactly when porcelain ware was first used in China. As far as can be ascertained from classical literature, the word *tse*, which now stands for porcelain, first appeared in an essay by Pan Yueh, a well known writer of the Chin dynasty (265–419 A.D.). The name of Changanchen, now Kingtehchen, appeared in history as a porcelain manufacturing center as early as the sixth century A.D., but some people are inclined to believe that modern porcelain was first made in the reign of Wu Teh (618–627 A.D.), of the Tang dynasty, when an inhabitant of this town presented to the Emperor a collection of "jadelike *tse*." During the reign of Cheng Tsung (998–1022 A.D.), of the North Sung dynasty, every piece of porcelain intended for the court was engraved with the characters "King Teh," which was the reigning title of the said Emperor. Through this association, the famous porcelain manufacturing center of Changanchen assumed its present name. Whether the Sung emperors had official kilns at Kingtehchen, historians did not make clear; but it is certain that there were no such kilns in the Yuan or Mongol dynasty, although private kilns already existed in large numbers. In the second year of Hung Wu (1369 A.D.), of the Ming dynasty, what were known as official kilns (*kuan-yao*) were first established at the foot of the Chushan Hill, near the town, to turn out porcelain wares exclusively for the imperial house. The industry reached the highest development during the following reigns, but declined toward the end of the dynasty. A fresh impetus was received in the early part of the Manchu dynasty, but again there was a set-back toward the end of the last century, when all the imperial kilns of former ages were left in ruins. In this town and its neighborhood there were only a little over one hundred private kilns, producing porcelain of ordinary grade. Although efforts have been made by both dealers and manufacturers to revive the industry under the Republic, and a few modern kilns were constructed there, their efforts were not crowned with success. The principal reasons are: (1) lack of transportation facilities between Kingtehchen and the outside markets, (2) lack of adequate capital on the part of the manufacturers, and (3) lack of close co-operation between the manufacturers and the dealers.

Porcelain clay is obtained in the neighboring quarries. About 10,000 diggers, breakers, and washers are engaged in preparing it for the kilns, but they still follow time-honored methods, and the clay is not ground to such fine particles as to suit foreign manufacturers. Proposals have recently been made to use modern machinery in this connection, but insufficient capital prevents their execution. Another separate class of manufacturers are the makers of the saggers, who numbered two hundred in

May, 1926, at the time of the investigation by the Bureau. A sagger-maker's workshop consists generally of a thatched hut, equipped with a variety of revolving discs or potter's wheels and wooden rings of different sizes. The average monthly output of each shop is about $400 worth of unfired saggers. Although apprentices serve terms of 4 or 5 years, the trade does not take much time to learn, and they are generally put on regular work after a short training. A mixture of two or more kinds of clay is reduced to a "slip" in large earthenware vessels, where it is thoroughly stirred with a wooden spade, and the fluid is removed to another vessel and filtered through a horse-hair sieve of great fineness. Then it is evaporated, yielding a fine clay, which is kneaded with a spade and later with the hand to produce the desired consistency. In making wares from the clay two different methods are used, one of which consists of throwing it on a potter's wheel where the workman shapes it with his hands into various kinds of shallow round vessels like dishes, plates, and bowls. Cylindrical, square, and hexagonal wares are made by building up the articles from a mass of clay, adding with the hand a piece here and removing one there until the desired shape is obtained. Glazing is done by brushing with a writing brush, blowing with a brass blow-pipe, or shaking the ware in a solution of glazing material. When fairly dry they are enclosed in saggers and fired in old-fashioned, vertical-type kilns, which look like huge cylinders lying horizontally on the ground. They are over 10 feet in diameter and about 30 feet long. They open at one end, and the chimneys, about 30 feet high, are at the other. Four classes of workmen are engaged at the kilns: (1) the porcelain placers who place the unfired wares into the saggers, (2) the sagger-placers who place the saggers in the kiln, (3) the firemen and (4) the drawers, who draw out the wares from the kiln after firing. All these processes need much skill, for the men must know where there is the highest temperature in the kiln, whether the firing should be "intense," "slow," or "open," how the saggers must be placed so as to suit the different kinds of clay, etc., lest the breakage of some saggers spoil the whole charge. Usually the burning of one charge of a kiln takes about 36 hours, and it is attended by thirteen or fourteen workmen of all four classes. As many porcelain manufacturers in Kingtehchen have no kilns, they often rent spaces in the kilns of others. The rent varies according to the nature, size, and other particulars of the biscuits, but they are definitely fixed by custom which no kiln owner can alter. Further glazing and decoration are done in still another set of workships, known as *hungtien*. Thus there are four classes of manufacturers in this industry: the producers of porcelain clay, the sagger-makers, the porcelain manufacturers, and the *hungtien*. The finished wares are sold to exporters at Kingtehchen through commission houses, and then distributed all over the country.

Although workshops prevail in indigenous industries which have not been affected by modern methods, some simple modern industries have been introduced into China and are carried on in the shops. Some of the Chinese laborers who returned from France after the great war and who learned something about modern machinery over there have opened small workships to manufacture machine parts and small machines. There are quite a few of them in Peking turning out knitting machines, small lathes, etc. The raw material is often imported, as are certain parts which they cannot manufacture or which can be bought cheaper from abroad, such as the knitting needles.

Modern bathroom boilers are also mostly products of similar workships. Such shops are usually owned and managed by a master-workman, although the work is not a handicraft, and they therefore constitute a cross between the old-fashioned workshop and the modern factory.[1]

### COTTAGE INDUSTRY

The manufacturing of knitted hosiery in certain localities illustrates another kind of Chinese industry—the cottage industry. In Pinghu, Chekiang, there were at the beginning of 1926 over 10,000 knitting machines producing approximately $4,-000,000 worth of hosiery. The industry was first introduced into that locality in about 1910, when it was not found anywhere in China except Shanghai. A Pinghu merchant named Kao saw the possibilities of the industry and bought some ten knitting machines from Shanghai and started business in his own town. Although the machines were then all imported, and cost $100 silver apiece, Kao was able to market his products at lower prices than imported hosiery, and gradually he expanded his factory by the addition of more machines, until in 1926 it possessed 1,000 of them, and was the largest factory in Pinghu. At first the female hands work in the factory, but as demand for its products grows very rapidly and the factory has no adequate space to take in more laborers, arrangement is made for the distribution of the machines to the laborers in their homes. The raw material—yarn—is also supplied by the factory, and for one catty of yarn supplied the laborer must turn in also one catty of knitted stockings. The wages are from 22 to 26 cents per dozen pairs, but the laborers must pay a monthly rent of $2 for the machine. At the beginning, a deposit of $8 must be made with the factory as a bond for the machine, for repairing which the factory, and not the laborer, is responsible. As the cost of the machine is now only $20, the $2 monthly rent is very profitable to the factory, and one having a thousand machines will derive $2,000 a month from this source alone. On the part of the laborers the arrangement is also agreeable. They can attend to their household duties while earning their living, and as an average worker can knit one dozen pairs every day, the monthly income, even after deducting the machine rent, would amount to about $5, fair earnings for a woman at home, especially as it takes so little time to learn the work. The industry also flourishes in Kashing, Kashan, Shihmen, and Kiashih, all of Chekiang Province, not far from Pinghu. Similar conditions exist around Foochow, Fukien Province.

Another example of cottage industry is cloth weaving, in and around Kaoyang, Chihli. In fact this is the place where the idea of renting out machines to laborers working in their own homes was first introduced. In 1902 some local gentry imported a few modern looms from Tientsin and started weaving cloth in imitation of imported varieties. The largest factory was Ho Kee, established in 1910 with a capital of $20,000. As its business began to grow it bought more and more looms, but kept only eight of them in the factory, the rest being all rented out. In 1913, when the Chihli Commercial Museum made an industrial survey of the province, it was found that Ho Kee factory had 200 looms rented out, producing about one hundred pieces of cloth every day. When a special investigator of this Bureau visited the district last

[1] When not stated otherwise, the information is taken from investigations of the Bureau of Economic Information.

August, the estimated total production of cloth reached at least $2,000,000 a year. The indusry was almost entirely carried on by farmers when they were not occupied with land cultivation, while in the five small factories then existing there were only some forty looms. The district has 144 villages, with a total population of 130,000, of which, it is said, about 90 per cent is engaged in the weaving industry. Cotton yarn is imported from Tientsin on junks along the Chulungho River to Tungkowchen, 30 li from Kaoyang, whence it is conveyed by mule carts to the district. When manufactured into cloth, it is carted to Potowchen on the Tientsin-Pukow railway and then shipped to Shangtung by train, or carted to Paoting on the Peking-Hankow railway, and then shipped to Peking, Kalgan, Shansi, Suiyuan, Honan, Shensi, Hupeh, and Mongolia. The industry is one of the largest in the province, and it has extended to the surrounding districts, as Jenchiu, Wenan, etc.

Somewhat different from the knitting industry of Pinghu and the weaving industry of Kaoyang is the artificial flower industry of Peking. According to an investigation made by this Bureau last June, there were about 1,500 families engaged in the making of such flowers, and they all lived along the Flower Market Street and the Second, Third, and Fourth avenues outside Hatamen. The street is so called because all buyers and sellers of paper and silk flowers gather near its east end at 6 o'clock every morning. These families bring their products to the market and sell them there, unless the products are made to the order of the small flower firms, of which there were about 130. With only a few workmen and apprentices, these firms manufacture and sell flowers in much the same way as the private families, although they sometimes obtain orders from outport purchasers and share them with the latter. Different kinds of flowers as well as different parts of a flower are often made by different families, each specializing in one line. The leaves are manufactured by another set of workers, the paper-wrapped wires used as flower stems are prepared by still another, and the bone hairpin, to which the flowers were attached when worn by ladies as hair ornaments, are made by special workships at Tamochang, which specialize in bone articles of all kinds. Indian silk, damask, silk waste, cloth, Chinese, and Japanese paper, araliaceoe (*Tungtsao*), paraffin, wheat flour, copper and iron wire, peacock feather, imitation silver thread, cotton, sawdust, and many kinds of native and imported dyes are among the raw materials used in this industry.

The chief difference between this and the Pinghu cottage industry is that here the working families are entirely independent of any factory or workship, although they may, when they choose, take orders from it. In the Pinghu industry the laborers are really employees of the factories and paid by them at piece rate, in spite of the fact that they work at home. In the Peking flower industry the workers buy their own raw materials and tools and dispose of the products at the market themselves. They are able to do so, perhaps, because the tools are simple and inexpensive and the raw materials can be bought from the local stores in small quantities. In Kaoyang there are also many independent families selling their own products at the local cloth market, and the conditions are therefore a combination of both Pinghu and Peking.

### MODERN FACTORIES

The third kind of industrial unit in China is the modern factory. As an example of this the cotton mill is perhaps the most important, as the cotton-spinning industry is now the largest modern industry in China. According to the latest statistical table of the Chinese Cotton Mill Owners' Association, which was for 1925, there were in that year 118 mills with 3,414,062 spindles in operation and a total capitalization of about $288,000,000. As far as could be ascertained, at least 720,000,000 pounds of yarn were produced in that year. The beginning of this modern industry was in 1890, when the well-known Viceroy Li Hung-Chang first established a cotton-spinning mill in Shanghai, with 65,000 spindles and 600 looms. A little later the weaving mill was burned down, and the government was reluctant to invest more money in the industry. The spinning plant was sold to a private company specially organized for the purpose, and was re-named Hua Sheng Cotton Mill. Since the conclusion of the

TABLE I

| Year | No. of Mills | Spindles | Looms | Approximate Total Capitalization |
|---|---|---|---|---|
| 1910*.......... | 23 | 587,646 | 3,066 | |
| 1918*.......... | 34 | 997,238 | 5,438 | $ 25,640,000§ |
| 1919†.......... | 29 | 659,752 | 2,650 | |
| 1920.......... | 37 | 856,894 | 4,540 | |
| 1921.......... | 51 | 1,238,902 | 6,650 | 90,130,000‖ |
| 1922.......... | 64 | 1,593,034 | 9,817 | |
| 1923.......... | 54 | 1,493,672 | 8,581 | |
| 1924.......... | 58 | 1,650,004 | 10,461 | |
| 1925‡.......... | 69 | 1,593,034 | 16,381 | 136,980,000¶ |

* Mills in Kiangsu only, but including both Chinese and foreign.

† Chinese-owned mills in all China, according to the statistics of the Chinese Cotton Mill Owners' Association.

‡ Not including four mills being installed.

§ Taels 14,689,000, $1,950,000, and Yen 9,000,000.

‖ Taels 31,685,000 and $45,770,800.

¶ Taels 46,215,000 and $72,280,000.

Sino-Japanese Treaty of 1896, foreigners obtained the right of establishnig factories in Chinese treaty ports, and the cotton mills of Jardine Matheson, Lao Kung Mow (both British), and Jui Kee (German) came into existence one after another. By 1896 there were nine mills in Shanghai and Wusih, of which the more important ones of Chinese ownership were Hua Sheng, Ta Shun, Yu Yuan (Shanghai), and Yeh Ching (Wusih). Su Lun, of Soochow, and Ta Sen, of Nantung, followed, while Ta Shun was soon sold to the Japanese and became Mill No. 1 of the Shanghai Cotton Manufacturing Company—the first instance of the purchase of Chinese mills by foreign interests.

After the Russo-Japanese War came to an end, cotton piece goods found a good market in Manchuria, and the cotton mills were induced to instal more looms to supply the demand, thereby utilizing also their own yarn in a more profitable manner. By 1908 there were already 23 mills in Kiangsu alone, with 587,646 spindles and 3,066 looms. In 1918 the number increased to 34, with 997,238 spindles and 5,438 looms. The total capitalization was about $35,000,000. The growth of the industry is shown in Table I.

During and immediately after the European war there was a great boom to the cotton industry of China because the supply of European yarn and piece goods was very much curtailed, if not entirely suspended. Many new mills were established by Chinese merchants, and a large number of spindles was being installed every year. A set-back occurred in 1923, when, instead of an increase, there was a decrease in the number of mills, spindles as well as looms, due to the closing down of some and the transfer of others to foreign companies. However, 1925 had more mills, spindles, and looms than 1922, and 1926 showed further progress, so far as Shanghai and Paoshan were concerned.

At first only very low counts of yarn were produced by Chinese mills, and none above 20's. Later new mills began to spin 32 and higher counts, although the majority of mills even now still produce coarse yarn. For such purposes Chinese and Indian cotton are quite well adapted, but for fine yarn American cotton, sometimes mixed with the indigenous Chinese variety, is generally used. The cultivation of a few American species on Chinese soil has been experimented with for some years, the Southeastern University of Nanking having done much, in distributing American seeds to Chinese farmers, to encourage their cultivation. Unfortunately, they produce good results only for a couple of years, and in the third or fourth year the cotton yielded is of about the same quality as the indigenous variety. In Chihli the farmers would not raise American cotton because the harvesting season is late and local time-honored custom allows anybody to pick cotton after the regular harvesting season of the indigenous species. Recently the Chinese mills are making use more and more of Indian cotton, which is much cheaper than that of America. As the former can be ginned only in English machines, it accounts for the installation of these machines in Shanghai and Tientsin mills during the last year or two.

As Shanghai is the principal center of the cotton industry, so it is also that of machine-milled flour. There are more flour mills in Shanghai than any other city, and the first mill, Tsen Yu, was established there by Germans in 1886. Foo Feng (1000), Hwa Hsin (1902), Li Ta (1906), and Sen Ta (1906) followed, and at about the same time the first Mow Sing Mill was established in Wusih, another important flour-milling center, as well as wheat market. Fu Sin (1900) is the first flour mill of Nantung, the home of the late industrial magnate, Chang Chien, and so far as can be ascertained, Hankow had its first mill in 1905—the Ho Feng Mill of joint Chinese and British ownership. Shwang Ho Shen, the oldest Chinese mill in Harbin, in the center of a large wheat belt, was established in 1908, and there are many Russian mills in North, and Japanese in South, Manchuria. Although Tientsin had eight mills toward the end of 1926, it did not make an early start, as the first mill—the Shou Hsin Flour Mill—was organized by Sino-Japanese interests as late as 1915. In 1919 it was affected by the anti-Japanese boycott, and the mill was closed up until 1925, when it was reorganized with purely Chinese capital under the name San Tsin Shou Feng. Tsinan is another milling center with ten mills (the number in existence when the city was visited by an investigator of this Bureau in 1924).

According to the same person, who compiled a list of flour mills in China in 1924 from books, newspaper reports, as well as personal investigation, there were in that year 116 mills capitalized at approximately $15,000,000 altogether, and having a daily producing capacity of about 39,453 piculs (of 100 catties or 133⅓ pounds). Besides the localities already mentioned, there were mills at Ningguta, Aigun, Lungtsingchun, Kirin, Changchun, Fushun, Szepingkai, Dairen, Liaoyang (all in Manchuria), Peking, Tatung (Shansi), Chefoo, Tsingtao, Tsining (all in Shantung), Kaifeng, Sinhsiang (both in Honan), Chengtu, Chungking (both in Szechwan), Changsha (Hunan), Kishui, Shasi (both in Hupeh), Wuhu (Anhwei), Haichow, Taichow, Kaoyu, Chinkiang, Tsingkiangpu, and Nanhwei (all in Kiangsu), and Yunnanfu (Yunnan). The list is admittedly incomplete, yet it includes most of the important Chinese mills and gives an idea of the total capitalization and producing capacity. It may be safely presumed that the actual figures are higher than those just given. Year-to-year statistics, like those of cotton mills, are not available.

The development of the industry depends very much on the supply of raw material. Tientsin, Harbin, Hankow, Wusih, etc., have become milling centers because they are centers of distribution for Chinese wheat. The wheat of North Manchuria is the best, and that of Shantung next, according to a Chinese authority. The product of northern Kiangsu, especially the region around Hsuchow, is comparatively hard, because the soil is not very well adapted to wheat production. Hankow wheat is also inferior to that of North China, and has the same defect as that of Kiangsu. Because Wusih is an important wheat market, Shanghai mills sometimes refuse to buy local wheat, but may be deceived into buying the same as Wusih wheat when it is first shipped to that city, where it is mixed with some low-grade wheat of Nanking or northern Kiangsu, and shipped back again to Shanghai. The machinery of these mills is nearly all supplied by American firms.

In Tientsin the wheat comes from Chihli, Shantung, Honan, and Manchuria. Some mills send purchasing agents to the producing centers, while others buy from the local cereal markets, of which there are two, at Sichi and Peichi, respectively. All wheat transported by junks along the Yu Ho River is concentrated at the former, and all by junks along the West River or by train along the Peking-Mukden railway, at the latter. There are five grades of wheat, but 100 catties of the average grade will yield 78 catties of flour, of which 70 per cent is of first grade, 10 per cent second, and 20 per cent third and fourth grades combined. The principal markets of Tientsin flour, outside of the city itself, are Peking and Tongshan, although great quantities are also sent to Jehol. Since the appearance of the modern mills in Tientsin the old-fashioned hand mills have gradually died out. There were over 400 workshops in this industry before 1916, with over 2,000 millstones, but last year their number had decreased to less than 200, and they had between them only 600 or 700 millstones. They now produce flour of corn, millet, bean; and kaoliang, instead of wheat and electric power, has taken the place of mules and horses. The eight modern mills consume every day about 10,000 sacks of wheat, each weighing 160 catties, and about 30,000 bales of flour (each weighing 49 pounds) are sold daily on the local market, of which about a half is the product of these modern mills.

Like the cotton mills, the Tientsin flour mills have gone over from the "foreman system" to the "supervisor system." When modern factories were established in China the managers did not know how to deal with the laborers, and they were generally hired through the foremen, who had full power of employing or dismissing the men as he liked. Now graduates of middle and vocational schools, who have learned something about the working of the machines, are employed as supervisors, and hands are hired directly by the management and put under their supervision. Many of these young men are intelligent, understand some English terms of machinery, and know the process. They also treat the laborers with more consideration than the former foremen, and it is very regrettable to find that most foreign-owned mills in China still persist in the old system of contract labor, which has caused many strikes during the last few years through the arrogance of the foremen toward the laborers. As is generally the case, the modern Tientsin mills do not supply food and lodging to the laborers as part of their wage payments, as in the old-fashioned workshops, although one of them at least maintains a restaurant from which the laborers may buy their own food. Apprentices are still kept in these mills.

### RAILWAYS AND INDUSTRIAL DEVELOPMENT

Among the factors that promote industrial development in China, railways are one of the most important. For instance, Chowkiakow, Honan, was formerly a very important trading center in the country, but now Chengchow has taken its place because it is at the juncture of the Peking-Hankow and Lung-Hai railways. Hsuchow, Kiangsu, where the Lung-Hai crosses the Tientsin-Pukow railway, has, due to the same reasons, superseded Tsingkiangpu on the Grand Canal as the leading town in northern Kiangsu. Although Tsinkiangpu is the northern terminus of steamship lines that navigate the Canal, the Lung-Hai railway does not pass through the town, and there is little hope of future development. On the other hand, if a good harbor is constructed at Haichow, the eastern terminus of that railway, now that the railway has reached the coast, that city may easily rival Nantung or Wusih of southern Kiangsu, if not Shanghai itself. The development of Shihkiachwang, at the juncture of the Peking-Hankow and Chengting Taiyuan railways, formerly a small market town, is another good example of the influence of railways on industrial development.

As special investigators have been twice sent to Tsinan, Shantung, by the Bureau, a more detailed account of its industrial development through the influence of railways will be here given. During the first visit, in the latter part of 1924, when a very careful study was made of industries in particular, there were forty-eight comparatively large Chinese factories devoted to the manufacturing of cotton yarn, beet sugar, paper, flour, matches, soap, vegetable oil, sewing needles, glass, bricks and tiles, enameled ware, cement, dyestuffs, leather, straw hats, hair nets, and knitted hosiery. The earliest of the then existing factories was an oil press established in 1909, while most of the others have come into existence since the Republic. It seems that wheat flour, leather tanning, matches, and paper manufacturing are among the earlier industries that had a foothold in that city, the first factories in these lines having been established before 1916. Straw hats and hair nets were also manufactured at an early date, but these are chiefly due to the influence of foreign trade, and will be discussed more fully in that connection. There were nine flour mills with a total capitalization of $5,900,000, not including one which is a branch of a Wusih mill. Tsinan would have had its share of cotton mills also if monopoly privileges had not been granted to the mill now in existence which prohibits the establishment of another mill within a radius of 30 li for 20 years. And all this industrial development has been due to the fact that the city is at the junction of the Tsingtao-Tsinan and Tientsin-Pukow railways. The former was completed in 1902, and the latter in 1911. The influence of the latter, which is a trunk line traversing four provinces, is much greater than that of the former, hence the more rapid developments since its completion.

The second conspicuous factor in China's industrial development is her foreign trade. This has three different aspects, which must be dealt with separately. In the first place, it is responsible for the industrial development of the treaty ports, which are the centers of foreign trade. Two generations ago Shanghai was little more than a fishing town, but today it has a population of approximately 1,500,000, and is the first industrial city of the country. At the same time about 40 per cent of China's foreign trade passes through Shanghai,[2] and in shipping tonnage it ranks among the first five ports of the whole world. The growth of foreign trade of Tientsin during

TABLE II

| Year | Total Tientsin Trade | Total Hankow Trade | Total Dairen Trade |
|---|---|---|---|
| 1925 | 287,704 | 288,761 | 273,709 |
| 1924 | 251,695 | 282,450 | 240,672 |
| 1923 | 238,407 | 239,745 | 230,549 |
| 1922 | 244,516 | 206,105 | 220,010 |
| 1921 | 224,779 | 173,546 | 210,431 |
| 1920 | 173,482 | 169,951 | 203,773 |
| 1919 | 189,775 | 200,398 | 210,748 |
| 1918 | 153,138 | 165,162 | 165,824 |
| 1917 | 142,360 | 170,730 | 135,945 |

the last few years has been very steady, and the port became a very close competitor of Hankow and Dairen for second place, Shanghai being always the first. Table II gives total trade figures (in 1,000 Haikwan taels) of Tientsin for the last nine years, compared with those of Hankow and Dairen.

From 1917 to 1919 the trade of Tientsin gradually increased, but there was a set-back in 1920, yet the set-back was even greater for Hankow, and during that year and the two following Tientsin got ahead of the latter port. There was another set-back in 1923, due to the Japanese earthquake, and then steady increase again. Turning now from foreign trade to industries, we find, according to the investigation of the Bureau, that the number of comparatively large factories established in Tientsin during the same nine years was as follows:

| | | | | | |
|---|---|---|---|---|---|
| 1925 | 5 | 1922 | 2 | 1919 | 6 |
| 1924 | 3 | 1921 | 10 | 1918 | 4 |
| 1923 | 4 | 1920 | 5 | 1917 | 2 |

The largest number of factories were therefore established in 1921, the year when foreign trade recorded the largest increase, namely, 50,000,000 taels. The increase of trade in 1919 over that of 1918 was the second largest, and in that year the increase of industrial establishments was also the second largest. There was a decrease in the number of new factories from 1919 to 1920, corresponding to the set-

[2] 41.9 per cent in 1924 and 42.4 per cent in 1925.

back in foreign trade. Similarly, other correspondences may be found for the years 1922–25, although there were more new factories in 1923 than were justifiable by trade developments, but they were probably brought into existence on account of the prosperous trade of the previous year, and at least the two flour mills established in that year were known to have been promoted in 1922. Three of the five cotton mills were installed in 1921, while of the nine flour mills, four were really organized during the flourishing trade period covering 1921 and 1922.[3]

The second aspect of the influence of foreign trade on industrial development is its effect on articles for export. The influence here is very direct, foreign demand being responsible for greater production, and greater production usually, if not always, means the establishment of more workshops and factories. The large number of bean-oil presses in Manchuria is a good proof of this statement. The rise of steam silk filatures in Shanghai is yet another. In Shantung the foreign demand for lace, strawbraid, and hair nets had resulted in the growth of three flourishing industries over a large part of the province, until the demand fell off in recent years, when these industries also waned. The fur industry of Suanhwa, described near the beginning of this paper, is also dependent to a great extent on the foreign market. In fact, there are quite a few articles of manufacture which would hardly be of any significance were it not for the demand in foreign countries. In recent years, however, as the Chinese people gradually take on foreign habits, a domestic demand is created for some of these articles, but this will be discussed under the next heading.

## FOREIGN TRADE AND CHINESE INDUSTRIES

Some very conspicuous instances of domestic demand for goods manufactured in imitation of imported articles are matches, cigarettes, canned food, cement, and knitted hosiery. Previous to intercourse with foreign countries there were no matches of the modern type, and flint and iron were the common means of ignition. But since the introduction of modern matches the flint and iron outfit has practically disappeared from cities and towns, and even in rural districts people prefer the matches. The Tan Hwa match factory of Peking, for instance, sells good matches in boxes to urbanites, and those that are partly broken, or otherwise not in good form, to dealers at so much a catty (measure of weight), and the dealers in turn sell them to the farmers at so many matches a copper. In Changsha special sulphur matches are manufactured for the farmers in the interior of the province, who still prefer these to ordinary matches. There are in China at present, so far as can be ascertained from the Bureau's records, 134 match factories and 15 factories making sticks, boxes, and other accessories.

Although China produces good raw material for making cement, such an article was never manufactured before it was imported, but a mixture of clay and lime was used for most construction purposes where cement is now used. Gradually the Chinese learned to appreciate the superior qualities of the latter, and now there are at least fifteen cement factories in China, of which Chee Hsin, at Tongshan, Chihli, is the oldest and largest. Of canned-food factories there are about 30, and they have been instrumental in preserving certain perishable goods which would otherwise have been

[3] Of course the number of factories is too small to make the conclusions final.

wasted. Changli, Chihli, for instance, produces large quantities of fruits, especially pears, but much had been left to rot on the trees before the Sing Chung canning factory was established. Now they are preserved in cans and marketed in Peking, Tientsin, and even far-away Shanghai.

At first the Chinese would not smoke cigarettes, because they were accustomed to smoking tobacco in pipes. A foreign importer of Shanghai (said to be the Mustard Company) started an "educational" campaign by distributing cigarettes free on the streets and having Chinese employees smoke them in the presence of other Chinese. Gradually the latter took to this form of smoking, and nowadays there is no place in China where one cannot find cigarettes on sale. The largest manufacturing company in the country is the British-American Tobacco Company, while the Chinese concern, Nanyang Brothers, runs a close second. Some forty other Chinese and foreign factories are found in various parts of the country, mostly in Shanghai, although there are some in such interior provinces as Shansi and Yunnan. The first two companies distribute American tobacco seeds to the farmers of Shantung, Honan, Anhwei, and other tobacco-producing provinces, and the industry has become more and more indigenous to the land. Of knitted hosiery much has already been said in connection with the cottage industries.

In order to encourage such manufactures, especially on the part of Chinese themselves, the government has regulations which exempt all machine-made articles in imitation of imported goods, generally called "factory products," or *chi-chih-yang-ho* from all likin levies, after having paid a tax of 5 per cent. This measure has produced good results, as will be further discussed under likin. When, for one reason or another, a boycott is declared by the people against some foreign nation, these Chinese factory products, as well as imports from other countries, are also much benefited. In fact, this was how the Hangchow umbrella industry gained its foothold. In 1908, on account of a dispute concerning a Japanese ship named "Er-chen-wan," there was a widespread boycott against Japanese goods. The urban population at that time used imported umbrellas, mostly from Japan, but the boycott made these very unpopular, and a small manufacturer of Chinese paper umbrellas in Hangchow whose workshop is named Sun Yuan Hsin, took this opportunity to improve his products to supplant the Japanese goods. The umbrellas were made smaller and lighter, hooked handles were substituted for the former straight ones, and the flowery designs on the paper were also improved. They immediately became very popular, many other manufacturers followed suit, and these improved paper umbrellas were marketed in many Yangtze provinces. At present there are about twenty manufacturers in Hangchow engaged in their production, making use of Fuyang (in Chekiang Province) bamboo for the ribs, and paper of eastern Chekiang districts for the shade. Later the Ming Sing and Sing Ya factories were also established, which manufactured silk and cloth umbrellas after foreign patterns, with steel ribs imported from Germany. Kaoyang cloth, referred to before in connection with the cottage industries, became popular also on account of a boycott against Japan in 1915, as a reaction to the Twenty-one Demands made by that country.

Some statistical data concerning the exportation of Chinese factory products are illustrative of the growth of such industries. Since 1921 the customs reports show the value of these products exported, and the increases in the following years are remarkable. The statistics follow:

| | Haikwan taels |
|---|---|
| 1921 | 3,724,813 |
| 1922 | 5,091,302 |
| 1923 | 12,145,616 |
| 1924 | 18,810,291 |
| 1925 | 15,378,913 |

The decrease in 1925 was probably due to the withdrawal of these products from the export trade to supply the domestic demand, as well as to the numerous strikes in Shanghai since the May 30th incident, which affected Chinese mills also. Exportation of cotton yarn fell from taels 7,500,000 to 3,700,000, and the decrease of cotton piece goods of various kinds totaled approximately taels 600,000. The other important factory products exported are socks, towels, gunny bags, candles, cement, electric lamps, machine-milled flour, soap, wood pulp, musical instruments, and matches. The exportation of the last article reached in 1923, when the industry was at its height, the value of taels 1,289,152. Although some of the factories are owned and operated by foreigners, the growing popularity of such "factory products" and the increasing quantities exported constitute the third important aspect of the influence of foreign trade on industrial development in China.

### OTHER FACTORS PROMOTING INDUSTRIAL DEVELOPMENT

Besides modern communications and foreign trade, three other factors have had much influence on China's industrial development. One is the availability of raw material, which explains the growth of the flour and bean-oil mills in Manchuria, the silk filatures and silk-weaving mills in Kiangsu and Chekiang, the iron works and wood-oil refineries in Hankow, the glass factories near Poshan, Shantung, the cane-sugar industry of Kwangtung, the vegetable-dyestuff industry of Kiangsi, etc. A second is the availability of skilled labor, which is particularly important where the industry is of a handicraft nature. The rug industry flourished in Peking because some Tibetan rug-makers first taught the art to Peking artisans, and it took a long time before the industry began to prosper there. Now, on account of the better facilities for foreign trade at Tientsin, the center of the rug industry has practically shifted to the latter city. For the same reasons concerning skilled labor, the cloisonné and artificial-flower industries have been confined to the national capital, and only recently Shanghai merchants offered very high wages to engage artificial flower makers from Peking, which involves a three-year contract at practically double pay and provision for passage both ways. The localization of the jade industry in Peking, Soochow, Canton, and a few other cities is due to the same cause, although the raw material comes principally from Burma, Yunnan, and Sinkiang, and so far as that is concerned, the industry might as well have been localized in the northwestern and southwestern provinces.

A third factor responsible for industrial growth is the effort of some individual or individuals in introducing an industry into a particular locality. Usually there are other factors favoring the introduction, but personal effort is responsible for the introduction into one place instead of another. For instance, Nanyang, Honan, is known for pongee silk because about 70 years ago a native of Tientsin named Yin Ju-pi became the city magistrate and taught the people to improve their silk fabrics because he himself came from a family which had long been in the silk business. The product of his improvement is known as Yin silk, and is marketed in many provinces. Had he been the magistrate of another district, Nanyang might never have become a producing center of pongee silk. Similarly, the industrial growth of Nantung, Kiangsu, is principally due to the efforts of Chang Chien, who is a native of that city, although the various industries he promoted there could have equally been established in any of the neighboring districts. Nanchung, Szechwan, has a flourishing industry in making noodles, because some of its merchants imported modern machinery from Hankow and started the industry there while other wheat-producing districts of the same province happened to be slow in promoting the business. Given a start by some individual, plus the momentum characteristic of industrial growth, and an industry takes root in a locality and a town grows steadily into an industrial city. Wusih, Kiangsu, owes a good deal to such circumstances for its rapid growth, and the members of the Lao family are among the individuals responsible for it.

In this connection a mistaken but popular notion of many foreign residents in China, and even of some Chinese also, may be discussed with advantage. Shanghai has become the principal industrial center of China, according to this notion, because there are foreign settlements under foreign rule, and foreign rule spells security of life and property. While such security is very important to industrial development, in general it is a mistake to consider it the cause of Shanghai's industrial growth. The flocking of refugees to Shanghai may cause a phenomenal rise in rent and prices, swell the pockets of the local landowners and tradesmen, and present superficial signs of prosperity, yet industries do not develop through mere congestion of population. No amount of security in a small area of a few square miles can make industries prosper if an adequate supply of raw materials is not maintained by good communication facilities, and the products marketed through the same means. The principal advantages of Shanghai are (1) its situation at the mouth of the easily navigable Yangtze River, which traverses some of the richest provinces of the country, (2) the possession of a good harbor where foreign and coastwise shipping lines converge, and (3) the modern transportation facilities of the Shanghai-Nanking and Shanghai-Hangchow railways. If, by blockade or other measures, all or even a large part of such communications were cut off, and with it the foreign and domestic trade, it would not take long to reduce the city to the fishing town which it used to be, or more probably, to a mere seaside resort of foreigners. The effect of the severance of economic relations between Canton and Hongkong in 1925 on the trade and industries of the latter place is sufficient proof of this statement. Finally, even the so-called "security" of Shanghai is more apparent than real, as there has been frequent fighting in and around the city during the last twelve years, and during peaceful times there are in Shanghai far more cases of kidnapping, murder, burglary, incendiarism, and other inherent evils of modern industrial cities than in most inland towns. Hence, in this paper, security of life and property, though important when reference is made to the general conditions of the country, is not considered a factor in the development of specific industries and cities, because it does not so apply.

OBSTACLES TO INDUSTRIAL DEVELOPMENT

Turning now from factors that promote industrial development to those which obstruct it, we shall first refer to likin and similar inland transit taxes as the greatest of all obstacles. The center of the rug industry, referred to a few paragraphs back, has shifted from Peking to Tientsin partly because of the facilities for foreign trade and partly because the manufacturers in the latter city can avoid three taxes which the Peking manufacturers must bear. Also, the raw material, wool, has to pay seven taxes and assessments when transported from Tatung, Shansi, to Peking, a distance of only 672 li (about 220 miles). Hankow brick tea, when transported to Kalgan, had to pay 13 levies of likin and native customs, and the tax burden on a box of tea valued at taels 7.5 (about $10.50) mounted to $3.19, or about 30 per cent. This was two years ago, and now the militarists are collecting more and heavier taxes on the way. On the other hand, the nominal 5 per cent tariff means so little burden on foreign imports that they can easily undersell Chinese products of the same grade. The Chee Hsin cement factory of Tongshan, near Tientsin, finds it cheaper to buy German gypsum than that produced at Yingcheng, Hupeh, because the latter has to bear much heavier taxes and monopoly fees than the 5 per cent tariff on the imported article. Japanese cotton yarn and piece goods compete very keenly with similar native products. The larger capital and lower production cost of large-scale industry in foreign countries give them an advantage over Chinese infant industries, and the low treaty tariff deprives China of one of the most important means of compensation. Also, there is the problem of competition of foreign factories in Chinese territory, which too are entitled to low tax rates by treaty stipulations. These must be dealt with through revision of the treaties and restoration of tariff autonomy to China. As there were simultaneous declarations at the Tariff conference by China and the treaty powers looking forward to restoration of tariff autonomy at the same time with likin abolition, these two questions are therefore closely related.

The second factor is the lack of uniformity in currency and in weights and measures. From the point of view of industry and trade, these two things—currency and weights—are essential measures in all transactions, the former fixing the value, and the latter, the quantity. When they are not uniform throughout the country, or even a large portion of the country trade cannot prosper and industry cannot develop along its natural course. A speculative element is introduced into all transactions which often incurs losses to traders, especially those who go into new markets, and this in turn means that sales of industrial products cannot be easily extended. Of course the Yuan Shih-kai dollar, or yuan, is gaining wider and wider circulation in the country, but there are still many different kinds of silver taels and paper money that circulate side by side with the dollar, and at certain cities they even form the standard of all values. The same is true with weights and measures, in spite of the fact that the government has adopted official standards, because they are maintained only in Shansi. Unfortunately, the importance of this factor is often overlooked.

Unsettled political conditions, together with frequent fighting in the country, are no doubt a most important obstacle to industrial development. They not only directly affect industries, but are also responsible for the maintenance of the obnoxious likin system and the lack of uniformity of currency and weights, and thus indirectly obstruct industrial development through these factors. Moreover, they prevent the proper maintenance and extension of railway lines, which, as was pointed out before, is perhaps the most important factor in promoting industrial growth. There are now altogether only about 9,000 miles of railways in China, which means approximately one mile of railway for every 475 square miles of territory, or 48,000 population. That this is absolutely inadequate is beyond question; but, partly due to unsettled political conditions and partly to contracts of concession with foreign companies, the extension of railway lines has been greatly hindered. The foreign concessionaires have contracted for many lines, but for one reason or another most of them have not laid a single mile of roadbed, while their contracts prevent others from undertaking the construction. In other cases the construction of one line prevents the building of others which may in any way be considered parallel to the existing one, or rather, which may compete for traffic with the other. To some extent certain foreign powers, for the protection of their economic interests in China, have exerted their influence on behalf of certain Chinese political parties and are instrumental in maintaining them in power, thus further complicating the political situation and often delaying its solution. As this paper does not purport to deal with political questions, it is sufficient to point out that Chinese politics has its international aspect, and that foreign economic interests in China—in trade, industries, and railways—while in some respects beneficial to China, are also in other respects responsible for obstructing the industrial development of this country. The treaty tariff, the railway contracts, and foreign influence in Chinese politics are some of the factors of the latter nature, and proper solutions must be found for them before Chinese industries can have untrammeled growth.

## SECTION 19

# THE LABOR MOVEMENT IN CHINA[1]

TA CHEN, Ph.D.
Professor of Sociology, Tsing Hua University, Peking

### CAUSES

Like other social movements, the awakening of labor in China is due to the interaction of economic and social factors. In the first place, China's industrial life is gradually passing from the handicraft to the factory stage. For the country as a whole this transition may seem slow, but in some industrial and commercial cities it is fairly rapid. Thus, during the closing days of the Manchu dynasty China had few flour mills, using modern machinery, but in 1923 no less than 160 factories were reported in all China. Again, before the Republic, electricity was considered a novelty, but in 1925 the country had about 400 electric companies and power plants. Then, too, the cotton industry has perhaps had the most rapid expansion. Before the Republican régime, the number of cotton mills in China was negligible, but toward the end of 1926 there were 122 cotton mills, having 3,414,062 spindles, 25,394 looms, and a total labor force of 209,759 men. These instances are sufficient to show the fairly rapid degree in which industrialization in parts of China is progressing. Simultaneous with this industrial change is the change of the personal status of the worker. Under the handicraft system there has been no clear-cut line of demarcation between the capitalist and the laborer, the master and apprentice indicating more the degree of skill in which one is proficient rather than one's economic status or social position. Between the master and the apprentice there has been fraternal relationship and personal attachment. As industries are gradually modernized, much of this personal relationship is being lost, and in its place there is a growing tendency of class cleavage between the employer and the employee. Of late these class distinctions are recognized not only by custom but by law as well. Thus, in an order of April 27, 1918, the Ministry of Agriculture and Commerce declares that since the interest of the employer and the employee is not always in harmony, each class should have its own organization; but that during the transitional period of industrial development capital and labor do not frequently have separate organizations as yet, and so the guild, which is generally undifferentiated respecting capital and labor, is still permitted. Thus, it is fair to state that the wage-earners in China are slowly assuming importance arising out of the gradual change from handicraft to modern industry.

The second cause which stimulates the labor movement in China is educational in nature. The Renaissance has popularized and simplified our language to a certain extent so that the acquisition of an elementary education is no longer a prohibitive

[1] Revised and expanded from the author's article in *International Labor Review*, Geneva, Switzerland, March, 1927.

task for the common laborer. Some forward-looking workmen thus avail themselves of this privilege to attend evening schools to learn to read newspapers or to keep simple accounts for the household. In addition, the idea of educational improvement of the workers has found sympathetic support of the liberal employers, and so a number of industrial and commercial establishments are providing fairly good educational facilities for their employees. To this educational program of the proletariat our student class has also made contributions. In vacation and on holidays squads of students often give popular lectures on liberty, equality, and the spirit of democracy, with the result that some workers gradually realize their rights and privileges in society. In some instances the workers themselves have brought educational enlightenment upon their fellow-workmen, such as Chinese seamen and also Chinese laborers in France during the World War. Chinese seamen on foreign vessels have had the privilege of visiting seaports in various countries and of associating themselves with foreign seamen and other laborers. In this way they have gained some knowledge of the labor movement in the west and then disseminate the information to their comrades at home. During the European war, Great Britain and France employed about 140,000 Chinese in France for industrial and agricultural labor. Since 1920 they have been gradually repatriated to their mother country, and some of the workers have organized themselves and made their influence felt among the rank and file of labor. Whenever their counsel and advice is sought, they avail themselves of the opportunity to educate and liberalize their fellow workers.

Thirdly, the social phase of the workers' movement should also be considered. Recently certain groups of our population have been engaged in a spasmodic fight for emancipation, demanding chiefly equality between the sexes and between the classes. The Cantonese workers have been leading a stubborn struggle for the right to vote, which, they contend, should be granted to every adult citizen regardless of sex, education, property, or religion. In this they have been partially successful, for at least they have obtained an explicit guaranty in the provincial constitution in addition to the one provided for in the provisional constitution of the Republic. Canton's example has been followed by workers in other provinces with varying degrees of success. Going a step farther than the legal recognition, female laborers in some cities have been struggling for entrance to trades and professions. In certain department stores in large cities the saleswoman is becoming gradually common. The woman doctor is no longer a curiosity, and the woman cashier begins to compete with men. In Shanghai girls and women practically monopolize the silk filatures. In Canton at one time girl waitresses in the tea houses became quite fashionable. Although the last instance aroused heated debates by the public on the question of sex morality, the orthodox view soon gave way to a more pragmatic consideration of giving women a livelihood. Women's entry into trades has modified our old folkways and created new social usage. To many people manual labor is no longer a despised occupation, and such expressions as the "love of work" and "sacredness of labor" become common assertions of the average workmen. With male laborers, however, the social phase of the struggle has been for the right to organize labor unions and to improve living conditions. In this changing Chinese society they find the ancient guild system inadequate for collective bargaining; and by trade-union they attempt to adjust themselves to the new standards of economic and social improvements.

Therefore from the foregoing consideration of industrial, educational, and social forces one is led to infer that the growing labor movement in China is but the natural consequence of the changing and changed conditions in the country. The principal characteristics of the movement are (1) class consciousness, (2) class organization, and (3) class struggle. As the workers' consciousness is already indicated in the foregoing discussion, our next attention will be directed to class organization and class struggle.

### LABOR ORGANIZATIONS

As the labor situation in parts of China is changing so rapidly at the present time it is quite difficult to give accurate and up-to-date information: All that is here attempted is a brief summary of general trends indicating the historical development, structural organization, and policies of the influential unions.

Relating to the history of the modern labor union in China, a sketch of labor activities in four industrial and commercial regions is of interest. Hongkong in the British Crown Colony and Canton in South China, the first region here considered, are reported to have adopted labor-union methods before the Republican régime. Toward the end of the Tsing dynasty, the machinists in Hongkong organized a club principally for educational and welfare work of its members. About the same time the barbers in Hongkong also had a friendly society, emphasizing more of the social and fraternal activities rather than economic improvement of the workers. Shortly before the establishment of the Republic the employees of foreign firms in Shamen were reported to have organized a club to hold occasional meetings and to give social entertainment to the members. At Canton the Chinese overseas have long maintained an industrial organization. But owing to internal dissensions it was broken up shortly after the Manchu dynasty was overthrown. Since then some of its enlightened members have organized the Chinese Labor Union, which was the only influential union of the modern type in Canton during the early period of the Republic. It had a program of rather wide scope, including the publication of a weekly bulletin of interest to labor. In more recent times the movement for local labor organizations has aroused keener interest. In 1917 Canton was said to have observed the first May Day celebration, which greatly encouraged the activities of local labor. Since the spread of the student movement, labor unions of various kinds came into existence. Labor organization received impetus from social unrest in recent times, especially the machinists' strike in Hongkong in 1920; the machinists' strike in Canton in 1921, and the seamen's strike in Hongkong in 1922. In 1922 the total number of unions in Hongkong amounted to about 100; in Canton, about 80. Evidently some of these unions have shown too rapid growth and are not built upon firm foundations. Consequently in recent years the unions in these two cities have shown considerable fluctuations. At present Hongkong claims a total of about 100 unions, and Canton, 300.

Tongshan, in Chihli Province, North China, is another pioneer industrial center. Its labor organization has had a unique growth. Toward the end of the Ming dynasty, about 285 years ago, the inhabitants of this district employed primitive methods to quarry the outcrop coal at the Tongshan mine. In 1878, when the country was still skeptical about occidental culture, Tongshan boldly introduced Western methods of mining, thus earning the reputation of having the first modernized mine in the nation. The great aggregation of workers soon called for group formation. Being village folks, the desire for democratic government was persistent, and in consequence a self-government club was formed. The heterogeneous subjects discussed by the club ranged anywhere from the worker's freedom to play the flute while off duty to his worship of Buddha in the clubhouse. The club was the common meeting place for the workers, and for a time it succeeded. In 1905 its membership included a considerable portion of the executive staff and employees of the Peking-Mukden Railway machine shops, the Kaipin mine, and a cement company. Slight friction between the native miners and the Cantonese soon developed into uncompromising sectional conflicts, resulting in the withdrawal of the latter from the club. Over a thousand Cantonese, constituting about one-sixth of the Tongshan industrial population, then organized the Kwangtung Provincial Guild to promote fraternal relations as well as industrial co-operation. Unlike the craft guild, which enrols workers of the same trade, this guild had for its sole standards neighborliness and townsmanship. The comradeship enjoyed through bringing to the same guild railway men and broom-makers was restricted to the provincials of Kwangtung. Liberal thinkers, who deprecated the narrow provincialism characteristic of this organization, immediately agitated for the creation of the Tongshan Labor Union, extending membership to all workers who cared to join. After the revolution of 1911 the union was firmly established and figured prominently in the labor movement at that time.

While the Tongshan Labor Union has been hampered by its connections with the Labor party and by political unrest in recent years,[2] a new development in the community is now discernible. Since the student strike, the employees of the Peking-Mukden Railway machine shops have organized the Comrades' Union to improve their working conditions as well as to equip themselves with an elementary education. This has stimulated similar organization on the part of the employees of the Kailan Mining Administration. They have a reading-room, a school for teaching the phonetic system of the Chinese language, and a magazine to popularize the use of the phonetics. Thirty years of industrial life have taught the Tongshan workmen, now numbering over 30,000, the importance of co-operation and combination. The recent organizations, with a broad educational program, clearly aim at equipping the workers with common intelligence for a persistent struggle with the capitalists.

Shanghai, the third industrial city here considered, has a more rapid development of labor unions than Tongshan. In February, 1919, the strike of the Sino-Japanese cotton mills which was a protest against the increasing cost of rice stimulated labor organization in Shanghai and vicinity. In January, 1922, when the Hua Shih cotton-mill strike in Changsha failed and its leaders were executed, the active members of the Hunan Labor Union fled to Shanghai and quietly worked among the factory laborers for more effective organization. About the same time Shanghai labor also received much impetus from the successful shipping strike in Hongkong, and a branch seamen's union was soon organized. These events precipitated in the sudden growth of labor unions which followed. In 1922 greater Shanghai boasted a total of about

[2] *Monthly Labor Review* (December, 1920), pp. 208, 209.

50 unions. But as most of them were loosely organized and ill-directed, a movement for consolidating them into one federation was started in May, 1922. This need was especially felt after the unsuccessful Peking-Hankow railway strike in February, 1923. In 1924 the agitation for consolidation bore fruition and the Federation of Labor Unions of Shanghai was created. In the manifesto it was declared that "since the World War, Chinese laborers, animated by the desire to relieve economic oppression of the capitalists as well as to maintain a decent standard of living, have been organizing themselves gradually, and that, based upon the spirit of mutual help and brotherly love, the Federation of Labor unions of Shanghai is created with the direct object of obtaining security of employment for its members and the indirect object of striving for social reforms in China." Among the federated unions should be mentioned the union of the Nanyang Brothers Tobacco Company, The Shanghai Spinners' and Weavers' Union, The Shanghai Metal Workers' Union, and the union of the Returned Laborers from France. The attitude of the federation is relatively conservative, and it has shown willingness to be affiliated with the right wing of the Kuomintang. The federation probably includes 40 unions aggregating about 50,000 workers.

This was the general situation of organized labor in Shanghai up to May, 1925. But when in that year the May 30th affair broke out, the labor world became increasingly more complicated. Nationalism, race prejudice, mob action, and intensified class hatred—these and other factors made the federation an inadequate organization to cope with the intricate situation. Under these circumstances the insurgents of the labor movement heralded a new movement, drawing some elements from the federation and recruiting others elsewhere. The general slogan of this new movement is couched in the phrase: "Down with capitalism, militarism, and imperialism." Stressing the importance of revolutionary tactics in labor, a militant organization entitled the General Labor Union of Shanghai was born. Its influential members include the union of the Naigai Cotton Mills, the Labor Union of Cotton Mills of Shanghai, the Shanghai branch of the Seamen's Union, the Union of the Tobacco Workers of the British Firms, the Foundry Workers' Union, and the Egg Factories Labor Union. Around September, 1925, this union probably had about 120 unions and a membership of about 200,000 men. When first organized it was engaged in active nationalist propaganda and was in deep sympathy with communistic theory and practice. Recently its influence is waning and its followers slowly diminishing.

From Shanghai, Canton, and Tongshan the labor movement spread to other commercial and industrial cities, including the districts of Changsha and Hankow upon the Yangtse River. In recent years Changsha has been progressive in social reconstruction and civic improvements. It has produced two prominent leaders in the revolution. Today its rising generation has an unfailing enthusiasm for liberal idealism. This is the fertile soil upon which the seeds of a liberal labor movement tinged with radicalism may grow. As early as in 1920 the Hunan Labor Union was organized, and in a brief period of two years no less than 20 unions came into existence. But when in January, 1922, the Hua Shih cotton mill strike was declared in Changsha and two of its leaders executed by the order of the provincial governor, labor activities were apparently suppressed. As a matter of fact, however, the influence of this tragic event upon the labor movement in China was far-reaching. Thus, in the recent organization of the Federation of Labor Unions of Shanghai, the labor elements from Changsha exerted considerable influence. Again, respecting the radical activities of the miners at Ping Hsiang and at An Yuen, Changsha labor leaders were in close touch with them. Even during the May 30th affair and its later developments, the part played by the laborites from Changsha was of considerable importance.

As to Hankow, although its present situation is too confusing for an objective analysis, its position in the history of Chinese labor may be briefly indicated. In December, 1921, over 6,000 ricksha men struck as a protest against the increase of ricksha rent imposed upon them by the ricksha owners. As the issues became complicated, the local authorities went in to arbitrate with the representatives of the consulates and the chambers of commerce. As the strike was partially successful, the ricksha pullers felt the utility of closer organization and the Ricksha Laborers' Union was organized. This event gave impetus to other workers in the city. In February, 1922, when the Peking-Hankow Railway strike was declared, Hankow was naturally an important center of the strike activities. But the strike was a failure and the Peking-Hankow Railway Union was suppressed. The civil and military authorities in the Hankow region have since adopted the repressive policy toward labor, and labor leaders have not been able to carry on their propaganda in the open. Powerful unions there are, but they hardly measure up to the commercial and industrial importance of the city. The Federation of Labor Unions of Hupeh province, though lacking definite policies at times, is a consolidation of the conservative unions in the district. Hankow, as well as Changsha, has the inclination toward radicalism, but the government has successfully checked it. Until recently, when the Kuomintang has established itself there, a liberal policy toward labor has been adopted and a rapid increase of labor organizations has taken place. A recent report states that the new unions in Hankow, Wuchang, and Hanyan during the last half-year that have been registered amount to about 200, with a total membership of over 100,000 men.

The foregoing paragraphs roughly indicate the history and development of the modern labor union in parts of China. As to the general principles upon which the workers are now organized, three typical tendencies may be mentioned.

One group of labor leaders contends that Chinese labor today is not yet able to fight its cause alone and must secure protection from a political party. The party platform should include provisions on social welfare and reform, emphasizing the need for improvement of the living conditions of the proletariat. The Kuomintang manifestly takes this stand. Its central executive committee has a special division on labor which is charged with the duty of giving counsel and advice to workers on matters affecting their interests. Recently numerous labor unions have sprung up in Canton, causing great confusion in industry. There has been no central organization which could command the confidence and respect of all the unions in the city for settling disputes or strikes. Although several efforts have been made to organize the important unions into a general federation of labor, no substantial result has been obtained. The Kuomintang has undertaken the task of consolidating the principal unions by the creation of the Association of Workers' Delegates. This Association was formed by asking each trade or industry to elect its representative to organize a central executive committee which should have authority to control the trades and industries by which it had been elected. Four groups of industrial workers were represented: (1) the transport workers, including those from the Yueh-Han Railway and the Canton-Kowloon Railway, seamen, telephone and telegraph operators, machinists on tug boats, boatmen, loading and unloading coolies, chauffeurs, risksha pullers; (2) factory workers, including workers in the municipal power company, arsenals, oil mills, rice mills, construction and building companies, foundries, and the textile trades; (3) handicraft workers, including tailors, carpenters, plumbers and tilers, carvers, ivory-ball workers, varnish men, blacksmiths, gold- and silversmiths; (4) miscellaneous workers, including unskilled workmen, casual laborers, and odd jobbers. The four general groups of workers elected their representatives to form the central executive committee, which appointed five subcommittees on education, publication, co-operation, political education, and military training, respectively. In addition there were four subcommittees, each looking after the interests of one of the groups (transport workers, factory workers, handcraft workers, and miscellaneous workers). As an example of the importance of the Association's activities those of 1924 may be mentioned. At its general meeting in May resolutions were passed in favor of the following: (*a*) the consolidation and reorganization of the employees of the Canton Telegraph Office and Telephone Company, the seamen's unions, and the transport workers; (*b*) the prohibition of night work by apprentices; (*c*) the standardization of wages in each trade and the elimination of unfair competition for employment agencies; (*e*) workers' education; (*f*) the organization of a committee on co-operation; (*g*) the strike fund. Recently, because of political changes and social unrest in Canton, part of this program has been held in abeyance. Promising beginnings have, however, been made along some lines. Thus the subcommittee on military training really helped to organize the labor corps, which was a serious attempt to train the workers for self-protection in emergency as well as a means of defense for the city. Experiments have been made in consumers' co-operation, with partial success.

The second general tendency in labor organization is represented by the left wing of the labor movement. The leaders of this group argue that the affiliation of labor with politics is not always helpful to the cause of labor, as party platforms are sometimes obliged to include compromises in order to pacify the conflicting elements in the party; they therefore wish to be more drastic and more uncompromising than a political party can be. They generally favor the strike, sabotage, direct action, and revolutionary tactics as weapons in the struggle between capital and labor. The program of this group is frankly communistic. They contend that the workers are deprived of rights and privileges in society which cannot be restored to them through parliamentary action or revolutionary social reforms, but must be sought through social revolution. Part of their propaganda is being carried on in close relation to the theory and practice of Bolshevism. Some labor organizations in Hongkong, Canton, Changsha, and Shanghai share the characteristics of this group. The labor union of the Pin-hsiang mines at An-Yuen, Hunan Province, may be taken as an illustration. This union, which was organized principally to strengthen the power of collective bargaining on the part of the workers, adopts an intransigent attitude toward the management and often resorts to strikes for settling labor disputes. At one time the miners virtually imposed their labor policy on the company and adopted certain features of syndicalism. They decided to work four or five hours a day instead of the normal long hours common to the mine workers in the country. As a result the daily output of coal was greatly reduced and the supply was far from sufficient to meet the needs of factories in Hankow and the vicinity. Communistic tendencies are also found in certain district unions of the Peking-Hankow Railway, as in the manifesto of these unions it is clearly stated that "the class war is inevitable and the most effective weapon for securing justice for the workers is direct action." Some members of the left wing of the Kuomintang are also in favor of this attitude and have been helping some labor men to propagate this idea. But at a conference of a group of the Kuomintang members held in Peking on November 23, 1925, it was decided to expel the communists from the Kuomintang on the following grounds:

1. That the Communists have been utilizing the party to strengthen their influence as well as that of Soviet Russia in China; (2) that while the Communists wish to be loyal to their ideals, the Kuomintang has principles of its own, and these two are not always harmonious, although both the Communists and the Kuomintang oppose imperialism and oppression; (3) that Russia and China have differences in national history and social life, and therefore communistic practices might not suit the Chinese people.

For these reasons it was felt that it would be beneficial to both sides to expel the Communists from the Kuomintang. Evidently this will mark an appreciable change of attitude of the party toward Communism on the one hand and its support of radical labor leaders on the other.

The third general tendency in labor organization is the belief that labor must fight its cause alone and work out its own salvation. Labor will not ask for help from politicians or radicals, but it will carry out its program by means of men experienced in social service, or by those who are truly interested in the welfare of the proletariat. The Machinists' Union of Hongkong may be cited as an example of this tendency. Its members now number about 60,000, including many Chinese in the islands of the Malay Peninsula, the Dutch East Indias, and the Philippines. These men, alarmed by the political unrest in their mother country, want their union to be entirely free from political entanglements. To their way of thinking, the advancement of the cause of labor must primarily depend upon the enlightened workers. Labor leaders of this frame of mind are still in the majority, but popular sentiment is steadily growing in their favor. This is mainly because of the bitter experience labor has recently undergone in relying upon outsiders to champion its cause. Occasionally shrewd politicians or scheming radicals have taken advantage of the opportunity of furthering their personal ambitions. Thinking men in the labor world therefore wish to organize independent unions, chiefly under the leadership of men of experience in social work, which shall have the economic and social improvement of the workmen as their sole aim.

### NATIONAL LABOR CONFERENCES

The trade-union movement of a really national character dates from the first national labor conference held at Canton May 1–6, 1922, at which 162 delegates from

200 unions in 12 cities, representing about 400,000 workers, were present. The Conference passed a number of resolutions, including those in favor of an 8-hour day, mutual aid to strikers, a permanent national organization of trade-unions, and the organization of unions on an industrial rather than a craft basis, and adopted as its general policy the promotion of the economic and industrial welfare of the workers, combined with abstention from political activity.

The second national labor conference was held at Canton May 1–7, 1925. Some unions pointed out that the conference was dominated by radicals; the Federation of Labor Unions of Hupeh Province went so far as to denounce the prime movers of the conference as having "sinister motives," stating that it considered the conference "unrepresentative of the Chinese proletariat as a whole." Nevertheless it was the second attempt to call together labor elements in different parts of the country for some common action and interest. The conference decided to create the General Labor Union of China in order to organize all the workers in the nation and to promote their general welfare. Membership was to be corporate rather than individual. Representatives of federations of labor unions became ipso facto members of the General Labor Union, while representatives of single unions might become members on the recommendation of the officers of the General Labor Union. The aims of the General Labor Union were to be: (*a*) to promote labor organizations in China, (*b*) to direct and unify the labor movement, (*c*) to promote friendship and education among the workers, (*d*) to formulate common aims and policies, (*e*) to arbitrate in labor disputes, especially between unions; and (*f*) to establish relations with international labor organizations. There was to be an executive committee of twenty-five members elected annually at the conference of the representatives of member unions. The decisions of the annual conference of the representatives and of the executive committee were to be binding on all member unions. Under the executive committee there were to be a secretariat, and a department each for organization, publications, and finance. Other important resolutions of the conference were in favor of: (*a*) the federation of laborers and farmers; (*b*) the federation of laborers and farmers with soldiers; (*c*) the promotion of workers' education; and (*d*) the consolidation of labor unions in Canton and Shanghai.

Reference may also be made to the proceedings of the third national conference, held at Canton May 1–12, 1926, at which 400 delegates, representing 1,240,000 organized workers belonging to 400 unions in 19 provinces were present. Reports were presented and resolutions passed on the following subjects: organization of the labor movement, reorganization and working of trade-unions, objects and program of the economic struggle, strikes, the relations between workers and peasants, workers' education, young workers and the trade-union movement, unemployment, co-operation, labor legislation, and the right of association and conditions of work.

### THE MOVEMENT FOR LABOR LEGISLATION

On the basis of information on labor conditions already published in English,[3] which is, however, far from complete, certain general statements may be made to indicate social tendencies in present-day China.

[3] Especially the following: J. B. Taylor and W. T. Zung, "Labor and Industry in China," *International Labor Review*, VIII, No. 1 (July, 1923), 1–20; "Labor Conditions

In the first place, money wages in recent years have shown an upward trend for the following main reasons: (*a*) Since the European war prices of commodities have generally risen. For example, in 1916 the cost of 200 pounds of polished rice in Shanghai was $7.78;[4] in 1923 it had increased to $12.45; over the same period and in the same city the price of potatoes rose from $3.09 per picul[5] to $3.40. This has increased the cost of living for the workers. (*b*) Realizing the foregoing situation, the workmen of the better organized trades have struck principally for economic reasons. Thus, between 1918 and 1925 there were in China 698 strikes; in 49 per cent of these, 1,273,606 workingmen were involved. (*c*) The depreciation of the copper currency has also had very serious results for the proletariat, as wages are customarily paid in copper coins. In Peking, for example, in August, 1923, one dollar exchanged for 195 coppers, but a year later it exchanged for 229 coppers, while early in 1926 the rate touched 340. Under these conditions wages have also increased. But whether the increase is sufficient to meet the rising cost of living is yet an open question.[6]

A second significant factor affecting labor conditions is the gradual decrease of the contract system in China. Up to very recently, foreign firms (and, to a lesser extent, Chinese firms), on account of unfamiliarity with the Chinese language and difficulties in knowing the habits and idiosyncrasies of the Chinese, have relied mainly upon the contractor for labor. The foreign company paid the contractor, who in turn paid his men. The management frequently used no pay-rolls and kept no records of its labor force. This practice has been found unsatisfactory for both employers and men. The workers suffered chiefly from the unfair practices of the contractor, including underpayment and inhumane treatment; the employers also considered it unsatisfactory, because the workers found it difficult to submit complaints to the company for redress and for the maintenance of just relations between the two parties, and the chasm between the management and the men was thus rendered unduly deep.

Under this system labor turnover was usually high. Today, although the practice still exists to a considerable extent, it is slowly decreasing in importance, and this among both foreign and Chinese employers.

---

and Labor Regulation in China," *ibid.*, X, No. 6 (December, 1924), 1005–28; Dame Adelaide Anderson, "The Recommendations of the Shanghai Child Labor Commission," *ibid.*, XI, No. 5 (May, 1925), 665–81; "Labor Conditions in China," *ibid.*, XII, No. 5 (November, 1925), 660–76; Dr. Ta Chen, "Wages and Hours of Labor in Five Chinese Cities," *Monthly Labor Review of the United States Bureau of Labor Statistics* (August, 1921), pp. 3–15; "Labor Conditions in China," *ibid.* (November, 1924), pp. 36–49; "Working Women in China," *ibid.* (December, 1921), pp. 142–49; "Labor Unrest in China," *ibid.* (August, 1921), pp. 16–30; "The Labor Situation in China," *ibid.* (December, 1920), pp. 207–20.

[4] The Chinese silver dollar is equivalent to 1.175 ounces of (standard) silver at par; the exchange rate fluctuates with the gold value of silver. At the time of writing this article the Chinese dollar exchanged for 54 cents gold.

[5] One picul = 133⅓ lb. = 60.48 kg.

[6] Cf. G. G. Dittmer, "Density of Population and Standard of Living in North China," *Proceedings of the American Sociological Society*, XIX (1925), 196–99; Maude B. Warner, "Living Conditions in China," *Annals of the American Academy of Political and Social Science* (November, 1925), pp. 167–73; Ta Chen, "Cost of Living in Japan and China since 1914," *Monthly Labor Review* (December, 1921), 1–7.

Thirdly, there is the regrettable fact that no substantial progress is now being made either in the reduction of hours of labor or in the improvement of working conditions. With the exception of a few modernized factories in commercial and industrial centers, the workers usually work long hours and have no rest on Sunday. The surroundings of the place of employment are generally unhygienic, ventilation is poor, working tools are inadequate, and sanitary equipment is frequently lacking. Social changes in China are manifestly slow, and rapid progress can hardly be expected in the near future in the improvement of working conditions, especially in the interior of the country.

Although working conditions are generally unsatisfactory, yet at the same time some valuable experiments along the lines of industrial welfare are being carried on. These are usually found among the larger undertakings and the relatively more enlightened employers, who are impelled by humanitarian motives to take adequate care of the workers and whose appreciation of modern welfare work encourages them to modify the antiquated systems of relief and charity practiced by the guilds.

In recent years the desire for protecting the workers' health and promoting their safety has found another channel of expression, namely, the movement for protective labor laws. In this movement various social forces have joined hands. Not only do the labor unions press for labor legislation, but national and provincial government departments and commercial, educational, and social welfare institutions are interested in it. Although no substantial progress has been made in the amount of legislation already in operation, yet public opinion is increasingly in favor of governmental action.

It may be well to outline recent attempts at enacting labor laws in China. At the annual meeting in 1919 of the China Continuation Committee attention was drawn to the existence of unsatisfactory labor conditions. Thereafter the Christian church took a sympathetic interest in the matter, and appointed a Commission on the Relation of the Church to China's Economic and Industrial Problems. In May, 1922, when the National Christian Conference met, three resolutions relating to labor were passed in the hope of promoting conformity with the standard set up by the first session of the International Labor Conference held in Washington in October, 1919. These resolutions advocated (1) the prohibition of the employment of children under twelve years of age, (2) one day of rest in seven, and (3) the safeguarding of the health of the workers by limitation of working hours, improvement of sanitary conditions, and installation of safety devices. In the same year a joint committee of women's clubs of British, American, Japanese and Chinese nationalities in Shanghai publicly declared their opposition to the employment of very young children in factories.

In addition, in some better organized trades and industries, the workers effectively expressed their discontent about working conditions. When the shipping strike in Hongkong, which lasted from January 13 to March 5, 1922, ended in a complete victory for the seamen, the Canton government became aware of the growing importance of the labor organizations and shortly afterward repealed section 224 of chapter xvi of the provisional criminal code, thus legalizing strikes and removing unnecessary shackles from the workers.

Throughout the rank and file of labor heated discussions on labor matters have also been going on. On September 4, 1922, the labor unions of Wuhan, in the province of Hupeh, sent a petition to the national parliament in Peking setting forth nineteen demands which were afterward indorsed by the labor unions throughout the nation. Although under existing conditions some demands were too idealistic for immediate realization, labor's earnest desire for protection is obvious. The workers' demands include freedom to hold meetings and to declare strikes, an 8-hour day and a 42-hour week, government regulation of farm products, abolition of usury and high rent in rural communities, prohibition of night work of women and children in factories, a minimum wage law, the establishment of wage adjustment boards, state insurance, and state education.

In February, 1923, when the Peking-Hankow Railway Union declared a strike which was suppressed by the government troops, the union pointed out that the right to organize and hold meetings was stipulated in the Provisional Constitution of the Republic, and was therefore inviolable. The strike was investigated by members of the House of Representatives, and debated at a joint session of the House and the Senate, attended by over one hundred members. Resolutions were passed and presented to the President urging the recognition of the right to organize labor unions. On February 22, 1923, a presidential mandate was issued ordering that labor laws should be drafted by the proper ministries and submitted to parliament for consideration. The President's order was strictly obeyed and speedy work was done. On March 29 the Ministry of Agriculture and Commerce promulgated provisional factory regulations[7] consisting of twenty-eight sections. The bill to convert these regulations into an act was not passed by parliament, but the regulations constitute the first ministerial order to lay down standards for the protection of factory labor. They contain provisions dealing with the following: Minimum age of admission to employment, limitation of hours of labor, prohibition of night work for young persons, and of certain kinds of work for women and children, compulsory education, and government inspection of factories. In certain respects the regulations differ both from an ordinance on the industrial employment of children which has been in operation in Hongkong since January 1, 1923, and also from the recommendations[8] of the Child Labor Commission contained in the report submitted to the Shanghai municipal council on July 9, 1924. But the main difficulties in the way of the effective operation of the ministry's factory regulations seem to consist in two conditions: (1) they apply only to factories which employ not less than 100 workers, or are dangerous or unhealthy, so that workshops and industrial establishments of smaller size which are not dangerous or unhealthy, but whose unsatisfactory labor conditions demand regulation, are excluded from their sphere; (2) no penalties are provided for violation of the regulations, and no adequate system of inspection exists, so that they cannot effectively be enforced.

A comparative statement of the main provisions of the provisional factory regulations (clauses affecting women and children), the Hongkong ordinance, and the recommendations of the Shanghai Labor Commission is shown below.[9]

[7] International Labor Office, Legislative Series, 1923, China. 1. Cf. *International Labor Review,* X, No. 6 (December, 1924), 1007 ff.

[8] *Ibid.,* pp. 1023–24.

[9] Adapted from *Monthly Labor Review,* November, 1924, pp. 40–41.

## COMPARISON OF PROVISIONAL FACTORY REGULATIONS

HONGKONG ORDINANCE, AND SHANGHAI RECOMMENDATIONS CONCERNING CHILD LABOR

| Item | Provisional Factory Regulations | Hongkong Ordinance | Recommendations of Shanghai Commission |
|---|---|---|---|
| Minimum age | Boys, 10 years; Girls, 12 years | 10 years; but no child under 12 to carry coal, building material, or débris | 10 years, rising to 12 within four years from promulgation of regulations |
| Proof of age | No provision | Child assumed to be under age if so appears to the judge | Some measure for proof should be adopted |
| Hours of labor | 8, exclusive of breaks* | 9, but no child to work more than 5 hours continuously | Children under 14: maximum of 12, including rest of 1 hour |
| Night work | None between 8 P.M. and 4 A.M. | None between 7 P.M. and 7 A.M. | Night work permitted now; to be reconsidered after 4 years |
| Rest days | Not less than 3 full days per month† | 1 day in 7 | 1 day in 14 |
| Prohibition of certain work | Women and young persons: cleaning, greasing, inspecting, and repairing about machinery in motion, minding winches and cranes, etc. Young persons: preparing poisonous, noxious, or explosive substances, or in unhealthy or dusty places | Carrying weight exceeding 40 catties‡ and at dangerous trades, i.e., boiler chipping, fireworks, and glass manufacture | Children under 14: work at dangerous unguarded machines, hazardous places or work likely to injure body or health |
| Compulsory education | At employer's expense | No provision | Outside commission's power, but commission favors it |
| Record keeping | No provision | Employer to keep current record of children employed | No provision |
| Inspection and penalties | Inspection, but no provision for penalties | Inspection; fine or imprisonment for violation | Inspection and penalties |

* Adults, 10 hours exclusive of breaks.

† Adults, at least 2 days per month.

‡ One catty = about 1⅓ lbs.

About the time when the provisional factory regulations were promulgated, the Ministry of Agriculture and Commerce also drew up a trade-union bill of fifteen sections and submitted it to parliament for consideration. The main provisions were as follows:

1. Recognition of the right of association of workers engaged in the same kind of employment;

2. Restriction of the unions to (*a*) mutual help among members, (*b*) improvement of conditions of employment, (*c*) investigation of labor conditions, (*d*) making proposals to the government with respect to labor legislation, and (*e*) answering inquiries made by the administrative authorities;

3. Stipulation that when a trade-union passes a resolution or carries one into effect which will produce any of the following results, the appropriate administrative authorities may order its dissolution: (*a*) disturbing the form of government, (*b*) disturbing the public peace, (*c*) endangering the life of any of the public, (*d*) obstructing communications or inflicting injury on the nation or society.

But before these regulations were passed by parliament, the coup d'état of June 13, 1923, took place in Peking, resulting in the deposition of President Li Yuanhung and the dissolution of parliament, and the agitation for national legislation on trade-unions temporarily subsided. In November, 1924, Dr. Sun Yat Sen promulgated trade-union regulations to cope with the situation in Kwangtung province. The preamble states that the main aims of the regulations are: (1) to recognize the status of labor organizations; (2) to grant them more rights and greater freedom; and (3) to remove obstacles that may hinder the organization and progress of the labor movement. The main principles of the regulations may be summarized as follows: (1) recognition that trade-unions and employers' associations are on an equal footing; (2) recognition that trade-unions shall have freedom of speech, of the press, and of educational work; (3) recognition that trade-unions shall have the right to conclude collective agreements with the employers' organizations; (4) recognition that in case of dispute a union shall have the right to ask the employers to set up a joint arbitration committee, and the right to apply to the appropriate administrative authorities to open an inquiry or institute arbitration proceedings; (5) recognition that unions have the right to declare strikes; (6) recognition that trade-unions shall have the right to participate with employers in regulating hours of labor, working conditions, and factory hygiene; (7) recognition of the principle that in disputes in a private industry (not a public utility) the administrative authorities shall only investigate or arbitrate, but shall not enforce their decisions by compulsion, in order to encourage the initiative of the trade-union concerned; (8) guaranties to trade-unions for the security of property belonging to them; (9) provision that the prohibition of meeting and of association contained in the criminal code and police regulations are not applicable to trade-unions; (10) encouragement of the principle of organization of trade-unions by industry with the possibility, in view of the importance of handicrafts among Chinese industries, of organization also by craft.

Toward the close of 1924 and throughout 1925 a period of active propaganda for labor legislation began anew. Strikes became more common and social unrest more widespread. Petitions to the government for equitable adjustments between capital and labor came from trade-unions, commercial associations, and educational organizations. In view of recent labor troubles, the Chinese government evinced a strong desire to enact appropriate labor legislation to govern the situation. Furthermore, with the approach of the seventh session of the International Labor Conference, China contemplated speeding up work on social reforms so as to present a constructive program at the Conference. A minor factor was the anxiety of a few political aspirants to have some sort of trade-union law enacted which would enable them to be elected to the provisional senate as representatives of legally recognized unions. When the incident of May 30, 1925, occurred in Shanghai, the cry for immediate legislation naturally became acute. Thus in a telegram of July 10, 1925, the Shanghai chamber of commerce stated that the episode of May 30 might be "partially due to the lack of trade-union laws, for had there been such laws the Japanese employers might have been willing to comply with them. Besides, in recent years China's delegates to the International Labor Conference have not always been able to represent the wishes of the workers." Under these circumstances the Ministry of Agriculture and Commerce drew up a new set of regulations embodying fourteen chapters and fifty sections and including the following provisions:

1. Trade-unions may deal with the following questions: (*a*) placing of members and mutual aid, (*b*) improvement of working conditions, (*c*) investigation of and reports on working conditions, (*d*) members' savings and workers' insurance, (*e*) consumers' co-operation and co-operative housing enterprises for members, (*f*) requests for arbitration of disputes between capital and labor, (*g*) proposals concerning the interests of labor and supply of information to the administrative authorities, (*h*) factory hygiene and technical training for the workers.

2. The promoters of a union must be fifty workers who (*a*) have been employed in the trade for three or more years, (*b*) are 30 years of age, and (*c*) can read and write simple Chinese.

3. When a union acts in contravention of any existing law or regulation, so as to disturb the public peace or endanger the public welfare, or does not observe the orders of the competent administrative authorities, these authorities may report the case to the Ministry of Agriculture and Commerce, or other appropriate government department, with a view to the dissolution of the union.

Some of these regulations met with opposition from various organizations. Certain trade-unions felt that their freedom of organization was curtailed. Thus in a telegram dated July 10, 1925, the General Labor Union of China raised the following objections: (1) organization of unions on a craft rather than an industrial basis is undesirable; (2) the conditions of age and education imposed on promoters are too rigorous; (3) the provision that the funds of the union must be deposited in a state bank is anti-democratic.

The original draft of the regulations was later modified by the Ministry of Communications and the number of sections was finally reduced to thirty-four. The main changes include the prohibition of strikes and lockouts in certain circumstances and the adoption of peaceful methods for the settlement of disputes between capital and labor. The Ministry of Communications also insisted upon the classification of industries into private and public, including in the latter category government undertakings, such as arsenals, public utilities such as water supply and telephones, and means of communication and transport such as railways. The Ministry was also in favor of adopting different regulations for the trade-unions in each of these four classes of industry.

Early in 1926, just before military hostilities broke out between the Kuominchun and the Fengtien troops, another set of regulations modifying the last-mentioned was drafted by the Ministry of Agriculture and Commerce. The significant provisions are as follows:

1. Unions may be organized on either a craft or an industrial basis.

2. A union may elect representatives to sit on a joint committee to settle disputes between capital and labor.

3. The promoters of a union must be thirty adult workers who are at present employed in the trade.

4. In case of a labor dispute the local authorities may, upon the request of the interested parties, hold an inquiry and act as conciliators. If necessary, the authorities may request both sides to appoint an equal number of experts to form an arbitration board, subject to the approval of the proper authorities. If a dispute arises in a public utility, the government department concerned must settle the dispute or request the local authorities to arbitrate and report their decision to the controlling government department for approval. If both sides are dissatisfied with the decision and the settlement of the case is thus delayed, the local authorities may enforce the decision by compulsion; in this case their action must be reported to the Ministry of Agriculture and Commerce and other appropriate government departments.

5. Lockouts and strikes are prohibited while inquiry and conciliation proceedings are in progress.

6. A trade-union in a public utility undertaking must be registered with the proper authorities.

7. These regulations, together with special rules for each case, shall apply to unions in government undertakings and in undertakings for communications and transport.

8. Resolutions or official acts of trade-unions or their officers which violate these regulations or other laws so as to endanger the public welfare or public peace shall be prohibited by the competent authorities. If the orders given are not obeyed the case shall be reported to the Ministry of Agriculture and Commerce, with a view to the dissolution of the union, or, in case of lesser seriousness, suspension of the union's activities for a period of from half a year to two years.

## STRIKES

When labor is fairly well organized in an industry on the lines before indicated, it gradually makes its grievances known as opportunity arises. In recent years, therefore, strikes have become more or less frequent. In order to show labor's activities in this direction, some strikes of special significance have been selected for discussion. The causes of strikes are complicated and their effects upon industrial life considerable. But, for the present purpose it may be noted that some strikes are dominantly economic in nature, such as the Hongkong shipping strike in 1922; some are in support of the right of association, such as the Peking-Hankow Railway strike in 1923; and some are due to a number of causes—racial, social, economic, and political—such as the Shanghai incident of May 30, 1925, and its later developments.

The initial trouble of the Peking-Hankow Railway strike began on February 1, 1923, the date chosen by the railway union for the celebration of its official opening and for the adoption of its constitution and by-laws. It had been arranged that 130 representatives of 35 local unions should attend the meeting in Chengchow, province of Honan, in addition to 65 representatives of the unions of other railways and 60 representatives of newspapers and schools in other cities. But on February 1 martial law was suddenly declared in Chengchow. The union's headquarters were guarded by armed police, and the hotels and restaurants in the city were forbidden to accommodate the union delegates. In protest the union men in the city walked out on February 4 and were soon joined by the railway workers on other sections of the same railway. Since this interfered with the operation of the railway, the police authorities forced the strikers to resume their work, killing three and wounding forty in so doing. Indignation was aroused among the rank and file of labor, and telegrams of sympathy were received from about a hundred unions throughout the country. The national parliament in Peking moved the impeachment of the military authorities, and at a session on "labor unrest" held in the House of Representatives four resolutions were adopted in favor of (1) the recognition by the government, in accordance with the Provisional Constitution of the Republic, of the workers' right to hold meetings, (2) release by the government of those workers who were under arrest, (3) the grant by the government of money to the families of the deceased or wounded, (4) the removal by the government of troops and police from the railway stations.

Strikes due to economic causes are relatively more numerous than those due to other causes. An example is the Hongkong shipping strike, which lasted from January 13 to March 5, 1922. Since 1914 the cost of polished rice in Shanghai had increased by 125 per cent; in Hongkong over the same period it had increased by 155 per cent. Prices of commodities had advanced too fast, and the slow increase in wages could not adequately meet the rising cost of living. This caused general discontent among the rank and file of labor. In Canton strikes were numerous, especially in 1921, when strikes occurred in almost every important industry. In Hongkong, since the strike of April 20, 1920, which involved 9,000 workers, local workers were increasingly dissatisfied with capitalists. This class feeling was intensified when, toward the end of 1921, foreign seamen in the colony, who already had a comparatively higher scale of wages, were granted a further increase of 15 per cent, whereas most of the Chinese seamen were still being paid at pre-war rates. Because of this discrimination the Chinese seamen had a general grievance against the shipowners. Since the shipping companies refused to consider the seamen's demands for a wage increase, the Chinese Seamen's Union on January 13 declared a strike, which was soon joined by sympathetic strikers from many trades and industries in Hongkong. At its most serious stage the strikers numbered about 50,000, and 166 steamers, with a total tonnage of 280,404, were tied up in the port. This caused direct losses of $5,000,000 to shipping companies, distributed among fourteen different lines; while the indirect losses, including loss of wages, destruction of property, injury to good will and credit, and interference with trade and commerce were enormous. For several weeks there was complete paralysis of the industrial life of Hongkong.[10]

The Shanghai incident of May 30, 1925, was the outcome of political, racial, and social-economic complications of long standing. The International Settlement of Shanghai is governed by a municipal council whose members are representatives of the British, American, and Japanese nationalities, the British predominating. Under its jurisdiction is a population of about a million, of which some 22,000 are foreigners, the remainder being Chinese. Yet the Chinese have no representative on the council, although it is they who pay the greater part of the taxes, and racial antipathy and racial discrimination have been common. Recently the situation has been further aggravated by unsatisfactory labor conditions. An ordinary factory worker works about 12 hours a day and receives not more than 50 cents; his earnings are not sufficient to meet the rising cost of living. Consequently, on May 4, 1925, the Chinese workmen of the Nagai Wata Kaisha Cotton Mills (of Japanese ownership) struck for an increase in wages. On May 15 a sympathetic strike was declared by the Chinese workers in five other mills, and the management of a seventh mill shut down the plant to avoid damage. A dispute arose and the management opened fire, wounding more than ten workers, one of whom was fatally wounded and died soon afterward. Indignation was at once aroused among labor organizations, student associations, and educational and commercial bodies. Popular demonstrations began. On May 30, in particular, a large demonstration paraded the streets, including students, artisans, factory workers, and others. A few of them were arrested by the foreign police; the demand for their release brought a large number of paraders to the municipal police station, whereupon the municipal police opened fire upon the unarmed crowd, killing six and wounding more than twenty. The tragedy of May 30 thus began.

From the Nagai Wata Kaisha mill strike to the end of 1925 a series of sympathetic strikes protesting against the shooting of May 30 took place in various places in China. According to a statistical study recently made by the writer there were 135 such strikes, distributed as follows: Shanghai, 104; Peking, 8; Hankow, Tsinan, 4 each; Tsingtao, Kaifeng, Chiocho, Nanking, 2 each; Fengtien, Tientsin, Chenkiang, Suikousan, Kongmoon, Swatow, 1 each; Canton-Hongkong, 1. Classified by industries, these strikes fell into eleven categories: (*a*) textile trades, 32; (*b*) foods, 14; (*c*) household goods, 6; (*d*) building and construction, 6; (*e*) tool-making and manufacturing, 18; (*f*) communications and transport, 12; (*g*) basic industries, 2; (*h*) educational undertakings, 6; (*i*) personal hygiene and public health, 7; (*j*) ornaments and luxuries, 5; (*k*) miscellaneous, 27. Of the 135 strikes, the number of strikers was reported in 94 cases (381,387 men, or 4,057 men per strike) and the duration of the strike in 25 cases (1,664 days, or 66.6 days per strike).

These strikes may be further analyzed as regards the causes, methods of mediation, and conduct of the strikers, and results. Excepting the Nagai Wata Kaisha Cotton Mill strike, the first in the series, the remainder were all protests against the events of May 30, together forming a forcible expression of the patriotic zeal which had grown out of the recent nationalist movement. In addition there were supplementary causes, such as demands regarding wages, hours of labor, and the social

[10] For further details cf. Dr. Ta Chen, "The Shipping Strike in Hongkong," *Monthly Labor Review* (May, 1922), pp. 9–15.

treatment of the workers. Strikes due to these other causes have yielded the following results: one case of complete success, 35 cases of partial success, one case of failure, and 98 cases not reporting. In 17 cases the right to organize trade-unions was recognized; in 16 cases the workers received a subsidy for the strike period in addition to an improvement in working conditions; and in 18 cases the strikers secured increases in wages.

The data regarding the methods of mediation and conduct of the strikers are incomplete: one case was settled by the management directly, one case by a mass meeting of the strikers, 7 cases by joint meetings of representatives of the management and of the workers, 11 cases by inviting disinterested individuals to arbitrate, 12 cases by inviting a chamber of commerce to arbitrate, 4 cases by inviting local officials to arbitrate, and 2 cases by inviting the federation of labor unions to arbitrate. The following information was obtained as to whether the strikers were riotous: In 3 cases the Chinese police were called out; in 2 cases the foreign police were called out; and in 3 cases there was injury to persons.

Space does not permit an outline of even the most significant strikes arising from the affair of May 30. A brief account may be given of one of the most remarkable, which occurred in the South and resulted in the boycotting of Hongkong by Canton. The seamen on a line of British steamers struck first (in June, 1925), and the strike quickly spread. Five days from the commencement of the strike, a parade including students, merchants, laborers, and soldiers was organized to demonstrate against Shameen, the foreign settlement at Canton. Firing broke out, with the result that many Chinese and a few foreigners were killed or wounded. Feeling was greatly inflamed and the Canton government (1) forbade the ships of Great Britain and Japan from entering South China ports, (2) gave the right to examine ships to the Federation of Anti-Imperialist Societies, and (3) set an embargo on the export of food and raw materials. The Cantonese laid down terms for the Hongkong government to accept as the condition of ending the boycott. The conditions for resuming work demanded by the Chinese laborers in foreign employ who had left Hongkong at the beginning of the boycott included, in addition to many political provisions, an 8-hour day, a minimum wage, collective bargaining with employers, the abolition of contract labor, improvement of the living conditions of woman and child labor, and compulsory labor insurance. For more than a year all attempts at negotiation failed, and the boycott was not called off until October, 1926. The losses to both Hongkong and Canton were enormous.

In Shanghai the changes in the labor situation following the original Shanghai incident of May 30, 1925, have had a less direct political effect, though they have not been without a bearing on the international situation; but they may yet prove to have been of more significance from an internal and purely labor point of view. But as the situation is still changing rapidly, it may be well to defer any attempt to describe it until greater stability has been reached.

### LABOR'S RELATION TO SOCIAL MOVEMENTS

From the foregoing it is clear that the labor question in China is causing considerable social unrest. In more recent times this question is further complicated by its relation to other social movements. First (*a*) Let us consider socialist and communistic propaganda. Toward the end of the Manchu dynasty, utopian socialism found its way to China chiefly through French Indo-China. Socialist clubs were organized in Canton, Nanking and Shanghai, and socialist literature occasionally appeared in print. Immediately after the overthrow of the Manchu dynasty, Shanghai became an important center of socialistic activities. Certain elements of the Kuomintang began to organize the national Labor party, with its headquarters in Shanghai and a branch in Tongshan, Chihli Province. In the platform the Labor party included socialist doctrines. But with the first political change that came to the Kuomintang, several of its members fled from Shanghai and the Labor party soon disappeared. In 1916 a member of the Kuomintang returned from Russia and organized the Federation of Laborers and Farmers in Shanghai, which advocated socialist principles. This temporarily revived socialist propaganda in the city, but the Federation was soon closed by the order of the local government. During that time socialist literature, including articles, pamphlets, and booklets, became gradually popular, and some of which were prohibited from circulation, such as the following: "Sufferings of a Laborer," "Proletarian Utopia," "Essentials of Socialism," "Common Sufferings," "Guide to Revolutionary Organs."

But socialist propaganda of a really radical character began with Dr. Sun Yat-Sen's activities in Canton. In 1922 Dr. Sun invited some of his followers to help him organize the Canton government. Among those who accepted his invitation were some communistically inclined who soon organized the Socialist Youth and the Marxian Society to discuss socialist teachings. Not long afterward communism gained strength in Canton and vicinity, and the Third Internationale at Moscow officially recognized the Communist party of China. In 1924 the Communist party was strong enough to persuade the Kuomintang to consolidate with itself in order to form a single party. This was agreed to, and since then communistic propaganda has been carried on in China in more systematic ways.

While communistic influences in China are thus pulling together, one should not overlook the part played by Russian communists, especially during the early period of communistic propaganda in China. In 1921 the Third Internationale held a conference on the Far Eastern peoples, at which a Russian delegate referred to the Chinese labor movement as in "the experimental stage of growth" and suggested that attention be directed toward "the organizing of the Chinese workers to prepare them for the people's revolution in China." Again, the executive committee of the Russian Communist party planned and directed the organization of the Communist Youth in China, which is essentially modeled after the same organization in Russia. In addition, some Russian communists have come to China to be engaged in the propagation of communistic ideas, as the recent raid of the Soviet embassy in Peking has revealed.

In the main, however, little information is now available regarding communistic activities in China. What the public knows is merely a broad outline of the manifold program of the communists which may be summarized under eight heads: (1) Part of their propaganda is being carried on through student organizations, as some of the student organs in China are radically inclined. (2) Similarly, some schools in China are also propagating communistic ideas through some teachers who offer courses or hold discussion conferences with students who show enthusiasm for extreme doctrines. (3) A certain degree of co-operation is effected through the agency of popular organizations such as the Anti-Imperialism Federation or the Anti-Religion Federation. (4) Some radical labor unions are also spreading communistic ideas such as the General Labor Union of China and its branch in Shanghai. (5) Some secret organizations are reported to be teaching communism in China, such as the D.S. club in Changsha, and the B.L.K. society in Loyang, Honan Province. (6) The Communist Youth, which is preliminary to enlisting members for the Communist party, is essentially an organization of young enthusiasts for communistic teachings, with the student class as the mainstay. (7) Although the Communist party officially affiliates itself with the Kuomintang, it privately conducts certain communistic practices. (8) The left wing of the Kuomintang is the most efficient organ for the spread of communist doctrines in China. Since 1924 the platform of the Kuomintang, especially the part dealing with people's livelihood, is modified to advocate (*a*) the limitation of capital and reform of wages for the laborers, and (*b*) the equalization of land and reform of village organization and life for farmers.

*b*) *The student movement.*—As the student movement is a very complicated affair, it is not attempted to do more than to sketch its chief relation to the labor movement. Popular lectures to the masses by small groups of students such as the "ten-men squads" are exerting far-reaching influence upon the laborers in opening their eyes to the great possibilities of a social revolt against existing evils. On holidays and during vacation energetic students often work among the workers either as counselors for drafting demands in labor disputes or as mediators between capital and labor. In more recent times the student unions are organized in most cities in China, and these organizations either issue manifestoes or pass resolutions to show sympathy or give support to the laborers and peasants.

*c*) *The peasant movement.*—As China is essentially an agricultural country, relatively more emphasis should be placed upon the elevation of the farmers if the labor movement is going to increase strength in society. This the labor leaders clearly see, and therefore both the communists and the left wing of the Kuomintang frequently advocate the joint movement of the workers and peasants. In January, 1923, when the Kuomintang held its first national conference in Canton, it declared its stand on the use of land and taxes on land. In the winter of the same year it began to encourage the farmers to organize farmers' unions, rural co-operative societies, and farmers' self-defense organizations, assisted with lecture groups and winter schools for farmers. In May, 1925, when the second national labor conference was convened in Canton, the farmers' unions were able to send delegates to participate in the discussion of problems affecting their welfare. At that time Kwangtung Province claimed a total of about 210,000 farmers who became members of the farmers' unions in twenty-two counties. Every year their numbers are increasing. The farmers' unions are organized to defend themselves against their common enemies, who, they contend, are undisciplined soldiers, corrupt officials, unscrupulous gentry, and greedy landlords. Their immediate objects are the building of roads, irrigation and drainage, rural education, reduction of rent, economic and social emancipation. Their ultimate goal is to co-operate with the urban workers for a common struggle for liberty, civil equality, and political franchise.

From Kwangtung the farmers' movement gradually spreads to other provinces, especially several provinces upon the Yangtse Valley. Wherever the influence of the Kuomintang reaches, there is the beginning of an agrarian revolt. The following is a typical instance. In 1923 Shensi troops were stationed at Low-shi County in Honan Province. In autumn of that year the county had a poor harvest, but the masses were still compelled to support the soldiers with food and shelter. The peasants revolted and the soldiers retreated into the city. As the city merchants were likewise unable to sustain financial losses, they urged the peasants to attack the soldiers for the second and third time!

### THE MAY DAY CELEBRATIONS

The activities of organized labor come to the notice of the public in yet another way, namely, the May day celebrations. On May 1, 1917, Canton was said to have observed the first May day celebration in China. From that time on the custom spread to other cities. On May 1, 1920, the cities of Peking, Shanghai, and Canton all had workingmen's demonstrations. Most of the handicraftsmen and organized workers in these cities had a holiday so that they could meet together for a parade and for meetings. Other social classes, such as student associations and chambers of commerce, either expressed their sympathy for labor or sent representatives to join the workers' celebrations. Handbills and pamphlets were freely distributed, some of them clearly showing the aims of the workers. One of them put forward the claim for "rice for all and labor for all"; another exclaimed "down with capitalism"; a third suggested "a union of all the workers"; a fourth advocated the division of the day into three equal portions, devoting eight hours to labor, eight hours to rest, and eight hours to education. In addition there were brief talks on the history of the May Day demonstrations in the West, the fundamentals of citizenship, and the aims of labor organizations. Since 1920 the custom has been observed every year in an increasing number of cities and an increasing number of workmen have joined in the celebrations. In 1924 the May Day celebration in Shanghai was notable for the presence of Dame Adelaide Anderson, formerly principal lady inspector of factories in Great Britain, Mr. Bunji Suzuki, president of the General Federation of Labor of Japan, and Mr. Wang Tsin-Wei, a liberal leader of the Kuomintang. More than 2,000 people, representing about fifty organizations, participated in the parade. A new "labor song" was sung. Committees were chosen to carry on propaganda for the cause of labor. Owing to political unrest, the May Day celebrations in 1926 were generally restricted by the local authorities.

### LABOR'S DEMAND FOR INTERNATIONAL REPRESENTATION

As the organization of Chinese labor is still in its infancy, it offers no persistent demand for international representation. Some demand there is, of course, and this is due to both internal and external reasons. Among some labor leaders and men who are interested in labor there is a natural desire that labor's views should be represented at meetings of international organizations. Then, too, from the international point of view, other countries certainly wish to procure economic, industrial, and social data about China in order to promote better international good will. In 1919, when the first session of the International Labor Conference was held in Washington, China had an official representative there. At recent sessions of the International Labor Conference in Geneva, the Chinese ministers to certain European countries and other diplomats have frequently acted as Chinese representatives. This method of representation, however, is unsatisfactory from several points of view. According to special provisions in Part XIII of the Treaty of Versailles, which created the International Labor Organization and laid down rules for the appointment of delegates from each state member to the annual International Labor Conference, it was stated that there should be delegates from each nation, representing the government, the employers, and the workers, respectively. Before the first session of the conference met in 1919, the Chinese Minister of Agriculture and Commerce declared that Chinese industry was still in the handicraft stage and had not yet reached such a stage of development as to warrant a delegate from labor. This immediately aroused opposition from a member of the House of Representatives, who asserted that the government was foregoing its privilege and would thereby lose its prestige in international affairs. Influential labor associations also contended that diplomatic representatives who might be handicapped by official duties and were out of touch with home conditions were sometimes not the proper persons to represent the interests of labor, and that labor must have its own representatives. The organizations of the overseas Chinese were especially determined on this point. Labor leaders and writers on social questions who hoped to stimulate industrial and social progress in the country also agreed with their view. But the Chinese government has not yet sent special delegates for labor, notwithstanding repeated requests from the International Labor Organization. Before the annual conference takes place, the program is sent to the Chinese government for suggestions and proposals. When the program of the sixth session of the conference (1924) came to Peking, the government was especially interested in the question of workmen's compensation for accidents and equality of treatment for national and foreign workers. Each year China submits her views to the conference on various problems which concern her.

In August, 1924, when the Red Internationale of Labor Unions met in Moscow, Chinese workers were represented at the conference. When called upon to make a report the Chinese delegates pointed out the growing strength of nationalism in China and stated that the leaders of the movement were fighting two monster evils of the times: militarism as a national evil, and imperialism as an international evil. In this struggle the Kuomintang is credited with having taken a leading part, as its party platform includes national and international reforms. Internationally it stands for the abolition of concessions, of extra-territoriality, and of unequal treaties. Nationally it is in favor of popular elections, freedom of speech, of the press, and of association, land reform, and the nationalization of the railways.

### LABOR MATTERS OF INTERNATIONAL SIGNIFICANCE

Closely associated with labor's demand for international representation are a series of labor matters of international relationships which have direct or indirect influence upon the labor movement in China. First, let us consider the case of Chinese laborers in France during the World War. During the years 1917 to 1920 there were about 140,000 Chinese laborers in France, chiefly in the employ of the British and French governments. Their terms of employment were stipulated in the Hui Min contract, which was drawn up by the Chinese emigration bureau. Their work varied from the loading and unloading of cargoes to the manufacture of airplanes and gun materials. When they were in France the Y.M.C.A. did considerable educational and social work for them. As a result their literacy was raised from 20 per cent to about 38 per cent. Since 1920 they have returned to Chihli, Shantung, Shanghai, and Canton. Some of them have resumed farm work, others have again engaged in industrial occupations. In the latter capacity they have made noteworthy contributions to the labor movement, for they insist: (1) that labor should be independent of politics, (2) that labor should pre-eminently strive for economic and social improvement, and (3) that the workers should abstain from drinking, gambling, and opium smoking.

Second, mention should be made of the massacre of Chinese laborers in Japan in 1923. During the World War Japanese industry and trade were developing at a rapid rate and Japan suffered a great shortage of labor. Chinese peddlers from Wenchow and Chuchow, Chekiang Province, who went to Japan to sell cheap wares, such as fans and seal stones, became struck with excellent opportunities for industrial employment. Some secured jobs for themselves; others induced their relations to emigrate to the Island Empire for employment. During the booming period this influx of Chinese workers was tolerated by the Japanese; but since the cessation of the European war there was in Japan a period of business depression coupled with low prices and unemployment. Then an agitation for ousting the Chinese began. An imperial ordinance of July 28, 1899, respecting the residences and business of foreigners who are not entitled to freedom of residence by the treaties and usages, states that "foreign laborers are not allowed to reside or do work unless they obtain a special permission therefor from the administrative office." Since the Chinese have not satisfied the foregoing condition, some Japanese agitators deem it a sufficient legal ground to exclude the Chinese laborers. Gradually friction and ill-feeling between the Japanese and Chinese became intensified. Around September 1, 1923, when the great earthquake broke out in Japan, the Japanese people were under a great emotional stress, and under this pretext they indiscriminately arrested and killed the Chinese. In Tokyo and Oshima the Chinese victims numbered about 340, or approximately 9 per cent of the total population of Chinese emigrant laborers who went to Japan during the World War. Protesting against this wanton atrocity of the Japanese, labor unions in China held many demonstrations. Nation-wide indignation was aroused, and the Chinese proletariat vigorously demanded redress. The Chinese government appointed a special commission to proceed to Japan to demand of the Japanese government to institute an investigation and publish its findings and to indemnify the families of the killed. As the commission's efforts were unsuccessful, the Chinese workers more keenly felt the impotency of governmental protection as well as the inadequacy of their own organizations. Therefore after the occurrence of this tragic event many enlightened workers clearly saw the urgent need of better organization among themselves and closer attention on international matters affecting the interest of labor.

Third, reference may be made to Chinese contract labor in the Pacific region. The question of Chinese contract laborers in the Pacific area forms an important chapter in modern immigration and emigration. Australia, New Zealand, the island of Nauru, Western Samoa, and Hawaiian Islands have at one time or another used Chinese contract labor, and some are still continuing it in a certain form, although attempts are being made in every country to stop it altogether. In Australia the literacy test is quite effective in barring Chinese emigrants seeking admission. Since 1907 this law has been adopted by New Zealand, after the heavy poll tax had proved ineffective in the latter country. Western Samoa has, since the World War, become a mandatory territory of New Zealand. The coconut and cocoa interests of the island have repeatedly petitioned the colonial government for the permission to import Chinese labor. But since 1915 Great Britain has prohibited the practice of contract labor in the Empire, so their requests were refused. However, recent negotiations between England, China, and Hongkong were in favor of the planters so late as 1920, and Western Samoa was able to get a fresh supply of Chinese laborers who embarked from Hongkong for Western Samoa. The former German island of Nauru is now a mandate of Australia. Although Chinese labor is being used, there are indications that the experiment will soon cease entirely. In fact, since 1924 the contract labor system in the island is prohibited by law. In the Hawaiian islands, though there are still Chinese laborers in the sugar and pineapple plantations, no further influx of Chinese labor is likely, because (1) in the Thirteenth Amendment of the federal Constitution of the United States there is a provision against involuntary servitude, and also there are several peonage statutes now in force in the United States; (2) the American Federation of Labor has always been against the importation of Chinese labor into Hawaii. At the first session of the Institute of Pacific Relations, held in Honolulu in July, 1925, the Australian and New Zealand delegations assured the members of the Chinese group that the practice of contract labor in their respective countries will soon discontinue in entirety. The Chinese members are pleased to have the assurance, for they firmly believe that the Chinese contract laborers in the Pacific area have been an important source of international misunderstanding between China and the Pacific countries. Public opinion in China is more and more against the existence of the system. Some labor organizations in China are even violently antagonistic to it, for, judging by past experiences, whether the Chinese were employed by a foreign government or a foreign private corporation, the result has been in the main unsatisfactory to the Chinese. Although the foreign government or the foreign capitalist employer were often enriched by employing Chinese labor, the Chinese workers themselves or their families received little material benefit therefrom. If their wages were higher than what they had been used to in the home country, it should be pointed out that their habits were also modified and wants increased so as to leave them a low margin of savings. Besides, the general neglect of the workers' social and educational needs by the labor administrators practically made no headway in improving the life of the Chinese laborers. Moreover, racial prejudice and discriminatory laws against the Chinese by foreign governments and nationals are more and more resented by the Chinese at home and abroad. Under these circumstances it seems wise to eradicate the system of contract labor altogether.

Fourth, as the nationalist movement in China is gaining strength, labor organizations in several foreign countries have shown sympathy and support. Since the Shanghai affair broke out on May 30, 1925, the Trades Union Congress and the Independent Labor party in England made strong representations to the British government to keep hands off in China in order not to hamper the natural growth of the nationalist activities. The American Federation of Labor went further, to suggest an international conference for the abolition of extra-territoriality in China. In May, 1927, a Pan-Pacific Conference on Labor was planned for in South China, to be attended by delegates from America, England, Soviet Russia, Australia, Japan, India, Korea, and the Philippines. It was reported that the idea first came from the Third International in Moscow, strongly advocated by certain labor leaders in Australia, indorsed by the Workers' and Peasants' party in Japan, and highly welcomed by the left wing of the Chinese labor movement. Although recent political changes in China have made it impracticable to realize the original aims of the promoters, such a move cannot fail to impress upon thoughtful men the great possibilities of international co-operation along the line of labor.

## CONCLUSION

In the light of the facts given, certain conclusions seem inevitable. In the first place, several factors are responsible for the labor movement in China today. Industrially, China is slowly emerging from the handicraft to the machine stage. With this change are also changes in social habits and educational methods. To precipitate these changes, radical ideas gradually find entry into China and socialist and communistic propaganda help to arouse the working population to a state of general unrest. Still another cause is found in a series of international labor events, some of which have educative influence, others serve as stimulants to the labor movement in China. Secondly, in order to strengthen the Chinese labor movement, labor must be divorced both from politics and radicalism, for in recent years political changes and communistic propaganda have adversely affected the cause of labor. Meantime, strenuous efforts should be made to recruit men of courage and determination to fight the cause of labor independently and unselfishly. Unless there are a considerable number of men with a strong conviction that social and industrial progress will come only through an emancipated proletariat, it will not be possible to carry on a fruitful labor movement. Thirdly, the predominant ambition of labor should be the social and economic improvement of the workmen, for their misery today is fundamentally due to combined social and economic causes. The main questions at issue include wages, hours of labor, conditions of employment, and social treatment by the employers. Only when the workers have an income adequate to maintain a decent standard of living can higher ideals of social life be discussed. The economic phase of the fight should precede any other consideration in a program of social reconstruction for present-day China. Lastly, unsound practices should be avoided. A general tendency today is to imitate the tactics of the labor movement in the West. Certain practices may have been successful for the struggle between capital and labor in Russia, Europe, or America, but may yet be ineffective in China. Regulations or policies of trade-unions may be efficient for one society but unsuitable for another. Certain aspects of the Chinese labor movement today are still too foreign in spirit. Trade-union methods and practices of Western countries should be so modified as to suit economic and social conditions in China. The 8-hour working day should not be blindly advocated when the 10-hour day would in many cases be a blessing to the workers. It is useless to agitate blindly for labor copartnership in industry when the majority of the workers are still illiterate and care little for such privileges. What is urgently needed, then, is a program of practical reforms based upon existing social conditions, which shall truly serve to promote the welfare and happiness of the workers. Some fundamental work must be done to build up an intelligent proletariat capable of appreciating and using wisely its just rights and privileges. Gradually its social standards should be raised, so as to insure industrial peace in the nation, and so ultimately throughout the world.

## SECTION 20

## THE FINANCIAL CRISIS IN JAPAN

JUNNOSUKE INOUYE
President, Bank of Japan, Tokyo

The recent runs on banks in Japan which started the middle of March and lasted till the latter part of April were the first bank runs, in the true sense of the term, that the country had ever experienced. Not infrequently in the past banks have been pressed for payment of deposits because of bad repute or for other reasons, but such runs were limited to the few banks concerned, not affecting others to any extent. The recent banking disturbances, however, covering the big cities of Tokyo, Osaka, Kyoto, Kobe, and Yokohama, and spreading throughout the country, resulted in the failure of no less than thirty banks.

No exact figures are available as to how much out of the total bank deposits of 11,400,000,000 yen was actually withdrawn during the panic, but Table I, indicating a sharp increase in the advances made by the Bank of Japan, which is the central bank, and also in the issue of bank notes, will throw some light on the amount involved:

TABLE I

(In Thousands of Yen)

| Date | Advances by Bank of Japan | Bank-Note Issue |
|---|---|---|
| March 15 | 234,940 | 1,095,631 |
| March 22 | 536,147 | 1,341,829 |
| March 31 | 538,744 | 1,355,036 |
| April 11 | 527,964 | 1,230,831 |
| April 15 | 554,031 | 1,203,829 |
| April 20 | 1,062,725 | 1,679,465 |
| April 25 | 2,095,992 | 2,659,543 |
| April 30 | 1,484,414 | 2,037,060 |

There were, of course, circumstances that may be counted as the direct causes of this nation-wide run on the banks, but underneath all those immediate causes we find some more fundamental circumstances of which the panic was only an unavoidable outcome. Any explanation of the recent banking crisis, therefore, must start from these fundamental causes.

During the past sixty or seventy years Japan has made remarkable progress in her economic life. Inasmuch as this progress has been within such a comparatively short period of time, a somewhat peculiar situation has resulted because of a disproportionate development of the different parts of the economic organization of the country. That is to say, the economic situation lacked stability, and as such is liable to disturbances.

It was after the Chino-Japanese War (1894–95) that Japan began to make notable progress along modern lines of economic activity. The Russo-Japanese War (1904–5), which broke out ten years later, marked the country's advance in the modern system of industry. The progress kept on unretarded on the whole during another ten year period that preceded the World War, yet the country's financial resources were still very much limited, Japan being far behind the industrial countries of the West in this respect. For instance, at the end of the year 1914 the gold holdings of the Bank of Japan and the government put together amounted only to 340,000,000 yen, and the bank deposits of the country did not exceed 2,300,000,000 yen. The total amount of foreign trade, both exports and imports, during 1914 was 1,200,000,000 yen. The World War that broke out in 1914 wrought a radical change in the economic life of the country. Until the great war our foreign trade had almost always shown an unfavorable balance, but the war reversed the situation, and in 1917 the exports amounted to 1,660,000,000 yen against the imports of 1,080,000,000 yen, leaving a balance of 570,000,000 yen in our favor. Thus in the four years of 1915–18, inclusive, the trade balance to our credit reached 1,400,000,000 yen. In addition to this there was an enormous amount of invisible exports due to the shipping activities of our mercantile marine. Putting both together, Japan's net gain in these years amounted to some 4,000,000,000 yen. The acquisition of such wealth quite naturally stimulated a rapid economic development of the country. The gold holdings of the Bank of Japan and the government at the end of 1919 had increased to 2,000,000,000 yen, or six times the pre-war figure, and the bank deposits of the country jumped to 11,000,000,000 yen, or five times the former amount. Parallel with this growth in resources, the prices of commodities advanced sharply and the standard of living of the people rose rapidly. In short, Japan's economic life has undergone a complete revolution during these past few years.

The extraordinary economic development which the war made possible produced a boom that was characterized by exceptionally large speculative activities, lasting from the latter part of 1919 till the spring of 1920. This boom terminated in a crash, which seriously affected and dealt a heavy blow to all branches of business. The fundamental cause of the present economic difficulties may be traced back to these circumstances.

Japan was not the only country that was visited by a post-war boom, for England, the United States, and other countries had the same experience. Then how is it that Japan alone suffers so severely from its consequences? The war, as mentioned before, brought about a complete change in our economic situation. The economic machinery of modern times became very much complicated and delicate in its working, and yet from the paucity of knowledge and experience the nation failed to handle the situation as it should have done. In other words, the people lacked the insight into the causes that bring about business cycles under the modern economic system, and in the intoxication of the boom failed to take the proper precautions against the business depression that comes afterward. How violent was the turn of the business cycle in this particular case may be seen in the increase of the index numbers of commodity prices and prices of securities during the boom of 1919 and after the reaction of 1920 (Table II).

In raw silk and cotton yarns, the two staple products of the country, we notice a striking instance of price movement at the turn of the business cycle. Raw silk, which was quoted at around 2,000 yen per 100 kin (1 kin equivalent to 1.32275 pounds) in July, 1919, rose up and up until it reached the height of 4,400 yen in February, 1920, only to precipitate down to 1,100 yen—one-quarter of the peak price—in July of the same year. In cotton yarn the fluctuation was not so violent, and yet in July, 1919, one bale of standard cotton yarn was quoted at the level of 500 yen; in November, the same year, 720 yen was the price recorded, and then after the collapse it fell down to the level of 200–300 yen—being from one-half to one-third of the high.

TABLE II

| | Prices of Commodities | Prices of Leading Shares |
|---|---|---|
| July, 1914.......... | 100 | 100 |
| July, 1919.......... | 254 | 222 |
| January, 1920....... | 317 | 250 |
| March, 1920........ | 338 | 225 |
| April, 1920.......... | 316 | 165 |
| June, 1920.......... | 261 | 113 |

No section of our business could have escaped the effects of such violent changes of commodity and security prices. The blow was severest on the industrial enterprises, which thus far had gone on expanding without interruption after the Armistice. The loss suffered was very big indeed. As the natural consequence, banks that had been financing those industries had the larger part of their funds tied up, which meant a serious loss to the banks involved. Had those bankers been more cautious and circumspect in the management of their business, or had they had more abundant resources in their hands, they might have better weathered the storm. Most of those banks, however, being lured on by the boom, granted accommodations rather freely and with but little precaution, some even going so far as to undertake the working of the enterprises themselves. Under these circumstances it was no wonder that they should have been hit seriously during the reactionary period.

Why, then, did not those banks that suffered great losses from the crash take immediate steps to radically readjust their affairs? This is a question that naturally comes up, and the explanation will made clear the fundamental causes of the recent banking crisis. For this purpose I shall describe below the business situation of our country since 1920 and up to the present time.

After the reaction of 1920, over two years of utter bewilderment as to the outlook elapsed, neither the bankers nor the industrial leaders being able to see what the future held in store; they therefore simply put off the necessary adjustments, keeping up their hope for the future. In 1923 things were gradually clearing up and a light became discernible in the financial horizon of the country, when suddenly there came the great earthquake which devastated Tokyo, Yokohama, and the adjoining districts.

The earthquake definitely drew a line between the businesses that had future possibilities and those that had none. The situation convinced the bankers of the necessity of taking a decisive step to clear off bad and doubtful assets carried by them. No bank, however, dared to adopt such a drastic measure, for they were afraid that, should they squarely face the facts, write off their capital losses, or even lower the rate of dividends, they would disclose their weakness, and then from the nature of business might lose public confidence and the consequent withdrawal of deposits. The bankers in those days were like a man hesitating with a heavily cracked vase. If left alone, the fissure will only extend, and the vase will finally be broken. In the same way the position of the banks became worse by concealing the weak points and putting off the necessary house-cleaning until the public began to look on them with misgivings. These conditions lasted for the two years of 1925 and 1926. Enlightened financiers and men with discerning eyes took the situation very seriously and closely watched developments. These circumstances will reveal how remote and deep rooted were the causes that brought about the recent banking disturbances of our country.

The banks were thus placed in a very delicate position when last February the government introduced into the Diet a bill relating to the liquidation of bills originating from the earthquake destruction. The debates on the bill in the Diet, however, incidentally bared the conditions of the banks holding such bills. The attention of the public was focused on the developments in the Diet, and the depositors' uneasiness was enhanced by the disclosures. The suspicious public was beginning to withdraw its money from all the banks. It was not until the sudden closing of a Tokyo bank on March 15, however, that depositors became really alarmed and the situation developed into bank runs. The withdrawal of deposits now extended in its scope and got so heavy that by the end of March 7 or 8 more banks had to close their doors. In the meantime, for the purpose of pacifying the excited depositors, the government and the Bank of Japan explained the actual state of the financial situation and announcing their willingness to give special accommodations to the banks in general. This measure proved effective, and a lull came in April; but runs on banks were resumed with fresh vigor and on a gigantic scale when, on April 18 the Bank of Taiwan, one of the chartered banks, and another big bank in Osaka suspended payments.

The Bank of Taiwan is a chartered bank established in 1899 under the Bank of Taiwan Act for the purpose of regulating the credit and currency of the Island of Taiwan (Formosa). It is vested with the right of issuing its own notes. Its business sphere originally comprised only the Island of Taiwan, South China, and the South Seas, where it carried on general banking business and foreign exchange. The Bank of Taiwan, however, gradually extended its foreign exchange business and soon became one of the leading banks in Japan proper. In the course of time the bank became closely connected with the Sudzuki & Company, which is a big and enterprising trading concern. After the armistice the company's business was unsuccessful and the bank's loans remained entirely unliquidated. Further, during the discussions in the Diet of the bill for liquidation of the earthquake bills, the Bank of Taiwan was made an object of much criticism because it was the largest holder of such bills. Public suspicion naturally centered on the bank. The Bank of Taiwan had hitherto been a large borrower of call money, so under the circumstances lenders began to call in the loans, which made the situation of the bank increasingly difficult, and by the middle of April the continuation of the business became almost hopeless. In view of the important position held by the Bank of Taiwan in Japan and abroad, the government, to save the situation, drafted an urgent imperial ordinance for authorizing the Bank of Japan to grant special advances to the bank and for indemnifying the Bank of Japan any loss thereby incurred up to 200,000,000 yen. The Privy Council, however, to which the draft was referred, rejected the measure, this causing the Bank of Taiwan to close it doors on April 18.

On the same day the Omi Bank, another big bank in Osaka, also announced suspension of payments. This bank was capitalized at 15,000,000 yen, with deposits amounting to 130,000,000 yen. The news of the failures of such big banks poured oil on the flames of public excitement, and April 21 witnessed another addition to the list of failures in the form of the Fifteenth Bank, which was one of the big banks in Tokyo, with a capital of 100,000,000 yen and deposits amounting to 360,000,000. Now the runs on banks became nation-wide, banks losing the confidence of their depositors. Even the first-rate big banks that boasted of the soundness of their position could not prevent long lines of people being formed before their doors. The number of banks that collapsed under the pressure reached thirteen in Tokyo and Osaka and seventeen in other places, making a total of thirty. So grave was the situation that should things have been left to take their own course, there would have been no knowing how large would grow the list of insolvencies. The government, therefore, by way of an emergency measure, decided upon the declaration of a moratorium. As a preparatory step to the moratorium all banks in the country announced a two days' holiday on April 22 and 23. The moratorium was proclaimed on the afternoon of the twenty-second by an urgent imperial ordinance. The purpose of the ordinance was to authorize general postponement of payments for three weeks from the day of the declaration. The banks, except for the withdrawals of less than 500 yen a day or for the payment of salaries and wages, were permitted to decline all withdrawal requests from depositors.

The moratorium served the purpose for which it was declared. The public had time to calm its excitement, the depositors getting more considerate, and the financial status of the country cleared up. The government, on the other hand, convened an extraordinary session of the Diet to pass two bills relating to special advances by the Bank of Japan under the government guaranty, one for banks in general and the other as a relief measure exclusively for Taiwan (Formosa). Both bills passed the two houses and were promulgated on May 9. These two laws were enacted to meet the situation after the termination of the moratorium. They provided for a government indemnity to the Bank of Japan to cover the losses that the bank might incur through special advances made by the bank regardless of its usual practices. The first of the said laws provides that when any bank applies to the Bank of Japan for an advance of funds needed for meeting the payment of deposits, the latter, for the period of one year from the date of the promulgation of the law, is authorized to grant the required accommodations, even if the securities offered be otherwise than those regularly accepted. The government guarantees to indemnify the bank to the extent of 500,000,000 yen if any loss is incurred through such operations. The other law provides that should it be deemed necessary by the government, for the purpose of preserving order in Taiwan or for the upholding of the country's credit abroad, financial institutions in Taiwan, whether banks or not, are allowed to approach the Bank of Japan for special accommodations during a period of one year; such advances shall be made regardless of the securities, and if the Bank of Japan incur any loss through such operations, the government guarantees to indemnify the bank up to the extent of 200,000,000 yen.

The enactment of these two laws proved reassuring. During the moratorium and even after its termination the public excitement subsided and calmness reigned over the country. Even the Bank of Taiwan, which had been the center of the whirlpool, reopened its doors on May 9, and thus to all appearances the crisis was tided over. This is reflected in the movements of the advances by the Bank of Japan, and the note issue. The highest mark was attained on April 25, since which date the figures have steadily declined, except for a slight advance again for a few days at the expiration of the moratorium (see Table III).

TABLE III

(In Thousands of Yen)

| | Advances by Bank of Japan | Amount of Notes Issued |
|---|---|---|
| April 25 | 2,095,992 | 2,659,543 |
| April 30 | 1,484,414 | 2,037,060 |
| May 5 | 1,237,006 | 1,684,567 |
| May 10 | 1,223,384 | 1,599,651 |
| May 14 | 1,250,291 | 1,629,026 |
| May 20 | 1,049,385 | 1,392,580 |
| May 31 | 991,094 | 1,426,912 |
| June 10 | 868,381 | 1,266,915 |

The special advances made by the Bank of Japan under these two laws represent only 97,000,000 yen of the figures in Table III. That is, the two laws largely achieved their purpose by their mere promulgation. Thus an inflation in consequence of the increase in the advances of the Bank of Japan, which was feared to follow the government guaranty of loss up to the total of 700,000,000 yen, has been avoided.

The recent financial crisis not only made inevitable the declaration of a three weeks' moratorium, but it forced the closing of many banks and there were grave disorders of credit; even now business, more or less, feels the effects of the shake-up of confidence. The cost to the country is calculated to be a considerable one. Yet, if the crisis brought home to our bankers and business men the pressing need of the long-delayed thorough house-cleaning, and if they have learned to seize the present opportunity as a starting-point for a sound and healthy development of their affairs in the future, the price will not have been paid in vain.

The exchange value of the yen was affected somewhat seriously by the disturbances. The American exchange, which prior to the panic was quoted at 49 dollars to 100 yen, dropped to 46 dollars, though the subsequent rally brought the rate up to 47 dollars. After the great earthquake of September, 1923, our exchange touched the lowest point of 38½ dollars, from which bottom it steadily recovered and pursued an upward course, along with the progress of the economic reconstruction of the country. During the latter half of the year 1926 there was increasing expectation of an early lifting of the ban on our gold exports, and the exchange advanced to 48 dollars. The upward trend continued to this year, and in March last it touched the level of 49 dollars. The recent collapse is no doubt an outcome of a loss of credit abroad, but it may be more pertinently explained by the reaction to the disappointed expectation of the removal of the gold embargo. This reaction in its turn was occasioned by the enormously increased note issue during the panic period and the apprehension of a currency inflation in the future.

The measures taken by the government and the Bank of Japan, as outlined previously, for dealing with the situation were of even greater effect than was expected, and the crisis has been completely overcome. Even the banks that are now suspending payments are expecting to resume operations sooner or later with the aid of the government and the Bank of Japan. Then will the main purposes of the measures for meeting the situation brought about by the panic have been accomplished. The recent panic, however, disclosed the defects and unsound features of our credit system and has taught us the necessity of its revision and improvement. The government had this last year already appointed a committee consisting of government officials and private persons for the purpose of reforming the banking and credit system of the country. It has also set about the study of the whole problem of our banking system. In view of the importance of its bearing on trade and business, the problem will now be given more urgent consideration from all parties concerned, and it is hoped that our recent bitter experiences will be fully turned into good account in that respect.

## SECTION 21

# THE RÔLE OF THE BANKER IN INTERNATIONAL RELATIONS

JEROME D. GREENE
Member of the firm of Lee, Higginson & Company, New York City

In choosing a title for this paper I have avoided the invidious term "international banker," which seems to have been invested with somewhat sinister implications. Moreover, the term is misleading in so far as it attributes to a banker in the foreign field functions peculiar to that field, and supposedly on an exalted plane of high finance to which only the ablest and shrewdest, if not the least scrupulous may aspire. The fact is, of course, that a banker is just a banker, good, bad, or indifferent, wherever his activities lie, and the principles, methods, and aims on which his service is based are simply the principles of ordinary business.

It is true that the word "bank" has different meanings in different countries. Some of the largest and best-known banks in Europe, especially in Germany, use their capital and deposits not only in the ordinary operations of loan, discount, and acceptance credits, but also in the promotion of new or speculative enterprises. In the United States banks are limited to the more strictly banking functions, and the capital necessary for promotions is commonly derived from groups of capitalists formed *ad hoc* and employing their own rather than borrowed money.

The functions of bankers in the broadest sense of the term may be classified under three heads, namely, (*a*) financing trade, that is, the supply of money or credit to cover raw materials and goods through the stages of production, transportation, and distribution; (*b*) investment financing, the loaning of money for a longer period than ordinary bank loans, usually to established industries, public utilities, governments, states, or municipalities; (*c*) promotions and developments requiring capital for enterprises during their initial or speculative stages.

Commercial financing is simply the instrument or vehicle of exchange which in the last analysis is essentially an exchange of commodities or services. In the very nature of the case international trade is a fifty-fifty proposition, and the banker's loans are automatically liquidated by the recurring cycle or turnover. Exports and imports must tend in the long run to balance, for any continued inferiority of the one must keep the other in check until equilibrium is approximately established.

Investment financing, with which this paper is chiefly concerned is for longer terms. If the loan is sound, it confers means whereby the debtor can create permanent assets or maintain or build up his earnings and thus insure his ability to pay interest and amortization at agreed rates, so that at maturity, when the loan has been fully paid, the lender has his money back with interest and the borrower has maintained or enlarged his assets and earning power. There should be a real mutuality of the benefits accruing from the transaction. The terms of the loan should be neither so oppressive as to make the borrower pay too dearly for the benefits received nor so lenient as to yield the lender a smaller return than that to which his money was entitled in view of the risk involved, the possible alternative uses for his money, and the rates prevailing in the money market.

In the realm of banking more accurately termed "promotion," there is perhaps the greatest opportunity for an inequitable apportionment of benefits and risks. Here lies the most danger of undue exploitation of natural resources with insufficient return to the country originally possessing them, and here likewise is the danger that obstacles placed in the way of operation, or the lack of a fair return for the risks involved, either keeps out capital entirely or handicaps its employment and prevents a due return upon it. But here again the ideal to be aimed at by intelligent self-interest is one of mutual benefit. If the pioneer who takes large risks wins the large reward to which he is entitled, he also correspondingly increases the wealth of the community served. His prosperity should promote rather than hinder the prosperity of the country.

In short, the various operations of banking and finance depend, or should depend, upon the complete mutuality of benefits which, as a practical matter can best be attained by the ordinary processes of bargain and trade within the limits of sound conservation policy with respect to natural resources. Single transactions of one-sided advantage may occur from time to time in this as in other realms of human activity, but the profits made by the swindler who has to seek a new field or a new victim for every transaction is not the profit in which the business community as a whole is interested. On the contrary, doing business at the old stand for satisfied customers is the only way to make a living, and for this the principle of mutual advantage must, in the long run, prevail. Those of us who are looking forward hopefully to the time when our present large trade with the Orient will become many times larger, have no idea that we can reap advantage from this growth in any other way than by honorable dealings continuously maintained for mutual advantage.

Before going further, let me say that in whatever references I make in this paper to the functions and purposes of American capital in the Pacific, and particularly in the Far East, I am expressing my own personal opinions and observations, and that I do not speak as the representative of any firm or banking group; and it goes without saying that nothing said or done at this conference can be taken as representing directly or indirectly any governmental authority.

Another point should be made clear which has often been the subject of misconception with regard to the function of bankers generally and especially with regard to foreign loans: The money available for large loans often described as coming from Wall Street or Lombard Street, or even from New York or London, does not represent accumulations in a few hands or taken out of some fantastically huge chest located in a great financial center. It is the money of the private investor whose name is legion—and nowadays a fairly small investor, at that. In the United States before the war the number of investors who were regular buyers of securities was estimated at a figure below half a million, and the average individual sale in the various bond issues as they came along and were taken up by the public was well over $10,000. Since the war, owing to the well-nigh universal subscription for war loans, the number of investors has gone into the millions and the average subscription for ordinary government, municipal, public utility, and industrial issues has been in the neighborhood of $3,000—sometimes less than that. The importance of this change can hardly be exaggerated, because it largely determines and limits the function of the banker. While the judgment and technical experience of the banker are indeed called into play, they are employed by him in his capacity as mediator between the investing public and the borrower. If terms are imposed with regard to security or with regard to the method of expending the proceeds of a loan, these terms are the expression, not necessarily only of what seems abstractly or intrinsically right and desirable, but also in some measure of what is necessary to make the bond saleable. The investor is naturally influenced by the banker's judgment or persuasion up to a certain point, but there is such a thing as a market taste or appetite with its likes and dislikes, which is at once too subtle and too real to be controlled by any man or small group of men. Take, for example, the question of security for a loan. It often happens that as between the banker, who has made a thorough study of a situation and who has entire confidence in the integrity and financial resources of the borrower, and the borrower himself, the formal, unsecured obligation to pay principal and interest is intrinsically sound and trustworthy. It might very well be, however, that a bond expressing such an obligation without security would, for market reasons, be wholly unsaleable; and, of course, if the banker, who is essentially a merchant, cannot sell the bonds to the public, he cannot buy them from the borrower and the loan cannot be made. The same principle applies not only as to whether there shall be security or not, but also to the amount and the nature of the security and to such other requirements as supervision of expenditure, the auditing of accounts, and the filing of periodical reports. In all this there need not be the slightest reflection on the integrity of the borrower, any more than in the case of an individual who makes a loan from the bank and is obliged to put up collateral: it is simply the ordinary practice of business. The banker may know that his friend in need of money is honorable and solvent, but if he makes a loan to him without security, he may have to account to his stockholders, if not to the courts. The banker may know that a foreign government or company is honorable and financially strong, but when the individual lender, a man of different language and race, lives thousands of miles away from the borrower, he may, until experience has educated him, impose terms and conditions that would otherwise be unnecessary. This is something that the banker may deplore or gradually help to remedy, but he cannot ignore it.

The practice of requiring government borrowers to hypothecate assets or to pledge revenues as security for loans has, however, in my opinion, a regrettable aspect. It being true, as a rule, that a sovereign government cannot be sued, the financial obligations of a government to those whose money it borrows rest ultimately on the value of its promise, or, in other words, on its will and capacity to pay principal and interest. The practice, doubtless justified in some past instances, of fortifying a government's promise by the hypothecation of its revenues has so accustomed private investors to regard such hypothecation as offering substantial protection that it has been demanded in cases where the merits of the situation did not require it. The inevitable result has been the impairment of what should be the most sacred of all obligations, the plighted word of a sovereign power or other governmental entity. Such impairment has a bad moral effect on both borrower and lender, and unquestionably hinders the desirable flow of capital in directions where it is legitimately desired. It may seriously be considered whether in a majority, if not in all, cases of public loans where revenues are now hypothecated, an equal safety for the investment might not be secured by the voluntary allocation of revenues, preferably those associated with the purposes of the loan; for example, a railroad, hydro-electric power, or other income-producing works, not as a matter of hypothecation but as a matter of budgeting, conforming to sound, business-like procedure. As a matter of fact, the so-called hypothecation of revenues, except where they are paid to a bank or other specified trustee for the bondholders, is not really anything more than a representation by the borrower that certain allocations of revenues will be made; and it is a pity, therefore, that the words "mortgage" or "hypothecation" should be used at all in such cases. In my opinion, bankers can confer a substantial benefit both upon debtor governments and upon bondholders by minimizing the resort either to real or to so-called hypothecation of revenues, so as gradually to put every governmental obligation on the highest plane of credit.

If it be true that the requirement of special security, or indeed any other method of enforcement, causes a regrettable impairment of the sanctity of government loan obligations, it is all the more incumbent upon governments so to control their receipts and expenses that the faithful performance of their promises may be assured. While the will to pay is important, no credit can be given for it if available means of assuring capacity to pay are not simultaneously envisaged and continuously employed. If due regard to national pride and self-respect require that the unsupported promise of the government be accepted as the basis of a loan, that same pride and self-respect should not only countenance but welcome the reasonable insistence *by bankers* on proper administration, supervision, audit, and report.

You will note my emphasis on the words "by bankers," and in this connection it may not be out of place to say that as a matter of voluntary bargaining a government may with perfect dignity accept, at the behest of bankers representing the bondholding public, stipulations with regard to administration and supervision which it might find more difficult to accept at the behest of foreign governments. In the concrete case of China, where so large a volume of capital will ultimately be required for the improvement of transportation, the prevention of flood and famine and the diffusion of such other material benefits as the Chinese people themselves may from time to time desire, I believe that many concessions to the reasonable demands of foreign bankers and investors in respect to the temporary employment of experts in the construction, operation, and supervision of railroads, waterways, and industries may be reasonably asked and honorably made, when the same concessions made at the behest of foreign governments would be painful if not intolerable.

This is but one instance illustrating the general fact that the intervention of governments in business, if sometimes a necessary evil, is nevertheless emphatically an evil; and if it has happened in the past that bankers have obtained or solicited the support of their own governments in the negotiation of loans to any other country, I believe they are now second to none in hoping that the time may soon come when government participation in business negotiations between bankers and a foreign government will be thought of, if at all, only as a last resort in exceptional circumstances. In saying this I do not forget that the governments of the countries represented in the present China consortium agreed to give the bankers "complete support." While it is not within my province to discuss either the past or the future policy of the consortium, a brief digression may be permitted: At the time when the present consortium was being organized, it seemed highly probable that large loans would be shortly forthcoming for railroad extensions and other purposes. Market conditions at that time were such that so far from there being any eager movement of American capital for the exploitation of China, grave doubts were entertained as to whether any large Chinese loans could be successfully floated in the United States. The American investor, conservative, if not timid, at that time with reference to all foreign investments, was not at all likely on his own initiative to put his money into the promotion of large enterprises in Asia, even with government guaranties. The only chance that a loan of this character would prove attractive to American investors lay in its indorsement by a group including most of the leading bankers in the United States, acting in harmony with corresponding groups in Japan, Great Britain, and France. The formidable array of banking strength represented by the thirty-odd members of the American group and their foreign colleagues was not the expression of a monopoly for the exploitation of China, but rather a measure to give a possible Chinese loan or series of loans sufficient prestige and attractiveness to make them saleable at all. It was a co-operative movement on the part of American and other bankers to accomplish what otherwise could not be done if the Chinese government was to have the money it needed. Nothing less would have had any chance of persuading the average American investor at that time to put large amounts of his money in China rather than into the countless opportunities for investment offered at home and, to an increasing extent, in Europe. The assurance "of complete support" was simply another element of security intended to make the investor feel that his money would be safe because it was, to a certain extent, limited by the vague phrase I have quoted, under the protection of the great powers.

Nevertheless, though I am perfectly convinced of the legitimacy of the aims of the China consortium and believe that all the prestige with which it could be clothed would have been necessary to insure the saleability of large loans under the conditions then existing, I am quite ready to agree with those who deprecate in principle the abandonment of private initiative and who desire to get back to normal conditions, free from the high diplomacy of consortiums, no less than from the high diplomacy of governments.

It must not be forgotten, however, that the organization of the consortium was one of the first practical steps directed against the policy of spheres of influence, for it embodied an agreement assuring to each of the member groups an opportunity for participation in loans secured by any of the others when such loans were based on the credit of the Chinese government or provinces, and issued to the public. In other words, the consortium was intended to be a practical expression of the Open Door. I mention the subject here not because it is of any immediate practical importance in the present confused situation, but merely to emphasize the fact that the tendency of the consortium, as opposed to the alternative course of scrambling for concessions in different spheres of influence, was a tendency no less in the interest of China than in that of foreign capitalists who hoped that through co-operation they could, as pointed out before, more confidently and effectively appeal to the investors of Europe and America. I am not suggesting that the foreign bankers were governed by altruistic motives. The benefits aimed at were mutual. If that were not true, there would be nothing to be said in favor of the business.

Bankers have often been accused of making loans to governments for the ulterior purpose of getting control of them, taking advantage for this purpose of periods of disorganization or disturbance; and much has been said of the interference by bankers in the foreign relations of their government for the purpose of safeguarding investments or of enlarging the field of future exploitation. My own observation has been, however, that in loaning to a government, as in loaning to a business corporation, the most important factor in determining the granting of credit is that of management. It is just as important as assets or earnings, for the latter are almost wholly dependent on management. The company or the government which enjoys the best credit is that one which is manifestly most capable of managing its own affairs, and the last thing that a banker wishes to contemplate when he makes a loan is the prospect that bad management will necessitate his subsequent exertions for the protection of bondholders. If such exertions do become necessary, it must be remembered that, as I have already said, the banker is loaning not his own money, but that of thousands of relatively small investors who relied on his judgment in making the investment, and toward whom he stands in a quasi-fiduciary relationship. He is doing less than his clear duty if he fails to take all legitimate steps to secure the punctual fulfilment of the obligations expressed in bonds which were sold to the public.

Nevertheless, I would adhere to the general proposition that the less that foreign bankers have to do with governmental policies, the better. A wise banker may be useful to a government as a financial consultant, and doubtless it is often impossible to separate matters of financial policy from those of national politics, but in general the banker's business is to consider matters of financial or political policy as they affect credit; and, if the credit is satisfactory, the banker should be relieved of responsibility for political consequences. To take a hypothetical case, let us suppose that a government makes a loan, the proceeds of which are designated for some constructive purpose, but that the money thus obtained has released other money which is employed, say, for purposes of dubious merit. Must the banker, regarding himself as the self-constituted guardian of the political policies of the borrowing government, withhold the loan for constructive purposes in order to check or prevent the questionable use of other money? To clothe the banker with a responsibility of this kind is, in my opinion, dangerous. In the long run it is better that the banker's rôle should be confined to the realm of business and that the responsibility for political results should be laid where it belongs. Such a general principle is not inconsistent with the banker's exercise of his discretion in associating himself with or dissociating himself from a governmental policy identified with proposed loan operations for questionable purposes; but in thus exercising his discretion he would have clearly in sight the responsibilities that go with his decision and be prepared to accept them.

Mr. Dwight W. Morrow, in his interesting article entitled "Who Buys Foreign Bonds?" published in *Foreign Affairs* for January, 1927, has given some interesting statistics and observations bearing out what I have said with reference to the wide distribution of foreign bonds among small investors in the United States, and he has also discussed in an illuminating way the delicate subject of the enforcement of foreign obligations in the event of default. He points out that cases in the experience of Great Britain and the United States where armed force has been employed explicitly and solely to enforce bond obligations have been hard to find, though it is admitted that where the interest of bondholders fell in with wider motives of national policy, the former may have sometimes benefited. I have no doubt that even a more exhaustive study than Mr. Morrow modestly claims to have made would justify his conclusions; but whether that is so or not, I have little fear of being challenged when I say that American bankers and investors, so far as they go into foreign investments at all, are content to rely upon international law, upon comity between nations, and upon the intrinsic justice of their claims as the ultimate resort for the payment of interest and principal, and that no intelligent banker or investor would for one moment rely upon the hope of the forcible collection of a foreign debt as a material element of security in the original contracting of a loan. If a foreign bond cannot be recommended to an investor on the faith and credit and material resources of the borrower with such guaranties, if any, as the borrower is willing to embody in the contract, no sensible banker would for a moment think of recommending it at all, and no investor would be justified in buying it.

On the other hand, no apology is needed for the efforts of the lender of money abroad to make every legitimate effort to secure the performance of obligations freely entered into by a foreign borrower; and while debt-collecting for its citizens is not the ordinary business of government, the principles of justice and equity, in the case of a default by which its nationals are injured, may justify a government in making the strongest representations in support of their claims.

Among causes of complaint that arise between nations, the wilful failure to discharge a valid debt incurred in good faith is by no means the least serious. The objection to going to war for the purpose of collecting debts is based not so much on the unworthiness or triviality of the cause as upon the barbarity and the usual futility of war as a means of settling disputes of any kind, and certainly disputes resting upon clearly ascertainable and adjudicable facts.

The rule of reason should apply here as everywhere else. A banker who rashly negotiates a loan under conditions that are obviously hazardous has little claim upon his government to pull him out of a hole into which he should never have fallen. Governments usually have discriminated, and always should, between the merits of claims submitted to them in determining the vigor with which those claims should be supported. The circumstances of different cases will indicate, as between bona fide claims, which should have official support as a matter of record and which should be made matters of major issue between the governments concerned.

During the process of education to which the American investor has been subjected since the war with regard to the foreign investment field much has been said, and I think properly said, with reference to the good effect of foreign loans in increasing the investor's knowledge of foreign countries, his interest in their affairs, and, on the whole, the liberality of his sentiments toward them. Of course I am speaking now of loans made by the investing public, and not of intergovernmental debts. A striking instance of this has been brought to my attention in one of the researches which has been made in preparation for this conference. One of the categories of persons to which the questionnaire "Orient and Occident" was sent a group of salesmen and other employees in a large investment house. That house had issued over two years previously the bonds of several important hydro-electric companies in Japan. The original sales of these bonds and the subsequent market operations had given the occasion for considerable instruction to the salesmen in regard to conditions in Japan, the characteristics of the Japanese people, and their general aims and aspirations. The returns from the questionnaire showed that this particular group were to a striking extent both better informed about, and more liberally disposed toward, the Japanese people than was true of the general average of those who answered the questionnaire in all other groups; and each salesman was in a position to influence many other persons. I regard this as the normal effect of good business relationships of this kind between countries.

These observations on the banker's functions in international relations may be summed up by saying the banker in international business performs an indispensable service by financing trade and by providing the vehicle or instrumentality—not his own hoard of gold, but the savings of hundreds of thousands of individual investors—necessary for the development of commerce and industry, the utilization of natural resources, and the improvement of transportation; that both enlightened self-interest and the interests of the countries concerned require a substantial mutuality of benefits derived from such operations; that the unsecured credit of a government or municipality should come to be regarded as the highest and safest form of credit available; that foreign credit operations should stand on a strictly business footing with the least possible governmental intervention; and finally that the wide distribution of bonds representing legitimate investment in foreign countries tends to promote a better understanding between peoples, and—the inevitable consequence of a better understanding—a more liberal and sympathetic attitude toward each other's national characteristics and aspirations.

# SECTION 22

# LEGISLATIVE ASPECTS OF ASIATIC MIGRATION

PREPARED BY INTERNATIONAL LABOR OFFICE (LEAGUE OF NATIONS)

## I. INTRODUCTION

Migration, which is a movement of population from one country to another affecting some millions of people every year, gives rise to a great many problems. From the practical point of view this movement of population affects particularly the workers—a fact which the Institute of Pacific Relations has recognized, e.g., by listing for discussion at its meeting problems such as the effect of migration on the standard of living of workers in the countries to which emigrants go and in the countries from which they come.

The International Labor Organization was established for the purpose of bringing about an improvement in the conditions of the workers and among the subjects specified in Part XIII of the Treaty of Versailles as requiring consideration by the organization as its contribution to the permanent peace of the world, mention is made of the regulation of the labor supply, the prevention of unemployment, the protection of the interests of workers when employed in countries other than their own. Further, Article 427 of the Treaty, which specifies certain methods and principles which seem to be "of special and urgent importance" and "well fitted to guide the policy of the League of Nations," enunciates the principle that "the standard set by law in each country with respect to conditions of labor should have due regard to the equitable economic treatment of all workers lawfully resident therein."

The International Labor Organization consists of an International Labor Conference and an International Labor Office under the control of a governing body. In this brief introduction considerations of space preclude any detailed account of the work of the annual conference and of the office and its governing body as regards migration problems but the following facts require to be recorded.

### A. THE INTERNATIONAL LABOR CONFERENCE

*Ascertaining the facts regarding migration.*—Realizing that an essential preliminary for the effective study of any question is adequate information, the conference in 1922 adopted a recommendation that governments "should communicate to the International Labor Office all information available concerning emigration, immigration, repatriation, and the transit of emigrants on the outward and return journeys, and the measures taken or contemplated in connection with these questions." The publication of the information thus received is undertaken by the International Labor Office and will be dealt with later.

*Employment of workers abroad.*—The draft international convention on unemployment adopted by the first session of the conference at Washington in 1919 contains an article by which governments agreed that the operations of the various national systems of employment exchanges should be co-ordinated by the International Labor Office in agreement with the countries concerned. This convention has been ratified by twenty countries.

The conference at the same session recommended that the recruiting of bodies of workers in one country with a view to their employment in another should be permitted only by mutual agreement between the countries concerned and after consultation of the employers and workers in each country in the industries concerned. This recommendation is applied very largely in continental migration in Europe.

*Treatment of foreign workers.*—The first (1919) session of the conference recommended governments, on conditions of reciprocity and on terms to be agreed upon between the countries concerned, to admit foreign workers and their families to the benefit of laws and regulations for the protection of its own workers.

The 1925 session adopted a draft convention on equality of treatment for national and foreign workers as regards workmen's compensation for accidents.

The foregoing recommendation concerning reciprocity of treatment has been applied in a number of bilateral treaties on various forms of social insurance and other branches of labor legislation. The convention on equality of treatment as regards workers' compensation has already been ratified by a certain number of countries and its application in the different parts of the British Empire was recommended by the Imperial Conference in November, 1926.

*Inspection of emigrants.*—At its 1926 session the conference adopted a draft convention concerning the general question of the organization of the inspection of emigrants on board ship, a recommendation concerning the presence of a woman inspector on ships carrying fifteen or more unaccompanied women and girls, and a resolution stressing the desirability of interpreters being provided where any considerable body of emigrants are carried belonging to a country other than that whose flag the ship flies.

B. THE GOVERNING BODY

*International emigration commission.*—In pursuance of a recommendation of the 1919 session of the conference, the governing body of the International Labor Office appointed an international emigration commission. This commission met in 1921 and the comprehensive report which it submitted on the various aspects of the problem (statistics, protection of migrants, finding of employment for migrants, equality of treatment of national and foreign workers, collective recruiting of workers for employment abroad, measures concerning the suppression of the traffic in women and children, application of laws restricting emigration and immigration taxes on foreign workers, state supervision of emigration agents, etc.) brought out the different subjects requiring consideration in the international sphere.

*Permanent migration committee.*—One of the recommendations of the international emigration commission was that a permanent committee, aided if necessary by experts, be set up to assist the office in its work and to follow the development of migration questions. This committee was appointed by the governing body in January, 1925, and consists of the chairman and the two vice-chairmen of the governing body, representing the governments, employers', and workers' groups, respectively. More than a hundred experts from practically every country have been attached to this committee, the function of which is to advise the governing body on migration questions.

C. THE INTERNATIONAL LABOR OFFICE

*International information.*—As has already been mentioned, the International Labor Conference adopted in 1922 a recommendation concerning the regular supply to the International Labor Office of statistical and other information concerning migration.

As a result of the adoption of this recommendation, the office now receives a steady stream of documents relating to international agreements, legislation, statistics, etc., on migration.

The information received is made available by the Office in the following manner: On the statistical side it published some years ago a brochure on methods of compiling emigration and immigration statistics, and after discussions with government services concerning improvements in methods of migration statistics, notably with a view to making the national statistics more readily comparable internationally, the office has published *Migration Movements, 1920–23,* and *Migration Movements, 1920–24,* being the first two in what it is intended to publish as an annual series in future. Monthly migration tables are published in the *Monthly Record of Migration,* while an historical inquiry into migration statistics from the time of their first publication in each country down to the present day has been undertaken at the suggestion of, and in co-operation with, the National Bureau of Economic Research of the United States, and the results will be published shortly.

Finally, reference must be made to the work of the office in providing information on the important subject of legislation affecting migration. In 1922 the office published a volume entitled *Emigration and Immigration: Legislation and Treaties,* containing information concerning a large number of countries. A second edition of this work, which will include new material not available in 1922, is now in preparation.

*The present note.*—The office has, of course, available in its records a large amount of material, which it has not so far published, on particular aspects of the migration problem. In accepting the invitation of the Institute to be represented by an unofficial observer at its meetings, it has occurred to the office that it would be of interest to members of the Institute if, in addition to the brief general statement contained in this introduction and having regard to the agenda of the meeting as communicated to the office, the latter submitted to the conference a résumé of laws dealing with the migration of Asiatics in the different countries bordering the Pacific, or other countries in which special legislation on this matter exists.

It wll be noticed how numerous these countries are. In the short note attached will be found an analysis of the legislation of as many as fifty countries and colonies which have studied this question with special interest. It will be seen that no European country appears directly in this list. This is because up to the present time the question has not been dealt with by any European legislature. On the other hand, various European countries have adopted such legislation for their colonies.

The study which the office thus submits to the conference does not pretend to be absolutely complete; nor does it always mention the latest changes in the laws. Particularly in connection with information from the countries most distant from Geneva, the laws described may not always be the most recent, and there may be gaps. Since the conference numbers among its members, some who are experts on the subject, the office hopes that these experts will be good enough to assist it by indicating any necessary modifications or additions to the present note. In any case the office asks that the note may be regarded as an earnest contribution to the proceedings of the Institute in its consideration of the facts of one of the great problems of the present time: the Pacific relations of the world.

### II. AUSTRALIA

Legislation: Immigration Act, 1901–25. Pacific Island Laborers' Act, 1901–6. Contract Laborers' Act, 1905.

*General restrictions on the immigration of Asiatics.*—The immigration of Asiatics and other colored persons into Australia is restricted by the Immigration Act of 1901–25, which provides, among other things, that any person who, when asked to do so by a public officer, fails to write out from dictation and sign in the presence of the officer a passage of more than fifty words in any prescribed language will be prohibited from landing in Australia.

*The Immigration Act, 1901–25, Art. 3 (a).*—This clause has been applied in such a way as virtually to prohibit Asiatic laborers from entering the Commonwealth. In 1905 it was decided after some correspondence between Japan and Australia that Japanese tourists, merchants, and students entering temporarily should be exempted from the test.

The exemption of special classes of persons from the dictation test was authorized by the insertion of Section 4A of the immigration act in 1905, which provides that arrangements may be made with the government of any country regulating the admission into Australia of the subjects and citizens of such country, and such persons are not required to pass the dictation test so long as the arrangement lasts. No regulations for prescribing languages have any force until they have been sanctioned by resolution of both houses of Parliament. At the present time merchants, students, and tourists of Japan, China, and India are admitted without the dictation test, but under a certificate of exemption which is renewable annually.[1]

The immigration of Asiatics is also indirectly restricted by the Contract Laborers' Act, 1905, which provides that no immigrant may enter Australia under contract to labor except with the permission previously obtained of the minister for external affairs, and the minister may approve the terms of the contract only if: (*a*) the contract is not made in contemplation of, or with a view to, affecting an industrial dispute, or (*b*) there is difficulty in the employer's obtaining within the Commonwealth a worker of at least equal skill and ability or, (*c*) the remuneration and other terms and conditions of employment are as advantageous to the contract immigrant as those current for workers of the same class at the place where the contract is to be performed (Art. 5 [2]).

[1] Institute of Pacific Relations, Honolulu Session, June 30–July 14, 1925, *History, Organization, Proceedings, Discussions, and Addresses* (1925), p. 148.

*Pacific island laborers.*—Under the Pacific Island Laborers' Act, 1901–6, no Pacific island laborer may enter Australia (art. 3), and any Pacific island laborer found there is liable to be deported (art. 8 [2]). The term "Pacific island laborer" includes all natives not of European extraction of any island, except the islands of New Zealand, situated in the Pacific Ocean beyond the Commonwealth (art. 2).

The minister for external affairs or any other officer authorized by him may grant a certificate to any Pacific island laborer exempting him from all or any of the provisions of the act. A certificate is issued to a Pacific island laborer who proves to the satisfaction of the minister: (1) that he was introduced into Australia prior to September, 1879; or (2) that he is of extreme age, or is suffering from such bodily infirmity as to be unable to obtain a livelihood if returned to his native island; or (3) that, having married before October 9, 1906, to a native of some island other than his own, he cannot be deported without risk to the life of himself or his family; or (4) that he was married before October 9, 1906, to a female not a native of the Pacific islands; or (5) that he was on July 1, 1906, and still is, registered as the beneficial owner of a freehold in Queensland, or (6) that he was continuously resident in Australia for a period of not less than twenty years prior to December 31, 1906 (art. 2 [1, 2]). The act does not apply to persons employed as the crew of a ship and persons possessed of certificates of exemption issued under the Immigration Act of 1901–25.

## III. CANADA

Legislation: Immigration Act and Regulations, 1910–24. Chinese Immigration Act and Regulations, 1923. Orders-in-Council P.C. 182, P.C. 1273, P.C. 23.

Agreements: Gentlemen's Agreement with Japan.

*General prohibition.*—By article 38 (*c*) of the Immigration Act of Canada (1910–24), the governor in council is empowered to prohibit the landing in Canada or the landing in any specified port or ports in Canada for a stated period or permanently of immigrants belonging to any specified class or nationality for any of the following reasons: (1) if restriction is desirable by reason of any economic, industrial, or other condition temporarily existing in Canada; (2) if the immigrants are deemed unsuitable having regard to the climatic, industrial, social, educational, labor, and other conditions or requirements of Canada; (3) if the immigrants are deemed undesirable owing to their peculiar habits, modes of life, and methods of holding property; (4) if the immigrants are deemed unable to become readily assimilated and to assume the duties and responsibilities of Canadian citizens within a reasonable time after their entry.

Under the authority of this section an order in council was passed June 9, 1919 (P.C. 1202) which prohibits the landing of any laborers, whether skilled or unskilled, at any of the following ports of British Columbia: Vancouver, Victoria, New Westminster, Nanaimo, Prince Rupert, Fort Simpson, Anyox, Comox, Ganges Harbour, Ladner, Ladysmith, Steveston, Chemainus, Powell River, Stewart, Union Bay, Whales Island, Newport, Alberni, and White Pass. In effect, the order restricts the immigration of Asiatic laborers into Canada, and it has been followed by a further order in council (P.C. 182, January 31, 1923) which regulates the immigration of Asiatics under the following terms:

From and after February 15, 1923, and until otherwise ordered, the landing in Canada of any immigrant of any Asiatic race is hereby prohibited except as hereinafter provided. The immigration officer in charge may admit any immigrant who otherwise complies with the provisions of the immigration act if it is shown to his satisfaction that such immigrant is: (1) a bona fide agriculturist entering Canada to farm who has sufficient means to begin farming in Canada; (2) a bona fide farm laborer entering Canada to follow that occupation who has reasonable assurance of employment; (3) a female domestic servant entering Canada to follow that occupation who has reasonable assurance of employment; (4) the wife or child under eighteen years of age of any person legally admitted to and resident in Canada who is in a position to receive and care for his dependents.

Every such immigrant, except those coming under Class 4, that is, the wife or child of any person resident in Canada, must possess in his own right, and as a condition to permission to land in Canada, the sum of $250. The regulation does not apply to the nationals of any country in regard to which there is in operation a special treaty or agreement or convention regulating immigration. This order in council covers the immigration of all Asiatic races which are not otherwise prohibited.

*Chinese restriction.*—Besides this general prohibition on "Asiatics," the immigration of Chinese into Canada is regulated by the Chinese Immigration Act of 1923.

1. *Restriction on entry.*—The Chinese Immigration Act of 1906–21 permitted the immigration of Chinese, but provided that every person of Chinese origin should pay, on entering Canada, a tax of five hundred dollars. This Act was repealed by the Act of 1923, article 5 of which provided that the entry or landing in Canada of persons of Chinese origin or descent irrespective of allegiance or citizenship should be confined to the following classes: (*a*) the members of the diplomatic corps, or other government representatives, their suites and their servants and consuls and consular agents; (*b*) the children born in Canada of parents of Chinese race or descent who have left Canada for educational or other purposes, on substantiating their identity to the satisfaction of the controller at the port or place where they seek to enter on their return; (*c*) (i) merchants; (ii) students coming to Canada for the purpose of attendance, and while in actual attendance, at any Canadian university or college authorized by statute or charter to confer degrees, who shall substantiate their status to the satisfaction of the controller at the port of entry subject to the approval of the ministry of immigration and colonization.

It is provided that no person of Chinese origin or descent shall enter or land in Canada except at a port of entry, and no person of Chinese origin or descent other than the members of the diplomatic corps or other government representatives, or children born in Canada of parents of Chinese race or descent, may enter the country otherwise than at the ports of Vancouver and Victoria (arts. 6, 7). All persons over fifteen years of age, physically capable of reading, must pass a dictation test in English or French or some other language or dialect (art. 3*a*–3*u*).

2. *Conditions of transport.*—No vessel carrying Chinese immigrants to any port in Canada may carry more than one such immigrant[2] for every 250 tons of its tonnage (art. 19). The master of any vessel or the conductor or other person in charge of any railway car or train bringing persons of Chinese origin or descent into Canada

[2] A "Chinese immigrant" is defined as "any person of Chinese origin or descent entering Canada for the purpose of acquiring Canadian domicile."

must, immediately on his arrival, deliver to the controller or other officer at the port or place of arrival a report containing a complete and accurate list of all such Chinese on board, showing their names in full, the country and place of their birth, their occupation and last place of domicile (art. 21). No Chinese, whether immigrant, passenger, stowaway, or member of the crew, may disembark from a ship before a permit to do so has been given by the controller (art. 20).

The order in council (P.C. 1273) laid down special provisions for the transport of Chinese immigrants in transit through Canada. All such immigrants are subject to medical examination for tuberculosis or leprosy in any form, or for a loathsome or contagious disease (art. 1). The transport company carrying such immigrants must give a bond or deposit to the value of $1,000 in respect of each Chinese person so carried that the provisions of the immigration act and regulations will be fulfiled (arts. 2–4). When the person enters Canada a manifest showing his full name and description must be furnished by the representative of the transportation company in triplicate. This manifest must be certified by the controller or officer in charge, and the "original" inclosed in a sealed envelope addressed to the controller at the intended port of exit from Canada and delivered to the conductor in charge of the train by which such individuals are despatched, who shall deliver it on arrival to the controller at the port of exit. A copy of the manifest must be mailed direct by the controller at the bonding port to the controller or officer in charge at the port of exit. The transportation company transporting such persons of Chinese origin must, while they are in transit through Canada, keep them in the car in which they embarked until the arrival at the designated port of exit, where they will be transferred to a depot for detention until the requirements of the act have been complied with and where they will remain until the vessel or vehicle in which they are to leave Canada is ready to depart, whereupon they will be taken directly on board after the controller or other officer has satisfied himself that the individuals produced are those named and described in the manifest (art. 5*b, c*). No person of Chinese origin or descent passing through Canada from one place or port out of Canada to another port or place out of Canada may be allowed to enter, land, or remain in Canada (art. 8).

3. *Registration of Chinese.*—Every Chinese immigrant who is permitted to land in or enter Canada is given a certificate containing a description and photograph of the individual, the date of his arrival, and the name of the port of his landing, and this certificate is prima facie evidence that the person presenting it has complied with the requirements of the immigration act. The certificate may, however, be contested by the government if there is any reason to doubt its validity or authenticity. The immigration authorities are bound to keep a register of all such certificates issued (Chinese Immigration Act, Art. 17 [1]). All Chinese who were in Canada at the time the act was passed (June, 1923), whether they were Canadian citizens or not, were likewise bound to register and to obtain a certificate (art. 18).

Every person of Chinese origin or descent lawfully resident in Canada who wishes to leave but intends to return, must register with the controller at the port or place at which he departs. The person so registered shall be entitled on his return, if within two years of such registration and on proof of his identity to the satisfaction of the controller, to re-enter; but if he does not return in Canada within two years from the date of such registration, he shall be treated in the same manner as a person making application for admission as an immigrant (art. 24 [1]). Every Chinese person who leaves Canada without registering shall be treated on his return as a first arrival (art. 24 [2]). Any person of Chinese origin who has been legally admitted to Canada and who is employed as a member of the crew of any vessel which operated between Canadian and United States ports shall, in order to retain his right of re-entry to Canada, register with the controller and obtain a certificate of registration (art. 25 [1]). A transportation company, master, agent, or owner of a vessel who employs a Chinese sailor who has failed to register is liable to a fine of $250 (art. 25 [3]).

4. *Procedure for admission and deportation of Chinese.*—The immigration act provides that the examination of persons of Chinese origin or descent applying for admission or entry into Canada shall be separate and apart from the public. If a decision is not reached at the preliminary hearing, the hearing may be adjourned for 48 hours or longer so that the person may seek legal advice (art. 10). Appeal may be made to the minister of immigration and colonization, except in cases where admission is refused on medical grounds (arts. 11, 12). Every Chinese ordered to be deported must be conveyed back to the place from whence he came by the transportation company which brought him to Canada (arts. 14, 16).

*Japanese restriction.*—Japanese immigration in Canada has been regulated by a Gentleman's Agreement, whereby the immigration of Japanese is kept within the limits agreed upon by the two governments and regulated by Japan. At first (1908), 400 laborers a years were allowed to enter. Owing to representation from Canada, the number has now been reduced to 150.[3]

*Indian restriction.*—There is no law or agreement which specifically limits the immigration of Indians in Canada, but, apart from the general restrictions on persons of Asiatic race (see foregoing), the immigration of Indians in Canada is in effect restricted by the Continuous Passage Ordinance (Order in Council P.C. 23). By this order the landing in Canada is prohibited of any immigrant who comes otherwise than by continuous journey from the country of which he is a native or naturalized citizen and upon a through ticket purchased in that country or prepaid in Canada.

## IV. NEWFOUNDLAND

Legislation: Consolidated Statutes of Newfoundland (1916), chapter LXXIX: "Of the Immigration of Chinese Persons."

There is no general restriction on the immigration of Asiatics in Newfoundland, but the immigration of Chinese is restricted by chapter LXXIX of the Consolidated laws of Newfoundland, 1916. The provisions of this act may be summarized as follows:

*a*) *Limitations on entry.*—No vessel carrying Chinese immigrants to any port in the country may carry more than one such immigrant for every 50 tons of its tonnage, and the owner of any such vessel who carries any number of immigrants in

[3] Institute of Pacific Relations, *op. cit.*, p. 67.

excess of the number allowed is liable to a fine of $200 for each Chinese immigrant so carried (art. 2).

*b*) *Prohibited classes.*—No Chinese person is permitted to land who is a prostitute, a person living on the prostitution of others, an idiot or insane, a person suffering from any loathsome, infectious, or contagious disease, a pauper or likely to become a public charge (art. 5*a, b, d*).

*c*) *Conditions of Entry.*—

1. Head Tax: Every person of Chinese origin entering the country must pay a tax of $300, except the following classes: (*a*) members of the diplomatic corps or other government representatives, their suites and servants, and consuls and their families. (*b*) Clergymen and their families, tourists, men of science and students, merchants and their families.

In the case of a person of Chinese origin who is the personal attendant or servant of a British subject, the tax payable may be refunded to the person paying it on his furnishing satisfactory evidence that the Chinese attendant or servant is leaving the port of entry with his employer or master on his return to China. A woman of Chinese origin is, for the purpose of the Act, considered to be of the same nationality as her husband (art. 1).

The master of any vessel bringing Chinese immigrants to the country is personally liable for the payment of the head tax (art. 8). He may not land any person of Chinese origin, or permit any to land, until a permit to do so, stating that the provisions of the Act have been complied with, has been granted to the master of the vessel by the proper officer. The landing of a Chinese person from a vessel is not held to mean the landing of him on a wharf or the placing of him in a proper building until the provisions of the Act have been complied with (art. 3).

2. Health Provisions: No subcollector at any port shall grant a permit allowing Chinese immigrants to land until the quarantine or health officer has granted a bill of health and has certified after due examination that no leprosy, loathsome, infectious, or dangerous disease exists on board the vessel (art. 4).

The provisions regarding the landing of persons of Chinese origin do not apply to the temporary landing of any Chinese sailor for the purpose of assisting in the lading or unlading of the vessel to which he belongs and for the purpose of his transfer to another vessel (art. 3 [2]).

*d*) *Registration of Chinese.*—The subcollector or other proper officer shall deliver to each Chinese immigrant for whom a tax has been paid, and who has been permitted to land, a certificate containing a description of such individual, the date of his arrival, the name of the port of his landing, and an acknowledgement that the duty has been duly paid. Such certificate should be evidence that the immigrant has complied with the requirements of the Act (art. 6). The assistant collector of customs and such other subcollectors as are authorized so to do shall each keep a register of all persons to whom certificates of entry have been granted (art. 7).

Besides the restrictive provisions given, the same Act empowers the governor in council to make such regulations as are necessary to prohibit the entry of any greater number of persons from any foreign country than the laws of the country permit to emigrate to Newfoundland (art. 18).

## V. NEW ZEALAND

Legislation: Immigration Restriction Act, 1908. Immigration Restriction Amendment Act, 1910. Immigration Restriction Amendment Act, 1920.

Under the Immigration Restriction Amendment Act, 1920, no person other than a person of British birth and parentage may enter New Zealand unless he is in possession of a permit. A person is not considered to be of British birth and parentage by reason of the fact that he and his parents are naturalized British subjects or by reason that he is an aboriginal native or the descendant of an aboriginal native of any dominion other than the Dominion of New Zealand or of any colony or other possession or of any protectorate of Great Britain (art. 5). Accordingly, an Indian would require a permit to enter New Zealand. In practice permits are issued (subject to the personal fitness of the applicant) in accordance with an indeterminate quota system.[4]

The governor-general may, by order in council, declare that the provisions relative to the permit shall not apply to certain nations or peoples. The minister of customs may exempt from the requirements referred to above any person or class of person entering or desiring to enter New Zealand (art. 6). The wives of Indians, Chinese, and Japanese already domiciled in New Zealand appear to be admitted when application is made, but subject to the state of the informal "quota."[5]

The Immigration Restriction Act, 1908, as amended in 1910, provides that if any ship arrives in any port in New Zealand having on board a greater number of Chinese than in the proportion of one to every 200 tons, the owner or master of the ship shall be liable to a fine not exceeding £100 for each Chinese so carried, provided that this ruling shall not apply in the case of any Chinese who is the bona fide holder of a through ticket to some place beyond New Zealand (art. 29).

Before any such aliens are permitted to land the master must pay to the collector £100 for every such Chinese, and no entry shall be deemed to have been legally made or to have any legal effect until such payment has been made (art. 31). This section, however, does not apply to any Chinese duly accredited to New Zealand by the government of China, or by or under the authority of the imperial government or on special mission. On the payment of this sum the collector must issue to each Chinese a certificate showing that the money has been paid (art. 33 [1]).

On the arrival at any port or place in New Zealand of a ship having Chinese on board as members of the crew, the master of the ship must summon the crew before an officer of the customs and give him the names and numbers of such members of the crew as are Chinese. Before the ship leaves the master must again summon the crew in the presence of an officer of the customs and satisfy him that all the Chinese mentioned in the list are still on board. Any Chinese sailor who is then found to be missing shall be deemed a Chinese who has landed in New Zealand in contravention of the Act (arts. 35, 36). No Chinese sailor may go ashore except in performance of his duties in connection with the ship (art. 37).

[4] Institute of Pacific Relations, *op. cit.*, p. 151.

[5] *Idem*, p. 152.

### VI. SOUTH AFRICA

The so-called "Asiatic problem" of South Africa affects Indians more than any other Asiatic race. The number of other Asiatics, indeed, is not considerable. The number of total Asiatics, Indians, and other Asiatics, respectively, in the various provinces of the Union as shown in the census of 1921 was as shown in Table I.

*Union legislation.*—The immigration of Asiatics into the union is restricted by clause 4 (1a) of the immigration law, 1913, which prohibits the entry of "any person or class of persons deemed by the Minister on economic grounds or on account of standard or habits of life to be unsuited to the requirements of the Union or any particular Province." According to the *Official Yearbook of the Union of South Africa, 1910–18,* No. 3, this clause was designed to prevent the entry of adult male Asiatics

TABLE I

| | Total Asiatics | Indians | Other Asiatics |
|---|---|---|---|
| Cape of Good Hope | 7,696 | 6,498 | 1,198 |
| Natal | 141,649 | 141,336 | 313 |
| Transvaal | 15,991 | 13,405 | 2,586 |
| Orange Free State | 395 | 100 | 295 |

(except to the extent allowed by the Transvaal under its registration act), and the clause further restricts Asiatics to the respective provinces in which they reside.[6]

The position of Indians already in the Union is regulated by the Indians Relief Act No. 22, of 1914, which was passed in accordance with the recommendations of the Indian Inquiry Commission of 1913 to redress certain grievances. Provision is made for the recognition of Indian marriages, and the immigration law of 1913 is modified to permit the entrance of the wife and minor children of an Indian resident in the Union, even though the marriage is not monogamous, provided that the Indian has no other wife or wives resident in any province of the Union, or no other offspring within any province by any other living women. The minister of the interior is empowered to grant free passages from any port in the Union to any port in India to an Indian who makes application for it, and signs an agreement abandoning on behalf of himself, his wife, and minor children, all rights to enter or reside in the Union.

Provincial Legislation.—

*a*) Cape of Good Hope: Besides the general restriction provided for by the Immigration Act of 1913, there is still in force in the Cape Province a Chinese Exclusion Act of 1904 which provides for the total exclusion of Chinese male adult immigrants and the registration of those resident already in the province at the time the Act was passed.[7]

*b*) Natal: The majority of Indians in South Africa are found in Natal, where they were imported in large numbers in the latter half of the last century for work on the sugar plantations. The Natal Indian Immigration Act of 1895 imposed a tax

[6] Union of South Africa. Office of Census and Statistics, *Official Yearbook of the Union,* No. 3 (1919), p. 189.

[7] *Idem,* p. 186.

of £3 on all Indians settling in the province, with the object of inducing them to return to India, but the Indian Inquiry Commission of 1913 found that the Act had failed to achieve its object and it was repealed by the Indians Relief Act of 1914, described previously.

*c*) Transvaal: A large number of Asiatics (mostly Indians) entered the Transvaal at the end of the last century and in the early years of the present century, but there are no exact records of their entry. After the South African War permits were granted to Asiatics who had left South Africa during the war, and who wished to return. As, however, the records of previous entry were incomplete, it is probable that a number of Asiatics entered South Africa and established themselves there who had no claim to previous residence. A system of voluntary registration was then initiated. Finally, compulsory registration of male Asiatics was effected under Act No. 36 of 1908.[8]

The Imperial Conference of 1918 recommended that Indians already permanently domiciled in other British countries should be allowed to bring in their wives and minor children on condition that (*a*) not more than one wife or her children should be admitted for each such Indian, and that (*b*) each individual so admitted should be certified by the government of India to be the lawful wife and child of the person in question. At a round-table conference between the South African and Indian governments which was held at Cape Town, December 17, 1926–January 12, 1927, an agreement was reached in accordance with this resolution. Minor children may not enter the Union unless accompanied by the mother (if alive), provided that the mother is not already resident in the Union. In the event of a divorce, proof of the divorce must be submitted before any other wife will be allowed to enter. The Conference also agreed to a scheme of assisted emigration of Indians from South Africa modifying that in force under the Indians Relief Act of 1914. Any Indian of sixteen years of age and over who returns to India will receive a bonus of £20, and each child will receive the sum of £10. The bonus is to be payable in India on the arrival of the emigrants. Adults who are decrepit and unable to earn a living are to receive a pension. Free passages to India and free railway facilities are provided. Any Indian over sixteen years of age may avail himself of the scheme, and in the case of a family, the decision of the father binds the wife and minor children. An assisted Indian emigrant will be allowed to return to South Africa within three years provided he pays back in full the bonus and the cost of the passage, but after that time he loses all right to domicile in the Union.[9] A bill providing for the carrying out of this agreement is being considered by the South African parliament at the present time.

### VII. BRITISH COLONIES

There is little legislation in the British Colonies restricting the immigration of persons on grounds of race. In Nyasaland and Northern and Southern Rhodesia the immigration is prohibited of any person who is deemed by the governor on account of standard or habits of life to be undesirable.

Nyasaland: Immigration Ordinance No. 17, of 1922, article 4.

[8] *Idem,* p. 187.

[9] *The Hindu,* February 24, 1927.

Northern Rhodesia: Immigrants' Regulation Proclamation No. 15, of 1915, article 2 (1).

Southern Rhodesia: Immigrants' Regulation Act No. 7, of 1914, article 2 (1).

In these same colonies also the immigration is prohibited of any person who is unable, by reason of deficient education, to read and write any European language to the satisfaction of an immigration officer, and this provision naturally restricts the immigration of Asiatics.

The colony of Papua has an immigration law, similar to that of Australia, by which a person of undesirable race can be excluded. The immigration is forbidden of any person who fails to pass a dictation test, that is, who, when an officer dictates to him not less than 50 words in any prescribed language, fails to write them out in that language in the presence of the officer. The lieutenant governor may, upon application by the owner or manager of a plantation, grant a certificate of exemption from the dictation test to any laborers of special skill whom the owner or manager may wish to bring in as overseers or foremen (Immigration Restriction Ordinance No. 2, of 1908, arts. 2–3).

Apart from this legislation, the regulation of the immigration of specified races into the crown colonies is based on economic considerations. Several of the colonies depend for their labor supplies on Asiatic immigration, and their policy is to encourage such immigration by offering special protection and advantages to immigrant laborers.

The labor codes of the Federated Malay States (1923), the Straits Settlements (1923), and the Unfederated Malay State of Johore (1924) contain detailed provisions for the reception and employment of both Chinese and Indians entering these colonies under contract. Funds are established for the payment of free passages to Indian laborers and their families. Any Chinese or Indian immigrant must be medically examined on arrival. If unfit for work, he must be sent to a hospital for treatment, and if found to be permanently unfit for labor he must be repatriated. In the case of Chinese immigrants special care is taken to see that an immigrant has not been brought into the colony by fraud or misrepresentation as to work or wages. On the other hand, an immigrant must fulfil the terms of his contract. Any Indian immigrant who has received a free passage under promise to labor in the colony, and who neglects or refuses to proceed to his place of employment is liable to a fine of £50. Further, Indian immigrant laborers may not leave the colony except to go to certain specified countries. Laborers from the Dutch East Indies are similarly protected by the Netherlands Indian Laborers' Protection Enactments of the Federated Malay States (1909), and the Straits Settlements (1908).

In the Unfederated Malay States of Perlis, Kedah, and Kelantan the immigration of Indians is regulated by the Indian immigration enactments. In these states, as in the Federated Malay States and Johore, Indians are introduced at the expense of an immigration fund. In Kedah and Perlis every contract is terminable by the immigrant or his employer at a month's notice. Every employer is bound to provide proper house accommodation, hospital facilities, medical attendance, and proper food and water.

Perlis: Indian Immigration Enactment No. 2, of 1329.

Kelantan: Indian Immigration Enactment, 1910.

Kedah: Indian Immigration Enactment No. 8, of 1328.

The immigration of indentured Indian laborers into British Guiana ceased in 1917, but a labor shortage in the colony was feared, and negotiations with the Indian government were commenced for the resumption of Indian immigration on a different basis. A colonization scheme was agreed upon in 1926 by which the government of British Guiana offers to any Indian immigrant an allotment of not less than five acres of good agricultural ground. The colonists are given free transport, free medical assistance, and free skilled supervision. On arrival in the colony they are housed and maintained without charge by the government for one month, and loans are made to them when necessary. Compulsory education is enforced on Indian children on the same terms as on children of other communities. Indian migrants under the scheme are free to take up work other than, or in addition to, cultivating a holding. They are entitled to repatriation at the cost of the government of British Guiana at the end of seven years or before that time under special circumstances.

In Fiji, as in British Guiana, the system of importing Indian laborers to work under indenture, which had been in force since 1879, came to an end in 1917, and has not at this time been resumed. The act of October 22, 1924, provided for the optional repatriation at the expense of the colony of any Indian immigrant who had resided continuously ten years in the colony, and any child of such an immigrant.

The influx of Indians into Mauritius took place between 1839 and 1909 under a system of indentured labor. The Labor Ordinance No. 12 of 1878 permitted re-indenture for a period not exceeding five years. Labor contracts were enforced by penal provisions. Assisted or free passages were allowed in necessitous cases. In 1909 a committee appointed to report on emigration from India to the crown colonies and protectorates recommended that the system of importing labor from India for Mauritius should be discontinued. The report was accepted and immigration of Indians ceased. In 1922 the system of indenture was definitely abolished.[10] Recruiting in India was resumed experimentally in 1923, but ceased after one year, and at the present time there is no immigration of Indian laborers into the colony.

### VIII. STATES OF CENTRAL AND SOUTH AMERICA

The immigration of Chinese is prohibited in various states of Latin America, Costa Rica, Cuba, Ecuador, and Peru. In Cuba the following classes are exempted: (1) Chinese business men returning to an established business, on proving their financial status and the nature and value of their business to the commissioner of immigration. (2) Chinese commercial travelers or merchants coming for business purposes on proving their bona fide status and the value of their business. They must obtain a special permit from the commissioner of immigration, who shall fix the duration of their stay and the amount of caution money required of them. They shall not be required to pay more than 1,000 pesos in metal as caution money.

In Costa Rica, Cuba, and Ecuador Chinese already in the country at the time the law was passed have the right to remain there.

[10] *Government of India,* report by Kunwar Maharaj Singh, M.A., C.I.E., on his deputation to Mauritius (Delhi, 1925), p. 7.

Costa Rica: Act of May 22, 1897, renewed January 15, 1917.

Cuba: Presidential Decree No. 570, of April 27, 1926.

Ecuador: Act of September 14, 1889. Provisions repeated in article 29 of the act of October 18, 1921.

Peru: Decree of May 14, 1909.

The immigration of coolies coming from India is prohibited in Costa Rica by the act of October 26, 1925. By the word "coolie" is meant "Indian laborers recruited under contract." Indians of good character may, however, enter Costa Rica with their wives and children under eighteen years of age if they are in possession of not less than 1,000 colones and are physically fit to work, but they must obtain special permission from the administrative authorities. The act of January 15, 1917, of the same state, which renewed the provisions already existing against the immigration of Chinese, gave power to the executive authority to restrict the immigration of other races when the progress and well-being of the country seemed to render such a course desirable.

In Uruguay, by the Decree of 1915, the authorities may, when they deem it expedient, prohibit the immigration of Asiatics.

Provisions for the registration of Chinese residents exist in Cuba, Costa Rica, Salvador, and Panama. In Panama all Chinese immigrants other than children under ten years of age and the wives of Chinese domiciled in the Republic must pay a head tax which varies according to the profession of the immigrant and the purpose for which he enters the Republic. Chinese immigrants must apply to the minister of foreign relations for special permission to enter. Chinese agricultural workers and commercial employees who change their occupation after their arrival in the Republic without previous permission are liable to deportation.

Cuba: Decree No. 570, of April 27, 1926.

Costa Rica: Decree of September 22, 1911, and December 11, 1924.

Salvador: Decree of November 28, 1925.

Panama: Decree No. 63, of September 18, 1923.

In contrast to the restrictive policies indicated, mention should perhaps be made of recent attempts in Brazil to encourage the immigration of Japanese and Indians by the offer of free grants of land.[11]

### IX. DUTCH EAST INDIES

The majority of immigrant laborers entering the Dutch Indies are Chinese, and although the ordinances of October 1, 1911, June 20, 1915, and November 14, 1924, which regulate the admission of coolie labor into the Dutch East Indies, do not specify any nationality, they are intended in effect to protect Chinese coolies and encourage their immigration.

By the ordinance of October 7, 1911, an employer is bound to pay wages regularly and to provide the laborers also with medical aid and drugs. When the contract expires he must transport the coolies at his own expense to the place whence they came. New regulations as to the contracts of coolies on the east coast of Su-

[11] See, for example, *International Labor Office Monthly Record of Migration No. 49* (October, 1926), pp. 381–83.

matra were introduced by the ordinance of June 21, 1915. The penalties on "excessive idleness" and "refusal to work" were abolished, but the penal sanctions relating to all violations of the labor contract were retained. The contracts, besides specifying the hours of work and rates of pay, provided for adequate housing, medical treatment, and administrative control over the execution of the contract. Contracts were signed for a maximum period of three years, and re-engagement contracts could be signed for eighteen months. By the ordinance of 1924 this re-engagement period was reduced to thirteen months, and it was provided that, if conditions in any undertaking were contrary to the provisions of the ordinance, or otherwise bad, the governor-general might decide that no workers might be engaged for that undertaking on a labor contract under the ordinance.

### X. FRENCH COLONIES

Although there are apparently no restrictions on the entry of Chinese or other Asiatic races into the French Colonies, there exist special regulations concerning their residence, and they are in some cases subjected to close supervision. In Indo-China, Chinese and Asiatics must, on arrival, be admitted into a congregation in order to receive a *permis de séjour*. These congregations are groups of persons composed according to country of origin, dialect, or religion, which are established in each administrative center. They are governed by elected chiefs who are responsible to the authorities of the colony. An immigrant who fails to join a "congregation" is liable to be deported, but the congregations, on their side, have the right to refuse admittance to any applicant. Asiatics and Chinese immigrants are obliged to pay a head tax which varies according to their occupation and residence.

Annam: Decree of April 28, 1926.

Cambodge: Decree of November 15, 1919, modified by Decree of March 30, 1925, on alien Asiatics.

Cochinchina: Decree of January 25, 1890, and October 16, 1908, on Asiatic immigration in Cochinchina.

Tonkin: Decree of December 12, 1913, modified by the decrees of August 19, 1920, and November 11, 1924, on Chinese immigration in Tonkin.

In several French colonies, Madagascar, New Caledonia, French Establishments in Oceania, Réunion, Guadeloupe, Martinique, Guiana, persons of Asiatic nationality are subjected to the conditions of *immigration réglementée* established by the decrees of February 13 and March 27, 1852.

No such immigrant may enter the colony except under a labor contract, and he must fulfil the terms of his contract before he can obtain permission to reside there freely. Absence from work is an indictable offense. Absence of more than three days is considered as desertion, and absence of more than one month as vagabondage, and severe penalties are imposed for these offenses.

Establishments of Oceania: Decree of February 24, 1920.

Guadeloupe: Decree of June 30, 1890.

Guiana: Decree of June 13, 1887.

Madagascar: Decree of May 6, 1903.

New Caledonia: Decree of July 11, 1893.

Réunion: Decree of March 30, 1881.

Further, in New Caledonia, by the ordinances of May 10, 1920, and March 3, 1923, it is provided that no Indian immigrant, Javanese, Tonkinese, or native of the New Hebrides or Wallis Island may be out after 8 P. M. unless his work necessitates it. On official fête days, however, such immigrants may obtain permission to be out up till midnight. By the decree of March 2, 1922, such races are prohibited from organizing native fêtes.

On the other hand, under these same decrees, immigrants of Asiatic and African nationality in Madagascar and the Pacific colonies are offered certain advantages. The government of the colony may place a representative on board any ship bringing immigrants to see that the regulations concerning the transport of immigrants have been carried out. Every ship on arrival in the colony is examined and the immigrants questioned, and opportunity is given them to make their complaints against the conditions of transport. Provision is made for hospital treatment of immigrants who are found on arrival to be unfit for work, and for their repatriation if permanently unfit. They have also the right to be repatriated with their wives and children at the end of their period of contract, at the expense of their employers. In Guadeloupe, by the decree of September 24, 1859, it is provided that commissioners and subcommissioners of immigration shall be in close touch with the immigrants and shall protect their interests.

In the French colonies in the Pacific, as in the British possessions and mandated territories, the native labor supply has proved inadequate for economic development and has been supplemented by Asiatic immigration. Since the war the labor shortage has become extremely acute and has resulted in agreements with the governments of Java (1922-26) and Indo-China (1923) for the recruitment of labor. These immigrants have been subject to the same conditions of the *immigration réglementée* described previously, but in the case of the Javanese the restrictions imposed on the immigrants are subject to conditions laid down by the government of the Dutch East Indies in the decree of April 18, 1922. The Javanese are recruited for employment in New Caledonia, and under the present arrangement they may enter into a contract for five years. Employers of Javanese are obliged to make a monthly contribution to a repatriation fund.

## XI. MANDATED TERRITORIES OF WESTERN SAMOA AND NAURU

Both in Western Samoa and the phosphate-bearing island of Nauru it has been found that native labor is insufficient for productive development. In Western Samoa, prior to the war, Chinese were introduced from Hongkong under indenture. The officers of the New Zealand government who administered the island during the war refused to allow a continuance of the policy, and the immigration of indentured Chinese labor ceased until 1919, when it was again permitted.[12]. Periods of indenture were for three years for a man without his wife, and for six years for a man who brought his wife with him. Refusal to work, absence from work, or illness caused by the laborer's own fault, were punishable by fines. A Chinese commissioner was

[12] Persia Crawford Campbell, *Chinese Coolie Emigration to Countries within the British Empire* (London, 1923), pp. 217–23.

appointed by the government of Western Samoa to care for the interests of the coolies. If at the end of his term of service the coolie did not wish to be reindentured, he had to be repatriated at his employer's expense. In December, 1923, this system was replaced by a free-labor system. Chinese laborers entering the territory obtain free-labor conditions by accepting an agreement with the Chinese commissioner in Samoa as representative of the government of Samoa and their future employers. The terms of the agreement, as laid down in the Chinese Free Labor Ordinance of 1923, provide for continuous employment for three years at 3*s* per day for a full day's work of 9–9½ hours, or for such other wage as may be agreed upon at the time of signing the contract. If the laborer wishes to change his employer, the commissioner will permit him to do so when practicable and if a valid reason is given. The government guarantees the fulfilment by the employer of certain specified conditions of work, housing, and maintenance. The Chinese commissioner in Samoa will investigate complaints made by laborers. The Chinese commissioner undertakes to repatriate a Chinese laborer at the end of the period of contract, unless the laborer wishes to renew the contract. If a laborer is certified as chronically unfit, he must be repatriated by his employer.

Chinese laborers in Nauru are employed under conditions laid down in the ordinance of November 18, 1922. On their arrival in the island the agreement is read to them, and the administrator of the island of Nauru must satisfy himself that each laborer understands the nature and terms of the agreement. The rates of pay, hours of work, and conditions of labor are subject to the approval of the administrator. The term of service is for three years. At the end of that time the employer must furnish the laborer with a free passage home and maintenance during the journey, unless the laborer wishes to renew his contract with his employer, which he may do for a further period of three years.

### XII. UNITED STATES

Federal legislation: (1) General—Naturalization Act, 1875; immigration acts of 1907, 1917, 1924. (2) Chinese restriction—Chinese restriction acts of May 6, 1882, July 5, 1884, September 13, 1888, May 5, 1892, November 3, 1893, April 29, 1902.

State legislation: Philippine Chinese Exclusion Act, 1903.

Treaties: United States and China—Burlingame Treaty, 1868; immigration treaties of 1881, 1894. United States and Japan—Commercial Treaty, 1894; Gentlemen's Agreement, 1908; Commercial Treaty, 1911.

*General restrictions on the immigration of Chinese, Indians and Japanese.*—Under article 13 (*c*) of the Immigration Act of the United States, 1924, any alien ineligible to citizenship is prohibited from entering the country unless he is: (*a*) an alien previously admitted to the United States who is returning from a temporary visit abroad, or (*b*) a minister of any religious denomination, a professor of a college, seminary, or university, who has been such for two years previously and seeks to enter the United States for the purpose of carrying on his vocation, and his wife and his unmarried children under eighteen years of age if accompanying or following to join him; (*c*) a bona fide student at least fifteen years of age who is seeking to enter the United States solely for the purpose of study at an accredited school, college, academy, seminary, or university; (*d*) a government official, his family, and servants; (*e*) an alien visiting the country temporarily either for business or pleasure; (*f*) an alien in continuous transit through the United States; (*g*) an alien lawfully admitted to the United States who later goes in transit from one part of the United States to another through foreign contiguous territory; (*h*) a bona fide alien seaman; (*i*) an alien entitled to enter the United States solely to carry on trade under, and in pursuance of, the provisions of a present existing treaty of commerce and navigation.

These provisions exclude persons of Chinese, Japanese, and Indian nationality, since the right of naturalization is confined to free white persons and aliens of African nativity and to persons of African descent (Naturalization Law, U. S. Revised Statutes, Section 2169, as amended, 1875).

The immigration of Asiatics, when no provision is made by treaty, is also prohibited by article 3 of the Immigration Act of 1917, which excludes all aliens coming from what is known as the "Asiatic Barred Zone," that is, "persons who are natives of islands not possessed by the United States adjacent to the continent of Asia, situate south of the twentieth parallel latitude north, west of the one hundred and sixtieth meridian of longitude east from Greenwich, and north of the tenth parallel of latitude south, or who are natives of any country, province, or dependency situate on the continent of Asia west of the one hundred and tenth meridian of longitude east from Greenwich and east of the fiftieth meridian of longitude east from Greenwich and south of the fiftieth parallel of latitude north, except that portion of said territory situate between the fiftieth and the sixty-fourth meridians of longitude east from Greenwich and the twenty-fourth and thirty-eighth parallels of latitude north."

*Chinese immigration: Historical review of legislation.*—The restriction of the immigration of Chinese into the United States was first provided for by treaties with China, the Burlingame Treaty of 1868, and the treaties of 1881 and 1894. Article 1 of the Treaty of 1881 empowered the government of the United States to regulate, limit, or suspend the coming of Chinese into the United States whenever the immigration of Chinese laborers affected or threatened to affect the interests of the United States or endangered the good order of the state. The American government, however, might not absolutely prohibit Chinese immigration. Teachers, students, merchants, or tourists should be allowed to come and go of their own free will (art. 2). The Treaty of 1894 provided that the immigration of Chinese laborers should be prohibited for a period of ten years, and China recognized the right of the United States to demand the registration of Chinese subjects in the United States, while the United States recognized the right of China to register its citizens in China.

The United States passed a series of acts prohibiting Chinese immigration. The Act of May 6, 1882, suspended the admission of Chinese workers for a period of ten years. It was amended by the Act of July 5, 1884. Both these acts were repealed by the Act of September 13, 1888, which re-enacted the main provisions and prohibited the return of Chinese who had already resided in the United States except under certain conditions. The Act of May 5, 1892, extended the period of exclusion to ten years from the passage of the Act. By the Act of April 29, 1902, the provisions of the previous laws were re-enacted, extended, and continued, and were applied also to the island territory under the jurisdiction of the United States. The existing legislation may be analyzed as follows:

*Numerical restriction.*—By article 5 of the Chinese Restriction Act of September 13, 1888, which was extended by the Act of April 29, 1902, the immigration of Chinese laborers, whether skilled or unskilled, is prohibited. Chinese teachers, officials, students, merchants, or travelers are exempted (art. 1). No Chinese laborer once resident in the United States who has left the country has the right to return unless: (1) He has a lawful wife, child, or parent in the United States, or (2) he has property of the value of $1,000 in the United States, or (3) he has debts pending settlement in the United States of not less than $1,000.

*Conditions of entry.*—By the same act it is provided that Chinese may enter only at specified ports and returning laborers must enter at the ports by which they have left (art 7). Immigrants must be supplied with certificates establishing their right to enter. In the case of the exempted classes (see preceding) these certificates are given by the United States consul when the immigrant has obtained the permission of the government (whether the Chinese government or a foreign government) to enter the United States. A copy of the certificate is given to the person and a copy to the captain of the ship bringing him to the United States. The captain also bears a sealed letter from the consul to the collector of customs at the port of destination saying that a permit to enter has been issued to such and such a Chinese person (art. 4). The certificate of a returning laborer is issued by the collector of customs for the district in which the laborer resides and the laborer must obtain it before his departure. It is valid for one year, but may be extended in special cases of sickness and disability (art. 7). The master of any vessel who knowingly brings to the United States and lands or attempts to land any Chinese laborer or other Chinese person in contravention of the act is liable to a fine of not less than $500 or more than $1,000 (art. 9). Every Chinese person, before being landed, must be examined by the collector or his deputy (art. 13).

*Registration of Chinese.*—The registration of Chinese laborers was provided for by the acts of May 5, 1892, and November 3, 1893. All Chinese laborers within the limits of the United States who were entitled to remain there were bound to apply to the collector of internal revenue of their respective districts within six months after the passage of the act for a certificate of registration. Any laborer who neglected or failed to obtain this certificate was liable to arrest and deportation. No Chinese person convicted in any court of the states or territory of the United States of a felony could register under the act (art. 1). The word "laborer" was defined to mean "both skilled and unskilled manual laborers, including Chinese employed in mining, fishing, huckstering, peddling, laundry men, or those engaged in taking, drying, or otherwise preserving shell or other fish for home consumption or exportation" (art. 2).

*Deportation of Chinese.*—The Chinese Exclusion Act, May 5, 1892, provides that Chinese persons arrested under the Act shall be deported either to China or to the country of which they are citizens or subjects. If such country demands a tax for their return they shall be deported to China (art. 2). (This obviously refers to Chinese citizens of Canada.) Bail is not allowed to persons under the Act (art. 5).

*Chinese in the Philippines.*—The Act of April 29, 1902, extended the provisions for the exclusion of Chinese to the island territory under the jurisdiction of the United States, and prohibited the immigration of Chinese laborers from such island territories to the United States. It also provided for the registration of every Chinese laborer other than a citizen rightfully in, and entitled to remain in, any of the insular territory of the United States (art. 4). In furtherance of this, the Philippine commission passed an act (March 27, 1903) making regulations and provisions necessary for the enforcement of registration. Every Chinese person having the right to be or remain in the Philippine Islands was obliged to obtain a certificate, and every Chinese person found without a certificate after the expiration of the time allowed by the law for registration was presumed in the absence of satisfactory proof to the contrary, to be a prohibited immigrant, to be deported (art. 5).

*Chinese in Hawaii.*—When Hawaii was annexed to the United States, a joint resolution was passed (July 7, 1898) to the effect that "there shall be no further immigration of Chinese into the Hawaiian Islands, except upon such conditions as are now or may hereafter be allowed by the laws of the United States; and no Chinese, by reason of anything herein contained, shall be allowed to enter the United States from the Hawaiian Islands." As cited previously, the Chinese Exclusion Act of the United States prohibited the immigration of Chinese from the island territories of the United States to the mainland.

*Japanese immigration.*—Japanese immigration into the United States was, until 1924, restricted by agreements between the United States and Japan.

In the Immigration Act of February 20, 1907 (art. 1), the president was authorized to refuse entrance to immigrants who, to obtain entrance to the mainland, were using passports originally issued to "any country other than the United States or to any insular possession of the United States or to the Canal Zone." Under this authority the president issued the proclamation of March 14, 1907, which ordered that "Japanese or Korean laborers, skilled or unskilled, who have received passports to go to Mexico, Canada, or Hawaii, and come therefrom, be refused permission to enter the continental territory of the United States." This stopped Japanese immigration from Hawaii and Mexico, but not directly from Japan. The Act of 1907, however, also authorized the president to enter into "such international agreements as may be proper to prevent the immigration of aliens who, under the laws of the United States, are or may be excluded from entering the United States and of regulating any matters pertaining to such immigration."[13] Accordingly, the United States entered into the Gentlemen's Agreement with Japan in 1907–8, the main features of which were as follows: (1) The Japanese government agreed not to issue passports to laborers, whether skilled or unskilled, for continental America except to those wishing to resume a formerly acquired domicile, and to parents, wives, and children under twenty years of age of such persons. (2) The Japanese government would continue to deliver passports to settled agriculturalists, but undertook to enforce

[13] Raymond Leslie Buell, "Japanese Immigration," *World-Peace Foundation Pamphlets Nos. 5–6* (1924), p. 288.

measures against fraud. (3) The Japanese government undertook to examine carefully the applications for passports of students, merchants, and tourists and to refuse passports to any Japanese likely to become laborers after their arrival in the Uinted States. (4) The Agreement was not applicable to Hawaii, but the Japanese government undertook to prohibit the emigration of Japanese workers to Hawaii under the same conditions. (5) As regards the emigration of Japanese laborers to territory contiguous to the United States, the Japanese government agreed to take measures to prevent their entering the United States without passports when passing by the frontier.[14]

In 1911 the Commercial Treaty of November 22, 1894, between Japan and the United States was replaced by a treaty which appeared to authorize the admission of Japanese only for purposes of trade.[15] Whereas article 1 of the Treaty of November 22, 1894, provided that "the citizens or subjects of each of the high contracting parties shall have full liberty to enter, travel, or reside in any part of the territories of the other contracting party and shall enjoy full and perfect protection for their persons and property," the Treaty of 1911 (art. 1) reads as follows: "The citzens or subjects of each of the high contracting parties shall have liberty to enter, travel, and reside in the territories of the other to carry on trade, wholesale and retail, to own or lease and occupy houses, manufactories, warehouses, and shops, to employ agents of their choice, to lease land for residential and commercial purposes, and generally to do anything incident to or necessary for trade upon the same terms as native citizens or subjects, submitting themselves to the laws and regulations there established." In the same treaty the Japanese government declared that it was fully prepared to maintain with equal effectiveness the limitation and control which it had for the past three years exercised in the regulation of the emigration of laborers to the United States.

Japanese nationals permitted by their government to enter the United States were subject to the ordinary immigration legislation and were subject to the literacy test enacted in 1917. In 1924 the American government passed the immigration act which prohibited the immigration of all aliens ineligible to citizenship. As the courts have declared in various decisions (Saito, 62 Fed. 126, June 24, 1894; Young, 195 Fed. 645, April 24, 1912; Takas Ozawa, 260 Fed. 178, November 13, 1922) that Japanese are ineligible to citizenship, Japanese are now excluded from the United States, with the exception of the classes given previously. The Japanese government protested against Section 13(c) of the immigration act as a discriminatory measure against their nation, and canceled the Gentlemen's Agreement in 1924.

## XIII. EMIGRATION LEGISLATION IN CHINA, JAPAN AND INDIA

The main principle underlying the regulation of emigration in China, Japan, and India is the protection of the citizen of the country as a laborer rather than as a subject of the state. At the same time the action of other countries in restricting the

[14] Raymond Leslie Buell, *op. cit.*, p. 290.

[15] Note of the Japanese ambassador, Mr. Masanao Hanihara, to the United States secretary of state, Mr. Charles E. Hughes, April 10, 1924.

immigration of these races and in imposing upon them grave disabilities, as described previously, may certainly be considered as a contributory cause of the close supervision exercised by the governments of India, China, and Japan over the emigration of their nationals.[16]

It is in India that emigration is most restricted. In that country, by the Act of 1922, emigration for the purpose of unskilled work is declared unlawful except to such countries and on such terms and conditions as the governor-general in council may specify (art. 10 [1]). The governor-general in council may prohibit from a date all persons or any specified class of person from emigrating to any specified country for the purpose of unskilled work (art. 13 [1]). Emigration for either skilled or unskilled work may only take place from certain ports (arts. 9 [1], 15). The countries to which at the present time emigration of unskilled laborers from India is authorized are Ceylon, the Federated Malay States, the Straits Settlements, and British Guiana.

It may perhaps be mentioned here that in 1924 the Indian legislature passed an act to regulate the entry and residence in British India of persons domiciled in other British possessions. This act empowered the governor in council to issue rules providing that persons of other than Indian origin domiciled in any British possession should only enjoy the same rights of entry or residence in India as are accorded to Indians in such possession.

In Japan and Korea every person wishing to leave the country must have special permission from the authorities to emigrate, and the permission to emigrate is invalidated by failure to depart within six months from the date at which the permission is granted. The administrative authorities may, with a view to the protection of emigrants or the maintenance of the public peace, or if they deem it necessary, having regard to foreign relations, suspend emigration and revoke the permission granted therefor. By the term "emigrant" is meant only "persons who emigrate for purposes of labor to foreign countries, and such members of their families as accompany them or emigrate to their place of residence." The administrative authorities may, according to the conditions of the place to which an emigrant desires to go, require him, if his emigration is not being arranged for by an agent, to appoint not less than two persons as sureties. These persons must be responsible for him if he is in need of assistance.[17]

Chinese laborers have complete liberty under Chinese law to emigrate where they will, but every laborer must be provided with a passport issued by the emigration bureau. They must fulfil certain conditions of physical well-being and good conduct imposed as a safeguard against their repatriation at the public expense. Apart from this, emigration from China is only regulated from the point of view of working conditions, and detailed provisions specify the conditions of recruitment, the type of labor contract, the maximum number of hours to be worked, etc.

Japan: Emigrants Protection Law No. 70, 1896, as amended by Law No. 23, 1901, Law No. 4, 1902, Law No. 33, 1907, arts. 1, 2, 3, 4.

[16] See, for example, the debates on the Indian Emigration Bill, March 21, 1921, *India Legislative Assembly Debates,* Vol. I, No. 13.

[17] Chinese Labor Emigration Law, April 21, 1918.

Korea: Notification No. 68, 1906, revised by notification No. 82, of 1908, arts. 1, 2, 3. Notification No. 75, of 1906, revised by notification No. 83 of 1908, arts, 1, 2.

### XIV. GENERAL EFFECT OF TREATIES ON THE MIGRATION OF ASIATICS

Reference has been made in the preceding pages to treaties which have had important effects on Asiatic migration. It is not within the scope of the present study, which deals exclusively with the legislative aspect of the problem of Asiatic migration, to analyze methodically the international regulation of this migration. It is important, however, to note in passing the part played by these treaties and to indicate the function they may fulfil in the future.

Agreements have been concluded to encourage Asiatic continental migration by determining conditions and assuring to the migrants equitable treatment in the country in which they settle. Such are the arrangements concluded by India for the recruitment of her unskilled laborers, and various other agreements, such as that concluded recently between Japan and Brazil, which reduces the difficulties of the emigration of Japanese.

Some indication has been given in the preceding pages of the manner in which the immigration of Asiatics is restricted by certain countries. In addition to this, persons of Asiatic race are in some countries subject to disabilities after entry, notably in matters of social insurance, education, landholding, trading licenses, etc. The subject is outside the scope of the present study, but it is one which undoubtedly deserves the earnest attention of all those who desire to bring about an amicable solution of the problems of the Pacific.

## SECTION 23

## RÉSUMÉ OF RESIDENT ORIENTALS ON THE AMERICAN PACIFIC COAST

ELIOT G. MEARS
Stanford University

Since this study is one of laws, regulations, and judicial decisions and their actual operation, the approach and treatment has been primarily from the legal standpoint. Furthermore, the point of view has been to make as broad a contrast as possible between the respective rights and privileges of citizens, of non-Asiatic aliens, and of Asiatic aliens. But the reader has doubtless been impressed frequently by the fact that law and justice are not synonymous terms.

This report throughout has been concerned, not with moral justice, but with the statement of the law and its actual operation.

### PARTIES CONCERNED

The country of emigration, China or Japan, retains control and a practical interest over its nationals. In some other matters, due perhaps to an unsympathetic public opinion abroad as applied to those of American citizenship but oriental ancestry a nation feels that it is but fitting and proper to guard what she regards as her just sensibilities.

The country of immigration, the United States of America, is rightly believed to be a democratic nation, "of the people, by the people, and for the people." She accords to aliens the full protection granted under the federal Constitution, which establishes treaties as "the supreme law of the land," and provides that no state shall "deprive any person of life, liberty, or property, without due process of law; nor deny to any person within its jurisdiction the equal protection of the laws." But the popular attitude toward one's government differs widely. "The Englishman," said a Japanese envoy at Washington, "reveres the state because it belongs to him; the Japanese because he belongs to it." Both are right,[1] one adds, in so far as they mean the same thing. The Chinese are an individualistic rather than a politically minded people. In America there is a laxness in regard for public authority[2] which applies jointly to the chief executive, whose personality is of great importance, to the legis-

[1] W. H. Hadow, *Citizenship* (Oxford University Press, 1923), p. 112.

[2] "But most significant of all political matters is the growing distrust of legislatures. Curiously enough, although there was a great distrust of the executive of the nation until within a very few years, that seems to have entirely passed away. Governors of states have too little power to inspire distrust in anybody. But that legislatures or representatives of the people should fail to inspire their confidence is one of the most curious developments of modern politics" (F. J. Stimson, *Popular Law-Making* [New York, 1912], p. 290).

lative branches of the government, and to the conduct of foreign affairs.[3] The courts are held in most esteem.

The component political entities, such as the states, counties, and towns, with inferior jurisdiction, are held in less popular esteem, yet frequently they are more loyally supported because they represent the sentiments of the local electorates. Resolutions and bills introduced, legislation passed, and acts of public officials are often less considered than is true of national authorities; many times petty politics are the guiding motive, but under the system of checks and balances the state occupies a strategic position which may be utilized to defy the federal authorities, even on questions which are primarily international and involve treaty rights.[4] Various remedies have been suggested,[5] while the existence of international law seems to be fairly well established.[6]

[3] "Most Americans who write of American foreign policy denounce their government. They take it as axiomatic that the Department of State is selfish and materialistic, that to differ proves their own beautiful idealism. They, of course, do not construct policy. They have the easier and more congenial task of pulling it to pieces. An Englishman or a Frenchman or a German seldom condemns his government in advance, especially in international dealings. His tendency is rather to support his government as long as he conscientiously can. I see no reason why Americans should be less patriotic" (article by N., "Our Much-Abused State Department," *Foreign Affairs* [New York, July, 1927], No. 4, 567).

[4] Article X of the Constitution, an amendment which became effective in 1791, provides, "The powers not delegated to the United States by the Constitution, nor prohibited by it to the states, are reserved to the states respectively, or to the people."

[5] "There would seem to be no valid constitutional objection to an act of Congress giving to the federal courts cognizance of all offenses for which the United States may according to the law of nations be held responsible to foreign powers" (W. W. Willoughby, *The American Constitutional System* [New York, 1904], p. 108).

"The economic and social problems faced by the people of the Pacific Coast, for example, can only in part be appreciated by the national government and its representatives. It would seem that California ought to be a part—if only a subsidiary one—to any diplomatic or other arrangement between the United States and Japan affecting the land legislation. At least no final conclusion should be arrived at unless through a conference in which California is more directly represented than by the state department. There is no constitutional difficulty in this procedure" (from article by Orrin K. McMurray, "Legal Aspects of the Japanese Question," *The Pacific Review* [December, 1920], pp. 402–3).

"New legislation on the subject has been vigorously recommended by President Harrison, by President McKinley, by President Roosevelt, and by myself" (from article, "The Treaty Rights of Aliens," by William Howard Taft, *International Conciliation*, No. 116 [New York, July, 1917]).

[6] "In modern times it is recognized that well-being rests largely upon law. Within a nation, law secures stability of relationships. Similarly, among nations, the provisions of law are necessary in order that international well-being may prevail. This law is called international law, and while the existence of international law has sometimes been questioned, the highest courts of nations, such as the Supreme Court of the United States, in the case of Paquete Habana, and the Judicial Committee of the Privy Council of Great Britain, in the case of Zamora, have recognized that international law does exist. The highest courts of other nations have taken similar action. And this is probably sufficient basis

American citizens determine conditions of their own well-being, in so far as they are able, either through or in spite of public authority. To the Californians, questions affecting the Chinese, and later the Japanese, centered around fresh racial problems.[7] The Californian's point of view is now incorporated into federal and state legislation. Unquestionably, sectional feeling has overshadowed considerations of international amity.[8]

First-generation Asiatic immigrants are ineligible to American citizenship; therefore their presence here involves frequent negotiations between American and foreign governments. The lot of those on American territory has been vastly improved because of the limitations imposed under the Immigration Act of 1924 upon prospective newcomers of an inferior standard of living. While the Chinese usually wish to return to their country, an increasing number of Japanese are loath to forfeit the higher living standards and comforts which they secure in America. Despite the discriminatory federal and state laws enacted since 1918, extremely few Asiatics have migrated to other states of the Union.

American-born persons of Asiatic parentage, commonly referred to as the second generation, are American citizens. Their relative, and probably their actual, numbers in the Chinese and Japanese groups, respectively, are on the increase. When subject to similar living conditions and advantages, they are worthy Americans; in this connection, the change in the Japanese citizenship laws is a favorable factor. To the second-generation Oriental, China or Japan is a strange land; English is often the only language he can read and write, and America is home and remains so even where living conditions and opportunities for improvement leave much to be desired.

### INFORMATION AVAILABLE

There is no authentic, factual history relative to the status of American aliens of whatever origin. This report, then, may serve as a suggestive background to the more

---

for confidence in the existence of this law" (from "Law and Treaties in the Pacific," by George Grafton Wilson, in *Proceedings of the Institute of Pacific Relations: Honolulu Session,* June 30–July 14, 1925).

[7] "It is the beginning of the biggest problem that ever faced the American people! . . . . Psychologically, this epitomized the whole question—the beginning of a race problem, multiplied in imagination by the possibilities of all the future; the challenge, which sort of a baby shall prefigure the future Californian" (Chester Rowell, in *World's Work,* June, 1913).

"The cardinal question relating to the Japanese population in California is the question of birth-rate. Immigration can be restricted, smuggling may be completely prevented, but the fact of the high birth-rate is something which cannot be very easily combated without infringing upon the traditionally sacred principles and personal freedom. . . . . Nor are the Japanese a race likely to amalgamate completely with Americans in a few generations. Thus the question of Japanese birth-rate in America becomes a vital matter, touching the fundamental questions of national and racial unity in the United States" (T. Iyenaga and Kenoske Sato, *Japan and the California Problem* [New York, 1921], pp. 109–10).

[8] Eliot G. Mears, "California's Attitude towards the Oriental," *Annals of the American Academy of Political and Social Science* (September, 1925).

significant relationships of a legal and economic character which exist in America between citizens and aliens, between Asiatic and non-Asiatic aliens, and between Americans and Asiatics.

The literature and the unpublished opinions on the particular subject of this report are almost invariably approached from interested and specialized points of view, which are surprisingly conflicting on the surface because no calm attempts have been made toward harmonizing them. There has existed almost a state of war because of the unwillingness[9] of either side to make concessions, or because the Christian spirit is lacking.[10]

The actual happenings, however, have been grossly exaggerated. The situation is surfeited with both misrepresentation and ignorance, the result of prejudice, the sensational press, high cable and wireless news rates across the Pacific,[11] which are apt to produce a brevity of news to the point of distortion, and the frequency of elections for public offices, in which race questions provide convenient campaign issues for unscrupulous politicians.[12] The facts have never been approached by the scientific method.

### LEGAL TREATMENT

From the legal standpoint, the discriminations to which Orientals in America claim to be subject, when closely examined, will be found to be based on solid precedent and on enactments which, in the main, antedate Oriental immigration.

Citizenship, marriage, and land ownership apart, what remains of legal disabilities of Asiatic aliens on the Pacific coast is not so inclusive as is sometimes supposed. Exclusion from public employment, from the privileges of hunting and fishing and carrying weapons, and some restrictions as to licenses—a denial of prerogatives that

[9] "The way we generally strive for rights is by getting our fighting blood up; and I venture to say that that is the long way and not the short way. If you come at me with your fists doubled, I think I can promise you that mine will double as fast as yours; but if you come to me and say, 'Let us sit down and take counsel together, and, if we differ from one another, understand why it is that we differ from one another, just what the points at issue are,' we will presently find that we are not so far apart, after all, that the points on which we differ are few and the points on which we agree are many, and that if we only have the patience and the candor and the desire to get together, we will get together" (Woodrow Wilson, in speech at the American Federation of Labor Building, Washington, July 4, 1916).

[10] Mr. Elihu Root, in accepting the award of the Woodrow Wilson Foundation, in New York, December 28, 1926, said: "I beg you to believe that I deeply appreciate the honor that you do me. The finest thing about it is the spirit in which it is done, which is able to brush aside as incidental long political opposition and not a few differences of opinion publicly avowed, and to rest upon fundamental identity of purpose with a sense of proportion suitable to the high distinction of the great President whose memory you celebrate, and suitable to the deep and permanent purpose of your organization. In foreign affairs it is peculiarly true that the spirit in which work is done is everything."

[11] V. S. McClatchy, "Communication as a Factor in International Relations," *Proceedings, First Institute of International Relations*, Riverside, 1926 (University of Southern California Press, 1927); also *San Francisco Business*, May 11, 1927.

[12] P. J. Treat, *Japan and the United States*, chap. xiii.

does not seriously interfere with the life and livelihood of most individuals—practically tell the whole story. These latter disabilities are not limited to Asiatic aliens: they extend to all aliens equally.

In America the general tendency during the past century has been to liberalize laws respecting rights of aliens. This result has been brought about by "aiding" statutes which have been more numerous than "restricting" ones, thereby giving the alien a better status than he formerly had under common law alone. This improving condition has come to Asiatic aliens as well as to non-Asiatics, although not to the same extent.

The citizenship status is entirely a federal matter. Intermarriage laws exist in California and Oregon. The alien land laws of the three Pacific coast states constitute the chief legal limitation to Orientals, who are deprived of some of the rights accorded to immigrants eligible for citizenship. It should be borne in mind, however, that the enactment of these laws was due, not to blind race prejudice, but to the strong desire on the part of the advocates to improve the rural community. The race problem which confronted the Western states appeared to them overwhelmingly serious and impelled them to pass laws which, to the outside world, seemed unnecessarily severe.

The classification adopted as the basis for these laws was set up by federal statutes long before any oriental problem appeared. Its application to persons ineligible to citizenship is not limited to Chinese or Japanese, but includes, according to the Supreme Court of the United States, native Hawaiians, Burmans, Canadian Indians, and Hindus.

The alien land laws do not violate any provisions of existing treaties with Asiatic governments. An analysis of coast legislation during recent years indicates this clearly, although undoubtedly the Pacific states framed laws which were directed at resident Orientals. It is to be noted that only one provision of the California Alien Land Law has been declared unconstitutional. That is the one relating to guardianship. In all other respects, whenever a case has raised a constitutional question as to any of its provisions, even in the Supreme Court of the United States, the law has been upheld. In fact, all the recent cases decided by the California courts against aliens have been upheld by the highest court. In one case, moreover, the Supreme Court of the United States was more strict in interpreting an agreement to work the land against the alien than the federal district court (N.D.) in California had been.[13]

Furthermore, the Washington supreme court has been overruled by the United States Supreme Court in only one recent important case,[14] which dealt with a license ordinance in Seattle. In no recent case has the California or Oregon supreme court been thus overruled on a resident alien question discussed in this report.

This evidence apparently proves that these state courts are as ready to protect the rights of aliens as is the Supreme Court of the United States. Aliens have been given every right to have their pleas heard, and most of the special provisions applicable to them have been tested in inferior and superior tribunals. The courts, state and federal alike, have been quick to discredit attorneys' arguments justifying dis-

[13] *O'Brien* vs. *Webb,* 263 U.S. 313 (1923).

[14] *Asakura* vs. *City of Seattle,* 265 U.S. 332.

crimination based on race,[15] color, language, personal privilege, or alleged inferiority. They have been and are above reproach in their handling of all alien problems arising from various laws and coming before them for decision. There is no denying that Orientals have had many just causes for complaint, but the inference that there may be a prejudiced judiciary on the west coast is not borne out by legal history.[16]

### OCCUPATIONAL OPPORTUNITIES

The problem of securing employment does not exist in the case of the first generation. The Chinese work in private homes, chop-suey houses, stores selling oriental goods, and in the establishments of Chinatown. The majority of the Japanese are working on farms,[17] but many are in grocery and produce stores, restaurants, hotels and lodging-houses, and in private homes. The Chinese are almost wholly in noncompetitive lines. The Japanese have been leaving the land, where their skill has been universally recognized by ranchers, to become more active in competitive city business. The majority of immigrants of both nationalities are past middle life. They command an adequate remuneration, and are very seldom out of work.

The second-generation Chinese seem to cling to Chinatown, where the opportunities are diminishing, partly due to its dwindling area and fewer activities. Relatively few of them are interested in business employment outside the racial colony, nor do they seem to care for agriculture. Their vocational status is less satisfactory than that of the second-generation Japanese, who are eager to secure any positions which appear to offer a promising future. The latter's inclinations are away from agriculture, a not unnatural situation with young Americans, who show an aversion to

[15] In June, 1927, a district federal court on the coast was censured by a higher tribunal because of its reference to the question of race—in this case, Italian.

[16] A leading California lawyer, William Denman, who has also served as chairman of the United States Shipping Board and president of the Emergency Fleet Corporation, remarked at an open meeting of the Commonwealth Club of California, San Francisco, May 19, 1927: "I have practiced for some twenty-seven years, very largely in the federal courts. We have had a very fine bench there. There have been no scandals. I do not think we have had any excess arbitrariness of mind or developing stiffness of mentality in any of the judges who have been there. Most of them have come from the state courts through the elective system, and that may have had something to do with it.

"But this has not been the experience throughout the United States. There are districts where, I am told by those wise men in Washington, the journalistic group, who are probably the best informed on personalities in America, that there have been arbitrary and oppressive federal judges, and we have known of impeachments of federal judges, for just that oppression and arrogance that certain kinds of minds develop in the exercise of power that is nearly arbitrary, under what is practically a life tenure. I believe that the fact that the judge has, back in his mind, the thought that, 'Now every so often I am going to be inspected, not by the litigants right in front of me, but by the community at large,' may bring an assurance of fair-mindedness and graciousness of contact which the Californian expects on the bench" ("Judicial Elections" number, *The Commonwealth,* Part II, Vol. III, No. 24 [San Francisco, June 14, 1927]).

[17] One of the leading coast Japanese, who has lived in San Francisco over forty years, told the writer in 1925 that the employment question for the Japanese in California would solve itself, provided the anti-alien land acts were not rigidly enforced.

start in farming by working from the ground up. Their ambition turns out in their case to be in the nature of a drawback, since for perfectly natural reasons employers give a preference to their own race, and thus far relatively few of the older generation have shifted from agriculture to consequential business positions.

The vocational problem for the American-born of oriental parentage is serious because of an assumption on the part of many employers, even when they are free from race prejudice themselves, that their employment of oriental workers would be criticized by others.

### RELATIONS BETWEEN AMERICANS AND ORIENTALS

The opportunities for close personal relations between white Americans and Orientals are few, though, considering the state of race feeling, there is surprisingly little objection to interracial contact in public and semipublic situations.

On the part of the Americans and unnaturalized foreigners in the country, there is a distinct prejudice on the Pacific slope which is the accumulated result of local experiences with Indians and foreigners. It is futile to deny that an antipathy exists on the coast, which is less marked, but not altogether absent, in other sections of continental America. But to compare the position of the American Chinese or Japanese with that of the American Negro is foolish. There is no doubt, moreover, that on the Pacific coast there have been afforded more opportunities for contact between Asiatics and natives than would have occurred under similar circumstances in the aristocratic South, where neither westerner nor northerner can easily break into society. As the record of the Western states unquestionably shows, dissimilarity inevitably provokes prejudice.[18]

### THE CHANGING SITUATION

On two most important features of the situation there is universal agreement, namely, that the nineteenth-century hostility toward the Chinese has given way to a tolerant, kindly feeling; furthermore, the prejudice against the Japanese, most marked from 1905 to 1925, has either practically disappeared or is quiescent. Doubtless the second alternative is more in accordance with the facts; but in any case the subject is hardly ever mentioned now. The "Survey of Race Relations" made this one of their main findings in March, 1925; a reading of the coast press and conversations with formerly outspoken individuals confirm this. The American Legion posts, the Native Sons, and the labor federations have not changed their well-known attitude regarding aliens. The California Joint Immigration Committee is still functioning.[19] On the other hand there are the church groups, China societies, Japan so-

[18] There must be the "recognition that races absolutely equal in character, intelligence, and culture may nevertheless be so far unlike that masses of voters, failing to discriminate between unlikeness and inequality, may surrender themselves to race prejudice; and that a government seeking to avoid so unfortunate an occurrence should not be presumed to be unwilling to treat all races equally" (Professor Franklin H. Giddings, in a reply to questionnaire. Tasuka Harada, *The Japanese Problem in California* [San Francisco], p. 36).

[19] It was announced on June 13, 1927, that "this Committee follows an established policy of assisting in securing for alien immigrants, ineligible for citizenship, every right and courtesy due them under treaty, or otherwise, while at the same time it insists on a rigid observance of national policy and law as to immigration."

cieties, chambers of commerce, etc., which are exceedingly friendly to the Orientals. Striking a general balance, on the further evidence, too, of letters from scores of people and organizations of widely different convictions, supplemented by personal interviews this spring with informed individuals in ten of the eleven western states, the writer is convinced that there is a more friendly feeling generally toward both the Chinese and the Japanese than has been true toward either race in the recent past.

This is further evidenced by the fact that there is a marked decrease in efforts to enforce the land laws. Many prominent citizens feel that any need for these laws is now past.

Among the reasons which can be cited for this kindlier feeling toward the Orientals are: the infiltration of Mexicans and Filipinos in large numbers, with whom the Chinese and Japanese are very favorably compared; the fairly recent action of the Japanese government relative to "picture brides," to domestic land laws, and to the right of expatriation; and the increased attention and interest in the export of Pacific coast products, notably canned goods, dried fruit, rice, flour, and lumber, which find important markets in China and Japan.

The rapid increases of the local Chinese population before 1882, and of the Japanese until recently, are not forgotten by the Pacific Coast states. Yet it is reasonable to expect that as soon as there is a general feeling of security against further oriental immigration there will be certain modifications of existing laws more in concord with international good will.

## SECTION 24

# AUSTRALIAN IMMIGRATION LAWS AND THEIR WORKING

A. H. CHARTERIS, M.A., LL.B.
Professor of International Law, University of Sydney

For an analysis of the Australian immigration laws, reference is made to *Proceedings of the Institute of Pacific Relations: Honolulu Session* (1925), 146.

In supplement of this analysis, the following information is given as to (*a*) the origin of the dictation test, (*b*) the "Gentlemen's Agreements" with Japan of 1904 and with other governments of subsequent date, (*c*) method of applying the dictation test, (*d*) the provisions for limitation of immigration by proclamation introduced by the immigration (amendment) Act, 1925, (*e*) numerical limitation effected by agreement in 1925 with statistics of immigration into the Commonwealth for 1926.

*Origin of the dictation test.*—The dictation test was first suggested to Australian colonial legislatures by the Imperial government in 1897 in order to spare the susceptibilities of British Indian subjects of the Crown as well as of foreign Asiatics, both of whom the legislatures of New South Wales, Tasmania, and New Zealand had by bills then awaiting the royal assent excluded as Asiatics from their respective territories. At the Colonial Conference in London in 1897, Mr. Joseph Chamberlain, secretary of state for the Colonies, had urged the colonial premiers to adopt the non-discriminatory method of a literacy test in the English language as contained in the Natal Act No. 1, of 1897, to which the royal assent had been given. The bills were accordingly amended in this sense. After federation in 1900, the literacy test in a modified form, which was thought desirable in order to prevent evasion of restrictions modeled on those of Natal was adopted by the Commonwealth parliament in the Immigration Act of 1901 (No. 17), which accordingly includes among "prohibited immigrants": "any person who fails to pass the dictation test; that is to say, who when an officer . . . . dictates to him not less than fifty words in any European language fails to write them out in that language in the presence of the officer" (Sec. 3a).

In view of representations by the Japanese government that insistence on knowledge of a European language operated discriminatively as against Japanese nationals, the act was amended in 1905 by the substitution of "any prescribed language" for "any European language," and by subjecting the prescribing of a language or languages to parliamentary approval by resolution of both houses. Pending such approval of a prescribed language, any language authorized by the s. 3 of the principal act as unamended was to be deemed to be a prescribed language in the sense of the amendment. In other words, the provisions of the original act remained *de facto* in force.

No regulations prescribing any language or languages have been in fact issued, as the objections of the Japanese government had already been met by an informal arrangement, in the nature of a Gentlemen's Agreement, made between the Australian and the Japanese governments in 1904.

*The Gentlemen's Agreement.*—By the agreement before mentioned, bona fide students, merchants (engaged in overseas trade), and visitors from Japan were permitted to enter the Commonwealth for a stay of 12 months without liability to the dictation test on passports issued by the Japanese authorities and viséed by the British consul at the port of embarkation. As from April, 1919, the permit may be extended beyond 12 months on application for a certificate of exemption. A similar arrangement was made with the Indian government permitting Indians of the specified classes to enter and remain indefinitely so long as they retain their original status. The amending act of 1905 legalized these arrangements in their original form and authorized the conclusion of others of the same nature (sec. 8). Special arrangements made in 1912 and modified in 1920 regulate in the same manner the admission and sojourn of Chinese students, merchants, and tourists. Similar arrangements, moreover, apply to individuals of the specified classes from the British possessions of Ceylon, Burmah, Hong-Kong and Straits Settlements, as well as from Annam, Egypt, the Philippine and Hawaiian islands.[1] Their importance lies, of course, in the fact that though terminable without notice, these arrangements signify the acquiescence, during their currency, of the foreign governments concerned in the application of the dictation test to all persons not falling within any of the exempted classes.

As used in Australia, the dictation test in a language selected by an immigration officer is understood to be unique. New Zealand, which adopted a dictation test from 1899, abandoned it in 1919. Canada enforces a reading test in order to exclude "illiterates," which the Canadian Immigration Act of 1919, section 3, defines as "persons over 15 years of age physically capable of reading, who cannot read the English language or the French language, or some other language or dialect." Under this provision the language for the reading test is selected by the immigrant, not the immigration officer. The Australian dictation test is thus not a test of fitness for admission but a flexible method of exclusion. Difficulty in applying it has occasionally arisen in regard to undesirables of unusual linguistic attainments. In one such recent case concerning an international rogue, recourse was had with success to Gaelic.[2]

Before the test is applied the immigrant is informed in his own language by the officer that the dictation test is about to be administered to him, and the language of the selected passage is named. Where necessary an interpreter is used for making this communication. The officer then, in the presence of the immigrant, reads out for the first time the selected passage slowly and clearly, and thereafter furnishes the immigrant with table, writing materials, and chair, and reads out the passage at a pace suitable for dictation. If the immigrant fails to write out and sign in the presence of

[1] For further details, see Mr. E. L. Piesse's article: "Australia and Japan," in *Foreign Affairs* (New York, 1926), p. 475, where the genesis, dates, and other particulars of these arrangements are, it is believed, published for the first time. Their existence appears to have been unknown to Professor A. J. Toynbee, whose admirable article on "Asiatic Migration," *Survey of Foreign Affairs, 1924* (Oxford, 1926), does not allude to them.

[2] The *Sun* (Sydney, August 23, 1921).

the officer the passage dictated, he is informed by the officer that he is a prohibited immigrant, and will not be permitted to land.

Where the language selected for the dictation test is a European language other than English, it is a translation into the foreign language of the English passage on the current official slip that is used in the test, but except in such cases the language used in the test is not mentioned in the officer's report.[3] That the dictation test operates as a "stand-off" signal is shown by the small number of persons who are excluded in virtue of it. For the year ending December 31, 1926, thirty-six persons were so excluded, comprising four British subjects, twenty-two Chinese, seven Papuans, and one Hawaiian.

Under section 4B of the Immigration Act, "any person who has resided in Australia for a period or periods in the aggregate of not less than five years" and who is about to leave the Commonwealth, is entitled to apply for a certificate which, if granted him, will exempt him from the dictation test on his return to Australia within the period specified therein, and must be produced and delivered to an officer. The number of Asiatics admitted to Australia without the dictation test, either in virtue of certificates of exemption or of passports issued under the Gentlemen's Agreement, was 2,538 in 1925.

*Methods of applying the dictation test.*—The method is as follows: The minister of home and territories, who is charged with the administration of the immigration act, selects and causes to be printed a passage of fifty words in the English language, which is issued in printed slips specifying the period during which it is valid for use by the customs officers, who are authorized to administer the dictation test on the minister's behalf. The following is a specimen passage:

[3] The following particulars are given in view of an error which has crept into *International Conciliation,* No. 218 (March, 1926), p. 14. It is there said that "the examination may be given in Latin, Greek, or Sanscrit. . . . ." I am informed by Mr. Merle Davis, the author of the paper referred to, that this statement is based on a passage in an address read at the Honolulu conference of the Institute in July, 1925, by an Australian delegate, and reading as follows: "For instance, in two well-known cases (1906–15) undesirable Germans were excluded by a test of 50 words in classical Greek, and it is conceivable that a person might be given a test either in the most technical botanical jargon or in 'Amharic' (*Proceedings,* p. 62). In the absence of the names of the Germans referred to, it has proved impossible to trace these cases in the records of the Ministry of Home and Territories. Nor is there any record that classical Greek has ever been used for the purpose of the dictation test. Moreover, the officer in charge of the administration of the act in 1906, of whom inquiry has been made, states that he would not have sanctioned the use of this language, had it been suggested. As regards the case in 1915, it is pointed out that a German national would have been excluded as an enemy alien under the War Precautions Act, 1914, without recourse to a dictation test under the immigration act.

The second sentence in the passage quoted is, as an interpretation of section 3 of the statute, doubtless correct: but, as stated before, a European language means in Australian official practice concerning immigration a living European language, and not a dead one. Both of the sentences quoted must, it is conceived, have been written under a misapprehension.

FROM JUNE 8 TO 15, 1926. No. '26/11

Wines are made by crushing the grapes and letting the juice ferment. The skins of the fruit may be fermented in the juice, thus making red wines that take their color from the pigment under the skin. Juice alone is used in making white wines. The sugar in grapes produces alcohol.

These passages are changed every fortnight.

In the case of passengers arriving by sea, it is the practice to apply the test on board the ship after it has reached the quarantine boarding station, but before the passengers have landed, so that in an appropriate case the shipmaster may be informed of the presence on board of a prohibited immigrant whom he must not allow to land.

The text may also be applied on land, since the act provides that it may be applied in the case of all immigrants at any time within three years after entry (sec. 5 [2]), and in the case of immigrants who have entered in evasion or violation of the act at any time after entry. In these cases, at any rate, if the immigrant passes the test in one language he seems to be liable under the words "at any time" to be tested again in another.

*Immigration (amendment) Act, 1925.*—Until 1925 the only departure made by the Australian parliament from the non-discriminatory or anonymous method of immigration restriction was to be found in a post-war measure of exclusion of ex-enemy aliens, which was embodied in the Immigration Restriction (amendment) Act, 1919. This Act provided that from December 2, 1920, and thereafter until the governor-general by proclamation otherwise determined, the term "prohibited immigrant" included any person who, in the opinion of an immigration officer, was of German, Austro-German, Bulgarian, or Hungarian parentage and nationality, or was a Turk of Ottoman race.[4] Except as regards Turks of Ottoman race, the ban on the immigration of ex-enemy aliens was raised as from December 2, 1925.[5]

Later in the same year, however, an important innovation on the Commonwealth's traditional policy of refraining from specifically excluding individuals of a named race or nationality was unobtrusively made in the Immigration (amendment) Act of 1925. In view of the considerable increase in the number of immigrants from countries in Southeastern Europe which had immediately followed the entry into force of the United States immigration act of July 1, 1924, clamor for increased restriction had arisen in the press and parliament. The government was urged to adopt on the United States model a quota system designed to prevent what was somewhat extravagantly described as the "influx" of undesirables. The government rejected

[4] Semble, under the double test of parentage and nationality a natural-born British subject of British parentage, who had acquired ex-enemy nationality by naturalization or marriage, would not be a "prohibited immigrant" within the meaning of this section. British-born women who had become nationals of any of the first four ex-enemy states by marriage were, doubtless, primarily in the contemplation of the legislature.

[5] By proclamation of the Governor-general of December 3, 1925, providing that the provisions of par (g. e.) of sec. 3 of Immigration Act of 1901–25 were declared not to apply to persons of German, Austro-German, Bulgarian, or Hungarian parentage and nationality on and after December 2, 1925 (*Commonwealth Gazette,* No. 103, of December 3, 1925).

these proposals on the double ground of the expense involved in establishing an immigration service for the Commonwealth in Europe and of the impolicy of giving possible ground of offense to foreign states. Nevertheless the latter objection applies to one at least of the three statutory grounds of exclusion which parliament in fact adopted, with the omission of certain important qualifying words, from the Canadian Immigration Act of 1919.

Section 3 of the amending act of 1925 adds the following provision to the Immigration Act of 1901–2:

3K: (1) The Governor-General may by proclamation prohibit either wholly or in excess of specified numerical limits and either permanently or for a specified period, the immigration into the Commonwealth or the landing at any specified port or place in the Commonwealth, of aliens of any specified nationality, race, class or occupation, in any case where he deems it desirable to do so. (*a*) on account of the economic, industrial, or other conditions existing in the Commonwealth; (*b*) because the persons specified in the proclamation are in his opinion unsuitable for admission into the Commonwealh; or (*c*) because they are deemed unlikely to become readily assimilated or to assume the duties and responsibilities of Australian citizenship within a reasonable time after their entry. (2) Any person who enters the Commonwealth in contravention of the prohibition contained.

The powers conferred by this Act have not so far been exercised. The three statutory grounds are, of course, additional to the existing grounds of exclusion, from which they differ in not relating to the personal qualities or attainments of the individual immigrant. Ground (*a*) is unobjectionable, relating as it does to the internal conditions of Australia. Grounds (*b*) and (*c*), however, may well cause international unpleasantness, if cited in their statutory baldness as justifying the exclusion of persons of a specified nationality or race. Doubtless the sting may be taken out of a possible affront by the addition of qualifying words like those in the Canadian statute.[6]

*Numerical limitation by agreement.*—Meanwhile, and independently of these statutory powers, the Australian government, in order to prevent an undue influx of immigrants from European countries principally affected by the operation of the United States Immigration Act of July 1, 1924, effected through the British diplomatic agents arrangements with the governments of Italy, Greece, Yugo-Slavia, and Albania and other countries in Southeastern Europe for limiting the number of passports to be issued in such countries with visa entitling the holders to travel to Austra-

[6] The Canadian Immigration Act of 1919 (9 and 10), Geo. V. c. 25, by sec. 13, repeals paragraph *c* of sec. 38 of the Canadian Immigration Act of 1910 and substitutes a paragraph on which the Australian provision is modeled (with better draftsmanship). The Canadian ground of "unsuitableness" (corresponding to *b* in the Australian act is qualified by the words: "having regard to the climatic, industrial, social, educational, labor, and other conditions or requirements of Canada" (omitted from the Australian act), and the ground of "undesirability" is qualified by the words (also omitted in the latter) "owing to their peculiar customs, habits, modes of life, and methods of holding property." The persons against whom the latter provision was aimed are understood to have been certain sects of peculiar people of the Doukebor, Hutterite, and Mennonite class, who had already given trouble in Canada by segregating themselves in prairie communities and holding themselves aloof from everything Canadian, even rates and taxes. By order in council made after the passing of the Act, persons of these three classes were denied admission to Canada.

lia. By regulation of December, 1924, the immigration of British subjects being Maltese is limited to 20 per month for each of the six Australian states, or 1,440 per annum; and of Yugo-Slavians, Greeks, and Albanians, to 100 per month for each nationality. The arrangement with the Italian government is that the latter undertakes not to issue passports with visa for travel to Australia except to migrants who can show that they possess at least £40 or its equivalent, or that some resident in Australia will be responsible for them on arrival. By these means a sensible diminution in alien European immigration to Australia has been effected.

The *Commonwealth Yearbook, 1926,* p. 897, shows the admission of Europeans without the dictation test for the period of 1922–25 (See Table I).

TABLE I

| | 1925 | 1924 | 1923 | 1922 |
|---|---|---|---|---|
| British | 82,662 | 88,335 | 85,440 | 84,263 |
| Italians | 6,102 | 4,540 | 1,739 | 3,367 |
| Greeks | 645 | 2,028 | 922 | 472 |
| Other Europeans | 1,397 | 2,735 | 587 | 339 |

*Admission as indentured laborers.*—The reference in section 5 (1*e*) of the immigration act to indentured laborers for service in the pearling industry requires explanation. By two acts of Queensland, 1888, and of West Australia, 1889, which had received the royal assent and were continued in force by section 7 of the Constitution Act, 1900, the pearl-shell and *beche-de-mer* fisheries in Australasian waters, even beyond the ordinary 3-mile limit, had been strictly regulated as regards *inter alia* the labor employed therein. In virtue of this legislation, the control of indentured colored labor employed is exercised by the Department of Home and Territories in connection with the administration of the immigration act. Under the regulations in force, a boat owner who proposes to introduce colored indentured labor for service in the pearl-shelling and trepang fishing industries must first obtain permission from the Department. If permission is granted he is required to furnish a bond in prescribed form for £100 in respect of every man indentured. Approved boat owners are permitted to introduce colored indentured labor on the basis of eight permits for an engine-pump boat and seven for a hand-pump boat (a permit representing authority to introduce one indentured laborer). Since January 1, 1924, it has been the rule that permits shall only be allowed to continue if the boat owners employ (with certain exceptions) not more than five indentured men of any one nationality on an engine-boat and four on a hand-pump boat. The usual period for which an indentured laborer is introduced is three years in the first place, but the period may be extended from time to time.

The center of the pearl-shell industry is at Broome, western Australia. The Asiatic population of about 2,200 greatly outnumbers the European, and consists principally of Japanese and Malays, with a sprinkling of Manila men. A royal commission appointed in 1913 to inquire into the industry gave reasons for retention of Asiatic laborers and made certain suggestions (see *Fed. Parl. Paper, 1914–16,* No. 326 F 12904).

## SECTION 25

# THE RESOURCES OF AUSTRALIA

PROFESSOR GRIFFITH TAYLOR
Department of Geography, University of Sydney

The Commonwealth has an area of 2,974,600 square miles—almost exactly the same as that of the United States, as Australian publicists frequently point out. Unfortunately there is no possibility of the southern continent developing to the enormous extent of the States, a development which can never be duplicated anywhere in the world. Before considering the present resources of Australia it will be helpful to consider the broader climatic and other physical controls in the two regions, for we can then obtain some idea as to how Australia may be expected to develop.

In the first place the United States lies wholly in the temperate zone, for Florida is over 100 miles on the cool side of the tropics. Australia has 1,150,000 square miles within the tropics, though very little of it is within 12 degrees of the Equator. Thus only the southern temperate portion of Australia is comparable with any part of the United States. Secondly, Australia has no high mountains, and indeed only about 4 per cent is above 2,000 feet, and only a few square miles above 6,000 feet. Perhaps half of the continent has a level over 1,000 feet. In fact it is a particularly stable portion of the earth's crust, long worn down to a low plateau (peneplain) and not affected materially by the folding forces which produced the Rocky Mountains, the Himalayas, and the Alps, etc.

As regards rainfall, the northern half for much of the year is swept by easterly trade winds, which bring some rain to the Queensland coast, but over central and western Australia tend to produce arid and even desert conditions. This part of Australia to some extent agrees in climate with Mexico, save that it is much wider and the arid area is correspondingly larger. The north coastlands are visited in the four hottest months by rain-bearing storms associated with the monsoons. Here there is, therefore, no rain for seven or eight months in the year, and the climate is to be compared with that of Central Nigeria. It is not suitable for agriculture by white folk, at any rate not until the empty areas of fair temperate land are settled. Cotton, millet, and ground nuts are possibilities in the far future, if cheap methods of agriculture can be made use of. The rain here is rather unreliable (as the writer has shown in various maps and graphs), so that it seems unlikely that the wheat which is grown to a small extent in Nigeria will pay. Much of the northern region is, however, good cattle country, as we shall see later.

The east coast is especially benefited by fairly numerous east-coast cyclones (which at infrequent intervals develop into hurricanes). These occur more or less through the year, so that there is a uniform rainfall region from Cooktown southward. The great farming belt extends more or less continuously from Cooktown to

Fowlers Bay (just east of the Bight in South Australia). After a gap it begins again near Albany, West Australia, and extends round the southwest corner to Geraldton. But somewhere near Melbourne the east-coast rain storms cease to benefit Australia, and all along the south coast it is Antarctic cyclones which bring the rains, and they occur almost entirely in winter. Hence the chief farming regions can be divided into three classes: (1) The Queensland littoral, with rather heavy uniform rains and tropical temperatures, where sugar is the main crop, but dairying, maize, and fruit are also important; (2) the New South Wales and East Victorian coast and hinterland, where maize, dairying, and oats and fruit are the chief crops, with sheep and wheat in the drier hinterlands; this is also a uniform-rain region; (3) the west of Victoria, east of South Australia, and southwest corner of West Australia, where the rain falls

TABLE I

Areas Climatically Suitable for Crops

| | Rain Control (Inches) | Total (Square Miles) |
|---|---|---|
| New South Wales.......... | Over 15 | 188,000 |
| Queensland (Temperate)..... | 20 | 134,000 |
| Queensland (Tropical)...... | 20 | 100,000 |
| Victoria................. | 15 | 68,000 |
| West Australia............ | 10 | 151,000 |
| Tasmania................ | Under 40 | 16,000 |
| South Australia........... | Over 10 | 60,000 |
| Northern Territory........ | ............... | nil. |
| Australia............. | ............... | 717,000 |

largely in winter and where wheat is the chief crop, though dairying and fruit are growing in importance.

We may tabulate these lands where the climate is suitable for agriculture (Table I), specifically stating that no allowance is made for rugged topography, for poor soils, or any other factors which will cut out much of the area (see Fig. 2).

Thus, out of a total of nearly 3,000,000 square miles there is about 24 per cent where the climate is fairly suitable for agriculture (though about one-quarter is too rugged for close settlement). It is very difficult to estimate how much of this can be used in the future, but the actual amount under agriculture today is almost negligible, reaching only 17,000,000 acres, or about 26,000 square miles.

O. E. Baker considers that in Europe 34 per cent of the climatically available wheat land is too hilly or rough for cultivation. In the wheat belt of the United States he considers that 300,000 square miles are too rugged—or 22 per cent. The writer has obtained a similar figure (30 per cent) for the part of humid New South Wales which receives over 25 inches of rainfall and yet is too rugged for settlement. In Victoria the proportion is about the same.

In the United States (out of 3,000,000 square miles) in 1923 farmers planted 341,000,000 acres, which equals about 500,000 square miles. If we take 78 per cent of the humid 2,600,000 square miles (so as to omit the 22 per cent of rugged humid country and about 300,000 square miles of arid country) we obtain a tentative estimate of 2,000,000 square miles of more or less suitable agricultural land in the United States. Only about half a million square miles was actually utilized in 1923, although a dearth of farmlands is being experienced. This is one-fourth of the land with suitable climate.

In Australia we may work out a similar proportion. If we omit arid and poor tropical lands, then one-fourth of 717,000 square miles is 179,000 square miles, or over six times as much as is now tilled (26,000). Thus Australian farmlands would seem to be capable of very much more intensive cultivation before they reach the density of tillage prevalent in America.

In Figure 1 the two small circular diagrams illustrate these proportions very tentatively. Some interesting comparisons are given approximately in Table II.

TABLE II

| | Australia | United States |
|---|---|---|
| Total area (*a*+*b*+*c*) | 2,975,000 | 3,000,000 |
| *a*) Desert | 600,000 | 300,000 |
| *a*) Sparselands | 660,000 | |
| *b*) Pasture | 1,000,000 | 300,000 |
| *c*) With agricultural climate: | | |
| Rugged | 215,000 | 300,000 |
| Used | 26,000 | 500,000 |
| Remainder | 474,000 | 1,600,000 |
| Total (*c*) | 715,000 | 2,400,000 |
| Portion of *c* with heavy uniform rain over 40 inches | 80,000 | 800,000 |
| Population, 1925 | 6,052,084 | 114,311,000 |

We may compare the 715,000 square miles in Australia with the 2,400,000 in the United States, both being mainly temperate, fairly watered areas. But we must also realize that of regions with a good rainfall (i.e., over 40 inches; where the chief dairying and mixed farming occurs) the proportions are very different. This is perhaps the chief guide to dense agricultural settlement. Australia has about 80,000 square miles of land with such a heavy fairly uniform rainfall; whereas the United States has about 800,000 square miles. The writer concludes from this tentative study that Australia can support about one-fifth or one-sixth of the population of the United States when it is as fully saturated as the United States is at present.

The relative importance of the units of agriculture in Australia for 1923–24 is shown in Table III.

This total of sixteen or seventeen million acres places Australia at present on a level with Japan or Roumania as an agricultural land. But Australia ranks ninth among the great wheat lands, being surpassed only by the United States, Canada, India, Russia, France, Argentine, Italy, and Spain. Her contribution to the world in other crops is negligible.

The wheat belt is bounded very approximately by the 10-inch winter-rainfall line. Within this line there is much empty wheat land, especially in West Australia. Advance into more arid regions may very slowly take place, but the possible increase is negligible when compared with the vast area of non-agricultural Australia.

In a survey made some years ago the writer attempted to classify the lands of Australia as regards potential occupation as shown in Table IV.

From Table IV it is readily seen that pastoral industries rank very importantly in Australia. The writer has shown elsewhere that few pastoral regions which contribute importantly to the total stock have been taken up in the last forty years. By

TABLE III

| | Acres | Percentage |
|---|---|---|
| Wheat | 9,540,000 | 57.7 |
| Wheat hay | 1,470,000 | 10.0 |
| Oats | 1,077,000 | 6.5 |
| Oaten hay | 1,663,000 | 10.6 |
| Green forage | 961,000 | 5.8 |
| Maize | 316,000 | 1.9 |
| Barley | 256,000 | 1.6 |
| Orchards | 274,000 | 1.7 |
| Sugar cane | 237,000 | 1.4 |
| Potatoes | 134,000 | .8 |
| Vineyards | 111,000 | .7 |
| Other crops | ............... | 1.3 |

TABLE IV

POTENTIAL OCCUPATION

| Class | Square Miles | Percentage |
|---|---|---|
| A. Pastoral lands, good | 1,009,000 | 34 |
| Pastoral lands, sparse (stock only) | 655,000 | 22 |
| B. Agricultural lands (i.e., suitable climatically) | 716,000 | 24 |
| C. Almost useless lands (deserts, etc.) | 590,000 | 20 |

1880 or so all the inhabited portion of Australia was sufficiently well known for it to be more or less occupied for agriculture or pasture. Certain large blocks of "sparse" pastoral country have been taken up in the arid regions; but, as stated, their aggregate contributions to the total number of stock in Australia are negligible. Out of the 13,500,000 cattle and 93,000,000 sheep, the greater proportion live either in the coastal dairy lands, in or near the wheat belt, or in the fairly well-watered areas of central Queensland.

Australia may be divided in a very striking manner (see Fig. 1) into two parts by a line from Geraldton, West Australia, passing near Kalgoorlie, Port Augusta, Broken Hill, and so north to the Gulf of Carpentaria. The drier northwest portion contains over 50 per cent of the area of Australia, but only about 20,000 white people live therein—or one-third of 1 per cent of the whole. Moreover, this arid moiety is not an important stock country, for it only contains about 11 per cent of the cattle and about 4½ per cent of the sheep.

Just as the agricultural lands are capable of much greater production, as I have indicated, so also are the stocklands. But it is not the "vast empty spaces" of Australia which are going to add to our population the many millions of the future. It is by filling up those portions of the land which are already more or less settled. It would be wrong to state that any of our pastoral lands are fully stocked, but it is

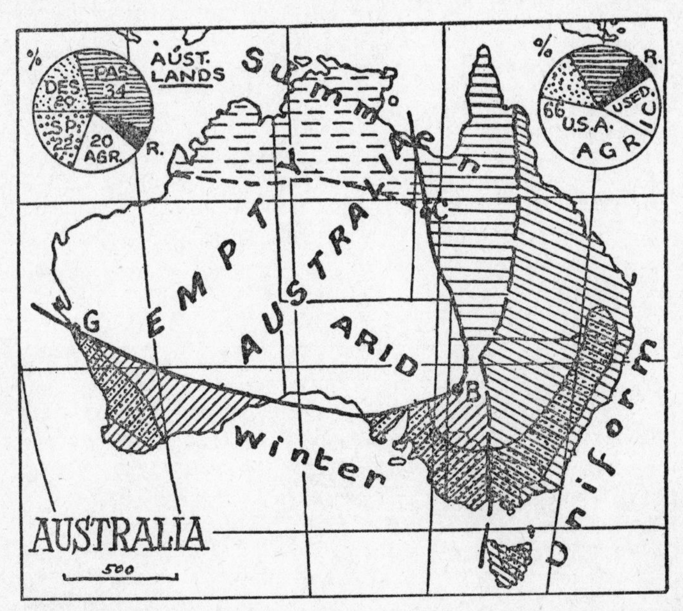


FIG. 1.—Empty and occupied Australia, separated by a line passing near Geraldton (*G*), Broken Hill (*B*), and Camoowest (*C*). Only about 20,000 people out of 6,000,000 live in the northwest half. Rain regions are indicated in generalized fashion. Wheat belt shown by dots. In the circular diagrams desert, pasture, rugged, and agricultural lands are compared.

clear, from the fact that sheep were more abundant about 1890 (when they reached 100,000,000) than they have been since, that the increase in flocks is not likely to be rapid. Cattle also have not increased much in numbers since the 12,000,000 figure of about that date, though they have recovered from the low figure of 6,000,000 which obtained after the great drought of 1902.

Table V shows the states in which the progress has been greatest (figures are percentages of whole).

Thus in the last twenty years the sheep have increased notably in Queensland and West Australia and diminished proportionately in Victoria and South Australia. Cattle have diminished relatively in New South Wales and especially in Victoria, but have increased in Queensland and Northern Territory.

Among the world's totals, Australia, with 13,500,000 ranks ninth as regards cattle, being surpassed by India (143,000,000), United States (60,000,000), Russia

(46,000,000), Argentine (37,000,000), Brazil (34,000,000), Germany (17,000,000), China (16,000,000), and France (14,000,000).

In sheep, however, Australia leads the world. In 1924 she possessed 93,000,000, while Russia had 67,000,000, United States, 41,000,000, Argentine, 36,000,000 and India, 33,000,000.

TABLE V

| | Year | N.S.W. | Vic. | Q. | S.A. and N.T. | W.A. | Tas. |
|---|---|---|---|---|---|---|---|
| Sheep... | 1904 | 52.5 | 15.5 | 16.4 | 8.9 | 4.3 | .2 |
| | 1924 | 50.4 | 13.6 | 20.4 | 6.8 | 6.9 | .2 |
| Cattle .. | 1904 | 27.4 | 21.6 | 34.7 | 6.6 | 7.1 | 2.6 |
| | 1924 | 21.6 | 12.0 | 48.5 | 9.4 | 6.7 | 1.7 |

In recent years there has been a tendency for sheep to replace cattle in the better pastoral country, since the former pay better. But in the arid "sparselands," trouble from wild dogs, and labor difficulties, etc., have caused cattle to replace sheep in many places. There is no marked tendency for the pastoral industry to give way to

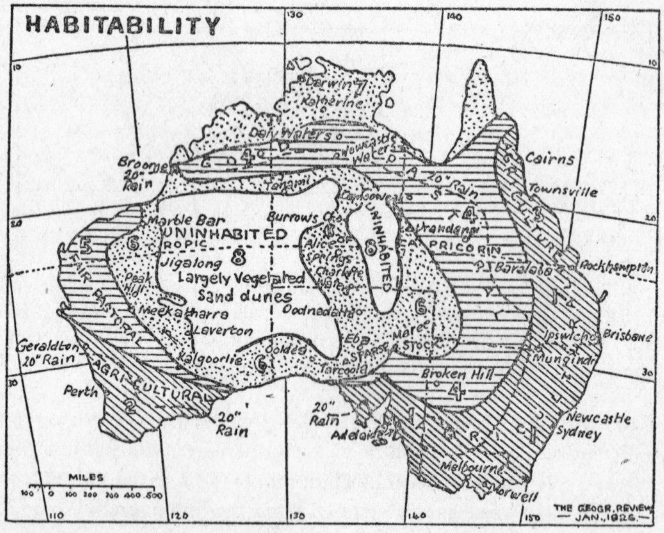


FIG. 2.—A generalized habitability map of Australia. The numbers show approximate values of land in descending order from 1 to 8. There are few sheep or cattle in 6 and 7, and none in 8. (From *Geographical Review*, January, 1926.)

agriculture except in the irrigated regions, which total only about 1,000 square miles in Australia. Unfortunately there does not seem to be much possibility of such progress by irrigation in arid or semi-arid lands except in the region already in part irrigated, i.e., in the southeast of Australia.

As regards the third great source of wealth, the mineral production is maintaining a steady annual output of some 25,000,000 sterling. The gold production has fallen notably from the prosperous days of 1903, and copper is temporarily under a cloud. But Broken Hill maintains its wonderful supply of silver lead, while coal has enormously increased in output since 1910 and now amounts to about 12,000,000 tons annually, worth about the same amount in pounds sterling. R. H. Cambage has estimated that there are 20,000,000,000 tons of extractable coal remaining in the Commonwealth (other estimates are much greater). This is the best supply in any country right on the coasts of the Pacific, though the United States has twenty-five times as much coal. It is, of course, impossible to predict the supplies of the precious metals which yet await the miner.

However, Australia ranks fourth in coal production, fifth in silver production, and tenth in copper in world supply.

In conclusion the writer may refer to his study of the "Future White Settlement of the World" (see reference 3). Assuming that Europe is "saturated" with about 400,000,000 white settlers, he has deduced that Australia can accomodate (almost entirely in the agricultural quarter specified in Fig. 2) about sixty or seventy millions of people before it arrives at the same stage of saturation as Europe.

REFERENCES

1. Griffith, Taylor, *Australia—Physiographic and Economic* (Oxford, 1925).
2. *Idem, Australian Meteorology* (Oxford, 1920).
3. *Idem, Environment and Race* (Oxford, 1927).
4. *Idem,* "Frontiers of Settlement in Australia," *American Geographical Review,* 1926.
5. C. Wickens, *Commonwealth Yearbook* (annual), Melbourne.

## SECTION 26

# JAPAN'S INTERNAL PROBLEMS AND HER RELATIONSHIPS WITH CHINA, RUSSIA, AMERICA, AND THE BRITISH COMMONWEALTH

YUSUKE TSURUMI
Tokyo

This is an age of unemployment: millions and millions of the unemployed. And I am one of them. However, unemployment is not always a handicap. It has some advantages. It gives one the privilege of speaking and writing frankly. Therefore I am going to take advantage of the position of a free lance and make a frank talk, with the understanding that I am making this talk with a sincere desire for international understanding and good will—malice for none and charity for all.

I have two objects in view. One is to explain the changing situation of Japan as briefly as possible, and the other is to connect this brief explanation with Japan's foreign policies toward China, Russia, America, and the British Commonwealth.

There are some people who think that the Japanese volcano is as quiescent as her symbolical mountain, Fuji, while her neighbor, China, is blazing with eruptions like Halemaumau. I hope it is. But who can tell?

Those who study the situation of Japan and know her problems seem to be inclined differently. By volcanic eruption, however, I do not mean a social revolution. There are changes that are more far-reaching and fundamental than a dramatic upheaval of social forces. And present-day Japan is undoubtedly undergoing some such changes, away from the gaze of human eye.

Let me paint a picture of modern Japan showing a few salient points, the results of the 60 years of her modernization. In the first place Japan won her place in the world. She formulated a continental policy and her territory was extended from the northern island of Sakhalien to the southern island of Formosa, embracing the peninsula of Korea and a small portion of Kwangtung peninsula in southern Manchuria. Her mandates in the South Seas extend to the equator. This gave Japan a strategic position in the Far East and a place in the council of nations. In the second place this political success gave Japan a spell of time to organize her human forces and mobilize her material resources. An industrial revolution took place and an agricultural nation became an industrial nation. In the third place these political and economic changes brought in their train a great increase of population and Japan's former population of thirty millions became sixty millions in sixty years. These three are the salient points in the field of material development.

Now let us turn our eyes to another side of the picture—I mean the world of spiritual forces. The continual peace and ensuing economic prosperity have brought about a number of changes, one of which is the spread of education. Although it may smack of boasting, I think the outstanding success of modern Japan is the spread of popular education. In a few decades Japan has reduced her illiteracy to less than 5 per cent of her entire population, and school attendance of the children of school age is somewhere around 99 per cent. Therefore Japan may be said to have fought one of the greatest enemies of humanity—ignorance—with some success. Another thing that has happened is the establishment of the principle of popular representation in politics. In 1925 Japan passed a law which gave universal manhood suffrage, and the voting population of Japan jumped from three to thirteen millions. They are going to vote on May 10, 1928—perhaps a new landmark for political Japan. Then, again, Japan has been undergoing a tremendous process of occidentalization. The cultures of Europe and America have flooded into the country. The upshot of it all is that Japan has obtained a scientific mind with analytical power and an unabating zeal for truth. With this scientific mind came another spiritual change, that is, the introduction of a new philosophy of life—individualism. This all tended toward a new system of political philosophy—democracy. How far is Japan going to adopt this new social principle and harmonize it with the traditional indigenous Japanese philosophy of collectivism based on the idea of family-nation? By this curious expression of "family-nation" I mean the Japanese conception of the state, that the whole nation is one family and all the citizens of the country are members of the same family.

Now at this moment of the ascendancy of democratic thought there appeared over the horizon a new system of thought, that is, socialism. Socialism has a history of its own in Japan because of an unfortunate incident in 1910, when the left wing of socialists attempted the wholesale murder of the imperial family and the word "socialism" came to mean a violent anarchical idea. It does not mean in Japan the moderate and idealistic kind of thought that it is in England. Socialism, as it is conceived by that term in Japan, means the system of thought originated by Karl Marx and expounded and applied by Nicolai Lenin. It is Germano-Russian materialistic communism. In Japan this system of thought has challenged the ideas of democracy, and, coupled with the changing social conditions brought about by industrialization, is gaining ground among the young people and the laborers. To sum up the situation: Japan now faces three systems of thought—traditional collectivist thought, individualistic-democratic ideas of liberalism, and communistic socialism. In other words, in the field of politics, that of economics as well as in that of speculative thought, Japan is witnessing a three-cornered fight—conservative nationalists, progressive liberals, and radical socialists.

This means that Japan is not a united nation so far as her political philosophies are concerned. This is an important point to bear in mind in studying the Japanese problems. For instance, compare the Japan of 1904 and the Japan of 1927. In 1904 the Japanese nation went into war with Russia as one man, with singleness of purpose and undisputed leadership. It was a strong Japan in a political sense. The Japan of 1927 is not a nation of united opinions and harmonious desires. It is a nation undergoing self-introspection and self-criticism. In a speculative sense the Japan of 1927 is deeper and more enlightened, but as a political unit Japan may not be a strong unit, as it used to be. Japan now needs one thing, that is, a new orientation of policies and a new leadership. Where will Japan get these? At this crucial point we are going to try a referendum by a general election next May.

Let me explain briefly here the political situation of Japan. The House of Commons is composed of 464 members, divided into two major parties and a few small groups. The largest party, the Constitutional Democratic party, has 227 members; and the second party, the Seiyu-Kai, has 184 members, and this party is in power with its leader, Baron Tanaka, as prime minister. In the forth-coming election these two major parties will be challenged by a number of new parties. There will be at least three small groups of liberals and four labor parties in the field. If one of the two major parties wins the majority of the members of the parliament, that party of course will go into power; but if no single party gets a majority, then one or two of the small groups will hold the balance in the ensuing political struggles of Japan. Then who will be these small groups who will be in the position of holding a casting vote in Japanese parliament? Here comes into play the importance of the three systems of thought. The two major parties are more or less conservative and tend to represent the conservative nationalistic school of thought and the small liberal groups will naturally represent the progressive yet moderate liberal ideas, and the labor parties will be inclined toward socialism. Therefore, the outcome of the next general election is not to be minimized, because it will not only decide the internal policies of Japan, but also her foreign policies.

Now let me take up Japan's foreign policies. First China. The most important part of Japan's foreign policy is of course China. The high spots of Japan's interests in China are two: the trade around the Yangtze River and the economic rights in Manchuria. It is a question of market as well as one of raw materials. Then again Japan has about 18,000 people scattered all over China, and 130,000 in Manchuria. She has also 1,000,000 Koreans in Manchuria to look after.

How can Japan protect the lives and properties of her citizens in China? How can she acquire raw materials from China to feed her industries at home? And how can she promote her trade in China? These are the material issues that face Japan.

Even viewed entirely from a materialistic point, Japan needs and covets the friendship of China. The problems of market and raw materials in themselves are imperative. This is the minimum desire of Japan and even the hardest-boiled nationalists of Japan agree in this point.

Why, then, this appearance of difference between Japan and China?

It is half psychological and half materialistic.

The psychological points are these: Japan as a whole, until a few years ago, did not hold present-day China in high respect. This naturally reacted on the Chinese mind. Japan up to 1918 was trained in the school of strong nationalism and measured the success of a nation by its attainments in the field of government and diplomacy. Judged by this criterion, China did not seem to rank very high.

This narrowness and self-conceit had a most deplorable effect on the relationship between Japan and China. And Japan is suffering from her fault even now. Her attitude toward China has changed greatly in recent years; but I must frankly admit that there is still a great deal of work to be done on our side.

Now let us turn our attention to the material problems.

A phase of China as Japan's military problem is Japan's fear that a strong foreign power may take advantage of the unsettled conditions in China and attack Japan. This leads us up to Manchuria. But before I go to Manchuria, let me discuss a few other things.

In 1915 Japan presented the so-called Twenty-one Demands to China. Twelve years have elapsed since then, and what is the actual situation of these Twenty-one Demands? There are only four in existence. The rest were either abrogated or fulfilled and exist no more. Three refer to Manchuria and one to a mine on the Yangtze River: (1) The lease of Kwangtung Peninsula and railway zone in South Manchuria. (2) The right to own and lease land (not yet decided). (3) The right to reside, travel, and trade in Manchuria. (4) The Sino-Japanese joint corporation of Han Yeh Ping iron mine.

When the World War ended in 1918 and Japan's psychology, as well as her actual policies, began to change, the change in her policy toward China was marked. It culminated in the Shidehara diplomacy. Baron Shidehara was perhaps one of the most popular foreign ministers in the past twenty years. He was particularly popular in his policy toward China. His fairness and sympathy toward the legitimate aspirations of the Chinese people was, I think, understood by fair-minded Chinese. He stood firmly for non-intervention.

Now let me take a few concrete incidents in order to explain Japanese foreign policies toward China and their reactions on the Japanese public. Late in March, 1927, the so-called Nanking Incident happened. The Southern army marched into Nanking and some Chinese broke into the Japanese houses and consulate and not only plundered, but treated the Japanese in a very violent manner. Fortunately there was no loss of life. When this news reached Tokyo the government was in a very delicate position because it had given out repeatedly that there was no fear of such a catastrophe. But Baron Shidehara stuck to his policy of non-intervention. This was supported by almost all the leading papers of the country. Here I may compare this incident with the similar incident that happened in Nanking in 1913. In 1913, when the news reached Tokyo, there was a riot. After a mass meeting and a number of inflammatory speeches by politicians, the mob surrounded the foreign office demanding a stronger policy toward China, and a few days later a high official in the foreign office was assassinated by a member of the mob. But when the trouble occurred at Nanking this year there was no ripple on the surface of Tokyo's political waters and no public protest over non-intervention. How may we account for this change? It was because in the first place the psychology of the people had changed. And in the second place there was a strong sympathy for the legitimate aspirations of the Chinese people embodied in the nationalist movement. And in the third place the sending of troops into a foreign country was disliked by the people after the experience of the Siberian expedition. In the middle of April the Seiyu-Kai came into power, with Baron Tanaka as the prime minister and the minister of foreign affairs. There was some popular apprehension as to the foreign policy it might adopt, owing to the repeated attacks the party had made while in opposition against the foreign policy of Baron Shidehara. But when the new Foreign Minister was interrogated in the House by a member of the opposition, he replied that he would continue the Shidehara policy. This was commented upon by all the newspapers very favorably.

I was in Peking late in May, 1927. When the news reached the town that the Southern army was fast approaching Tsinan it gave rise to great anxiety on the part of the Japanese residents. They were afraid there might be some looting either by the retiring or the entering troops. The government faced a delicate situation. In view of the Nanking incident there was reason to fear some injuries to the Japanese residents in China. There were two alternatives before the government: Either the Japanese residents had to be taken out of these affected cities, or the Japanese government had to send troops to protect the lives and property of the Japanese citizens in China. Opinions in Peking among the Japanese were divided. The government took the second alternative and decided to send troops. At that moment Baron Tanaka made a public statement and said that the object of the despatch of troops was strictly for the protection of the Japanese, and as soon as the government felt that the danger was gone, these troops would be withdrawn. He sent 2,000 soldiers to Tsingtao early in June. I went to Tsingtao on the seventh of June and talked with the Japanese consul and military officers. I want to state emphatically that there were not more than 2,000. The newspapers accepted this new step as inevitable, but warned the government not to overstep the limit of necessity. Early in July, in view of a change in the military situation, these 2,000 were sent to Tsinan and 2,300 more were despatched from Manchuria to Tsingtao. Although there are rumors to the contrary, I can state that the Japanese troops in Shantung number 4,300 and no more. This is the limit that Baron Tanaka could go in view of the public opinion reflected in all the papers of Japan.

Now I am coming to an important subject, that is, Japan's policy concerning Manchuria. Japan's fundamental policies in Manchuria are equal opportunities and the open door for all the nationals and economic developments of this area. The economic interests are the primary and sole interests of Japan. But unfortunately China's unsettled political situation makes it difficult to dissociate economic interests from political rights. Because of this fact Japan has been subjected to criticism by foreign students in diplomacy. However, when one studies the actual conditions in Manchuria more closely, the clouds of suspicion undoubtedly disappear. Manchuria is a problem for the Japanese statesman, not only because of its economic importance, but also because of the psychological aspect it has in the minds of the Japanese. The memories of the gigantic struggle with the Russians in 1904–5 are not entirely forgotten. Therefore it is quite easy to arouse public sentiment on matters pertaining to Manchuria. This makes the situation more delicate and difficult for Japanese statesmen. There is also the unfortunate suspicion that Japan is supporting Chang-Tso-Lin. You might be surprised to know who is the most popular Chinese in Japan at present. It is General Chiang-Kai-Shek, the leader of the Nationalist army. Here is an interesting sidelight on the contact of the Japanese with the Chinese. Chiang-Kai-Shek studied in the Military School at Tokyo. He understands the Japanese language as well as the Japanese psychology. He is putting up a gallant fight which appeals to the imagination of the Japanese people. There is also another situation which makes the Manchurian problem still more complex, that is, the existence of the Soviet government in the North.

Now let me pick up a few salient factors bearing on the Manchurian situation. One, and perhaps the most important one, is the problem of railways. Besides the lines of the South Manchuria Railway Company, there are three or four important branch lines which are drawing the attention of the world. There are the political rights, such as the lease of the Kwantung Peninsula and that of the railway zone. Then again there are a number of unsettled legal problems, such as the liberty of domicile, travel, and trade. The problem of the lease of lands by negotiations has not yet been settled. An important item in the Manchurian problems seems to me the mixing of races which is taking place at present. There are at present over 1,000,000 Koreans and about 130,000 Japanese in Manchuria. Owing to the political disturbances, a great number of Chinese are leaving the province of Shantung and migrating into Manchuria and Mongolia. Their number has been estimated as between 300,000 and 500,000. The original Manchus are not growing in number. This mingling of races will gradually complicate the problem in the future. Then again there is a problem of exploiting the coal mines and developing the trade with Japan.

What is the attitude of the Japanese people toward these problems? Japan, on this point again, is not united. The Nationalists would take a very firm stand, and the Communists would not care a bit whatever happened to Manchuria. But the Liberals, who are larger in number, have no decided opinions yet. Their decision would depend on developments. The government policy will therefore change according to the situation. By this I mean Japan has not a rigid and fixed policy on Manchuria, as some outsiders are inclined to think. But she has never questioned the sovereignty of China over this region, and hopes that all the complicated problems can be solved by patience and fair play.

The next country on my list is Russia, that is, U.S.S.R. There is a fundamental Russian policy among a certain group of Japanese statesmen. According to them it is not so much a matter of Russia as of China. The basic policy of Japan is to keep peace on the Asiatic continent—in China. To attain this end the next important thing is to come to an understanding with Russia in regard to the policy toward China. The late Prince Ito conceived this idea and started for the then Petersburg to negotiate an understanding. He was assassinated on his way in Harbin. That was in 1909. In 1912 this attempt was taken up by the late Prince Katsura and by Viscount Goto. On their arrival in Petersburg the news of the Emperor's sudden death in Tokyo prevented them from carrying the matter farther. Viscount Goto's invitation of Joffe to Tokyo in January, 1923, was prompted by the same motive.

What are the people of Japan thinking about Russia? The popularity of Russian literature among the Japanese young men is something you can scarcely imagine. The Russian interpretation of socialism is gaining ground among the more limited academic young men. Then again there are the trade interests, fishing interests, and oil and other mineral interests in Siberia. There is also another factor, that is, the increasing number of Koreans in the Maritime Province of Russia. Therefore, contrary to the rumors spread in southern quarters, the Japanese people cannot be considered as contemplating a clash with Russia in Manchuria.

Then comes the question of America. The American influence in Japan can scarcely be overemphasized. It is in evidence all over the country. Films, motor cars, baseball, office buildings, newspapers, to cite only a few examples. Trade interest is growing, and the English language is spreading far. There is also a very important factor in Japan's interest in America, that is, silk. During my speaking tours in Japan I could wake up the interest in America of the people in any rural district by mentioning the simple word "silk." Almost every peasant in Japan is raising silk to make good the deficiency in farm products, and they all know where the silk is going.

The keen interest of the Japanese people in America is not confined to the material realm. There is an intellectual aspect to it. You will be surprised at the extent to which names like Washington, Lincoln, Roosevelt, and Wilson are known and respected. Next only to China, therefore, we read and hear constantly about America. If I may cite a personal experience, on my return from America I gave a lecture on America last year in May. It was in the auditorium of a newspaper building, with six hundred seats. And how many turned up? Four thousand. They would not go away, so we had to jam as many as we could in the small room and distribute tickets to those who were standing outside for the second speech. I was on my feet for four hours and some of the audience waited for five hours to get in. Anybody can get a good crowd talking on America.

The good effect of the Washington Conference and the sad effect of the immigration law need not be repeated here. The most serious problem, next only perhaps to the immigration issue, is America's policy toward China. Rightly or wrongly, some Japanese feel that America has been supporting China in order to weaken Japan, and it is very desirable for Americans to keep this in mind and try to clear the clouds of suspicion by their fair statement of policies.

I have at last arrived at the last topic of this evening, that is Japan's attitude toward the British Commonwealth. The Japanese people as a whole know rather little about the British dominions south of the Equator. But their interest in Great Britain is very deep. The Japanese people entertain a kind of historical affection for the British people. English gentlemen were often compared to Japanese samurai. We felt that there were some common traits, owing to the insular nature of the two countries, and some similarities in their system of government. However, the apparent lack of interest among the Japanese young people in English literature and English history is changing the situation. The abrogation of the Anglo-Japanese alliance did not work in a favorable direction. The pin pricks of the Singapore naval base are also another deplorable point. The increase of interest in socialistic literature among the young men is not favorable to Great Britain or America. They consider these two countries as the citadels of capitalism. There is no particular issue between Great Britain and Japan at present. I, for one, am one of those who lament the lessening of interest of the Japanese in Great Britain and British culture.

## SECTION 27

## DRAFT TREATY OF PERMANENT PEACE BETWEEN THE UNITED STATES OF AMERICA AND . . . . .

JAMES T. SHOTWELL AND J. P. CHAMBERLAIN
Columbia University

### PART I. RENUNCIATION OF WAR

*Article 1.* The United States of America and———[1] mutually undertake that they will in no case attack or invade each other or resort to war against each other.

Renunciation of war (General Treaty of Locarno, Art. 2)

*Article 2.* The stipulation in the above article shall not, however, apply in the case of: (*a*) The exercise of the right of legitimate defense, that is to say, resistance to a violation of the undertaking contained in the previous article, provided that the attacked party shall at once offer to submit the dispute to peaceful settlement or to comply with an arbitral or judicial decision; (*b*) action by the United States of America in pursuance of its traditional policy with reference to the American continents, provided that the United States will use its best endeavors to secure the submission to arbitration or conciliation of a dispute between an American and a non-American power.

Legitimate defense permitted (Treaty of Locarno, Art. 2)

And defined (Treaty of Locarno, Art. 5)

Monroe Doctrine

*Article 3.* For the furtherance of universal peace among nations, the High Contracting Parties agree: That in the event of a breach of a treaty or covenant for the compulsory peaceful settlement of international disputes other than this covenant, each of them undertakes that it will not aid or abet the treaty-breaking Power. In the event that the treaty-breaking Power is one of the High Contracting Parties, the other Party recovers full liberty of action with reference to it.

General provisions

The measures to be taken in this regard shall be determined in the case of the United States of America by the action of its own government, in the case of———[2] in accordance with its existing treaty obligations.

*Article 4.* Recognizing the importance of accepted rules of law in the preservation of peace, the High Contracting Parties agree that they will undertake to further a progressive codification of international law based upon the renunciation of war as an instrument of policy, as set forth in this treaty.

Codification of international law

*Article 5.* In view of the greater degree of security provided by this treaty, the High Contracting Parties undertake to co-operate with one another in furthering the progressive reduction of armaments and to that end to study the appropriate ways

Disarmament

[1] Insert here the name of the other signatory. The draft treaty is drawn with especial reference to those powers which are signatories to the General Treaty of Locarno, but is also capable of extension to other powers. The text of the stipulation providing for the renunciation of war is literally that of the Treaty of Locarno; with this the Monroe Doctrine, as worked out historically in relation to non-European powers, is stated in parallel terms.

[2] Insert here the name of the other signatory.

and means in international conferences on disarmament which shall meet at regular intervals.

PART I. ARBITRATION AND CONCILIATION

*Article 6.* The High Contracting Parties agree to submit disputes arising between them to arbitration, judicial settlement, or conciliation as set forth in the following articles of this treaty, provided that the dispute does not concern a matter which under international law is solely within the domestic jurisdiction of one of the High Contracting Parties; nevertheless in every case the provisions of Part I shall apply.

ARBITRATION

Adapted from the existing arbitration treaty between the United States of America and France, expiring February 27, 1928. The similar treaty with Great Britain will expire June 4, 1928, that with Japan, August 24

*Article 7.*[3] Differences which may arise of a legal nature, or relating to the interpretation of treaties existing between the two Contracting Parties, and which it may not have been possible to settle by diplomacy, shall be referred to the Permanent Court of Arbitration *or to the Permanent Court of International Justice,* established at The Hague, provided, nevertheless, that they do not affect the vital interests, the independence, or the honor of the two Contracting States, and do not concern the interests of third Parties.

*Article 8.* In each individual case the High Contracting Parties, before appealing to the Permanent Court of Arbitration *or to the Permanent Court of International Justice* shall conclude a special agreement defining clearly the matter in dispute. If the matter is referred to the Permanent Court of Arbitration, the special agreement shall also define the scope of the powers of the Arbitrators and the periods to be fixed for the formation of the Arbitral Tribunal and the several stages of the procedure.

It is understood that on the part of the United States such special agreements will be made by the President of the United States, by and with the advice and consent of the Senate.

CONCILIATION

*Article 9.*[4] *Subject to the conditions of Article 6,* any disputes arising between the government of the United States of America and the government of ———[5] of

[3] The text is identical with that of the existing treaty except for the possible reference to the Court of International Justice, as an alternative to the Court of Arbitration. The inserted text is given in italics.

[4] The text of this section follows literally that of the Bryan treaties except where indicated by italics. Four changes have been made. (1) The Bryan treaties covered "any disputes of whatever nature they may be"; this section applies only to those which lie outside of the field of domestic law. (2) The Bryan treaties provided only for inquiry as to the facts; this section provides for "recommendations for settlement," which may enable the parties to adjust their difficulties but do not bind them to do so. (3) In the last article of the section the Bryan treaties allowed the parties to recover full liberty of action, but here (under Article 13) the provisions of Part I still apply, so that they do not recover liberty to go to war. They may not agree as to the settlement, but in that case they simply leave matters unsettled awaiting some more favorable basis of future agreement. (4) The provision in the second section of Article I of the Bryan treaties, that neither Party "shall resort to any act of force" during the period of investigation has been here transferred to a separate article (Art. 14), so as to apply as well to arbitration procedure.

[5] Insert here the name of the other signatory.

whatever nature they may be, shall, when ordinary diplomatic proceedings have failed and the High Contracting Parties do not have recourse to arbitration, be submitted for investigation and report *and recommendations for settlement* to a Permanent International *Conciliation* Commission constituted in the manner prescribed in the following article.

**Adapted from the (Bryan) Treaty between the United States of America and France for the Advancement of General Peace (Arts. 1, 2, 3, 4, 5)**

*Article 10.* The International *Conciliation* Commission shall be composed of five members appointed as follows: Each government shall designate two members, only one of whom shall be of its own nationality; the fifth member shall be designated by common consent and shall not belong to any of the nationalities already represented on the Commission; he shall perform the duties of President.

In case the two governments should be unable to agree on the choice of the fifth commissioner, the other four shall be called upon to designate him, and failing an understanding between them, the provisions of Article 45 of The Hague Convention of 1907 shall be applied.

The Commission shall be organized within six months from the exchange of ratifications of the present convention.

The members shall be appointed for one year and their appointment may be renewed. They shall remain in office until superseded or reappointed, or until the work on which they are engaged at the time their office expires is completed.

Any vacancies which may arise (from death, resignation, or cases of physical or moral incapacity) shall be filled within the shortest possible period in the manner followed for the original appointment.

The High Contracting Parties shall, before designating the Commissioners, reach an understanding in regard to their compensation. They shall bear by halves the expenses incident to the meeting of the Commission.

*Article 11.* In case a dispute should arise between the High Contracting Parties which is not settled by the ordinary methods, each Party shall have a right to ask that the investigation thereof be entrusted to the International Commission charged with making a report. Notice shall be given to the President of the International Commission, who shall at once communicate with his colleagues.

In the same case the President may, after consulting his colleagues and upon receiving the consent of a majority of the members of the Commission, offer the services of the latter to each of the Contracting Parties. Acceptance of that offer declared by one of the two governments shall be sufficient to give jurisdiction of the case to the Commission in accordance with the foregoing paragraph.

The place of meeting shall be determined by the Commission itself.

*Article 12.* The High Contracting Parties shall have a right, each on its own part, to state to the President of the Commission what is the subject-matter of the controversy. No difference in these statements, which shall be furnished by way of suggestion, shall arrest the action of the Commission.

In case the cause of the dispute should consist of certain acts already committed or about to be committed, the Commission shall as soon as possible indicate what measures to preserve the rights of each Party ought in its opinion to be taken provisionally and pending the delivery of its report.

*Article 13.* As regards the procedure which it is to follow, the Commission shall as far as possible be guided by the provisions contained in Articles 10–34 and Article 36 of Convention 1 of The Hague of 1907.[6]

The High Contracting Parties agree to afford the Commission all means and all necessary facilities for its investigation and report.

The work of the Commission shall be completed within one year from the date on which it has taken jurisdiction of the case, unless the High Contracting Parties should agree to set a different period.

The conclusion of the Commission and the terms of its report shall be adopted by a majority. The report signed only by the President acting by virtue of his office, shall be transmitted by him to each of the Contracting Parties.

*Subject to the provisions of Part I,* the High Contracting Parties reserve full liberty as to the action to be taken on the report *and recommendations for settlement* of the Commission.

INTERIM MEASURES[7]

**Adapted from the Bryan Treaty (Art. 1, sec. 2) and the Locarno Arbitration Treaties (Art. 19)**

*Article 14.* During the procedure of conciliation or arbitration or judicial procedure, the High Contracting Parties agree: (*a*) not to resort with respect to each other, to any act of force, and in general to abstain from any sort of action whatsoever which may aggravate or extend the dispute. (*b*) to abstain from all measures likely to have a repercussion prejudicial to the execution of the decision or to the arrangement proposed by the Conciliation Commission or Court.

PART III. RATIFICATION

**Adapted from the (Bryan) Treaty between the United States of America and France for the Advancement of General Peace (Art. 6)**

*Article 15.* The present treaty shall be ratified by the President of the United States of America, with the advice and consent of the Senate of the United States, and by the ———[8] in accordance with the constitutional laws of ———.[9]

It shall go in force immediately after the exchange of ratifications, and shall remain in force until the expiration of a period of twelve months after either Party shall have notified the other of the intention to terminate it.

In witness whereof the respective plenipotentiaries have signed the present treaty and have affixed thereunto their seals.

Done at Washington this day of , the year ninteen hundred and .

## An American Locarno: Comment on the Text[10]

When on the sixth of April last, on the tenth anniversary of America's entrance into the World War, M. Briand, Foreign Minister of France, stated in an interview with the Associated Press, in Paris, that France would willingly subscribe publicly

[6] There is a slight change here from the Bryan treaties. In the Bryan treaties the reference is to Articles 9–36. This has been changed so as to exclude Articles 9 and 35 of the Hague Convention which limited the scope of the Commission to fact finding, so that these two articles were not applicable to a Conciliation Commission with power to recommend terms of settlement.

[7] The provision of the Bryan treaties preventing measures of force during the period of investigation is here extended to apply to the cases of arbitration or judicial procedure, using the text of the Locarno treaties literally.

[8] Insert here the name of the other signatory.

[9] Insert here the name of the other signatory.

[10] By James T. Shotwell.

with the United States to the outlawry of war as between the two countries, few at first in either France or the United States paid any attention to this most remarkable utterance. After attention had been called to it, however, by President Nicholas Murray Butler, favorable comment by statesmen and in the press generally indicated a wide and growing interest in the proposal. But there was a question in many minds as to what the offer meant. In the first place, it was addressed to the people of the United States, rather than to the government through diplomatic channels. In the second place, it used a formula unfamiliar to French diplomacy, and the implications and bearing of it were not quite clear. This Draft Treaty is an effort to state just what the French offer would mean in the light of the existing treaty obligations of the United States and France. At least, this was originally the purpose of the present draft; but as work upon it proceeded, it became clear that the treaty might be framed in terms applicable to any other signatory of Locarno and to other non-American powers as well, including even Japan. Viewed in this light, the draft became not merely an effort to clarify the offer of M. Briand, but to state the possibilities of an American Locarno.

It is doubtful if this drafting would have been undertaken if it had not been for a conversation which I had with M. Briand on March 22, last, in which the general subject was discussed of the possibility of a joint statement by France and America of common ideals and attitudes in France and America as to the elimination of war. It was evident from this conversation that M. Briand was already studying the ways and means by which to give expression to this feeling of solidarity in fundamentals between the two great democracies in spite of all the technical difficulties which might arise, and were then in fact arising, over the question of disarmament. When, therefore, M. Briand, in the course of his tribute to America's participation in the war, stated these common ideals as the basis of a program for future policy, it seemed to call for some more definite understanding upon our part of so far-reaching a proposal. Consequently, in response to the request of some of my friends, to whom I expressed my conviction that the speech of M. Briand was in reality a serious offer and not merely a gesture of friendship, I have undertaken, in collaboration with Professor Joseph P. Chamberlain, to state the meaning of the Briand offer in the most definite terms possible, in the shape of a draft treaty which embodies all the mutual obligations which the adaptation of the principles of Locarno to America would imply. For the text itself, Professor Chamberlain and I are jointly responsible.

The Draft Treaty consists of two main parts: Part I, on the renunciation or "outlawry" of war is in its main terms, taken literally from the Treaty of Locarno. Part II, providing for arbitration and conciliation, is taken almost literally from our two existing treaties with France—all that we have bearing on this subject—the Arbitration Treaty of 1908 which expires automatically February 27, 1928, and the so-called "Bryan" treaty "for the Advancement of General Peace." Both of these are adapted with very few verbal changes to fit in with Part I.

While this text has been prepared so as to apply to civilized states, it is perhaps necessary to say frankly that a treaty of this kind will hardly be found suitable for application with nations which have widely different conceptions of political institutions and varying degrees of political development. The "renunciation of war as an instrument of policy" should not be made a formula so all-inclusive as to prevent civilized powers from measures of an international police under certain circumstances. This is perhaps the most difficult problem left us in the development of international justice. The Draft Treaty has been prepared with an eye to its possible application as between civilized powers equal in sovereignty and capable of ensuring respect for law and treaty obligations. If it were to be made a precedent for universal application, some further consideration would have to be given to this problem. But the very merit of the Treaties of Locarno lay in the clarity of obligations as between states of equal political development, whose ideals were fundamentally similar. It is surely not a valid objection to a document of this kind that it does not attempt to make provision for universal application, if by so limiting its scope it can apply definitely as between the great civilized powers. It is, after all, by steps such as these that the instruments of universal peace may finally be discovered.

The following document, therefore, is simply an attempt to set forth in the plainest language suitable to such matters what it would mean to the United States if it were to bind itself to policies of peace and not to resort to war as an "instrument of policy," to use the phrase in M. Briand's offer. A study of this document will show that it involves no real departure from our settled policies, and that an American Locarno could be made the basis of an adjustment of the United States with all the existing instruments of peace that have gone into operation in recent years. Until now we have not found the way to make this adjustment. This Draft Treaty provides a program. It is a program which carefully safeguards American sovereignty with reference to every other prerogative except that of aggressive war. Surely any American who considers the proposals laid down here would find it hard to deny their validity without at the same time denying the traditional policies and repeated statements of ideals of the United States with reference to this fundamental world-problem of peace and war.

The fact that there is no real crisis in world-affairs at the present moment does not argue that America has no immediate need of any such framework of peace as is proposed in this treaty, any more than it would argue our giving up armies and navies. The strategy of peace includes both; and the history of 1914 clearly showed that the need of a definite agreed program for times of international crisis was even more important than the timetable of the General Staff. Only last March the Foreign Minister of Germany stated in the presence of the foreign ministers of France, England, and Belgium that there could hardly have been a world-war in 1914 had the nations been provided with the implements of international understanding which are embodied in the Treaty of Locarno and the Covenant of the League. This Draft Treaty does not go so far in its provisions as the Treaty of Locarno, and has avoided all the entanglements of the League Covenant. At the same time it provides against the use of war as an instrument of policy, and if adopted by the United States and the other powers, including Japan, would so extend over the world the spirit of Locarno as to insure, not only effective measures of disarmament, but world-peace in so far as it is possible to guarantee peace by such measures of international insurance.

### PART I. RENUNCIATION OF WAR

Articles 1 and *2a* are taken from the Treaty of Locarno with hardly a word changed. However, the renunciation of war is stated much more clearly here by the elimination of details in the Locarno Treaty.

These three paragraphs contain three fundamental stipulations. Article 1 is the sweeping statement of the renunciation of war. But this would not and could not stand unless at the same time "the right of legitimate defense" was asserted with equal definiteness. Neither of these, however, would mean anything unless defense (and by implication aggression as well) were defined in terms recognizable by the world at large or at least by a third party. For most wars among civilized nations are wars of defense in the eyes of those who wage them, or are so camouflaged as to be presented to the world under the color of defense. The definition of a defensive war, as set forth here, is adapted from Article V of Locarno, without which it would have been impossible for Great Britain to have signed that Treaty. As it is, the whole situation is set forth in the simplest possible way. That nation is really exercising legitimate defense which offers to submit the dispute to peaceful settlement when attacked by another. The aggressor is naturally the nation which goes to war refusing to meet the request for peaceful settlement or arbitration, or the court. This does not imply that in every case they must go to court, as we shall see later on.

Section *b* of Article 2 is a statement that the United States is not bound by this Treaty with reference to any action which it may take in pursuance of its traditional policy under the Monroe Doctrine, "provided that the United States will use its best endeavors to secure the submission to arbitration or conciliation" in case the dispute is between an American and a non-American power. This Treaty, therefore, does not touch such questions as our own relations with other American states. All such matters are definitely and distinctly reserved from the action of the Treaty by this clause. It would not be impossible to draft the additional clause or clauses which would make a treaty like this applicable to the Americas. The present Treaty, however, provides only for cases arising under the Monroe Doctrine when the other party is a non-American power; this was the original purpose and direction of the Monroe Doctrine, rather than the problems of inter-American politics.

Article 3 deals with the relations of the signatories of this Treaty to other states which have signed similar treaties, such as the European Locarno. It introduces the principle of a very important reform: that nations signing such documents as this "will not aid or abet the treaty-breaking power." It recognizes a moral duty not to help an aggressor. As stated in this Treaty, this principle does not call for any change in international law. But some day, in connection with the provision for the reduction of armaments in Article 5, or through some other connection, the civilized powers will naturally proceed to give this principle a more far-reaching effect by denying the right of private shipment of arms on the part of neutrals to such treaty-breaking powers. As this Treaty stands, it does not affect the private shipment of arms, unless the individual governments choose so to interpret it. Its legal obligation is limited to the action of the government itself and it does not cover the action of private citizens.

The next sentence in the Treaty is a very important one, "In the event that the treaty-breaking Power is one of the High Contracting Parties, the other Party recovers full liberty of action with reference to it." This is the American alternative to the much stronger obligations which members of the League of Nations have assumed. In the League of Nations a state which is attacked by another state in violation of the Covenant is assured the support of the other members of the League, who are supposed to join in an attack upon the aggressor. The clause in this Treaty is very different indeed from the obligation of the Covenant; nevertheless it is of real importance and value. The proposition which it embodies was first made in the "Draft Treaty of Disarmament and Security" which was submitted to the League of Nations in 1924 by an informal American committee. That was the first time that the proposal was made to inaugurate a method of treaty enforcement which both leaves the high contracting parties free to apply the enforcement or not as they see fit, and yet at the same time puts a deterrent upon aggression by denying the aggressor any certainty of the continuance of friendly action toward it.

The next paragraph more definitely still insists upon the free prerogative of the United States in measures of general treaty enforcement, such as those envisaged in this Article. It should be stated, however, for the other nations involved, and perhaps in the form of an exchange of notes accompanying a treaty of this kind, that the United States has in the past found a way for furthering peace in other countries by way of a joint resolution of both houses of Congress and the proclamation of the president. In the case of other powers, existing treaty obligations should be noted, for some of them have treaties which definitely prescribe the mode of action in the event of a violation of a treaty of compulsory peaceful settlement. The United States, having no such treaty obligations, decides what it will do on its own account. There is no disharmony between these two, since in the Treaties of Locarno the tests of aggression are those of this Treaty. The only thing is that the United States would not go so far in the general maintenance of peace as the other powers have gone.

Article 4 recognizes the importance of accepted rules of law in the preservation of peace. There can be no disputing the importance of this principle nor of the need of a "progressive codification of international law based upon the renunication of war as an instrument of policy, as set forth in this treaty."

Article 5. The provision for "the progressive reduction of armaments" is made, not simply bilateral but general as among nations, and to that end the signatories will "study the appropriate ways and means." This could only be done in regular systematic meetings, in conferences on disarmament at which the question of reduction will be discussed point by point in proportion to the steady increase of the "will to peace" which is bound to flow from the enactment of such provisions as those of this Treaty.

These international conferences are expressly limited to technical study. They are not meetings of plenipotentiaries with power to bind the nations concerned, but will leave the final arrangements to the governments themselves. This is a minimum requirement, but it might well turn out to be more effective than a provision for a more ambitious scheme which, under the present conditions, operates to some extent under conditions of mutual distrust. Fitted in to the whole of this Treaty the provision for disarmament is really more effective than any spasmodic efforts can ever be, however dramatic at the time.

### PART II. ARBITRATION AND CONCILIATION

This part of the Treaty contains two sections: one dealing with arbitration, and the other with conciliation. A study of the text will show that the Treaty is decidedly not an effort to bind the United States to compulsory measures in either case. The Draft Treaty frankly admits in principle that there may be questions for which there is at present no known solution. It leaves these questions therefore unsolved, and does not provide for them except the sweeping statement in the last clause in Article 6: "Nevertheless in every case the provisions of Part I shall apply;" that is to say, that the signatories will not go to war about the questions at issue. The only war that is permitted is a war of defense. No war of policy can stand in a treaty based on the Treaties of Locarno.

Article 6 is a general article accompanying the whole of Part II and is inserted for the purpose of giving effect to a general provision that "a matter which under international law is solely within the domestic jurisdiction of one of the High Contracting Parties" is not necessarily to be taken to arbitration or conciliation. This means in plain English that the United States need not take questions of immigration to arbitration or conciliation unless in some future day and generation this question passes from domestic law to international law.

As in Part I an exception was made of the Monroe Doctrine, so in Part II an exception is made of the chief problem between ourselves and Asiatic countries. It is of some interest that the text of the exception which here safeguards the United States is almost literally that which Japan insisted upon to safeguard its interests at the time the Geneva Protocol was being discussed in 1924.

Articles 7 and 8 contain the arbitration treaty now existing between the United States and France, Great Britain, and Japan. The text is literally unchanged, with the one slight exception that it permits reference to either the Court of Arbitration or to the Permanent Court of International Justice. The latter was not in existence when these treaties were drawn up in 1906.

As these treaties all fall due in 1928, the occasion will present itself for some such slight modification as is here made in any case.

From Article 9 to the close, we have the so-called "Bryan" treaties. The text of this section follows literally that of the Bryan treaties except where indicated by italics. Four changes have been made.

1. The Bryan treaties covered "any disputes of whatever nature they may be"; this section applies only to those which lie within the field of domestic law.

2. The Bryan treaties provided only for inquiry as to the facts; this section provides for "recommendations for settlement," which may enable the parties to adjust their difficulties but do not bind them to do so.

3. In the last article of the section the Bryan treaties allowed the parties to recover full liberty of action, but here (under Article 13) the provisions of Part I still apply, so that they do not recover liberty to go to war. They may not agree as to the settlement, but in that case they simply leave matters unsettled, awaiting some more favorable basis of future agreement.

4. The provision in the second section of Article I of the Bryan treaties, that neither party "shall resort to any act of force" during the period of investigation, has been here transferred to a separate article (Article 14), so as to apply as well to arbitration procedure.

These relatively simple changes do, however, radically alter the setting of the Bryan treaties. They were intended as "cooling-off" treaties providing a period during which the signatories should not go to war, but at the end of this period of investigation they were to be left free to fight if they still wished to do so. Now they are no longer left this freedom to go to war because of the provisions of Part I. The Bryan treaties, therefore, are simply used to provide the machinery for conciliation commissions similar to those of Locarno.

Looking back over the whole Treaty, one finds that the structure is exactly similar to that of Locarno, which also falls into three parts: the renunciation of war and provisions for arbitration and conciliation. The Locarno Treaties, however, have behind them the sanction of the League of Nations, which makes them more ironclad than this Treaty, which attempts to state a compromise between American history and precedent and the new experiments of Europe. The greater degree of elasticity which is implied in the arrangement may ultimately offer some new suggestions to the solution of this world-old problem.

## SECTION 28

## NOTES ON CERTAIN ASPECTS OF THE WORK OF THE LEAGUE OF NATIONS OF INTEREST TO THE PACIFIC COUNTRIES

PREPARED UNOFFICIALLY BY MEMBERS OF THE LEAGUE SECRETARIAT

### I. INTRODUCTORY NOTE

The Institute of Pacific Relations, having invited the Secretariat of the League of Nations to send observers to the forthcoming session of the Institute at Honolulu, the following documents have been prepared with a view to collating information on certain aspects of the work of the League which, it is thought, are of particular interest to the Pacific countries. It is very far from giving, even in a summary form, any complete view of the work of the League, and is intended merely to bring into relief certain selected subjects. Three of the chapters—those on health, traffic in drugs, and mandates—have been written because what the League does in these domains has a special application to the Pacific area. Chapters have also been written on the economic work of the League and its work for disarmament, both of which are at present being very actively pursued, and which though general in scope, are certainly of no less interest to Pacific countries than to others. In view of the last item on the Agenda of the Institute, a note has been added on the Press Conference summoned by the League for August, and finally there is a chapter on the work of the League for intellectual co-operation.

The work has been done by members of the Secretariat in their individual capacity and must not be regarded as engaging any official responsibility.

The League of Nations having been founded "to promote international co-operation and to achieve international peace and security," there is no need to emphasize the sympathy with which those who serve it must regard the efforts now being made by non-official organizations in various parts of the world to insure that international problems may be studied in a thorough and objective manner and with a will to find their peaceful solution, and, in view of the particular importance to the present epoch of problems of the Pacific, the calling of the July conference at Honolulu "to give an opportunity for the full and frank discussion of the principal problems of mutual interest and concern among the peoples of the Pacific area" is especially welcome.

Since it has been thought worth while to bring together the information on certain of the League's activities contained in these documents, it may be useful to illustrate them in this introductory note by one or two comments of a general nature on the functions of the League. These comments may appear to have little or no bearing on the immediate work of the Institute; but should the time come when the discussion of Pacific problems should point toward the concerted action by the governments of the Pacific nations, the position of the League, whose method is essentially to secure such common governmental action on a large scale, is naturally to be taken into account.

The first point to be noticed is the great extent to which the promotion of general international agreements is facilitated by the existence of the permanent machinery of the League of Nations. The calling of international conferences, their adequate preparation, and the following up of their decisions can now be carried out much more simply and much more quickly than when, as before the war, the initiative had to rest with a single government and no international facilities were available. The "success" of the League in the fundamental sense of actually achieving the common action desired naturally varies in proportion as states are more or less willing to co-operate. What it is desired to emphasize here is that nowadays where there is a will for that kind of international co-operation to which effect can be given by international agreements there is a much straighter way than ever before.

The fact that several states, including two very big ones, still remain outside the League has in fact invalidated to a surprisingly small extent the usefulness of the League for promoting these universal agreements. It is usual for states not members to be invited to general conferences convoked by the League, and at many of them the United States of America has been represented, and at the last (the International Economic Conference), the Union of Socialist Soviet Republics.

The League has had less experience, though what it has had has been of a promising kind, in promoting what may be called "regional international agreements." It did, for instance, summon a conference of European states which drew up a convention on the measurement of vessels employed in inland navigation. Similarly, the Advisory Council of the Eastern Epidemiological Bureau at Singapore, consisting of representatives of the health administrations of practically all the Pacific countries, is annually convoked by the League to meet at Singapore. It may be assumed that, if any important group of states, such as the Pacific group, were to desire to settle some common problem in an official conference, the machinery of the League would be at their disposal for the convocation, staffing, and following up of such a conference. Needless to say, also, the committees and other standing organs of the League frequently (as may be seen from the chapters on health and opium) deal in the course of their current business with problems specially or exclusively affecting a restricted number of states.

It would be wrong to suppose that the work of the League in "promoting international co-operation" consists only in the framing of conventions or other international agreements. This is merely the culmination of a long process of preparation and study, whether by the standing technical organs of the League or by *ad hoc* expert Committees. This preparatory work insures that the international problems dealt with by the League will be considered in a scientific and objective manner; and it is always on the basis of such expert opinion that the governmental conferences summoned by the League arrive at their final decisions. Nevertheless, it is generally true —and to understand the true position of the League in international affairs it is useful to realize this—that the League's work on given international problems is all related more or less directly to common action by the governments of its members.

Most people interested in the League will agree that this promotion of common action by states for the solution of concrete problems which concern them is useful, not only because of its immediate results, but also because successful international co-operation in a variety of such questions cannot but contribute to a certain degree to the cause of peace in general. Nevertheless, however, much the habit of international co-operation may in the future grow, and however much its technique may be improved, the solution of dangerous political crises as they arise must continue to be a primary care of an organization set up "to achieve international peace and security."

As will be seen both from the Covenant and from the history of the League, the essential principle for which it stands, as regards the settlement of grave political disputes not settled by diplomacy or voluntarily submitted to arbitration, is that the parties thereto must consent to consideration of the dispute by the Council of the League. It is interesting to note that the desire which underlies this principle, namely, the desire to remove disputes from the plane of competition between the parties and the alliances they may invoke to the plane of general international consideration, has found special recognition in the "Washington Treaty" between the United States of America, the British Empire, France, and Japan relating to their insular possessions and insular dominions in the region of the Pacific Ocean.[1]

Though, as the following pages show, the League has done certain things of special interest to the Pacific region, and though it offers facilities for co-operation on a regional as well as a universal scale, it is not a collection of separate regional groups, but an institution imposing obligations and affording benefits in which all its members share. Therefore, instead of attempting to assess the value of the League to the Pacific countries, or the part they have played in it, it will suffice here to let these be inferred from a statement of the bare facts that of the fifty-five members of the League, thirteen—Japan, China, Siam, Australia, New Zealand, Chile, Peru, Colombia, Panama, Nicaragua, Salvador, Guatemala, and Canada—belong to the Pacific, and three more—Great Britain, France, and the Netherlands—have special interests there; that of the fourteen present members of the Council, five—Japan, China, Chile, Colombia, and Salvador—are Pacific countries; that there are many nationals of these countries (and of the United States) in the Secretariat and the various commissions of the League, and in its sister institutions, the International Labour Organization and the Permanent Court of International Justice; finally, that the establishment of the League, with Japan as an original permanent member of the Council (together with Great Britain, France, Italy, and subsequently Germany), and the self-governing dominions of the British Empire as original members of the League, has brought into relief certain features of the new international order of equal importance to the Pacific and the world.

With aims and functions as approximately described previously, the League has

[1] "If there should develop between any of the High Contracting Parties a controversy arising out of any Pacific question and involving their said rights which is not satisfactorily settled by diplomacy and is likely to affect the harmonious accord now happily subsisting between them, they shall invite the other High Contracting Parties to a joint conference to which the whole subject will be referred for consideration and adjustment."

developed its work in response to practical needs, and above all has been careful to preserve its elasticity. In political disputes its object is not necessarily to demand that a solution be reached through its own institutions (though several disputes have been so settled), but to assist in seeking a solution where it may best be found; and in continuing the work of international co-operation it collaborates easily with those who in various ways pursue the same ends as itself.

## 2. THE LEAGUE OF NATIONS AND THE MANDATES IN THE PACIFIC

### HISTORICAL INTRODUCTION

Article 22 of the Covenant of the League of Nations provides as follows:

> To those colonies and territories which as a consequence of the late war have ceased to be under the sovereignty of the States which formerly governed them and which are inhabited by peoples not yet able to stand by themselves under the strenuous conditions of the modern world, there should be applied the principle that the well-being and development of such peoples form a sacred trust of civilisation and that securities for the performance of this trust should be embodied in this Covenant.
>
> The best method of giving practical effect to this principle is that the tutelage of such peoples should be entrusted to advanced nations which, by reason of their resources, their experience or their geographical position, can best undertake this responsibility, and which are willing to accept it, and that this tutelage should be exercised by them as Mandatories on behalf of the League.

It is further stated that "securities for the performance of this trust should be embodied in this Covenant." These securities, as laid down in the same article, fall into three categories.

In the first place, there are definite prescriptions forbidding some abuses which have been found in the past to result from the contact between backward and advanced peoples.

In the second place, there are provisions to secure that the administration shall promote the welfare of the indigenous population, and shall have due respect for the rights and interests of the other members of the League.

In the third place, the mandatory powers are to make annual reports to the Council of the League and, in order that the Council may be able adequately and fully to examine these reports, provision is made for a Permanent Commission to advise it on all matters relating to the observance of the mandates.

As the territories to which the mandate system is applied differ greatly, the Covenant recognizes that the character of the mandate must vary according to the degree of development of the people, the geographical situation of the territory, its economic conditions, and other circumstances. The territories are accordingly divided into three classes—the so-called A mandates (Palestine, Syria, and Iraq), B mandates (Togo, Cameroons, Tanganyika, and Ruanda-Urundi, all situated in Central Africa) and C mandates (Southwest Africa and the former German colonies in the Pacific), varying in respect of the powers of administration conferred upon the mandatory.

As a result of the provisions of Article 22 of the Covenant and Article 119 of the Treaty of Versailles, in which "Germany renounces in favour of the Principal Allied and Associated Powers all her rights and titles over her overseas possessions," the mandates system is at present applied to all the former German colonies in the

Pacific. The German possessions in this part of the world comprised the Caroline, Marshall, and Marianne islands, except Guam, all north of the Equator, and to the south of the Equator, a part of the island of New Guinea, the Bismarck Archipelago with adjoining islands, the western islands of the Samoan group, and the Island of Nauru. All these territories were occupied by Allied forces (despatched by Australia, New Zealand, and Japan) shortly after the outbreak of the war in 1914, and were afterward under a provisional military administration.

On May 7th, 1919, the Allied Supreme Council reached the following decisions regarding the mandatories for the former German colonies in the Pacific:

| | |
|---|---|
| The German Samoan Islands . . . . . . . | Mandatory (New Zealand) |
| Nauru . . . . . . . . . . . . . . | Mandatory (British Empire)* |
| The other German Pacific possessions south of the Equator (excluding the German Samoan Islands and Nauru, and including German New Guinea) . . . . | Mandatory (Australia) |
| German Islands north of the Equator . . . . . | Mandatory (Japan) |

* The administration of Nauru is in fact, according to agreements between them, vested in the governments of Australia and New Zealand, together with Great Britain and Northern Ireland. The Australian government was appointed by the three parties as their agent to administer the island for the first five years —an appointment which was subsequently prolonged for another five years. In all matters relating to major policy, however, reference is made to all three governments concerned, whose concurrence is essential.

On December 17, 1920, the Council of the League of Nations confirmed the mandates for the various territories in the Pacific. In the Covenant itself, certain general principles for the administration of these territories, as well as for the other territories under mandate (in the Near East and Africa), were laid down. It was particularly provided that the mandates in the category C (Southwest Africa and the former German possessions in the Pacific) should be administered under the laws of the mandatory as integral portions of the territory, subject to certain safeguards in the interests of the indigenous population. The mandates as confirmed by the Council contain a series of provisions reaffirming with greater detail and precision the principles laid down in the Covenant. Certain clauses are common to all the mandates: full power of legislation and administration is given to the mandatory, subject to the provisions of the mandate; the mandatory is to present to the Council of the League an annual report containing full information concerning the measures taken to carry out the provisions of the mandate; the mandatory agrees that disputes arising with other members of the League regarding the interpretation or the application of the mandate which cannot be solved by negotiation shall be submitted to the Permanent Court of International Justice. The consent of the Council is required for any modification of the terms of the mandate.

For all the C mandates, the terms of the mandates are almost identical and fairly simple. The mandatory is given the right to administer the territory as an integral portion of its home territory, and may apply its laws, subject to the necessary local modifications.

As a general principle, it is laid down that the mandatory "shall promote to the utmost the material and moral well-being and the social progress of the inhabitants of the territory subject to the present mandate."

In accordance with the provisions of the Covenant, the mandate particularly provides that the slave trade shall be prohibited and no forced labor be permitted except for essential public works and services, and then only in return for adequate remuneration. A strict control must be exercised over the traffic in arms and ammunition, and the supply of intoxicating spirits and beverages to the natives shall be prohibited. Military training of the natives, otherwise than for purposes of internal police and the local defense of the territory, and the erection of military or naval bases and fortifications, are not allowed. The mandatory must insure freedom of conscience and the free exercise of all forms of worship, subject, however, to the maintenance of public order and morals; all missionaries nationals of any state member of the League may enter into, travel, and reside in the territory for the purpose of their calling.

The C mandates, as well as the mandates for the territories in the Near East and Central Africa, contain no provisions regarding economic equality or freedom for trade and commerce of all Members of the League. On this point the Japanese government, at the moment when the C mandates were confirmed by the Council, made the following Declaration:

> From the fundamental spirit of the League of Nations, and as the question of interpretation of the Covenant, His Imperial Japanese Majesty's Government have a firm conviction in the justice of the claim they have hitherto made for the inclusion of a clause concerning the assurance of equal opportunities for trade and commerce in C mandates. But from the spirit of conciliation and co-operation and their reluctance to see the question unsettled any longer, they have decided to agree to the issue of the mandate in its present form. That decision, however, should not be considered as an acquiescence on the part of His Imperial Japanese Majesty's Government in the submission of Japanese subjects to a discriminatory and disadvantageous treatment in the mandated territories; nor have they thereby discarded their claim that the rights and interests enjoyed by Japanese subjects in these territories in the past should be fully respected.

### PROBLEMS, METHODS, AND RESULTS

The main principle of the mandates system is national administration and responsibility by the mandatory powers, but in conformity to certain special international obligations. How has the application of this system worked out in practice, particularly as far as the mandates in the Pacific are concerned?

The mandates system has only been in force for a very short time, although longer for the C mandates than for the others, it is true, the former having been confirmed by the Council in December, 1920, while the latter only took effect from July, 1922 (B mandates), September, 1923 (Palestine and Syria), and September, 1924 (Iraq). The first regular reports (all on territories under C mandates) were examined at the second sessions of the Permanent Mandates Commission in August, 1922, and submitted to the Council and Assembly in September of the same year. It would therefore seem too early to draw any definite conclusions as regards the practical working of the system and its general value.

I. As regards one side of the mandates system—the actual administration of the territories itself—it is difficult to say what difference is made by the fact that they are administered under mandate, there being no adequate basis for comparison. If the present administration is compared with the administration of the same territories as colonies before the war, it may be said that conditions have changed in many ways apart from the transfer from the pre-war colonial administration to the administration under mandate. If, on the other hand, the administration of the mandated territories is compared with the present administration of other territories administered as colonies proper, it is certain that the wide differences in local conditions (geographical, ethnographical, etc.) will disturb our judgment.

Is it possible to say that a particular legislative measure or administrative practice which is being applied in a mandated territory at present would not have taken place under the ordinary colonial system? Again, can it be established that there are certain abuses which have actually been avoided by the fact of the territory being under the mandates system? It is evident that any effort to pronounce upon such questions must more or less be regarded as conjecture.

II. The advantages resulting from the League's supervision of the mandates are easier to determine. In practice they apply to all categories of mandates, not only to the territories in the Pacific, and it is therefore necessary to say a few words regarding the organization of the control by the League and the general experience gained in this respect, especially through the work of the Permanent Mandates Commission.

*a*) According to Article 22 of the Covenant, each mandatory power must submit an annual report to the Council. These reports, which as a rule have been printed by the mandatory powers, are public documents, and, thanks to an arrangement made at the suggestion of the Assembly, are made available to the governments and to the general public through the Secretariat of the League. (The observations of the Mandates Commission, the minutes of the meetings at which the reports are discussed, and the relevant resolutions of the Council are also published in due course.) As a matter of fact, the annual reports contain considerably more information than the ordinary administrative reports submitted by colonial governors to their home authorities. There is no doubt that this is the result of the requests made by the Permanent Mandates Commission for more complete information on various points. As a general indication of the amount of information which the reports contain, it may be said that the first five reports of the following territories contain the number of pages given below:

| | Number of Pages |
|---|---|
| New Guinea | 1,101 |
| Nauru | 213 |
| Western Samoa | 253 |
| Japanese Islands | 699 |
| Total | 2,266 |

and this does not include special reports, such as the annual reports on public health forwarded by the administration of Western Samoa, and reports on inquiries, such as that of Colonel Ainsworth on the administration of New Guinea. For anyone who in the future would wish to make a study of conditions in the Pacific, these reports, as well as the relevant minutes of the Permanent Mandates Commission, contain invaluable material. From a historical point of view, they constitute a complete annual record of the administration since the occupation by Allied forces in the early days of the war. Several of the reports also contain information of considerable scientific value (geographical, linguistic, and ethnological observations).

*b*) All the reports of the mandatory powers are forwarded to the Secretariat of the League and to the members of the Permanent Mandates Commission, who study them individually at home and examine them in common at one of the two annual sessions of the Commission.

In accordance with its constitution, the Commission, which at present consists of ten members chosen in their individual capacity and not as representatives of governments, examines and discusses each report in the presence of a duly accredited representative of the mandatory power who supplies any supplementary information required. The Commission not only takes cognizance of the contents of the reports, but asks for supplementary information as regards the points dealt with and also raises questions which may not be referred to therein. Further, a right of petition as defined by the Council is recognized, not only for inhabitants of mandated territories, but also for outside persons and organizations who may wish to raise questions concerning the administration of mandated territories. Such petitions may also give the Commission information which may lead it to ask supplementary questions of the accredited representative or of his government. In the report which, at the end of each session, the Commission presents to the Council (the Commission is an advisory body and only the Council has executive power), observations are generally found on the administration of each territory the report on which has been examined during the session. Such observations may consist of requests for additional information, points raised as regards the interpretation of certain stipulations of the Covenant and the mandates, or various suggestions.

On the other hand, the examination of one or more reports may give rise to observations or suggestions of a more general character applicable to all or most of the mandated territories. In practice, the Commission has often been able to make helpful suggestions and to contribute to the solution of difficult problems to which the interpretation or application of Article 22 of the Covenent, and of the mandate, have given rise. Such matters have in several cases been brought to the attention of the Commission by the spontaneous action of various mandatory powers which have asked for the assistance of the Commission. As examples of important problems of a general character which have been brought out in the report of the Commission to the Council and which have found a solution thanks to co-operation between the Commission, the mandatory powers, and the Council, the following may be mentioned: (1) the nationality of the inhabitants of mandated territories, (2) the extension of special international treaties (treaties of commerce, navigation, etc.) to the mandated territories in order that the latter may have the same benefits as the colonies of the mandatories, and (3) investment of public and private capital in mandated territories. On the latter point, the Council, on the proposal of the Commission in September, 1925, adopted a resolution calculated to allay certain fears which had been expressed concerning the security of title in mandated territories and the responsibility of mandatory administrations for the financial obligations of such territories. The Commission has also in various instances acted as a friendly mediator in questions concerning the tracing of frontiers which might seem to be contrary to the interests of native tribes or of good administration.

*c*) An effect of the mandates system which was perhaps not directly contemplated at the moment when it originated is the increased friendly co-operation and exchange of experience in colonial matters in general which is facilitated by the rendering of accounts to the League of Nations in accordance with the mandate by various governments which are also colonial powers and by the discussions with the accredited representatives which take place at the sessions of the Permanent Mandates Commission.

The mandatory powers, which in the beginning were mostly represented by officials of the home government, now often send to the Commission senior officials of the administrations of the mandated territories. At the fourth session of the Commission, in 1924, the South African government appointed as its representative the Administrator of Southwest Africa. In its report to the Council, the Commission marked its appreciation of this measure and laid stress on the value of direct relations between the Commission and the responsible administrators of the mandated territories. It expressed the hope—indorsed by the Council and the Assembly—that other mandatory powers would follow this example.

Since then the High Commissioner for Palestine, the High Commissioner for Syria, the High Commissioner for Iraq, the commissioners for the French Cameroons and Togoland, the Commissioner for Ruanda-Urundi, and other high officials have traveled to Geneva for the purpose of furnishing the Commission with first-hand information on their administration. No local officials actually in service in the territories under mandate in the Pacific have up to the present attended the meetings of the Commission, but the governments of New Zealand, Australia, and Japan have on one or more occasions detailed one of the officials in the government department specially dealing with these matters to come before the commission and furnish it with particularly valuable information.

It is evident that the personal contact thus established between the Commission, partly composed of former governors with a varied and wide experience of colonial matters, and officials directly responsible for the administration of the mandated territories is a further and valuable result of the mandates system. The members of the Commission in this way get a clear view of the particular problems and special difficulties of the administration of these various territories; and on the other hand, the local officials, through the contact with the members of the Commission, become acquainted with the general spirit in which the supervision of the obligations of the mandate is carried out by the organs of the League, and often get direct benefit from suggestions made on the basis of previous experience by recognized colonial authorities.

Another factor in the promotion of a better understanding and the exchange of experience through the agency of the mandates system is the distribution of mandates documents which is actually taking place in most of the territories under mandate. Acting on the suggestions made by Mr. Ormsby Gore, accredited representative of the British government and former member of the Commission, the Commission, at its meeting in July, 1925, proposed that the Council should recommend to the various mandatory powers to forward to officials in the mandated territories the documents of the League concerning mandates, particularly the minutes of the Mandates Commission. This recommendation has since been carried into effect by most of the mandatory powers. There is no doubt that the fact that such documents are brought to the knowledge of local officials is important in several respects. It is a good means of exchange of experience already referred to. On the other hand, the perusal of the minutes of the Commission would seem of a nature to give some encouragement to officials in mandated territories by showing them what is being accomplished is in fact widely known and appreciated. From the study of the minutes which they now get they will be able to realize that the reports they are asked to prepare, often at the cost of considerable effort and time, are not shelved, but are really made use of, discussed by a body of men far removed from their daily problems, it is true, but who have nevertheless, through their own previous administrative experience, acquired the ability of appreciating their task and its difficulties.

This latter fact may perhaps, from the point of view of the League, be specially emphasized as regards Pacific mandates. The mandatory powers in the Pacific have great problems to solve which are not only of direct interest to them, but which from a general point of view it is important that other members of the League should understand. Distance makes this effort of mutual comprehension harder, but perhaps even more necessary.

It is an important result of the mandates system that such problems, the difficulties certain Pacific nations are trying to overcome, and the result of their work should be explained to an international audience. At present the League, through its Mandates Commission, gets at least an idea of such great problems of the Pacific as the various aspects of a better health organization and its effect on the development of population, immigration of Asiatics into territories under European control, labor questions (such as the system of indentured labor to make up for the deficiency of native labor in certain Pacific islands), reorganization of native education, and the work of missionaries in the mandated territories.

On the other hand, the Pacific countries, which often remark on their remoteness from European problems, are, as a result of their new duties as mandatory powers, getting a direct contact with such colonization problems as have for a long time been preoccupying the Europeans in Africa.

Another more internal aspect of the mandates system may also be emphasized. The fact that the government of a country has to report to an international body, and that its administration in the mandated territory must conform to standards laid down internationally, which constitute an international obligation, may also have a certain influence upon public opinion in those countries themselves. Experience has already shown that, at least in certain mandatory countries, the national parliaments take an active interest in the way in which their government is carrying out the "sacred trust" confided to their country. Various discussions—for instance, in the Parliament of the Commonwealth of Australia—demonstrate this, and the press of such countries as Australia and New Zealand not infrequently contain articles about conditions in the mandated territories under their control, and comments on the administration by the mandatory governments.

From a League point of view, this can only be greeted with satisfaction, for it becomes more and more evident that the essence of the mandates system is publicity and the support of an active, well-informed public opinion.

SPECIAL PROBLEMS OF EACH OF THE TERRITORIES UNDER MANDATE IN THE PACIFIC

Certain aspects of the mandates system which are common to all the mandated territories in the Pacific have already been dealt with. Various geographical, ethnographical, and political conditions account, however, for the particular problems which have arisen for each of them.

*Western Samoa.*—The total area of this island is 1,133 square miles, while the population consists of about 34,817 natives and 3,048 non-natives.

As was once said at a session of the Assembly, the Samoans may perhaps be regarded as the "aristocracy of the Pacific," being more highly developed than most of the other populations of the Pacific islands. The policy of the mandatory administration has in general been to develop the existing native institutions for self-government, to give certain powers to the chiefs and other local native officials, and to give the Samoans collectively the possibility of expressing their views through the council of native chiefs, the Fono of Faipules. On the other hand, it has not been thought advisable to give the Samoans representation on the legislative council which, in addition to official and nominated members, comprises three unofficial members elected by the European population.

The general conception of the mandates system as applied to Samoa was formulated in a speech by the governor-general of New Zealand, Sir Charles Fergusson, given at Samoa in June, 1926, in the course of which he stated:

> It is not always remembered that there is a distinction between such a task [administration of a territory under mandate] and that of administering an ordinary dependency of the Empire. In the latter we are responsible to ourselves; in the former our honour is at stake. It is a trust, and our duty is to administer it in the interests of the people to whom the country belongs, and to fit them as far as may be for self-government. Western Samoa is not an integral part of the British Empire, but a child of which we have assumed the guardianship. . . . .
>
> For these reasons the Government is bound to consider everything from one single point of view—that of the ultimate benefit of the Samoan people, and not from the point of view of our national interests. Still less can personal or private interests be allowed to weigh in the scale. That does not mean that the Administration will not give full and impartial consideration to all, of whatever race they may be, who have interests in the Islands, but it does mean that where interests conflict, as in some cases it is inevitable that they must do, then the deciding factor is consideration for the interests and the good of the Samoan people. The responsibility rests not on the Administration alone, but on every individual of the community, and it is the bounden duty of all to support the Administrator in the policy which under the Government of New Zealand it is his duty to carry out and in the steps which he takes to enforce it.

This statement was noted with particular satisfaction by the Permanent Mandates Commission during its tenth session in November, 1926.

The general principle thus laid down has found practical application in various fields. One point which has given rise to some controversy and criticism amongst the Europeans in Samoa is the method by which the New Zealand government has carried out the provisions of the mandate, acccording to which "the supply of intoxicating spirits and beverages to the native shall be prohibited." The mandatory administration, being convinced that it would not be possible or reasonable to enforce prohibition as regards the natives only, has introduced total prohibition for all the inhabitants of the territory.

The Mandates Commission has expressed its appreciation of the measures taken by the mandatory administration to develop the educational facilities—in which respect its work has been greatly assisted by the missions which, during the past decades, have obtained very satisfactory results in Samoa—and the public health services.

A problem which Western Samoa has in common with other countries of the Pacific is that of imported Asiatic labor. Both during the pre-war administration and under the mandate, it has been found necessary, in order to cultivate the plantations under European ownership for which the labor supply available in Samoa is not sufficient, to import and employ a certain number of Chinese laborers on the islands, sometimes as many as three or four thousand. Arrangements for their recruitment have been made with the assistance of the Chinese authorities, and the interests of the laborers in Samoa are looked after by a Chinese consul. The number of Chinese workmen in Samoa has been somewhat diminished since the transfer of the administration of the island to New Zealand; and furthermore, important reforms have been effected in the labor regulations. By the "Free Labour Ordinance," the indentured system, according to which the laborers were bound by long-term contracts with the same employer, has been abolished, and any laborer dissatisfied with his employment may now at any time give notice to terminate his services and be free to obtain other employment. At the same time the wages were increased, and shortly afterwards the system of bringing matters of breach of labor contracts before a penal court was abolished; they are now dealt with as civil cases. From the recent annual reports of the mandatory power, the Permanent Mandates Commission has been able to note that the new system seems to give good results.

The Commission is following with interest the recent plans of the New Zealand government to develop gradually the system of individual property in land on the islands.

*Islands under Japanese mandate.*—These islands, belonging to the groups of the Marianne, Caroline, and Marshall islands, are numerous (about 600, and in addition 700–800 islets and reefs) and are scattered over a large area of the Pacific (about 1,200 miles from north to south and 2,500 miles from east to west). Their total area is only 2,158 square kilometers, and the total population about 56,000, of which 7,500 are Japanese. Owing to these geographical conditions, the administration presents particular difficulties and must necessarily be rather costly. The Japanese government has, in fact, given a considerable subsidy annually for the administration.

The problems to which the Mandates Commission, in examining the annual reports of this territory, has particularly called attention are:

1. Japanese immigration.—The Japanese population has, since the beginning of the war, increased from almost nothing to 7,500. The Commission has asked for information regarding the conditions of recruitment and the regulations which govern

the work of the Japanese immigrant workers, and has also, in view of the many cases of venereal diseases amongst them, expressed the hope that the mandatory power would take particular care in order to protect the native population from the spread of these diseases. In general the Commission has expressed its appreciation of the measures taken by the Japanese government to improve the health services in the islands.

2. Another point to which the Commission has given some attention is the working of the important phosphate deposits and mines, in which the mandatory government has acquired a preponderant financial interest.

3. The production of sugar cane has been developed considerably, thanks to special subsidies and particular arrangements made with Japanese tenants and workers. The Commission is following closely the development of this system.

4. The question of state domain in the territory had been repeatedly discussed in its legal and budgetary aspects, which have both been dealt with by the Commission in a general way by recommendations applying to all the mandated territories.

5. Finally, the Commission has asked for further details as regards the importation and manufacture of spirituous liquors, which, according to the mandate, must be prohibited as far as the native population is concerned, but which takes place in order to supply the Japanese inhabitants.

*New Guinea.*—From a geographical and ethnographical point of view, the territory of New Guinea under Australian mandate is much less homogeneous than Western Samoa under mandate of New Zealand. It comprises a part of the main island of New Guinea (the rest of it being administered respectively as a colony of Australia—Papua—and by the Netherlands), and, further, the islands of New Britain, New Ireland, and several others. The total population is not exactly known. but is estimated at about 400,000. Only a part of the territory, the total of which is 91,300 square miles, is under effective administration, the rest being either under the partial control only or entirely outside the scope of the mandatory authority. The Mandates Commission has on several occasions (see the minutes of its sixth and tenth sessions) called attention to the desirability of bringing a larger part of the territory under more effective control, but the mandatory power has pointed to the circumstances which for the present make any development in this direction difficult.

Before the war, a considerable number of European plantations had been created in the territory. In accordance with the terms of the Peace Treaty, their German owners have been repatriated and the plantations expropriated by the Australian government. Since then most of them have been administered by an expropriation board, but efforts are being made to dispose of them by sale or lease. A considerable number of native workers (about 30,000) are working on these plantations. The Mandates Commission, in the report on its ninth session, pointed out that thus apparently over one-eleventh of the total enumerated population were working as indentured laborers. At a previous session it had called attention to the possibly unfavorable effects of this system on the development of the population in the territory.

The Australian immigration laws enforcing the "white Australia" policy have been applied in New Guinea. The Mandates Commission, at its third session, asked whether, in view of the scarcity of the population and its stationary character, it would not be possible for the mandatory power to contemplate a less restrictive system in the mandated territory. The Australian government has, however, on various occasions stated that it did not contemplate any change in its present policy.

Various criticisms of the administration of New Guinea having been made, both in the Australian press and elsewhere, the Australian government in 1924 asked Colonel Ainsworth, former native commissioner in Kenya, to undertake a general inquiry into the administration of the country, particularly from the point of view of the welfare of the natives. His report was submitted to the Australian government, published, and copies forwarded to the Mandates Commission. At its sixth session the Commission took note of this report and questioned the accredited representative of the Australian government regarding the extent to which it had decided to give effect to the recommendations made by Colonel Ainsworth. It noted with interest that the mandatory power had already approved some of the suggestions made, such as: the creation of an advisory council, the adoption of a policy of native agriculture, an annual grant by the commonwealth of £10,000 for the betterment of the conditions of the natives, the abolition of a fixed minimum wage for native laborers, and the appointment of an inspecting district officer. The Commission noted, on the other hand, that the government was unable to agree with other proposals of Colonel Ainsworth, including: changes in the existing immigration regulations, the suppression of the present system of education, and the abolition of the system of deferred pay to native laborers. On the same occasion the Commission noted that the Australian Navigation Act had been extended to New Guinea and that consequently the shipping of the territory was in practice restricted to Australian bottoms, which, according to Colonel Ainsworth, would appear to hamper the economic development of the territory. Afterward, however, the Australian government, by a telegram dated September 12, 1925, informed the Council of the League that the application of the Navigation Act to the territory had been discontinued as from September 1, 1925.

*Nauru.*—This small island (8 square miles), with a total population of only 2,200, of which 961 are non-natives, has particularly attracted the attention of the Mandates Commission by the special arrangements made for its administration and for the exploitation of its natural resources. On July 2, 1919—thus before the issue of the mandate—the governments of Great Britain, Australia, and New Zealand concluded an agreement (later supplemented by another agreement) providing (*a*) for the administration of the island and (*b*) for the exploitation, division, and disposal of the phosphate rock, of which the island contains a considerable quantity and which makes it very valuable from a financial point of view. The agreement provided for an administrator to be appointed for a first period of five years by Australia, and thereafter as should be agreed upon by the three governments; the administrator to have sole legislative, executive, and judicial authority in the island. On the other hand, the three governments having purchased as from June 25, 1920, from the British Phosphate Company its whole right, title, and interest in Nauru (as well as its plant on that island and on Ocean Island) for the sum of £3,500,000, being contributed in the proportion of 42 per cent each for Great Britain and Australia and 16 per cent for New Zealand, a British Phosphate Commission of three members, one to be appointed by each of the three governments, was intrusted with the charge of exploiting the deposits and distributing the output. Each of the three governments has a claim on the annual output for home consumption only, not for export, the quota being in the same ratio as their respective contributions to the purchase price. At its second session the Mandates Commission called attention to the fact that the agreement just quoted had not been made the subject of any notification to the League of Nations. The Commission felt some uncertainty as to whether the mandate for the island of Nauru, with the responsibility which it entails, was to be considered by the League as having been in effect transferred to the Australian government. It also wished to bring to the notice of the Council the question of the relation of the authority responsible for the administration of the island under the conditions of the mandate to the British Phosphate Commission, especially in view of Article 13 of the agreement, which lays down that: "there shall be no interference by any of the three governments with the direction, management, or control of the business of working, shipping, or selling the phosphates, and each of the three governments binds itself not to do or to permit any act or thing contrary to, or inconsistent with, the terms and purposes of this Agreement."

The question therefore arose as to whether the conditions of labor employed, whether imported or local, were under the control of the administrator, and through him of the mandatory power or were under the control of the three phosphate commissioners, who would appear to be vested with powers subject to little, if any, government control. The Commission hoped to find, in the next annual report, information which would remove any apprehensions arising from this fact. As a great part of the island consisted of phosphate deposits, it seemed that the conditions of life and the future well-being of the Nauruan natives, whose lands were used by the phosphate commissioners, merited the continuous attention of the Commission, and it was hoped that the exploitation of the mineral wealth of the island would not entail any undue restriction of the area open to native habitation or cultivation.

In the observations which the accredited representative of the mandatory power, Sir Joseph Cook, presented on the report of the Commission, he pointed out that there was no evidence to justify the apprehensions entertained by the Commission, no profit accruing to the three governments concerned in the exploitation of the phosphates, and hence there was no motive to subordinate the interests of the people. The real benefit to the governments was that their farmers were assured of a supply of the best phosphate at less than world-price.

As regards the question of the relations between the Phosphate Commission and the administrator, Sir Joseph Cook pointed out that the powers of the commissioners referred to in the agreement related only to their functions as directors of a business corporation, and that their freedom from governmental control in the business of working and selling the phosphates was not interpreted by the governments concerned to include freedom of control by the administrator in regard to conditions of labor, etc. He also stated that, in view of the importance of the deposits, there was no ground for assuming that, at the present rate of production, the agriculture on the island was being interfered with or that there was any cause to fear for the development of the native population in future.

The discussions and observations of the Commission on this point attracted considerable attention at the moment and were mentioned both at the second session of the Assembly and in the press of various countries. At later sessions no particularly important debates have arisen on these general matters.

Most of the other questions raised by the Commission in connection with the administration of Nauru concern the measures taken for the protection of the imported Chinese laborers, and the suggestion has been made whether it might not be possible, as in Western Samoa, to abolish the system of penal sanctions for breach of labor contracts and to substitute civil action in such cases.

TABLE I

| Territory | Date | Population | | | | Source of Information |
|---|---|---|---|---|---|---|
| | | Natives | Europeans | Asiatic | Total | |
| New Guinea (91,300 sq. miles)....... | 1922–23 | 359,959 (partly counted, partly estimated) | 1,565 | 1,414 | 362,938 | Report 1922–23, pp. 94–95 |
| | 1923–24 | 403,676 (*ibid.*) | 1,555 | 1,389 | 406,620 | Report 1923–24, pp. 67–69 |
| | 1924–25 | 402,122 | 1,688 | 1,357 | 405,167 | Report 1924–25, pp. 53–55 |

TABLE II*

| Territory | Census | Population | | | Source of Information |
|---|---|---|---|---|---|
| | | Natives | Non-Natives | Total | |
| Western Samoa (1,133 sq. miles).. | 30. XII. 20 | 32,479 | ....... | ....... | Statistical tables forwarded by the New Zealand Government's letter of February 1, 1927 |
| | 17. IV. 21 | 32,601 | 3,821 | 36,422 | |
| | 31. XII. 22 | 33,685 | 3,716 | 37,401 | |
| | 31. XII. 23 | 33,800 | 3,299 | 37,099 | |
| | 31. XII. 24 | 34,817 | 3,048 | 37,865 | |

* Note by the New Zealand Government.—The gradual decline in the non-native population is explained by the fact that, since the beginning of 1921, the number of imported laborers has been steadily decreased. On April 17, 1921, the total number of imported laborers was 1,755, whereas on December 31, 1924, this number was reduced to 919.

The area and population of mandated territories in the Pacific are shown in Tables I–IV.

## 3. THE HEALTH ORGANIZATION OF THE LEAGUE OF NATIONS WITH SPECIAL REFERENCE TO ITS WORK IN THE PACIFIC

### ORGANIZATION OF THE HEALTH WORK OF THE LEAGUE

The Health Organization of the League of Nations is so organized as to represent in the international field the large majority of public health administrations.

It has an Advisory Council in the Permanent Committee of the Office International d'Hygiène Publique, which has a membership of forty-one states and meets twice yearly in Paris. Among the members of this Committee are delegates from countries in the Pacific zone and from other countries having similar public health problems (Australia, Chile, French Indo-China, India, Japan, Netherlands East Indies, New Zealand, Peru).

The Health Committee, which consists of twenty members and four expert assessors (who participate in the sessions in an advisory capacity, but have no vote), advises the Assembly and the Council of the League in all health questions and directs the technical work of the Health Section. The Health Committee usually meets

TABLE III

| Territory | Approximation | Population | | | Total | Source of Information |
|---|---|---|---|---|---|---|
| | | Natives | Europeans | Chinese and Kanakas | | |
| Nauru (8 sq. miles) | 24. IV. 21 (Census) | 1,084 | 119 | 863 | 2,066 | Report 1920–21, p. 6 |
| | 31. XII. 22 | 1,156 | 128 | 872 | 2,156 | Report 1922, p. 15 |
| | 31. XII. 23 | 1,179 | 110 | 720 | 2,009 | Report 1923, p. 20 |
| | 31. XII. 24 | 1,219 | 125 | 796 | 2,140 | Report 1924, p. 18 |
| | 31. XII. 25 | 1,239 | 124 | 837 | 2,200 | Report 1925, p. 19 |

TABLE IV

| Territory | Date | Population | | | Source of Information |
|---|---|---|---|---|---|
| | | Natives | Non-Natives | Total | |
| Islands under Japanese mandate (833 sq. miles) | Oct. 1920 | 48,505 | 3,717 | 52,222 | Statistical tables forwarded by the Japanese government's letter of March 1, 1927 |
| | 30. VI. 21 | 48,494 | 3,248 | 51,742 | |
| | 30. VI. 22 | 48,487 | 3,470 | 51,951 | |
| | 30. VI. 23 | 47,916 | 4,090 | 52,006 | |
| | 30. VI. 24 | 48,797 | 7,496 | 56,293 | |

twice a year, and its members are chosen, not as government representatives, but as experts. The presence of members from countries either bordering on the Pacific or having similar public health problems (India, Japan) is an assurance that such questions will receive intelligent consideration. The Health Committee has a number of subcommittees (known as commissions) of experts in various fields of public health. For instance, there is a Commission on Plague, with a membership drawn mainly from the Far East, where problems of plague are so important (see description of Eastern Bureau of the Health Organization at Singapore), and one on malaria, on which many countries from different parts of the world where malaria exists are represented. Other commissions on problems of particular interest to the Far East and to some Pacific areas, such as cholera, will probably be set up in the future.

The Health Section, the third division of the Health Organization of the League, is a small body of technical officers (medical) with the necessary clerical assistants, forming part of the Secretariat of the League of Nations and working under the direction of a medical director.

### WORK OF THE HEALTH ORGANIZATION OF THE LEAGUE

Succinct descriptions of the work of the Health Organization of the League may be found in its published annual reports. The following summary touches only on its more important aspects.

A. *Epidemiological intelligence service.*—This service seeks to collect and to distribute all available information in regard to the movement and prevalence of disease. A large majority of the countries submit voluntarily to the Health Section information of this character by cable (Eastern Bureau) and post. The information so collected is disseminated to the various public health administrations by wireless, cable, and post. There are two weekly printed bulletins (Geneva and Singapore), a monthly, and an annual report.

The service also seeks to bring about international comparability of statistics of disease and death. For instance, a commission of the Health Committee prepared a definition of still-birth, the adoption of which would assist in the comparability of infant mortality rates. By order of the Council, this definition was circulated to all the governments and replies have been received from twenty-three, including Australia, Japan, and New Zealand.

The Health Organization is also engaged in preparatory work incident to the revision of the international list of causes of death. Should this list be generally adopted, it would mean greater comparability of vital statistics and a wider possibility of taking advantage of improved methods for preventing disease and death. Governments of all countries in the Pacific zone have been consulted on this subject, and many have submitted replies (Japan, New Zealand, United States of America, and various Latin-American countries).

Handbooks on the vital statistics of various countries have been published, or are in course of preparation, for the purpose of explaining how the foreigner may use the statistics of these countries for comparative purposes. Such a volume on the statistics in the United States of America is in course of preparation, and arrangements have been made for the publication of a volume on Australia. It has been decided to publish a similar volume on Japan, and one on the vital statistics of New Zealand is in contemplation.

Surveys of public health organization and administration in a number of countries have been published by the Health Organization; these include volumes on Australia, the French colonies, and Japan. These publications have a different purpose from the annual reports of public health administrations; the latter do not furnish the kind of information needed by the outsider who wishes to understand the organization and functioning of the various public health administrations.

B. *Interchanges of public health personnel.*—The system of interchanges of public health personnel has been extended to the Far East, including the Pacific zone. In the autumn of 1925 such an interchange was held at the invitation of the Japanese government in Japan, Manchuria, and Korea. Seventeen public health officers from eleven administrations, practically all from the Pacific area, were enabled to study in detail the public health services of Japan, and members of that service expressed the view that the interchange gave them an opportunity of surveying their own position and furnished an impetus for certain new developments.

An interchange in India of Far-Eastern public health officers, many from the Pacific zone, has been arranged for January, 1928.

A collective study tour restricted to health officers from Latin-American countries was held in 1925. Ten health officers from as many countries participated. After studying public health organization and administration in North America, the group spent some weeks in European countries and dispersed at Geneva to continue their studies individually before returning to America.

C. In addition to collective interchanges, a number of individual missions have been granted to public health officers from the Pacific zone. Thus four Japanese officers are studying in Europe at the present time venereal-disease control, photonutrition, the preventive aspects of health insurance, and parasitology, respectively, while European health officers are studying similar subjects in Japan, all under the auspices of the Health Organization. Health officers of Australia and New Zealand have also been granted such fellowship missions for the study in Europe of subjects of particular interest to their administrations, and fellowships have also been granted to American medical officers.

D. Various missions to the Pacific have been undertaken by members of the staff of the Health Section for particular purposes. The mission of Dr. Norman White, which led to the establishment of the Singapore Bureau, is described in the chapter on that subject. Dr. Norman White also represented the Health Organization at the Melbourne Conference (December, 1926) convened by the Australian government to consider methods of securing and exchanging epidemiological information of local interest from and among the Pacific islands. He studied the public health problems of a number of these islands at the invitation of the governments concerned, and made a report to the Health Committee. The medical director, Dr. Ludwik Rajchman, visited Japan and China in 1925 and 1926 in connection with the interchange in Japan. His mission enabled him to take account of the public-health problems in these countries and to make recommendations which were later adopted by the Health Committee, with the result that collaboration between Eastern and Western public health administration was greatly improved. Dr. Rajchman found that the results of much valuable medical research in Eastern countries was not known to Western medicine, mainly because of language difficulties. To remedy this condition, the Health Organization has already published volumes on cholera, plague, and nutrition written by Eastern workers.

E. The *International Health Yearbook,* published annually by the Health Organization, seeks to give a summary of public health progress in the various countries. The last volume has chapters on twenty-one countries, and, while only one of these is within the Pacific zone (United States of America), yet the material must be of interest to all countries, particularly those who have felt the need of developing their public health services and wish to take advantage of the experience of the older countries with long-established systems.

F. It is not necessary to describe in detail the work of the Health Organization to show that it is of interest to countries within the Pacific zone. The examples given will suffice, with a word about several of the remaining activities.

1. *Standardization work.*—From the beginning, the Health Organization has sought to standardize the biological preparations used in medicine, such as sera and vaccines. For instance, it is important to have all producing countries adopt the same unit for diphtheria antitoxin, in order that, in countries which import the preparation, there shall be no confusion as to the proper dosage. The Health Organization has succeeded in standardizing units of diphtheria antitoxin and tetanus antitoxin. Progress has been made with dysentery serum and with a number of preparations requiring biological methods of testing (insulin, digitalis, ergot, arsenicals used in the treatment of syphilis, etc.).

2. *Antimalarial work.*—The Malaria Commission of the Health Organization has sought to study the methods for malaria control practiced in various countries, and has published reports enabling malariologists to take account of the value of methods used in other countries. It has also enabled a number of governments to train malariologists by study tours and courses arranged at important antimalaria institutes.

Finally, it has co-ordinated antimalaria researches, particularly with regard to the use of alkaloids other than quinine in cinchona bark. The results of this work are of value to all public health administrations faced with a malaria problem.

3. The remaining branches of work of the Health Organization are alike in their interest to the public health administration of all countries, but they need not be detailed here. They include the preventive activities of health insurance, tuberculosis, infant mortality, sleeping-sickness, smallpox and vaccination, rabies, cancer, etc.

A detailed description of the Eastern Bureau of the Health Organization at Singapore follows.

### THE DEVELOPMENT AND WORK OF THE EASTERN BUREAU OF THE HEALTH ORGANIZATION AT SINGAPORE

In the world at present the chief battle-ground for the more important epidemic diseases lies in the Far East. The diseases which prevail there, particularly plague and cholera, constitute much more important problems for the Far East itself than they do for the other portions of the globe. Nevertheless, enlarging and changing methods of transportation increase the possibility that, in the not-far-distant future, the threat of epidemic disease now so common in certain Far-Eastern countries will be a real danger to Europe and the Americas. This has been obvious for a number of years, and in the reports of various Far-Eastern public health officers this fact has been emphasized and the conclusion reached that a clearing-house for information in regard to the spread of the major epidemic diseases in this area was the first logical step in any campaign of prevention. However, it was not till the League was established and machinery provided for international co-operation in various fields that the need for such a clearing-house of information was satisfied.

In August, 1922, the Japanese member of the Health Committee of the League of Nations proposed that a small mission should be sent to the Far East to collect information concerning the incidence and prevention of the more serious epidemic diseases which constitute international problems. With the approval of the Council, the Health Committee despatched its epidemic commissioner, Dr. Norman White, on a tour of the principal ports of the Far East from November, 1922, to July, 1923. His report, which contained a large amount of information in regard to the sanitary equipment of ports and the epidemiological intelligence which was available for collection, recommended the establishment of a bureau in the Far East, and suggested that representatives of the public health administrations of the principal countries concerned should be convened at Singapore to consider the work of the proposed bureau and to frame its budgetary estimates. After consideration and approval by the Health Committee and the Council, the steps recommended in the report were carried out and a conference was held at Singapore, February 4–13, 1925. Delegates from twelve[2] public health administrations attended and agreed on the importance of the bureau, which, in their opinion, should receive from the public health administrations of countries having ports in Asia and Australasia east of Suez immediate telegraphic notice on the first appearance of cholera, human or rat plague, smallpox, yellow fever, or unusual prevalence of or mortality from any other infectious diseases.

In addition to the despatch of a telegram on the first appearance of plague and the other diseases mentioned, it was recommended that the continued presence of these diseases should be indicated telegraphically at weekly intervals, and that letters confirming the telegrams should include additional information on mortality, the graver epidemic diseases, and particulars of the movements of infected ships. The conference further recommended that a summary of all the information received should be sent to all the public health administrations of the Far East by wire or wireless in code, and suggested that an endeavor be made to obtain and distribute regular reports in regard to pilgrimages which might be instrumental in the spread of epidemic diseases.

A budget was drawn up, and this, together with the report of the conference, was presented to the Health Committee of the League of Nations, which, during the regular session held in April, 1925, adopted the budget and other proposals of the conference. The Bureau itself started work on March 1, 1925, and began immediately to receive information from thirty-five ports of the twelve countries represented at the first Conference. In order to be of real value to the Far-Eastern public health administrations, it was clear that information from a much larger number of ports must be collected and distributed. This was done by getting in touch with different administrations, and at the end of December, 1925, epidemiological intelligence was being received and transmitted regularly from approximately seventy-six ports belonging to twenty-seven countries and including the principal ports of Asia, the east coast of Africa, and Australasia.

On March 1, 1927, the second anniversary of the first functioning of the Bureau, it was in regular communication with 135 ports in the area, and the total number of ports with which it is hoped that communication may be established eventually is only 150.

[2] Dr. H. F. Smith, of the United States Public Health Service, stationed at the Philippine Islands, attended the conference as an observer.

*How the Bureau is organized, administered, and financed.*—The staff of the Bureau consists of a director (a Swiss physician from the Health Section at Geneva), an assistant director (a Japanese public health officer), a statistician (a Polish member of the staff of the Health Section) and the necessary clerical staff. The whole staff numbers sixteen. The first director of the Bureau was Dr. Brooke, chief medical officer of the port of Singapore, who is largely responsible for the rapid development of the Bureau during the first two years of its existence. The appointments to the staff are made by the Secretary-General of the League, and indeed the staff is an integral part of the General Secretariat of the League. The medical director of the Health Organization of the League is responsible for the administration of the Bureau. Once a year delegates from the public health administrations of the important Far-Eastern countries meet at Singapore to review the work of the Bureau, to establish its budget for the coming year, and to make recommendations regarding the extension of its activities. This assembly, known as the Advisory Council, functions as a subcommittee of the Health Committee, to which its reports and recommendations are forwarded. Delegates to the Advisory Council have come from the public-health administrations of Australia, Ceylon, China, Korea, Dutch East Indies, Federated Malay States, Formosa, French Indo-China, Hong-Kong, India, Japan, Macao, North Borneo, the Philippines, and Straits Settlements.

The financial support of the Bureau is drawn from three sources. First, a contribution is made from the budget of the League. Secondly, the governments participating in the work of the Bureau have promised certain contributions. Finally, the International Health Board of the Rockefeller Foundation made the organization of the Bureau possible by a contribution of $125,000 (gold) to be spread over a period of five years.

*Work of the Bureau.*—So far the main work of the Bureau has been to collect and transmit information in regard to the prevalence and distribution of the most important epidemic diseases, notably plague, cholera, smallpox, and yellow fever, but it has already begun to take on other functions and should eventually carry on for the Far East the whole program of the Health Organization of the League of Nations.

The collection and distribution of epidemiological intelligence is carried on by means of cables, wireless, and the post. Telegrams are received from ports (at the expense of the administrations concerned) on the first appearance of cholera, human or rat plague, smallpox, yellow fever, or unusual prevalence of, or mortality from, any other infectious disease. A weekly telegram is received from each public health administration relating to the week ending Saturday, midnight, and containing the following information in regard to its ports: (1) total deaths from plague, (2) plague infection found in rats, (3) total deaths from cholera, (4) total deaths from smallpox, (5) particulars of any unusual epidemics in any part of the country, (6) incidence of yellow fever.

The weekly telegram is confirmed by the first available post and further particulars are given, such as: (1) total deaths from all causes in important ports; (2) number of cases of, as well as deaths from, the before-mentioned diseases; (3) supplementary information regarding plague, cholera, smallpox, or other unusual epidemic; (4) particulars of any infected ships which have arrived.

The Advisory Council recommended that the Bureau should also secure copies of documents possessing public health interest, such as sanitary legislation, annual reports, meteorological reports, and reports of research.

The information received by wire is summarized and coded (using a code developed for the purpose and known as the A A code), and then broadcast by wireless from powerful wireless stations at the following places: St. Denis, Saigon, Bandoeng, Shanghai, Bombay, Madras, Sandakan, and Nauen (Germany). During the early history of the Bureau, many administrations experienced difficulties in picking up these broadcasts, and it was necessary to send a large number of cable messages. With increasing experience these early difficulties are being overcome, and the number of cables required has materially lessened. Arrangements have been made so that one administration which receives the broadcast will post it to its close neighbors which are not equipped for such reception.

The broadcast or cabled message is confirmed by a printed *Weekly Fasciculus* posted each week to each public health administration and others concerned. This *Fasciculus* contains, besides the broadcast message, information with regard to the movements of infected ships, general death-rates, prevalence and mortality of the important epidemic diseases in the hinterland, and meteorological reports. There is also a semiannual report containing material of public health interest, and the director issues a report to the Advisory Council on the work of the Bureau during the year.

*Other work of the Bureau.*—It was early recognized by the Advisory Council that the Bureau was peculiarly adapted to act as a co-ordinating center of public health work in the East. Resolutions were adopted recommending: (1) that information in regard to pilgrimages (from Camaran, El Tor, Jeddah, and Mecca) be collected and distributed; (2) that the bureau should collect and distribute information with regard to quarantine notifications and legal requirements by the various administrations—in a word, such information as may be of use to shipping; (3) that the bureau should be used as a center for co-ordinating the scientific studies of the many unsolved problems of epidemiological importance; (4) that the bureau be utilized as an instructional center for Eastern health officers interested in statistical work; (5) that the literature and publications of the League of Nations be distributed from the Bureau; (6) that the Bureau be used as an information center for technical and scientific visitors passing through Singapore.

The Advisory Council has emphasized on various occasions "that the Bureau is designed to represent an extension to the Far East of the epidemiological intelligence service of the Health Organization of the League of Nations." Resolutions have been adopted and approved by the Health Committee and the Council of the League providing for studies and investigations by the Eastern Bureau of the great problems of public health in the East, including malaria, plague, tuberculosis and vaccination against cholera and dysentery by mouth. The Advisory Council proposed that subcommittees on these subjects should be set up.

A subcommittee on plague will meet at Delhi in December, 1927. This Committee consists of certain members of the Advisory Council and a number of experts from Europe and the Far East.

Steps have been taken to test the efficacy of vaccination by the mouth against cholera and dysentery. Professor Shiga, the Japanese scientist, has already begun his experiments on this subject. This work is also being carried on at Singapore, India, the Philippines, the Dutch East Indies, and French Indo-China. Should these trials be crowned with success, the method could be utilized to great advantage because of the facility with which large numbers could be protected against these diseases.

This general work of the Bureau in the field of co-ordination of national public health effort has only begun, and its possibilities have not even been explored. It must be remembered that the public health problems of the East are of extreme importance, that the distances are great, and that collaboration between the public health administrations is difficult. The Bureau has already shown that such collaboration is possible and useful.

*The new international sanitary convention and the Eastern Bureau.*—During the international sanitary conference held in Paris in May and June, 1926, the importance of the Eastern Bureau was fully recognized and, indeed, a statement to that effect was incorporated in the text of the international sanitary convention, which it is expected will shortly be ratified and will replace the 1912 convention. The new convention contains an article (Article 7) providing that the Office International d'Hygiène Publique may conclude an agreement with the Health Organization of the League whereby the Eastern Bureau at Singapore may carry out in its area certain of the more important duties imposed on the Office International by the convention. These duties relate mainly to the rapid collection and distribution of information in regard to the four diseases mentioned by the convention, namely, plague, cholera, smallpox, and typhus fever. Such an agreement has actually been drawn up and only awaits approval by the Council of the League and the ratification of the convention to become operative. The actual text of the article mentioned reads: "In order to facilitate the accomplishment of the task entrusted to it by the present Convention, the Office inernational d'hygiène publique, because of the value of the information which is furnished by the Service of Epidemiological Intelligence of the League of Nations, including its Eastern Bureau at Singapore, . . . . is authorized to negotiate necessary arrangements with the Health Committee of the League of Nations. . . . ."

The arrangement concluded with the Office International will not interfere with the present work of the Bureau, but will, indeed, add somewhat to its scope.

*Results secured by the Bureau.*[3]—The results secured by the Bureau may be summarized under three heads:

1. It has succeeded in establishing a rapid and useful interchange of epidemiological intelligence in an area which is the source of most of the major epidemic diseases, especially plague, cholera, and smallpox. Its success in this regard has stimulated the collection of such information within countries, as, for instance, China,

[3] It should be noted that the information regarding epidemic diseases is sent voluntarily by the public health administrations. Under the convention, the governments will be obliged to send this information in regard to plague, cholera, smallpox, and typhus. When the duties of the convention are assumed by the Bureau, it will have the authority to require the transmission of this information.

where on the suggestion of the Bureau, the National Epidemic Prevention Bureau now gathers reports of important diseases from all provinces.

2. It has succeeded in inaugurating the co-ordination of national researches in subjects of major importance to the East, such as oral (mouth) vaccination against cholera and dysentery, problems of plague prophylaxis, etc.

3. It has promoted collaboration between the public health administrations of Eastern countries, bringing the chiefs of these administrations together annually to discuss international health problems of mutual importance.

Finally, a recommendation of the last session of the Advisory Council throws some light on the importance it attaches to the Bureau as a means of preventing disease. It had been proposed to provide shipping companies with copies of the code used for broadcasting the weekly message in order that they might supply information to the captains of their larger ships in regard to the presence or absence of epidemic disease at their ports of call. It was unanimously decided that there was no reason why this information should be kept secret and that one of the wireless stations should begin broadcasting the message in clear every week. This means that the information will be available to every ship possessing wireless equipment in the East, as well as to shipping companies, the press and all other interested persons.

Documents which may be referred to concerning the Eastern Bureau at Singapore: *Annual Report of the Eastern Bureau of the Health Organization* (1924); minutes of the conference held at Singapore, February, 1925; *Annual Report of the Eastern Bureau of the Health Organization* (1925); *Annual Report of the Health Organization of the League of Nations* (1925, 1926).

### 4. THE WORK OF THE LEAGUE FOR THE SUPPRESSION OF THE TRAFFIC IN OPIUM AND OTHER DANGEROUS DRUGS

The opium problem which first aroused public opinion was the problem of opium-smoking as it existed in the Far East and principally in China. Alarm at its extent and the ravages it caused led to a conference being held in Shanghai in 1909. A further conference in 1912 was held at The Hague, which resulted in an international convention, which, up to the present, remains the only opium convention in force.

In the preamble to the convention, the signatory powers are described as "determined to bring about the gradual suppression of the abuse of opium, morphine, and cocaine, as also the drugs prepared or derived from these substances, which give rise or might give rise to similar abuses," and as convinced that "in this humanitarian endeavor they will meet with the unanimous adherence of all the states concerned."

The actual provisions of the convention are of a more radical character than would appear from the preamble. These may be briefly described as "control of production" in the case of raw opium, "gradual and effective suppression of the manufacture, internal trade in, and use of" in the case of prepared opium, whilst in the case of morphine, cocaine, and their respective salts their manufacture, sale, and use are to be "limited exclusively to medical and legitimate purposes."

As a result of the insertion in Article 23 of the Covenant of the League of Nations of a provision intrusting the League with the duty of supervising the execution of agreements with regard to the traffic in opium and other dangerous drugs, the first assembly of the League of Nations, in November, 1920, decided to establish an Advisory Committee on Traffic in Opium and other Dangerous Drugs. The Committee is an advisory body to the Council of the League of Nations, its secretarial work being performed by the opium section of the Secretariat, which by an assembly resolution is intrusted with the duty of collecting information on the arrangements made in the various countries for carrying out the opium convention and on the production, distribution, and consumption of the drugs, together with other data necessary for the purpose of enabling the League to exercise general supervision over the execution of the arrangements concluded.

Consisting originally of representatives of China, France, Great Britain, India, Japan, the Netherlands, Portugal, and Siam, and of three expert assessors not representing governments, the Advisory Committee has gradually been enlarged by the addition of representatives of the United States of America, Germany, the Kingdom of the Serbs, Croats and Slovenes, Switzerland, Bolivia, and, most recently of all, Italy. Mainly concerned with the study of the manner in which more effective execution of the provisions of the international opium convention of 1912 might be secured, the Committee has nevertheless not lost sight of the necessity for a more comprehensive policy destined to supplement the provisions of that convention in such a way as to lead to a more rapid suppression of the illicit traffic in narcotics.

The Committee's study of questions, such as that of the world's estimated requirements for medical and scientific purposes, of international control by the adoption of an import certificate system, increased penalties, exchange of information concerning seizures, control in free ports and free zones, control over narcotics in transit, leads it to include in its reports to the Council suggestions and recommendations which the Council, if it approves them, brings before the various governments. The task of the Advisory Committee is facilitated by the regular supply of information sent in the form of annual reports by governments parties to the Hague convention. These annual reports summarized by the Secretariat and accompanied by statistical tables, enable the Committee to follow the world-narcotic situation both as regards production, manufacture, and international movements.

By its reports and recommendations to the Council of the League, the Advisory Committee has, to an extent unknown before, exposed the details of the illicit traffic in drugs and made known the measures which, if adopted by the governments, would be most likely to suppress it.

Directly arising out of the work which the Advisory Committee had been doing since its creation, two international conferences on opium and dangerous drugs were held at Geneva, November, 1924, to February, 1925, in pursuance of resolutions adopted by the Assembly of the League of Nations at its meeting in September, 1923.

The first conference concerned with opium-smoking assembled on November 3, 1924. All the powers having territories in the Far East in which the use of prepared or smoking opium is temporarily continued, i.e., China, France, Great Britain, India, Japan, the Netherlands, Portugal, were represented. The conference surveyed the existing situation and examined and considered measures which could be taken to carry out more effectively the policy of gradually suppressing the use of opium for smoking. It discussed such questions as government monopoly, registration and rationing of smokers, smuggling, the opium situation in China, the application of opium revenues. The conference gave rise to an agreement which has been ratified by France, Great Britain, India, the Netherlands, Portugal, and Siam. The second conference, at which forty-one states were represented, met on November 17, 1924, and considered the whole question of the production, manufacture, and control of narcotic drugs. It drew up a convention which—although it has not up to the present received a sufficient number of ratifications to bring it into force—may, at a not too distant date, become effective. The convention provides for the more effective restriction of the production or manufacture of narcotics and establishes closer control and supervision of the international trade. Certain states represented at the conference were in favor of inserting in the convention provisions for the limitation of the production of the poppy to the amount required to meet the medical and scientific needs of the world. Agreement could not, however, be reached on this point, though the Conference as a whole admitted the vital necessity of putting a stop to overproduction of the raw material.

Much has been done toward establishing an enlightened public opinion on the question of opium and dangerous drugs by the open discussions during the sessions of the Advisory Committee, the Council, the Assembly committee meetings and the plenary sessions of the Assembly, and the meetings of the conferences.

What will the League of Nations do in the future in connection with the opium and drug problems if already their causes and remedies are known and the application of the remedy lies with the individual contracting powers? The League can continue to enlighten public opinion as to the nature and extent of the danger and the nature of the remedies, and it can suggest measures to assist governments in the discharge of the obligations which they have assumed. To hasten successful action by governments, the League may in future work out in detail all the phases of control necessary to bring about a limitation in conformity with the provisions of the existing Hague convention and second Geneva convention. But the League, though it can inspire and co-ordinate, cannot compel the necessary action. In the last instance the responsibility will always remain with the individual governments parties to the conventions.

Every phase of the work done by or with the assistance of any of the League's organs in connection with the suppression of the illicit traffic in opium and narcotics is of special interest for Pacific countries. Opium-smoking, which can be considered as almost entirely a Pacific problem, was considered in detail during the first Geneva opium conference. The rapid spread in certain Pacific countries of the use of narcotic drugs such as morphine, heroin, and cocaine, the enormous existing illicit traffic of such narcotic drugs from European countries to certain Pacific countries, and their reshipment to other countries cannot but be of the greatest interest to all of those Pacific countries whose long seaboard favors the trafficker, and whose population, barely, if at all, aware of the deadly danger of these narcotics, falls an easy victim. With these and other problems connected with the traffic in drugs, the second Geneva opium conference occupied itself. It devised measures which were embodied in a convention which will, when applied, prove of inestimable value as a safeguard against the spread in Pacific countries of what is threatening to become a world-wide danger.

Nearly all of the countries specially concerned with Pacific problems were present at, and rendered material assistance to, that conference, thus contributing to the elaboration of a convention which, by reinforcing the Hague convention of 1912, promises to be of the greatest value to Pacific countries.

### 5. THE WORK OF THE LEAGUE FOR THE REDUCTION AND LIMITATION OF ARMAMENTS

At the time this note is written (June, 1927), a draft convention for general disarmament[4] has been passed, in first reading, in the circumstances described below, by the Preparatory Commission for the Disarmament Conference, set up by the Council of the League of Nations, and the "conversations" between the three great naval powers are due to begin in Geneva on June 20. The position is therefore somewhat fluid, and nothing final and definite can be expected before the June conversations have taken place on the one hand, and before the Preparatory Commission before mentioned meets again for its second reading before the close of the present year.

The task of disarmament imposed on the League of Nations by Article 8 of its Covenant was, in the circumstances in which the League of Nations was born, a counsel of perfection. In the turmoil which followed the war, and which, save for open hostilities, so closely resembled the war itself, it was hopeless to expect that so high a standard of international relations as that laid down by Article 8 of the Covenant could be immediately applied. States members of the League were not only required to reduce their armaments to the minimum level compatible with their national security and their international obligations, but they were also to exchange full and frank information as to their military, naval, and air programs and as to the condition of such of their industries as are adaptable to warlike purposes. The difficulties inherent in a post-war situation were considerably increased by the fact that two of the greatest powers in the world remained outside the League, and therefore free from the obligations of the Covenant: the United States of America and the Soviet Union.

In these circumstances, the Council of the League of Nations, which had direct responsibility for the application of Article 8, might excusably have claimed that there was wisdom in delay. Yet it decided to begin work immediately. In May, 1920, it created the Permanent Advisory Commission on Military, Naval, and Air Questions provided for in Article 9 of the Covenant. In 1921, at the suggestion of the first session of the Assembly, it appointed a Temporary Mixed Commission, which started work at once. While the Permanent Advisory Commission was constituted on the basis of technical and official delegations of the governments represented in the Council, the Temporary Mixed Commission was composed of political, economic, financial, industrial, labor, and military personalities chosen by the Council on account of their own competence, but free from all governmental control. It was evident that all that could be done at the moment was to explore the means of approach toward the problem in the hope that in time a better international atmosphere would permit of a more direct treatment. In this first phase of the disarmament work the Temporary Mixed Commission did valuable work. Nevertheless, the outcome of this work—a

[4] The word "disarmament" is used as a convenient substitute for the more correct expression "reduction and limitation of armaments."

treaty of mutual guaranty, which embodied the principles laid down by the Assembly and particularly that which linked up disarmament and security by laying down that there would be no disarmament without guaranty and no guaranty without disarmament—did not meet with general acceptance.

The Assembly of 1924 inaugurated a second phase in disarmament work. This Assembly, through its third committee, acted, it might be said, as a specialized disarmament organ, since it set up during its short session what was called the Geneva Protocol, an instrument aiming at the solution of the preliminary problems of security and arbitration considered as indispensable before a disarmament convention could be prepared and accepted. As the Assembly and its committees are composed of government representatives, this work might be considered as the first step in a new period of direct government work. A comparison between the Protocol and the treaty of mutual guaranty will show that the first phase, that of preliminary studies carried out by a Commission of individual experts, had been most valuable as the preparatory phase towards the Protocol.

Though the Protocol was not finally adopted, it provided the necessary moral atmosphere for the groups of treaties signed at Locarno, which constitute an application of its principles to an area of the world, if limited in extent, most important on account of the political problems which are centered in it. This result was generally considered as a sufficient advance in international relations to justify the creation of a Commission specialized in the problem of disarmament in order to prepare the political and technical conditions under which a convention on the general reduction of armaments might be accepted by the governments. Such a Commission was appointed by the Council in December, 1925. It was composed of representatives of twenty governments, including that of the United States of America.

This is the third phase in disarmament work carried out under the aegis of the League of Nations.

The first phase might be described as that during which political and technical experts chosen by the Council, but not representing their governments, dealt with general disarmament questions; the second, as that during which government representatives dealt with general preliminary questions; the third and present, that during which government representatives are dealing with the actual problems of disarmament.

It is evident that this final phase is the most difficult of all. For, even if no political considerations were present, the technical difficulties would be considerable. Each nation has a different outlook in matters of defense, owing to an aggregate of political, geographical, historical, and economic conditions. The point of view of a small nation placed in the midst of a highly populated and differentiated continent such as Europe can hardly be compared with that of a big insular nation in the Pacific—to take two extreme cases. Even within Europe a country with a secular tradition of neutrality, such as Switzerland, will obviously consider disarmament questions from quite another point of view than that of a reconstituted country reborn in a war, such as Poland.

Moreover, each country has to adapt the general rules adopted by the Conference to its own internal organization. Professional armies, standing armies, militia, combinations of some or of all of these systems, can be found in one or other of the would-be signatories to the convention. Long and short systems of service, differences in parliamentary control over army organization and army expenditure, land-locked countries, insular countries, countries depending for their life on sea communications, have to be considered each according to its requirements, and, finally, each state brings to the discussions a different tradition which tends to enforce its own particular point of view and transform it in its own eyes into a kind of permanent standard.

Such a maze of technical difficulties would suffice to justify long and arduous work even if the matter had no political implications. If a question of trade or industry, of communications or of international health, bristling with similar difficulties were in discussion, no one would expect a solution in a short period of time; and yet the political implications of such questions would be trifling compared to the immense importance of those which are raised by the problem of disarmament. For disarmament aims at reducing the very force in which for centuries nations have been accustomed to see the basis of their sovereignty, of their independence, and even of their international prestige.

If the evolution of the question of disarmament since its official inception in the Covenant of the League of Nations is thus considered in its entirety, surprise at its rapidity, rather than at its slowness, should be felt. The very fact that the governments members of the League in collaboration with the government of the United States of America should be engaged in an official consideration of a convention on the reduction of armaments is in itself a proof of the immense progress which this difficult problem has already achieved. The Preparatory Commission appointed by the Council began work in May, 1926. After a short preliminary survey of the ground, it decided to submit to its technical subcommissioners the problems briefly outlined before, with a view to studying the possibility of reaching an understanding satisfactory to all with regard to the different systems of defense in operation. The work of the technical commissions lasted for the rest of the year, and resulted in the preparation of several voluminous reports which were immediately submitted to the governments represented in the Commission. After the necessary time had been given to these governments for the consideration of these reports, the Preparatory Commission met again in March, 1927.

During this second session, the Preparatory Commission decided to draft the result of all the previous work in the form of a draft convention, and this text, as drafted at the first reading, is now submitted to the respective governments. It is as yet little more than a repertory of alternative proposals, with the exception of its first chapter, dealing with the limitation of effectives, which is, with some reservations, unanimous. It contains chapters on the limitation of effectives, of war material (including land, sea, and air armaments), and of military expenditure, on chemical warfare, and on general miscellaneous clauses. There are two reasons why it was indispensable that, between the first and the second readings of the Commission, a considerable time should elapse. The first is that the very importance of the report prepared made it necessary that the governments themselves and the public opinion of the several nations should bring their collaboration to the work of the Commission.

In matters so intimately connected with the political life of every nation the work of specialized bodies such as League of Nations commissions would be useless and sterile without the active co-operation of every government, with a strong backing of public opinion. Such co-operation requires time.

But there is a second reason for such delay. It is well known that, at the beginning of the year, the President of the United States of America suggested to some governments that a certain number of naval matters raised in the course of the work of the Preparatory Commission should be considered by the principal naval powers in the course of direct conversations between them, to take place in Geneva. These conversations will begin in Geneva, at the offices of the League of Nations, on June 20. The debates of the Preparatory Commission have shown that the success of these conversations will be a considerable contribution to the success of the second reading of the Preparatory Commission.

### RELATION OF LEAGUE'S WORK ON DISARMAMENT TO PACIFIC COUNTRIES

The object of the task of progressive disarmament undertaken by the League being the reduction of the chances of war, it may be assumed that the Pacific nations will have the same interest as all others in its ultimate success. It may, however, be expected that their interest in the immediate problem of disarmament will bear on the question of the limitation or reduction of naval armaments rather than on any other form of disarmament, and for this reason the results of the Three-Power Conference which is to meet in Geneva at the end of June and the effect that such results may have on the naval chapter of the League's General Convention on the Reduction of Armaments will be of primary importance to the Pacific countries.

### SPECIAL QUESTIONS RELATING TO ARMAMENTS DEALT WITH BY THE LEAGUE

1. *Traffic in arms.*—After a long period of preliminary work, an International Conference of forty-four states (including the United States of America) met at Geneva in May, 1925, to draw up a convention on the international traffic in arms. The convention, the object of which is to establish a general system of supervision and publicity over international trade in arms, ammunition, and implements of war, and a special system for certain areas, will come into force when ratified by fourteen powers.

2. *Private manufacture of arms.*—In accordance with Article 8, paragraph 5, of the Covenant, the League is also engaged in examining the question of the private manufacture of arms.

3. *"Armaments Yearbook."*—Article 8, paragraph 6, of the Covenant of the League of Nations states that "the members of the League undertake to interchange full and frank information as to the scale of their armaments, their military, naval, and air programs, and the condition of such of their industries as are adaptable to warlike purposes." To assist in the execution of this obligation, the Disarmament Section of the Secretariat of the League of Nations publishes yearly an *Armaments Yearbook,* which gives general and statistical information on the organization, effectives, material, and budgets relating to the military, naval, and air establishments of

fifty-nine countries members and non-members of the League. The *Yearbook* also includes statistical information on the trade in arms, ammunition, and implements of war.

6. THE ECONOMIC AND FINANCIAL WORK OF THE LEAGUE OF NATIONS

A clear and concise survey of the whole of the economic work accomplished by the League of Nations up to the present and of the different stages of this work will be found in the three following documents (see Bibliography): "Report on the Economic Work of the League of Nations" (document C.E.I. 41), "Guide to the Preparatory Documents of the Conference" (document C.E.I. 40), "The World-Economic Conference: Final Report" (document C.E.I. 44).

The first document (C.E.I. 41) summarizes the work done by the competent organizations in the financial and economic sphere and in connection with transport and communications up to the summoning of the International Economic Conference.

The other two documents (C.E.I. 40 and C.E.I. 44) relate exclusively to the preparation and work of the Economic Conference which has just been held, and which forms a fresh starting-point for the League's economic work.

The first of these two documents, i.e., the "Guide to the Preparatory Documents of the Conference," gives, in concise form, some idea of the long and careful preparation which preceded the summoning of the Economic Conference.

Any further information which may be required as to this preparatory work will be found in document C.E.I. 6, agenda of the Conference.

The last document, C.E.I. 44, contains the general report of the Conference and the conclusions reached. It will be noted that the work of the Conference is summarized in the closing speech of the President of the Conference.

While document C.E.I. 41, "Report on the Economic Work of the League of Nations," summarizes what has already been done, the report of the Conference is mainly concerned with indications as to future work.

A special article on the International Economic Conference follows:

THE INTERNATIONAL ECONOMIC CONFERENCE

The International Economic Conference, summoned by the Council of the League of Nations, met at Geneva in May, 1927, under the presidency of M. Theunis, former prime minister of Belgium.

It was a world-conference, attended by delegates from fifty countries, including states members and non-members of the League,[5] amongst the latter of which might be specially mentioned the United States of America and the Union of Socialist Soviet Republics. The members, except a few appointed direct by the Council, were

[5] Abyssinia, South Africa, Albania, Australia, Austria, Belgium, Brazil, Great Britain, Bulgaria, Canada, Chile, China, Colombia, Cuba, Czechoslovakia, Danzig, Denmark, Egypt, Estonia, Finland, France, Germany, Greece, Guatemala, Hungary, India, the Irish Free State, Italy, Japan, Latvia, Luxemburg, the Netherlands, New Zealand, Nicaragua, Norway, Paraguay, Persia, Poland, Portugal, Roumania, Salvador, the Kingdom of the Serbs, Croats, and Slovenes, Siam, Sweden, Switzerland, Turkey, the Union of Socialist Soviet Republics, the United States of America, Uruguay, and Venezuela. Mexico sent observers.

chosen by the governments on the basis of technical and personal qualifications, and not as the spokesmen of official policies. They included industrialists, merchants, bankers, economists, agriculturists, officials with experience of commercial policy, representatives of workers' and consumers' organizations, co-operative societies, and three women specialists appointed by the Council after consultation with the appropriate women's organizations.

Over a year had been spent in preparation by a committee which was in itself a miniature conference, including, as it did, thirty-five experts drawn from twenty-one countries and appointed on the same basis as the members of the Conference. This preparatory committee had collected and published in about sixty memoranda a large amount of material, compiled with the aid of official and private organizations throughout the world and covering a wide range of subjects.

The main object of the Conference was to bring about a general exchange of views on existing economic difficulties and the means of overcoming them; to evoke collective opinion on the conditions, principles, and guaranties which might serve as a starting-point for the improvements and progress necessary to restore greater freedom to international commerce. As the preparatory committee had pointed out in its report, the Conference was not to be regarded as an isolated event, but as a stage in the continuous work of collaboration in the economic sphere which had begun before the project of a general conference was launched, and would continue when the Conference itself was over.

The first part of the agenda included a general discussion of the economic tendencies capable of affecting the peace of the world, and also a general survey of the principal features and problems of the international economic position. The second part of the agenda came under three main heads—commerce, industry, and agriculture—and it is in the three chapters of the final report under these titles that the principal recommendations of the Conference appear.[6]

### COMMERCE

The central point is shown in the following extract from the report:

> In spite of the variety of questions raised, the diversity of theories, and the legitimate national sentiments of all those who took part in the discussion, one important and extremely encouraging fact has emerged, and, having emerged, has become increasingly manifest as the work has advanced. This fact is the unanimous desire of the members of the Conference to make sure that this Conference shall, in some way, mark the beginning of a new era, during which international commerce will successively overcome all obstacles in its path that unduly hamper it and resume that general upward movement which is at once a sign of the world's economic health and the necessary condition for the development of civilisation.

The following further extracts indicate the position of the Conference on this question:

[6] In the final report, see especially: pp. 5, and 6, 12 and 13 (president's survey and summary); pp. 14–18 (short picture of world-economic situation); pp. 20 (commerce); pp. 29–31, 32 (tariffs and trade barriers); 40 (the industrial situation); pp. 43–44 ("cartels").

The Conference is convinced that a return to the effective liberty of international trading is one of the primary conditions of world prosperity (p. 22).

The Conference unanimously recognised the desirability of *simplifying* customs tariffs as far as possible, particularly by avoiding unwarranted subdivisions (p. 25).

Tariffs . . . . which in recent years have shown a tendency to rise, are for the most part higher than before the war, and are at present one of the chief barriers to trade. The increase in most countries is almost wholly due to higher duties on manufactured articles (p. 29).

In Europe the problem has been complicated by political readjustments which have changed many frontiers and increased the number of separate customs units from 20 to 27, all of which strive for an independent national economy which they defend by means of tariff barriers.

The harmful effect of these tariffs upon trade has in many cases been increased through their constant changes, which have created an element of uncertainty and made it impossible to place long contracts. The nations have failed to deal with this situation by long-term contracts (p. 29).

Tariffs, therefore, are higher, more complicated, more numerous, and less stable than before the war. In all these respects the Conference unanimously urges reform.

The Conference also strongly condemns the practice of imposing excessive duties as a basis of bargaining (*tarifs de combat*).

After searching analysis of the present position, the character of which is shown by the foregoing extracts, the conclusions, unanimously adopted, come with great force:

In view of the fact that harmful effects upon production and trade result from the high and constantly changing tariffs which are applied in many countries; and since substantial improvement in the economic conditions can be obtained by increased facilities for international trade and commerce; and in view of the fact that tariffs, though within the sovereign jurisdiction of the separate states, are not a matter of purely domestic interest but greatly influence the trade of the world; and in view of the fact that some of the causes which have resulted in the increase of tariffs and in other trade barriers since the war have largely disappeared and others are diminishing; the Conference declares that the time has come to put an end to the increase in tariffs and to move in the opposite direction.

The Conference recommends: (1) that nations should take steps forthwith to remove or diminish those tariff barriers that gravely hamper trade, starting with those which have been imposed to counteract the effects of disturbances arising out of the war.

Moreover, in order to insure that this action is continuously pursued, the Conference recommends: (2) that states should proceed to the conclusion of commercial treaties on lines and under conditions calculated to insure the attainment of the aims mentioned herein; (3) that, in future, the practice of putting into force, in advance of negotiations, excessive duties established for the purpose of bargaining, whether by means of *tarifs de combat* or by means of general tariffs, should be abandoned; (4) that the Council of the League of Nations should be requested to instruct its economic organization to examine, on the basis of the principle enunciated by the present Conference, the possibility of further action by the respective states with a view to promoting the equitable treatment of commerce by eliminating or reducing the obstructions which excessive customs tariffs offer to international trade.

*Prospects for the recommendations.*—The crucial question is whether the recommendations of the Conference will in fact be followed.

The following considerations need to be taken into account:

1. The recommendations of the Brussels Conference of 1920 were, like those of this Conference, taken unanimously by persons chosen by governments, but not representing governments; and they were also in striking contrast with the actual policies of governments at that date. But little by little, over these six and one-half years, the recommendations have been put into effect. In 1920 only four European countries had succeeded in balancing their budgets. Now nearly every country has established its budgetary equilibrium. For some years currency fluctuations were by far the greatest impediment to economic recovery. Now they are "not a factor of primary importance."

Immediate and dramatic results are scarcely to be expected. But a gradual movement, extending over years and of increasing effect, may reasonably be hoped for.

This hope is confirmed by other considerations:

2. The report brings out very clearly that the "causes which have resulted in the increase of tariffs and in other trade barriers since the war have largely disappeared and others are diminishing."

Fluctuating and depreciating currencies were a principal cause, and this cause has almost ceased.

The general dislocation resulting immediately from the war resulted in tariffs to protect industries that had grown up under war conditions and would, without protection, have been destroyed instantly with great consequent unemployment. This cause again, in the nature of the case, is a diminishing one.

Many tariffs have been due to the general sense of political insecurity resulting from the war. This cause again is happily diminishing. Moreover, the policy which it has caused is becoming recognized to be largely fallacious. "The effort to attain self-sufficiency cannot hope to succeed unless it is justified by the size, natural resources, economic advantages, and geographical situation of a country. There are very few countries in the world which can hope to attain it." Moreover, as the report continues, "it cannot be denied that this argument (the need of protecting industries required for national defense) . . . . has often been abused to cover exclusively economic objectives."

The effects have unhappily lasted longer than the causes. But the fact that these causes have ceased or are diminishing gives ground for a real hope that the effects may now also cease or diminish. It is one of the great merits of the Conference to have secured a clear recognition of these causes and of the fact that the reasons which perhaps justified the present tariff situation no longer exist.

This, indeed, constitutes the chief ground for hoping that the Conference will inaugurate a new era.

3. The time of the Conference was well chosen. The cessation of currency fluctuations had brought out the true importance of trade barriers. All over Europe people were beginning to say, "This has gone too far"; signs of this were to be found in Pan-Europe and similar movements, in the Bankers' Manifesto, in the International Chamber of Commerce reports, etc. These were all sectional only. Only a fully representative conference could reveal the full extent of the forces involved. The conference itself could not have *created* a sufficient force. What it has done is to reveal,

express, and consolidate forces already in existence—and of unexpected strength—and thus to make it effective. It has released a pent-up and hitherto inarticulate demand. This is its strength.

4. The composition of the Conference gives it enormous collective influence. It included leading representatives of industry, commerce, agriculture, and finance, officials with experience of commercial negotiations, economists, representatives of workers' and consumers' organizations. These members, numbering 194, though not in the strictest sense official representatives, were, with very few exceptions, chosen by governments. It is a great mistake to think of them as irresponsible or academic. They were, in fact, grouped for the most part in "national delegations," and very definitely conscious of national policies and national interests and points of view.

Their attitude may be fairly compared with that of the "Dawes experts," who were also not government representatives, but whose main task was really to make recommendations which, though at variance with the existing policies of the different governments, might be accepted by these governments if framed with all the authority of a collective international expert body.

In these circumstances, unanimous recommendation of the kind indicated previously is at once a very remarkable achievement, and likely to have a most powerful influence on policy.

The Conference deliberately put aside the question of abstract principle which divides free-traders from protectionists. Perhaps the most surprising and remarkable fact about the Conference is the extent of the common ground of policy and reform on which free-traders and protectionists alike, without prejudice to their basic principles, were found to be agreed upon.

### INDUSTRY

While the Conference must, in the main, stand or fall by the results which follow from its commerce resolutions, it made important recommendations as regards both industry and agriculture.

In industry it first warmly recommended methods of "rationalization," and passed a number of specific resolutions. Chief interest perhaps attaches to its attitude toward "international industrial agreements" (cartels, etc.).

The report reflects some conflict between opposing views. Its general effect, however, is to give both a more restricted importance, and a more conditional approval, than would have been suggested by the discussions of six months ago.

They must be "considered as good or bad according to the spirit which rules the constitution and the operation of the agreements, and in particular according to the measure in which those directing them are actuated by a sense of the general interest."

The Conference considers that the field of operation for agreements, both national and international, is usually limited to branches of production which are already centralised and to products supplied in bulk or in recognized grades, and that, consequently, they cannot be regarded as a form of organisation which could by itself alone remove the causes of the troubles from which the economic life of the world and particularly of Europe is suffering.

Nevertheless, in certain branches of production, they can—subject to certain conditions and reservations on the one hand, secure a more methodical organisation of production and a reduction in costs by means of a better utilisation of existing equipment, the development on more suitable lines of new plant, and a more rational grouping of undertakings, and, on the other hand, act as a check on uneconomic competition and reduce the evils resulting from fluctuations in industrial activity.

By this means, they may assure to the workers greater stability of employment and at the same time, by reducing production and distribution costs and consequently selling prices, bring advantages to the consumer. It is generally recognised that in this way agreements may in some cases be useful, not only to producers, but also to consumers and the community in general.

Nevertheless, the Conference considers, on the other hand, that such agreements, if they encourage monopolistic tendencies and the application of unsound business methods, may check technical progress in production and involve dangers to the legitimate interests of important sections of society and of particular countries.

It consequently appears to the Conference that it is entirely necessary that agreements should not lead to an artificial rise in prices, which would injure consumers, and that they should give due consideration to the interests of the workers. It is further necessary that they should not, either in intention or effect, restrict the supply to any particular country of raw materials or basic products, or without just cause create unequal conditions between the finishing industries of the consuming and producing countries or other countries situated in the same conditions. Nor must they have for their object or effect any reduction in the economic equipment which any nation considers indispensable, nor should they stereotype the present position of production, whether from the point of view of technical progress or of the distribution of industries among the various countries in accordance with the necessities imposed upon each by its economic development and the growth of its population.

The Conference, while taking note of the different measures taken by different governments controlling the operation of cartels, etc., did not recommend an international control.

It considered, however, that the "League of Nations should closely follow these forms of international industrial co-operation and their efforts upon technical progress, the development of production, conditions of labor, the situation as regards supplies, and the movement of prices, seeking in this connection the collaboration of the various governments. It should collect the relevant data with a view to publishing from time to time such information as may be of general interest. The Conference is of the opinion that the publicity given in regard to the nature and operations of agreements constitutes one of the most effective means, on the one hand, of securing the support of public opinion to agreements which conduce to the general interest, and on the other hand, of preventing the growth of abuses."

The Conference also includes in its report an authoritative analysis of the principal causes which are causing depression in a number of industries.

Finally, the Conference made very strong and comprehensive recommendations as to the necessity for obtaining and publishing fuller industrial statistics and information, and suggested a considerable extension of the work of this kind already undertaken by the League.

AGRICULTURE

For the first time at this Conference, agriculture was represented side by side with industry and commerce in such a way as to take its place in a general review of the economic situation of the world.

The Conference noted that the economic depression in agriculture was "characterized by the disequilibrium which has arisen between the prices of agricultural products and those of manufactured products."

It recommends that:

> It is desirable that all hindrances to the free circulation of and trade in agricultural products should be removed, in so far as their removal does not endanger the vital interests of the different countries and their workers.
>
> In those states in which customs protection is maintained it should be reduced both for industry and agriculture, to the lowest possible point indispensable to production; care should be taken to assist in the maintenance of an equitable balance between industry and agriculture and not to stifle one to the advantage of the other.
>
> The system of export prohibitions and export duties (with the exception of taxes levied for the benefit of the industry concerned) and frequent changes in customs tariffs, which long experience has shown to be ineffectual and dangerous, should be definitely abandoned.

Further resolutions recommned an extension of agricultural co-operation, including the development of relations between agricultural co-operative societies and consumers' co-operative societies—a study of the possibility of facilitating agricultural credits—the conduct of the campaign against diseases affecting plants and animals, and the improvement of information and statistics on agricultural questions.

In addition, the Conference passed a few general resolutions, one of which calls attention to the heavy burden of armaments expenditure upon national finances, "entailing heavy taxation which reacts upon their whole life and lowers their standard of living."

Lastly, the Conference passed a resolution, to which the President gave special prominence in his closing speech, as dealing with one of the two principal objects of the whole Conference, on the relation between economic policies and the peace of the world:

> The Conference, recognising that the maintenance of world-peace depends largely upon the principles on which the economic policies of nations are framed and executed, recommends that the Governments and peoples of the countries here represented should together give continuous attention to this aspect of the economic problem, and looks forward to the establishment of recognised principles designed to eliminate those economic difficulties which cause friction and misunderstanding in a world which has everything to gain from peaceful and harmonious progress.

The adoption in practice of the recommendations of the Conference would mean a considerable transformation of the economic policies of the world. The process can only be gradual, but it may in time be complete, and progress may be cumulative. Certainly the recommendations come at a particularly favorable moment, expressing and strengthening forces already in existence, and with unexampled weight and authority.

It may indeed be, as the Conference states, that all its members unanimously desire "the beginning of a new era."

### 7. THE WORK OF THE LEAGUE FOR INTELLECTUAL CO-OPERATION

The question of the international organization of intellectual work was brought before the League during the first year of its existence. It was said, to quote the words of M. Léon Bourgeois, that "if the League concerned itself with improving the exchange of material products, it should surely also study the methods of accelerating the exchange of ideas between nations. Without a spirit of mutual understanding between nations, the League cannot live." As practical methods for promoting this kind of international co-operation, the importance of developing contact between intellectual workers, scholars, thinkers, writers, artists, together with the communication of the results achieved in scientific work in different countries, has been emphasized.

In order to study the means of strengthening and extending intellectual relations between different countries—efforts in this direction had of course been made before the war, but little had been done to co-ordinate them—an advisory committee was set up by the League. This committee, called the International Committee on Intellectual Co-operation, composed originally of twelve, now comprises fifteen members.[7] The first chairman of the Committee was the French philosopher, Henri Bergson, and among the members representatives of various cultures and important schools of thought and scientific work are included. The secretarial work of the Committee was carried out under the direction of the Japanese scholar, Dr. Nitobé, under-secretary-general of the League of Nations, until his resignation from the Secretariat early in 1927.

The first session of the Committee was held in August, 1922. Since then it has met, sometimes once, sometimes twice, a year, and it will have its ninth plenary session in July of this year.

At the outset of its work, the Committee received numerous proposals for its future activity. The questions selected for further study and action were the following:

1. A general inquiry into the present conditions of intellectual life in various countries was instituted, and as a result, several monographs were published containing information on various aspects of intellectual life in a given country as well as on some special problems of intellectual work.

2. As a result of the war, the development of intellectual life and especially of research work was endangered in certain countries by unfavorable rates of exchange, which made it difficult to obtain foreign publications, material for laboratories, and instruments.

[7] The present members of the Committee are: Professor Lorentz (Dutch), Chairman; Professor Gilbert Murray (British), Vice-Chairman; Mlle Bonnevie (Norwegian); Sir J. Bose (Indian); M. J. Casares (Spanish); M. de Castro (Brazilian); Mme Curie (French); M. Destrée (Belgian); Professor Einstein (German); M. Lugones (Argentinian); Professor Millikan (American); M. Painlevé (French); M. de Reynold (Swiss); M. Rocco (Italian); Professor Tanakodaté (Japanese).

The Committee, in the early years of its work, appealed to learned institutions and similar societies in different countries in order to obtain assistance for universities and individual intellectual workers in the most afflicted countries.

To promote this work, national committees on intellectual co-operation, generally composed of representatives of the principal scientific associations and institutions, were formed in several countries. The activities of these committees, which at present number thirty-two, have since, however, been extended beyond this problem of assistance to intellectual workers.

3. The Committee decided to take up the study of questions relating to intellectual property, and a subcommittee was formed to study both the best means of protecting scientific property and also special questions such as the right of the scientist to his invention, on the principle that there might be extended to scientific discovery the same guaranties which underlie the copyright protecting artistic creation and patents protecting technical inventions.

4. In order to study the question of inter-university co-operation, another subcommittee was constituted. One of the first achievments in this domain was the formation of an International University Information Office, originally in connection with the Secretariat of the Committee and later as a section of the Institute of Intellectual Co-operation (see below, 7). This office publishes a periodical bulletin in which special attention is given to the curricula of different universities, to international courses and lectures, as well as to the international recognition of courses of study, diplomas, and degrees in various countries. The subcommittee co-operates with the international organizations of students and pays particular attention to the question of facilitating the interchange of students. It also collaborates with the national university information offices. In order to facilitate scientific research and at the same time develop international contact between intellectual workers, the question of international post-graduate scholarships is the object of special attention.

5. A third subcommittee deals with the study of bibliographical questions with a view to facilitating research work for the scientists of various countries. It decided on the publcation of an *Index bibliographicus,* which was issued in 1925. The *Index* is an international catalogue of sources of current bibliographical information. The subcommittee has studied, with the assistance of several committees of experts, the organization of co-operation between libraries and the interchange of publications (international conventions of 1886 and 1925). Information regarding the loan of books and manuscripts between libraries in different countries and the accessibility of archives has been collected and is being published in the *Bulletin* of the Institute of Historical Research, London. For the co-ordination of the work of analytical bibliography with reference to specified subjects, four expert committees have been working: namely, on physics, Graeco-Roman antiquity, economic sciences, and biology.

6. In addition, the Committee has been active in developing international relations in the field of arts and letters. It has created an international museums office in connection with the Institute of Intellectual Co-operation and is preparing an international congress on popular arts to be held in Prague in 1928.

7. Since the end of the year 1925, the Committee has possessed a valuable organ

in the form of the International Institute for Intellectual Co-operation in Paris, which carries on research work and inquiries and maintains permanent relations with intellectual centers in different countries. This Institute is subsidized in the main by the French government, but receives some grants from other countries.

8. The most important work attempted by the League in this field is undoubtedly that of inspiring young people in all countries with the ideals of international interdependence and co-operation. It is evident that the future of an institution like the League depends on the attitude of the coming generation. In order to pave the way for a better understanding of its aims and of international co-operation in general, the Assembly of the League has adopted several resolutions inviting the member states to give young people instruction on these subjects.

A subcommittee of experts was appointed in 1926 to study and to report upon suitable methods for such instruction. The provisional recommendations of this subcommittee (see Bibliography) have been widely distributed and have been instrumental in provoking action by governments and responsible educational authorities. Some twenty-five non-official international associations (e.g., the International Association of Teachers, the Boy Scouts, and Girl Guides, etc.) were consulted by the subcommittee and have actively assisted in this work.

## 8. THE LEAGUE AND THE PRESS

### CONFERENCE OF PRESS EXPERTS

The League of Nations has summoned a Conference of Press Experts to meet at Geneva August 24, 1927, to consider a series of technical questions concerning facilities for the press on an international scale.

The idea was first presented by M. Yanez, a Chilian delegate at the 1925 Assembly, the proposal being: "(1) to inquire into means of insuring more rapid and less costly transmission of press news with a view to reducing the risks of international misunderstanding; and (2) to discuss all technical problems the solution of which, in the opinion of experts, would be conducive to the tranquilization of public opinion in various countries."

The Council, to which the suggestion was referred, instituted a consultation with the press, decided as a result of these inquiries that a meeting of press experts was opportune and desirable, and instructed the Secretary-General to proceed with the preparatory work. Three preliminary meetings have been held, the first consisting of directors of news agencies, the second, of directors of press bureaus, and the third, of journalists.

The first preliminary meeting consisted of representatives of sixteen large news agencies in America, Asia, and Europe. It drew up a series of recommendations, dealing generally with rates for press communications, improvement of communications, and the protection of property rights in press news.

The second preliminary meeting comprised the directors of sixteen European press bureaus. It had a general discussion of telegraph and telephone tariffs, news copyright, and facilities for journalists, and drew up a questionnaire with the object of collecting more detailed information on these different points. The replies to this questionnaire provide a basis for wider discussions of the subject.

The third preliminary meeting comprised a number of journalists chosen from those obliged by their profession to live abroad or travel frequently. They drew up recommendations regarding facilities which they considered necessary for their work.

On the basis of these reports, the replies to the questionnaire, and the general consultation conducted by the Secretariat, a provisional agenda for the Conference has been prepared on the following questions: press rates, coding of press messages, improvement of communications, transport of newspapers, postal subscriptions to newspapers, protection of news, professional facilities for journalists, censorship in peace time, information on the latest technical improvements of interest to the press.

The documentation for the Conference contains an analysis of the questions on the agenda with a record of the present position. The League Secretariat, during the course of the preliminary meetings, was asked to undertake various preliminary tasks, including the preparation of a memorandum on the protection of news.

The Conference, which will meet under the presidency of Lord Burnham, will include about sixty experts representing every continent of the world.

BIBLIOGRAPHY

1. The Covenant of the League of Nations.
2. The League of Nations: A Survey (January, 1920–December, 1926).
3. Weekly Fascicule of Epidemiological Intelligence received by the Eastern Bureau of the Health Organization of the League of Nations.
4. Preparatory Commission for the Disarmament Conference, Report on the Third Session.
5. Report on the Economic Work of the League of Nations.
6. Guide to the Preparatory Documents of the Economic Conference.
7. The International Economic Conference: Final Report.
8. Recommendations of the Subcommittee of Experts for the Instruction of Children and Youth in the Existence and Aims of the League of Nations.

## SECTION 29

# THE RADIO SITUATION WITH REFERENCE TO THE UNITED STATES, CHINA, AND JAPAN

MANTON DAVIS
Radio Corporation of America

How can mankind learn to see large not small, telescopically not microscopically, how can each of the earth's peoples know and be brought sympathetically to consider the other's point of view, are questions with which the Institute of Pacific Relations concerns itself.

Communications, certain, speedy, and cheap, manifestly must precede and inevitably would promote mutual understanding between nations. The latest born and the most lusty in the communications family is radio. It has not merely grown; its growth has rather been explosive in character. Probably no other instrumentality of commerce has ever more intrigued the world's imagination.

The vast distances of the Pacific Basin encourage the development of radio and discourage the building of cables.

This Institute can advance its own purposes and will serve mankind by helping to settle discords in the world-wide wireless field.

These considerations may perhaps justify us in examining certain radio questions microscopically in the hope that we may, by helping to find a solution for such questions, promote the creation of facilities by means of which other questions may be seen in the largest possible way.

Radio service between Japan and the United States was opened November 15, 1916. Messages were relayed via Hawaii. The American and Hawaiian stations were then owned and operated by the Marconi Wireless Telegraph Company of America. The Japanese stations which worked with the American and Hawaiian stations were owned and operated by the Japanese government. In consequence of the war, the American Marconi stations were taken over by the government of the United States on April 7, 1917, and were operated by the government until March, 1920.

During the war the great American electrical companies co-operated, at the urgent request of the government, in the development of devices useful in radio communication. The inventions of all these companies were used by the government in war-time radio service, the government undertaking at the conclusion of the war to return to each company its inventions and to make due compensation for patent rights used without licenses.

When the war was done and the government was ready to return to the respective owners the radio inventions it had been using, no one of the companies was in a position to take over and operate the radio system then in use by the government. A number of companies had contributed to the system, but each company lacked inventions owned by others and necessary to the system in use, or to any efficient system of radio communication.

To break this deadlock, and hoping to avoid interminable patent litigation, there was organized October 17, 1919, the Radio Corporation of America.

The great American electrical companies transferred to this corporation all their inventions in the radio field, and the corporation acquired not only all the patents, but also the physical properties of Marconi Wireless Telegraph Company of America. The Radio Corporation of America, since March 1, 1920, has owned and operated all the commercial radio stations in the United States engaged in overseas service.

The rate for ordinary traffic to Japan was originally 80 cents per word. This rate was early reduced to 72 cents. A deferred rate of 36 cents was introduced January 1, 1925. An urgent service at triple rates was put into effect in 1921. The cable across the Pacific was a tardy follower of radio in the matter of rates. This has always been true when radio and cables have come into competition.

The radio press rate, United States to Japan, was originally 40 cents per word, reduced to 36 cents in 1920, to 27 cents in 1921, to 18 cents in 1926. In November, 1926, the Radio Corporation of America proposed a press rate between Japan and the United States of 10 cents per word, but the Japanese government, owning the other end of the circuit, was not able at the time to agree, and the rate therefore as yet has not been applied.

The Japanese circuit has been successful. It carries more than 60 per cent of the traffic against the cable's less than 40 per cent. The success of this circuit through co-operation between Japanese and Americans suggests a clue for the solution of the Chinese wireless controversy, the principal subject discussed in this paper.

Other transpacific services of the Radio Corporation of America are: to Hawaii, the corporation owning both ends of the circuit; to Dutch East Indies, in connection with the Dutch East Indies government telegraph administration, which owns the other end of the circuit; to French Indo-China, in connection with the Compagnie Générale de Télégraphie sans Fil, Paris, which owns the other end of the circuit.

The Radio Corporation of the Philippines, a subsidiary of the Radio Corporation of America, has just completed its overseas station in Manila. Service began on June 26, 1927. The ordinary commercial rate is 60 cents; the deferred rate, 30 cents; the urgent rate, $1.80, and the press rate, 8 cents per word between Manila and San Francisco.

The new press rate to Manila is low. It compares favorably with transatlantic rates, being the same as the press rate between the United States and France.

Rate-making in radio is difficult. In international services the two ends of a circuit are under different ownership, frequently a government owning one end and a private corporation the other. Governments have not always accepted the commercial principle that a small margin of profit and a large volume of traffic means satisfactory service and commercial success. It was easy, however, to apply the low press rate between Manila and San Francisco, since the Radio Corporation of America controls both ends of the circuit. This rate, and the traffic resulting from it, will doubtless exercise a profound influence to further better understanding between the peoples of the United States and the Philippines.

The interest of the Institute of Pacific Relations in radio is centered not so much in international co-operation as in international controversies. This brings us to China.

I shall endeavor to discuss China's wireless contracts objectively, as becoming a member of this Institute. My connection with this matter is, however, well understood, and it is generally known that the Radio Corporation of America controls the federal wireless contracts and the American radio contracts with China.

The Radio Corporation, however, is engaged in creating and carrying on international radio communication circuits, and those who serve the corporation know full well that real success cannot be attained unless arrangements be made which are and continue to be profitable and satisfactory to all concerned. I represent that Corporation, but not at this Institute, where, like other members, I represent no one and speak my own opinions. My effort, like that of all members of the Institute, will be to discuss these matters frankly but fairly, to help create a spirit of accommodation and mutual understanding, and thus to further the finding of a solution at another time and place.

The radio *impasse* in China results from three contracts each made by the Republic of China, but represented in one instance by its ministry of the navy contracting with a Japanese company, in another by its ministry of communications contracting with an American company, and in yet another by its ministry of war contracting with a British company.

On February 21, 1918, the Chinese ministry of the navy entered into an agreement with the Mitsui Bussan Kaisha, a Japanese company, for the erection near Peking of a wireless station, capable, according to the contract, of direct communication with Japan, America, and Europe. The purchase price for this station was to be paid in thirty annual instalments. The contractor undertook that the payments the contract required could be made from earnings of the station. The government agreed that the contractor should, for the period of thirty years, manage and operate the station. After the contract had been executed, the government seems to have adopted a resolution which provided: "During the period of thirty years mentioned in Article 4 of the contract, the government shall not permit any other person or firm to erect, nor shall it erect by itself, any wireless station in China for the purpose of communicating with any foreign country."

The execution of the principal contract with the Mitsui company was generally known, but the resolution quoted, purporting to give to the Mitsui company a monopoly, was a secret arrangement not published until long after the publication of the original agreement.

Certain American parties in January, 1921, not knowing of Mitsui company's claim to a monopoly, negotiated on behalf of the Federal Telegraph Company, an American company, with the Chinese government, through its ministry of communications, a contract for the erection of five wireless stations. One great station with two complete units was to be erected at Shanghai, one station at Harbin, one at Peking, and one at Canton, together with a smaller unit at Shanghai for communication within the country. The Chinese government agreed to issue bonds for the whole contract price of these stations. Provisions were included in the contracts for a joint administration for the operation of the stations during the period of ten years, within which it was estimated that the net revenues of the stations would retire the bonds. This joint administration was named the China Federal Radio Administration.

In 1918 Marconi's Wireless Telegraph Ltd., a British company, made a contract with the Chinese ministry of war for the sale of certain wireless field sets. Later, and in May of 1919, the Marconi company and the Chinese government united to form the "Chinese National Wireless Company," to which the Chinese government gave an undertaking which read:

> If goods supplied by the Chinese company are not lower in quality nor higher in price to those offered by other companies, the government will purchase exclusively from the Chinese company all of its present and future requirements of wireless telegraph and telephone apparatus, materials and supplies, and further, if the government suffers no loss by giving such work to the Chinese company, the Chinese company shall be exclusively intrusted with the repair and maintenance of all wireless telegraph and telephone apparatus and equipment in China.

The British government has contended that the rights of the British Marconi Company as stated in the contract quoted were infringed by China when the American radio contracts were made.

But the history of the transaction, the ministry concerned in it, and the language just quoted seem to indicate that purchases and sales of portable radio devices were under consideration, and the parties were not contracting concerning great radio stations to be constructed for overseas communication.

In 1923 the Mitsui company agreed to turn the Peking wireless station over to a company to be formed by Mitsui, British Marconi, and the French radio company, Compagnie Générale de Télégraphie sans Fil. This agreement was conditioned upon the parties being able to make necessary arrangements with the Chinese government. The contract further provided: "The three parties also agree to use their best efforts and exercise their influence to avoid possible competition in future and consequent waste of capital, staff, and materials in China."

Since the execution of the contract last quoted, the British have the more supported the Japanese claims and the less urged their own. It would therefore appear that the Chinese radio controversy concerns the Japanese and the American contracts.

The Japanese contract provides for a monopoly. The erection and operation of the Japanese station is not inconsistent with the American contracts, but the erection and operation of the American stations would violate the monopoly asserted by the Mitsui company.

The Japanese government has consistently supported the Mitsui company's contract, and the American government has given like support to the federal contracts. The American companies concerned contend that the monopolistic provisions of the Japanese contract violate the principle of the "Open Door"—the principle of equal opportunity in China for the commerce and industry of all nations—a principle to which the Japanese government, many times prior to the execution of the Mitsui contract, had given its adherence, and to which, many times since, it has subscribed.

The American companies concerned believe the Mitsui claim of monopoly is inconsistent with many international undertakings and declarations, among them the following:

Article XV of the Sino-American treaty of 1844, which provides that American citizens in China shall not be "impeded in their business by monopolies or other injurious restrictions."

The Anglo-Japanese treaty of January 30, 1902, which provides for "the preservation of the common interests of all powers in China by insuring the independence and integrity of the Chinese Empire and the principle of equal opportunity for the commerce and industry of all nations in China."

The Anglo-Japanese treaty of July 13, 1911, which repeats the language last quoted.

The Franco-Japanese agreement of June 10, 1907, by which the parties undertook to respect the independence and integrity of China as well as "the principle of equal opportunity in that country for the commerce and subjects or citizens of all nations."

The Root-Takahira agreement of November 30, 1908, between Japan and the United States, in which the parties assert their determination "to preserve the common interests of all powers in China by supporting by all pacific means at their disposal, the independence and integrity of China and the principle of equal opportunity for commerce and industry of all nations in that Empire."

The speech of Viscount Ishii, delivered in New York, September 29, 1917, during the visit of the Imperial Japanese Mission. The distinguished diplomat said:

> I am persuaded that the grumblings and the whisperings about a door closed in China by the Japanese against America did not come from the broad and generous heart of the enterprising American in New York or elsewhere, but is the result of ten years of an enemy's effort to create prejudice and distrust. Gentlemen, I assure you that a closed door in China has never been and never will be the policy of my government. The door is open. The field is there. We will welcome co-operation and competition, all tending to the betterment of the equal opportunity.

Contention has been made that the American contracts themselves attempt to create a monopoly. This is based upon Article XIV of the agreement dated September 19, 1921, which reads:

> The government agrees that all monies and income accruing to it from the operation of said stations or from the operation of the China Federal Radio Administration shall be immediately upon receipt thereof deposited in the Asia Banking Corporation or such other bank or banking institution as may be from time to time designated by the Federal Telegraph Company, and that all radio messages from China and for the United States of America are to be handled exclusively by the Federal Telegraph Company for a time twenty years from the date of the completion of the last station erected and provided for under the agreement of the 8th day of January, 1921.

Eminent authorities, official and other, have construed this language to mean merely that the China Federal Radio Administration in operating the stations to be built under the Federal contracts should send all messages coming into its hands and destined for America to the American company which was to furnish the money and build the stations. The China Federal Radio Administration is to be a joint partnership created by the contracts, to the end that the American company which was to furnish the money to build the stations should, while the debt for the stations was being paid, participate with the Chinese government in operating the stations.

The language quoted merely stipulates that the Chinese end of the circuits to be created should work with, and not against, the American interests which were to create those circuits.

There is no provision forbidding anyone erecting and operating wireless stations in China, and no provisions forbidding anyone erecting and operating wireless stations in America or elsewhere. It takes two ends to make a radio circuit, and a monopoly would not seem to be created by an undertaking that one end of a particular circuit be required to operate exclusively with the other end of that same circuit. Consistent with the American contracts, anyone may establish circuits with China and the American companies contend that the Chinese circuit they create should not be divided against itself.

It is not intended, however, too narrowly to discuss the American and Japanese contracts. They are inconsistent, and from this the controversy arises.

The Institute of Pacific Relations seeks to find the facts concerning international controversies, and with the facts ascertained, to consider how honorable adjustment might be made, irritating differences accommodated, and good will established where ill will existed or might arise.

Further discussion will be addressed to suggestions for settlement.

The Japanese and the American radio interests, strangely, have never met face to face in an endeavor to adjust their differences concerning radio in China. Both have carried on long negotiations with China; and China, in a vain effort to satisfy both, has satisfied neither. The Japanese and American governments have had much correspondence on the subject, and the fact that the issues were pending between the governments has prevented direct negotiations between the parties. Both Japanese and Americans have made suggestions for a solution.

The American companies concerned believe that a comprehensive and efficient wireless service could be formed in China by co-operation between the Mitsui and the Federal projects, both completed and brought up to date. They have suggested as a solution that both projects be completed; that the necessary modifications in plans and installations be made so that each station, whether Mitsui or Federal, shall be modern and be equipped with the latest devices; that the smaller or feeder stations of the Federal system be connected with, and shall serve, the Mitsui station at Peking as well as the two overseas units of the Federal station at Shanghai; that the radio stations of the world be divided as correspondents between the Mitsui station in Peking and the two units of the Federal station in Shanghai, so that each of the stations in China engaged in overseas service shall have as few correspondents as possible and therefore shall be required to break circuits as infrequently as possible; that the Mitsui and the Federal projects each retain their separate managements and be operated as required by their respective contracts; and finally, the gross receipts from all the stations be pooled and divided on an equitable basis, as, for example, in proportion to the debts incurred by China for the respective installations.

The Japanese have suggested that both the Mitsui and the Federal companies surrender their contracts and consent that they be canceled; that an international consortium be formed consisting of the great radio interests of Japan, Great Britain, France, and America, which consortium shall lend money to China to buy the Mitsui station already built, and to erect additional radio stations in China as need for additional stations develops; that the consortium supply the engineers and accountants necessary for the operation of the radio installations financed by it. In practice the stations would be operated by such engineers and accountants.

A consortium of interests and efforts is an appealing suggestion as a solution. But to be acceptable, the arrangement proposed must offer such equitable adjustments that the parties will be disposed not only to accept, but to carry them out with good will.

The Japanese, in their suggestions, refer to the Mitsui station as having been already completed. The completion of the Mitsui station, while the building of the American stations has not even been begun, is the principal fact which may make the Japanese suggestion difficult of acceptance by the Americans. Cancellation of the Mitsui contract would not cancel the completed station. The Mitsui company would properly expect payment for the station it had built. Under its contract with the Chinese government payment is the only right the Mitsui company now has. The monopoly asserted is not a right in itself, but is only a security by which the right of payment is guaranteed. If through the organization of an international consortium the Mitsui company should secure payment for the station it had already built, then all its rights under its contract with the Chinese government would have been realized. For this the Japanese suggest that the Americans abandon all their rights and surrender their contracts to be canceled. Such a course would seem not only to save for the Japanese their every right and take from the Americans every right they possess, but in addition would require the Americans to make large financial contributions for the payment of the insecure debt the Japanese are now carrying for the station they have built.

The suggestion of the American companies, it is to be observed, accepts the consortium principle, but they propose a consortium for final results; not a consortium for construction of the stations, and not a consortium for their operation.

If construction were undertaken through the instrumentality of a consortium, each of the four interested parties would strive with the others to furnish the equipment. Compromises would be inevitable, and the hodge-podge result would be installations less efficient than any one of the parties would produce working alone.

Under a consortium operations would be managed by a board composed of representatives of five different nationalities, each controlled from a different world-center and each ordered by a radio company concerned more with problems at home than with problems in China. English, French, Germans, and Americans tried construction and operation of radio stations in South America by a consortium. Radiograms passing from South America to London, Paris, Berlin, and New York attempting to settle managerial disputes were said to have equaled in volume the traffic paid for by the public. The poor quality and high cost of service resulting from stations so operated and controlled would surely preclude such a method furnishing the practical and helpful solution so much desired by all the parties concerned.

Under the solution suggested by the Americans, not one, but three, great units would be engaged in China's overseas radio service. The Japanese suggestion contemplates China depending for overseas wireless service upon the Mitsui station alone until the pressure of traffic would seem to require additional installations. The American companies concerned believe that if China depends for her overseas wireless service upon the Peking station alone the development of radio service will be retarded to the injury of China and to the injury of other countries and their nationals. The Peking station is no longer new. It is not now modern, and it is not thought to be technically efficient; it is badly located; but a small portion of China's overseas traffic originates in the Peking area; the station must depend for the greater part of its traffic upon the land lines, and would in consequence incur for its messages additional expense, delay, and liability to mutilation. The station cannot furnish effective competition with the cable, and perhaps would never develop revenues sufficient to pay for itself. One receiver and one transmitter alone could not establish efficient circuits with the many wireless stations of the world. The delays on such a circuit would discourage, not encourage, development of the service. In radio, much more even than in telephone service, delays are occasioned by making and breaking circuits. A circuit can handle a vastly greater volume of traffic if it be established between two stations only. In any radio system adding additional units and reducing the number of other stations with which each unit of the system must communicate increases the volume of traffic that can be handled, not arithmetically, but geometrically.

Japanese have expressed fear that the completion of both radio projects in China would unduly burden the Chinese treasury. The American companies are not without information concerning the financial difficulties of the Chinese government at this time; but they are nevertheless willing to build the stations required by their contracts, believing that the stations will pay for themselves. They further believe that were the two projects operated as parts of a co-ordinated system, each would be more valuable than if operated alone; that the system would produce revenues sufficient to pay for both projects. The fears the Japanese entertain perhaps do not take sufficiently into consideration the increased revenues sure to result from new facilities of high efficiency. American communication companies find that facilities newly created create revenues by which they are sustained and stimulate rather than diminish the revenues of those facilities which existed before.

Co-operation is normal in radio. Japanese and Americans successfully co-operate in maintaining the Japanese-American circuit. They could be mutually helpful in their wireless projects in China. The American companies believe that the system of co-operation herein suggested is sound and fair and offers a solution consistent with the interests and the dignity of all the parties concerned; but above all, these companies believe that no solution can be found until the interested parties shall come together and discuss their problems face to face.

The International Radio Telegraphic Convention will meet in Washington October 1, this year. All the nations of the world interested in radio communication and all the great companies engaged in international radio service will be there represented. It is expected that treaties and agreements governing such service will be there concluded.

What a notable achievement if frank and friendly discussions here might pave the way for a mutually satisfactory settlement there of the long-drawn-out Chinese wireless controversy.

## SECTION 30

# CHINA'S RADIO COMMUNICATION PROBLEM

AKIRA ISHII
Formerly Vice-President of the Nippon Yusen, Kaisha

The establishment of radio communication between China and the rest of the world is highly desirable, both for economic and political reasons, not only to China herself, but also to those other nations having definite relations with her as well. And though preparations for the realization of this enterprise had been completed three years ago, still to this day it has failed to materialize. We therefore propose to enumerate the conditions that have so long obstructed this work.

On February 21, 1918, the Mitsui Bussan company, of Japan, entered into a contract with the navy department of the government of China, which contract contained the following provisions: (1) that the Mitsui Bussan company construct, on behalf of the government of China, a wireless plant capable of communicating with Japan, America, and Europe; (2) that the government of China reimburse the Mitsui Bussan company for the construction of this plant in thirty annual payments; (3) that such annual payments be made out of the net profits secured from the operation of this wireless plant; (4) that the Mitsui Bussan company retain the privilege of operating this wireless plant, this privilege to be turned over to the government of China, upon her demand, following total reimbursement of the cost of the plant; (5) that the government of China permit the Mitsui Bussan Kaisha, in order to realize the revenues of the plant as much as possible, to establish connection between this plant and others, so that it might secure the transit of a maximum of messages, both in point of number and of revenues.

On January 8, 1921, the Federal Telegraph Company of the United States entered into a contract with the commerce department of the government of China, which contract awarded the Federal Telegraph Company the privilege to construct a high-powered radio plant at Shanghai and subsidiary plants in other parts of China wherever necessary.

It was obviously certain that the Federal contract would jeopardize the Mitsui contract. Moreover, the Mitsui contract was essentially and admittedly monopolistic in character, the government of China having agreed to grant no other franchise in view of the fact that without such a guaranty the investment on the part of the Mitsui Bussan company of so much capital under such an obviously heavy risk would hardly be consistent with safety. The Mitsui Bussan company, aided by the government of Japan, immediately protested to the government of China, demanding cancellation of the Federal contract for the above reasons. The government of China, however, seemed unable for some reason to comply with this legitimate demand. The government of the United States, to which a similar note of protest was sent, not only refused to abrogate the Federal contract, but also took definite steps in hastening the fulfilment of this contract.

In the meantime, the Mitsui Bussan company, in accordance with the terms of its contract, completed the construction of the radio plant in 1924, and several experiments were made with radio stations in Europe and America to test its capacity for service, and it was ascertained that it worked splendidly. Everything, moreover, was in readiness at the plant to begin operation. Owing, however, to the tripartite negotiations over the abrogation of the Federal contract being still pending, the government of China refused to permit the Mitsui Bussan company to start operation. For the same reason the Federal Telegraph Company has been unable to enforce upon China the fulfilment of its contract.

In other words, China today possesses a huge radio plant, but because of her infidelity to the fulfilment of her contract with the Mitsui Bussan company, she is unable to utilize it to her advantage. As a result her own inconvenience is apparent, and the loss she has thus incurred upon the Mitsui Bussan company is a huge one.

In attempting to seek a solution to this problem, the governments of the United States and China should particularly bear in mind that, under the terms of the Mitsui contract, the government of China granted an exclusive monopoly to the Mitsui Bussan company to build the Peking radio plant, and that the Mitsui contract antedated the Federal contract by three years, and that this monopoly is national and necessary in view of the fact that the huge outlay of capital for the construction of the radio plant is to be reimbursed to the Mitsui Bussan company by the government of China out of the net operating profits in annual payments extending thirty years, the Mitsui Bussan company sustaining the loss of any amount outstanding at the end of that period.

This form of monopoly is recognized by all countries. Even the Washington Conference definitely recognized its validity. Moreover, it is in accordance with the principles of open door and equal opportunities.

The government of Japan seems to be convinced of the validity of the Mitsui contract and of the invalidity of all contracts entered into by the government of China with any other party in violation of the terms of the Mitsui contract.

China's loss as a result of the fulfilment of the Federal contract will amount to $6,500,000.00. With the construction of other radio plants by the Federal Telegraph Company, the Peking radio plant built by the Mitsui Bussan company will not only become unnecessary to China, but the capital invested in its construction and the interest accruing thereon will have to be reimbursed to the Mitsui Bussan company, and with the inability of the government of China to meet this debt out of the net operating profits of this plant, the deficit will have to be made up by revenues from other governmental sources.

Obviously China's requirements do not call for any radio plant other than the one constructed at Peking. It is equally obvious that the fulfilment of the Federal contract would only increase the heavy financial burden of the government of China.

## SECTION 31

## THE MANAGEMENT OF DISCUSSION

WILLIAM H. KILPATRICK
Teachers College, Columbia University

Can the experience of the recent Conference be so used as to tell us how better to run the next Conference? The effort is here made to do this. This paper seeks to use the experience of the Conference so as to attain a clearer and more consistent view of the purpose and function of the Institute, and then to get, both from the experience and from clearer view of the aim, light on the management of discussion in the Conference.

### THE NATURE OF THE INSTITUTE

The Institute concerns itself with the points of international difficulty and potential friction in the Pacific area. It aims by study to improve these conditions. This statement of aim would probably be accepted by the members generally, and study is well stressed as the chief function of the Institute; but so brief a statement fails to differentiate adequately the Institute from other agencies at work in the field. It fails further to furnish the guidance that we seek for the management of discussion. From consideration it appears that the Institute differentiates itself principally by the way in which its study is mainly done and by the subsequent ways in which this study is expected to make for peace and co-operation.

As to method of study, the Institute aims to bring together in Conference equal national groups equally concerned to study afresh their situations of international difficulty. In this study the members seek such common understandings and such mutual sympathy as will best make for a practical clearing of the difficulties which menace. The study of the Institute is thus done largely under conditions of personal contact, the members of the various national groups meeting together in conference on equal terms. True enough, study in advance of the Conference is expected both from individuals and from the groups, and research of a high order is provided for by the Institute; but all such prior study—apart from further resulting study later to be noted—will find its characteristic functioning in the actual discussions of the Conference. In this procedure of joint-conference study, conducted mainly in round tables shared in common by the members of the participating national groups, we have a characterizing and differentiating feature of the first importance.

It will perhaps repay us to look further at this conception of joint study. Study, real study, study in its best and truest sense, and in fact the study of the Conference, does not contemplate the acceptance by learners of conclusions known in advance to others and by them expounded to those who would learn. It is not through lectures, nor even in seminars, that the study of the Conference is done. Rather does the Conference study mean a shared activity in which, as already stated, the members meet on equal terms, with the discussion leader serving, not as a professor in charge of a class, but at most as a moderator to help the round table do its own thinking. And search, joint search, is the characteristic of this shared study, a real search in which prior views are now honestly held plastic and subject to change and reorganization as the developing discussion may find and exhibit better and truer views. *Shared actual search* and *developing discussion* are here the significant conceptions indicating respectively the necessary attitude on the part of the members and the resulting successful procedure. Of course, so long as men are human, prior views will resist change and group attachments will obstruct; so that the ideal here presented will always fail, in some measure, of attainment. But the ideal remains clear. The Conference means through its discussion to conduct such real and impartial study as will reach fresh conclusions. It will hope also in the process to bring the participating members approximately together both in opinion and in attitude, or at any rate to bring them to a sympathetic understanding and appreciation of honestly held differences of opinion or attitude.

It may help our search to consider that discussion of the kind indicated above is properly called educative in the highest and best sense of that term. The members of the several national groups come together not in a contest to foist prior chosen views on each other. This would approximate propaganda, not education. In the aim of the Conference each member comes anxious only to see that pertinent facts are properly considered and related. Even if a member thinks that he has achieved better insight than have others, it is still true, in the ideal of the Conference, that he will wish his views to be considered only on their merits, and that he will hold these views as tentative, subject to the testing of the best available data. In the degree, then, that the members meet with such aims and seek thus the truth, in like degree will they in the process probably undergo change of both opinion and attitude. Such changes so sought and so affected are of the kind properly called education, and that of the highest type.

Propaganda, even of the better sort, stands in contrast with such an education. Good propaganda and bad agree in not expecting a change of view during the effort at propagandism. Bad propaganda will seek by deceit to persuade to its view. Even good propaganda so assumes the correctness of its own view as not to provide in the process place for a change of opinion. Opinions may change during the process, but propaganda as such is not concerned. Men, however, are fallible. The need for change may arise at any stage, and conscious thought should be given to it. Clearly higher then than any propaganda is the conference type of study which is consciously entered upon with intent to re-examine all positions, including one's own, and to "follow the argument" at whatever cost of prior opinion. It is on these grounds that the Conference can claim to be educative in the highest and best sense.

It will hardly need to be said that such educative discussion is possible only under favorable conditions. And the consideration of these conditions will in turn help us to see better the nature of the Conference. First of all, the Conference must know that while it may decide on researches and perhaps even on experiments, still, as regards any of its proper problems, it will reach no formal conclusions, adopt no resolutions, and formulate no programs. It may be that other discussion assemblies need not be so strictly bound, but it seems clear that if this Conference did any of these things, its discussions would no longer be a search only for the truth. They would cease to follow the argument. Frankness would disappear. Bargaining would ensue. So, further, if any member had official relationship with any foreign office, his own frankness—if no other's—would suffer. If all had such relationship, the Conference would entirely change its character. Publicity at the Conference also finds in this a limit set for itself, otherwise frankness is lessened. If everything said were liable to be published, members could hardly forget distant groups. A partisan press, both at home and elsewhere, stands ready to seize selfish advantage. The penalties and prizes which such a press offers would make honest and frank talking too hazardous to prevail. All these specific conditions thus set out as necessary to successful educative discussions in the Conference help us to conclude that the essential nature of the Institute is to be found in its educative character, and further, to see that certain conditions must be met if the Institute is to be itself.

If the method of the Institute in conference is thus essentially educative, so also, it would seem, does the hope of the Institute for further results remain dependent on education. This we must now consider.

As regards results, it may well be asked, How can any feasible changing of opinion or attitude at the Conference be expected to help the international situation? The members of the Institute are few in numbers and they stand in no official governmental relationship. How, then, can practical results be expected? For answer we may say that success at the Conference, in the degree that it has been attained, has meant not only common understanding and mutual sympathy; it has meant quite as much that the members of the Conference have returned home emotionally stirred to help forward the cause of international co-operation and good will. It is this further work and influence that can and should remain educative in character. Certain of the members, favorably connected, may quite immediately influence governmental action. If so, a better insight founded on the better-seen merits of the case will pass thus from conference to government official: an essentially educative process. Certain other members will use platform and press, while still others will influence schools, study groups, and other kindred organizations. But in all this the approach can be and should be educative rather than propagandic. It can be the process of impartial study that is promoted, rather than specific programs. The widening range of others so reached can be and should be encouraged to study and conclude for themselves. Any other procedure would be untrue either to the spirit of the Institute or to the best of ethics.

Still further, as has been suggested elsewhere recently, the Institute can perform a most significant service to the Pacific countries if its several constituent groups will resolutely study the movements and conduct of the various Pacific governments and peoples with their probable outcomes and faithfully report for criticism and amendment the results of their studies to each other in conference assembled. In the degree that this work can be well and faithfully done, in like degree may the Institute hope to influence the conduct of peoples and government and so help in bringing a real Pacific community into existence. But here again the hope is in the educative effect of what is done.

We may conclude, then, of the Institute, whether we look to its immediate method or to its further results, that it is essentially educative in character. If so, we should find in this the guidance we seek for the management of the Conference. As the aim is education and the method is study and discussion, our next inquiry may well be how to make the study and discussion most educative. For this purpose we may profitably make use of results worked out in the study of modern educational procedure.

### HOW TO MAKE DISCUSSION EDUCATIVE

In the treatment of this specific aspect of our topic, as elsewhere in the paper, apology should perhaps be made for the inclusion of the obvious. It seems wiser at times, even though most may not need it, to call to mind well-known matters which bear on the problem at hand. Here we are concerned with some facts about learning.

From what has already been said, discussion in the Institute has a twofold aim: first, to make the most effective possible study of the problem at hand, objectively considered, so as best to promote a satisfactory solution; second, to secure to all the participants the best attainable growth as concerns both their intellectual grasp of the matter at hand and their attendant attitudes of sympathy and appreciation. It is at once clear that the second aim states the educative outcomes sought, while the first gives the means through which these results must be attained. Educationally, then, we seek "intellectual grasp" and "attitudes of sympathy and appreciation." How, now, can the discussion be so conducted as to secure this "grasp" and these "attitudes"? How is grasp got, and how are attitudes built?

First, we acquire only as we practise. If we would acquire grasp, we must practice grasping. If we would acquire sympathy for others we must actually share their feelings. If we would acquire appreciation for the position held by another, we can fix such appreciation as a habitual attitude in character only through actually appreciating the other's position.

Second, it seems further true that the degree in which or with which any response is made affects the rapidity and the lastingness of the learning involved. If the stove is hot enough to burn sharply, the child learns the more quickly and permanently to keep his fingers away. Fulness of response helps the learning process. Thus, the more wholehearted one is in doing anything and the more he approves it during and after his doing, the more certain and lasting will be the learning.

These things will help us to decide how to manage the discussion in the round tables and forums. If we are seeking intellectual grasp, and are seeking it for all the members, then we shall wish the fullest possible participation of each and all in the discussions. We must know that the more fully each member can himself think through and appreciate each point as it comes up, the more will he get the point and the better will he organize it with other points to make a consistent and effective whole. The good discussion leader will then consistently refrain from telling the group what to think, and he will not allow such in others. Each one educates himself by the thinking he himself does. There is, moreover, a peculiar stimulation to think which comes from the give and take of face-to-face discussion, and in this quickness and brevity are essential factors. The good leader will therefore frown upon long statements. They benumb thinking. So also with statements prepared in advance. Not only are they generally too long and likely not to stick to the point; but, even more, their lack of present freshness often destroys their stimulating effect. The greatest stimulation the discussion can get comes from something said now because it is pertinent now. Widely shared, short and pithy give and take, properly directed as the subject unfolds, will as a rule bring best results to all concerned. It is in this way that the fullest and widest—and in the long run the most effective—thinking can be secured. It is thus that we shall attain in greatest degree the most widespread intellectual grasp of the matter at hand.

As regards building attitudes, there is little to add. At least some of the members will come to the discussion with the active wish to understand hitherto opposed positions, the wish so to locate and define differences as to make the why of difference easier to see and appreciate. Such a spirit at work will as a rule call out more of the same spirit in response. It is the hearty exercise of the spirit of sympathy and appreciation and the hearty approval of it when exercised that will build the attitudes we seek. It would seem then to follow, first, that members should as far as feasible be initially so chosen that they can and will come together in this spirit, and, second, that the discussion leader shall see to it as far as he can that the members so speak and act toward each other as best to call out the desired response attitudes. In such ways may we hope to make the discussion of the Conference best attain its educative needs.

### PRACTICAL MANAGEMENT OF THE ROUND TABLE

In the matter of size, it is easy to see that the round table should be neither too large nor too small. How large it can be will depend in part on the efficiency of the leader, in part on the difficulty of the topic, in part on the expertness of the membership. If the round table is too small, chance attitudes of individuals may prove overdominating. Besides, there will be too little variety of opinion and too little mutual stimulation.

As regards composition, the round table, since it is the Conference most characteristically at work, should as nearly as feasible be a cross-section of the entire Conference. Of course where different round tables are simultaneously discussing different topics this will be more difficult of accomplishment.

The choice of problems is a matter of no small moment. Not all matters are equally suitable for discussion. To be thus suitable a problem must be of general and real concern, else no widespread interest or effort. It must be single and definite, else the discussion will lack goal and criterion. It may happen that a situation of difficulty will upon examination yield more than one problem. If so, these several problems should be analyzed out, if possible in advance of round-table discussion, and arranged in some proper order for separate attack. Nothing is more ruinous to discussion than not to be able to settle down to one exclusive line of attack. To be suitable for discussion a problem must, further, lie within average grasp of the members, else there can be no inclusive discussion. A discussion limited to experts cannot be satisfactory. Problems, however insistent, that do not meet the conditions here laid down are probably better cared for elsewhere than in round tables.

### THE CHOICE AND PREPARATION OF DISCUSSION LEADERS

So strategic is the work of the discussion leader in the success of the Conference that this office should be considered solely as an expert service, and not at all as an honor or courtesy to be apportioned among the several national groups. The leaders should therefore be chosen exclusively for fitness to perform their specific work as guides to the discussion groups. Their national affiliation should not be considered. To lessen the ascription of honor it might be well never to publish either the name or nationality of the discussion leaders as such.

If danger arise that one nation or language hurtfully monopolize the post of leader, it might be well, where there are several parallel round tables, to appoint, in addition to the expert discussion leaders, a chairman for each such set of round tables. If care be taken to appoint to this post someone of assured ability in the field under discussion, he can render a real service in the pertinent deliberations before and after the round-table meetings. Under such circumstances this office of chairman would justly be considered an honor, and could be apportioned and published accordingly.

The qualifications of the successful discussion leader are more easily felt in the success of his performance than analyzed for helpful description. As regards a knowledge of the subjects to be discussed by the round tables, the leader need not be an expert in all or even in any of these specific subjects, though he will find ample opportunity to use all the pertinent knowledge that he may possess. This knowledge, however, he will use, not as an authoritative expert in the field. There is positive danger to the leader who thinks of himself as an expert lest he overmaster the discussion. Rather should the leader's knowledge of the subject help him to analyze fruitfully the developing discussion and thus to sense more quickly and surely the pertinence and significance of suggestions made and data proffered or withheld. The leader will accordingly need broad human interests and a criticized knowledge of human relationships in the field in which the problems are located, rather than expert knowledge of the specific problems under consideration. In a word, the leader's business is, not to supply the needed data for the discussion of the problem, but to sense the pertinence, or its lack, in the suggestions and data offered by others. Only in this way can he decide what is "the point" to which discussion must be held.

More important than knowledge are the personal qualities of the leader. He must be quick, though not hasty, to think and speak. Otherwise the discussion may run away with him and come to grief. He must be tactfully persistent in holding the discussion "to the point." The word "tact" here speaks volumes. Without it, irritation may ensue and disaster follow. Also, proper persistence must be fairly determined and not confused with the leader's private wishes or personal opinions.

Great pains must thus be taken in the choice of discussion leaders. Personal qualifications must be carefully canvassed and fitness evaluated. On this selection hangs much of the success of the conference.

Now it is a fact that both knowledge and technique can be improved by proper effort. The suggestion therefore seems good that the discussion leaders be chosen well in advance, as soon as the main lines of the program are fixed, and in number rather more than the maximum number of simultaneous round tables to be held. So chosen, the leaders can begin in advance to study for their duties. In particular, however, they should be assembled some days in advance of the Conference in order to study together, possibly under expert leadership, both the conduct of round tables and the specific topic to be discussed. These persons so selected and prepared should then be set aside to serve exclusively as discussion leaders for all the round tables and forums conducted by the Conference.

### THE SYLLABUS: HOW MADE AND HOW USED

It has seemed best to prepare a syllabus for each round-table meeting. This syllabus will serve two main functions: one to direct the thinking and study of the members of the Conference in advance of the round-table meeting, the other to help steer the process of discussion in the round table. Probably both functions are best served by putting the syllabus in the form of questions. To help in the advance study, suitable reading references should accompany the questions. Since, unfortunately, little time will be available for study, these references should be as easily accessible as possible, and fairly specific as regards chapter or page to the several questions on the syllabus.

To serve both of the functions named, the questions of the syllabus should be such as will in fact best call into play the thinking of the participants. To this end they must call attention to, and lay bare to thought, the several successive significant aspects of the problem under consideration. However, in framing questions to attain this aim great care must be taken not to supply ready-made thinking for the participants, in particular not to try to lead the discussion to any predetermined end, and of course to avoid every appearance of partiality as regards the merits of any matter likely to be in dispute.

The formulation of a syllabus may be the work of various hands. In general two sets of thinkers must co-operate. First will be those who, as experts in the subject matter, know so well the situation of difficulty that they can with reasonable probability foretell the most important problems that will emerge, and within like limits can anticipate the most promising attack or attacks upon these problems. The second group to help make the questions will be those who are so familiar with discussion work that they will know how to frame such questions as will effectually cause the members of the round table to think through the matter set for discussion.

Probably in most cases questions can be made in advance which will with fair success both lead the advance study and guide the resulting discussion. But each discussion leader must be free to let the discussion develop along other lines than those written down in advance, if at the time another course seems better. Always the discussion leader and round-table members must together have final authority to decide the course they will follow.

### THE MANAGEMENT OF DISCUSSION

A well-chosen problem for a conference round table is one which has its setting and matrix in some situation of international difficulty, some sore spot where contrary interests clash and the opposed sides are at least in danger of failure to understand and sympathize with each other. The direct business of the round table, as opposed to its indirect aim of building attitudes, is thus through its discussion to compass three successive steps: (1) to understand the opposed difficulties of the situation, (2) to come to clear consciousness of the problem thus set, and (3) to move as far as possible toward a solution of the problem satisfactory to all concerned.

These three steps should as a rule be followed consciously and in the order named. While so doing the discussion leader will hold in mind certain conditions necessary to success: one, to keep vigorous discussion going; another, to enlist as many members in the discussion as possible; a third, to make sure that each side or party to the difficulty feels that all the significant aspects of its case are adequately presented. Some chairmen, in order to make sure both that nothing drags and that a full opening case is made out, will ask certain better-informed members to prepare in advance statements to be presented to the round table. This type of advance preparation is, as has already been suggested, generally a mistake, defeating its own aim. Most such statements are lengthy and dull, and give the round table a bad start. As a rule it will suffice for the discussion leader to elicit directly from the round table the several counts, one by one, in the situation of difficulty, one count from one member. "Divide and conquer" holds here as elsewhere. It seems probable that the several items are usually better seen and grasped if they are brought out in this fashion. Any doubt or obscurity regarding any one can be cleared then and there. Also, being better grasped, the counts are better remembered. Further, more members having participated, more members have profited. Whoever contributes in a discussion thereby gives hostages to further interest and participation. Moreover, as we have seen, to participate is as a rule the shortest road to appropriation. Personal action helps personal grasp. Contrariwise, merely to listen with no thought of other or further reaction is as a rule the poorest road to personal grasp. It may be added that, other things being equal, a voluntary contribution is superior to one elicited by the chairman. Having the tang of personal initiative, it proves more stimulating both to speaker and to hearers.

In spite, however, of all the foregoing consideration, it may at times happen that certain necessary facts are not sufficiently widespread among the members to be thus elicited. In such case recourse must be had to some authoritative statement. This may be demanded by any one round table or by all in joint session. If a joint meeting is to be held, it may prove administratively easier to hold it at the beginning, before the round tables begin their work; but from considerations of interest and learning effects it would as a rule be far better to hold such a meeting after the need has been felt.

The task of the first step as just given is essentially that of locating the problem, finding the generating situation and cause of the difficulty or divergence under consideration. It may be that the opposed groups are looking at different sets of facts, or that they are differently interpreting the same set of facts. It may be that one group has misunderstood the position of an opposed group. More usually there is actual conflict of interests which manifests itself also in one or more of the foregoing differences. Whatever be the opposed elements in the situation, where ever the difference may lie, it is the task of this first step so to locate the opposition and difference as to define more clearly the problem and difficulty for more hopeful attempts at solution. For the sake of facilitating practical solutions it is also important to seek and note here and elsewhere in connection the points of agreement both among the members and among the various parties concerned with the issue.

One result of discussion under this head may be to single out areas for subsequent research. An impartial study of pertinent facts by the appropriate experts may ultimately give such light and confidence as will lead both sides far along the road to agreement. Herein is to be found the principal justification of research as a main function of the Institute.

The second step in our analysis, the formulation of the problem, needs little discussion. It is usually wise to formulate the problem consciously and formally. A proper statement of the problem is necessary both to facilitate the search for a solution and to furnish a criterion for testing solutions. Here especially, but in lesser degree throughout, regard must be had to terms to see that all are using them in the same sense.

The third step, the proposal and evaluation of solutions, will naturally require the most of the available time. Under fortunate conditions actual lines of a solution may be found. More usually, however, the best that can be hoped for is to discover and state in a satisfactory manner the conditions which seem necessary to be met if a permanent solution of the problem is to be attained or a proper community of interest is to be established. In all of this the discussion leader must have a defined procedure, else confusion may reign amid many proposals and shifting criticisms. It matters little what precise procedure is followed, provided it cover the ground, be known and accepted by the round table, and be in fact followed. The leader must, however, be alert not to adhere to his defined plan in such way to lose a really promising lead through any bare mechanics of discussion management.

In connection with all the foregoing it may be stated that in general the discussion leader exists to help the round table mobilize its own thought resources and direct these to the attack of the problem at hand. As one member of the round table, he has a right to the expression of his own opinion, but the exercise of this right is limited by his duties as leader. In particular he must not lecture. He must not use his position of authority to secure for his own opinions a favored hearing. It of course follows from the nature of the Institute that the leader is not to control or guide the discussion to any prior and externally chosen end. On the contrary, it is his specific function so to sense the current of thought developing freely among the members as to find in it his lead and criteria for guidance.

If the discussion leader is sufficiently skilful, he can help significantly in this process by making from time to time summaries of progress to date. These may indicate the trend of discussion and agreements apparently reached or they may indicate significant differences of opinion that seem to be emerging. At times even capable members will lose the wood for the trees. If the leader can succeed in making summaries that do in fact bring to clearer consciousness the group's own thinking or lack thereof, a signal service has been rendered. An inclusive summary at the close will, if well made, bring to many members a surer satisfaction of achievement accomplished and give them something more definite to take away as a result of discussion. The part of the discussion leader is thus to help an internally developing process to direct itself more truly and adequately from within. Those who believe in democracy will see in this how essentially identical is the democratic process at its best with the process of group thinking here upheld.

In conclusion, one important function of the tactful leader requires a second mention. He must see to it that as large a proportion as possible of the members participate fruitfully in discussion. This as a means and measure of success ranks almost equally with the actual emergence of excellent ideas. As suggested earlier, voluntary contributions are the best; but many members are hesitant. Oftentimes the leader may by a glance or word induce some reticent member to contribute information or doubts which would otherwise be repressed. In particular the leader must see to it that those whose English is uncertain shall not thereby be kept from participating effectually in the discussion. In an extreme case it may be necessary to make special arrangements for this in advance, even to the extent, if necessary, of having a short statement written out in advance for reading to the round table. So far as is humanly possible, no national group should ever have occasion to feel that it is denied fair participation in the consideration of a problem in which it feels concern.

### THE PLACE OF THE EXPERT

The function of the expert has perhaps been sufficiently misunderstood to demand a word as to his proper part in the round-table discussion. Considering the aim of the Institute and the educative process by which the round table works toward this aim, we may say, negatively, that the expert is not to furnish an authoritative solution to the problem under discussion. If he were in fact capable of doing this and it were only necessary for him to inform others of his solution, then there would be no need for a round table on that topic. His written or oral statement of the solution should suffice. Nor are two opposed, and thus, fallible, experts to be pitted against each other to conduct a high grade dialogue and contest in which the lesser members of the round table shall be informed what to think. If the matter at hand be so technical that only the experts can discuss it intelligently, then it is of doubtful fitness for the ordinary round table; some other way should be contrived for treating such a topic. The expert is not to take the "spot light" in either of these fashions.

In a word, the expert as such is present to furnish more exact knowledge when and because it is needed as data in the course of discussion. The solution belongs to the members themselves. The chairman or any member should feel free to appeal to the expert to furnish knowledge; and the expert himself should feel free to volunteer it when he conceives the discussion to be going astray through lack of it. Of course, as a member of the round table the expert enjoys all the rights of any member to express himself properly on any matter under discussion. It is only as expert that his duties limit this right.

### THE PRESENCE OF "DIE-HARD" ADVOCATES

Question has arisen as to whether the Conference has included sufficient variety of position, in particular whether care should not be taken to include within the membership certain of those determined advocates popularly known as "die-hards."[1] As to this two positions are possible and both actually do present themselves. One position is that until the Institute has gathered fuller momentum the presence of "die-hard' advocates as full members of the Conference would, though otherwise desirable, too much hurt the discussion. The argument for this is that the best results depend on a general step-by-step reconstruction of opinion and attitude among the participants as the discussion advances. In this process of reconstruction, so it will be urged, no ultimate "die-hard" will share. Moreover, his discussion may easily prove so irritating to some as to make their reconstruction less probable. Those who

[1] "Die-hard" is here used to describe a state of mind, not any particular political or economic point of view. The "die-hard" mind-set may characterize people whose opinions may be regarded as either conservative or radical.

hold this position thus question the advisability of admitting thoroughgoing "die-hards" to full membership in the Conference. The other, and probably the majority, position is that without full and actual representation of all pertinent opinions, "die-hard" included, there cannot be adequate consideration of the really difficult problems that face the Conference. In fact, so it will be urged, if the Conference is to face the actualities of this world and not merely engage in wishful thinking, the presence of the "die-hard" is a most essential factor. Morover, if such be excluded because they are difficult to convince, the world at large may well question the seriousness of the Institute's purpose. While the two positions are here stated as if they were precisely mutual exclusives, it does not seem necessary so to conclude. Probably the best plan, as often happens, is to seek such an intermediate course as promises to get as much as possible of the good desired by each side with as little as possible of the evil feared. Tact and consideration for the feelings of others, and even open-mindedness, are quite consistent with deep-seated convictions. Proper care in the choice of membership may go far toward meeting all the needs of the situation.

### THE FORUM

So far the Conference has not succeeded so well with its forums as with its round tables. Possibly in the nature of the case it never can. At any rate it seems probable that further experimentation will be necessary before a reliable procedure is established. For purposes of the present discussion it is necessary to distinguish the forum from other types of joint meetings. The forum may be either a joint session of parallel round tables or it may be the whole Conference attacking some problem independently of round-table discussion, whether preceding or succeeding. The essence of the forum is thus large-scale discussion. It will differ from the round table in size. Also it may, but not must, differ in that it expects the major part of the discussion, either the exchange of opinion or the giving of data, to be more limited to the better informed than is proper for the round table. There may also be a prearrangement of program not suitable in the round table. Clash of opinion with spontaneous discussion, however, should always be sought. Without this a forum can hardly be a success.

If a forum is then to succeed other than as a debate or as a series of interesting addresses, that is, if it is to succeed as a forum, it must meet several conditions. First, in addition to whatever report of round-table progress may be made there must emerge a real conflict of opinion about a matter of common concern. Second, there must be, both in expectation and in resulting fact, a spontaneous participation of members, and the more widespread this can be the better. Third, the discussion must not be haphazard; it must "get somewhere"; that is, it must proceed in orderly fashion toward completeness.

Can any suggestions be made for meeting these conditions? At the outset, in the judgment of this writer, it should be understood that no forum will be held simply as a matter of course. Unless there is something that needs to be discussed in forum fashion there should be no forum. The burden of proof is on those who propose to hold one. And "face" is not an argument. The time of the Conference is too valuable and failure is too hurtful. If a forum is to be held independently of round-table discussion the Program Committee will, of course, be the agency to provide for it. Most forums, however, will grow out of the work of the round tables and be arranged for in conference of the chairman of the round tables with the discussion leaders and secretaries and one or more representatives of the Program Committee. At such a conference each forum may report its definition of the problems distinguished and of terms used, a statement of its agreements, a diagnosis of its significant differences, and such constructive suggestions as may have emerged. If upon consideration a forum seems desirable, this conference will then proceed to make one joint report to be presented to the forum. This report will show especially significant agreements, distinguishing probably those common to all round tables from those reached only in some. It may also show divergences of opinion, including some not expected to provoke discussion. This report should be printed and distributed at the forum. The main preparation for the forum, however, will be the finding or selection of certain concrete issues or suggestions that demand further discussion before the whole Conference. It is this which must justify holding a forum.

As discussion is thus an essential feature of the forum, care must be taken to secure the most competent management possible. The proper person will usually be the most skilled of the discussion leaders acquainted with the matter under review. The chairman of the Conference, perhaps better the chairman of the round tables, will open the meeting, introduce the discussion leader, and formally give to him full charge of the discussion. This leader, in company with others best acquainted with the matter, should in advance of the forum have already come to agreement as to the field of the discussion for the meeting, and he should, under all ordinary conditions, hold the discussion within the field and see that development takes place. The whole point is to have under competent leadership a real discussion of developing character on a topic of genuine interest. The forum, of course, may or may not be open to the public, depending upon the topic under discussion. For many reasons it is desirable to have as many meetings open as possible, but some certainly will have to be closed.

### INFORMAL DISCUSSIONS

In the degree that the Conference succeeds with round table and forum, in like degree should there result a demand for all sorts of informal "follow up" discussions of interests aroused by the more formal discussions. In fact, the number and seriousness of these informal discussions may well be taken as the measure of the immediate success of the Conference. This being so, it would seem wise to see that more free time should be available for such. Adequate free time might be found in the afternoons and evenings. This would be feasible in the afternoons if the social entertainments were sufficiently abridged. As regards the evening, time would be available if the evening meetings were often of a more popular character. The Conference could then split. Those so wishing could hold their informal discussions. Others would find interesting entertainment at the popular lectures.

## SECTION 32

# THE HUMAN POTENTIAL IN PACIFIC POLITICS

HERBERT CROLY
Editor, *New Republic,* New York

## I

Last summer there assembled in Honolulu a body which called itself the Institute of Pacific Relations. It consisted of delegations from many of the countries which inhabit the shores of the Pacific Ocean or exercise power upon its waters. There were representatives present from China, Japan, New Zealand, Australia, Korea, the Philippines, Canada, Great Britain, and the United States.[1] I have called them representatives, but the representation was wholly unofficial. The delegates were members of national groups who had reason to be interested in the economics and politics of the Pacific and hoped by study and conference to increase their insight into the conditions of human life and intercourse throughout that vast area. The organizers of the conference had planned to assemble a body of men and women who belonged to all the nations of the Pacific and who took part in most of the essential activities of their respective communities; but they did not wholly succeed. There was a preponderance of intellectuals and reformers and a scarcity of men or women of affairs. But they were an unusually able, well-informed and disinterested lot of people, who brought more candor and fewer ulterior purposes to a discussion of the politics of the Pacific than would any body whose members had been more formally and officially chosen.

With the process, the story, and the results of the conference, I do not propose, except incidentally, to deal. They are of interest and value chiefly to the people who participated in the gathering, and it is only a pallid or perverted version of them which can be passed on to an absent spectator. In fact, I doubt the possibility of fairly summarizing the proceedings of such a miscellaneous, informal, discursive, and loosely organized body, and my personal interpretation of what took place could not be properly checked save by somebody else who was also present. But it is possible and worth while to call the attention of people who did not attend the conference, but are interested in its subject matter, to the meaning which the Institute of Pacific Relations came to have for some of the conferees. It seems to be, when you examine it carefully, a new thing in the universe of politics. If such is the case, I should like to distinguish wherein it is new and what the opportunities and penalties of its novelty may be.

The Institute of Pacific Relations proposes for the first time a political function

[1] Invitations were sent to appropriate persons in Mexico and the Soviet Republic, but it was impossible for them to accept.

for an exclusively inquisitive and deliberative international parliament which, from a severely practical point of view, may seem to be of doubtful utility. Politics is, of course, chiefly a matter of getting things done. It proceeds by means of legislative and administrative acts, of decisions, or, in self-governing communities, of discussions which result in resolutions and decisions. But the conference of the Pacific Institute, instead of, as is usual with political bodies, acting without sufficient deliberation, deliberates without any attempt to act and without any intention of acting or deciding. It is, if you please, a lily in the farmyard of politics. It toils not, neither does it spin, in the ordinary sense of indorsing expedients or outlets which may be of comfort to a statesman who is harassed by the exigency of events or puzzled by a conflict of counsel. Its members plumed themselves on its sterility in this respect. They investigated and discussed elaborately and solemnly a multitude of questions; they decided none. They did not pass any resolutions except an explicit one to adjourn and an implicit one to congratulate themselves on their own urbanity and humility.

The Institute believes that it cannot conscientiously and intelligently carry on its work of deliberation and investigation without renouncing the attempt to reach decisions. It is justified in this belief. It does not form a body which is adapted to action or capable thereof. Its members, either as individuals or as collected into national groups, do not represent anything in particular. They do not represent their governments or the policy of their governments. They do not represent any common set of interests, activities, convictions, traditions, or culture. They are not united by any recognized legal economic responsibilities. Having no meaning or focus as a vehicle of action, they properly avoided the attempt to reach decisions or to pass resolutions which, in the circumstances, would have been equivalent to action. So far as I know, there was no dissent among any members of the conference against the limitation of its function to that of "study," mutual consultation, and research.

On the other hand, here was a difference of opinion among its members as to the meaning of its indecisive activities. Many of them believed, or at least acted on the belief, that, although the conference did not commit itself to specific decisions or resolutions, its work was preparing the way for specific action by official agencies. They talked a good deal about proposing "constructive solutions" for critical economic and political problems. They assumed that any sprigs of understanding that the Conference gathered during its deliberations might be planted in the popular mind and developed into propaganda for the benefit of particular acts by particular governments. They conceived the Institute as a sort of general counsel for a society of Pacific peoples which an official department of operations would subsequently bring into existence.

This interpretation of the functions of the Institute appears to me doubtful, and, if acted on, may lead it astray. The Institute should, I think, refrain from toiling in order to spin political fabrics, even by indirection. Its function is really novel and more radical than these delegates seemed to realize. It is an experiment in the use of the understanding in elucidating and integrating political relationships. If it carries on its work with any success, it may eventually exercise an important influence on the world of affairs in the Pacific; but considering the extent to which, at present, action in politics tends to corrupt understanding, it should, if it is in earnest about exploring its subject matter, avoid any primary concern with the specific exigencies of politics. It is, at bottom, trying to find out whether an experiment in understanding among peoples of a particular area may not, by a beguiling and a discipline of the popular imagination, eventually result in the birth of a new kind of community—a community in which government would be divorced from authority, statecraft from party politics, officialism from prestige, and society from any explicit obligations or compulsions except the obligations of its members somehow to live together. Such is the only kind of community which can be formed, for the present, out of the raw materials of the Pacific area.

## II

Let us consider, for a moment, the significance of the selection by the Institute of the Pacific Ocean as an area of profitable political association, consultation, and deliberation. Political communities have come into existence, for the most part, through the habitation of adjacent neighborhoods by people who, as the result of having to live together, developed a common language, a common culture, and some measure of common allegiance. Large bodies of water have placed obstacles in the way of political association among the peoples who navigated their highways. These obstacles were so considerable that they could be overcome only by prolonged intercourse, by elaborate organization, by an advanced political technique, and by a consciousness of common interests and destiny. The Mediterranean was the first of the seas or oceans which served as a means of educative communication among the inhabitants of its shores. It enabled peoples with wholly different economies, cultures, and loyalties to exchange products, inventions, methods, and ideas without, in the beginning, entering into political responsibilities one toward another. Classic civilization was, more than anything else, Mediterranean. It could have come into existence only as the result of many kinds of intercourse by water among societies which themselves were local territorial products. But the members of these communities went to sea in ships not only to trade, to colonize, and to satisfy their curiosity, but, as they became politically more self-conscious, to plunder and subjugate one another. Classic civilization culminated politically in the Roman Empire, which profited by the previous cosmopolitanism both of Carthage and Magna Graecia. It was a water-made community. Its symbol, the Roman eagle, was, it is true, a bird of prey, but, being a bird, it also symbolized flight and seeing from afar, and a dominion which was derived from exploration.

The Roman Empire and classic civilization finally succumbed partly to internal decay and partly to a deluge of invading peoples who traveled in hordes and by land only. The invaders created a new community, Europe by name, whose conscious bond was, in the beginning, religious rather than political, and which continued for centuries to be formed almost entirely by territorial intercourse among a variety of peoples. Prompted both by restlessness and religion, they tried to override their territorial limits by marching against the Mohammedans on their eastern frontiers, but they were thrown back. They could not escape from Europe by a land route. After, however, a thousand years of self-regarding provincialism, which is one result of intercourse with others only or chiefly by land, they did finally escape by sea. Improvements in the art of navigation changed the Atlantic Ocean from an impassable barrier into a water highway which opened up communications with both the East and the West. It served as the water area about which progressive human beings traded, colonized, explored, and fought. Modern Europe owes almost as much to the Atlantic as the Roman Empire and classic civilization did to the Mediterranean.

Europe, however, in spite of its Atlantic voyages, has not yet freed itself from the remnants of its ancestral provincialism. Their relations to their neighbors on the Continent formed the conscious political outlook of its peoples and the politics of its governments. When European navigators embarked upon Atlantic voyages, they did so either to get away from Europe or to promote European interests. They occupied the unoccupied territory on the other side of the Atlantic for the founding of European colonies. They exterminated or subjugated the inhabitants of the occupied territories. They conceived the New World as a minor subdivision of the old. This attitude toward America, which was an inevitable result of the aboriginal savagery of the new continents, outlasted, however, the conditions out of which it had sprung. Throughout the nineteenth century, although the era of American colonization was over, Europeans still envisaged the Atlantic Ocean as a European area, bounded on the west by certain American tributaries. Europe recognized, of course, the political independence of some of these American communities, but it was recognition with reservations to which Americans subscribed. It was generally, but not too explicitly, assumed that, no matter how explosively Americans asserted the right to govern themselves, they had not achieved equality at the same time as independence. Their peoples were culturally European. Proud as they were of their political autonomy, they agreed with Europeans in acting and thinking as if Europe were the exclusive home of high and mighty politics.

Their cultural colonialism as well as their political and economic immaturity prevented the American communities, the United States included, from presuming to assert themselves in Atlantic affairs in any but a negative way. In so far as the Atlantic Ocean was not a liquid extension of Europe, it was not dominated by any positive political ideas. It was patrolled by the British fleet, whose overlords in London believed the maintenance of the balance of military power in Europe to be the one all-important international political interest. If, now and then, European statesmen allowed the New World on the other side of the Atlantic to enter into their calculations, they invoked it, as Canning did, to restore the balance in the old, or, like Louis Napoleon, to provide an opportunity for an increase of European empire. The retort of the United States was, of course, the Monroe Doctrine; but its proclamation was no more than a defensive reaction. It separated the presumably superior international politics of Europe from the presumably inferior international politics of the Americas. Thus the Atlantic Ocean, while it united the two continents for purposes of trade, divided them for purposes of politics. No European or American political speculator proposed an institute of Atlantic relations. From the point of view of the controlling political ideas, such an institute would have been, at best, a well-intentioned absurdity.

The World War brought to an end the efficacy and the authority of European domination in the Atlantic. The United States, when it entered the war as a protest against the interference by the German submarine with the customary highways of trade between America and Europe, intervened, indeed, in the ostensible interest of British sea power, which had been the instrument used for subordinating the politics of the Atlantic to European continental interests; but European statesmen suddenly revolutionized their ideas about the essential nature of European interests and American obligations. Both groups of belligerents insisted on fighting for a victory which was bound to destroy rather than to preserve any balance of military power in Europe. The Allies were victorious, and by annihilating, with the help of the United States, this old and powerful dragon of European politics, they entirely altered the political significance of the Atlantic highway. This result was no part of the war aims of the American people. They had intervened from sympathetic and sentimental motives, which their cultural colonialism had enabled French and British propaganda skilfully to kindle into a conflagration. The policy of emasculating Germany, which was implicit in the knockout blow of Lloyd George and *la victoire intégrale* of Clemenceau, was more congenial to the average American than Wilson's Fourteen Points. As soon as the danger of defeat for the Allies and the romance of the crusade were over, the Americans immediately felt ill at ease in Europe and far from home. The expeditionary force, in crossing the Atlantic, had violated an alien body of water. America might be a part of Europe; but Europeans had never admitted, nor had Americans imagined, that Europe might be part of America. The tradition of separatism resumed its former authority. The New World, in the person of the United States, withdrew precipitately to its side of the dividing water.

The withdrawal brought upon the American people bitter criticism at home and abroad, and it was, undoubtedly, a cheap and easy way of shifting a responsibility which they had assumed with sufficient solemnity. But it was also an instinctive retreat on their part from an exposed and costly position which they had entered in an excited and perverted moment, without understanding what they were doing. Their discomfiture was clearly a consequence of the failure of European statesmen during the nineteenth century to move in the direction of an international system which envisaged the Atlantic Ocean as a highway of communication among political equals. Yet, in unconditionally withdrawing, the American nation had acted to prolong European pretensions which, although they had not been expressly abandoned, the War had tended to deflate. It was no longer possible to conceive the Atlantic Ocean as a gusty pool of European politics, tempered by the Monroe Doctrine. The Washington Conference subsequently divided power in the Atlantic between Europe, represented by Great Britain, and America, represented by the United States. For the present, the United States insists on preserving this division; but eventually it will have to adjust itself to the assumption of co-operative, even if expressly limited, liabilities in Europe.

It is profoundly significant that the Washington Conference of 1921, which, by dividing sea power between the British Empire and the United States, destroyed the physical basis of the traditional conception of the Atlantic Ocean as a liquid extension of Europe, looked in the direction also, of a new conception of the Pacific. During the nineteenth century European statesmen had treated the Pacific as a vast and distant, but less troublesome, bay of the Atlantic—an Atlantic minus the Monroe Doctrine. Politics in the western Pacific was either frankly predatory or it was subordinated to the exigencies of a conflict between two groups of powers in Europe which, after 1900, rapidly became increasingly dangerous and tense. British sea power furnished the physical major premise of Far Eastern politics. Early in the twentieth century it employed the Japanese fleet as its local partner, the understanding being that Japan would share in the game of European imperialism and take part in the European effort to transfer to the Far East the methods and interests of European international politics. The Far Eastern system collapsed, of course, with the collapse of its model in the Atlantic. As the result of American pressure, Great Britain abandoned the Japanese alliance, and Japan soon thereafter ceased to pursue a policy in China which imitated the former policies of the European powers and which she could not pursue without the connivance either of the United States or Great Britain. The Washington Conference treated the Pacific, for the first time, as a somewhat independent political and economic area. It even outlined the sketch of a Pacific regional community, which, if it could be realized and developed, would neutralize the Pacific highway as an instrument of predatory politics. As a result partly of the Four Power compact, and partly of the limitations imposed upon the battle fleets of Japan and the United States, it practically excluded from the navigation of the Pacific (except in Chinese waters) vessels which were bound upon errands of political and military aggression—unless Great Britain, Japan, and the United States all agreed to the aggression and participated in it.

This beginning of a Pacific society of nations, rudimentary and frail though it was, introduced into maritime politics a novel principle which it applied to the largest, most varied, and most important oceanic area in the world. From the beginning of international law there had been many attempts to neutralize the ocean, but they had not succeeded to any great extent. During the great war, as during the French Revolutionary and Napoleonic wars, the oceans were treated as part of the territory of the power which possessed the dominant fleet; and since the League of Nations was formed, it has never presumed to claim jurisdiction even of the European waters and to label them as an international area. The Washington Conference, on the other hand, did in some measure internationalize the Pacific. If the waters of that ocean were, by virtue of an international agreement, not in the future to be troubled by ships which were bound on aggressive or predatory errands, its navigation would become in every respect an agency of positive human intercourse and understanding. The Pacific would serve as the inviolate highway of a society of nations whose members on its shores would all enjoy some measure of political security, autonomy, and equality. No doubt powerful maritime nations, such as the United States, Japan, and Great Britain, would continue to possess legal rights in the territory of Pacific islands and in Eastern Asia, which derived from predatory expeditions of the past, and the beneficiaries of these pockets of imperialistic politics would have an interest in contesting the future development of a Pacific society of nations. But these powers, however any one or all of them behave in the future, have consented to the first essential step. The peoples of the Pacific are partially protected in theory against any further aggression, and in this sense they are by way of forming a community of political equals which are obligated to consult one another about their common political and economic difficulties and policies.

The Pacific society of nations remains, however, a sketch which may easily be wiped out. It is, in fact, certain to be wiped out unless the Pacific peoples are fascinated by the advantages and the possibilities of the sketch and do something to substantiate it. Their governments are not disposed or qualified to undertake the job. Like all governments, they do not act until they have to act; and, when they act, they are inevitably more preoccupied by their existing legal rights than by revolutionary visions of experimental communities of nations. If, in the meantime, the work of filling in the sketch is to be carried on, unofficial agencies which will act, not in opposition to existing governments, but wholly independent of declared national policies, will have to do it. The Institute of Pacific Relations has elected itself to this position. Its object is to give reality to the vision of the Pacific as an area of positive political association among the inhabitants of its shores, and in this respect it is, as I have said, a political novelty. It is not only attempting to bring into existence a new political community bound together by an internationalized body of water, but it is forced by its own nature to invoke for its purposes a method exclusively of inquiry, study, and consultation which heretofore has never been employed successfully in order to create a going political concern.

## III

An institute of this kind has, of course, an obvious justification. If a regional community of Pacific peoples be a desirable international society and if the governments of the more powerful Pacific nations have, by issuing a self-denying ordinance against aggression, rendered such a community possible, why not anticipate further action on the part of these governments in a constructive direction by setting up an international agency whose business it will be to compare the vision of the new society with the facts of existing political and economic policy and life in the Pacific? Assuming that it includes representatives from all the important peoples of the Pacific and covers in its surveys all their important political and economic activities, such an institute is peculiarly adapted to explore the idea of such a community, and to comprehend the activities which are helping to make or unmake it. If the institute summoned periodic conferences to compare and discuss the experience and the inquiries of its national groups, its gatherings would literally play at being parliaments of a Pacific society of nations. They would go through all the motions of a parliament in dealing with these questions, except the costly final motion of reaching or recommending decisions. Thus they would diagnose for the benefit of statesmen, and dramatize for the benefit of public opinion, the conception of the Pacific as the connecting medium of an international community whose parts could not obtain unity save by conscious co-operation.

This description of Pacific conferences as assemblies which play at being parliaments will not recommend the institute to the man of affairs, whether in business or politics. He can demur with a great deal of force that, in refusing to pay the price of reaching decisions, a conference of the Pacific Institute will expose its deliberations to an extreme danger of unreality. In politics it is usually compulsory to reach decisions, and the compulsion is very often urgent. Particularly when a question of war or peace is involved, the decision is likely to demand a choice between two partial evils or partial goods, and these choices, when they go wrong, bring with them the most disastrous and irrevocable consequences. A parliament which, in dealing with vexatious questions of this kind, avoids decisions and falls back, let us say, on further investigation and consultation is evading the spearhead of the problem. Practical politics, like war, is largely made up of snap decisions which have to be taken on insufficient evidence and in an atmosphere vitiated by greed, ignorance, hurry, propaganda, passion, intolerance, and exclusive interests. Would not a political lily, such as an institute of this kind, need a glass case in order to protect it from rough weather; and, in that event, would it not be smothered for lack of air?

This objection is not fatal, but it contains an amount of truth which the friends of the Institute will do ill to ignore. It is not fatal, because the partial internationalization of the waters of the Pacific and the disposition to safeguard its peoples against aggression will diminish the number, the urgency, and the exclusiveness of the choices which may be necessary in conducting the politics of the Pacific. Knots which formerly would have been cut by intervention will be given a chance to unravel. If they will not unravel and intervention is supposed to be necessary, it probably will not take place except by the unanimous consent of the nations with fleets. Interference from abroad has not as yet interrupted or frustrated the Chinese Revolution, as it would have done before the war. But while exclusive decisions no longer make up the stuff of politics in the Pacific, as they formerly did both in the Pacific and the Atlantic, they reman for the present the terminal realities of practical politics. An institute which will not pay the price of precipitating decisions, but which is, nevertheless, trying to spin a political fabric for early use, will not avoid the penalties of playing politics; while the kind of politics which it plays will, as a consequence of its virtuous intentions, compromise the thoroughness of its inquisition. In the case of China, for instance, it is probable that the question for or against intervention, with or without the company of all the other maritime powers, will, during the next fifty years, have to be decided several times by the Japanese, the British, and the American governments. A society of Pacific nations will be promoted or retarded, perhaps even made or unmade, as the result of these decisions. If the Institute is playing politics even indirectly it will try to influence decisions of this kind which will have to be reached to a large extent in the dark.

The existence of this dilemma was recognized by the conference of the Institute in certain of its proceedings; but it was not, I think, recognized in its full force. Nor was the better way out of it sharply enough distinguished. Probably a majority of the conferees believed that, while the Institute could not survive if it sought to reach decisions, it could inoffensively perform at least three highly realistic services. It could dig up information which would help statesmen to reach sound decisions; it could indicate the direction which a decision should take; and in certain cases it could, by the weight of its testimony and authority, affirm principles which would have a salutary influence on particular decisions. A case in point was the behavior of the conference toward the question of feeding the inhabitants of an island like Japan, who are increasing at the rate of almost 900,000 a year and who cannot, because of the policy of other Pacific nations, export in sufficient quantities either population or goods. The conference did not, of course, explicitly recommend any way of dealing with this problem, but the various speakers tended to indorse the Japanese contention that the other Pacific peoples ought to modify their own policies in order to take care of the Japanese increase in population. If they were not willing to accept Japanese immigrants, it was their duty to provide Japan with raw materials and to buy from her more and more manufactured products, and thus help her to support her increasing population.

This, as it seems to me, is a good illustration of a doubtful way of trying to give reality to the proceedings of the Institute. While the Institute did not explicitly act, it did, by the emphasis of its discussion, affirm a certain problem of Japanese policy to be primarily international. It implied, consequently, that in any future recognized scheme of international obligations the Japanese could fairly demand a market for either their population or their products in other countries up to the limit of their own self-determined necessities. In implicitly affirming this principle, it was, I think, perverting its own proper function and misleading the Japanese. For the Japanese surely are not entitled to export either their population or their manufactures to other countries in larger quantities than those countries are disposed to take, unless they have tried persistently and intelligently to reduce the volume of their surplus population; and this is precisely what the Japanese have not as yet done. Doubtless they cannot do it without experimenting with social control in a realm of individual conduct which, from the point of view of Japanese social ethics, should be inviolate; but if the Japanese are unwilling or unable to regulate their increase in population, they cannot reasonably ask another country to modify its tariffs or its immigration laws in order to take care of the fruits of Japanese irresponsibility. It is beginning to look as if there can be no effective future socialization of human life and no stable international pacification unless the progressive societies set up an intelligent censorship over the increase of population. If this is true, and the Japanese are unable or unwilling to play their part in controlling the menace of overpopulation, it is they, rather than their associates in the Pacific, who are ignoring international obligations.

The conference would, I think, have behaved more realistically if, instead of practically succumbing to the Japanese contention, it had taken the opportunity to reaffirm its own inquisitorial function. All that the Japanese can fairly ask of such a body as the Institute is a dispassionate, an exhaustive, and a continuing study of the extremely important question which they had raised. The Institute cannot give reality to its own proceedings and to the idea of a society of Pacific peoples either by proposing or accepting solutions for particular problems chiefly on the ground of international generosity. If its members assume it to be in search of solutions which can be labeled international and allow their minds to be influenced by this assumption, they are almost certain, when they collide with the ugly and unmanageable dilemmas of practical politics, to indulge in the historic weakness of liberal politicians and publicists. They will try to avoid the dilemmas and satisfy their own consciences by proclaiming pious aspirations or ambiguously virtuous principles, and allegiance to these principles will prevent them from examining disinterestedly the consequences of particular proposals or decisions.

A research institute which is devoted to the exploration of a lofty but remote and unprecedented vision of a Pacific community is, in truth, not equipped to extricate governments from international crises, particularly when they arise from the faulty past experience of the Pacific peoples. It may and should help to create the inquisitive public opinion in the various countries of the Pacific which may prevent the precipitation of these ugly crises. It may and should insist that, unless the waters of the Pacific come to be an international medium, there can be no Pacific community. But beyond that it will guard its conduct from being unreal, not by trying to contribute to practical political solutions, but by keeping, no matter what happens, the lamp of disinterested and thorough inquiry ablaze. International crises are fatalities which are themselves indications of political barbarism on the part of governments. When they occur in the Pacific area they will call for exclusive choices which must be reached largely in obscurity. The members of the Institute cannot, as citizens, avoid taking sides in these controversies. They will have to indorse the policy of their own government or oppose that policy, according to the verdict of their individual consciences; but in either event they have a more important service to perform. As the members of a Pacific Institute they are pledged to watch the conduct of the several governments and peoples and to understand their different motives and proceedings. Unless they keep their own judgment disinterested, alert, and well informed, they will paralyze their own ability to bring a Pacific community into existence.

The limitations which I am indicating of the function of an Institute of Pacific Relations are merely a reflection of the limitations of the wholesome operation of understanding and conscience in human affairs. The spokesmen of understanding and conscience have assumed too often that their essential function is legislative. They have supposed themselves to be sufficiently righteous and wise to proclaim principles which were entitled to preside over the destinies of peoples and nations. But legislation, even through the medium of principles, is a rough, peremptory, and exclusive activity which can never be more than partially adjusted to its supposed object. The spokesmen of understanding and conscience would do better, consequently, to dissociate themselves, in part at least, from the business of dictating to people how they must or ought to behave. They will be more effective and more consistent if they will confine themselves to the exercise of a more modest function: the function of helping themselves and other people to attain an increasing awareness of the consequences of their acts, and particularly of acts which embody purposes and principles, upon the lives both of individuals and of society. They may, if they like, think of themselves as angels, but as recording angels rather than angels of judgment and righteousness. Theirs is a work of methodical inquiry, of indefatigable exploration, of inveterate attention. They fulfill their mission by watching without prejudice what is taking place, by anticipating consequences, detecting latent conflicts, suggesting clues for understanding them and perhaps devices for reconciling them, but in any case by continuing to occupy themselves primarily in observing and cross-examining the event.

## IV

In order to understand what the Pacific Institute can do, it is necessary to keep in mind what the Pacific area is. It is at present only a geographical expression. Its peoples do not dwell in relatively permanent or in legally and morally definable relations one to another. Neither can these relations be analyzed into problems of mutual adjustment which are capable of early and satisfactory treatment. The Pacific peoples are only beginning to find one another out. They dwell in and around the largest oceanic area in the world, and amidst the utmost possible diversity of climate and physical surroundings. Their cultures are both more primitive and more worn out, both more ancient and more modern, than those of any European countries. They exemplify every stage of economic growth, every variety of political and social institutions and racial stocks, and every contrast of religious outlook. They are associated only by one important fact. The Pacific Ocean provides them with a common and an increasingly intimate medium of communication. If anything of importance happens to one of the Pacific peoples, the events will react favorably or unfavorably upon the others. Yet, like the Mediterranean communities, but unlike those of the Atlantic, they originated as states without any reference one to another.

At present the various Pacific peoples are, more than the Atlantic peoples, unconscious of their origin, their destiny, the changing channels of their lives, and their possibilities of future growth or decay. Yet they are well launched on a period of rapid, drastic, and incalculable change. Whatever their relations are supposed to be at present, they will soon be entirely transformed. The creation of a Chinese fleet and army comparable to those of Japan would, for instance, paint the whole Pacific area a different political color. So would the economic development of the Philippines by American capital, parallel to the existing development of the Hawaiian Islands. It is wholly impossible to predict what these transformations will be or how they will be brought about. There is no existing center of authority which knows how these affairs ought to be managed. They are bound to run their own course; and yet they cannot be left wholly to chance.

If these transformations are thoroughly watched while they are running their course, they will not be left to chance. Human beings can only modify those processes of which they are conscious. Whenever they seek to ameliorate processes of individual and social life, their first job is to devise a technique of becoming conscious of what they propose to regulate. That, in relation to the Pacific area, is a definition of the work of the Institute of Pacific Relations. I like to think of it as an entirely realistic experiment in unpractical politics. Its way of playing the game will be to sit on the side lines and watch, but watch eagerly, systematically, and associatively. It will watch, through its national groups, the policies of the different governments in so far as they react on the welfare and the states of mind of the people of other Pacific states. These national groups should consider it their most important job to report the result of their scrutiny to the other national groups at periodic conferences. The value of these conferences will depend partly upon the candor and thoroughness of these reports and partly upon the candor and the thoroughness of the comments by the groups from other parts of the Pacific. In this way the associated experiences of the several Pacific peoples will be uncovered, recorded, and, in a sense, pooled.

The Institute would conduct the equivalent in one political area of a cost-accounting system in a vast and complicated business. The United States Steel Corporation could not be operated without a system of keeping accounts which recorded fully and accurately the behavior of every branch of the business and the extent to which each plant or department contributed or did not contribute to the welfare of the whole corporation. This system of accounts is one method which the centralized management uses to keep the different parts of the business together without destroying the independence of these parts. No similar system of accounts is as yet possible in politics. Statesmen or political philosophers are not agreed upon any method of measuring political welfare. Yet a research institute can watch and record, even if it cannot measure. The watching and recording will help, if it is thoroughly and disinterestedly done, to create out of the peoples of the Pacific area a going political concern.

Such an institute cannot, however, if it is to perform its job of accounting conscientiously, afford to let itself get entangled in the responsibilities of legislation and government. Its members will constantly be tempted to believe that it is capable of some salutary intervention in a critical dilemma. It will be continually solicited to take sides in some particularly ugly controversy. Sooner or later it will probably yield to one of these temptations or solicitations and undertake to place its authority as a research institute behind some piece of practical political advice. But I hope not. If it does commit itself to particular policies it can hardly fail to become propagandist, and it will measurably disqualify itself for the more permanently important task which no other organized body is in a position to perform. It cannot afford to indorse or to participate in any policy that is not frankly experimental, and the effect of its own attitude of watchfulness is to attach an experimental significance to policies which may be intended to be conclusive.

I have called the Institute, as it calls itself, a research body; but it is only partly engaged in digging up information about what has already happened. It is, in reality, far more occupied in searching the careers of those events which are now happening. It is chiefly an instrument of discovery. The vital ingredient in its work consists in practicing an impassioned and tireless curiosity which will feed upon the very processes of life in the different parts of the Pacific. Curiosity is an activity which submits other activities to inveterate cross-examination, on the general theory, as Socrates says in the Apology, that an unexamined life is not worth living. It is by virtue of the exercise of this activity that other human activities become manageable; but the control, in that case, is not entitled to be presumptuous. Beware of the pretensions of the alleged social or spiritual achitect. The salutary awareness is not merely constructive. Its effect is at times likely to be destructive. It does not plan for the future, except occasionally and for limited purposes. But for that very reason it may work the more creatively. It provides a spiritual medium which is favorable to discovery, to invention, and to intuitive revelations; and it is by discovery, and invention, and imaginative revelation that human beings alter the channels through which their lives flow and develop new possibilities of intercourse and conduct.

## V

Liberals need a new figure in which to envisage the creative increment which takes place when human beings, by conscious effort, add a cubit to their stature. Until recently they have compared the creative process both in individual and social life to some kind of political or social engineering, born of an alliance among expert knowledge, definite purpose, and good will. But this analogy assumes an excessive confidence in the intellect and its particular resources. Regeneration demands a synthesis between life and truth, not the dictation of one to the other. Liberals will have to trust the success of their aspirations more to the operation of vital processes whose outcome they cannot foresee and whose actualities they may not approve. The goal will not dictate the route; but by feeling out the route without too much presumption, they may come upon surprising glimpses of the goal. It will be their lot to tread in the footsteps of Saul, who went out in search of an ass, and, by searching, came into a kingdom. They might compare what they are doing, not to the building of a bridge from a design, but to a well-known chemical process which would, until recently, scarcely have seemed symbolic of a desirable social or spiritual synthesis.

When oxygen and sulphur dioxide are mixed in the presence of a filament of platinum they form sulphurous acid. This combination takes place only if the platinum is present. Nevertheless, the newly formed acid contains no trace of platinum, and the platinum itself is not diminished or transformed as the result of the new synthesis which its presence had brought into existence. The platinum has been active and powerful, but at the same time neutral with respect to the two chemicals, and disinterested with respect to the result.[2] Now, what we need in order to cultivate more successfully the art of fulfilling individual and social life is a spiritual catalyst—an activity, that is, which by its presence will modify unexpectedly, but not arbitrarily, customary behavior, without itself planning or insisting what form the modification will take, and without becoming identified with the success or failure of the new synthesis.

The human spirit is not, apparently, capable of any activity which meets these requirements, except the activity of becoming thoroughly aware of the processes through which its life is realized. This awareness is, I think, in its primary expression, personal and religious, but inveterate and methodical curiosity about what is actually happening to social bodies, both after it has happened and as it is happening, will, if focused in public opinion, act as a catalytic agent with respect to political and social development. The agent will not pretend to predict or dictate the particular form the development will take. It will itself remain disinterested and unconcerned about the specific issues and incidents which may seem of transcendent importance to the more passive actors in the drama of the moment. But it would, by virtue of this very enlightened neutrality, exercise a more profound influence on the outcome of the affair than if it had interfered too officiously and too irretrievably to bring about a specific result. It is an infusion of this kind which social intelligence needs in order to free itself from the domination of particular interests, arrogant rationalizations, cultivated stupidities and a general disposition to act as a lord rather than a leaven of social and political events.

[2] I have borrowed this particular illustration from Mr. T. S. Eliot.

Perhaps I am attaching too much importance to the unpredictably formative effect upon social and political activities which a ruthlessly attentive and inquisitive public opinion may have; but it offers, I think, the only possible way of accomplishing the traditional liberal aspirations. Certainly, if something of the kind cannot be brought to bear on political life, or if, after being brought to bear, it fails to act as a catalytic agent, I doubt whether an institute such as that of Pacific Relations will survive as a positive element in Pacific politics. It cannot act as general counsel for a corporation of Pacific powers. No such corporation exists or anywhere nearly exists. It is quite impossible to overestimate either the unmanageability, the novelty, or the contentiousness of the specific problems which the future politics of the Pacific will throw up. But if it is content to act as a watchman, and to keep its flag as a watchman flying, in spite of every temptation to run after the red herrings which provide the diet of practical politics, then it will have a chance to survive and to perform a unique service for the Pacific community. Such a community can only come into existence freely and consciously. No one Pacific people is going to conquer the others as Rome conquered the Mediterranean area, and they will not be forced to combine, as the European nations are now being forced, by outside pressure. Yet if they are to take advantage of their opportunities of intercourse over an international highway, if they are to save themselves from the expense of interfering with one another's development, and if they are to develop their varied and rich social and political possibilities, then they must form a community.

This community can, in the circumstances, be born only of a germ which is somehow both creative and conscious—a rare combination in human life, but perhaps not impossible. So far as I can see, the only chance which we as conscious human beings have to become creative is to fasten our attention on the very processes of life, in the hope of comprehending them rather than dictating to them. If the Institute can comprehend the lives and policies of the Pacific peoples, partly by watching them and partly by comparing different national interpretations of what has happened, it will do its utmost to bring a Pacific community into existence. It should, consequently, be quite content to play the rôle of lily in the barnyard of the Pacific. If it can only succeed, by paint or otherwise, in keeping the lily white, it may do something to transform the barnyard into a garden and to give the more highly colored flowers of humanity a better chance to grow.

## SECTION 33

## REPORT OF COMMITTEE ON PERMANENT ORGANIZATION

J. MERLE DAVIS
General Secretary, Institute of Pacific Relations

The 1925 conference of the Institute of Pacific Relations appointed a Committee on Permanent Organization with responsibility to create a Pacific Council, establish a headquarters, employ a secretariat, raise funds, and prepare for a second Institute conference. The members of this committee were: President R. L. Wilbur, of the United States, chairman; Mr. F. C. Atherton, of Hawaii, vice-chairman; Mr. John Nelson, of Canada; Mr. Y. Tsurumi, of Japan; and Dr. S. T. Wen, of China.

The Committee on Permanent Organization held three meetings, two of which took place at the close of the 1925 conference in Honolulu and the third in San Francisco in the following October.

It was decided to organize for a five-year period, which would include two more conferences; to make Honolulu the headquarters; and to secure Messrs. J. Merle Davis and Charles F. Loomis as executive secretaries. In January, 1926, these appointments were changed to general secretary and associate general secretary. It was further decided to raise a budget of $90,000 for 1926, to hold the next conference in Honolulu in 1927, and to have the secretariat visit the participating groups in the various countries in preparation for that meeting. It was voted to ask the Canadian group to take steps toward securing British participation in the next Institute. It was further voted to secure a research secretary as soon as feasible.

Through the autumn of 1925, Secretary Davis assisted President Wilbur and members of the American group in forming an American National Council and in raising funds. Among the substantial gifts which were made to the 1926 Institute budget were $15,000 from the Carnegie Endowment for International Peace, and $10,000 from the Laura Spelman Rockefeller Memorial. During the fall and winter of 1925–26, President Wilbur made two visits to Canada and assisted in bringing the work of the Institute to the attention of leaders in Toronto and Montreal and Vancouver.

The General Secretary spent the greater part of the year 1926 in a tour of visitation of the Institute groups in Japan, China, Philippines, Australia, New Zealand, Canada, and the United States. He also visited the Dutch East Indies.

During the summer of 1926, Mr. Loomis proceeded to New York and co-operated with the honorary secretary of the American Committee, Mr. E. C. Carter, in a reorganization of that national group.

In October President Wilbur sailed for Japan to attend the Pacific Science Congress in Tokyo. This journey enabled the Chairman of the Pacific Council to have conferences with the leaders of the Japanese Institute Branch and to meet Institute leaders attending the Science Congress from Australia, Canada, and New Zealand. Dr. Wilbur also visited North China and promoted the interests of the Institute there.

The Institute has made a substantial start in research. The promise of an annual grant of $15,000 per year by the Laura Spelman Rockefeller Memorial for a three-year period beginning with January, 1927, made possible the calling of Dr. J. B. Condliffe, of Canterbury College, New Zealand, as Research Secretary. Dr. Condliffe has recently returned from a journey of visitation and study in Canada and the United States, and expects to continue this preliminary survey of his field by proceeding to the Orient in the autumn.

Another impetus to the research work of the Institute has been a *liaison* effected between the American Institute Council and the Social Science Research Council of the United States. The latter body has created a special committee to co-operate with the research activities of the Institute.

In February, 1927, Mr. John Nelson, honorary secretary of the Canadian group, proceeded to London for a conference with the Royal Institute of International Affairs regarding a possible relationship between the Canadian branch of that organization and the Institute of Pacific Relations. Mr. Nelson also assisted the Pacific Council by discussing the question of British participation in the conference of the Institute of Pacific Relations with members of the Royal Institute of International Affairs.

Summing up the work of the two years covered by this report, National Institute Councils have been organized under strong leadership in six countries of the Pacific area, namely, Australia, Canada, China, Japan, New Zealand, and the United States. The Australian council is composed of two regional or local councils, in Melbourne and Sydney. In Canada, three local groups are functioning—Montreal, Toronto, and Vancouver. New Zealand reports three regional Institute Committees, at Wellington, Auckland, and Christchurch, under a national council centering at Wellington. In China, Japan, and the United States a national council is functioning in each country. Institute groups have also been organized in Seoul, Manila, and Hawaii, the latter being designated the Hawaii Council of the Institute of Pacific Relations.

The chairmen of the national councils, together with the chairman of the Central Executive Committee, form the Pacific Council, which is the controlling body of the Institute. The members of the Pacific Council are: chairman, President R. L. Wilbur, United States; vice-chairman, F. C. Atherton, Hawaii; Sir Mungo MacCallum, Australia; Sir Robert Borden, Canada; Dr. David Yui, China; Hon. J. Inouye, Japan; Sir James Allen, New Zealand.

The responsibility for the administration of the Institute has been relegated by the Pacific Council to a Central Executive Committee in Hawaii, composed of nine members. Local resident nationals of some of the participating countries have been appointed by their respective national councils to serve upon the Central Executive Committee. The chairman of the Committee is Mr. F. C. Atherton.

The growth of the Institute is to a striking extent indigenous. There has been no outside promotional work in the various participating countries. The local and national groups have been formed spontaneously. The national councils are working according to policies of their own shaping, and, in four instances, under their own constitutions and by-laws. These national constitutions have been used as a basis for the forming of a general constitution and by-laws for the Institute which will be submitted for the consideration of the Pacific Council at the present conference.

The Institute expended in 1925 a sum amounting to $50,418.24, and in 1926, $32,022.99. Both fiscal years were closed without a deficit. The accepted budget for 1927 was $98,000 (including $40,000 for the conference). On June 30 this was revised to $77,200. The first six months of the year show an expenditure of $31,860.45.

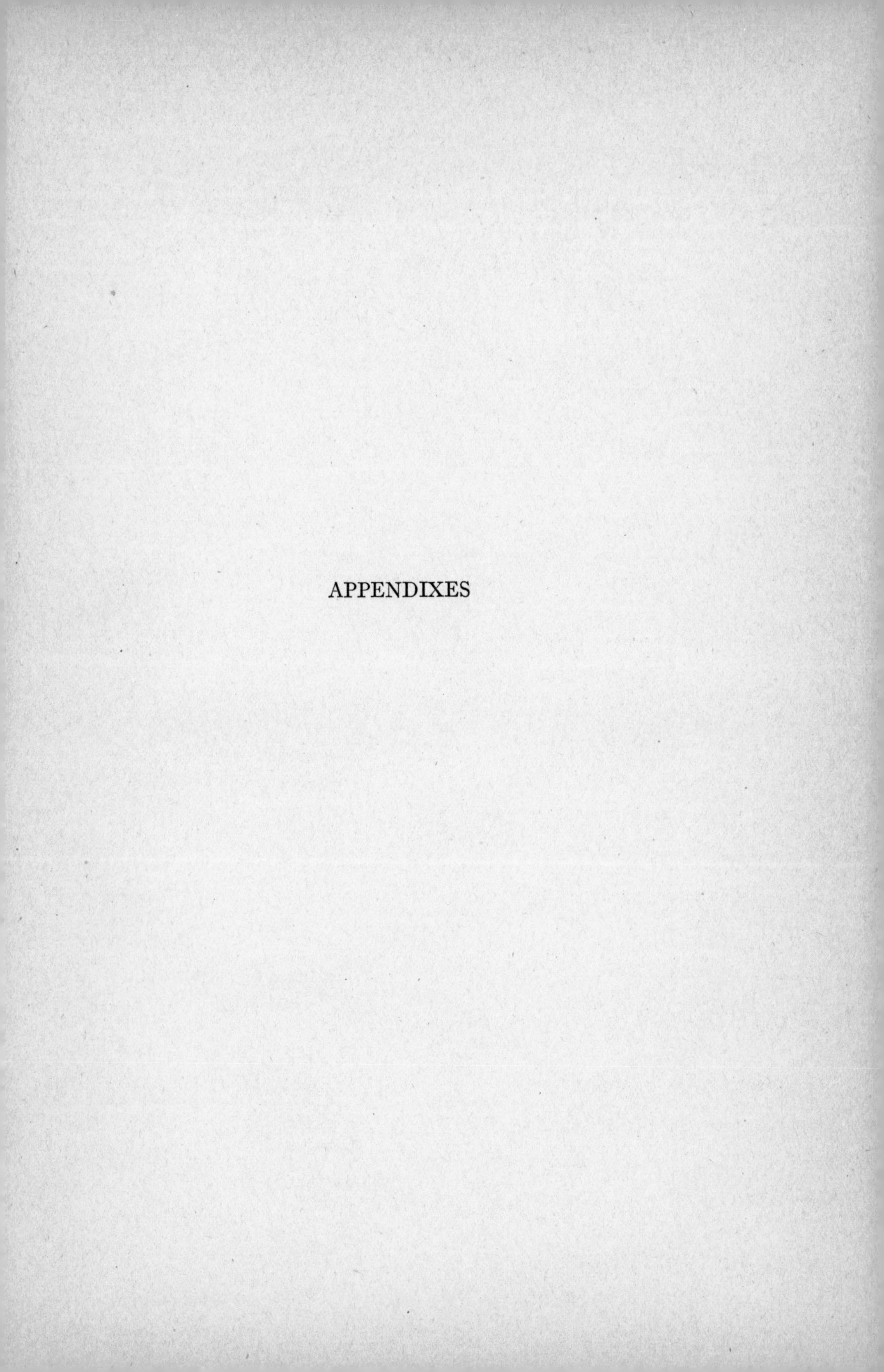

APPENDIXES

# APPENDIX I

## MEMBERS OF THE 1927 CONFERENCE

### AUSTRALIA

HON. F. W. EGGLESTON, formerly attorney-general and minister of railways for Victoria, Melbourne; chairman of the group.

MISS PERSIA CAMPBELL, assistant research officer of the New South Wales Industrial Commission, Sydney; secretary of the group.

C. H. CURREY, lecturer in Modern History, Teachers' College, Sydney.

H. DUNCAN HALL, professor of International Relations at the School of Citizenship and Public Affairs of Syracuse University, Syracuse, New York.

G. L. WOOD, lecturer, School of Commerce, University of Melbourne.

### CANADA

GENERAL SIR ARTHUR CURRIE, G.C.M.G., K.C.B., principal and vice-chancellor, McGill University, Montreal; chairman of the group.

JOHN NELSON, supervisor, Department of Public Relations, Sun Life Assurance Company of Canada; secretary of the group.

J. W. BEATON, general secretary, Metropolitan Board, Young Men's Christian Association, Montreal.

VINCENT BLADEN, lecturer in Economics, University of Toronto.

C. A. BOWMAN, editor, *The Citizen,* Ottawa.

STANLEY BRENT, general secretary, Young Men's Christian Association, Vancouver.

R. W. BROCK, dean of the Faculty of Applied Science (Geologist), University of British Columbia, Vancouver.

W. W. GOFORTH, assistant professor of Economics, McGill University, Montreal.

MRS. W. W. GOFORTH, Montreal.

W. B. LANIGAN, former general freight superintendent of the Canadian-Pacific railway.

GEORGE C. MCDONALD, of McDonald, Currie & Company, vice-president, Montreal Board of Trade.

T. F. MCILWRAITH, assistant professor of Anthropology, University of Toronto.

MRS. T. F. MCILWRAITH, 46 Summerhill Gardens, Toronto.

JOHN MACKAY, principal, Manitoba College, Winnipeg.

HENRY T. ROSS, K.C., secretary, Canadian Bankers' Association, Montreal.

### CHINA

DAVID Z. T. YUI, general secretary of the National Committee of the Young Men's Christian Association of China, Shanghai; chairman of the group.

L. T. CHEN, secretary of the National Committee of the Young Men's Christian Association of China; secretary of the group.

MINGCHIEN JOSHUA BAU, professor of Political Science, Peking National Normal University and Peking National College of Law and Politics.

GEORGE HOH, address care of W. W. Ahana Company, Honolulu, Hawaii.

WILLIAM HUNG, professor of History and dean of the College of Arts and Science, Yen Ching University, Peking.

T. Z. KOO, associate general secretary, National Committee, Young Men's Christian Association of China.

SHAO CHANG LEE, professor of Chinese History and Language, University of Hawaii, Honolulu, Hawaii.

O. S. LIEU, proprietor and general manager, Shanghai Cement Company, Shanghai.

KO FONG LUM, secretary, Nuuanu Young Men's Christian Association, Honolulu, Hawaii.

W. S. NEW, physician, formerly professor in the Peking Union Medical College.

MRS. W. S. NEW, 329 Bubbling Well Road, Shanghai.

MRS. C. F. WANG, formerly dean, Women's Department, Canton Christian College.

CHARLES WONG, cashier and manager, Chinese-American Bank Ltd., Honolulu, Hawaii.

MRS. SOPHIA CHEN ZEN, author and publicist, formerly professor of History, National University of Peking.

GREAT BRITAIN

SIR FREDERICK WHYTE, K.C., S.I., formerly president of the National Indian Legislative Assembly; chairman of the group.

MALCOLM MACDONALD, joint secretary of the group.

THE HONORABLE W. W. ASTOR, New College, Oxford, joint secretary of the group.

VISCOUNT CASTLEREAGH, formerly honorary attaché, British Embassy, Rome.

LIONEL CURTIS, honorary secretary of the Royal Institute of International Affairs, London.

W. J. HINTON, Department of Political Economy, University of Hongkong.

HENRY T. HODGKIN, secretary of the National Christian Council of China, Shanghai.

MRS. HENRY T. HODGKIN, Shanghai.

MISS MARION J. HUNTER, formerly honorary secretary, V.A.D., Central Selection Board for Scotland, British Red Cross Society; formerly honorary assistant secretary, Missions and Governments Committee, International Missionary Council, London.

WILLIAM P. KER, C.M.G., formerly of the British Consular Service, China.

MRS. R. MACGREGOR MILLS, Calle Napoles 11, Mexico, D.F.

C. K. WEBSTER, Woodrow Wilson Professor of International Politics, University of Wales, Aberystwyth, South Wales.

MRS. C. K. WEBSTER, Aberystwyth, South Wales.

THE HONORABLE HUGH A. WYNDHAM, formerly member of the House of Assembly, Union of South Africa.

HAWAII

FRANK C. ATHERTON, vice-president and manager, Castle & Cooke Ltd.; chairman, Central Advisory Committee, Honolulu; treasurer, Pacific Council of the Institute of Pacific Relations.

ROMANZO ADAMS, professor of Sociology, University of Hawaii, Honolulu.

AKAIKO AKANA, pastor, Kawaiahao Church, Honolulu.

MISS BEATRICE CASTLE, 1301 Victoria Street, Honolulu.

C. MONTAGUE COOKE, JR., Bishop Museum, Honolulu.

DAVID L. CRAWFORD, president, University of Hawaii, Honolulu.

ARTHUR L. DEAN, director, Experiment Station, Association of Hawaiian Pineapple Canners, Honolulu.

JAMES D. DOLE, president, Hawaiian Pineapple Company Ltd., Honolulu.

HON. WALTER F. FREAR, president, Bishop Trust Company Ltd.; ex-governor and formerly chief justice of Hawaii, Honolulu.

HERBERT E. GREGORY, director, Bishop Museum, Honolulu; chairman, Committee on Pacific Investigations, National Research Council.

RIGHT REV. JOHN D. LAMOTHE, St. Andrews Cathedral, Protestant Episcopal Bishop of Hawaii.

KARL C. LEEBRICK, professor of History and Political Science, University of Hawaii, Honolulu.

I. MORI, physician, 1481 Nuuanu Street, Honolulu.

MISS ELSIE WILCOX, school commissioner for Island of Kauai, Lihue.

Y. C. YANG, physician, 491 South Beretania Street, Honolulu.

JAPAN

HON. MASATARO SAWAYANAGI, member of the House of Peers; president of the Imperial Educational Association, Tokyo; chairman of the group.

SOICHI SAITO, general secretary of the Young Men's Christian Association, Tokyo; secretary of the group.

TANEO TAKETA, executive secretary of the Japanese Council of the Institute of Pacific Relations, Tokyo.

ROY HIDEMICHI AKAGI, general secretary of the Japanese Students' Christian Association in North America, New York City.

INO DAN, lecturer at the Imperial University of Tokyo.

TASUKU HARADA, ex-president of Doshisha University, Kyoto, and professor of Japanese History and Literature, University of Hawaii, Honolulu.

MISS AIKO HOSHINO, acting president of the Tsuda Women's College, Tokyo.

AKIRA ISHII, formerly vice-president of the Nippon Yusen Kaisha, Tokyo.

SHIROSHI NASU, professor of Rural Economics, Imperial University of Tokyo.

MASAMICHI ROYAMA, assistant professor of Political Science, Imperial University of Tokyo.

MRS. MASAMICHI ROYAMA, No. 3343 Nakano, Tokyo.

BUNJI SUZUKI, president, General Federation of Labor of Japan, Tokyo.

YASAKA TAKAKI, professor of American Constitution, History, and Diplomacy, Imperial University of Tokyo.

KENZO TAKAYANAGI, professor of Law, Imperial University of Tokyo.

MRS. KENZO TAKAYANAGI, 431 Zushi, Kanagawa, Ken.

YUSUKE TSURUMI, author, 53 Sangenya, Azabu, Tokyo.

MRS. YUSUKE TSURUMI, 53 Sangenya, Azabu, Tokyo.

NAOMASA YAMASAKI, professor of Geography, Imperial University of Tokyo.

### KOREA

UCK KYUM YU, dean and professor of Law, Chosen Christian College, Seoul; chairman of the group.

MISS HELEN K. KIM, dean of Ewha College, Seoul.

KWAN SOO PAIK, editor, *Korea Daily News,* Seoul.

### NEW ZEALAND

WALTER NASH, secretary of the New Zealand Labor Party, Wellington; chairman of the group.

PETER HENRY BUCK (TE RANGIHIROA), formerly director of Maori hygiene; new member of staff of Bishop Museum, Honolulu, Hawaii.

WILLIAM HOLLIS COCKER, barrister and solicitor, Auckland.

WILLIAM MAWSON, Presbyterian missionary, formerly of Canton, China.

HUGH C. TENNENT, Tennent & Wright, Honolulu, Hawaii.

### PHILIPPINES

FRANCISCO BENITEZ, dean of the College of Education, University of the Philippines, Manila.

NICOLAS C. DIZON, pastor, United Filipino Church, Honolulu, Hawaii.

FRED C. FISHER, former justice of the Supreme Court of the Philippines, Manila.

### UNITED STATES

RAY LYMAN WILBUR, president of Stanford University, California; chairman, Pacific Council of the Institute.

E. C. CARTER, secretary, *The Inquiry,* New York; honorary secretary, United States group.

MISS CATHERINE PORTER, secretary, United States group.

MISS GRACE ABBOTT, chief of the Children's Bureau, United States Department of Labor, Washington, D.C.

WALLACE M. ALEXANDER, president of Alexander & Baldwin Ltd., of Honolulu, San Francisco.

CARL L. ALSBERG, director, Food Research Institute, Stanford University, California.

O. E. BAKER, economic analyst, Bureau of Agricultural Economics, United States Department of Agriculture, Washington, D.C.

GEORGE H. BLAKESLEE, professor of History and International Relations, Clark University, Worcester, Massachusetts.

MRS. CARRIE CHAPMAN CATT, chairman, National Committee, Conference on the Cause and Cure of War, New York City.

MISS ADA COMSTOCK, president of Radcliffe College, Cambridge, Massachusetts.

MISS MABEL CRATTY, general secretary of the National Board, Young Women's Christian Association, New York City.

HERBERT CROLY, editor, *New Republic,* New York City.

HON. FREDERICK M. DAVENPORT, congressman, and professor of Political Science, Hamilton College, Clinton, New York.

MANTON DAVIS, legal staff of the Radio Corporation of America, New York City.

STEPHEN P. DUGGAN, director of the Institute of International Education and professor of Political Science, College of the City of New York.

ALFRED C. ELKINTON, president of the Philadelphia Quartz Company, Berkeley, California.

GALEN M. FISHER, executive secretary of the Institute of Social and Religious Research, New York City.

DANIEL J. FLEMING, professor of Missions, Union Theological Seminary, New York City.

JEROME D. GREENE, member of the firm of Lee, Higginson & Company, New York City.

ARNOLD BENNETT HALL, president of the University of Oregon, Eugene, Oregon.

MOST REVEREND EDWARD J. HANNA, archbishop of the Diocese of San Francisco, and president of the National Catholic Welfare Council of America, San Francisco.

MRS. WILLIAM G. HIBBARD, regional director, National League of Women Voters, Chicago, Illinois.

ALFRED HOLMAN, San Francisco correspondent for the *New York Times,* San Francisco, California.

STANLEY K. HORNBECK, lecturer on History of the Far East, Harvard University, Cambridge, Massachusetts.

EDWARD H. HUME, M.D., formerly president of Yale in China, Changsha, New York City.

JEREMIAH W. JENKS, research professor of Government and Public Administration, New York University, New York City.

WILLIAM H. KILPATRICK, professor of the Philosophy of Education, Teachers' College, Columbia University, New York City.

IVY LEE, 4 East 66th Street, New York City.

ROBERT NEWTON LYNCH, vice-president, San Francisco Chamber of Commerce, California.

R. D. MCKENZIE, professor of Sociology, University of Washington, Seattle, Washington.

MRS. ALFRED MCLAUGHLIN, 3537 Clay Street, San Francisco, California.

ELIOT G. MEARS, professor of Economics, Graduate School of Business, Stanford University, California; honorary secretary, Survey of Race Relations on the Pacific Coast.

FRANK A. MILLER, Mission Inn, Riverside, California.

PAUL MONROE, director of The International Institute, Columbia University, New York City.

WILLIAM F. MORRISH, president, First National Bank in Berkeley, vice-president, California Bankers' Association, Berkeley, California.

W. J. PAPE, vice-president, Associated Press of America.

HENRY S. PRITCHETT, president of the Carnegie Foundation for the Advancement of Teaching, Santa Barbara, California.

CHESTER H. ROWELL, writer, and formerly editor of the *Fresno Republican,* Berkeley, California.

John A. Ryan, professor of Moral Theology and Industrial Ethics, Catholic University of America, Washington, D.C.

Paul Scharrenberg, secretary and treasurer of the California State Federation of Labor, San Francisco.

James T. Shotwell, professor of History, Columbia University, New York City.

George Grafton Wilson, professor of International Law, Harvard University, Cambridge, Massachusetts.

Miss Mary E. Woolley, president of Mount Holyoke College, South Hadley, Massachusetts.

Quincy Wright, professor of Political Science, University of Chicago, Chicago, Illinois.

## OBSERVERS

Setsuichi Aoki, director of the Tokyo branch of the League of Nations.

William Caldwell, International Labor Office, Geneva.

H. R. Cummings, representing the Secretariat of the League of Nations, Geneva.

## CONFERENCE STAFF

| | |
|---|---|
| Arthur A. Hauck | *Buildings and Grounds* |
| Mrs. Doremus Scudder | *Hostess* |
| Galen R. Weaver | *Editorial Bureau* |
| Elizabeth Green | *Press Bureau* |
| Carol Remele | *General Office* |
| Elsie Baum | *General Office* |

## PERMANENT SECRETARIAT, INSTITUTE OF PACIFIC RELATIONS

J. Merle Davis, *General Secretary,* Honolulu.

Charles F. Loomis, *Associate General Secretary,* Honolulu.

J. B. Condliffe, *Research Secretary,* Honolulu.

## APPENDIX II

### THE CONFERENCE PROGRAM

|  |  |  |
|---|---|---|
| July 15 | 8:00 P.M.–10:00 P.M. | The Geography of the Pacific |
| | | Herbert E. Gregory |
| | | The Races of the Pacific |
| | | Peter H. Buck |
| | | The Pacific Problem as I See It |
| | | Chester H. Rowell |
| July 16 | 9:00 A.M.–12 NOON | Report from Committee on Permanent Organization |
| | | J. Merle Davis |
| | 2:00 P.M.– 4:30 P.M. | Opening Statements Giving the Outlook on Pacific Affairs of Each of the Institute National Groups: |
| | | 1. The Viewpoint of Australia on Pacific Affairs |
| | | F. W. Eggleston |
| | | 2. Canada and Pacific Relations |
| | | General Sir Arthur Currie, G.C.M.G., K.C.B. |
| | | 3. China and Pacific Relations during 1925–27 |
| | | David Z. T. Yui |
| | | 4. Opening Statement for the British Group |
| | | Sir Frederick Whyte, K.C., S.I. |
| | | 5. The General Features of Pacific Relations as Viewed by Japan |
| | | M. Sawayanagi |
| | | 6. Pacific Relations from the Viewpoint of the Korean Group |
| | | Helen K. Kim |
| | | 7. A New Zealand Outlook on Pacific Affairs |
| | | Walter Nash |
| | | 8. Present-day Problems of the Philippines |
| | | F. C. Fisher |
| | | 9. An Interpretation of America in Pacific Relations |
| | | Ray Lyman Wilbur |
| July 17 | 7:30 P.M.–10:00 P.M. | Addresses on the Aims and Aspirations of the Pacific Countries |
| | | Australia |
| | | C. H. Currey |
| | | Canada |
| | | Henry T. Ross, K.C. |
| | | China |
| | | T. Z. Koo |

Great Britain
Lionel Curtis
Japan
Yusuke Tsurumi
Korea
Uck Kyum Yu
New Zealand
W. H. Cocker
Philippines
Nicolas Dizon
United States
Mrs. Carrie Chapman Catt

| DATE | TIME | LECTURES, ETC. | ROUND TABLES | FORUMS |
|---|---|---|---|---|
| July 18 | 9:00 A.M.–10:30 A.M. }<br>10:45 A.M.–12:15 P.M. } | | Tariff Autonomy in China (4) | |
| | 7:45 P.M.– 9:15 P.M. | | | Tariff Autonomy in China |
| July 19 | 9:00 A.M.–10:30 A.M. }<br>10:45 A.M.–12:15 P.M. }<br>7:45 P.M.– 9:15 P.M. } | | Extra-territoriality in China (4) | |
| July 20 | 9:00 A.M.–10:30 A.M. }<br>10:45 A.M.–12:15 P.M. } | | Foreign Concessions and Settlements in China (4) | |
| | 7:45 P.M.– 9:15 P.M. | | | Foreign Concessions and Settlements in China |
| July 21 | 9:00 A.M.–10:30 A.M. }<br>10:45 A.M.–12:15 P.M. } | | Population and Food Supply (1)<br>The Pacific Mandates (1)<br>International Education and Communications (2) | |
| | 7:45 P.M.– 9:15 P.M. | | | International Education and Communications |

| DATE | TIME | LECTURES, ETC. | ROUND TABLES | FORUMS |
|---|---|---|---|---|
| July 22 | 9:00 A.M.–10:30 A.M.<br>10:45 A.M.–12:15 P.M. | | Population and Food Supply (1)<br>Foreign Missions and Pacific Relations (2)<br>International Education and Communications (1) | |
| | 7:45 P.M.– 9:15 P.M. | | | Population and Food Supply |
| July 23 | 9:00 A.M.–10:30 A.M.<br>10:45 A.M.–12:15 P.M. | | Industrialization and Foreign Investment (1)<br>Foreign Missions and Pacific Relations (2) | |
| | 7:45 P.M.– 9:15 P.M. | | | Industrialization and Foreign Investment<br>Foreign Missions and Pacific Relations |
| July 24 | Sunday | No Program | | |
| July 25 | 9:00 A.M.–10:30 A.M.<br>10:45 A.M.–12:15 P.M. | | Industrialization and Foreign Investment (2)<br>Diplomatic Relations in the Pacific (1) | |
| | 7:45 P.M.– 9:15 P.M. | Yusuke Tsurumi | | Industrialization and Foreign Investment |

| DATE | TIME | LECTURES, ETC. | ROUND TABLES | FORUMS |
|---|---|---|---|---|
| July 26 | 9:00 A.M.–10:30 A.M.<br>10:45 A.M.–12:15 P.M. | | Immigration and Emigration in the Pacific (3) | |
| | 7:45 P.M.– 9:15 P.M. | | | Diplomatic Relations in the Pacific |
| July 27 | 9:00 A.M.–10:30 A.M.<br>10:45 A.M.–12:15 P.M. | | Immigration and Emigration in the Pacific (3)<br>Diplomatic Relations in the Pacific (1) | |
| | 7:45 P.M.– 9:15 P.M. | Mrs. Sophia Chen Zen | | Immigration and Emigration in the Pacific |
| July 28 | 9:00 A.M.–10:30 A.M.<br>10:45 A.M.–12:15 P.M. | | The Future of the Institute (4) | |
| | 7:45 P.M.– 9:15 P.M. | Closing Addresses<br>Sir Frederick Whyte<br>William Hung<br>Yusuke Tsurumi<br>Jerome D. Greene<br>Ray Lyman Wilbur | | |

## APPENDIX III

## CONSTITUTION
## OF THE
## INSTITUTE OF PACIFIC RELATIONS

### ARTICLE I
NAME

The name of this organization shall be Institute of Pacific Relations.

### ARTICLE II
OBJECT

The object of the Institute is to study the conditions of the Pacific peoples with a view to the improvement of their mutual relations.

### ARTICLE III
MEMBERSHIP

1. Subject to the provisions hereof the Institute of Pacific Relations is constituted by the national units the names of whose representatives are appended to this Constitution and by such other national units as may hereafter be admitted to membership as provided herein.

2. A national unit as comprehended by Section 1 of this article shall be a National Council organized for the purpose of the Institute, or an organization of similar purposes, in any sovereign or autonomous state lying within or bordering the Pacific Ocean or having dominions, colonies, dependencies, territories, mandated or otherwise, in the Pacific area, subject to its being approved and admitted to membership by the Pacific Council as hereinafter constituted. Each constituent country shall have one National Council or equivalent organization, hereinafter referred to as the National Council. With the approval of the Pacific Council, independent Local Groups may be organized in an eligible country which has not created a National Council.

3. To encourage at Conferences of the Institute the fullest self-expression of distinct racial or territorial groups existing within an eligible country as defined in Section 2 of this Article, the Pacific Council and the Secretariat may, with the assent of the National Council of such country, enter into direct relations with such groups in making arrangements for their representation and participation in Conferences.

4. Each National Council shall determine its own constitution and rules of procedure and shall file with the Secretariat of the Institute a certified copy thereof and of any subsequent amendment.

### ARTICLE IV
PACIFIC COUNCIL

1. The Institute shall be directed by a Pacific Council consisting of one member duly appointed by each National Council, together with the Chairman of the Advisory Committee. The members of the Pacific Council shall each have one vote.

2. The officers of the Pacific Council shall consist of a chairman, a first Vice-Chairman, and a second Vice-Chairman, who shall be, ex officio, the Chairman and Vice-Chairman, respectively, of the Institute. They shall be elected by the Council at a meeting held during the stated Conference, or at an adjourned meeting held thereafter, to serve until the close of the next stated Conference or until their successors have been elected. The Pacific Council shall appoint the General Secretary and the Treasurer of the Institute. The General Secretary shall act as secretary of the Pacific Council.

3. A stated meeting of the Pacific Council shall be held during the period and at the place of the Institute Conference. Special meetings may be called by the Chairman on not less than fifteen days' notice by telegram or two months' notice by post, and they shall be so called at the request of three members.

4. In the event of the inability of a member of the Pacific Council to attend a stated meeting his place may be taken by an Alternate designated by his National Council. In the event of the inability of a member to attend a special meeting his place may be taken by an Alternate designated as above or by a Proxy appointed by the member himself; but the vote of a Proxy shall be valid only as to proposals of which his principal has been informed at least ten days before the special meeting is held or as to which the principal's instructions governing the voting of the Proxy are received before a vote is taken.

5. A quorum of the Pacific Council shall consist of not less than four members including a member or his Alternate or Proxy from each of the following: a member of the British Commonwealth, China, Japan, and the United States.

6. A majority vote of the members present shall determine the action of the Pacific Council except as otherwise expressly provided.

7. A copy of the minutes of each meeting of the Pacific Council shall be sent to each National Council.

### ARTICLE V

### SECRETARIAT

The Secretariat shall be the instrument of the Pacific Council for carrying on the work of the Institute. It shall be directed by the General Secretary who shall be responsible to the Pacific Council for all its activities. The General Secretary shall be assisted by a staff appropriate for the direction, supervision or execution of the several activities of the Institute in accordance with the policies and regulations of the Council.

### ARTICLE VI

### ADVISORY COMMITTEE

The Pacific Council shall appoint a Committee the advice and assistance of which shall be available to the General Secretary in the discharge of his functions and to which the Council may delegate such authority as shall seem expedient. So far as practicable the personnel of the Committee shall represent the countries having members on the Pacific Council; but at least three of its members shall reside sufficiently near the Secretariat to be able to attend meetings of the Committee and to inform themselves of the condition of the Institute's affairs. The Advisory Committee shall report to the Chairman of the Pacific Council at least once in six months, and at any time upon his request, with regard to the administration and activities of the Institute.

### ARTICLE VII

#### CONFERENCES

1. Conferences of the Institute shall be called by the Pacific Council at stated intervals, which, however, may be changed from time to time as the Council may see fit. In addition to such regular Conferences the Council may call special Conferences. The location of Conferences shall be fixed by the Council.

2. The arrangements for Conferences shall be in charge of the General Secretary acting in co-operation with the Committees concerned with the program and other preparatory work and with the National Council within whose territory the Conference is held.

3. The members of the regular Conferences shall be appointed by the National Councils and independent Local Groups, except as otherwise provided in Article III, Section 3 hereof, the quotas whereof shall be fixed by the Pacific Council.

### ARTICLE VIII

#### FINANCE

1. The expenses of the Institute shall be met by an international budget to which contributions shall be invited from all National Councils and from other sources, but in such manner and to such an extent as to safeguard in the highest possible degree the international character and control of the Institute.

2. The Pacific Council shall fix the fiscal period to be covered by the budget, beginning with the calendar year. At a suitable time prior thereto, as determined by the Council, the General Secretary shall submit a budget for the following fiscal period; and upon the adoption of such budget by the Council, with any necessary modifications, all expenditures shall be made in conformity therewith subject to any subsequent amendments thereof by or under the authority of the Council.

3. The property of the Institute shall be vested in the Pacific Council and the custody and disbursement of its funds and the accounting therefor shall be under the control of the Council.

4. A copy of the budget and of any amendment thereof and a semiannual statement of receipts and expenses shall be sent to each National Council.

5. Each National Council and independent Local Group shall be responsible for its own expenditures.

### ARTICLE IX

#### BY-LAWS AND REGULATIONS

The Pacific Council shall have power to make such By-Laws and Regulations for the conduct of its business and of the affairs of the Institute generally as are not consistent with the provisions of this Constitution.

### ARTICLE X

#### AMENDMENTS

This Constitution may be amended or repealed by an affirmative vote of not less than two-thirds of the members of the Pacific Council provided that notice of the proposed amendment shall have been given by the General Secretary to each National Council not less than four months if by mail and not less than two months if by telegraph, in advance of the meeting at which the amendment is presented.

### ARTICLE XI

#### RATIFICATION

This Constitution shall take effect upon its ratification by the several National Councils provided, however, that the failure of any National Council so to ratify it shall not invalidate it as between the other parties thereto. The vote of each National Council ratifying this Constitution shall be attested by a competent officer of such Council and filed with the Secretariat.

#### SIGNATURES

The undersigned, by authority of their several groups assembled at the Conference of the Institute of Pacific Relations in Honolulu, Territory of Hawaii, U. S. A., hereby approve and adopt the foregoing Constitution of the Institute of Pacific Relations, subject to the ratification of the said Constitution by the full authority of their respective National Councils.

(Signed) FRED W. EGGLESTON (Australia)
A. F. WHYTE (for the British Group)
A. W. CURRIE (Canada)
DAVID Z. T. YUI (China)
A. ISHII (Japan)
W. NASH (New Zealand)
RAY LYMAN WILBUR (United States of America)

July 29, 1927

# APPENDIX IV

## LIST OF PAPERS DISTRIBUTED TO MEMBERS

|  |  |
|---|---|
| The Viewpoint of Australia on Pacific Affairs | Eggleston[1] |
| Canada and Pacific Relations | Currie[1] |
| China and Pacific Relations during 1925–27 | Yui[1] |
| Opening Statement for the British Group | Whyte[1] |
| The General Features of Pacific Relations as Viewed by Japan | Sawayanagi[1] |
| Pacific Relations from the Viewpoint of the Korean Group | Kim[1] |
| A New Zealand Outlook on Pacific Affairs | Nash[1] |
| Present-Day Problems of the Philippines | Fisher[1] |
| An Interpretation of America in Pacific Relations | Wilbur[1] |
| The Aims and Aspirations of Australia | Currey[2] |
| Aspirations and Ideals of Canada | Ross[2] |
| British Aspirations and Ideals | Curtis[2] |
| The Ideals and Aspirations of Japan | Tsurumi[2] |
| Aspirations and Ideals of the Korean People | Yu[2] |
| The Aims and Aspirations of New Zealand | Cocker[2] |
| The Aspirations of the Filipino People | Dizon[2] |
| Ideals and Aspirations of the United States | Catt[2] |
| Notes from a Pacific Circuit | Davis |
| The Geography of the Pacific | Gregory[3] |
| Races of the Pacific | Buck[4] |
| Tariff Autonomy and Its Exercise | Bau[5] |
| Extra-territoriality and Its Relinquishment | Bau[6] |
| Concessions and Settlements and Their Transference to Chinese Rule | Bau[7] |
| Documents Relating to the Chinese Question | Bau[8] |
| Report of the Commission on Extra-territoriality | [9] |
| China and Foreign Powers | Whyte[10] |
| China Today | Hornbeck[11] |

[1] *Institute News-Bulletin* (August–September, 1927).

[2] *Ibid.* (October, 1927).

[3] Below, Documents, Section 1.

[4] *Ibid.*, Section 2.

[5] *Ibid.*, Section 3.

[6] *Ibid.*, Section 4.

[7] *Ibid.*, Section 5.

[8] *Ibid.*, Section 6.

[9] Published by United States Government Printer, Washington, D.C.

[10] Published for the Royal Institute of International Affairs by the Oxford University Press.

[11] Published by World-Peace Foundation, Vol. X, No. 5.

| | |
|---|---|
| Official Statements on China by the Japanese Government . . . . . . . . . . | Japanese Group[12] |
| Trend of Editorial Comment on Problems of China | Japanese Group[13] |
| Missions as a Cultural Factor in the Pacific . . | Beach[14] |
| The Relationship of the Protestant Mission Boards in America to the Churches in Japan, Korea, China, and the Philippine Islands . . . | Warnshuis |
| Memorandum on Missions . . . . . . . | Hodgkin[15] |
| Facing the Future of the Missionary Movement . | Hume[16] |
| Suggestions for a Code of Ethics between Religions | Fleming[17] |
| Some Missionary Problems from an Anthropological Viewpoint . . . . . . . . . . | McIlwraith |
| The Missionary of the Future . . . . . . | Saito |
| The Status of Missionaries in China . . . . . | Warnshuis[18] |
| The Problem of Population and Food Supply in Japan | Nasu[19] |
| A Note on the Geographical Distribution of the Density of Population, Birth- and Death-Rates of Japan . . . . . . . . . . . | Yamasaki[20] |
| Japan's Fuel Supply . . . . . . . . . | Oshima |
| Land Utilization in China . . . . . . . . | Baker[21] |
| Some of China's Food and Mineral Resources . . | Lieu |
| The Australian Aborigines . . . . . . . | Radcliffe Brown |
| Aspects of Australian Population . . . . . | Wood |
| The Progress of Population . . . . . . . | Baker[22] |
| The Factors that Govern Population Growth . . | Alsberg[23] |
| Resources and Possibilities of New Zealand—Food and Fuel . . . . . . . . . . . . | Nash |
| Graphic Summary of American Agriculture . . | Baker |
| Statement on the Effects of the Industrial Development of the Orient on European Industries . | Hinton[24] |
| China's Industrial Development . . . . . . | Lieu[25] |
| Some Practical Problems in Industry and Foreign Trade in China . . . . . . . . | Lieu |
| The Labor Movement in China . . . . . . | Chen[26] |

[12] Documents, Section 7.

[13] *Ibid.*, Section 8.

[14] Published by the American Group of the Institute.

[15] Documents, Section 9.

[16] *Ibid.*, Section 10.

[17] *Ibid.*, Section 11.

[18] Preliminary Paper, Conference on American Relations with China (Baltimore, September, 1925).

[19] Documents, Section 15.

[20] *Ibid.*, Section 16.

[21] *Ibid.*, Section 14.

[22] *Ibid.*, Section 13.

[23] *Ibid.*, Section 12.

[24] Documents, Section 17.

[25] *Ibid.*, Section 18.

[26] *Ibid.*, Section 19.

|  |  |
|---|---|
| Child Workers in China | Friedlander |
| Brief Review of Japan's Industries | Ishii |
| Review of the Shipping Industry of Japan | Ishii |
| The Financial Crisis in Japan | Inouye[27] |
| The Industrialization of Canada | Brock |
| Australian Secondary Industries | Wood |
| Human Resources and Occupations in New Zealand | Nash |
| Industrialization in New Zealand | Nash |
| The Rôle of the Banker in International Relations | Greene[28] |
| Some Political and Economic Effects of International Movements of Capital | Copland |
| The Australian Public Debt | Mills |
| Australia and Capital Investment | Wood |
| Social Effects of the Industrialization of the Far East | Nasu |
| Resident Orientals on the Pacific Coast | Mears[29] |
| Oriental Exclusion | McKenzie[30] |
| Treaty Laws and Rules Governing the Admission of Chinese | U.S. Department of Labor |
| Immigration Laws and Rules of March 1, 1927 | U.S. Department of Labor |
| Admission of Aliens into the United States | U.S. Department of State[31] |
| Immigration Laws of Australia, Canada, New Zealand, and Japan | Wilson |
| Orient and Occident, a Preliminary Study of Opinions and Attitudes | Watson |
| The Second Generation Problem | Akagi[32] |
| Legislative Aspects of Asiatic Migration | International Labor Office[33] |
| The International Labor Organization and Its Contacts with the Countries and Problems of the Pacific | Caldwell |
| The Superiority of Race | Faris |
| Some Reasons for the Importance Attached by Americans to the Standard of Living | Dean |
| The Japanese Race from an Anthropological Point of View | Matsumura |
| Statistics of Japanese Abroad | Japanese Group |
| Australian Immigration Laws and Their Working | Charteris[34] |

[27] *Ibid.*, Section 20.

[28] *Ibid.*, Section 21.

[29] Published by the American Group of the Institute; for résumé of same, see Documents, Section 23.

[30] *Ibid.*

[31] Published by United States Government Printer, Washington, D.C.

[32] Published by Japanese Students' Christian Association in North America.

[33] Documents, Section 22.

[34] *Ibid.*, Section 24.

| | |
|---|---|
| Effect of Migration on the Economic Condition of Laborers in the Lands to which Migrants Go | Wood |
| Differences in Standards of Living as a Barrier to Immigration | Wood |
| The Resources of Australia | Taylor[35] |
| Asiatic Immigration into New Zealand | Scholefield and Hall |
| The Chinese Immigrant in New Zealand | Mawson |
| The Education and Economic Outlook for the Boys of Hawaii | Adams |
| The Social Status of the Japanese in Hawaii | Harada |
| The Second Generation Oriental in America | Smith |
| The Outstanding Cultural Assets of the Chinese People | Zen |
| The Chinese Point of View of the So-Called Material Civilization of the West | Zen |
| Brief Interpretative Outline of Chinese Culture | Lee |
| Japanese Art and Its Modernization | Dan |
| Naval Disarmament in the Pacific | Eggleston |
| Japan's Internal Problems and her Relationships with China, Russia, America, and the British Commonwealth | Tsurumi[36] |
| Analysis of the Existing Machinery for Settling International Disputes in the Pacific | Hall |
| Draft Treaty of Permanent Peace | Shotwell[37] |
| Remarks on the Proposed Draft Treaty of Permanent Peace | Takayanagi |
| The Imperial Conference and Dominion Status | Corbett |
| The British Empire and the League of Nations | Corbett |
| Appendixes to "British Commonwealth of Nations" | Lowell and Hall[38] |
| Preliminary Textbook Study | Hawaiian Group |
| How Japan Is Trying to Develop the International Mind of Her Young People | Hoshino |
| Summary of Legislation concerning Public Control of Private Schools and the Teaching of Religion in Public Schools in the United States | Wilson |
| Notes on Certain Aspects of the Work of the League of Nations of Interest to the Pacific Countries | League of Nations[39] |
| The League of Nations and Intellectual Co-operation | League of Nations |
| International Committee on Intellectual Co-operation | League of Nations |

[35] *Ibid.*, Section 25.

[36] Documents, Section 26.

[37] *Ibid.*, Section 27.

[38] Published by World Peace Foundation, Vol. X, No. 6.

[39] Documents, Section 28.

|  |  |
|---|---|
| Public Opinion and International Relations | Lee |
| Communications | Rogers[40] |
| Communications | Pape |
| The United Press | Bickel |
| The Radio Situation with Reference to the United States, China, and Japan | Davis[41] |
| China's Radio Communication Problem | Ishii[42] |
| Australia's Communications with Other Pacific Countries | Australian Postal Department |
| Communications on the Pacific | McClatchy[43] |
| The International Labor Organization and Labor Problems in Mandated Territories | Caldwell |
| Micronesia and Micronesians | Yamasaki |
| Samoa and Other South Sea Islands as a Problem of the Pacific | Tennent |
| The Mandated Territory of Western Samoa | N.Z. Group |
| Memorandum on American Samoa | Elkinton |
| The Mandates of New Guinea and Nauru | Eggleston |
| Selected Bibliography on Australian Political, Economic, and Social Questions | Campbell |
| Report of Committee on Permanent Organization | Davis |
| Closing Address | Whyte[44] |
| Closing Address | Hung[44] |
| Closing Address | Tsurumi[44] |
| Closing Address | Greene[44] |
| Closing Address | Wilbur[44] |

[40] Reprint of a paper presented at the Conference on American Relations with China (September, 1925), with a preface by the United States Navy Department (June 20, 1927).

[41] Documents, Section 29.

[42] Documents, Section 30.

[43] Reprint from *San Francisco Business* (May 11, 1927).

[44] *Institute News-Bulletin* (October, 1927).

INDEX

# INDEX

PRINTED IN U·S·A